Lecture Notes in Computer Science 2722

Edited by G. Goos, J. Hartmanis, and J. van Leeuwen

T0142027

Springer
Berlin
Heidelberg
New York
Hong Kong
London
Milan
Paris
Tokyo

Juan Manuel Cueva Lovelle
Bernardo Martín González Rodríguez
Luis Joyanes Aguilar
Jose Emilio Labra Gayo
María del Puerto Paule Ruiz (Eds.)

Web Engineering

International Conference, ICWE 2003
Oviedo, Spain, July 14-18, 2003
Proceedings

Springer

Series Editors

Gerhard Goos, Karlsruhe University, Germany
Juris Hartmanis, Cornell University, NY, USA
Jan van Leeuwen, Utrecht University, The Netherlands

Volume Editors

Juan Manuel Cueva Lovelle
Bernardo Martín González Rodríguez
Jose Emilio Labra Gayo
María del Puerto Paule Ruiz
University of Oviedo, Department of Computer Science
C/Calvo Sotelo S/N, 33007 Oviedo, Spain
E-mail: {cueva, martin, labra}@lsi.uniovi.es
paule@pinon.ccu.uniovi.es

Luis Joyanes Aguilar
Universidad Pontificia de Salamanca, Campus de Madrid
Departamento de Lenguajes, Sistemas Informáticos e Ingeniería del Software
Paseo Juan XXIII, 3, 28040 Madrid, Spain
E-mail: joyanes@retemail.es

Cataloging-in-Publication Data applied for

A catalog record for this book is available from the Library of Congress

Bibliographic information published by Die Deutsche Bibliothek
Die Deutsche Bibliothek lists this publication in the Deutsche Nationalbibliographie;
detailed bibliographic data is available in the Internet at <http://dnb.ddb.de>.

CR Subject Classification (1998): D.2, C.2, I.2.11, H.4, H.2, H.3, H.5, K.4, K.6

ISSN 0302-9743
ISBN 3-540-40522-4 Springer-Verlag Berlin Heidelberg New York

This work is subject to copyright. All rights are reserved, whether the whole or part of the material is
concerned, specifically the rights of translation, reprinting, re-use of illustrations, recitation, broadcasting,
reproduction on microfilms or in any other way, and storage in data banks. Duplication of this publication
or parts thereof is permitted only under the provisions of the German Copyright Law of September 9, 1965,
in its current version, and permission for use must always be obtained from Springer-Verlag. Violations are
liable for prosecution under the German Copyright Law.

Springer-Verlag Berlin Heidelberg New York
a member of BertelsmannSpringer Science+Business Media GmbH

http://www.springer.de

© Springer-Verlag Berlin Heidelberg 2003
Printed in Germany

Typesetting: Camera-ready by author, data conversion by PTP-Berlin GmbH
Printed on acid-free paper   SPIN: 10928981   06/3142   5 4 3 2 1 0

Preface

In the last decade, we have seen tremendous successes in World Wide Web and Internet technologies. Traditional development techniques had to be adapted to this new situation, and at the same time new techniques emerged. Many research teams began to investigate different ways to adapt classic – but still effective – software engineering design and development techniques to the Web and Web engineering emerged as a new research field that relates several subject areas, including agents, e-commerce, e-learning, human-computer interaction, mobile technologies, security, quality and testing, the Semantic Web, etc.

The International Conference on Web Engineering (ICWE) continued the tradition of earlier conferences with the aim of bringing together researchers and practitioners in these areas, trying to offer a good environment where people with different backgrounds could exchange their insights in this area.

The success of this conference generated an incredible amount of work for the Program Committee members and the External Reviewers, lead by the Program Committee chairs Oscar Pastor López, Luis Olsina Santos and Martín González Rodríguez. We are immensely grateful for the effort they put into the process of selecting the very best papers. There were 190 papers submitted, with 25 papers accepted (13%) as long papers. A large number of papers describing ongoing research were included as short papers or posters. Unfortunately, we were forced to reject many good papers. Paper selection is always a difficult task.

We want to thank all the members of the Object-Oriented Technologies Laboratory of the University of Oviedo (http://www.ootlab.uniovi.es) for their daily support and encouragement for this enterprise. The School of Computer Science Engineering of Oviedo gave its full support to the conference and we want to take this opportunity to congratulate it on its 20th anniversary celebration. In fact, this conference was part of that celebration. We also want to acknowledge the Department of Software Engineering research group at the Pontifical University of Salamanca, Madrid Campus, for its support in the organization and other practical matters. Thanks also to the Department of Computer Science of the University of Oviedo. We are also very grateful to Steven Furnell and Dieter Fensel for agreeing to deliver keynote lectures at the conference.

May 2003

Juan Manuel Cueva L.
B. Martín González R.
Luis Joyanes A.
Jose Emilio Labra G.
María del Puerto Paule R.

Organization

Organizing Committee

Organizing Committee Chairs	Luis Joyanes A. (Pontifical Univ. of Salamanca, Madrid)
	Juan Manuel Cueva L. (Univ. of Oviedo)
Co-ordinator	B. Martín González Rodríguez (Univ. of Oviedo)
Management	Daniel Gayo A. (Univ. of Oviedo)
	Jose M. Redondo (Univ. of Oviedo)
	Jose M. Morales (Univ. of Oviedo)
	T.H. Sagastegui (Univ. of Oviedo)
	M.E. Alva (Univ. of Oviedo)
Sponsorship	M. de los Ángeles Díaz F. (Univ. of Oviedo)
	Alberto M. Fernández (Univ. of Oviedo)
	M. Cándida Luengo (Univ. of Oviedo)
	Agustín Cernuda (Univ. of Oviedo)
Networks and Communications	Benjamín López P. (Univ. of Oviedo)
	Néstor García F. (Univ. of Oviedo)
	Luis Vinuesa (Univ. of Oviedo)
	J. Arturo Pérez (Univ. of Oviedo)
Paper Submission	David Tuñón F. (Univ. of Oviedo)
Graphic Design	Marcos González G. (Univ. of Oviedo)
	Aitor de la Puente S. (Univ. of Oviedo)
Call for Papers	Juan Ramón Pérez P. (Univ. of Oviedo)
	Francisco Ortín S. (Univ. of Oviedo)
Publication	Jose E. Labra G.(Univ. of Oviedo)
	M. del Puerto Paule R. (Univ. of Oviedo)
	Oscar San Juan (Pontifical Univ. of Salamanca, Madrid)
	Javier Parra (Pontifical Univ. of Salamanca, Madrid)
	Juan Manuel Lombardo (Pontifical Univ. of Salamanca, Madrid)
	Salvador Sánchez A. (Pontifical Univ. of Salamanca, Madrid)
Finance	Darío Álvarez G. (Univ. of Oviedo)
	Aquilino A. Juan F. (Univ. of Oviedo)
	Lourdes Tajes M. (Univ. of Oviedo)
Logistics	Fernando Álvarez G. (Univ. of Oviedo)
	A. Belén Martínez P. (Univ. of Oviedo)
	M. del Carmen Suárez T. (Univ. of Oviedo)
	Raúl Izquierdo (Univ. of Oviedo)
	Almudena García (Univ. of Oviedo)

Keynote Speakers

Steven Furnell (Univ. of Plymouth, UK)
Dieter Fensel (Leopold Franzens Universität Innsbruck, Austria)

Program Committee

Program Committee Chairs

Oscar Pastor L. (Polytechnic Univ. of Valencia, Spain)
Luis Olsina S. (National Univ. of La Pampa, Argentina)
Martín González R. (Univ. of Oviedo, Spain)

Tutorials

Jose E. Labra G. (Univ. of Oviedo)
Mar Escribano (Pontifical Univ. of Salamanca, Madrid)
César F. Acebal (Univ. of Oviedo)

Program Committee

Gustavo Rossi (National Univ. of La Plata, Argentina)
Juan Manuel Cueva L. (Univ. of Oviedo, Spain)
Daniel Schwabe (PUC Rio, Brazil)
Luisa Mich (Trento Univ., Italy)
Ana Regina Cavalcanti da Rocha, (UFRJ, Brazil)
Symeon Retalis (Cyprus Univ., Cyprus)
Daniel German (Victoria Univ., Canada)
Manuel Pérez Cota (Univ. of Vigo, Spain)
João Falcão e Cunha (Porto Univ., Portugal)
San Murugesan (Southern Cross Univ., Australia)
Luis Joyanes Aguilar (Pontifical Univ. of Salamanca, Spain)
Julio Abascal (Univ. of the Basque Country, Spain)
Jaelson Castro (Federal Univ. of Pernambuco, Brazil)
Jürgen Hauser (Deutsche Telekom, Germany)
Fernando Sánchez (Extremadura Univ., Spain)
George Fernandez (RMIT Univ., Australia)
Yogesh Deshpande (Univ. of Western Sydney, Macarthur, Australia)
Mario Piattini (Castilla-La Mancha Univ., Spain)
Paul Dowland (Univ. of Plymouth, UK)
Martin Gaedke (Univ. of Karlsruhe, Germany)
Antonio Vallecillo (Univ. of Malaga, Spain)
Fernando Orejas (Polytechnic Univ. of Catalonia, Spain)

Miguel Katrib (Univ. of La Habana, Cuba)
Ramon Puigjaner (Univ. of the Balearic Islands, Spain)
Steven Furnell (Univ. of Plymouth, UK)
Dieter Fensel (Leopold Franzens Universität Innsbruck, Austria)
Jesús Lorés (Univ. of Lleida, Spain)
Analia Amandi (National Univ. of Centro de la Pcia, Argentina)
Enrico Motta (Knowledge Media Institute, The Open Univ., UK)
Juan Manuel Corchado (Univ. of Salamanca, Spain)
Frank van Harmelen (Vrije Universiteit Amsterdam, The Netherlands)
Carole Goble (Univ. of Manchester, UK)
Daniel Riesco (San Luis National Univ., Argentina)
Gaston Mousques (ORT, Uruguay)
Asunción Gómez Pérez (Polytechnic Univ. of Madrid, Spain)
Bebo White (Stanford Linear Accelerator Center, USA)
Franca Garzotto (Polytechnic Institute of Milan, Italy)
Arno Scharl (Vienna Univ. of Economics and Business Administration, Austria)
Marcelo Visconti (Technical Univ. Federico Santa María, Chile)
Ricardo Orosco (UADE, Argentina)
Kathia Marçal de Oliveira (Catholic Univ. of Brasilia, Brazil)
Emilia Mendes (Univ. of Auckland, New Zealand)
Riccardo Rizzo (Institute for Educational and Training Technologies of Palermo, Italy)
Nora Koch (Ludwig-Maximilians-Universität München, Germany)
José Carlos Ramalho (Univ. of Minho, Portugal)

Special Reviewers

Ana Pont (Polytechnic Univ. of Valencia, Spain)
Jose A. Gil (Polytechnic Univ. of Valencia, Spain)
Carlos Guerrero (Univ. of the Balearic Islands, Spain)
Ivana Carla Miaton (Univ. of Trento, Italy)
Sean Bechhofer (Univ. of Manchester, UK)
Martin Dzbor (Knowledge Media Institute, The Open Univ., UK)
Dnyanesh Rajpathak (Knowledge Media Institute, The Open Univ., UK)
Liliana Cabral (Knowledge Media Institute, The Open Univ., UK)
Daniela Godoy (ISISTAN Research Institute, UNICE, Argentina)
Silvia Schiaffino (ISISTAN Research Institute, UNICE, Argentina)
Alejandro Zunino (ISISTAN Research Institute, UNICE, Argentina)
Adolfo Lozano (Univ. of Extremadura, Spain)
Roberto Rodríguez (Univ. of Extremadura, Spain)
Julia González (Univ. of Extremadura, Spain)
Emma Tonkin (Univ. of Karlsruhe, Germany)
Nuno Nunes (Univ. of Porto, Portugal)
José Magalhães Cruz (Univ. of Porto, Portugal)

Horst Treiblmaie (Vienna Univ. of Economics and Business Administration, Austria)
Myriam Arrue Rekondo (Univ. of the Basque Country, Spain)
David del Rio Angulo (Univ. of the Basque Country, Spain)
Sergio Escribano de Paula (Univ. of the Basque Country, Spain)
Jorge Tomás Guerra (Univ. of the Basque Country, Spain)
Daniel Gayo Avello (Univ. of Oviedo, Spain)
María del Puerto Paule Ruíz (Univ. of Oviedo, Spain)
Juan Ramón Pérez Pérez (Univ. of Oviedo, Spain)
Darío Álvarez Gutierrez (Univ. of Oviedo, Spain)
María de los A. Martin (National Univ. of La Pampa, Argentina)
Federico Kovak (National Univ. of La Pampa, Argentina)
Carlos Maffrand (National Univ. of La Pampa, Argentina)
Guillermo Lafuente (National Univ. of La Pampa, Argentina)
Guillermo Covella (National Univ. of La Pampa, Argentina)

Table of Contents

E-learning

Human-Computer Interaction

Languages and Tools

Mobility and the Web

Multimedia Techniques and Telecommunications

Security

Web Quality and Testing

Semantic Web

Web Applications Development

Semantic Web Services: A Communication Infrastructure for eWork and eCommerce

Dieter Fensel

Institut for Computer Science (IFI), University of Innsbruck
Technikerstrasse 25, 6020 Innsbruck, Austria
Tel.: +43-512-5076485/8 Fax: +43-512-5079872
http://www.google.com/search?q=dieter or
http://informatik.uibk.ac.at/nextwebgeneration

"The Semantic Web is an extension of the current web in which information is given well-defined meaning, better enabling computers and people to work in co-operation." – Tim Berners-Lee, James Hendler, Ora Lassila, The Semantic Web, Scientific American, May 2001

The computer has been invented as a device for computation. Today it is also a portal to cyberspace, an entry point to a world-wide network of information exchange and business transactions. The Internet and its most popular application, the World Wide Web, have brought about this change. The World Wide Web in particular, is an impressive success story, both in terms of the amount of available information and the number of people using it. It has reached a critical mass very rapidly and now starts to penetrate most areas of our daily life as citizens and professionals. Its success is based largely on the simplicity of its underlying structures and protocols which make for easy access to all kinds of resources. However, this simplicity may hamper the further development of the Web. Indeed, as will be explained below, current web technology has severe shortcomings. While it works well for posting and rendering content of all sorts, it can provide only very limited support for processing web contents. Hence, the main burden in searching, accessing, extracting, interpreting, and processing information rests upon the human user.

Tim Berners-Lee created the vision of a **Semantic Web** that enables automated information access and use, based on machine-processable semantics of data. In his informal 'Semantic Web Road Map' note[1] he outlined possible future directions for the evolution of the World Wide Web. These ideas, partly based on previous content and resource description activities, have met with growing enthusiasm of researchers and developers world-wide, both in academia and in industry. They encourage the integration of efforts that have been ongoing for some time in many R&D communities, involving specialists in various computer science disciplines. These efforts are aimed at capturing the semantics of digital content of all sorts and origins, and at devising ways of acting sensibly upon the formal knowledge representations thus gained.

---

[1] http://www.w3.org/DesignIssues/Semantic.html

J.M. Cueva Lovelle et al. (Eds.): ICWE 2003, LNCS 2722, pp. 1–7, 2003.
© Springer-Verlag Berlin Heidelberg 2003

The explicit representation of the semantics of data, grounded in domain theories (i.e., Ontologies), will enable a qualitatively new level of service. It will weave together a huge network of human knowledge, complement it with machine processability, and allow for automated services that support people (from all walks of life) in carrying out tasks that are contingent on the expedient use of information and knowledge. Access to these services may become as crucial as access to electric power.

Ontologies are the backbone technology for the Semantic Web and - more generally - for the management of formalised knowledge within the technical context of distributed systems. They provide machine-processable semantics of data and information sources that can be communicated between different agents (software and people). Many definitions of "Ontology" have been given in the past. One that in our opinion, best characterises its essence has been proposed by Gruber, 1993: *An Ontology is a formal, explicit specification of a shared conceptualisation.* A 'conceptualisation' refers to an abstract model of some phenomenon in the world which identifies the concepts that are relevant for that phenomenon. 'Explicit' means that the type of concepts used and the constraints on their use are explicitly defined. 'Formal' refers to the fact that the Ontology should be machine-readable. Different degrees of formality are possible. Large Ontologies like WordNet comprise a thesaurus of over 100,000 natural language terms explained in natural language. At the other end of the spectrum is CYC, that provides formal axiomatic theories for many aspects of common sense knowledge. 'Shared' reflects the notion that an Ontology captures consensual knowledge: consensus is usually reached through cooperation and communication between different people who share the same or similar interests. People who agree to accept an Ontology are said to *commit* themselves to that Ontology. Basically, the role of Ontologies in the knowledge engineering process is to facilitate the construction of a domain model. An Ontology provides the required vocabulary of terms and the relations among them. Ontologies and other technologies underlying the Semantic Web support access to unstructured, heterogeneous and distributed information and knowledge sources. They are now as essential as programming languages were in the 60's and 70's of the 20th century.

Semantic web technology is still in its early stages. We are focusing on building its basic -- and mostly static -- infrastructure. The next step will be to produce active components that use this infrastructure to offer human users intelligent services. **Web services** aim to support information access and e-business. Examples include UDDI, a repository for describing vendors, products, and services. It uses WSDL to describe its entries, and SOAP as a protocol to define how they can be accessed. At present, none of these service description elements are based on semantic web technology. As a result, it requires tremendous human effort to perform such tasks as: searching for vendors, products, and services; comparing and combing products; and forming coalitions of vendors, etc. **Semantic web-enabled web services** can provide a higher level of service by mechanizing many of these aspects. Steps in this direction are being taken by projects, such as DAML and Ibrow. Within DAML, a service description language called DAML-S has been developed. This language allows formal competence descriptions that enable automatic inference as a means of selecting and combining services. Ibrow developed a language called UPML that can be used to describe static and dynamic aspects of a semantic web. UPML offers features that describe Ontologies, heuristic reasoners (called problem-solving methods) and methods to interweave them. Based on these descriptions, an automated broker provides support in component selection, combination, and execution.

Web services described by WSDL are individual message exchanges. They can be synchronous or asynchronous one-way messages between a sender and a receiver or a pair of messages following a request/reply pattern between a sender and a receiver. While these two patterns are sufficient in many cases they are insufficient for more complex message exchange patterns (called public processes) like a purchase order (PO) and purchase order acknowledgment (POA) exchange whereby the PO message as well as the POA message are acknowledged individually by low-level message acknowledgements confirming the receipt of the message. WSDL is not able to define those public processes. If trading partners try to match their complex public processes in order to conduct business with each other they might encounter a mismatch of their public processes. For example, one trading partner expects message acknowledgments but the other trading partner does not provide them. Above mentioned languages do not support at all the compensation of these public process mismatches. In a peer-to-peer environment no third party mediator can be asked to compensate for the process mismatches. The trading partners have to do the compensation themselves in their environments. To implement the vision of mechanized support of public process integration the appropriate concepts as well as an approach for automatic and semantics preserving public process semantic web technology has to be applied to web services. Currently, all these service descriptions are based on semi-formal natural language descriptions. Therefore, the human programmer need be kept in the loop and scalability as well as economy of web services is limited. Bringing them to their full potential requires their combination with semantic web technology. It will provide mechanization in service identification, configuration, comparison, and combination. **Semantic Web enabled Web Services** have the potential to change our life in a much higher degree as the current web already did.

No technology can survive without convincing applications. Therefore, we will sketch three broad application areas. However, the reader should also be aware of the time span of innovation. For example, it took 30 years before the most prominent application of the Internet, the World Wide Web, came of age. Perhaps the kinds of application we are going to discuss will lead to major breakthroughs much faster.

Knowledge Management. The competitiveness of companies in fast changing markets depends largely on how they exploit and maintain their knowledge (their corporate memory). Most information in modern electronic media be it on the Internet or on large company intranets, is rather weakly structured. Finding relevant information and maintaining it is difficult. Yet, more and more companies realize that their intranets could be valuable repositories of corporate knowledge. However, raw information does not by itself solve business problems; it is useless without an understanding of how to apply it effectively. Turning it into useable knowledge has become a major problem. Corporate knowledge management is about leveraging an organization's data and information sources for innovation, greater productivity, and competitive strength. Due to the globalization and the impact of the Internet, many organizations are increasingly geographically dispersed and organized around virtual teams. Such organizations need knowledge management and organizational memory tools that enable users to understand better each other's changing contextual knowledge, and that foster collaboration while capturing, representing and interpreting the knowledge resources. Of course, knowledge management has dimensions that take it way beyond the needs of commercial enterprises. This concern in particular scientists, scholars, educators and other professionals, and their specific knowledge resources (of all kinds of media). Yet the basic problems these *communities of practice* face when it comes to creating and exploiting their resources, are quite similar to those that "knowledge workers" in companies big and small have to tackle. A fair number of knowledge management systems are already on the market, designed to deal with operations of relevance to the "knowledge lifecycle" within a given organization or community of practice. However, these systems still have severe limitations, e.g.:

- **Searching information**: Existing keyword-based search retrieves irrelevant information due to term ambiguity, and misses information when material related to similar concepts is stored under quite different terms.

- Extracting information: Currently, people have to browse and read extensively in order to extract relevant information from textual or other representations. Software agents do not possess the common-sense knowledge required to assist effectively in tasks of this type, let alone automate them. Moreover, they fail to integrate information from different sources.

- Maintaining large repositories of weakly structured text is a difficult and time-consuming activity.

- Adaptation and dynamic reconfiguration of information repositories (e.g. web-sites) according to user profiles or other aspects of relevance, hinges on **automatic document generation** and is not yet fully mastered.

Semantic Web Service technologies and especially the use of Ontologies, are expected to enable a much higher degree of automation and scalability in performing operations pertaining to the above mentioned tasks. For instance, in order to keep weakly structured collections consistent, or to generate information presentations from semi-structured data, the semantics of these collections and data must not only be machine-accessible but also machine-processable. In other words, the semantics must be represented based on formal Ontologies.

Enterprise Application Integration. For a number of reasons the integration of data, information, knowledge, processes and applications within businesses becomes more and more important, e.g.:

- Company mergers often require large-scale integration of existing information technology (IT) infrastructures;

- within existing corporate IT infrastructures new software solutions often have to integrate existing legacy software;

- for reasons of cost and quality a company may decide to adopt products (e.g. for Customer Relationship Management/CRM and Enterprise Resource Planning/ERP) from different vendors; these products need to work together;

- companies are forced to adapt to ever changing IT standards.

Recent studies by Gartner and Forrester estimate that a significant share of future IT budgets will be spent on Enterprise Application Integration tasks. This may seriously hamper progress in IT: if most of a company's resources are spent on integrating existing solutions little is left to develop new approaches.

Up until now, many companies have been trying to meet their integration needs through adhoc projects. Adhoc integration, however, does not scale. Global integration platforms on the other hand, require major investments and are often likely to fall behind the current state-of-the-art very fast.

A successful integration strategy must combine the advantages of adhoc and global integration. It must be driven by business needs (identified in terms of business processes and available information sources) but also address the all important issues of extendibility and reusability:

- **Extendibility** can be achieved through the use of Ontologies to prevent adhoc integration and to ensure that the integration effort can be extended in response to new and changing business needs. Ontologies provide the necessary controlled terminologies based on structured and well-defined domain theories.

- **Reusability** is greatly enhanced through the use of web service technology in combination with Ontologies to meet further integration needs based on standardisation.

We expect that Semantic Web technologies will greatly benefit Enterprise Application Integration before they are successfully applied to tackling problems at the next higher level: the integration of several organisations, for instance in eCommerce environments.

eCommerce. eCommerce in business-to-business (B2B) relationships is not new. Initiatives to support electronic data exchange in business processes between different companies already existed in the 60's of the last century. To perform business transactions sender and receiver had to agree on common content formats and transmission protocols. In general, however, these arrangements did not live up to the expectations of their proponents: establishing an eCommerce relationship required a major investment and it was limited to a predefined number of trading partners, connected via a specific type of extranet.

Since then, the Internet and the World Wide Web have drastically increased the online availability of data and the amount of electronically exchangeable information. Internet-based electronic commerce now allows for more *openness, flexibility* and *dynamics*. This will help to improve business relationships in many ways, e.g.:

- Instead of implementing one link per supplier, a supplier can be linked to a marketplace with a large number of potential customers.

- Consequently, suppliers and customers can choose between a large number of business partners, and

- they can update their business relationships as the markets evolve.

In a nutshell, web-based eCommerce makes it possible to contact a large number of potential clients without running into the problem of having to implement as many communication channels. Hence, virtual enterprises can form in reaction to demands from the market and large enterprises can break up into smaller units, mediating their eWork relationship based on eCommerce relationships.

Achieving the desired level of openness and flexibility is not an easy task. The integration of various hardware and software platforms and the provision of a common protocol for information exchange might in fact be among the lesser problems to be solved. The real problems are in the openness, heterogeneity (in terms of *product*, *catalogue*, and *document* description standards) and dynamic nature of the exchanged content.

- **Openness** of eCommerce cannot be achieved without standardisation, a lesson learnt from the success of the web. In eCommerce, however, the requirements on standardisation are much stricter: they extend to the actual content exchanged and thus go far beyond the requirement of standardising protocols and document layouts.

- **Flexibility** of eCommerce cannot be achieved without multi-standard approaches. It is unlikely that a single standard acceptable to all vertical markets and cultural contexts, and covering all aspects of eCommerce will ever arise. And in any event a standard does not free us from the need to provide user-specific views on it and on the content it represents.

- **Dynamism** of eCommerce requires standards to be like living entities. Products, services, and trading modes are subject to frequent change. An electronic trading arrangement must reflect the dynamic nature of the processes it is supposed to support.

Again, given these requirements, Ontologies and other Semantic Web technologies are the most likely candidates to provide viable eCommerce solutions: Ontologies span networks of meaning where heterogeneity is an essential feature. Tools for dealing with conflicting definitions, as well as strong support for interweaving local theories, are essential in order to make this technology work and scale. Ontologies are used to exchange meaning between different agents. By definition an Ontology is itself the result of a social process. Therefore, it is not static. While Ontologies are required in order to exchange meaning the very exchange of meaning may impact on an Ontology. Ontologies evolve. Hence, capturing the time dimension is an essential requirement if Ontologies are to be useful mediators of the information needs of eCommerce processes. It follows that Ontologies must have strong versioning support and the underlying process models should cater for evolving consensus.

Books covering the issues discussed above are: [1, 2, 3, 4, 5]

References

1. D. Fensel, J. Hendler, H. Lieberman, and W. Wahlster (eds.): Spinning the Semantic Web: Bringing the World Wide Web to its Full Potential, MIT Press, Boston, 2003.
2. J. Davis, D. Fensel, and F. van Harmelen (eds.): Towards the Semantic Web: Ontology-Driven Knowledge Management, Wiley, 2002.
3. D. Fensel, B. Omelayenko, Y. Ding, E. Schulten, G. Botquin, M. Brown, and A. Flett: Intelligent Information Integration in B2B Electronic Commerce, Kluwer, 2002.
4. D. Fensel: Ontologies: Silver Bullet for Knowledge Management and Electronic Commerce, Springer-Verlag, Berlin, 2001.
5. D. Fensel: Problem-Solving Methods: Understanding, Development, Description, and Reuse, Lecture Notes on Artificial Intelligence, no 1791, Springer-Verlag, Berlin, 2000.

Cybercrime: Vandalizing the Information Society

Steven Furnell

Network Research Group, Faculty of Technology, University of Plymouth,
Plymouth, United Kingdom
sfurnell@plymouth.ac.uk

Abstract. Cybercrime has received significant coverage in recent years, with the media, law enforcers, and governments all working to bring the issue to our attention. This paper begins by presenting an overview of the problem, considering the scope and scale of reported incidents. From this, a series of common attack types are considered (focusing upon website defacement, denial of service and malware), with specific emphasis upon the potential for these to be automated and mounted by novices. Leading on from this, the problem of policing cybercrime is considered, with attention to the need for suitable legislation, and appropriate resourcing of law enforcers. It is concluded that that cybercrime is an inevitable downside of the information society, and that organizations and individuals consequently have a stake in ensuring their own protection.

1 Introduction

Cybercrime is now recognized as a major international problem, with continual increases in incidents of hacking, viruses, and other forms of abuse having been reported in recent years. Although the problem of computer crime has been apparent since the early days of computing, the difference today is the increased scope available to would-be attackers – largely due to the popularity of the Internet. The numerous benefits offered by the Internet and, in its turn, the World Wide Web have now led to their widespread public adoption. At the same time, however, their increased usage has also amplified the accompanying problems, and not a day seems to go by without a cybercrime incident of some kind being reported.

The majority of Internet users, whether corporate or consumers, have little appreciation of the online world in which they participate. They do not understand how the system works, and quite legitimately they have no wish to. However, although a detailed understanding of the technology is not necessary, Rheingold observes that the opportunities it offers can only be realized by an informed population [1]. Similarly, an uninformed population is more likely to find itself vulnerable to the risks. As such, an awareness of cybercrime problems is not only prudent, but also increasingly essential.

J.M. Cueva Lovelle et al. (Eds.): ICWE 2003, LNCS 2722, pp. 8–16, 2003.
© Springer-Verlag Berlin Heidelberg 2003

2 The Cybercrime Problem

At the most basic level, cybercrime is clearly a crime involving the use of computers. However, this is obviously a very broad classification, and in order to define the topic more precisely, it is useful to sub-categorize the issue. A useful classification is provided by the UK Audit Commission, which has been conducting computer crime and abuse surveys since the early 1980s. In the most recent version of their survey, released in September 2001, the Commission suggested the categories and associated definitions below [2]. This is by no means the only classification, and various other views are possible [3], but this provides a manageable list that does not group too many distinct issues together.

- **Fraud:** Private gain or benefit by: altering computer input in an unauthorized way; destroying, suppressing or stealing output; making unapproved changes to stored information; or amending or misusing programs (excluding virus infections).
- **Theft:** Theft of information.
- **Use of unlicensed software:** Using unlicensed copies of software.
- **Private work:** Unauthorized use of the organization's computer facilities for private gain.
- **Invasion of privacy:** Breaches of data protection legislation.
- **Hacking:** Deliberately gaining unauthorized access to an information system.
- **Sabotage:** Interfering with the computer process by causing deliberate damage to the processing cycle or to equipment.
- **Introduction of unsuitable material:** Introducing subversive or pornographic material, for example, by downloading from the Internet.
- **Virus:** Distributing a program with the intention of corrupting a computer process.

Having introduced the scope of the problem, another relevant factor is the scale. Some specific statistics are presented in the later discussion of common attacks, but it is useful to get a general overview that includes some evidence of the pattern over time. A good example in this respect comes from the Computer Security Institute (CSI), which has been conducting annual surveys in the United States since 1996. As Fig. 1 illustrates, there has been a notable increase in the proportion of organizations experiencing unauthorized use of their computer systems.

In total, the CSI's 2002 survey reported losses approaching $171 million, from 41 respondents who were willing and able to quantify the financial impacts of their incidents [4]. With an average loss per incident of over $4.1 million, this is not a problem that one should dismiss lightly. It is also worth noting that financial loss is merely one type of impact that may result from cybercrime. Other impacts, such as disruption to services, loss of data or damage to reputation, are more difficult to quantify and may actually be more significant in many contexts.

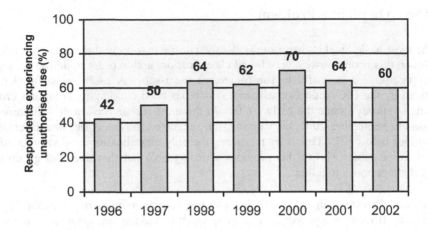

Fig. 1. CSI/FBI Computer Crime and Security Survey results 1996-2002

3 Common Forms of Attack

As the classifications in the previous section have identified, cybercrime can manifest itself in a number of guises. This section considers some of the most commonly encountered incidents – namely website defacements, denial of service, and malware – that frequently occur in the Internet environment.

3.1 Defacing Web Sites

The defacement of web sites has become very popular in the last five years, and is an attack that falls quite literally under the heading of vandalism suggested by the title of this paper. Defacing a site enables hackers to leave their mark in a very visible manner. While such an attack does not necessarily result in any breach of privacy, financial loss or even significant disruption, it does have the potential to cause significant embarrassment to the affected organization. In addition, to the casual observer who logs into the site during the period in which it has been affected (or hears reports about it in the media), the nature of the breach may seem more significant. Results from the CSI/FBI survey [4] suggest that vandalism is the most common form of web-related security incident. In the 2002 survey, 166 organizations indicated that their web sites had suffered some form of unauthorized access or misuse within the previous year. Of these, 70% cited the problem of vandalism [4]. Numerous high-profile organizations have suffered such attacks, including the CIA, the US Department of Justice, the New York Times, and online auction site eBay. An illustration is provided in Fig. 2, which depicts a fairly early website defacement, targeting the UK Labour Party back in 1996.

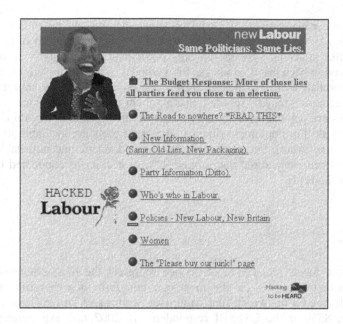

Fig. 2. The hacked UK Labour Party web site (6 December 1996)

Over the years, a number of websites have been created to monitor and record defacement activities, maintaining mirror versions of defaced pages. A notable example was Alldas.org, which began in 1998 – recording 74 defacements during the entire year. By 2001, however, this figure had risen to 22,379 defacements, and by February 2002 the volume of incidents became too much for Alldas to handle, and it ceased its mirroring activity (as a similar site, Attrition.org, had been forced to do the previous year for the same reason). One reason that so many defacements are possible is that web sites are being run on systems with vulnerable operating systems and servers. Hackers utilizing appropriate scanning tools can easily identify such systems, and then exploit the vulnerabilities in order to gain access (the exploitation is often handled by automated tools as well, removing the requirement for technical skill). Many systems continue to be vulnerable even when patches are made available, often because administrators are unaware of problems or have not prioritized the task of addressing them [5].

3.2 Denial of Service

The CSI/FBI findings suggest that denial of service (DoS) incidents represent the second most common form of website attack – with the aforementioned survey indicating that they were experienced by 55% of the 166 respondents. DoS attacks can range from fairly simple techniques, such as Ping of Death or SYN flooding, to more advanced distributed methods – all of which intend to undermine access for legitimate users. A significant example of the distributed DoS (DDoS) approach was witnessed back in February 2000, with sustained attacks that targeted Yahoo!, eBay,

Amazon and other major sites [6]. A DDoS attack may involve potentially hundreds of computers, which then bombard other Internet sites with thousands of requests for information (the attacking systems typically participate unwittingly, with the DDoS attack code having been installed via stealth methods). The distributed attack is more difficult to combat, as the malicious traffic comes in from many sources and, in addition, the addresses may be spoofed, making them even harder to trace.

DoS attacks are popular with novice hackers, in the sense that they do not require any significant skill to implement (indeed, numerous tools are available to automate such attacks in software), but can nonetheless have dramatic and noticeable effects. Indeed, it has been conjectured that around 90% of hacking is conducted by people using such methods [7].

3.3 Malware

Although defacements and denial of service represent the most common targeted attacks against systems, by far the most common form of cybercrime relates to malicious software (or malware), such as viruses, worms and Trojan Horse programs. For example, 85% of the CSI/FBI respondents in 2002 had experienced a virus incident [4]. As of February 2003, anti-virus vendor Sophos was citing over 80,000 known virus strains [8], and the company claimed to have detected 7,825 new strains in 2002 – suggesting that the problem is far from disappearing. One of the significant reasons for this is the lower entry requirement placed before would-be malware writers. Related information and tools are now readily available on the Internet, including toolkits that enable someone with no technical skill whatsoever to create and release their own program. As with automated DoS and cracking tools, the problem with malware toolkits is that they make the task of releasing a virus or worm so easy that a complete novice could do it. An example of such a tool is the VBS Worms Generator, pictured in Fig. 3, which was used to create the so-called Anna Kournikova worm in February 2001 [9]. Creating a worm using this tool can be as simple as running the application, giving the worm a name, and selecting a payload for it to execute when it is triggered. The whole process (including locating, downloading and installing the application) can be accomplished in less than 5 minutes.

It may be noted that automation of the attacks has been a common theme in all of these cases, lending the techniques to script kiddies (novice hackers, lacking technical skills, but typically prone to causing mischief and malicious damage). The problem is that the ease of launching the attack does not reduce the damage and inconvenience that it can cause; it just makes it more likely that attacks will happen.

4 Problems of Policing Cybercrime

Given the problems that cybercrime can cause for organizations and individuals, it is unsurprising that society has been obliged to respond through legislative and policing initiatives. Many developed countries have now introduced relevant legislation to address the problem of cybercrime and associated activities. An example is the UK's Computer Misuse Act 1990, which can be considered reasonably representative of the issues that other countries have also taken into account when enacting cybercrime laws. The CMA introduced new three offences [10], as below:

1. "Unauthorised access to computer programs and data"
2. "Unauthorised access with intent to commit or facilitate the commission of a further crime"
3. "Unauthorised modification of computer material, that is programs or data held in a computer"

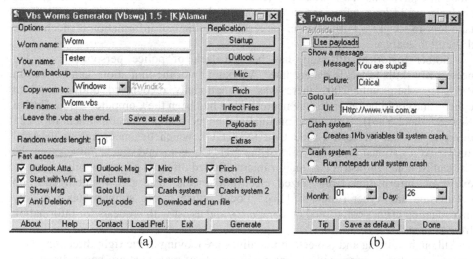

Fig. 3. The VBS Worms Generator (a) main options and (b) payload selection

The law has been successfully used a number of times during the last decade or so, and other countries with similar legislation have had comparable experiences. However, some more recent categories of attack do not fit comfortably within existing laws. For example, Denial of Service does not clearly fit as an offence under any of the Computer Misuse Act sections above − if all the attacker is doing is requesting a web page, then this clearly is not an unauthorized access, because the web server invites public access. Similarly, by simply requesting information, there is no modification of data involved. Consequently, laws need to be able to keep pace with the fairly dynamic landscape of new attacks. Another fundamental problem is that while computer crime is international, the jurisdiction of the law is not. Indeed, many countries have no cybercrime law at all (a situation that, in 2000 at least, applied to 60% of Interpol member countries). Unsurprisingly, this can cause difficulties if a crime is committed from within a country lacking appropriate legislation. For example, the alleged author of the Love Bug worm (which caused estimated worldwide damage of $7 billion in 2000) was traced to the Philippines. However, the authorities were forced to release him because the country had no relevant law in force at the time of the incident. This is not to say that things cannot be done to improve the situation. An example here is the European Convention on Cybercrime [11], which was devised by the 41 member countries within the Council of Europe (along with and representatives from the United States, Canada, South Africa, and Japan), with the specific intention of reducing inconsistencies in the handling of cybercrime.

Considering the perspective of those responsible for enforcing the law, the issue of investigating cybercrime has become much harder. Not only has the range of potential attacks increased, but the dramatic increase in desktop computing capabilities has also influenced the magnitude of the investigator's task. For example, whereas a typical computer in 1990 would hold an average of around 3,000 files, their modern equivalents hold around 25,000. So, whereas copying the contents for analysis would have taken one to two hours a decade ago, it is now more likely to take four to six [12]. Furthermore, the resulting volume of information is much more difficult to analyze.

Another historical difficulty has been a lack of police personnel with the necessarily skills to tackle cybercrime. An example of the limitations can be seen in the UK, where until 2001 there was no nationally recognised body to whom cybercrime could be reported (the nearest thing had been the Computer Crime Unit at New Scotland Yard). This situation finally changed with the establishment of a £25 million National Hi-Tech Crime Unit (NHTCU), which began operation in April 2001. At a national level, the role of the NHTCU is to investigate "attacks on the Critical National Infrastructure; major Internet based offences of paedophilia, fraud or extortion; information from seized electronic media; and gather intelligence on cybercrime and cybercriminals" [13]. Local police forces support this work by investigating crimes committed on computers and assist with requests for information from abroad.

Although policing and protection initiatives are moving in the right direction, there are still questions over whether appropriate levels of resources are being directed at the cybercrime problem. In the US, for instance, Gartner Group Inc. suggests that around 97% of all law enforcement funding for cybercrime is spent on about 300 federal agents (which represents less than 0.1% of the 600,000 agents that are funded in total). Furthermore, of the estimated $17 billion in federal discretionary spending that is directed towards law enforcement, only £10 million goes towards training, staffing, and support relating to cybercrime. This represents less than 0.1% of the total spending. As a result, Gartner concludes that the majority of Internet crime goes unpunished, and that cyber criminals know that they have little to fear from law enforcement [14].

Policing activities are also complicated by the fact that many incidents do not get reported (estimates have suggested that the level of reporting may be as low as 5% [15]). There are three general reasons why this may be the case. Firstly the organizations concerned may not consider the incidents to be significant enough to warrant concern or further action. A second potential reason is that the victim may lack confidence in the ability of the authorities to deal with the matter, and may feel that there is little to gain by getting them involved as few cases result in convictions (e.g. the chances of prosecution for hacking in the US are claimed to be one in 10,000 [16]). However, research suggests that the third explanation is the most likely -

namely, that organizations do not wish to report crimes as they are concerned about the adverse effects that widespread knowledge of such incidents could have upon their business [17]. Organizations are generally keen to avoid adverse publicity, as this may risk losing the confidence of the public or their shareholders. In addition, certain incidents could (if publicized) lead to a risk of legal liability. From a more personal perspective, those responsible for maintaining security may prefer to hush things up rather than report an incident in order to avoid potential ridicule by peers. The result of all this is that, in many cases, incidents are not willingly reported. It is, of course, easy to appreciate the company perspective in these situations – particularly in cases where the loss or disruption is ultimately perceived to be negligible or, at least, manageable. It may simply not be worth the effort, or indeed the risk, for them to report an incident. At the same time, those that keep quiet can be considered to be helping to hide the extent of the problem – which ultimately makes life more difficult for others. If the overall extent of the problem is underestimated, it will certainly receive less attention than it actually deserves. This may be manifested within individual organizations, as well as at higher levels, such as the level of funding allocated by governments to cybercrime prevention initiatives.

5 Conclusions

Widely reported incidents of computer abuse can do nothing but give the information society a bad reputation. It is often hard enough for new users to be faced with the task of becoming IT literate, without feeling that they are entering an unfriendly environment in which others may damage their systems or steal their data. Many organizations and individuals can see benefits that the Internet and the web will offer them. However, along with the good things, some of the most memorable net-related headlines have come from cybercrime incidents such as the Love Bug – which is somewhat off-putting.

It would be unrealistic to expect a complete removal of the criminal element from the information society – within any society there will always be elements that are unethical or disruptive. As such, we must change our attitudes and give the issue a similar level of consideration to that which we already afford to other types of crime, such as theft from our properties. In addition, an increase in the instances of computer crime must be seen as inevitable. As the technology itself becomes more pervasive, cyberspace will become a natural environment for criminal opportunities. The widespread acceptance of this fact will be the first step in ensuring that the information society is a safe place to be. Having said this, many of the common problems that enable cybercrime *can* already be solved with existing IT security measures. Security technologies, such as intrusion detection systems, are continually improving, with more advanced capabilities that will limit the future opportunities. So, with the technologies available or in place, the main ongoing problem is again linked to the attitudes and awareness of the people involved. Organisations must find a way to configure and maintain their systems securely. Everyone else must take their share of responsibility too, following good security practice where possible and ensuring that their own actions do not compromise protection.

Acknowledgement. The content of this paper is largely based upon material from the author's book, *Cybercrime: Vandalizing the Information Society*, published by Addison Wesley.

References

1. Rheingold, H. The Virtual Community – Finding Connection in a Computerized World. Secker & Warburg, London. (1994)
2. Audit Commission: yourbusiness@risk – An Update on IT Abuse 2001. Audit Commission Publications, UK. September (2001)
3. Furnell, S.M.: Categorising cybercrime and cybercriminals: The problem and potential approaches. Journal of Information Warfare, Vol. 1, No. 2. 35–44.
4. Power, R.: 2002 CSI/FBI Computer Crime and Security Survey. Computer Security Issues & Trends, vol. VIII, no. 1. Computer Security Institute. (2002)
5. Alayed, A., Furnell, S.M. and Barlow, I.M.: Addressing Internet security vulnerabilities: A benchmarking study. In Ghonaimy, M.A., El-Hadidi, M.T. and Aslan, H.K. (eds): Security in the Information Society: Visions and Perspectives. Kluwer Academic Publishers, Boston. (2002) 121–132
6. McCullagh, D. and Arent, L. 2000. "A Frenzy of Hacking Attacks", Wired News, 9 February 2000. http://www.wired.com/news/print/0,1294,34234,00.html
7. Akass, C.: On the straight and narrow – not. Personal Computer World, February (2000) 57
8. Sophos: Top ten viruses and hoaxes reported to Sophos in February 2003. Press Release, Sophos, UK, 3 March 2003
9. Greene, T.C.: Anna-bug author OnTheFly 'fesses up. The Register, 13 February 2001
10. HMSO: Computer Misuse Act 1990. Her Majesty's Stationary Office, UK (1990)
11. Council of Europe: Draft Convention on Cyber-Crime (Draft No 19), Council of Europe, PC-CY (2000) Draft No 19. Strasbourg 25 April (2000)
12. British Computer Society: Partner in crime, The Computer Bulletin, May (2000) 23–25
13. Home Office: New Hi-Tech Crime Investigators in £25Million Boost to Combat Cybercrime, News Release, 13 November 2000. http://wood.ccta.gov.uk/homeoffice
14. Garner Group Inc.: Gartner Says Most Internet Crime Goes Unpunished, Press Release, 7 December 2000
15. Blake, C.: Casting the Runes, Seminar presentation, British Computer Society Information Security Specialist Group seminar, London, UK, 7th February (2000)
16. Bequai, A.: Cyber-Crime the US Experience. Computers & Security, Vol. 18, No. 1 (1999) 16–18
17. Parker, D.B.: Consequential loss from computer crime. In Grissinnanche, A. (ed.): Security and Protection in Information Systems. Elsevier Science Publishers B.V., North-Holland (1989) 375–379

Agent-Based Web Engineering

J.M. Corchado[1], R. Laza[2], L. Borrajo[2], J.C. Yañez[2], A. de Luis[1] and
M. Gonzalez-Bedia[1]

[1]Departamento de Informática y Automática, University of Salamanca, Salamanca, Spain
corchado@usal.es
[2]Departamento de Informática, University of Vigo, 32004, Ourense, Spain

Abstract. Technological evolution of the Internet world is fast and constant. Successful systems should have the capacity to adapt to it and should be provided with mechanisms that allow them to decide what to do according to such changes. This paper shows how an autonomous intelligent agent can be used to develop web-based systems with the requirements of today users. Internet applications should be reactive, proactive, and autonomous and have to be capable of adapting to changes in its environment and in the user behavior. The technological proposal presented in the paper also facilitates the interoperability and scalability of distributed systems.

1 Introduction

Internet is growing and evolving continuously. Web pages and applications needs to be updates and most of the web sites are dynamic. Such systems needs to be redesigned frequently and adapted to the technological changes and requirements. Successful web-based systems should have the capacity to adapt to changes automatically and should be provided with mechanisms that allow them to decide what to do according to environmental and user changes. Such mechanisms are known as autonomous or intelligent agents [21]. This paper presents an autonomous agent architecture that may be used to construct dynamic, scalable, intelligent, autonomous, reactive, and proactive Web-based systems.

Agents and multiagent systems have evolved substantially in the last decade in parallel to the Internet explosion and expansion. In most computing systems, all the executed actions are previously planned and encoded by a programmer [2]. However, in our present-day world, where technological evolution is fast and constant, it is necessary to build up systems with the capacity for adaptation and provided with mechanisms that allow them to decide what to do according to their objectives. Such systems are known as agents [26]. This paper shows how to build automatically autonomous agents for the Internet, using a case-based reasoning (CBR) system. The proposed method facilitates the automation of their construction and provides them with the capacity of learning and therefore of autonomy. These agents will facilitate the construction of dynamic and intelligent application for the Internet.

Autonomous agents and multiagent systems should be able to reply to events, which take place in their environment, to take the initiative according to their goals, to interact with other agents (even human), and to use past experiences to achieve

J.M. Cueva Lovelle et al. (Eds.): ICWE 2003, LNCS 2722, pp. 17–25, 2003.
© Springer-Verlag Berlin Heidelberg 2003

present goals. These properties may be very beneficial to Internet applications. There are different types of agents and they can be classified in different ways [27]. One way is the so-called deliberative agents with a BDI architecture, which have mental attitudes of Beliefs, Desires and Intentions. In addition, they have the capacity to decide what to do and how to get it according to their attitudes [15], [20], [26]. The paper describes how intelligent Internet systems may be constructed with autonomous agents that reason with the help of a CBR system [8], [14].

This paper reviews first the concept of autonomous deliberative agents. Then the proposed model is outlined, and it is shown how a CBR system is used to operate the mental attitudes of a deliberative agent. Several Internet and Wap applications have been constructed with this technology and this paper presents a case study: a sales support e-business system. Finally the proposal is evaluated and some conclusions are exposed.

2   Autonomous Agents for the Internet

As mentioned above, autonomous deliberative agents, with a BDI architecture, are composed of beliefs, desires and intentions. The beliefs represent their information state, what the agents know about themselves and their environment. The desires are their motivation state, what the agents are trying to achieve, and the intentions represent the agents' deliberative states. Intentions are sequences of actions; they can be identified as plans. These mental attitudes determine the agent's behaviour and are critical to attain proper performance when the information about the problem is scarce [2], [17]. A BDI architecture has the advantage that it is intuitive, and it is relatively simple to identify the process of decision-making and how to perform it. Furthermore, the notions of belief, desires and intentions are easy to understand. On the other hand, its main drawback lies in finding a mechanism that permits its efficient implementation. The formalisation and implementation of BDI agents constitutes the research of many scientists [4], [12], [15], [16], [20], [23]. Some of them criticise the necessity of studying multi-modal logic for the formalisation and construction of such agents, because they have not been completely axiomatised and they are not computationally efficient. Rao and Georgeff [21] state that the problem lies in the big distance between the powerful logic for BDI systems and practical systems. Another problem is that this type of agent is not able to learn, a necessary requirement for them since they have to be constantly adding, modifying or eliminating beliefs, desires and intentions. It would be convenient to have a reasoning mechanism which would enable the agent to learn and adapt in real time i.e. as the computer program is executing rather than have to recompile such an agent whenever the environment changes.

It has been demonstrated that BDI agent implemented using a case-based reasoning system can substantially solve the two problems previously mentioned [8], [14]. Implementing agents in the form of CBR systems also facilitates their learning and adaptation. Among the different disciplines of cognitive science, cognitive psychology has widely shown the importance of learning from experience [3]. If the proper correspondence between the three mental attitudes of BDI agents and the information manipulated by a case-based reasoning system is established, an agent with beliefs, desires, intentions and a learning capacity will be obtained. Although the relationship between agents and CBR systems has been investigated by other researchers [1], [10], [19], [26], we have proposed an approach, whose main characteristic is its direct mapping between the agent conceptualisation and its implementation, in the form of a CBR system [8], [13], [14]. Intelligent and autonomous agents may then be implemented for working on the Internet automatically, in an unsupervised way, and then may be capable of evolving without supervision. The concept of case based reasoning system is presented and then it is shown how this methodology may be used to construct autonomous agents.

2.1   Case-Based Reasoning Systems

Case-based reasoning (CBR) is used to solve new problems by adapting solutions that were used to solve previous similar problems [22]. To reach this objective, CBRs are based on the knowledge stored in their memory, in the form of cases or problems. Figure 1 shows the reasoning cycle of a typical CBR system that includes four steps that are cyclically carried out in a sequenced way: retrieve, reuse, revise, and retain [24]. Each of the reasoning steps of a CBR system can be automated, which implies that the whole reasoning process could be automated to a certain extent [7], [11]. This assumption means in our opinion, that agents implemented using CBR systems could be able to reason autonomously and therefore to adapt themselves to environmental changes. The automation capabilities of CBR systems have led us to establish a relationship among cases, the CBR life cycle, and the mental attitudes of BDI agents. Based on this idea, a model that facilitates the implementation of the deliberative BDI agents (for the Internet) using the reasoning cycle of a CBR system is presented.

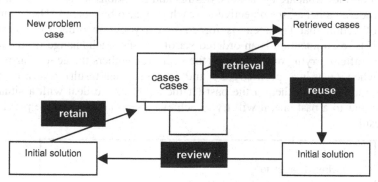

Fig. 1. CBR Cycle of Life

2.2   Automating the Construction of Agents Using CBR Systems

This section identifies the relationships established between deliberative BDI agents and CBR systems, and shows how an agent can reason with the help of a case-based reasoning system. Our proposal defines a direct mapping from the concept of an agent to the reasoning model, paying special attention to two elements: (i) how the mapping should allow a direct and straightforward implementation of the agent and (ii) how the agent is able to learn and evolve with the environmental changes. Properties that may be very useful to dynamic Internet applications. In the presented model, the CBR system is completely integrated in the agents' architecture, referring to the above-mentioned works, in which the agents see the CBR system just as a reasoning tool. Our proposal is also concerned with the agent's implementation and presents a "formalism" easy to implement, in which the reasoning process is based on the concept of intention. In this model, intentions are cases, which have to be retrieved, reused, revised and retained [8], [13].

```
Case: Problem, Solution, Result
      Problem: initial_state
                                       *
      Solution: <action,[intermediate_state]>
      Result: final_state
```
*Where <>: Sequence, []: Optional, *: 0 or more repetitions*

Fig. 2. Definition of a case in a case-based reasoning system

To achieve both goals, the structure of the CBR system has been designed around the concept of a case. The problem, the solution and the result obtained when the proposed solution is applied make a case. Figure 2 shows these components: the problem defines the situation of the environment at a given moment, the solution is the set of states undergone by the environment as a consequence of the actions that have been carried out inside it, and the result shows the situation of the environment once the problem has been solved.

Figure 3 defines what are the beliefs, desires and intentions for a BDI agent. Each state is considered a belief; the objective to reach may also be a belief. The intentions are plans of action that the agent is forced to carry out in order to achieve its objectives [2], so an intention is an ordered set of actions; each change from state to state is made after carrying out an action (the agent remembers the action carried out in the past when it was in a specified state, and the subsequent result). A desire will be any of the final states reached in the past (if the agent has to deal with a situation, which is similar to a past one, it will try to achieve a similar result to the previously obtained result).

```
Belief: state
                        *
Desire: <final_state>
                     *
Intention: <action>
```
*Where   <>: Sequence, *: 0 or more repetitions*

Fig. 3. Definition of the mental attitudes of a BDI agent

The relationship between CBR systems and BDI agents can be established implementing cases as beliefs, intentions and desires which caused the resolution of the problem. The obvious relationship between BDI agents and CBR systems can be identified by comparing Figures 2 and 3.

Using this relationship we can implement agents (conceptual level) using CBR systems (implementation level). Then we are mapping agents into CBR systems. The advantage of this approach is that a problem can be easily conceptualised in terms of agents and then implemented in the form of a CBR system. So once the beliefs, desires and intentions of an agent are identified, they can be mapped into a CBR system. The case based reasoning system may use then a Variational Calculus based planner (VCBP) to identify its actions plans in execution time using past experiences and the user feedback [13]. Variational calculus can be used to obtain the most adequate plan to achieve a goal in environment with uncertainty, during the CBR retrieval and reuse stage. The case-tool VCBP-Agents automates the implementation of such Internet agent based systems and the specifications of the believes, desires and intentions of the agents [14].

3   A CBR-BDI Based Engineering Sales Support System

The construction industry is an information intensive economic sector. This activity, as many others, require the use of a great amount of data, ranging from product data to technical publications, from buildings regulations to best practice guides. This section describes an information system that has been developed for a construction company, D&B Constructions, in which a the previously mentioned agents have been used. This distributed agent based system helps the company to make as much profit as possible from the information published on the Internet and the information that the company holds, and to reuse it as much as possible especially to estimate budgets.

The e-business engineering sales support system incorporates several specialised agents that search for and organise information and data, and several assistant sales support agents. The multiagent system has been implemented in Java using servlets (running in an Apache, Tomcat, jserv and Linux environment). The specialised agents are Java applications that run on the company Intranet and the assistant agents run in a portable computer connected to the Internet via a mobile phone.

The D&B Constructions deals with medium to small construction problems and it specialises in installing heating and air conditioning systems in a wide area of the Northwest of Spain. They have a sales force that is growing continuously, which implies that continuously new salesmen are taken on board without much experience in many cases. Until now the salesmen had to visit the clients on demand, had to take notes of their problems and then they had to contact an engineer or an experienced salesman, which had to estimate the work price and personnel and material required to carry on the work. The system here outlined was developed to aid the sales force, and in particular the inexperienced personnel, in the estimation of costs, thus reducing the process bureaucracy.

3.1   The System Architecture

In the expansion policy of B&D Constructions one of the main points is its incorporation of new technologies. Several steps will be taken in this direction for developing a web based information system that allows the company to publish information about their activities and that facilitates the communication between the administration, the sales force, the providers and the clients.

Figure 4 presents the architecture of the multiagent system. The planning agent has been implemented with the architecture described in [8], [14]. It estimates the construction cost, and the personnel and material required to carry out a construction project. It also generates reports about clients (or potential clients) using the information stored in the company databases and the one obtained by the Web search agent from the web. The planning agent generates working plans using their incorporated CBR system. The Web agent incorporates a web search engine that looks continuously for potential clients, information about them, new providers and products. This agent starts looking from a predetermined web address and searches for new ones using natural language processing strategies, optimised for the Web, based on the combination of the grammatical characterisation of words and statistical decision techniques [5]. This agent is monitored and guided by a marketing expert. Assistant agents (they can be as many agents as salesmen) are interface agents that facilitate the communication between the salesmen and the planning agent, they also hold summary information about the clients visited by its salesman owner and by the rest of the salesmen.

Before a salesman visits a client, he/she interrogates his/her assistant agent providing a description of the client (Name, Address and Activity). The assistant agent compares this data with previous queries and stored knowledge, using the VCBP incorporated by the CBR system, to identify the most suitable installation. This information is related to previous building work carried out for the client, his financial status, comments about him, noted by the firm's personnel during previous relations with this client, location information and other potentially useful data. This information is valuable especially when an inexperienced salesman starts a negotiation process. If the assistant agent cannot help the salesman or if the salesman demands more information, his assistant agent contacts the planning agent, which searches for information about the client in its case-base. This agent also interrogates the Web search agent asking for information about clients. The Web search agent obtains information from the web, analyses and indexes it using natural language processing algorithm optimised for Internet, as mentioned above. Information about potential clients, new materials and providers is sent to the administration agent, which can be interrogated by any of the Construction Company managers, engineers or sales supervisors. They can, then, use this pruned information to target new business. The administration agent is an interface agent that facilitates the interaction between the users (Company managers) and the rest of the elements of the system: agents, databases and even salesmen.

As mentioned above, the multiagent [25] system has been built using a Java-based library. This library is an extension of the one used to implement the STEB (Simulated Tactical Environmental Bubble) system [6], [7]. The STEB system was designed to forecast the temperature of ocean waters ahead of ongoing vessels. It is a multiagent system composed of several software agents that co-operate between them and that are operational in different locations: war/oceanographic vessels and in an Oceanographic Laboratory (Plymouth Marine Laboratory). The agents installed on the vessels use hybrid Case Based Reasoning-Artificial Neural Network (CBR-ANN) system [1] to forecast and communicate with the rest of the agents using Knowledge Query and Manipulation Language (KQML) performatives.

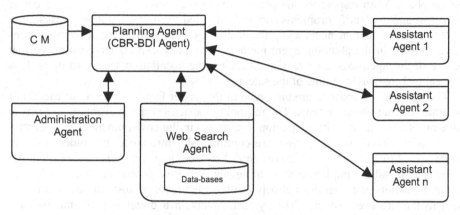

Fig. 4. Agent-oriented architecture

Similarly to the STEB system, when constructing the e-business multiagent system here presented, a decentralised architecture was selected, in which agents interact between one another when they require information or need to share data. The agents communicate with each other using a message passing protocol. Such messages are KQML performatives. The agents of this system collaborate between each other sharing information and working together to achieve a given goal. They use a simple collaboration mechanism. For example, if Salesman A is associated with the Assistant Agent A, and visits a Client X, the Assistant Agent A has to contact (send the problem of the Client X, via a performative) the Planning Agent. Then the Planning Agent generates the solution plan, and sends it back to the Assistant Agent [14].

In a system of these characteristics, data security has to be taken into consideration. A Role-based Access Control with elements that allow the certification of operations has been implemented to guarantee the data security and the information protection [9]. This security system protects the knowledge-base and the information stored in the system from external "agents" or non accredited personnel.

4   Results and Conclusions

The acceptance of this agent-based distributed system, by the Company staff, has been excellent. The system has been used in 1450 potential sales. D&B Constructors hold a data base with over 7810 installations from January 1997 till now.

In 92% of the system interrogations the estimation of the CBR-BDI agent differed by less that 3% of the one given by an expert salesman, and in the 6% of the enquires, it differed by less than 7%. Only in 2% of the occasions the agent output differed in more than 7% to the expert estimation. These deviations were caused by two reasons: the client required a combination of installations and equipment, which did not appear in any of the cases stored in the agent case-base, or there were errors in the system communication or in the data collection. This errors may be minimised during the review phase. With respect to this point, strategies are under investigation to detect such error and to identify problems and/or "generated plans" with potential risks.

It is expected that the accuracy of the business solution will increase as more cases are introduced in the planning agent memory. Company experts have estimated that the use of this agent-based system could reduce the installation sales cost up to 42% of the actual cost, and the time of the sale up to 45%.

The agent-based architecture presented in this paper facilitates the construction of dynamic Internet based systems. The reasoning capacities of the agents help them to solve problems, facilitate its adaptation to changes in the environment and to identify new possible solutions. New cases are continuously introduced and older ones are eliminated. Mora *et al.* [18] have described the gap that exists between the formalisation and the implementation of agents. What we propose in this article is to define the beliefs and intentions clearly (with a high level of abstraction), and to use them in the life cycle of the CBR system, to obtain a direct implementation of a autonomous agent. This paper has shown how agents can be developed with this technology, and how such agents can be successfully used to construct autonomous agent based system for the Internet.

Acknowledgement. This work has been partially supported by the CICYT projects TEL99-0335-C04-03 and SEC2000-0249, the PGIDT00 project MAR30104PR and the project SA039/02 of the JCyL.

References

1. Bergmann R and Wilke W. (1998) Towards a New Formal Model of Transformational Adaptation in Case-Based Reasoning. European Conference an Artificial Intelligence (ECAI'98), John Wiley and Sons.
2. Bratman M.E., Israel D., and Pollack M.E. (1988) Plans and resource-bounded practical reasoning. Computational Intelligence, 4. pages 349–355.
3. Caplan L.J. and Schooler C. (1990) Problem Solving by Reference to Rules or Previous Episodes: The Effects of Organized Training, Analogical Models, and Subsequent Complexity of Experience. Memory & Cognition, 18(2). pages 215–227.
4. Cohen P.R. and Levesque H.J. (1990) Intention is choice with commitment. Artificial Intelligence, 42(3).
5. Corchado J. M. (2001) CBR Agents in an e-commerce environment. Proceedings of WOOPS-ECOOP, Budapest, June.
6. Corchado J. M. and Aiken J. (2003) Hybrid Artificial Intelligence Methods in Oceanographic Forecasting Models. IEEE SMC Transactions Part C. Vol.32, No.4, November 2002: 307–313.
7. Corchado J. M. and Lees B. (2001) A Hybrid Case-based Model for Forecasting. Applied Artificial Intelligence. Vol 15, no. 2, pp105–127.
8. Corchado J. M., Laza R., Borrajo L., Yañes J. C. and Valiño M. (2003) Increasing the Autonomy of Deliberative Agents with a Case-Based Reasoning System. International Journal of Computational Intelligence and Applications. In press. ISSN: 1469–0268.
9. Corchado J.M., Aiken J, Rees N. (2001) Artificial Intelligence Models for Oceanographic Forecasting. Plymouth Marine Laboratory. ISBN-0-9519618-4-5.
10. Feret M. P. and Glasgow J. I. (1994) Explanation-Aided Diagnosis for Complex Devices, Proceedings of the 12th National Conference an Artificial Intelligence, (AAAI-94), Seattle, USA, August 94.

11. Fyfe C. and Corchado J. M. (2001) Automating the construction of CBR Systems using Kernel Methods. International Journal of Intelligent Systems. Vol 16, No. 4, April 2001. ISSN 0884-8173.

12. Georgeff M. P. and Lansky A.L. (1986) Procedural knowledge. In Proceedings of the IEEE Special Issue on Knowledge Representation, volume 74. pages 1383–1398.

13. Glez-Bedia M. and Corchado J. M. (2003) Constructing autonomous distribted systems using CBR-BDI agents. Innovation in knowledge Engineering. Faucher C., Jain L. and Ichalkaranje N. (eds.). Springer-Verlag. In press.

14. Glez-Bedia M, Corchado J. M., Corchado E. S. and Fyfe C. (2002) Analytical Model for Constructing Deliberative Agents, Engineering Intelligent Systems. Vol 3: 173–185.

15. Jennings N.R. (1992) On Being Responsible. In Y. Demazeau and E. Werner, editors, Decentralized A.I. 3. North Holland, Amsterdam, The Netherlands.

16. Kinny D. and Georgeff M. (1991) Commitment and effectiveness of situated agents. In Proceedings of the Twelfth International Joint Conference on Artificial Intelligence (IJCAI'91), pages 82–88, Sydney, Australia.

17. Kinny D., Ljungberg M., Rao A.S., Sonenberg E.A., Tidhar G, and Werner E. (1994) Planned team activity. In Artificial Social Systems. Lecture Notes in Artificial Intelligence (LNAI-830). Amsterdam, Netherlands. Springer Verlag.

18. Mora M. C., Lopes J. G., Viccari R. M. and Coelho H., (1998) BDI Models and Systems: Reducing the Gap. ATAL-98.

19. Olivia C., Chang C. F., Enguix C.F. and Ghose A.K. (1999) Case-Based BDI Agents: An Effective Approach for Intelligent Search on the World Wide Web", AAAI Spring Symposium on Intelligent Agents, 22–24 March 1999, Stanford University, USA

20. Rao A. S. and Georgeff M. P. (1991) Modeling rational agents within a BDI-architecture. In J. Allen, R. Fikes, and E. Sandewall, editors, Proceedings of the Second International Conference on Principles of Knowledge Representation and Reasoning. Morgan Kaufmann Publishers, San Mateo, CA.

21. Rao A. S. and Georgeff M. P. (1995) BDI Agents: From Theory to Practice. First International Conference on Multi-Agent Systems (ICMAS-95). San Franciso, USA, June.

22. Riesbeck, C. K. and Schank, D. B. (1989) Inside Case Based Reasoning. Erlbaum.

23. Shoham Y. (1993) Agent-Oriented programming. Artificial Intelligence, 60(1): pages 51–92.

24. Watson I. and Gadingen D. (1999) A Distributed Case-Based Reasoning Application for Engineering Sales Support. In Proceedings of IJCAI-99. Morgan Kaufmann Publishers Inc. Vol 1, pp 600–605.

25. Weiß G. (1996). Adaptation and learning in multi-agent systems: some remarks and Bibliography. Proceedings IJCAI95 workshop. Montreal, Canada. August, 1995.

26. Wooldridge M. (1999) Intelligent Agents. Multiagent Systems. A modern approach to Distributed Artificial Inteligence. Edited by Gerhard Weiss. Pages 27–77.

27. Wooldridge M. and Jennings N. R. (1994) Agent Theories, Architectures, and Languages: A Survey. Procs. ECAI-94 Workshop on Agent Theories, Architectures, and Languages.

Assisting Database Users in a Web Environment

Silvia Schiaffino[1,2] and Analía Amandi[1]

[1]ISISTAN Research Institute – Univ. Nac. del Centro Pcia. Bs. As.
Campus Universitario, Tandil, 7000, Bs. As., Argentina
[2] Also CONICET
{sschia,amandi@exa.uncen.edu.ar}

Abstract. Intelligent agents assisting users with repetitive tasks learn how these users perform these tasks and then they help users by making suggestions and, sometimes, by executing tasks on behalf of the users. Making queries to a relational database system is a repetitive and time-consuming task in which intelligent agents can be very helpful. In this work we present QueryGuesser, an intelligent agent with the capability of generating personalized queries according to a user's working habits and information needs. This agent observes a user's behavior while he is working with a database system and builds the user's profile. This profile is used to generate and execute personalized queries in advance, reducing the amount of time the user has to wait for the answers and offering the user the information he needs before he has to ask the system for it.

1 Introduction

The revolution in technologies and communications we have been experiencing in the last decade has left us a great volume and variety of information available in different electronic media. A big part of this information is recorded in relational databases, which are manipulated by information systems through query languages. With the growing of the WWW several companies have leveraged their database systems to Internet and Intranet contexts. Managing the information contained in databases in these new contexts has become a progressively more complex process that demands many time and effort from users [1].

In this context consider, for example, those users who regularly make queries to a given database system (within an Intranet or via Web) searching for information relevant to their interests. For example, consider a set of technicians working at a laboratory in a petrochemical plant. These employees are in charge of tracking and analyzing information about samples of different products. This information is stored in the laboratory database system. In their daily work, these technicians make queries to this database to get the information they need. Making queries is a time-consuming activity for these users, since they generally have difficulties in getting the information they need in a rapid manner due to network connections and server delays and they have to wait for it more than they would want to. Making queries is also a routine task since these users make similar queries in different opportunities to get the information they

J.M. Cueva Lovelle et al. (Eds.): ICWE 2003, LNCS 2722, pp. 26–29, 2003.
© Springer-Verlag Berlin Heidelberg 2003

usually work with. In consequence, users spend their time performing repetitive and time-consuming tasks instead of working productively with these information systems.

In this work we present an intelligent agent that acts as a personal assistant of a database user. This agent, named QueryGuesser, is capable of determining the queries a user commonly executes when he has certain information needs. Then, our agent can assist the user with his database work by suggesting him the execution of queries and by executing some of these queries on the user's behalf.

In order to achieve its goal, our agent has to solve some problems. First, it has to learn which queries the user generally makes to obtain information relevant to his interests and information needs. Second, the agent has to learn when the user executes each type of query, i.e. if there exist some kind of behavioral pattern in the user's actions. Finally, the agent has to detect changes in both a user's interests and working habits.

Our agent attacks these problems by utilizing a technique we have developed to build user profiles that combines Case-Based Reasoning (CBR) and Bayesian Networks (BN). QueryGuesser observes a user's behavior while he is making queries and records each querying experience as a case. Those cases representing similar queries are clustered in order to determine the various information needs the user has and his different querying habits. The agent uses the information contained in the case base to build a BN that models the relationships among query features. The BN allows the agent to deal with uncertain information about the user's information needs and the relationships among them.

This paper is organized as follows. Section 2 presents an overview of QueryGuesser. Section 3 describes some experimental results. Finally, Section 4 presents our conclusions.

2   The QueryGuesser Agent: An Overview

QueryGuesser is an intelligent agent that assists users who work with a relational database system through Web or Intranet applications. The QueryGuesser agent has the capability of managing personalized queries according to the information needs (or interests) and working habits of a given user. QueryGuesser's goal is to obtain this information about a user from the queries he generally makes. Once the agent has obtained this information, it can assist the user with the operation of the database.

QueryGuesser can help the user in two ways: it can suggest the user the execution of queries according to his interests and needs, and it can perform some of these queries in advance in order to save the user's time. Then, the agent processes the feedback the user provides regarding the assistance it has given him. The user can explicitly evaluate the quality and relevance of the queries the agent has suggested him and the behavioral patterns the agent has inferred. Besides, the agent can observe the user's behavior after assisting him to detect some indirect (or implicit) feedback, such as the user making a query different to the one suggested by the agent.

In order fulfill its tasks, a QueryGuesser agent must have the capability of building a user profile, which represents the user's habits and information needs in a given database domain. These information needs or interests are represented by the attributes or keywords involved in the user's queries. Thus, each topic of interest is described by a set of attributes and the values these attributes take, as well as an importance value or weight associated with each attribute and attribute value. The user's working habits are described by a set of situations in which the user makes queries. Each situation is associated with one or more topics of interest, and vice versa. For example, a situation may indicate that a user makes a certain type of query every morning or at the end of the month.

QueryGuesser learns about a user by observing his behavior while he is working with a database application and by recording data obtained from this observation process. This information is stored in the form of cases, according to the CBR paradigm. CBR means reasoning based on previous cases or experiences [3]. In CBR, a reasoner remembers previous situations similar to the current one and uses them to solve a new problem. In this work, each case records information about a particular user query, i.e. the attributes or keywords used by the user to make the query and temporal information describing the moment in which the query was executed (e.g. date, time, shift). We use interpretive CBR to classify a new query according to its similarity with previous recorded ones. Similar queries are clustered, forming different topics of interest. The agent classifies the queries considering two different criteria: content similarity and temporal information similarity.

In addition to storing a user's queries in a case base, the agent also builds a Bayesian model of the user's interests. A BN models the relationships among items of interest and the strength of these relationships. A BN is a directed acyclic graph that represents a probability distribution, where nodes represent random variables and arcs represent probabilistic correlation between variables [2]. The BN is dynamically updated as new information is obtained from the observation of the user's behavior. The information stored in the case base and in the BN of a given user is used to build the user profile.

3   Experimental Results

We implemented the QueryGuesser agent in Java and we used JavaBayes[1] to manipulate the BN. The QueryGuesser agent was tested while assisting a set of 20 users that operate the subsystem in charge of sample tracking within a LIMS (Laboratory Information Management System). The main goal of these tests was to analyze if the content of user profiles improved as the agent interacts with the user, tending to the user's needs. We studied the effects of user feedback in the profile building process, since we can view the evolution of user profiles in this way.

In order to make the tests, we asked each user to make twenty queries. At certain points, which were different for each user, the user required the agent's assistance.

---

[1] http://www.cs.cmu.edu/~javabayes/Home

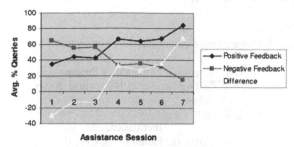

Fig. 1. Evolution of User Profiles

Then, we asked each user to provide feedback for each query suggested by the agent, rating them as relevant or irrelevant. The graph in Figure 1 plots the performance of the QueryGuesser agent. The graph plots, for each session, the average percentage of suggested queries that received positive feedback, the average percentage of suggested queries that received negative feedback and the difference between them. We can observe that there is a pattern of improving performance in the queries suggested by the agent. We can observe a soft learning curve in the initial states, since the first feedback values are mostly negative. This situation arose because we did not wait until the agent had learned something about the users' preferences to start testing it. In this way, the agent gave assistance to the user having information about a few queries made by the users. But then, due to the users' feedback, the agent stopped suggesting general (irrelevant) queries and feedback values became positive.

4 Conclusions

In this paper, we have presented QueryGuesser, an agent developed to assist users in their work with a database system. Our agent has been successfully tested in a LIMS, assisting users who made queries from distant places in a petrochemical plant. These users had considerable delays in getting the information they needed. Thus, our agent was very useful to them. The experimental results obtained so far have proved that our agent is good (and promising) at determining a user's topics of interest.

References

1. Y. Han and L. Sterling: Agents for citation finding on the World Wide Web. In PAAM 97, pages 303–318, 1997
2. J. Kolodner. Case-Based Reasoning. Morgan Kaufmann Publishers, 1993
3. P. Haddawy. An overview of some recent developments in Bayesian problem-solving techniques. AI Magazine, pages 11–19, 1999

The PSI3 Agent Recommender System

Jorge J. Gómez-Sanz[1], Juan Pavón[1], and Áureo Díaz-Carrasco[2]

[1]Dep. Sistemas Informáticos y Programación,
Univ. Complutense, 28040 Madrid, Spain
{jjgomez,jpavon}@sip.ucm.es
http://grasia.fdi.ucm.es
[2] Ibermatica,
Avda. del Partenón, 16 - 18, 1º
28042 Madrid, Spain
adiazcar@ibermatica.es
http://www.ibermatica.es

This paper presents a multi-agent system (MAS) that implements a recommender system, essentially using collaborative filtering techniques. The design of the MAS is flexible to support the implementation of different filtering strategies and to control the global behavior of the system and its users. It has been applied in the PSI3 project to implement a personalized information dissemination service. Personalization requires some feedback from users in order to obtain some rating of their satisfaction with the information they receive. But, in order to make this effective, it has to be done with minimum disturbance to them. One way to achieve such purpose is by associating a personal agent for each user (to build and manage the user's profile) and a community agent for each group of users (to manage the dissemination and evaluation of information in the group, improve system performance, and prevent malicious behavior).

1 Introduction

The context of this work is the European project PSI3 (Personalized Services for Integrated Internet Information, *www.psi3.org*), whose main purpose was the provision of a set of tools for personalization of web sites. An important feature for personalization of a web site is the capability to suggest information of interest to users, based on their preferences (this is also known as *recommender systems* [1]). Basically, the problem consists on filtering from a set of elements those which may be of interest to the user, taking into account the matching of attributes of the user and the type of information (*content-based filtering*) or the experience from other users with similar profile (*collaborative filtering* [2]).

Collaborative filtering implies the classification and combination of preferences and opinions from users to determine groups of users with certain similarity. Then, the information of interest for a specific user can be derived from what is well rated in the groups to which the user is associated. The difference with content based filtering is that the answer of the system is determined by the behavior of the group, instead of a simple matching for a user profile with item attributes. Collaborative filtering is

J.M. Cueva Lovelle et al. (Eds.): ICWE 2003, LNCS 2722, pp. 30–39, 2003.
© Springer-Verlag Berlin Heidelberg 2003

adequate, for instance, to recommend products such as books, movies, or web pages, where there is a significant degree of subjectivity in the user's choice.

There are already several agent-based systems implementing some collaborative filtering algorithms (for instance, [3] or [4]). Although they solve satisfactorily some specific problems, the architecture of these agent systems is not very flexible as all agents have strong dependencies between them in order to implement some concrete algorithm. The multi-agent system (MAS) presented in this paper intends to offer a more flexible architecture that would allow the implementation of different collaborative filtering algorithms, and even the possibility to combine these with content-based mechanisms, as it has been suggested in [5].

In this work, the collaborative filtering tool is conceived as a MAS, whose purpose is to provide users of a web community with personalized information. As such, the system needs to obtain some rating of the information presented to the users, but with minimum disturbance to them. This is achieved by associating a personal agent for each user, to build and manage the user's profile, and a community agent for each group of users, to manage the dissemination and evaluation of information in the group.

The interest of the proposed approach with respect to others is that this MAS is defined in terms of an organization and the associated workflows. These describe the collaborative filtering process and can be configured in different ways, not only by assigning values to certain parameters, but also by introducing social rules that determine the behavior of the group. This clarifies the design of the system since in the definition of the workflow we use simple terms and concepts closer to the intuitive definition of a process. It also provides flexibility because the workflow can be configured to behave in different ways, according to the kind of results that system administrators expect. Finally, this workflow can evolve. Actors in this workflow may change along the time. Therefore the behavior of the system can change too, but we can control its evolution to maintain some basic features. For instance, we can prevent from malicious behavior that could be (intentionally or not) introduced in the system by certain users (e.g., users doing spam or similar). Another characteristic of this system is the support for scalability, as the MAS is a distributed solution, which can support an arbitrary number of users. This is achieved by allowing system administrator to add new agent nodes for load sharing MAS components.

The organization of the MAS and its agents is described in section 2. There is special emphasis on the description of the main workflow in the organization and the parameters for its configuration, as the basis to structure the collaborative filtering algorithm. The complete design of the system, using the INGENIAS methodology [6], is available at http://grasia.fdi.ucm.es/ingenias/ejemplos/.

Section 3 discusses the definition of social rules to manage the behavior of a community. These can be used, for instance, to monitor the participation of users in the information filtering process and support the evolution of the community to some specific model, in which all the community users behave following certain patterns.

This system has been tested at two web sites (more information at www.psi3.org). Section 4 presents some results from this experimentation, which show that the application of the social rules described in section 3 contributes to reduce the number of interactions (i.e., improves system performance) and facilitate the evolution of the community of users to the desired configuration in a reasonable time.

Based on the results of this work, the conclusions, in section 5, argue that the application of agent concepts facilitates the development, monitoring and evolution of recommender systems. These concepts, such as organization, social rules, workflows, goals, interactions, etc., can be used both at system level (e.g., configuration of workflows) and locally (e.g., personalization of the behavior of each agent). These ideas can be also applied to the design of other distributed applications that interact with a diverse and changing environment, involving different types of users.

2   Organization and Workflows in the Design of the MAS

The organization of the MAS is derived from the main workflow of the recommender system. Users with common interests are grouped in *communities*. Members of a community provide information to other members, who may find this information interesting or not. This information provision process can be understood as a document dissemination workflow. Participants in this workflow will determine agents in the system, their role (functionality), and interactions.

Users participate in the workflow through *personal agents*, one per user. Personal agents keep record of the experience of the user and some other attributes, and may act (with autonomy) on behalf of the user, thus minimizing user interactions with the system (for instance, in the process of rating the adequacy of a certain document, the personal agent can make the evaluation of the document). This means that the system can work whether the user is present or not. On the other hand, *community agents* act as group representatives, aim at reducing the number of interactions required between personal agents, and define policies for information dissemination and community membership. *Community Agents* are responsible of managing the information flow among *Personal Agents*.

There are several ways to improve the performance of the recommender system. First of all, by reducing the dissemination of irrelevant documents. This requires the participation of a subset of the members of the community in an evaluation process. If the evaluation is successful, then the document can be distributed to the community. In order to avoid too much involvement of users in this process (which could be annoying for them), personal agents can do such work. Personal agents build a user profile by taking into account those documents that were annotated positively by the user in the past. Example of annotations are: the user visited the document twice, the user recommended the document to other communities, or the user rated the document as good. Then, personal agents can check the adequacy of suggested documents against those of the user profile by means of text mining tools. Similarly, community agents can also check the adequacy of a document to the community.

This workflow, with the participation of agents, is shown in Fig. 1. It starts with a user or an agent, providing a document to the user's community. This document is checked against the profile of the community and if it passes the test, it is evaluated by a subset of the members of the community. If members evaluate it positively, the community disseminates the document to the rest of the members. The opinion of the members is an additional feedback for the document evaluation. Along the way, the document is compared against a user profile or the community profile, which are expressed here as a set of documents, using automated analysis (text mining tools such as Rainbow [7] in our case). This comparison occurs when the community receives the document and when an evaluator or a suggestion receiver receives the document.

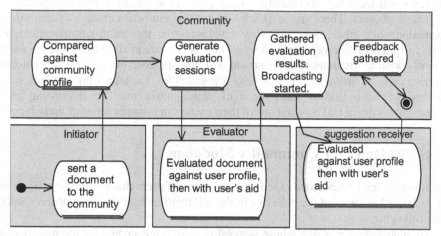

Fig. 1. Workflow implemented by agents to support collaborative filtering. Four actors execute the workflow: the initiator of the workflow, the community, the evaluator, and the suggestion receiver.

The workflow identifies the activities in the collaborative filtering process and the roles, which are responsible for them. Agents play roles, so they have the responsibility for performing the tasks that are assigned to the corresponding roles. In this system, personal agents undertake the roles of Initiator, Evaluator and Suggestion Receiver, whilst community agents undertake the role of Community. In this way, the identification of activities in the workflow and their assignment to roles is useful for defining which tasks and goals are assigned to each agent in the system.

The workflow can be configured at specific points with parameters (1), algorithms (2), and some rules (3 and 4):

1. The number of members who evaluate the information. The quality of the document depends highly on the number of users that have reviewed it.
2. Decision criteria for the autonomous evaluation of documents. These criteria determine whether the document fits into a profile (from the community or the user). A profile is initially defined as a set of positively evaluated documents. The default criterion is to consider the profile as a category and use a *k-nearest neighbor* algorithm with key word extraction [7] to obtain a degree of relevance to the profile. This degree has to be higher than a configurable threshold.
3. Decision criteria to consider evaluation results. Once users have evaluated documents, these criteria are used to decide whether or not dissemination should progress. The default criterion is to check if the number of positive evaluations is greater than the number of negative evaluations.
4. Criteria to act when a user ignores the document. Default behavior is to consider that the user is not interested in the document.

These workflow configuration features are those considered for the system that has been implemented in the PSI3 project and others could be considered. Each feature influences the behavior of the communities of users in which the workflow is executed. Users participate in the information flow because they benefit from the information received. If they do not feel satisfied with the documents they receive, then users will leave the community. However, there are many subtle differences in the attitude of users. There are users who do not feel confident enough to share their information with other users, but may collaborate in the information evaluation. Others just want to receive information and not collaborate at all. Also, there are users who only wish to disseminate information that perhaps does not interest other users, advertisements of products or services, for example. To take into account such attitudes, we have studied what types of communities may be interesting in a recommender system and how to control their evolution towards some of these types.

3   Social Rules for Community Modeling

A community can be described in terms of the types of users that constitute it. Type of user is defined in terms of the behavior in the information dissemination process, such as the following:

- An *annoying user* is one whose suggestions are not accepted by the majority of users.
- A *passive user* is one that does not review nor evaluate any document, but reads the supplied documents.
- An *active user* is one that participates in the evaluation workflow. It may be:
  - o   An *active reviewer*, one that provides an evaluation on a document.
  - o   An *active suggestor*, one that frequently provides documents to the community.

In order to improve the efficiency of the system, some types of users, e.g., annoying users, should be discouraged to participate in the community. Depending on the strategy of the recommender system, the ideal community can be defined as composed of users of specific types, for instance:

- A community where all users are *active suggestors* or *active reviewers*. The percentage of active reviewers should be higher than active suggestors so that reviewers are not overloaded by the amount of information to process.
- A community where all users are *active suggestors, active reviewers* or *passive users*. Ideally, there should be much more active reviewers than passive users. When there are more *passive users* than *active reviewers* and the number of reviewers is low, it is difficult to ensure document quality without overloading the reviewers.

Initially the system starts with any kind of community, as users subscribe to the community. By applying some social rules it is possible to evolve the community towards an ideal composition. A way to achieve this goal is with a rejection mechanism based on accumulated negative votes. The more negative votes a user provides, the more he is eligible for rejection. This policy is implemented in the form of rules managed by *Community Agents*. These rules are called *social rules* because their purpose is to tune the behavior of the community of agents attending to the social behavior of each one. Examples of such rules are:

1. When the user does not review a document after a certain time, it means that there is a negative vote. Such users may be *passive users*. The interpretation is that the system punishes the *passive user* increasing the chance of rejection for that user.
2. When a user provides a negative evaluation for a document that is finally accepted by the community, it means that the user may be showing prejudices. Prejudices are punished with the assignment of negative votes to the user.
3. When a user suggests documents that are being badly evaluated, that means that there is a possible *annoying user*. In this situation, negative votes are generated.

The policy can be customized by system administrators to determine how many negative votes are needed to reject users, to ignore suggestions from *annoying users* or what is the punishment for *passive users*. Also, the number of rules can be increased at any time. So, system administrators can define new rules to deal with specific situations.

In this case, there is no rule that decreases the amount of negative votes (i.e., a kind of positive vote). Therefore, the system may end up rejecting members of the community that provide good information and with a very active participation in the community. To deal with this situation, personal agents can be programmed to subscribe again to the community that rejected them. This can be done transparently to the user. The community agent, instead of admitting them directly, inspects new subscribers to check if their profiles match those of the existing members of the community. Matching is performed with text mining tools [7]. This ensures that the community will accept users who provided good documents in the past.

The mechanism for the selection of reviewers is also important to determine the evolution of the community:

- Selecting the same person (for instance a community administrator) as a reviewer makes the community become a *tyranny* (a government in which a single ruler is invested with absolute power). This is usually the situation in moderated distribution lists. Depending on the skills of the moderator, this procedure may or may not work well. If the subject of the community is politics, the actuation of the moderator will undoubtedly influence the kind of documents that will be distributed. Also, the moderator becomes a bottleneck in the flow of information inside a community.
- Selecting among a fixed sub-set of users, who may be experts in the field, leads to *oligarchy* (government by a small group). This situation is desirable as long as selected users perform well.
- Voting who will act as reviewer leads to a *democracy* (government by the people, exercised either directly or through elected representatives). The reviewer role should be temporal and community members should present themselves as candidates for reviewing. Without a reward policy, we do not expect such collaboration from the members of a community. Another issue is that this solution overloads the users of the community.

The selection policy must ensure equality in information overload and provide participative evaluation criteria. This can be achieved by selecting a random set of users to act as reviewers. The selection process ensures that all users participate in a similar number of evaluation processes. This policy has been implemented in the PSI3 system, and the experimentation shows that with this simple policy the overload is low while the evaluation ratio can be kept high.

4 Testing PSI3 Agent Recommender System

The final implementation of the recommender system in the PSI3 project, following the strategy discussed in the previous section, demonstrates that the policy of random selection of reviewers leads to low information overload and that the punishment policy leads to ideal communities for information dissemination.

To simulate exhaustive work of the system, the experiments run simulations of users accessing the PSI3 system. Each user is simulated by an agent whose profile is defined by a list of documents from the Reuters-21578 collection. These documents, which are marked with tags, represent the preferences of the simulated user and are used to simulate human decision criteria (*I like this document if its topics match those of my profile*). The generation of the profile is done by selecting a distribution of documents (see table 1) according to a predefined set of categories. Each category corresponds to a topic keyword from the Reuters collection.

Table 1. Categories of users. The column on the left is the percentage of users that belong to each category. The top row indicates the categories of documents.

Percentage/Categories	Soy-bean	Housing	Money-supply	Corn	Wool
25	0	0	0	100	0
50	50	0	50	0	50
25	0	0	100	50	0

Initially the community under test is formed by 25% of users whose profile consists 100% of documents talking about *corn* (i.e., they are only interested on documents from this category), 50% whose profile consists of 50% of documents about *soy-bean* and 50% about *money-supply*, and 25% who are interested only in *money-supply* documents.

The tests start with a community composed of 30% of *active suggestors* (suggests, reviews and evaluates), 30 % of *active reviewers* (reviews and evaluates) and 20% of *passive users*. The community uses 7 members to evaluate documents. These members are randomly selected.

The purpose of this experiment is to check whether the composition of the community evolves to a community where there are only *active users* who are interested in the topics of the community. The behavior of this community along the time is described in Fig. 2.

As it was expected the number of *passive users,* as well as the number of *active users* (*suggestors* and *reviewers*) that do not share common interests, decreases with time. Note that the number of *active reviewers* is related with the number of *active suggestors*. When the first increases, so does the second. Also, *passive users* influence negatively in the number of *active suggestors*. When the number of *passive users* increases, the number of *active suggestors* decreases. This means that in the workflow it is important to reject as soon as possible *passive users* so that *active reviewers* can support *active suggestors* with positive votes. This can achieved by modifying the number of negative votes that are needed to reject a user.

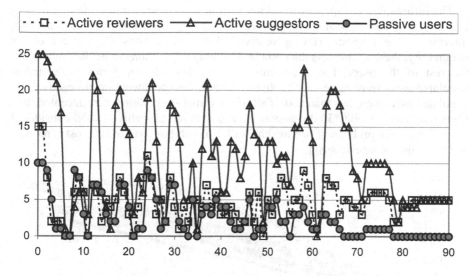

Fig. 2. Evolution of *active users* and *passive users* in the experiment. The X-axis represents time in minutes and the Y-axis represents the number of users in the experiment.

The system for the experiments was a Pentium III at 500 MHz and 300 MB, running Linux. Agents were programmed with Java and the JESS rule engine system, which has considerable impact on performance. With this configuration, it took seventy minutes for the system to become stable with no *passive users* and ten *active users*. To achieve this state, the majority of the members in the community should evaluate some documents positively. These documents can be taken to build the community profile and are used to evaluate new candidates. This information is used by the community agent to determine whether new subscription requests may be accepted or not taking into account their potential to contribute with relevant documents to the community.

Another issue is how to measure the performance of the workflow. Traditional measurement in information retrieval establishes a widely accepted method (recall and precision). However, in real systems, such a measurement would not work because the user may simply have forgotten to review a piece of information that according to the system is highly rated. That is why in this case we preferred to collect how many times:

- A document was recognized as good and the user recognized it as good too.
- A document was recognized as good but the user did not think so.
- A document was recognized as good but the user did not review it.

On the other hand, it is also interesting to measure how good community agents are acting as filters. Again, similar measurements are applied:

- How many users have rated a piece of information (any) as good.
- How many users have rated a piece of information (any) as bad.
- How many users have rated a piece of information as good after the evaluation.
- How many users have rated a piece of information as bad after the evaluation.
- How many users have not reviewed the information.

The information gathered by the system about these points appears in Fig. 3. As it was expected the ratio of users that received a suggested document is drastically inferior to the original. Having received 1400 suggestions from users of the community, these enable less than 400 high quality suggestions to be disseminated to the rest of the users. The documents that matched the categories associated to simulated users were more than 1100; meanwhile the documents rated negatively by simulated users were less than 600. If all of the initial suggestions were accepted, then users may receive 1400*50 documents what would not probably be well considered. Also, there is the problem of bandwidth. With this solution, bandwidth cost is reduced and users do not receive spam.

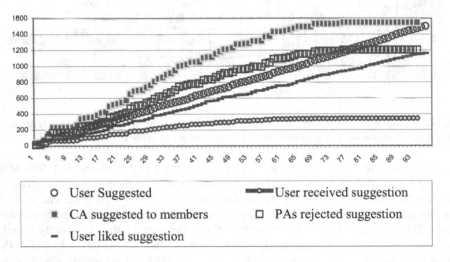

○ User Suggested		▬●▬ User received suggestion
▪ CA suggested to members		□ PAs rejected suggestion
– User liked suggestion		

Fig. 3. Statistics on the performance of the workflow. These data represent accumulated values at a specific moment. The X-axis represents time in minutes and the Y-axis represents the accumulated number of times an event occurred.

5   Conclusions

The design of an agent-based recommender system around the specification of its workflows provides great flexibility. This is because the behavior of the MAS can be configured at different points in the workflow with parameters, algorithms, or rules. This enables experimentation until the desired behavior of a community of users is achieved. As an example, this paper shows the use of social rules to evolve a community of several types of users into a community of *active users*.

Social rules can be used to regulate the flow of information and community membership in the recommender system. This provides flexible ways to control some undesirable behavior by some users, for instance, those who insert advertising as interesting information. Social rules can specify how to detect people who annotate documents negatively too many times or who supply documents that are not considered as interesting by other members, and take the appropriate actions with them (for instance, ignore them or reject from the community).

User modeling can be quite simple, as in this case, where user profile consists of a collection of documents that were positively evaluated by the user. As already mentioned, this has the advantage of allowing the use of text mining tools for matchmaking agents.

Although current tests do not ensure that users will accept the results from this system better than others, experiments show that communities evolve to a number of users who are satisfied with the results, because the system promote users to participate proactively in the evolution of the community composition and improves the quality of the information received. We have focused on an evolution of the communities to relatively small communities where users are satisfied with the results they obtained from them, but other behaviors could be developed taking into account different strategies for recommender systems.

Acknowledgment. This work has been supported by the projects PSI3, a shared-cost RTD project under the 5th Framework Program of the European Commission (IST-1999-11056), and INGENIAS, a project funded by Spanish Ministry of Science and Technology (TIC2002-04516-C03-03).

References

1. Resnick, P. and Varian, H. R.: Recommender systems. Communications of the ACM, vol. 40, no. 3 (1997) 56–58.
2. Goldberg, D., Nichols, D., Oki, B. M., and Terry, D.: Using collaborative filtering to weave an information tapestry. Communications of the ACM, vol. 35, no. 12 (1992) 61–70.
3. Delgado, J. and Ishii, N.: Multi-Agent Learning in Recommender Systems for Information Filtering on the Internet. International Journal of Cooperative Information Systems, vol. 10, nos. 1&2 (2001) 81–100.
4. Lashkari, Y., Metral, M., and Maes, P.: Collaborative Interface Agents. In Proc. Twelfth National Conference on Artificial Intelligence. AAAI Press (1994).
5. Schein, A., Popescul, A., Ungar, L., and Pennock, D.: Methods and Metrics for Cold-Start Recommendations. To appear in Proceedings of the 25'th Annual International ACM SIGIR Conference on Research and Development in Information Retrieval (SIGIR 2002).
6. Gómez-Sanz, J., Pavón, J.: Meta-modelling in Agent Oriented Software Engineering. In Proc. 8th Ibero-American Conference on AI (Iberamia 2002), LNAI 2527, Springer Verlag (2002) 606–615.
7. Andrew McCallum's: Bow: A Toolkit for Statistical Language Modeling, Text Retrieval, Classification and Clustering. http://www-2.cs.cmu.edu/~mccallum/bow/

Mob: A Scripting Language for Mobile Agents Based on a Process Calculus

Hervé Paulino[1], Luís Lopes[2], and Fernando Silva[2]

[1] Department of Informatics. Faculty of Sciences and Technology.
New University of Lisbon. 2825-114 Monte de Caparica, Portugal.
herve@di.fct.unl.pt
[2] Department of Computer Science. University of Oporto.
Rua do Campo Alegre, 823, 4150-180 Porto, Portugal.
{lblopes, fds}@ncc.up.pt

Abstract. Mobile agents are the latest software technology to program flexible and efficient distributed applications. Most current systems implement semantics that are hard if not impossible to prove correct. In this paper we present MOB, a scripting language for Internet agents encoded on top of a process calculus and with provably sound semantics.

1   Introduction

This paper presents a scripting language, MOB, for programming mobile agents in distributed environments. The semantics of the language is based on the DiTyCO (Distributed TYped Concurrent Objects) process calculus [1], whose implementation provides the run-time for the language. In particular, we rely on it for interprocess communication and code migration over the network.

The development of mobile agents requires a software infrastructure that provides migration and communication facilities, among others. Current frameworks that support mobile agents are mostly implemented by defining a set of Java classes that must then be extended to implement a given agent behavior, such as Aglets [2], Mole [3], or Klava [4]. MOB, on the other hand, is a simple scripting language that allows the definition of mobile agents and their interaction, an approach similar to D'Agents [5]. However, MOB applications may interact with external services programmed in many languages such as Java, C, TCL or Perl. The philosophy is similar to that used in the MIME type recognition. The runtime engine matches a file type against a set of internally known types and either launches the correspondent application or simply executes the code.

MOB also differs from other mobile agent frameworks in the fact that it is compiled into a process-calculus core language, and its semantics can be formally proved correct relative to the base calculus. Thus, the semantics of MOB programs can be understood precisely in the context of concurrency theory.

J.M. Cueva Lovelle et al. (Eds.): ICWE 2003, LNCS 2722, pp. 40–43, 2003.
© Springer-Verlag Berlin Heidelberg 2003

2 Language Description

In this section we describe the basic language abstractions.

2.1 Agents

The MOB programming language is a simple, easy-to-use, scripting language. Its main abstractions are mobile agents that can be grouped in communicators allowing group communication and synchronization. Programming an agent involves implementing two steps: the **init** and the **do** methods. Method **init** consists of a setup that will execute before the agent starts its journey. It is usually used to assign initial values to the agent's attributes. The **do** method defines the agent's actions/behavior on the journey.

Agents have several built-in attributes: **owner** carrying the identification of the agent's owner; **itinerary** carrying the agent's travel plan; and **strategy** carrying the definition of a strategy of how the itinerary must be traveled. The programmer may define as many new attributes as he wishes. Their usefulness is to hold state to be retrieved when the agent migrates back home. The following example presents the skeleton of a MOB agent definition, Airline. Beside the built-in attributes, a new one, named price, has been defined.

```
agent Airline {
    price;
    init { price = 0 }
    do { // Implementation of the agent's actions/behavior }
}
```

Once the template for an agent is defined an undetermined number of agents can be created. The following example creates an agent named airline owned by johndoe and with **home** hosts host1 and host2. One can also launch several agents at once using the **-n** flag. airlineList will contain the list of the agent's identifiers. Notice that the attribute initialization supplied in the agent constructor will not override the ones in the **init** section.

```
airline = agentof Airline -u "johndoe" -h "host1 host2"
airlineList = agentof Airline -n 10 -u "johndoe" -h "host1 host2"
```

Each agent must be associated to an owner, defined in an entry of the Unix-like file named passwd. An entry for each user contains login, name, password and group membership information. Following the Unix policy for user management, users may belong to groups defined in the groups file, sharing their access permissions. Each MOB enabled host must own both files in order to authenticate each incoming agent. As featured in FTP servers, an agent can present itself as anonymous for limited access to local resources.

2.2 Communicators

Communicators are conceptually equivalent to MPI communicators [6] and allow group communication and synchronization. The **communicator** construct requires the list of agents (eventually empty) that will start the communicator. Other agents may join later.

2.3   Instructions

Most of the statements included in MOB are common in all scripting languages (**for**, **while**, **if**, **foreach** and **switch**), the only difference lies in the **try** instruction, a little different from the usual error catching instructions found in, for instance, TCL. Its syntax is similar to the try/catch exception handler instruction of Java, allowing specific handling of different types of run-time system exceptions. MOB provides instructions to define a mobile agent's behavior and its interaction with other agents and external services. These commands can be grouped in the following main sets:

1. agent state (**email**, **owner**, **home**, **itinerary**, **strategy**, **hostname**, etc) and creation (**clone**).
2. mobility: **go**.
3. checkpointing: **savestate** and **getstate**.
4. inter-agent communication: asynchronous (**send**, **recv**, **recvfrom**), synchronous (**bsend**, **brecv**, **brecvfrom**), communicator-wide (**csend**) and multicast (**msend**). There are variants of these functions for use with the HTTP and SMTP protocols (e.g., **httpcsend**; **smtprecv**). These variants are useful to bypass firewalls that only allow connections to ports of regular services.
5. managing communicators: **cjoin** and **cleave**.
6. execution of external commands: **exec**. This functionality allows the execution of commands external to the MOB language. The MOB system features a set of service providers that enable communication through known protocols, such as HTTP, SMTP, SQL and FTP. The interaction with these providers is possible through **exec**'s protocol flag.

MOB's input/output instructions are implemented as a syntactic sugar for the **exec** instruction. **open** filename could also be written as **exec** -p fs open filename. MOB features all the common file input/output commands.

3   Programming Example

The example defines a network administration agent that performs a virus check by perpetually moving through the hosts. If a virus is found and the installed version of the anti-virus cannot solve the problem, the agent updates the anti-virus software and retries to remove the virus. If the problem remains an email is sent to the administrator. This implementation considers that all the anti-virus software is present, thus not protecting the **exec** calls with **try** instructions.

```
agent Antivirus {
    init { strategy = "circular" }
    do {
        if ([exec viruscheck] == -1) {
            version = exec viruscheck -version
            host = hostname
            try {
                go -h updates
```

```
                update = exec getupdate version
                try {
                    go -h back
                    exec applyupdate update
                    if ([exec viruscheck] == -1)
                        exec -p smtp email "Cannot erase virus on " + host
                } catch exec -p smtp email "Cannot connect to repository"
            } catch {
                exec -p smtp email "Cannot connect to " + host
                go -h back
            }
        }
    }
}
agentof AntiVirus -i "host1 host2" -u "Admin" -e "admin@mob"
```

When the agent reaches the end of the **do** code it migrates to the next host resulting of the application of the strategy over the itinerary. In this case, a circular strategy that moves accross all nodes of the itinerary forever. Although MOB features several strategies, it allows the programming of new ones. An agent's itinerary is seen as an object that can be managed through an iterator. The methods fand **previous** of the iterator define the MOB traveling strategy.

4   Future Work

MOB is currently under implementation. Future work will focus on features such as the implementation of a local exception handling mechanism and the development of external services, such as, recognition/execution of programs in several high-level languages (e.g. Java, C, TCL).

Acknowledgments. This work is partially supported by FCT's project MIMO (contracts POSI/CHS/39789/2001).

References

1. V. Vasconcelos, L. Lopes, F. Silva: Distribution and Mobility with Lexical Electronic Notes in Theoretical Computer Science 16(3), Elsevier Science Publishers, 1998.
2. Lange D.: Java Aglet Application Programming Interface. IBM Tokyo Research Laboratory. 1997.
3. Straber K., Baumann J., Hohl F.: Mole – A Java Based Mobile Agent System. Inst. for Parallel and Distributed Computer Systems, University of Stuttgart. 1997.
4. Bettini L., De Nicola R., Pugliese R.: Klava: a Java Framework for Distributed and Mobile Applications. Software – Practice and Experience, 32(14):1365–1394, John Wiley & Sons, 2002.
5. Gray R.: Agent TCL: A flexible and secure mobile-agent system. Department of Computer Science. Dartmouth College. 1996.
6. MPI Forum: The MPI Message Passing Interface Standard. www-unix.mcs.anl.gov/mpi/. 1994

Putting Together Web Services and Compositional Software Agents*

Mercedes Amor, Lidia Fuentes, and José María Troya

Depto. Lenguajes y Ciencias de la Computación
Universidad de Málaga
Campus de Teatinos s/n 29071 Málaga
{pinilla, lff, troya}@lcc.uma.es

Abstract. Web services are the newest trend in information technology, being considered the most used alternative for building distributed open systems. Although currently Web services involve a single client–server access, the market is demanding cooperative Web services to provide a global solution. Recently software agents appear as a good option that can cope with the control of Web services composition, obtaining an integral solution. This paper presents an approach to integrate Web services and software agent technologies. The basis of our approach is the use of the component technology for the development of adaptive software agents. Our compositional software agent performs automated software composition based on the flexibility provided by the component orientation, which makes possible to plug Web services into the agent functionality and compose them during the agent interaction.

1 Introduction

Computer industry increasingly focuses on Web services as an alternative to build distributed open systems above Internet. Any Web-accessible program can be considered one of this kind of services. Web services are the newest trend in information technology, because they are XML-based, can operate through firewalls, are lightweight, and are supported by all software companies. Web services are accessible through standardized XML messaging, with no care about how each Web service is implemented. Web services use and support an important set of new standards proposals, such as XML Schema [1], SOAP [2] (Simple Object Access Protocol), UDDI [3] (Universal Description, Discovery and Integration), and WSDL [4] (Web Services Definition Language. Besides these standards, Web service developers and users need to broadly agree on the semantics of specifics domains. The Resource Description Framework (RDF) [5], DARPA Agent Modeling Language (DAML+OIL) [6], and ontologies in general support this agreement.

---

* This work has been partially supported by CYTED project VII.18 ("WEST: Web Oriented Software technology").

J.M. Cueva Lovelle et al. (Eds.): ICWE 2003, LNCS 2722, pp. 44–53, 2003.
© Springer-Verlag Berlin Heidelberg 2003

But Web services technology also presents some shortcomings [7]: a Web service is not so adaptable, and it is unable to benefit from new capabilities of the environment to provide improved services; commonly Web services are not designed to use ontologies, and if the service provider and the client happen to use different ontologies the result of the service invocation could not be satisfactory; Web services are passive until they are invoked, and they are not able to provide alerts and updates when information becomes available; and finally, the most important drawback is that currently there is no standard to support composing functionalities among Web services. Concluding, although currently Web services involve a single client–server access, the market is demanding cooperative Web services to provide integral solutions.

Agent technology is now being used to interact with Web services on behalf of a customer, trying to overcome some of these Web services drawbacks. For instance, software agents can send alerts and updates when Web service information becomes available, and they can manage the correct use of ontologies. Above all, software agents are able to integrate different Web services into a unique solution. Software agents make use of a Web service by accessing to its semantic description, especially in terms of an ontology specified in a well-known language. That is, a software agent needs a computer-interpretable description of the service, for example in DAML-S [8].

Some efforts have recently started to integrate the software agent and the Web service communities. The FIPA services group has initiated a specification that enables FIPA agents to use Web services infrastructure (e.g. the message transport service), and propose to extend the Web services model with the benefits of agent technology [9]. Similarly, AgentCities has established a working group to integrate Web services architecture into their AgentCities framework [10]. This working group is examining the complexity of service descriptions and the dynamic composition of Web services in open environments. On the contrary, however, the Web service community does not seem to be interested in integrating agent technology into its infrastructure.

We propose to integrate Web service and software agent technologies through our component-based architecture for developing software agents [11][12], where agent behaviour is provided by different plug-ins components. In order to improve agent modularisation we also apply the separation of concerns technology [13]. Concretely, functionality and coordination issues are separated internally in different entities inside the architecture. The composition between agent internal components is performed at runtime, allowing the reconfiguration and adaptation of agent behaviour to support new interactions, for instance with Web services.

The benefit of component-oriented systems lies on their increased flexibility: a system built from components should be easier to recompose to address new requirements [14]. A compositional design may allow software agents to be dynamically adapted to support new negotiation protocols and new functionality, by plugging new software components.

Since agent functionality is provided by in-house and/or Commercial-Off-The-Shelf (COTS) components, a Web service can be considered as a special kind of a software component. Likewise components, Web services represent black-box functionality, and can be reused without worrying about how the service is implemented, being really loosely coupled. While a software component provides its functionality through well-defined interfaces, a Web service is offered through a XML standard service description, which provides all the necessary details to interact with the service. A Web service interface is defined strictly in terms of the messages the Web service accepts and generates as response, the message format (e.g. inside SOAP) and the transport protocol (normally HTTP).

In addition, we propose a single interface description of all the components, without taking care of how a component is accessed or implemented. In order to make possible components and agents interoperability it is needed a syntactic and a semantic agreement of component provided interfaces. We use a subset of DAML-S, an ontology for services description, as our component interface description language.

2   Software Agent Compositional Architecture

In this section we describe the core of our approach, a compositional architecture for software agents. Software agents are systems that perform actions or tasks autonomously to reach a set of goals. Software agents are able to perform complex interactions including negotiation and collaboration. The main characteristic of our model is that encapsulates agent functionality in software components. Modelling agent functionality as components we found out that a software agent contains components for data storing (e.g. to store its internal goals, facts, etc.), for providing application domain functionality (e.g. buy, bid, search actions), and components that coordinate the agent internal and external execution.

To improve agent functional decomposition we apply the principle of separation of concerns, that is, we model the coordination issue separately in a new entity called connector. We mean by coordination, the flow control between agent inner components and/or external agents. Thus connectors may model negotiation protocols. We have already successfully applied the Aspect Oriented Programming (AOP) to separate the coordination issue in some previous works [15][16], so we endow the connector concept to agents, mainly to increase their adaptability. In this case, we improve the agent dynamic adaptation to a new interaction protocols through the runtime composition of components and connectors inside the software agent. Fig. 1 shows the UML class diagram of the proposed compositional architecture of a software agent based on components and connectors. We use UML stereotypes for modelling the principal entities of our model, which are Component, Connector, Mediator and Interface. To simplify Fig. 1, we represent data and behaviour classes that model components as a subsystem, and connector class as a coordination subsystem ([12] contains a more detailed description of the UML class diagram). Connectors coordinate the different interactions the agent is involved. An agent can participate in more than one conversation simultaneously, and one protocol connector controls each conversation. Connectors coordinate dialogues according to a specific interaction protocol (e.g. English Auction Negotiation Protocol). These connectors differ only in the coordinated protocol, given by a template filled by the protocol specific rules, transitions and constraints.

Components encapsulate data and behaviour. Some behavioural components are always presented in the architecture providing generic agent functionality, such as to send a message, or to store general data. Domain specific behaviour is provided also by components. Specific components offer functionality to perform, for example, e-commerce tasks, such as to generate a bid. Components will be plugged into agent functionality on demand, and are changeable over the lifetime of the agent. Hence, domain specific behaviour can also be provided by Web services or COTS components.

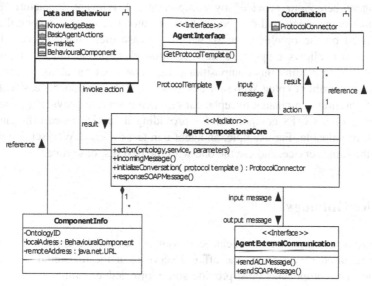

Fig. 1. Compositional Architecture for Software Agents.

Interface components manage the interactions of the agent. The *AgentExternal-Communication* (*AEC*) component processes the input messages and sends replays to an agent platform for delivery. Incoming messages are first processed by this component, and it may discard messages that are not syntactically well formed. The component *AgentInterface* (*AI*) contains the public agent interface, which is an extension of the traditional IDLs of software components. For instance, *AI* includes, in addition to the provided services descriptions, a list of public negotiation protocols, etc., (the agent interface description is beyond the scope of this paper). Concerning this paper, this component mainly stores the templates of the supported protocols, and the ontologies committed by the plugged components.

The *AgentCompositionalCore* (*ACC)* mediator component mainly performs the dynamic composition of components and connectors. The *ACC* receives input messages from the *AEC* component, dispatching them to the appropriate conversation according to the conversation identifier contained in the message. In addition, this component launches the connector that encapsulates a specific protocol as a new interaction is initiated. The mediator also maintains the relevant information about components that provide agent functionality. This information is represented in the architecture by the class *ComponentInfo*. Each component is registered within the agent architecture with a kind of role name, which is used to identify the component for late binding purposes. Since the role a component plays inside an agent is determined by the ontology it commits, we use the ontology name for identifying components. In addition it is necessary to indicate the location of the component. If the component is an internal instance, the *localAddress* field contains the local reference of the component. In other case, that is, the component is an external COTS component or a Web service, the *remoteAddress* field will contain the URL to access to component services.

Dynamic composition is used for the late binding between coordination connectors and the agent behaviour provided by components. A relevant characteristic of our model is that components and connectors have no direct references among them (they are referenced by the ontology name), which increase their independency. Dynamic composition also allows plugging a new component implementation into the agent dynamically, or upgrading this compositional agent without replacing the agent. This feature makes feasible to plug Web services and/or COTS components easily. Even the agent configuration can change to replace a registered service provider (a component, Web service, or a COTS component) for providing a service more efficient, with a lower cost, or valuable. For example, an agent can test different Web service providers that offer the same service, and use the one with the best response time.

3   Service Ontology

For composing coordination and agent behaviour at runtime the agent has to match up connector required services with the offered services of the registered component. In order to do that, components must provide some knowledge mainly about the services they provide. Web services, COTS components, and in general software components provide their functionality through well-defined interfaces. The way the connector requests the services is through the Mediator component, which knows registered components and their interfaces, since the connector must be unaware of the type of the plugged components. Consequently we need to use a common access method independent of the implementation language and location of the component, unifying the interface description of different software components that provide agent functionality. A simple solution could be to match connector service request by using just the syntactic description of component public methods, i.e. their signatures. However, it is required to share a common agreement about the meaning of the terms used in the interfaces, i.e. a common vocabulary. Since most IDLs only include a syntactic definition of the offered services, and any semantic information, we will enrich component interfaces with a semantic description of the services.

We consider the use of ontologies for describing components public interfaces. Ontologies are a powerful tool to enable knowledge sharing, and reach semantic interoperability. Actual ontologies in use focus on service advertising and discovery [17]. We propose to use DAML-S to describe components provided and even required functionality. DAML-S is a DAML+OIL ontology for describing the properties and capabilities of Web services, and it is as part of DARPA Agent Markup Language program. DAML-S complements low-level descriptions of Web services describing what a service can do, and not just how it does it. DAML-S is a Web markup language that provides a declarative, computer-interpretable API for executing function calls. The description of a service using DAML-S comprises three different views of the service:

what the service requires and provides the user, or agent is described in the service profile; how the service works is given in the process model; and, how to use the service is described in the grounding.

In our model, if an agent commits a given ontology means that there is a local component that implements the functionality required by the ontology, or knows an external component (e.g. a Web service) that provides it.

Now, we will walk through a small example to show how to define and describe a service using DAML-S. Consider the case of a Web service that provides an account transfer service, accessible through a WSDL description (WDSL is an XML-based language used to define Web services and describe how to access them). Apart from grounding we need to provide the DAML-S profile and process model of the Web service to describe a service in DAML-S. The profile and the process ontologies define classes and properties that must be specialized to describe a particular service.

The first step is to declare each distinct public service of a component as an instance of Service class. Fig. 2 shows how to declare the service to transfer money (*Express-BankTransferService*) as a DAML-S service.

Fig. 2. Declaration of Transfer as a DAML-S Service.

The Service class is at the top of the DAML-S ontology. Service properties at this level are very general. The property *presents* refers to the profile that describes the service capabilities; the property *describedBy* refers to the service model that describes how the service works; and the property *supports* refers to the description of how to invoke the service, given by the grounding.

A service profile provides a high level description of a service and its provider (the service profile for the transfer service in the example of Fig. 3). It is used to request or advertise services for service discovery and registry purposes. Service profile consists on three types of information: a description of the service and the service provider (in this case, the Web); the functional behavior of the service; and several functional attributes for automated service selection. In the service profile input and output parameters are described, and additional information, such as the response time, or the cost of the service.

Notice that service providers use the service profile for advertising purposes, but software agents also use this profile to specify their needs and expectations. For instance, a provider may advertise a software component that provides services for accessing an auction house catalog, whereas a software agent may also look for an auction service but with a cheaper access. Since in our approach we consider that agent functionality may be provided by an external Web service or COTS component, before registering a software component we launch a component discovery task. The software agent fulfills a service profile for the searching, demanding a specific functionality including also some requirements about quality of service (QoS). DAML-S service profiles focus on the representation of what the service does rather than where to find the service, which improves service discovery.

The profile of the bank transfer file (see Fig. 3) contains three input parameters (the amount to be transferred, the target account number, and the user personal identification), and one output parameter (the invoice).

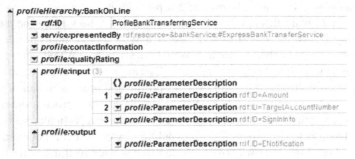

Fig. 3. Bank transfer service profile in DAML-S.

The third step is to provide a declarative description of the service properties, that is, the process model. Actually, the process model describes the individual programs that comprise the service, and conceives each program as an atomic process, a simple or a composite process. In DAML-S, a non-descomposable program is described as an atomic process, which is characterized by its ability to be executed by a single call, as methods in a software component interface.

	process:ProcessModel		
	≡ *rdf:*ID	ExpressBankTransferProcessModel	
	☑ *service:describes* rdf:resource=&bank;#ExpressBankTransferService		
	☑ *process:hasProcess* rdf:resource=#ExpressBankTransfer		
	daml:Class		
	≡ *rdf:*ID	ExpressBankTransfer	
	☑ *rdfs:subClassOf* rdf:resource=&process;#AtomicProcess		
	rdf:Property (2)		
	≡ *rdf:*ID	() *rdfs:subPropertyOf*	() *rdfs:domain*
1	TransferAmount	☑ *rdfs:subPropertyOf* rdf:resource=&process;#input	☑ *rdfs:domain* rdf:re
2	TransferSignInInfo	☑ *rdfs:subPropertyOf* rdf:resource=&process;#input	☑ *rdfs:domain* rdf:re

Fig. 4. Transfer service process model in DAML-S

Accordingly, the transfer service is described in the process model as an atomic process, as Fig. 4 shows: Each process has a set of subproperties to describe input and output parameters (for example the properties *TransferAmount* and *TransferSignInInfo* in Fig. 4). DAML-S let us to describe conditional outputs, to express, for example, when you search for product in a catalog, and the output may be a detailed description, or may be an "unclassified product" response.

Finally, the grounding is given by the WSDL description. The grounding details about service access can be considered as a mapping from the general description given in the process model to a concrete implementation of services. Thus, the Web service developer can reuse the WSDL description of the Web service as the grounding. Specifics details for this relation are given in [18].

We want to point out that using DAML-S as interface description language different types of software components, such as COTS components, Web services, or in-house components, can provide a unified description of their interface. They only differ in the grounding specification, which depends on the component implementation.

4 Service Invocation

Suppose a software agent that is participating in an electronic auction on behalf of a user. Suppose also that the auction rules say that if the auction winner has not enough money in the account, he or she will be sacked the winner would be the second finalist. Hence, the negotiation is not finished until the money transfer is done. Generally the final payment in e-markets is done by credit card, but in this case is necessary to connect to the bank Web site to perform the money transfer. For security issues, the operations over a bank account (consult, transfer) are available only through a Web service offered by the bank Web site. This way, the server can establish a secure connection to keep the data protected.

Requests to agent functionality are done during a negotiation protocol execution that controls the participation of the agent in a given interaction. Inside the agent, a protocol connector coordinates each interaction. Every time a message is received, this connector changes its state and executes a set of actions, implemented inside software components registered in the agent.

The collaboration diagram given in Fig. 5 shows the composition of the connector that coordinates the auction (the instance labelled as *Auction* in Fig. 5) with the Web service that realizes the money transfer (modelled as an instance of Actor and labelled as *BankWebService*). When the agent receives from the auctioneer a message informing that it has win the auction and has to transfer the money to a given bank account, the protocol connector will invoke the action to transfer the money to a given bank account (*action (Bank ,transfer, {amount,account})* see an example in Fig. 5). The protocol connector that coordinates the interaction does not directly invoke the action, but it forwards the request to the Mediator component (step 1 in Fig. 5). This component works, in some way, as a service broker. The Mediator component will forward the service request to the component that provides that service and will send the result back to the connector. Notice that the Mediator performs the dynamic composition of components and connectors by handling the connector's output calls, and delegating them to the appropriate software component.

As we told above registered components are addressed by the identifier of the ontology they commit, and the Mediator only has to retrieve the component reference from the *ComponentInfo* class that provide that functionality (step 2 in Fig. 5). Since there can be more than one software component registered for a given ontology. The Mediator will choose the best component according to a rule. If none of the components satisfy some QoS requirement, or rule associated to a kind of interaction, then the Mediator will initiate the searching of a better component. For example, it will choose the component that offers the lower cost service, or the Web service nearest to the current agent location. This is a very powerful feature of our model that can be used to build more adaptable agents.

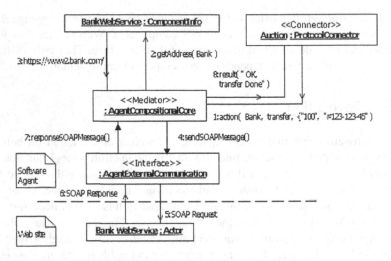

Fig. 5. Service Invocation Collaboration Diagram

Coming back to our example, since the Mediator has the URL of the bank Web service, it maps the general request "action" to a concrete invocation, after consulting the grounding for the selected component. In this case, the Mediator component constructs a SOAP Message, which is sent through the AEC component to the Web service (step 4 and 5 in Fig. 5). The AEC component has the capability of sending any kind of message through any transport protocol or component platform. Finally, the Mediator (again through the AEC component –step 6 in Fig. 5) will receive the result of the operation (step 7 in Fig. 5), and will pass it to the connector that continues the protocol execution (step 8 in Fig. 5).

5 Conclusions

In this paper, we propose integrating Web services by a component-based architecture for software agents that combine component orientation and separation of concerns. Domain specific functionality of agents and the coordination issue are modelled in separated entities. Functional components (e.g. Web services) are bound at runtime and composed with the corresponding negotiation protocol connector.

Due to the flexibility provided by the component orientation we are able to plug Web services into the agent functionality coordinating them to accomplish complex tasks. For composing coordination and agent behavior at runtime the agent has to match up connector required services with the offered services of registered components. In order to do that, both components and connectors must provide some knowledge about the services they provide and demand. Web services, COTS components, and in general software components provide their functionality through well-defined interfaces. We need to use a common access method independent of the implementation language of the component, and describe components interfaces using a shared vocabulary. As a result we propose to use DAML-S for describing the provided interfaces of software component. DAML-S provides an ontology for describing the functionality of agent inner components. Now we are developing a FIPA compliant working prototype of a generic software agent using the compositional architecture showed in previous sections.

References

1. W3C Consortium, XML Schema. http://www.w3c.org/XML/Schema
2. W3C Consortium,Simple Object Access Protocol (SOAP).
    http://www.w3.org/TR/2002/CR-soap12-part1-20021219/
3. Microsoft, UDDI, Universal Description, Discovery and Integration of Web Services. The UDDI Whitepaper. http://www.uddi.org.
4. W3C Consortium, Web Service Definition Language (WSDL).
    http://www.w3c.org/TR/wsdl
5. W3C Consortium, Resource Description Framework. http://www.w3c.org/RDF
6. The DARPA Agent Markup Language Homepage. http://www.daml.org
7. M. N. Huhns, "Agents as Web Services", IEEE Internet Computing, July/August 2002
8. DAML Services. The DARPA Agent Markup Language Homepage.
    http://www.daml.org/services/. 2002
9. FIPA Services. http://www.fipa.org.docs/input/f-in-00050/f-in-00050.html
10. AgentCities Web Services Working Group.
    http://www.agentcities.org/Activities/WG/WebServices
11. M. Amor, M. Pinto, L. Fuentes, J.M. Troya, "Combining Software Components and Mobile Agents", ESAW 2000, LNAI 1972, Springer-Verlag, 2000.
12. M. Amor, L. Fuentes, J.M. Troya, " Training Compositional Agents on Negotiation Protocols". Iberagents 2002, Proceedings of the Fourth Iberoamerican Workshop on Multi-agent Systems, 2002.
13. G. Kiczales et al. "Aspect-Oriented Programming", Proceedings of ECOOP'97, LNCS 1241, Springer-Verlag, 1998.
14. O. Nierstrasz, L. Dami, "Component-Oriented Software Technology", Object-Oriented Software Composition, eds. O.Nierstrasz and D. Tsichritzis, Pp. 3–28, Prentice Hall, 1995.
15. L. Fuentes, J.M. Troya, "A Java Framework for Web-based Multimedia and Collaborative Applications", IEEE Internet Computing, 3(2): pp. 55–64, April 1999.
16. L. Fuentes, J.M. Troya, "Coordinating Distributed Components on the Web: An Integrated Development Environment", Software Practice & Experience, 31(3), pp. 209–233, 2001.
17. J. Hendler, "Agents and the Semantic Web", IEEE Intelligent Systems, March/April, 2001.
18. A. Ankolekar et al, "DAML-S: Semantic Markup for Web Services", in *Proceedings of the International Semantic Web Working Symposium (SWWS)*, July 30-August 1, 2001.

Mobile Agents Markup Language[1]

Roberto Carlos Cascos Fernández[1] and Jesús Arturo Pérez Díaz[2]

[1] University of Oviedo, Computer Science Department
C/ Calvo Sotelo S/N, 33007 Oviedo, Asturias, Spain
Tel. (34) 985-206118
rcascos@gmx.net
[2] ITESM Campus Cuernavaca, Electronics and Communications department
Av. Paseo de la Reforma# 128-A. Temixco, Morelos, 62589. México
Tel. (777) 329-7163 Fax. 329-7166
jesus.arturo.perez@itesm.mx

Abstract. The aim of this paper is the definition of a data and instructions interchange language for mobile agents which belong to different mobile agents systems with the goal of allowing the information interchange between these applications and improving students learning in distributed environments.

1 Mobile Agents

Mobile agents are autonomous and intelligent programs that roam throughout a net gathering information and interacting with different services desired by its programmer [1]. They are mainly used for: monitoring, data compilation (searching and filtering), massive distribution of information and supercomputer emulation [2].

A mobile agent system is a set of programs and tools that allow the programming, execution and monitoring of mobile agents.

1.1 Communication between Mobile Agents

There are many different mobile agent systems. All of them provide simple tools for communication between their own agents, but also most of them are incompatible with other systems, which generates a lack of interoperability when mobile agents of different platforms try to exchange information.

Since messages in plain text are required to allow communication among agents of different mobile agent systems, a common directory will be used where agents which want to establish communication can send and leave their messages and other who want to get information can retrieve and read their messages.

Although this method is limited, it is similar to the method in any other mobile agent system. Messages can be sent only by the agents programmed to do so, similarly only the agents programmed to listen messages can do it.

---

[1] This paper has been supported by the ITESM inside the research project of Distributed collaborative systems for teaching.

J.M. Cueva Lovelle et al. (Eds.): ICWE 2003, LNCS 2722, pp. 54–57, 2003.
© Springer-Verlag Berlin Heidelberg 2003

2   MAML

The acronym MAML stands for "Mobile Agents Markup Language" and it will be the name that we give to the message interchange language.

The first thing to be done is to delimit the information that an agent owns and that could be useful to other agents. This information can be classified in several groups:

The description of this language will be based on a DTD, part of it is given in this chapter. The name of the different DTD elements tries to describe its content.

The XML root element simply includes a reference to each of the five internal elements, being the last four optional. It will be as follows:

```
<!ELEMENT MobileAgent (GeneralInformation, Security?,
Mobility?, Data?, Methods?)>
```

2.1   General Information

In this category, the following information could be included:

- Name of the agent: This name must be a global and unique identifier.
- Author: name of the author/authority and other important information about him.
- Creation date of the agent; hour of execution, lifetime, system which it belongs to.
- Creation date of the XML file.
- Agent description: a brief description of its goal.

```
<!ELEMENT GeneralInformation (AgentName, Author?,
Date?, AgentSystem?, Description?)>
```

2.2   Security

Usually, part of the information of the XML document must be hidden to some agents and this information can only be known by other agents that have been programmed by us. Besides, the authenticity of the information included in the file must be ensured. Finally, modification of these files by other agents or by the server cannot be allowed, in order to avoid that other agents change it and write false information.

To solve these problems, information about the security system used is included in the file. Also, private data will be encrypted. The agents that read these files must know the proper public keys to decrypt these data. These keys will be used according to the specified security policy.

In order to ensure that data has not been modified a digital signature containing the hash of the file can be included, in this way, if the public key of the agent's creator entity is known, the destination can ensure that the file has not been modified.

- Creator entity/authority: it will be necessary only if this field does not match up which the data given in the general information.
- Digital signature: with a hash of the message and information about the entity.
- Used method for the hash: by using this field, any method is allowed.

An attribute which indicates the encryption algorithm, will be used to mark an element as "encrypted". Agents, which want to read that field, must recognize de encryption algorithm mark and decrypt the field content by using this algorithm.

```
<!ELEMENT Security (CreationEntity, DigitalSignature?,
HashMethod?)>
```

2.3   Mobility Information

The agent can use this element to write the list of the servers it has been through, as well as the list of the servers it plans to visit.

- Visited servers: for each server several data can be considered, for example IP address, URL, if the address has been useful, etc.
- Server to visit: in the same way that the visited servers list, the IP address, URL and additional information can be included.

```
<!ELEMENT Mobility (VisitedServers?, Path?)>
```

2.4   Data

The agent can cooperate with other agents and tell them the data it has found. To make them possible to understand each other, the other agents must know what the searching agent is looking for. Data is one of the elements that should be keep it encrypted so that not all the agents are able to know what has been found it by others.

```
<!ELEMENT Data (#PCDATA)>
<!ATTLIST Data encoded CDATA #IMPLIED >
```

2.5   Methods

Commands that an agent can give to others are included here. An agent should only perform the instructions given by a trusted agent (verifiable by the digital signature).

A programming language could be developed so that we would be able to create our own methods, but in order to simplify the process, it is going to be considered that all functions are already pre-programmed. In this way just a few of the more used functions in mobile agents are going to be described.

A method has three parts (if it is considered that it does not return a value):

- Name of the function.
- Name (identification) of the target of the function (one agent or many).
- List of parameters.

As an example of functions that can be necessary we can consider the following:

- Add the following URL to the list of server that will be visited.
- Indication that the searched information has been found.
- Show an element on the screen.
- Load a file. The parameters would be the name and location of the file to load.

The number of functions that could be specified could be very big and they should be programmed on the agent who receives the command. The four previous functions are an example of four very simple functions that an agent could require from another. Other functions could be of the type "look for this thing", the destination agent must know how to perform that search. One search that can be executed by mobile agents is the search of other agents (location system). This system could be used to give instructions to other agents by finding them first.

```
<!ELEMENT Method (MethodName, TargetAgent,
ParametersList?)>
```

3 Conclusions

The MAML language is only an example of a possible utilization of XML in the construction of data interchange languages among mobile agents.

MAML represents an efficient solution to the interoperability problem among mobile agent systems since it allows the sharing of information, data and instructions in a secure way to create a secure interchange environment. This environment can be used to develop collaborative systems that allows students to get a higher learning in distributed environments.

In order to make the language completely efficient the agent system must know all methods (commands) that can be used. Agents could then consult to the agent system which it belongs to. A common directory must be included programmatically in all the agent systems. In this place messages are going to be left and read by agents.

Before the language can be used, it would be necessary an extended list of all the commands that agents could require, as well as encryption and hash methods that could be used by the agents, so that they could create the digital signature and the hash of the message.

References

1. Cetus Links, 18,199 Links on Objects and Components / Mobile Agents [http://www.cetus-links.org/oo_mobile_agents.html]
2. Venners, B.: Solve real problems with aglets, a type of mobile agent [http://www.javaworld.com/javaworld/jw-05-1997/jw-05-hood.html]
3. Finin, T., Fritzon R., Mackey, D. and MacEntire, R.: KQML as an agent communication language, [http://www.csee.umbc.edu/pub/ARPA/kqml/ papers/kqmlacl.pdf] (1995)
4. Cabri, G., Leonardi, L., Zamboneli. F.: XML Dataspaces for Mobile Agent Coordination. ACM Symposium on Applied Computing (2000)
5. Pérez Díaz, J. A.: Tesis Doctoral: SAHARA: Arquitectura de seguridad Integral para Sistemas de Agentes Móviles basados en Java. University of Oviedo, Spain (2000)
6. Petrie Charles J.,: Agent-Based Engineering, the Web, and Intelligence. IEEE Expert, (1996)

Building Wrapper Agents for the Deep Web

Vicente Luque Centeno, Luis Sánchez Fernández, Carlos Delgado Kloos,
Peter T. Breuer, and Fernando Paniagua Martín

Departamento de Ingeniería Telemática
Universidad Carlos III de Madrid,
Avda. Universidad, 30, E-28911 Leganés, Madrid, Spain

Abstract. The Web has rapidly expanded not only as the largest human
knowledge repository, but also as a way to develop online applications
that may be used for many different tasks. Wrapper agents may automate these tasks for the user. However, developing these wrapper agents
for automating tasks on the Web is rather expensive, and they usually
require a lot of maintenance effort since Web pages are not strongly
structured.
This paper introduces two programming languages for automating tasks
on the *legacy* Web developing low cost, robust wrapper agents that may
navigate the Web emulating browsers and may process data from the
Web automating some user's behaviours. These languages are based on
formal methods and W3C standards and are suitable for the legacy *deep
Web*, automating tasks like data mining or information integration from
different sources. A platform providing execution support to agents developed in these languages has been provided.

1 Introduction

In order to automate user's navigation tasks on the Web, agents that navigate
through Web pages can be used. An agent can integrate data gathered from
heterogeneous Web sources and process them properly by just emulating the
behaviour of a user behind a browser. With such agents, less user interactivity
is required during navigation, larger amounts of Web data can be managed and
complex data processing can be performed without overwhelming the user during
the navigation process.

Robots like [2,1,18,3] may be used for some simple specific tasks. However,
these *crawlers* are oriented to a specific task, and can not be used to navigate
through the *deep Web*, i.e., the Web which is dynamically built according to
user's requests by querying server side databases and other online applications.
Agents being able to navigate through the *deep Web* in order to perform a
specific task must properly automate, not only the behaviour provided by the
user to the browser, i.e., selecting which links are to be followed, which forms are
to be submitted, how form fields must be filled in and when to stop navigation,
but also other kind of actions not so well directly supported by browsers, like
relevant data extraction, and data processing.

However, developing these agents is rather expensive for many reasons.

J.M. Cueva Lovelle et al. (Eds.): ICWE 2003, LNCS 2722, pp. 58–67, 2003.
© Springer-Verlag Berlin Heidelberg 2003

- Web pages usually have similar markup style for similar data within the same source. This can be used to build data extraction rules that can extract relevant data embedded within retrieved HTML pages. However, Web pages are visualization oriented, irregular semi-structured sources of information [9], so the step of extracting relevant data embedded in HTML pages is not simple.
- Many Web sites have been designed to be used only by specific browsers. These sites may not be properly navigated by other browsers, because accessibility guidelines like [19,17] were not considered by their designers. This implies that agents will have accessibility problems too.
- Agents should be able to automate tasks for the user, not only on experimental simple XML-based environments, but also on the legacy Web, i.e., the visualization-oriented Web which has been built during the last few years on Internet. This involves dealing with large differences across Web sites.

Developing an automated navigation agent for the Web involves a great programming effort. Web data are embedded in visualization oriented, badly structured, heterogeneous and difficult to be processed HTML pages. The ever changing Web may easily stop these programs from running properly, so a great maintenance effort is also needed. As a result, methods for easily developing agents that may robustly navigate through the *deep Web* are needed. These methods should allow programmers to reduce maintenance costs by improving readability and simplicity, allowing the user to encapsulate code in user defined functions and using standards-based, simple but powerful, components that can be easily combined to build easily any extraction rule or data processing behaviour without having to write too many lines of code.

2   Related Work

Most software engineering techniques oriented to the Web have been applied to the development of Web enabled applications running on the *server side*. The purpose of these projects, like [5] is to develop efficient applications able to process user's requests correctly, without providing pages with error messages and maintaining internal data structures in a consistent state.

Some projects, however, have been oriented to facilitate the development of *client side* Web applications. Data extraction from HTML pages has traditionally been implemented with custom-defined languages based on lexical analyzers and parsers, where regular expressions are applied to detect expected parts of a HTML document, treating Web pages just as plain text files. Examples of this approach can be found in [4,6,7,15,11] . In these cases, special care must be taken in order to avoid that extraction rules may be broken by simple internal representation changes at Web pages, like spacings, case sensitiveness or attribute orderings. This approach, yet powerful, since it can be applied to any text file, not only HTML pages, can be considered as a low level solution because the tree-like structure of the page is not considered and rules can't be applied only to selected nodes. Another problem is that most of the proposed regular expression based rules, appear quite complex to many users (programmers included), since many of these projects define their own extraction language.

Recent projects [16,8] prefer to approach this issue by applying XML techniques, like DOM [21] programming or XSLT [20] transformation rules, to dynamically XML-ized Web pages. XSLT is then used to transform incoming XML-ized Web pages into well formed documents that can be processed further. This is a higher level approach, but something more than simple XML transformation is usually needed to properly process document's information. In fact, better than well formed XML documents, structured data directly processable by user defined computation routines are often preferred. DOM is a much more powerful solution which can solve this issue, but since it has a lower level of abstraction, more lines of code are required to be developed and to be maintained when a simple modification in the markup design of a Web site may appear. XPath has been designed as a language for addressing parts of XML documents. XPath expressions may easily fit in a single line and are well understood by many people. XPath 1.0 is a good option for selecting nodes in a document only if no complex processing need to be specified, so it becomes a good option for XSLT. More complex treatments can be specified with the new XPath 2.0 draft [22], but most of its new capabilities, have not been completely defined yet.

None of the approaches above have adopted a well known formal method as a software engineering technique for simplifying the development and reducing the maintenance costs of these agents. Software engineering techniques to develop robust agents able to navigate in a browser-oriented Web are needed nowadays to reduce navigation costs for many users who find tasks on the Web difficult.

3   Types of Automated Navigation

Manual navigation, i.e., navigation with browsers is based on interaction with the user. Users are required to build navigation paths by selecting which links are to be followed. Users need to visualize data on the screen in order to decide which action should be next performed. Browsers have no user autonomy and are unaware of the user's targets, but they can be used on any Web site. Manual navigation with browsers may be compared to sea-diver's costumes. Users may navigate through the *deep Web*, but they can visit only small depths and explore short navigation paths.

With generic non-site-adapted robots, some simple tasks can be automated. These robots use to visit all pages in a domain in order to perform the same simple predefined action over all those pages, without considering their particular semantics or structure. Robots can be compared to ships. They can be used on any Web site, and explore long navigation paths, but they can only explore its surface, without having deep access to the contents of online databases.

With generic site-adapted agents, more complex tasks can be automated. Generic agents are configured with external parameters in order to perform a specialized task on the Web. The Semantic Web [12] could be considered as an example. With external declarative metadata, ontologies and semantic rules associated to Web pages, intelligent agents are required to find the results of a user's query within a page in a domain. These agents have no *a priori* navigation path to be followed, so they have to build it dynamically (like users in manual navigation), every time trying to choose the best promising link in a target guided basis. However, these agents can only navigate through metadata-enabled pages, so not all paths can be followed. These metadata guided navigation could be similar to built-in tunnels under the sea. They allow users to inspect the *deep Web*, but only metadata-enabled paths can be followed. Paths are implicitly defined in external metadata and there is no guarantee that the same path ending to a correct solution can be followed again in the future, unless recorded.

With task-customized agents, tasks involving a big amount of data and long navigation paths may be efficiently performed. By pre-programming a site-customized static (but flexible with alternatives) navigation path, specialized code can have programmed access to HTML pages retrieved during navigation, emulating user's behaviour completely, including choices and repetitiveness. Implicit programmed semantics allows data to be properly processed according to the user's wishes. No metadata is needed and well known paths will be followed in a deterministic way, without needing to infer which is the best link to be followed next. However, these programs, usually called *wrapper agents*, are usually difficult to be programmed and maintained, and can only be used on the Web site they were designed to navigate. Wrapper agents could be compared to small non tripulated remote-controlled submarines or *bathyscaphes*. They can navigate farther and deeper than humans. Since they don't need external metadata, they can navigate anywhere, taking into account particular programmer's preferences. However, they are very expensive to build and maintain, and a path to be followed has to be specified according to the Web site. Table 1 summarizes major differences among different kinds of Web navigation agents.

Table 1. Classification of Web navigation agents

	Manual	**Generic non adapted**	**Generic adapted**	**Customized**
Example	Browsers	Robots	Semantic Web Agents	Wrapper agents
Algorithm	User	Simple action	Target guided	Pre-programmed
Semantics	User	None	Declarative metadata	Implicit in program
Path building	User	Cover all pages	Dynamic	Static, but flexible
Maintenance	None	None	Easy (declarative)	Difficult (program)
Deep Web	Yes (small depths)	No	If metadata enabled	Yes (any depth)
Suitable	Any Web	Any Web	If metadata enabled	A particular Web site
Metaphor	Sea-diver's costume	A ship	Tunnel under the sea	Bathyscaphe

4 Steps of Automated Navigation

Navigation through the Web involves several actions that have to be executed sequentially. Basically, these actions can be classified as implicit or explicit. Implicit actions should be transparently performed by the agent's platform execution. Explicit actions need to be explicitly declared in a task specification.

4.1 Implicit Actions

Actions can be considered implicit if the user is not supposed to be aware of them. They are typically transparently managed by browsers without requiring user intervention. Management of HTTP headers and the cookies' database, SSL support, internal reparation of badly constructed pages, query-string coding and execution support for scripting languages (like JavaScript) embedded in HTML pages are some representative examples.

4.2 Explicit Actions

Actions can be considered explicit if the user can be considered responsible of their execution. Browsers can't execute these actions by their own, so they require user intervention in manual navigation. Tasks can be described as a sequence of explicit actions.

Data extraction. Data extraction involves selecting relevant data from Web pages and extracting them for being further processed. Data extraction is the most critical action involved in task's automation on the Web, because it plays a relevant role on every navigation step. Following a link firstly involves selecting which relevant link should be followed and extracting the URL it contains. Submitting a form firstly involves selecting all form fields contained within and filling in them accordingly to their nature and user's aims. Other user defined processings, like data integration, comparisons and other behaviours, also need complex data extractions to be previously performed.

Data extraction is performed visually on the screen by the users, requiring them to visualize several windows and perform some scrolling. In automated navigation, data extraction can be automated by selecting relevant data from semi-structured documents. This is not always easy, and is clearly dependant on the page's structure. This task can be challenged by data extraction rules based on markup structure and its regularity, selecting those data that match some *expected* format. However, this markup structure is usually too much visualization oriented and may be changed with no advice, so these rules need maintenance to keep on working properly. Techniques mentioned on section 2 which can be used for developing these rules are suitable for keeping these efforts reduced. Programming mechanisms for keeping data extraction rules simple, robust and easy to maintain are highly recommended.

Data structuration. Relevant data extracted from a page might be processed several times during navigation, so they should be conveniently stored in a structured repository. In manual navigation, users are usually required to do this by their own. That's why they use to memorize data (usually in the short-term user's memory), write them in a paper or saving them wherever the user might consider. However, user's memory nor papers nor editor's windows are adequate repositories for being accessed during automated navigation. Computer's memory variables or structured files are preferred instead. Web pages might be internally saved as trees or as a sequence of bytes, depending on the platform's capabilities. Tree-like structuration, like [21] is usually preferred because it provides better capabilities for document inspection.

When saving selected parts of a document to specialized repositories, textual data obtained from semistructured documents might be transformed into suitable data types for computation, like numbers, dates, booleans, strings or perhaps, nodes in a tree-like structure. Programming effort is then reduced to the management of these simple and already known repositories and performing these simple transformations, so just a few lines of code can solve this issue. Manual navigation has no support for this, so the user is supposed to apply his own contextual semantics during navigation.

Follow links. Data are usually distributed among several documents that have to be retrieved by following links. This is an easy to do action in both manual and automated navigation. In manual navigation, it is a semiautomated action where the user just has to click in a link with her pointing device. In automated navigation, this involves a single call to a GET primitive, available in several libraries for multiple programming languages. Programming effort is reduced to set expected parameters to this primitive.

Fill in forms. Filling in form fields is a relatively easy to do action in both manual and automated navigation. In manual navigation, it is a semiautomated action where the user just has to set up proper values on every viewable field, guided by the browser. In automated navigation, this usually involves establishing a mapping between form fields and their values. Programming effort can be reduced to code a single sentence for each form field modifying it's default value, according to the values selected by the user and the form field's nature. This is usually performed within an internal structure representing the page's form, usually a list of form fields.

Submit forms. Submitting forms is an easy to do action in both manual and automated navigation. In manual navigation, it is a semiautomated action where the user just has to click on a submit button with her pointing device. In automated navigation, this involves a single call to a GET or POST primitive, available in several libraries for multiple programming languages. Programming effort is reduced to set expected parameters to this primitive.

Data processing. Finally, structured data can be processed according to the task's aims, without being dependant on the Web sites' singularities. Data processing involves data comparisons, aggregation, text processing, sorting data and producing some computed results. Data processing might be rather heterogeneous according to the task which is being performed, so it is usually performed by the user directly with her mental capabilities on manual navigation, but programmable in user defined code in automated navigation. For example, finding the best hotel for the user taking into account several criteria (price, place, distance to relevant places, breakfast included, sauna, spa, ...) can only be performed if the user specifies relevance for those criteria. These user defined computing can be programmed, not only in user defined routines, but also on external programs.

As can be seen in table 2, only three from six actions are supported by browsers during manual navigation. Users need to participate in all of them during manual navigation, but semiautomated support from browsers can only be found at simplest actions. For automated navigation, a single line of code can easily implement also the simplest actions. However, more complex actions need to be programmed completely by the user, so they usually require more lines of code.

Table 2. Explicit actions for Web tasks

Explicit action	Manual Navigation	Automated Navigation
Data extraction	User	Data extraction rules based on markup
Data structuration	User	Structured repositories
Follow links	User + Browser	Call to GET primitive
Fill in forms	User + Browser	Metadata, programmer's code
Submit forms	User + Browser	Call to POST/GET primitives
Data processing	User	User defined routines, external programs, ...

5   XTendedPath: A XPath 2.0 Extension for Extraction and Manipulation of XML Documents

XTendedPath has been designed as a XPath 2.0 [22] extension for extracting data from XML documents. XPath-like data extraction rules may be easily specified in a single line, taking also into account the internal tree-like structure of XML documents. However, XPath only allows addressing whole XML nodes within that tree, their whole text or their attributes, so it results difficult to express other portions of XML documents. XTendedPath provides a set of simple yet powerful primitives which implement most of the main XPath features, like axis, predicates, variables, sequences, quantification, conditional and iteration in a functional notation. However, some features not considered in XPath 2.0 have been added to provide new functionalities like addressing ranges (parts of a document not fully attached to nodes), manipulating document or user supporting user definable routines.

- XPointer's ranges and points [23] have been included as a XTendedPath data type. These data types are not considered in XPath, but they provide great flexibility to address small pieces of text.
- With document manipulation, XTendedPath expressions may change document's internal structure by adding or removing nodes within the document or changing attribute values within nodes. This is useful to eliminate non desired parts of documents or to fill in forms.
- With user definable routines support, XTendedPath programmers may encapsulate their own reusable lambda expressions [14]. By allowing lambda expressions to be considered as a first order data type, a higher order set of functions may be applied to solve some common tasks by manipulating sequences of data extracted from Web sites.

6   XPlore: A MSC-Based Language for Navigation and Data Processing on the Web

XPlore has been designed as a programming languages suitable for processing data obtained from the Web by XTendedPath expressions and defining explicit navigation paths for automating tasks on the Web. XPlore is based on the well known MSC [10] formal method from the ITU (Telecommunication Union). MSC graphs provide a high level specification of behaviours expected by distributed components exchanging messages. Since their birth in 1992, MSC specification have received important enhancements for improving its ability to describe complex communication systems. XPlore is a Web adapted language based on MSC. With XPlore, the programmer can easily define his own specific navigation paths for traversing links in a pre-programmed way in order to automate well known tasks on the Web. XPlore also provides suitable mechanisms for processing all those data obtained from those visited pages.

6.1   Navigation Paths

Building well known navigation paths is not difficult with XPlore. XPlore provides easy-to-call and detail-enabled primitives for sending HTTP commands like GET or POST to Web servers and receiving their responses, a desirable feature according to table 2. However, GET and POST primitives are not enough for building longer-than-one-step session based navigation paths. Complex navigation paths can be considered as the skeleton of a task on the Web. Navigation paths must be properly specified prior to data processing. For that reason, it is required that these GET and POST primitives may be properly parameterized with URLs which may not be a priori known and which must be obtained during the navigation process. These links can be obtained with XTendedPath rules, except for the first URL to be visited. Without such rules, the program would not be able to select the proper link to be followed. It is also needed to adjust low level parameters like some HTTP headers for maintaining a session with the server. A fully detailed navigation path is a guarantee that all needed documents can be retrieved from the Web.

6.2 Data Processing

Once relevant data are extracted from visited pages with XTendedPath data extraction rules, extracted data must be properly structured and stored in a convenient repository. XPlore provides typical programming data types for storing atomic values like numbers, booleans, strings or complex structures like lists and objects. XPlore also manages references to nodes in a document. User defined routines written in Java can take those data as arguments and process them according to the programmer's aims. However, simple arithmetical or string data processing may be specified with some pre-defined in-line XPlore primitives, so simple processing need not always be specified in user defined routines. External processes may also be called for invoking legacy programs.

A fully commented example of a XPlore program accessing a Yahoo! mail account can be found at [13].

7 Conclusions

Information retrieval is only the first step towards Web task automation. Once all relevant pages are retrieved, further computing needs to be applied to the data embedded in those pages. Integrating data from Web pages into a program requires giving structure to those data, according to extraction rules which are usually based on markup regularities. These extraction rules, which enclose some semantics for the task of the user, can be easily broken when expressed in general not XML suitable formalisms, like regular expressions. XML related standards like XPath have been defined to solve many issues, but they can poorly be applied to define complex computing. In this paper, a well known formal method (Message Sequence Charts) has been adapted for the construction and maintenance of Web clients that automate the Web and a extraction language has been based on several W3C Recommendations.

Acknowledgements. The work reported in this paper has been partially funded by the project *TEL1999-0207* of the Spanish Ministry of Science and Research.

References

1. Altavista. www.altavista.com.
2. Google. www.google.com.
3. Wget tool. sunsite.auc.dk/pub/infosystems/wget/.

4. A. S. F. Azavant. Building light-weight wrappers for legacy web data-sources using w4f. *International Conference on Very Large Databases (VLDB)*, 1999.
5. J. Baeten, H. van Beek, and S. Mauw. An MSC based representation of DiCons. In *Proceedings of the 10th SDL Forum*, pages 328–347, Copenhagen, Denmark, June 2001.
6. S. Chawathe, H. Garcia-Molina, J. Hammer, K. Ireland, Y. Papakonstantinou, J. D. Ullman, and J. Widom. The TSIMMIS project: Integration of heterogeneous information sources. In *16th Meeting of the Information Processing Society of Japan*, pages 7–18, Tokyo, Japan, 1994.
7. C. P. David Buttler, Ling Liu. A fully automated extraction system for the world wide web. *IEEE ICDCS-21*, April 16-19 2001.
8. D. Florescu, A. Grunhagen, and D. Kossmann. Xl: An xml programming language for web service specification and composition. In *WWW 11th conference*, 2002.
9. R. Goldman, J. McHugh, and J. Widom. From semistructured data to XML: Migrating the lore data model and query language. In *Workshop on the Web and Databases (WebDB '99)*, pages 25–30, 1999.
10. ITU-T. Recommendation z.120: Message sequence chart (msc). In *Formal description techniques (FDT)*, Geneva, Switzerland, 1997.
11. L. Liu, C. Pu, and W. Han. XWRAP: An XML-enabled wrapper construction system for web information sources. In *ICDE*, pages 611–621, 2000.
12. S. Lu, M. Dong, and F. Fotouhi. The semantic web: Opportunities and challenges for next-generation web applications. *Information Research*, 7(4), 2002. Special Issue on the Semantic Web.
13. V. Luque-Centeno, L. Sanchez-Fernandez, C. Delgado-Kloos, P. T. Breuer, and M. E. Gonzalo-Cabellos. Standards-based languages for programming web navigation assistants. In *5th IEEE International Workshop on Networked Appliances*, pages 70–75, Liverpool, U.K., October 2002.
14. G. Michaelson. An introduction to functional programming through lambda calculus. In *Addison-Wesley, XV, 320 S. - ISBN 0-201-17812-5*, 1988.
15. I. Muslea, S. Minton, and C. A. Knoblock. Hierarchical wrapper induction for semistructured information sources. *Autonomous Agents and Multi-Agent Systems*, 4(1/2):93–114, 2001.
16. J. Myllymaki. Effective web data extraction with standard XML technologies. In *World Wide Web 10th Conference, Hong Kong*, pages 689–696, 2001.
17. W3C. Policies relating to web accessibility. http://www.w3.org/WAI/Policy/.
18. W3C. W3c link checker. validator.w3.org/checklink.
19. W3C. Web content accessibility guidelines 1.0. *W3C Recommendation 5-May-1999*, 1999.
20. W3C. Xsl transformations (xslt) version 1.0. *W3C Recommendation 16 November 1999*, 1999.
21. W3C. Document object model (dom) level 2. *W3C Recommendation 13 November, 2000*, 2000.
22. W3C. Xml path language (xpath) 2.0. *W3C Working Draft 15 November 2002*, 2002.
23. W3C. Xml pointer language (xpointer). *W3C Working Draft 16 August 2002*, 2002.

Agent-Based Privilege Negotiation for E-commerce on World Wide Web

Richard Au, Ming Yao, and Mark Looi

Information Security Research Centre
School of Software Engineering and Data Communications
Queensland University of Technology
Brisbane, Qld 4001, Australia
{w.au, m.yao, m.looi}@qut.edu.au

1 Introduction

The World Wide Web (Web) is an important channel for business-to-customer transactions in E-commerce. Most commercial organisations have the basic goal to outreach as many potential customers as possible and establish business relationships with them. Before granting privileges to access some protected resources, organisational systems must facilitate the ability to assess the trustworthiness of entities (users or applications) they encounter. For E-commerce on the Web, a typical service provider faces a wide spectrum of potential users without any pre-existing relationship. The question of interest is how these processes of trust establishment and authorisation can be conducted effectively and efficiently.

2 A New Agent-Based Authorisation Framework

Applying the concept of mobile agents, we design a new authorisation architecture that supports automated privilege negotiation in the Web environment.

Referring to figure 1, our framework consists of four main components:

- An infrastructure of domain-based security servers for trust distribution across different administrative domains [3].
- Authorisation tokens for secure delivery of user credentials [1].
- Secure Client Agent Environment(SCAE) for hosting multiple agents and providing them with execution resources and security protection [2].
- A family of privilege negotiation agents for establishing trust and authorisation.

2.1 Privilege Negotiation Agents for Distributed Authorisation

In this paper, we propose a novel family of *Privilege Negotiation Agents* which can migrate from various servers to the client's secure agent platform. These agents are trusted representatives of their parent servers and they work collaboratively in the negotiation process for trust establishment and authorisation. The family consists of three types of members:

J.M. Cueva Lovelle et al. (Eds.): ICWE 2003, LNCS 2722, pp. 68–71, 2003.
© Springer-Verlag Berlin Heidelberg 2003

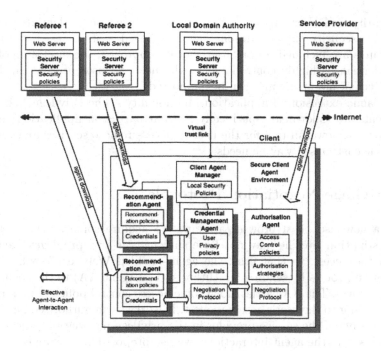

Fig. 1. Agent-based Authorisation Framework

- **Authorisation Agent(AA) from Service Provider** – It performs the enforcement of access control with functions of:
  - Assessing authorisation credentials from client.
  - Providing access control and resource information to clients.
  - Making authorisation decision.
  - Keeping authorisation states in the workflow of the access.
- **Credential Management Agent(CMA) from Client** – It works on behalf of the user and performs the following tasks:
  - Managing the credentials delivery and storage.
  - Making requests to referee servers for recommendations.
  - Enforcing user privacy policies.
- **Recommendation Agent(RA) from Referee Server** – It provides certified credentials according to its recommendation policies and CMA's request.

2.2 Advantageous Features

Our user-centred and agent-based approach to authorisation can enhance distributed access control systems in the following ways:

- User Customisation - The use of agents provides better support for heterogeneous environments as it can express more the user's context and provide more interactions with the servers.

- Security and User Privacy - Authorisation based on credentials can be of higher security than traditional identity-based systems as more user attributes are included. In our user-centred approach, the disclosure of user's credentials is highly controllable by the user. So user privacy can be well protected and anonymity can be supported.
- Dynamic extension of application functionality - The Privilege Negotiation Agents are tailor-made specifically for that particular application and they provide a powerful tool for the user to access remote services and resources in the customised way he needs.

3   Privilege Negotiation Protocols

When a new user at a browser attempts to acquire some services/resources at a destination site, he may not have sufficient, if any, privileges/credentials to gain the access. In that case, the agent-enabled Web server will start the registration process by sending an Authorisation Agent(AA) to the client secure agent platform. The AA carries along some access control policies and strategies corresponding to the user's access request. It works as an authorised and trusted representative of the service provider in the privilege negotiation process.

To illustrate the agent interactions, we use propositional symbols to express various services and credentials.

$$S \leftarrow P (C_1,....,C_n)$$

The above expression denotes that resource/service S has an authorisation policy $P(C_1,....,C_n)$ and P is a Boolean expression involving user credentials, $C_1,....,C_n$, required. If sufficient credentials are submitted so that P becomes true, then S is granted. It is also possible to have $C \leftarrow P(C_1,....C_n)$, which shows a policy P for combining a number of credentials into another one, C. In practice, a policy may be either *public* (i.e. can be disclosed to users at any time) or *confidential* (i.e. disclosure are restricted).

Based on the client's request for service S, AA can ask for the necessary credentials according to its authorisation policy P_{AA}.

$$\mathbf{AA} : S \leftarrow P_{AA}(C_1,....,C_n)$$

On the client platform, the Credential Management Agent(CMA) works on behalf of the user. It enforces the user privacy policies and manages credential delivery and storage, etc. CMA holds information of a finite set of credentials that are kept by the user and/or the referee servers.

$$\mathbf{CMA}: \{C_1,......C_m\}$$

Upon receiving the credential requirements from AA, CMA can contact the appropiate referee servers and invite download of Recommendation Agents

(RA). When all the agents AA, CMA and RA are present on the client platform, they can work collaboratively and conduct privilege negotiation dynamically. RA provides recommendation (certified credential) R according to the user's request Q, his existing credentials C_m and local recommendation policy P_{RA}. (Note: C_m may be submitted by client or stored in the server repository, depending on individual system.)

RA: $R \leftarrow P_{RA}(C_m, Q)$

When necessary, RA or AA can make suggestions to CMA for inviting more RA to join in the negotiation. Based on the user privacy policy P_{CMA}, CMA can either discard or forward the recommendation R to AA as certified credential C. It is also possible to develop mechanisms to allow CMA to forward only a selected portion of R to AA and hide the other parts [4]. With CMA as an intermediary, trust establishment and authorisation can be completed without revealing irrelevant credentials to the service provider. Also user privacy can be well protected.

CMA: $C \leftarrow P_{CMA}(R)$

AA can collect a set of submitted credentials from a user, $\{C_1,....C_k\}$, and evaluate it using all the authorisation policies. When $P_{AA}(C_1,....C_n)$ becomes true, access right to service S will be granted to the client by AA itself or the service provider server. Otherwise AA can make further request to the client asking for extra credentials.

4 Future Work and Conclusion

In this paper, we have proposed a new credential-based authorisation framework using *Privilege Negotiation Agents* to enhance the authorisation service in the Web environment. For further research, we can put efforts to develop an universal set of languages with formal semantics for expressing policies and credentials for interactions between various agents and servers.

References

1. Au, R., Looi, M. & Ashley, P. (2000) *Cross-Domain One-Shot Authorisation Using Smart Cards*. Proceedings of 7th ACM Conference on Computer and Communication Security, pages 220–227.
2. Au, R., Yao, M., Looi, M. & Ashley, P. (2002). *Secure Client Agent Environment for World Wide Web*. Proceedings of Third International Conference on E-commerce and Web Technology, LNCS 2455, Springer, pages 234–244.
3. Au, R., Looi, M. & Ashley, P. (2001) *Automated Cross-organisational Trust Establishment on Extranets*. Proceedings of the Workshop on Information Technology for Virtual Enterprises(ITVE' 2001), pages 3–11.
4. Brands, S. (2002) *A Technical Overview of Digital Credentials*. URL: citeseer.nj.nec.com/brands02technical.html

An Automated Negotiation Model for M-commerce Using Mobile Agents

Fernando Menezes Matos and Edmundo R.M. Madeira

IC - Institute of Computing
UNICAMP - University of Campinas
13083-970 Campinas, SP, Brazil
{fernando.matos, edmundo}@ic.unicamp.br

Abstract. This work proposes an automated negotiation model between two participants, for m-commerce, using mobile agents and considering the mobile device personalization through the use of profiles in the negotiation.

Keywords: M-commerce, Mobile Agents, Automated Negotiation

1   Introduction

Due to the growing number of cellular phones and PDAs, more and more people desire to perform activities using them. One of these activities is mobile commerce (m-commerce), where a user can buy a product or service no matter where he is.

However, to do this it is necessary to develop techniques and communication mechanisms for mobile commerce, which satisfy the requirements and the limitations of the mobile infrastructure, like the reduced screen size of the cellular phones and the low bandwidth of the wireless networks [1].

Another issue to take into account in mobile commerce is the fact that mobile devices are personal. Due to this, it is interesting the development and use of a user profile. If the transactions could be performed using this profile, they will become more similar to what is done in the real life, guaranteeing a great purchase personalization.

This paper proposes an automated negotiation model for mobile commerce using mobile agents based on a preexisting negotiation model for electronic commerce [2]. The extensions presented here, take into account the low processing power of the portable devices, the small screen size of these devices, the low bandwidth of the wireless networks and mainly the user profile.

2   The Negotiation Model for Mobile Commerce

2.1   Model

The model works as follows. There is an application in the mobile device, called *BuyApplication*, used by the client to make purchases. Each time a mobile network user wishes to make a purchase, *BuyApplication* connects to another application called *CallApplication*, which is hosted in a server in the fixed network,

J.M. Cueva Lovelle et al. (Eds.): ICWE 2003, LNCS 2722, pp. 72–75, 2003.
© Springer-Verlag Berlin Heidelberg 2003

and sends information about the product which the user wants, like its features, the desired price and the maximum price to offer. After that, *CallApplication* creates an original buy agent for each incoming request. Fig. 1(a) shows the creation of n original buy agents due to n buy requests. Each original buy agent creates a certain number of buy agent copies to negotiate with the sell agents. Fig. 1(b) illustrates that the original buy agent A1 created two buy agent copies that negotiate with two sell agents, related to an incoming request. The proportion between sell agents and buy agents is one to one

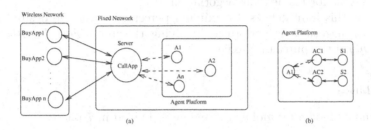

Fig. 1. Communication in the Proposed Model.

After the buy agents have been created, they move to the host of the selected sellers to negotiate with them. Once there, they start to negotiate until they reach an agreement, or one party rejects the other's offer. At the end of the negotiation, each buy agent sends its results to the original buy agent to present to the user.

2.2 Profiles

One of the inherent features of mobile devices is their customization. Hence, the creation of a user profile for mobile commerce is important. In this work, we have created two types of profiles. The first one is related to the user and contains the following items:

Number of Negotiations: this item defines the maximum number of buy agent copies created by the original buy agent to negotiate;
Number of Results: this item defines the maximum number of responses that will return to the user;
Automatic Purchase: this item defines if the original buy agent must perform the purchase after all results have returned, without previous consultation to the user.

The other profile type is the purchase profile and contains the following items:

Fast Negotiation: if this item is enabled, the original buy agent performs the purchase of the first incoming result below the desired price plus a percentage (*variation*), without informing the user about the negotiation results, and it informs all other buy agents to stop the negotiation;

Fidelity: this item defines if the user wants to keep fidelity to a seller. The
original buy agent performs the purchase of the first incoming result if its
price is lower than the desired price plus a percentage and if it is a result
from that specific seller;

Connected: this item defines if the user wishes to keep connected to the server
during the negotiation. In this case, the original buy agent informs the
user about the results. Otherwise, information of any pending negotiation
is recorded in the fixed network, and made available when the user recon-
nects. Then, the user can establish connection with the original buy agent
responsible for his pending negotiation;

Variation: this item defines a maximum percentage over the desired price to
offer in negotiations performed involving the items *Fast Negotiation* and
Fidelity of the purchase profile.

2.3   Phases

The proposed model for mobile commerce is divided in 7 phases.

Connection Phase: when the user wants to start a new negotiation, he sends
a message to the fixed network, requesting a new negotiation process. This
message contains the desired product price and its features. When the request arrives, the application in the fixed network creates an original buy
agent responsible for performing the negotiation.

Call Phase: in this phase a multicast message is sent by the original buy agent
to the sell agents, in order to verify which of them have the desired product.

Selection Phase: in this phase, the original buy agent selects which sell agents
it will negotiate with, amongst the sell agents which responded affirmatively
in the prior phase.

Negotiation Phase: in this phase, a copy of the original buy agent is sent for each
host of the sell agents selected in the previous phase. After that, the price
negotiation is performed. This is done using proposals and counterproposals
between the agents. The agreement between the agents occurs when the price
offered by the sell agent is lower than or equal to the price proposed by the
buy agent. An agreement finishes the negotiation. Another way to terminate
the negotiation is when the buy agent should propose a price higher than
the maximum the client would pay.

After an agreement is reached, the buy agent requests a discount to the sell
agent upon the agreed price, through the *Discount* message. The sell agent
may grant the discount or not, depending if it is using any fidelity service
and if the buyer is its client or not.

Analysis Phase: this is the phase where decisions are made taking into account
almost every information contained in the user and purchase profiles. The
possibilities are as follows.

Fast Negotiation: The original buy agent doesn't wait for the return of all
responses. When the first result from a buy agent, in which the obtained
price is lower than the desired price plus a percentage (defined in the user
profile by the *variation* item) returns, the original buy agent performs

the purchase and informs all other buy agents to stop the negotiation. This kind of negotiation is extremely useful in mobile commerce since mobile devices have little autonomy due to its dependency on batteries;

Fidelity: if this item is enabled, when the first result in which the obtained price is lower than the desired price plus a percentage (defined in the user profile by the *variation* item) returns and the result came from a seller the user wishes to keep fidelity to, the original buy agent performs the purchase;

Automatic Purchase: if this option is enabled, the original buy agent waits the return of all responses and then it asks for the copy that got the lower price to perform the purchase. If it is not enabled, the original buy agent sorts the offers in increasing order of price and sends them to the application hosted in the mobile device to be presented to the user, considering the number of results defined by the user.

Presentation Phase: this phase starts when an original buy agent has all results and it has already taken the decisions about them, using the user and purchase profiles. If the *Connected* item is enabled, the agent sends the results to the user. Otherwise, it waits for the user to establish a connection and to request the results.

Conclusion Phase: in this phase the negotiation is concluded. Either the user chooses one of the presented proposals or is informed about the purchase that was performed.

3   Conclusion

This paper proposes an automated negotiation model, using mobile agents, for mobile commerce. The contributions are: a-) the definition of user and purchase profiles. That are used mainly in the Analysis phase to make decisions about the product purchase; b-) all the heavy computation is performed in the fixed network, by the CallApplication and the agent platform, and do not overload the mobile device. It also does not overload the communication channel, because it imposes a small data traffic between the mobile device and the fixed network; and c-) the user doesn't need to be connected during the negotiation, since he can request the results afterward.

References

1. Tsalgatidou, A., Veijalainen, J., Pitoura, E.: Challenges in Mobile Electronic Commerce. In: Proceedings of Iec 2000. Third Internacional Conference on Innovation through E-Commerce. Manchester England (2000) 169–174
2. Ueyama, J., Madeira, E.R.M.: An Automated Negotiation Model for Electronic Commerce. In: Proceedings of the Fifth IEEE Internationl Symposium on Autonomous Decentralized Systems – ISADS'01. Dallas USA (2001) 29–36

A Fully Anonymous Electronic Payment Scheme for B2B[*]

Josep Lluís Ferrer-Gomila, Magdalena Payeras-Capellà, and Ll. Huguet-Rotger

Universitat de les Illes Balears
Carretera de Valldemossa km. 7.5, Palma de Mallorca, 07122, Spain
{dijjfg, mpayeras, dmilhr0}@clust.uib.es

Abstract. In this paper we present a fully anonymous (for payer and payee) electronic payment scheme for B2B transactions involving high amounts, without using tamper resistant devices, without pseudonyms, and preventing double spending. Schemes with detection of double spending at deposit are not well suited for high amount transactions (merchants and banks don't want to assume potential high losses). Our scheme allows anonymity revocation in case of illegal activities (using prevention techniques).

1 Introduction

B2B transactions demand a specific electronic payment scheme, because amounts can be high (more than 1000 dollars). It should be "impossible" to counterfeit money. It should not be based on tamper resistant devices [1, 4] (an attack could be very attractive). Nobody wants to assume possible double spending (with high amounts). So, it is not useful to detect double spending a posteriori, and we can not use transferable [5, 9] and/or off-line [2, 3, 7, 8] schemes. The anonymity should be absolute (as in paper-based transactions, e.g., for undeclared earnings). Otherwise, merchants will continue using paper money. We have to achieve the untraceabilty property (not achieved in [1, 6]). We don't want to use pseudonyms because it is not a real anonymity. The behavior of the bank has to be verifiable. Merchants and the bank have the necessary communications infrastructure to carry out on-line transactions. Finally, anonymity should be revocable if the appropriate authorities order it. In fact, some of the previous requirements were listed in [9]. But we have to keep in mind that this electronic payment scheme is specific for B2B and for high amounts.

Here we present a scheme that avoids counterfeiting, forgery and double spending, without using tamper resistant devices (nobody assumes undesirable risks). Untraceability and anonymity are guaranteed without using pseudonyms. Finally, our scheme allows the anonymity revocation in case of illegal activities (using prevention techniques when the illegal activity is suspected).

---

[*] This work has been partially supported by the Balearic Islands Government under project PRDIB-2002GC3-18.

J.M. Cueva Lovelle et al. (Eds.): ICWE 2003, LNCS 2722, pp. 76–79, 2003.
© Springer-Verlag Berlin Heidelberg 2003

2   Fully Anonymous Electronic Payment Scheme

The presented scheme includes *withdrawal, transfer* and *deposit* sub-protocols. We use the term *e-note* to refer to the electronic bank notes. In the description of the protocol A is a merchant acting as a payer, B is the payee and F is the bank. Other notation and elements are as follows:

ID_X	identity of actor X
Q_i	amount to be withdrawn, transferred or deposited
Y, Z	concatenation of two messages (or tokens) Y and Z
$Sign_i(Y)$	digital signature of principal i on message Y
$i \rightarrow j: Y$	principal i sends message (or token) Y to principal j
$E_K(M)$	symmetric encryption of message M with key K
$PU_F(K)$	key K enciphered with the public key of the bank
$SN_i=H(SP_i)$	serial number (SN_i) of an *e-note*, hash of a random secret proof (SP_i)
$M_i= Sign_{Fx}(SN_i)$	signature on SN_i with a private key indicating value x

2.1   Withdrawal Sub-protocol

In the *withdrawal* sub-protocol, a merchant, A, requests an *e-note* to F. F creates an *e-note* and debits A's account:

1. $A \rightarrow F$: $ID_A, Q_1, SN_1, Sign_A(Q_1, SN_1)$
2. $F \rightarrow A$: Q_1, SN_1, M_1

A generates a random number SP_1 (the secret proof to validate the *e-note*), and it must be kept secret. SN_1 (the serial number of the future *e-note*) is a hashing of SP_1. A proves ownership of his account signing the serial number and the amount, Q_1. F's signature on SN_1, and SP_1, is the *e-note*. SN_1 will be used to prevent double spending of the *e-note*. A can prove the ownership with the knowledge of SP_1 and M_1.

To redeem an *e-note*, the owner must show the knowledge of the *e-note* secret proof (SP_1), but he is not forced to reveal his identity. If F saves all available information about the *e-note*, it could recognise that *e-note* at deposit, but thanks to the use of the *transfer* sub-protocol (see section 2.2), the bank (or the collusion of the bank and the merchant depositing the *e-note*) cannot reveal where A spent it. So payments will be anonymous and untraceables. And the scheme is secure against money forging.

2.2   Transfer Sub-protocol

When A wants to pay to B, A executes the following sub-protocol:

1. $A \rightarrow B$:   Purchase_order
2. $B \rightarrow A$: $Q_i, SN_i, Sign_B(Q_i, SN_i)$
3. $A \rightarrow F$: $PU_F(K), E_K(SN_j, M_j, SP_j, Q_i, SN_i, SN_r)$
4. $F \rightarrow A$: M_i, M_r
5. $A \rightarrow B$: SN_i, M_i

B sends to A a serial number (SN_i), the price of the item (Q_i) and the digital signature of the previous information, as a response to the *Purchase_order*, without revealing the secret proof (SP_i). A will request to F an *e-note* to pay B, with the serial number given by B (SN_i). A sends her *e-note* M_j to the bank, with the associated secret proof (SP_j). The request is encrypted with a session key (K), so nobody can intercept SP_j. A indicates the amount (Q_i) of the *e-note* M_j to be converted in the new *e-note* using SN_i. The remaining fraction Q_r (if $Q_i < Q_j$) will be used to create another *e-note* with serial number SN_r. F cannot find out the identities of the merchants.

If SN_j is found in the list of spent *e-notes*, F has detected a double spending attempt, and will abort the operation. If the *e-note* (SP_j, M_j) is valid, F creates the new *e-notes* M_i and M_r, and sends them to A. A knows the *e-note* M_i and SN_i, but A doesn't know SP_i. A stores the information related to the payment during an established period. This information can be requested in case of anonymity revocation. The scheme is anonymous for A, because B doesn't know the identity of A.

B checks the validity of the *e-note* M_i (verifying the signature of F). Only B knows SP_i and he is the only one that can spend that *e-note*. He doesn't need to contact F. Now, B has an *e-note* with the same properties that a withdrawn one. B can deposit it identifying his account. Also, B can use the *e-note* for a new payment, but a collusion between A and F will be able to trace B. To solve this problem B has to use the auto-transfer sub-protocol.

Transfer Sub-protocol Applied to Auto-transfer. A knows SN_i and B's identity. So, payments with that *e-note* could be traced by the collusion of A and F. The solution is the auto-transfer operation:

1. $B \rightarrow F$: $PU_F(K), E_K(SN_i, M_i, SP_i, Q_s, SN_s, SN_t)$
2. $F \rightarrow B$: M_s, M_t

B calculates SN_s and SN_t from the random secret proofs SP_s and SP_t, respectively. B requests F that a specific *e-note* is going to be transferred. B sends SP_i encrypted with a session key (and other information analogous to the previous case).

If the *e-note* is valid (e.g., not double spent), F creates two new *e-notes* with the new serial numbers and the required values, and SP_i is appended to the list of spent *e-notes*. F doesn't know who is the user auto-transferring the *e-note*. Furthermore, F cannot distinguish if the user is auto-transferring the total amount of the *e-note*, or if he is preparing a payment with a fraction of the *e-note* and auto-transferring the remaining part, or if he is preparing two payments.

2.3   Deposit Sub-protocol

In the *deposit* sub-protocol, it is necessary an identification of the merchant's account:

1. $B \rightarrow F$: $PU_F(K), E_K(ID_B, SN_i, M_i, SP_i, Q_i), Sign_B(ID_B, SN_i, M_i, SP_i, Q_i)$

B sends the secret proof SP_i, and some identifying information (to deposit money in the right account), all encrypted with a session key K. F checks the validity of the *e-note*, and if it is correct then credits B's account.

3 Conclusion: Fraud Protection and Privacy

We have achieved security requirements: *e-notes* cannot be counterfeited (thanks to the use of the bank private keys), overspending and double spending are avoided (*e-notes* are created after a debit in an user account, and the bank saves the list of redeemed serial numbers, deposited and transferred, with their secret proofs), and stolen *e-notes* cannot be redeemed (it is necessary the secret proof, and it is encrypted when is transmitted). On the other hand, our scheme provides anonymity and untraceability to payers and payees, thanks to the *auto-transfer* subprotocol. *E-notes* can be transferred multiple times without depositing and without any identification. Payments between the same pair of merchants are unlinkable. There isn't any relationship between them: new serial numbers are used in each payment.

Our scheme prevents illegal activities (as blackmailing, money laundering and illegal purchases/sales). For example, if blackmailing is suspected or reported, the appropriate authority will allow to the bank to demand the identity of the user who will try to *transfer* or *deposit* the suspicious serial number (*SN*). We don't use blind signatures to achieve anonymity, and so a blackmailed user always knows the serial number of the money given to the blackmailer. If money laundering is suspected, the authority will allow to the bank to demand user identification when this user is going to transfer the money.

We want to remark that we don't use tamper resistant devices, nor pseudonyms. The possibility of anonymous payment and redemption, the double spending prevention and other security properties, makes this scheme suitable for anonymous payments of high amounts in B2B transactions.

References

[1] Anderson, R., et alter: "NetCard - a practical electronic cash system", 4th Security Protocols International Workshop, LNCS 1189, pages 49-57, Springer Verlag, 1996.

[2] Brands, S.: "Untraceable off-line cash in wallet with observers", Crypto'93, LNCS 773, pages 302-318, Springer Verlag, 1993.

[3] Chaum, D., et alter: "Untraceable electronic cash", Crypto'88, LNCS 403, pages 319–327, Springer Verlag, 1988.

[4] Chaum, D. and Pedersen, T.: "Wallet databases with observers", Crypto'92, LNCS 740, pages 89–105, Springer Verlag, 1992.

[5] Eng, T. and Okamoto, T.: "Single-term divisible electronic coins", Eurocrypt'94, LNCS 576, pages 306–319, Springer Verlag, 1994.

[6] Medvinsky, G. and Neuman, B.C.: "Netcash: A design for practical electronic currency on the internet", 1st ACM Conference on Computer and Communication Security, pages 102–106, 1993.

[7] Mu, Y., et alter: "A Fair Electronic Cash Scheme", ISEC 2001, LNCS 2040, pages 20–32, Springer Verlag, 2001.

[8] Nakanishi, T. and Sugiyama, Y.: "Unlinkable Divisible Electronic Cash", ISW 2000, LNCS 1975, pages 121–134, Springer Verlag, 2000.

[9] Okamoto, T. and Otha, K.: "Universal electronic cash", Crypto'91, LNCS 576, pages 324–337, Springer Verlag, 1991.

An Efficient Anonymous Scheme for Secure Micropayments[*]

Magdalena Payeras-Capellà, Josep Lluís Ferrer-Gomila, and Ll. Huguet-Rotger

Universitat de les Illes Balears
Carretera de Valldemossa Km. 7.5, Palma de Mallorca, 07122, Spain
{mpayeras, dijjfg, dmilhr0}@uib.es

Abstract. Micropayment systems allow payments of low value. Low cost for transaction is the main requirement for micropayments. For this reason, anonymity, a desired feature, is difficult to implement in micropayment systems. This paper presents an anonymous and untraceable micropayment system that offers low transactional costs while the use of secure protocols avoids financial risks. The efficient anonymity is achieved thanks to the use of a double spending prevention technique. Finally, the bank behavior can be verified.

1 Anonymity in Micropayments

The ideal features of micropayments are: low transactional costs, financial risks control, atomic interchange, privacy and velocity. The achievement of these features requires adjustment in: number of interactions among parties, volume of information, use of asymmetric cryptography, storage requirements, use of tamper resistant devices, anonymity and use of specific coins. As a consequence, there is a relaxation in security and privacy aspects, and because anonymity and efficiency are in conflict, micropayment systems are rarely anonymous. Privacy can be achieved with the use of pseudonyms [3, 6], but when anonymity is implemented [7], the high computational cost associated is not suitable for low valued payments. In the existing proposals, we can distinguish systems that use universal coins and systems that use specific ones (can be spent only at a defined merchant [2, 4, 9]).

Neither on-line nor off-line systems are suitable for anonymous micropayments. On-line systems aren't efficient. In other hand, off-line systems with specific coins [8, 9] can't be anonymous (credit systems) and off-line systems with universal coins require double spending detection or tamper resistant devices. Another approach is the use of semi-offline systems [2, 3, 5]. The better combination of efficiency and anonymity in micropayments appears in systems that use semi-offline payments, and more exactly in those that achieve *double spending prevention* without the need of hardware devices. We present a micropayment system that allows anonymous payments while maintains the associated costs at a low level, using specific coins (formed by a chain of *coupons* that can be used in independent payments [4, 9]), and semi-offline payments. Customers only need to communicate with the bank when they have to create a new chain of coupons (coin). In order to maintain efficiency our scheme presents a new algorithm for *double spending prevention*. This way, anonymity doesn't need to be revocated and coins don't include identifying information.

[*] Partially supported by the Balearic Islands Government under project PRDIB-2002GC3-18.

J.M. Cueva Lovelle et al. (Eds.): ICWE 2003, LNCS 2722, pp. 80–83, 2003.
© Springer-Verlag Berlin Heidelberg 2003

2   Efficient Anonymous Micropayment Scheme

In the description of the scheme, A realizes a payment to B, with a coin obtained from F (a financial entity that uses the key K_{sfQ} to create coins with value Q). The notation $H(\ )$, $Sign_i(\ )$, K_{pi} and K_{si} will be used to represent a hash function, a digital signature and the public and secret key of user i, respectively. The withdrawal coins are $M = K_{sfQ}(W_0) = Sign_{fQ}(W_1)$, in where W_1 and $W_0 = H(W_1)$ are the secret proof and identifier of the coin, respectively. The withdrawn universal coins can be changed for specific coins: $K_{sfQ}(W_{0b}, W_{0a}, n)$.

2.1   Withdrawal Subprotocol

A requests a new coin to F, proving ownership of his account. A random number W_1 that must be kept secret will be the proof to validate the coin. W_0 is used to prevent double spending. In order to avoid traceability, a blind signature [1] is used. A includes the amount Q and the blinded identifier W in the request to F. F validates the identity of A, and encrypts the blinded identifier. A calculates de coin M_1 from the blinded coin M_1'. The identifier is the digest of the secret proof W_1, so M_1 is a signature on W_1. Now, the coin is universal. Only A can prove the knowledge of W_1.

This withdrawal provides anonymous universal coins, security against counterfeiting and authentication of the account's owner. Moreover, the subprotocol uses a secret proof of validity that will be required for the redemption of the coin.

$$A \rightarrow F: \quad \{Q, W, Sign_a(Q, W)\}$$
$$F \rightarrow A: \quad M_1' = K_{sfQ}(W)$$

2.2   Pre-payment Subprotocol

When A wants to realize a payment to B, A changes a universal anonymous coin for a coin specific for B. With this purpose, B generates a new pair of identifier and secret proof W_{1b} and W_{0b}, then sends to A the signed identifier and his certificate. A generates a chain of coupons from a random number, applying successively a hash function $(W_{na}, \ldots, W_{0a} = H^n(W_{na}))$ and sends to F the amount (Q_2), the identifier (supplied by B), the secret proof of the universal coin (W_1), the last item of the new chain $(W_{0a}$, it is possible to calculate an element W_{ia} from another element W_{ja} only if j is greater than i), the number of coupons (n) to be generated and a new identifier (W_{0x}) to create a new coin with the remaining value (Q_3). The secret proof W_1 is encrypted to avoid counterfeiting. F checks the validity of the coin using W_1.

$$B \rightarrow A: \quad \{W_{0b}, Cert_b, Sign_b(W_{0b})\}$$
$$A \rightarrow F: \quad \{M_1, K_{pf}(W_1), Q_2, W_{0a}, W_{0b}, n, W_{0x}\}$$
$$F \rightarrow A: \quad \{M_2 = K_{sfQ2}(W_{0b}, W_{0a}, n), M_3 = K_{sfQ3}(W_{0x})\}$$

2.3   Payment Subprotocol

Once executed the pre-payment subprotocol, A knows the coin M_2 and its identifier W_{0b}, but A doesn't know the proof of validity W_{1b}. Only B knows W_{1b} and for this reason, he can be sure that the coin has not been spent before the payment. There is no need to contact the bank on-line to check double spending. A sends a message formed by the coin (M_2), a coupon of the chain and the order number of this coupon. A can send an arbitrary pair of coupon and order number. The difference between this number and the last spent one multiplied by the value of each coupon represent the amount transferred. B checks the validity of the coin and saves M_2 and W_{0a}. These operations are done only once. M gets the order number i and applies i times the hash function over W_{ia}. If the result is the value W_{0a} the payment is valid. The elements of the customer's chain are revealed in upward order, so if an element with an order number minor than a used element is presented, the merchant detects a double spending attempt. In later payments the same operations are done with the last used order number (j, W_{ja}) instead of W_{0a}.

$$A \rightarrow B: \{M_2, W_{ia}, i\}$$

2.4   Deposit Subprotocol

B can deposit the received coupons although he hasn't received all n coupons of the coin. F checks the secret proof (W_{1b}), the relation between W_{ia} and W_{0a} and the list of spent coupons of the coin comparing the value of the order number of the last deposited coupon (j) with the included in the deposit message (i). F will credit B's account with the value of the group of deposited coupons $(i-j$ coupons$)$. If i is lower or equal to j, then double deposit is detected. Only B, with the knowledge of the coin's secret proof, is able to deposit.

$$B \rightarrow F: K_{pf}(M_2, W_{ia}, W_{1b}), ID_b$$

2.5   Verificability of the Bank

It is possible verify the behaviour of F modifying the scheme. A specific proof must be generated for each coupon in the chain. B uses a hash function to generate a chain of proofs. When A requests the conversion of coin M_1 in the pre-payment, F checks if the coin has been converted or deposited before, preventing double spending. If the coin is valid, F sends an Ack (Ack = $Sign_f(W_0, W_{0b})$) to A, declaring that it will refresh a valid coin M_1. If F detects a double spending attempt, he sends a $Nack$ (Nack=$Sign_f(W_1)$), showing the secret proof given by A when the coin was first deposited. The Payment doesn't suffer changes. Each element in the chain will be used to deposit payments with each coupon of the coin. For each deposit of coupons of the same coin, B shows a different secret proof. F needs to prove the knowledge of the right secret when detects double spending or double deposit and can't claim a non-existent reutilization: the bank is verifiable.

3   Conclusions

Although our payment subprotocol presents a minimised number of interactions, in the semi-offline system has to be considered, for each payment, the proportional part of transactional cost involved in the pre-payment (amortised in a high number of payments using coupons of the same coin). The use of asymmetric cryptography is minimised (withdrawal, transmission of the identifier between receiver and payer and transfer of secret proofs) and it's not used in the payment stage.

Counterfeiting, overspending and robbery are avoided. All parties can be sure the payments can be redeemed. In order to prevent double spending, the receiver maintains a list of identifiers together with their secret proofs until the reception of all coupons of the related coin or their expiration date. When payments are received, the receiver adds to the list the order number and the value of the last received coupon. The bank prevents double deposit listing the identifiers (secret proofs in the verifiable scheme) only for those unexpired coins received in deposit or pre-payment. If the receiver detects a payment with a double spent coupon (the order number of the coupon is lower than the stored one), the receiver prevents the double spending rejecting the payment. If a coin is reused, the related identifier is not found in the list of valid coins.

Anonymity in an off-line payment without the inclusion of identifying information in coins is possible due to our double spending and double deposit prevention technique. The traceament of payments is not possible even by a collusion between the receiver and the bank.

The presented micropayment scheme has a high degree of efficiency together with control of financial risks and anonymity (and untraceability) of the payer in front of the receiver and the bank. Finally, we have presented a solution in where the bank is verifiable.

References

[1] Chaum, D.: "Blind signatures for untraceable payments", Crypto'82, pages 199–203, Springer Verlag, 1982.
[2] Glassman, S. et Al.: "The Millicent protocol for inexpensive electronic commerce", 4th International World Wide Web Conference Proceedings, pages 603–618, O'Reilly, 1995.
[3] Gabber, E. and Silberschatz, A.: "Agora: A minimal distributed protocol for electronic commerce", 2nd USENIX workshop on Electronic Commerce, pages 223–232, 1996.
[4] Hauser, R., Steiner and M. and Waidner, M.: "Micro-payments based on iKP", 14th Worldwide Congress on Computer and Communication Security Protection, pages 67–82, 1996.
[5] Jarecki, S. and Odlyzko, A: "An efficient micropayment system based on probabilistic polling", Financial Cryptography'97, LNCS 1318, pages 173–191, Springer Verlag, 1997.
[6] Lipton, R.J. and Ostrovsky, R.: "Micro-Payments via efficient coin flipping", Financial Cryptography'98, LNCS 1465, pages 1–15, Springer Verlag, 1998.
[7] Mao, W: "A simple cash payment technique for the Internet", ESORICS'96, LNCS 1146, pages 15–32, Springer Verlag, 1996.
[8] Rivest, R.: "Perspectives on financial cryptography", Financial Cryptogaphy'97, LNCS 1318, pages 145–149, Springer Verlag, 1997.
[9] Rivest, R. and Shamir, A.: "Payword and Micromint: two simple micropayment schemes" 4th Workshop on Security Protocols, LNCS 1189, pages 69–87, Springer Verlag, 1996.

User Parameter Tunning for VoD Service Users

A. Echavarren, C. Zubieta, J. Villadangos, and M. Prieto

Área de Ingeniería Telemática, Departamento de Automática y Computación.
Universidad Pública de Navarra Campus de Arrosadia, 31.006 Pamplona.

Abstract. This work has been focused on the design of a VoD parameter-measuring tool. This tool works as a video client and additionally provides a set of measurements used to define different user parameters in different network conditions.

1 Introduction

The operation of a VoD service involves a number of engineering decisions that affect the VoD quality of service. Some papers in the literature consider the system perform-ance [1, 4], others, that the bottleneck of the VoD service is the I/O bandwidth [1,2], and there are different proposals to optimise the video server performance by applying different scheduling algorithms to serve the movies [2, 3].

However, there are other parameters that should be taken into account both in the client as in the network side. The client usually uses a pre-load buffer to store the first bytes of the movie to avoid starvation during video playback and there is also a very important decision about the size of the playback buffer of the client player. In the same way, it is necessary to measure the effect of the network during the movie transmission.

2 Measuring Tool Architecture

The measuring tool has been developed based on the DirectX graph filter architecture for Windows [5]. It provides a flexible and adaptive tool as it can works with all the registered filters in Windows.

The measuring tool consists on a filter graph built by the filter manager (see figure 1). An asynchronous input filter has been developed ad-hoc to provide the measuring tool characteristics (see figure 1). The other necessary filters are the same to those needed to play the file from the hard disc.

The asynchronous input filter manages the data transmission between the video server and the player. The received data from the network is stored in a circular buffer and when the next filter asks an amount of data the developed input filter gives the data from the circular buffer. Consequently, DirectShow is used to make the necessary

J.M. Cueva Lovelle et al. (Eds.): ICWE 2003, LNCS 2722, pp. 84–85, 2003.
© Springer-Verlag Berlin Heidelberg 2003

conversions and to render the samples correctly. In addition, the input filter allows monitoring parameters as the bytes/s, packets/s, and so on. In addition, it provides the graphical representation of the parameters. Moreover, the developed input filter manages different possible critical circumstances (see figure 1 a, b).

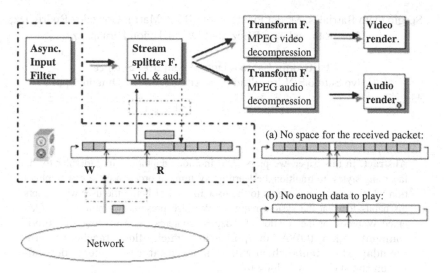

Fig. 1. A filter graph built in the video client to play an MPEG video file

3 Conclusions

This experience has shown from the point of view of the client that many points have to be considered in a VoD service. The developed tool allows setting different user parameters and evaluating the VoD service.

References

1. Sudhanshu Aggarwal and Juan A. Garay and Amir Herzberg. *Adaptive video on demand.* Proc of the 13th annual ACM symposium on Principles of distributed computing, 1994
2. Min-You Wu, Su-Jun Ma, Wei Shu. *Scheduled video delivery for scalable on-demand service* Proc of the 12th International Workshop on Network and Operating Systems Support for Digital Audio and Video, 2002
3. Emmanuel L. Abram-Profeta and Kang G. Shin. *Scheduling video programs in near video-on-demand systems.* Proc of the fifth ACM international conference on Multimedia, 1997
4. N. Judice, E. J. Addeo, M. I. Eiger, H. L. Lemberg. *Video on Demand: A Wideband Service or Myth?* Proc. of ICC'86, June 1986
5. *Use Multimedia Streaming in DirectShow Applications.* MSDN Library January 1999. Microsoft Corporation.

IOWA: Intuitive-Use Oriented Webtool for the Creation of Adapted Contents (in an E-learning Environment)

Sergio Ocio Barriales, Mª del Puerto Paule Ruiz, Martín González Rodríguez, Juan Ramón Pérez Pérez, and David Tuñón Fernández

HCI Group- Labtoo- Dpto. Computer Science
C/Calvo Sotelo S/N Facultad de Ciencias. 33007 Oviedo. Spain
djrekcv@terra.es,{paule,martin, jrpp}@pinon.ccu.uniovi.es,
davidtf@telecable.es

Abstract. In this paper, we propose to include adaptation, in particular to the laearning styles, to traditional e-learning systems in order to get a new application which adapts its contents to the user instead of being the user who adapts his habits to what the system requires. We also present the Intuitive-use Oriented Webtool for the creation of Adapted contents (in an e-learning environment), a.k.a. IOWA, an application which allows teachers to create adapted contents which will be showed later to students depending on the style they belong to.

1 Introduction

Nowadays, there are many applications which allow to offer distance learning (e-learning) as another system which can be used by the teaching community to accomplish their task. However, these systems are not fully perfected, because they force both students and teachers to change their normal behavior to work as the system requires. Due to these limitations, actual e-learning does not reach the level effectiveness got by traditional teaching, in which there are a wider freedom to work as each wants to.

Feijoo.net has being developed to cover these deficiencies, offering in a single system all that was offered by traditional distance learning systems and a model of adaptation to the learning styles. This makes the system to adapt to its users' neccesities rather than the inverse way. IOWA is the component of Feijoo.net which task is the creation of contents, so it will be mainly used by teachers.

J.M. Cueva Lovelle et al. (Eds.): ICWE 2003, LNCS 2722, pp. 86–89, 2003.
© Springer-Verlag Berlin Heidelberg 2003

2   A Model of Adaptation: CHAEA's Test

Each person has his own way to learn new concepts, which makes the learning be successful in less time or easier. This 'tricks' are called learning styles [1]. Basing on this concept, we need a classification which allows us to group people depending on their learning style.

CHAEA's test [2] offers a classification that divides all the possible ways to learn in four groups: theoretician, active, reflexive and pragmatic. CHAEA's test in focused in how teachers would work with students in a class.

In addition, this test is leaned to university students and has been proved in Spanish Universities, so we have decided to use this classification instead of others like VARK [3].

3   System's Architecture

Our system's architecture is made following the pattern model-view-controller. The core of IOWA is composed by four subsystems:

3.1   Creation of Contents Subsystem

As in all e-learning systems, contents are a key part of Feijoo.net. IOWA provides editors to create both text contents and to purpose exercises to strengthen student's knowledge. The biggest difference is that, while other system's contents are common for all their users, in Feijoo.net there can be a common part and a specific part. When a student requested these contents, the system will show automatically the common part and the specific for that kind of user (depending on the learning style), creating this way different contents for each style without bothering teachers as they do not need to worry about how adaptation is actually done.

Our studies have demonstrated that presenting information that is adapted to the learning style of the user improves learning. However, with exercises this is not this way, because any student can do any exercise even if that exercises was not planned for that kind of user; when a concept is assimilated, it does not matter how a student is asked about it, because he/she should know the answer. So, exercises will be common to all users in Feijoo.net.

3.2   Organization of Contents Subsystem

Once all contents have been created, the teacher can create a new planning for the didactic unit he is working with. This way, he/she can control in which order the contents may be shown to his/her students, how can a student go through those contents and even decide if certain contents are interesting or not to a specific learning style. Using an acyclic graph, which can be easily created through an editor, provided by IOWA, this planning, is described. There must be a planning for each learning style. This gives the teacher another tool to create contents that are even more adequate to his/her students. This planning concept fits with context concept from OOHDM [4]. In Feijoo.net, each learning style has its own context for each didactic unit, as for each style it will be specified what contents will be shown and in which order.

3.3 Templates of Visualization Subsystem

All Feijoo.net data is saved as XML. This is very beneficial, because data can be process in a very easy way.

This subsystem takes advantage of this property, providing a simple wizard-like interface to create a XSLT template that, applied to the XML obtained from our database produces that contents can be shown as the teacher wants.

Although a default template is provided to teachers, they can create all the ones they want. Then, they can select one of these templates to be used with a course. Teachers have the option to preview what format any existing template applies.

3.4 Preview Subsystem

This subsystem will allow the teacher to "visit" the didactic unit's contents as if he/she was a student. After selecting a learning style to preview, IOWA will generate the final results after linking contents, planning and template, offering the possibility of checking if everything is as the teacher wanted.

Providing this subsystem completes the tool and makes the teacher to feel more comfortable with IOWA, as she/he can see what the result of his/her work is.

3.5 Other Components

IOWA has other secondary components to offer a full editing system:

- *System's help*: IOWA has a context-sensitive help system in which teachers can learn to do any action offered in the application, though all the system has been developed having its users in mind; usability is one of its improved features.
- *Error manager*: it provides explanation for each error that can be present in the system and avoids the system to crash.
- *Teacher-guide system*: as its name points, this system guides the teacher through each step at the time of offering new contents to students. It remembers where a teacher has left his/her work last time when he/she reenters the system and advises him/her about what is the best path to follow to accomplish his/her task.
- *Database-access web service*: in order to centralize all the access to Feijoo.net database, we have created a Web Service built on .NET framework. It accepts a SQL sentence as input and outputs the query's results as XML. Teachers will not know how the system works internally, but this system is one of the most important components of all Feijoo.net.

4   Conclusions and New Features

Adding some kind of adaptation to distance learning systems can improve a lot the quality of this kind of teaching, as Feijoo.net tries to demonstrate.

IOWA gets that the task of creating new on-line contents could be much more powerful, because the behavior of the system when it is being used by some kind of student can be determined and, despite this, the task does not get more work to be done, because a great part of this adaptation is made automatically by the system.

We think that adaptation is the next way to follow in e-learning systems if they want to offer teaching with the same quality it would have if it was given in a traditional way.

References

1. Learning Styles. http://galeon.hispavista.com/pcazau/guia_esti01.htm.
2. CHAEA's test. Deusto University. http://www.ice.deusto.es/guia/test0.htm.
3. VARK. http://www.vark-learn.com.
4. The Object-Oriented Hypermedia Design Model (OOHDM). Rossi, G.; Schwabe, D.. http://www.telemidia.puc-rio.br/oohdm/oohdm.html

Other References

5. Paul De Bra and Licia Calvi. "Towards a Generic Adaptive Hypermedia System" in Proceedings of the Second Workshop on Adaptive Hypertext and Hypermedia, Pittsburgh, PA, 5–11, 1998.
6. Del Moral Pérez and et.all (2002):"Rur@lnet: Un espacio para la teleformación y el trabajo colaborativo". En 2nd European Congress on Information Technologies in Education and Citizenship: a critical insight.
7. Del Moral Pérez, M. Esther; Álvarez Fernández, Susana (2002): "Generación de entornos de teleformación y atención a la diversidad cognitiva de los usuarios". En Comunicación y Pedagogía .

Reaching Agreements through Fuzzy Counter-Offers

Javier Carbo[1], Jose M. Molina[1], and Jorge Dávila[2]

[1] Computer Science Department, Univ. Carlos III,
28911 Leganes, Madrid, Spain
jcarbo@inf.uc3m.es, molina@ia.uc3m.es
[2] Computer Science Faculty, Univ. Politécnica de Madrid,
28660 Boadilla, Madrid, Spain
jdavila@fi.upm.es

Abstract. Automated negotiations require a more elaborated dialogue where agents would explain offer rejections in a general and vague way. We propose to represent the disappointment about an offer through fuzzy logic. Specifically we study two alternatives: a piece-wise fuzzy set or a linguistic label applied to each attribute of the offer. These alternatives are evaluated comparing the performance of both types of counter-offers with a classical approach based on linear programming. Therefore, the media of negotiation length, benefits and percentage of agreements allow us to conclude the accuracy of the alternatives proposed.

1 Introduction

Several types of automated negotiations have been proposed. Among them, agent-mediated auctions have become relatively popular [1]. Nevertheless auctions are very different from the daily bargain of markets. Most people is not familiar with their rules. If agents intended to reflect the real behavior of human society, then a human-like negotiation would be searched. The most human-like negotiation scheme proposed involves the use of arguments in order to persuade the other part of improving the offer [2].

We propose the use of fuzzy sets to express the counter-offer of buyers in a negotiation. Each attribute of the agreement to negotiate has associated a fuzzy set to persuade the merchant to improve the offer. Both linguistic and numerically defined fuzzy sets were applied to compare with corresponding negotiations where buyers reject the offer of merchants in a concrete way.

2 Fuzzy Counter-Offers in Automated Negotiations

The negotiation setup proposed defines the preferences function of each part as a boundary value and a weight for each negotiation attribute. Therefore an agreement is reached when the offer satisfies the next requirements:

J.M. Cueva Lovelle et al. (Eds.): ICWE 2003, LNCS 2722, pp. 90–93, 2003.
© Springer-Verlag Berlin Heidelberg 2003

$$\forall i \in \text{Attributes, and weight[i]>0: offer[i] > threshold[i] ,} \tag{1}$$
$$\forall j \in \text{Attributes, and weight[j]<0: offer[j] < threshold[j] ,}$$
$$\forall k \in \text{Attributes: benefit} > \Sigma_k \text{ weight[k] ·offer[k] .}$$

The weights and thresholds of each part are chosen with certain random but in a way that agreements are possible, satisfying the next condition:

$$\forall i \in \text{Attributes, and weight[i]>0, } \forall j \in \text{Attributes, and weight [j]<0 :} \tag{2}$$
$$| \text{ peso[j] · threshold[j] } | > \text{peso[i] · threshold[i] .}$$

Finally, the initial offer from the merchant is computed from the next equation:

$$\forall i \in \text{Attributes, offer[i]= threshold[i] + } \frac{benefit}{weigth\ [i] \cdot \dim} . \tag{3}$$

To obtain a crisp counteroffer, we use parameter λ in simplex method in lineal programming with several goals [3]. The goals are: maximize benefits and minimize the distance with the offer of merchants. Some restrictions were posed over such goal function:

$$\Sigma_i \text{ weight[i] · } x_i >= \text{benefit - } \Sigma_i \text{ weight[i] · offer[i] .} \tag{4}$$
$$\forall j \in \text{Attributes, and weight[j]>0:}$$
$$x_j >= \max (0, \text{threshold[j]-offer[j]}) ,$$
$$x_j <= \text{offer[j] · } \lambda \text{ · weight[j] / (weight[j]-weight[k]) .}$$
$$\forall k \in \text{Attributes, and weight[k]<0:}$$
$$x_k >= \max (0, \text{offer[k]-threshold[k]}) ,$$
$$x_k <= \text{offer[k] · } \lambda \text{ · | weight[k] / (weight[j]-weight[k])| .}$$

The first of the alternatives proposed is a piece-wise definition of a trapezium over a dominion of fictitious values. Then, the shape and relative position of the trapezium should reflect in an indirect way the preferences of the buyer over such attribute. So buyers assign his own scale to the dominion of fictitious values using a value called m. The corresponding dominion results then from offer[i]-m to offer[i]+m. The value m is computed from:

$$m = \max (\text{ |offer[i] - threshold[i] | , | benefit / weight[i] – offer [i] |) .} \tag{5}$$

Therefore the four points that define the fuzzy set are the next ones:

$$\forall j \in \text{Attributes, and weight[j]>0:} \tag{6}$$
$$x_j^0 = (m + \text{threshold[j]-offer[j]})\cdot 100 / m\cdot 2$$
$$x_j^1 = (m+ \max (\text{threshold[j], benefit/(weight[j] ·dim))-offer[j]) · 100 / m·2}$$
$$x_j^2 = 99.999, \quad x_j^3 = 100$$
$$\forall k \in \text{Attributes, and weight[k]<0:}$$
$$x_k^0 = 0, \quad x_k^1 = 0.001$$
$$x_k^2 = (m+ \min(\text{|benefit / weight[k] – offer[k]|/dim, offer[k]) -offer[k])}$$
$$\cdot 100 / m\cdot 2$$
$$x_k^3 = (m+ \text{threshold[k]-offer[k]) ·100 / m·2x + y = z .}$$

The second alternative proposed uses two linguistic labels per each attribute. One of them represents one of the fuzzy set, and the other label represents a linguistic modifier where modifiers only changes the gradient of the sides of the trapezium. In order to generate this pair of labels from an offer of the merchant, two values are computed: distance and gradient with the next equations:

$$\forall j \in \text{Attributes, and weight[j]>0:} \tag{7}$$
$$\text{distance= offer[j]} \cdot \text{weight[j]} \cdot \text{dim / benefit ,}$$
$$\text{gradient=} \frac{\textit{offer } [j] - \textit{threshold } [j]}{\textit{benefit} \Big/ (\textit{weight } [j] \cdot \dim) - \textit{threshold } [j]} ,$$

$$\forall k \in \text{Attributes, and weight[k]<0:}$$
$$\text{distance= 1 + offer[k] weight[k]} \cdot \text{dim / benefit ,}$$
$$\text{gradient=} \frac{\textit{threshold } [k] - \textit{offer } [k]}{\textit{benefit} \Big/ (\textit{weight } [k] \cdot \dim) + \textit{threshold } [k]} .$$

Distances determine the first linguistic label, while gradients determine the linguistic modifier. When the merchant receives such linguistic labels, a graphical interpretation of the linguistic label is drawn over the dominion scaled with the preferences of the merchant. The crossover of the fuzzy set built up the preferences of the merchant and the fuzzy set corresponding to the interpretation of the linguistic labels, is then re-scaled to obtain a crisp offer answering to the previous fuzzy counter-offer based on linguistic labels.

3   Experimental Results

We have tested an illustrative example of 100 negotiations about two issues: price and quality. In each of these 100 negotiations, buyers and merchants use different preferences functions computed randomly (essentially weights and thresholds of the negotiation attributes). It is also stated that negotiations fail after a sequence of 10 pairs of offers and counter-offers. With all these conditions we obtained the next results:

Table 1. Agreements, benefit and messages involved in negotiations.

	Messages needed	Benefit obtained	% of agreements
Crisp	2.82	80.10	44%
Fuzzy Set	1.79	73.09	86%
Fuzzy Label	5.58	80.29	48%

As we can see in table 1, for the negotiations involving fuzzy sets, a higher percentage of success is reached wasting less computational resources, although the benefit obtained is lower than the other two alternatives. So it seems that fuzzy sets are specially useful to face fast negotiations and to avoid failed negotiations. Furthermore, the velocity of convergence of this alternative does not mean an easier acquisition of buyers' shopping profile as it is shown in [4]. On the other hand, negotiations involving fuzzy labels last much more than the others, and obtain a percentage of success similar to negotiations involving crisp counter-offers. Nevertheless the final agreement obtained satisfies better the preferences of buyers. So this type of counter-offer obtains better agreements lasting more time.

4 Conclusions

The main contribution relies on the application of fuzzy logic to agent-mediated negotiations. Our proposal first shows how to make negotiation dialog more human, and second, how to make negotiations more profitable for buyers without wasting computational resources in no-way-out negotiations.

References

1. Rosenchein, J. Zlotkin G.: Rules of Encounter: Designing conventions for automated negotiation among computers, MIT Press 1994
2. Sierra C., Jennings N.R., Noriega P., Parsons S.: A framework for argumentation-based negotiation. Intelligent Agents IV, number 1365 in LNAI, Springer (1997) 177–192
3. Zadeh L.A.,: Fuzzy Sets Information and Control, n° 8, (1965) 338–353.
4. Carbo, J., Ledezma A.,: A machine learning based evaluation of a negotiation involving fuzzy counter-offers. In Procs. Int. Conf. on Atlantic Web Intelligence (2003).

A Dynamic Replication Service for XML-Documents to E-commerce

A. Córdoba[1], J.J. Astrain[1], J.E. Armendariz[1], and J. Villadangos[2]

[1] Dep. de Matemática e Informática
[2] Dep. de Automática y Computación
Universidad Pública de Navarra
Campus de Arrosadía, E31006 Pamplona (Spain)
{alberto.cordoba, josej.astrain, enrique.armendariz, jesusv}@unavarra.es

Abstract. E-commerce transactions informations is traditionally stored in RDBMS. In this paper we consider that transaction tracking information is stored as XML documents in RDBMS geographically distributed. In order to support fault-tolerance and persistent storing service we propose a replication service. It provides a high available document retrieval against possible server failures, granting the access to the last version of the document. The service also allows to perform queries over the persistent data store in order to recover commercial transaction information from the replicated persistent store.

1 Introduction

E-commerce is one of the major concerns playing on the minds of corporate executives the world over. In interview after interview, senior managers say one of the biggest challenges facing their organizations is how effectively leverage the Internet, to give them a competitive advantage [1]. Each commercial transaction data of an e-commerce system is stored as XML documents, because this tag language is well suited to map it on Relational Database Management Systems (RDBMS) and to look for specific information in them. Tags are pattern elements that can be easily used to select the desired information, reducing the search space. Data in XML format is permeating all corners of the computing milieu: e-commerce, data streaming, web content, messaging, data interchange, database management. Many of these areas require breaking up XML into fragments and combining pieces of XML into larger documents, for purposes such as querying, stream monitoring, incremental updates and producing "recombinant documents".

Many authors have persistently stored the XML schemas in *Database Management Systems* (DBMS). Many works can be found for RelationalDBMS [2,3,4] (mapping XML structures into tuples), Object-RelationalDBMS [5,6] (mapping XML structures into objects), applications in FederatedDBMS [7] and mixed solutions [8]. Our implementation uses as storage system a relational database as is depicted in [4].

J.M. Cueva Lovelle et al. (Eds.): ICWE 2003, LNCS 2722, pp. 94–97, 2003.
© Springer-Verlag Berlin Heidelberg 2003

The Object Group Service (OGS) [9] provides replication for CORBA applications through a set of CORBA services. Replica consistency in ensured through group communication based on a consensus algorithm implemented through CORBA service objects. OGS provides interfaces for detecting the liveness of objects, and mechanism for duplicate detection and suppresion, and for the transfer of application-level state. This approach has been followed by different works, which uses the OGS or bases its group communication service on it [10,11,12,13]. However, this implies [14] that the Object Request Broker (ORB) should be modified. In [14], it is proposed an alternative based on an interception mechanism whose major advantage is that it does not require to modify the ORB.

We propose a CORBA application to provide high available XML documents containing e-commerce transactions. The replication service is based on the use of a replication manager and a set of geographically distributed repositories where documents are replicated.

The replication manager stores for each document its template (DTD), its current version and its repository owner. The replication manager is in charge of the correct replication of the commercial transactions and its management, that is, the creation, modification and deletion of XML documents stored in the repositories geographically distributed.

Each repository consists of an RDBMS and a local agent of the replication service, called Local Interface (LI), which translates XML documents to tables and viceversa. While there is at least one active repository, the replication service ensures that users get the last version of the document. It also supports failures at the local manager level and at the RDBMS.

The manager replicates asychronously the XML documents. Each operation over a document is always performed firstly in the repository owner of the document. Once it is done, the manager updates asynchronously all the replicas in the remainder repositories. Moreover, the manager follows a passive replication policy. Whenever a document access fails, the manager receives an exception. This leads it to a state which, by means of its local infomation, tries to recover the document from other repository of the system. The system tolerates repository failures: LI and RDBMS stop failures.

2 System Model

E-commerce systems generate an important amount of relevant information that must be appropriately managed. Because of the relevance of the information generated by the business logic of the e-commerce system, it is usually saved in a persistent storage system. From the user point of view users interacts with the e-commerce system to do a commercial transaction (CT). The user connects to web services to perform a CT. These services provide the interface between the user and the e-commerce system. In commercial systems, different kind of CT can be issued. Each one contains a set of information that constitutes its template. Whenever a CT is performed, a set of information corresponding to its template is persistently stored by way of CTs and XML documents.

This paper proposes the use of XML schemas to store both CT information and CT templates. Each template has associated a XML schema. The use of XML schemas allows to store properly the information and to recover it from the storage system when needed. In order to perform the storage of the XML documents generated in each CT, the system implements a storing service that allows to keep the different XML documents according to their templates.

Commercial data and XML schemas are stored in a repository, each one is composed of an RDBMS (where data is stored) and its local interface (LI). The LI is the interface (by way of CORBA) between web services and RDBMS that allows applications to manage the commercial transaction documents. The LI receives storing/recovering requests of XML documents and translates locally these documents to a set of SQL sentences. An XML2SQL parser is used to do that, as it is shown in [15] . LI demands to the RDBMS the execution of the SQL sentences in a transactional way, which allows the LI to store/recover the requested information. It inserts a new database register when storing information and provides an XML document for the web service when recovering the information. The system stores/recovers XML documents that users/applications can update using web services. The LI component provides the translation from XML to a set of SQL sentences. These sentences, executed by the RDBMS, allow to store/recover XML persistent documents of an e-commerce system.

However, the system is prone to fail-stop or crash errors. In order to improve the fault-tolerance of the e-commerce system we propose and implement a replication service (RS). The RS is designed to ensure consistency and high availability of CT information by replicating repositories working in a replicate all policy. So, all available (non-faulty) repositories eventually will contain the same set of information. The RS is composed by two basic elements: the replication protocol (RP) and the information storage manager (ISM) that stores information processed by the protocol. RS interacts with the ORB agent and manages the replicas throughout all the Internet, being this process totally transparent to the users. LIs register to the RS in order to be considered for the replication process. The RS service can be implemented in anyone of the LIs that compose the system. The unique difference between an LI and the RS is the performance table employed by the RS to store information related to the performances and availability of the LIs composing the system. As the RS is the kernel of the proposed system, it is necessary to ensure fault-tolerance making use of UPS and RAID disks.

The RP protocol is composed by the system control protocol (SCP), and by the document storing protocol (DSP). The SCP establishes channel communications with the LIs of the system and detects failures in the replication system. The DSP protocol manages the storage of the XML documents into relational tables.

3   Conclusions

This paper introduces an on demand replication service, which allows the persistent storage of XML documents into RDBMSs, and their recovery whenever a repository crashes (LI or/and RDBMS). This service uses CORBA and is about to be a liable alternative to the protocols supported by the CORBA standard, avoiding node grouping and multicast when connections are established in order to know the state of the system.

References

1. Reynolds, M.: Beginning e-commerce. Wrox Press (2000)
2. Kanne, C., Moerkotte, G.: Efficient Storage of XML Data. In Proceedings of the 16th International Conference on Data Enginnering (2000)
3. Florescu, D., Kossmann, D.: Storing and Querying XML Data Using an RDBMS. Data Engineering Bulletin, 22(3) (1999)
4. Shanmugasundaram, J., Tufte, K., He, G., Zhang, C., DeWitt, D., Naughton, J.: Relational Databases for Querying XML Documents: Limitations and Opportunities. In Proceedings of the 25th VLDB Conference, Edinburgh, Scotland (1999)
5. Klettke, M., Meyer, H.: XML and Object-Relational Database Systems – Enhancing Structural Mappings Bases on Statistics. Int. Workshop on the Web and Databases (WebDB), Dallas, (2000)
6. Shimura, T., Yoshikawa, M, Uemura, S.: Storage and Retrieval of XML Documents using Object- Relational Databases. In Database and Expert Systems Applications, Springer (1999)
7. Dittman,L, Frankhauser, P., Maric, A.: AmetaCar a Mediated eCommerce-Solution for the Used-Car-Market. In Ralf-Detlef Kutsche, Ulf Leser, and Johann Christoph Freytag, editors, 4. Works. "Federated Databases", Berlin, Germany (1999) 18–33
8. Tufte, K., Maier, D.: Merge as a Lattice-Join of XML Documents. In Proceedings of the 28th VLDB Conference, Hong Kong, Chine (2002)
9. Felber, P., Guerraoui, R., Schiper, A.: The implementation of a CORBA object group service. Theory and Practice of Object Systems, 4(2) (1998), 93–105
10. Vaysburd, A., Birman, K. : The Maestro approach to building reliable interoperable distributed application with multiple execution styles. Theory and Practice of Object Systems, 4(2) 1998, 73–80
11. Cukier, M., Ren, J., Sabnis, C., Sanders, W. H., Bakken, D.E., Berman, M.E., Karr, D.A., Schantz, R. : AQuA: An adaptive achitecture that provides dependable distributed objects. Proc. of the IEEE 17th Symposium on Reliable Distributed Systems (1998), 245-253
12. Natarajan, B., Gokhale, A., Yajnik, S., Schmidt, D.C.: DOORS: Towards high performance fault tolerant CORBA. Proc. of the International Symposium on Distributed Objects and Applications (2000), 39–48
13. Marchetti, C., Mecella, M., Virgillito, A., Baldoni, R. : An interoperable replication logic for CORBA systems. Proc. of the International Symposium on Distributed Objects and Applications (2000), 7–16
14. Narasimhan, P., Moser, L.E., Melliar-Smith, P.M : Strongly consistent replication and recovery of fault-tolerant CORBA applications. Journal of Computer Systems Science and Engineering, (2002)
15. Keller, W.: Mapping object to tables: a pattern language (2000). http://ourworld.compuserve.com/homepages/WolfgangWKeller/

Planning: An Intermediate Solution to the Problems in Design

J. Bravo, M. Ortega, M.A. Redondo, and C. Bravo

Castilla-La Mancha University, Paseo de la Universidad, 4
10071 – Ciudad Real - Spain
{Jose.Bravo,Manuel.Ortega,Miguel.Redondo,
Crescencio.Bravo}@uclm.es

Abstract. A great variety of simulation environments aim at supporting education through a modelling process. However, there are certain problems associated to modelling environments. We intend to build the solution model to every problem through plans based on intermediate languages outlined by the students. These learner plans are abstract solutions to the design problems. Our proposal consists in a tool, Plan Editor, to help the students design a domotic environment, following the intermediate language approach as a first step in the resolution of the problem. In the end, the student will be able to more efficiently simulate the plan proposed.

1 Introduction

A great variety of simulation environments aim at supporting education. There are obviously multiple advantages in them. But there is not an evident conclusion on their effectiveness since, while some authors show its excellences [20] [10], others do not believe in it [7][17]. However, everybody agrees that these environments motivate the learner [1], since the achievement of the goals produces their satisfaction [5] and the knowledge adquired through the simulation is more intuitive and efficient [2].

Simulation environments can be used to promote discovery learning. The concepts of exploration and discovery greatly motivate the learner who has the initiative. However, they bear the responsibility in the learning process [8]. Here, the teacher is just an adviser in those situations in which the learners doubt about their own performance [16].

There are certain problems associated to discovery environments. To mention some, we can start with the incorrect execution of the exploratory processes of learning. De Jong finds out that only 50% of the processes by discovery are fulfilled in an efficient way. Another problem is the incorrect relation between hypothesis and experiments [13]. Wason [22] demonstrated by means of a series of experiments that students do not often follow logical thought. Finally another problem we found in this type of environments is that the students' knowledge of the model is not precise enough. Besides, the degree of freedom in knowledge acquisition in this kind of learning does not suggest any ordered mechanism or guidelines that the students must follow. So, responsibility together with freedom of action can, in some cases, frustrate the learner, preventing the training goals from being successfully achieved.

J.M. Cueva Lovelle et al. (Eds.): ICWE 2003, LNCS 2722, pp. 98–107, 2003.
© Springer-Verlag Berlin Heidelberg 2003

There are certain simulation environments that require the previous modelling of the scenario to be simulated. At this stage we should notice the role of the computer as a student, a metaphor mentioned by Paper [15]. Here we must tell the computer what to do in order to construct the scenario where the simulation will take place. Unlike simple simulation environments, in these cases the student can modify not only input data to the system but also the model itself.

A crucial element of the constructivist learning environments is the specification and use of complex activities during the learning process [11]. It is necessary for the learner to solve subproblems of less complexity before trying the real problem [9]. Schank proposes Project-Based Learning and Goal-Based Scenarios [18][19]. These approaches present the context, the motivation and the necessary material for the learner to build specific projects in the same system.

To organise the solution to complex problems, a common approach is to establish a series of schemes or stages represented in different intermediate languages of growing precision. This produces an optimum outcome, or at least a better solution than other techniques which do not use this approach. This technique is based upon the supposition that the important thing is not only the reached solution, but also the path taken until the final product is achieved. One of the main conclusions taken from Brown's article [6], is the necessary change from the formal learning based on textbooks to the more informal "learning by doing" or to the "learning while doing" methods. The other conclusions, which are equally important, are centred on the emphasis proposed on the learning of independent abilities of the domain (for example, the generic solution of problems or the search for information) as well as of the metacognitive abilities (those related to learning how to learn, for example, drawing conclusions from our own mistakes).

The introduction of intermediate languages with the objective of finding solutions to proposed problems can be found in [21] [3]. Both authors present tutors for the learning of programming, although they lack debugging mechanisms.

In [21] a series of methods of plan composition are described. Sequencing, looping, mixing or tailoring are the ways in which each created subproblem can meet. The use of dynamics opposite to the static design implied in the use of these techniques is also recommended. Consequently, the dynamic perspective has to do with the simulation of the created assumptions.

The ideas of Soloway are developed in the work of Bonar and Cunningham [3]. These authors suggest an intelligent tutoring system (called Bridge), with the purpose of teaching how to program. This tutoring system not only finds out and informs about the mistakes committed by the student, but it partially understands the designs carried out by the student and fills the developing programs.

The intermediate languages are considered a helping step between the goals to develop and the final product as these are initially quite distinct. These languages help us write the goals and their later refinement leading to the final product. In the case of this article, the code in Pascal.

We intend to build the solution model to every problem through plans based on intermediate languages outlined by the students. These learner plans will be abstract solutions to the design problems. The planning requires a strong knowledge of the domain to study [14], so we think that the system assistance is positive during the creation of the plan. The system guides the student when he/she needs it, relying on a case memory [12]. This case memory is made up with the plan proposals that the teacher includes in the system. These cases must have certain degrees of freedom to choose among several solutions to a particular plan.

Every plan is a sequence of instructions and actions compatible with the goals [23]. In this way, the learner mistakes in the elaboration of the model and the failure in the use of this kind of educative tools in complex domains are reduced.

In this paper we present a proposal of intermediate solution. This proposal consists in a tool called Plan Editor to help the students design a domotic environment. In the next point we present the matching between the plan proposed in the first stage and the final design made at the subsequent stage. In section 4 we focus the process on matching with the simulation environment. Finally, we give the test results of an experience made in a real learning situation.

2   The Plan as a Proposal of Intermediate Solution

Our core aim is that the student learn to plan the actions of modelling. To do this, it is necessary to have a previous knowledge in the domain to study related to the domain objects, the objects characteristics, the relations between the objects and the actions to carry out over object.

Once this knowledge has been acquired by the student, he/she will be able to build the sequence of instructions that will constitute his/her plan. These instructions are obtained through combinations of objects and actions on them. His/her plan must be in accordance with the proposal that the teacher outlined about the problem to study.

The contribution of our proposal is that the instructions of the plan are abstract actions whose aim is to allow the learner to obtain a first approximation to a modelling problem solution. Each instruction can match with several actions in the modelling phase. The solution to the problem proposed by the teacher should be flexible enough to allow the student to choose among several options.

Our solution consists of educational environments composed of Simulator and Plan Editor [4]. The Plan Editor is the tool that will facilitate the intermediate solution as a previous step towards the final solution. We should mention the permanent matching between both tools. Thus, at the end of the design the student will have the information about the possible inconsistencies between plan and design.

In this learning environment the students have a collection of problems classified in different levels of complexity. They also have a structure of the domain so that they can make use of different instruction levels to compose the steps of their plan. The plan monitoring will be carried out by means of the comparison with the plans of the expert. The revision of their incorrect actions will be recorded in the plan trace, and, finally, the plan and the scenario design will match.

3   The Plan Editor

Our study domain is Domotics, this is, the integral automation of buildings and housing. We can define it as: "A set of elements that, when installed, interconnected and controlled automatically in a building, save the users worrying about routine everyday actions, providing improvement in their comfort, in energy consumption, in security and in communications as well".

Previous to the simulation stage, a domotic simulation environment requires a phase of design of the scenario where it will be carried out. Before this phase of design we expose our monitored planning tool so that the student can cope with this intermediate solution leading to an acceptable design of the scenario to simulate.

Speaking about domotic design implies the management of several objects. These objects are classified into the ones which are strictly objects in domotics (such as radiators, the thermostat, sensors of fire, alarms, etc.), and those backgrounds where these will be inserted.

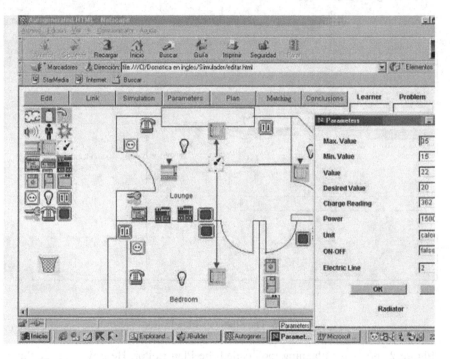

Fig. 1. Basic actions of the domotic design.

The domotic objects are grouped into the so-called management areas. There are different areas such as thermic comfort, lighting, security and the energy control. These areas include three kinds of domotic objects regarding their behaviour: the receivers that capture information, the actuators activated or inhibited when they receive a command, and the systems, taking the information from the receivers and sending commands to the actuators. This is the basic behaviour of a management area.

We have studied the actions of design as shown in Figure 1, which shows the simulation interface. In this figure we can see how the student should compose the scenario to simulate.

These actions refer to aspects such as:

- Selecting the background among a given set at the student's disposal.
- Extracting items from the tool bar and inserting them into the selected background.
- Relating them by means of visual connecting elements with compatible direction.
- Parameterisation of the domotic objects (providing the variables with their values) and, on the other hand, parameterisation of the environment.
- Showing the simulation behaviour.

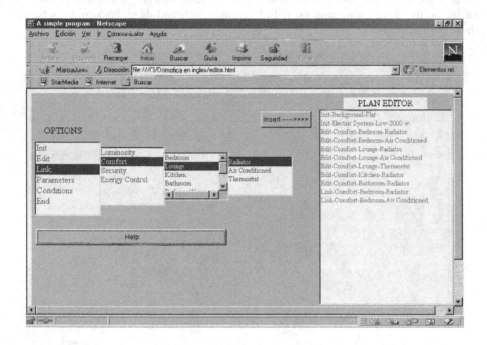

Fig. 2. The Student's Plan Editor.

Figure 2 shows the planning tool, called the Plan Editor. Here we can see the way in which the commands are included in the Student's Plan. As we can see, there is a series of instructional levels assembled in several menus. The first menu called OPTIONS contains the General Plan of Action, while the ones following can contain management areas, background items, domotic objects or variables of these objects or variables of the environment. Each menu is compounded according to the criteria mentioned before and is displayed gradually when the student selects each of the actions that it contains. Once completely displayed, the system, by means of certain mechanisms of comparison with the Expert's Plan, will accept or refuse each of the commands in the Student's Plan. In each case it will be able to request the appropriate help and, as we can also see in the figure, the system will offer some advice to the student.

Table 1 shows the Expert's Plan. The column on the left shows the sequencing of the General Plan of Action with the basic actions of design over the different parts of the background object study case, or over the variables of the environment. The column on the right shows the domotic objects with the aforementioned characteristics of mandatory (M) or optional (O).

Table 1. Expert's Plan (Study of the Bedroom Background Item Comfort and Energy Control).

Action[Subsystem] [Variables]	[Set of Objects][Set of Variables]
Initialise – Select Background	Bedroom
Edit – Comfort – Bedroom	Heater(M)–AirCond. (M)–Thermostat(M)
Edit – Energy Control– Bedroom	TV (O)-Video (O) - Hi-fi (O) -Plug(M)
Link – Comfort – Bedroom	Heater(M) – Air Conditioned (M)
Link – Energy Control– Bedroom	Plug(M)
Parameterise – Desired value	Thermostat (M)
Parameterise - Power/Consumption	TV (O)- Hi-fi(O)
Conditions	Exterior Temperature (M)-Load. Lines (O)

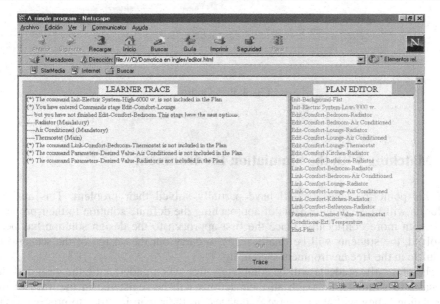

Fig. 3. Plan Trace

As an aid, the system offers the students the trace of the plan (Fig. 3), in which they are provided with the aspects of the plan where they should improve their knowledge of the domain. These aspects include warnings about the erroneous instructions they tried to include in their plan, incorrect sequencing, or some advice when including the appropriate domotic objects according to the problem to study.

In the same way (Fig. 4), in order to help the student at the design stage, the system automatically elaborates a scheme of the plan carried out. In it, the student will be able to observe the sequencing and its flexibility when inserting an item in a management area. This flexibility leads to an unordered insertion but it should be completely fulfilled.

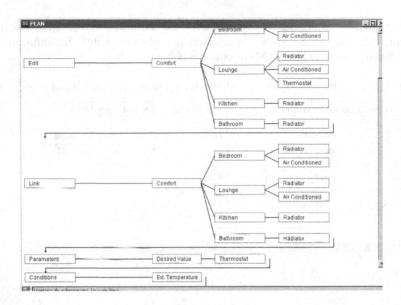

Fig. 4. Plan Outline

4   Matching with the Simulation Environment

At this point the students will have partially solved their problem. This abstract solution will make them capable of approaching the definite solution to their problem of design more confidently. Once the first approach to the design solution has been resolved, the students will be finally ready to carry out the design of the scenario to simulate in the free environment seen in fig. 1.

Therefore, the students will be completely free when undertaking the design of the scenario to simulate, although all their actions will be registered in the trace of the simulation. They will always have free access to their plan in order to proceed along the design. The matching between the planned actions and the freely fulfilled ones in the simulation environment is received by the students as a conclusion comparing the plan and the design.

Once the design has been completed in the simulation environment, the student plan should also be integrated in the working process. Therefore, their actions of free design in the simulation environment will match the ones previously planned.

As a result we propose a matching between both solutions in order to improve the knowledge of the domain in those actions with a higher level of detail, previously seen in a more abstract way in the plan. So, feedback is provided when the student considers re-planning the initial plan. Figure 5 shows the different user interfaces of the Plan Editor (up and left), the simulation environment (right) with a previously designed domotic scenario and finally the conclusions offered by the system (below) combining the design and the plan.

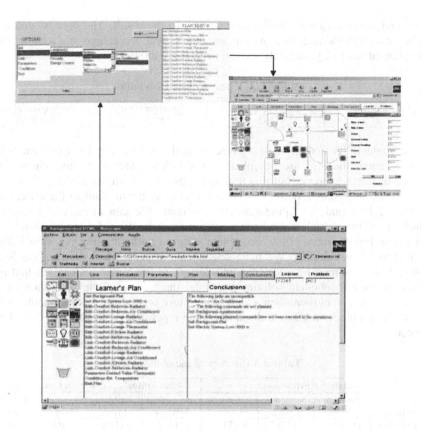

Fig. 5. Plan - Simulation Matching

The system has been designed to work on the Web. This will enable the student-teacher collaboration by including the student's actions in both traces (the plan trace and the design trace), the student's plan and its identification in a database available for that purpose. This database has a range of options (training levels), sets of problems, domotic items, compatibility tables, backgrounds, alternatives to the plan, etc.

5 Evaluation and Conclusions

In order to evaluate DOMOSIM-TP we used a database in which, together with all the data managing the teaching environment, the students' experiences have been recorded within that environment. So, there are tables containing data on their performance regarding these two tools, the Plan Editor and the Simulation Environment.

Regarding the exercises done by the students, we have taken two aspects into consideration. On the one hand, we have evaluated the impact of the new tool, its monitoring and consequently its acceptance. On the other hand, we have carried out a study of the contrast between the freedom of action that the Simulation Environment offers and the planning + simulation approach to the result. The data related to this test are shown in Table 2. In it, we can see that a great percentage of students finished their plan satisfactorily, and only a small percentage did not.

Table 2. Acceptance of the Plan Editor

Students	Plans	Complete plans	Incomplete plans
87	152	122 (80%)	30 (20%)

The students have done a first exercise in the Simulation Environment without knowing about the tool used to plan their solution. Later they have carried out a second different exercise, but this time using the Plan Editor previously. The results are reflected in Table 3. With the second exercise we try to contrast the efficiency of the Plan Editor and the Simulation Environment. We can observe a considerable reduction of the mistakes appearing when using the Plan Editor previous to the Simulation Environment (79% incomplete solution without using the Plan Editor in contrast to 32 % using it). We have selected the aspects of monitoring the Student Plan and the matching between plan and design. In this sense we can see that in the aforementioned incomplete solution example, the failure in the resolution of each problem is reduced in more than a half. Other more precise aspects of this monitoring, such as the problem mistakes and sequence and repetition errors are also considerably reduced.

Table 3. Efficiency of use of the model

Simulation Environment				Plan Editor + Simulation Environment			
Incomplete Solution	Problem Errors	Sequence Errors	Repetition Errors	Incomplete Solution	Problem Errors	Sequence Errors	Repetition Errors
19 (79%)	11 (49%)	8 (33)%	9 (38%)	10 (32%)	3 (10%)	5 (16%)	3 (10%)

We think that building a plan, i.e., an intermediate solution, helps the student to break the complexity of the modelling task and make learning through this kind of simulation environments much more effective. The students first build a more abstract, and consequently easier, solution and then, with an adequate design plan, they proceed to build a model. This model is the final solution to be tested by simulation.

Our proposal for the future includes peer collaboration for planning as much as for simulation. Members of our team are working to deal with this approach so that groups of students can work together in solving both the intermediate solution (plan) and the final solution (model). We thing this collaborative planning and simulation can improve the final solution due to the positive interaction that the classmates can produce through collaboration and negotiation.

References

1. Ajewole, G.A. (1991), "Effects of discovery and expository instructional methods on the attitude of students to biology". Journal of Research in Science Teaching, 28, 301–409.
2. Berry, D.C. & Broadbent, D.E. (1984), "Explanation and verbalization in a computer-assisted search tsak". The Quarterly Journal of Experimental Psychology, 386, 209–231.

3. Bonar, J. G. & Cunningham, R. (1988), "Intelligent Tutoring with Intermediate Representations" ITS-88 Montreal.
4. Bravo Rodríguez, J. (1999), "Design Planning in Simulation Environment for Distance Learning". Doctoral Dissertation, Madrid.
5. Brennenstuhl, D.C. (1975), "Cognitive versus effective gains in computer simulations". Simulation & Games, 6, 303–311.
6. Brown, J.S., (1983), "Process vs product: a perspective on tools for communal and informal electronic learning", report from "The learning Lab: Education in the electronic age".
7. Carlsen, D.D. & Andre, T. (1992), "Use of a microcomputer simulation and conceptual change text to overcome students preconceptions about electric circuits". Journal of Computer-Based Instructions, 19, 105–109.
8. de Jong, T., van Joolingen, W., Pieters, J. & van der Hulst, Anja. (1993), "Why is discovery learning so difficult? and what can we do about it?". EARLI conference. Aix-en-Provence.
9. Duffy, T., Jonassen, D. (1992), "Constructivism and the Technology of instruction". Lawrence Erlbaum Associates, Hillsdale, New Jersey.
10. Faryniarz, J.V. & Lockwood, L.G. (1992), "Effectiveness of microcomputer simulations in stimulating environmental problem solving by community college students". Journal of Research in Science.
11. Fishman, B.J., Honebein, P.C., Duffy, T.M. (1991), "Constructivism and the design of learning environments: Context and authentic activities for learning". NATO Advanced Workshop on the design of Constructivism Learning.
12. Hammond, K.J. (1990), "Case-Based Planning". In Cognitive Science, vol 14, pp. 385–443.
13. Lavoie, D.R. & Good, R. (1988), " The nature and use of predictions skills in a biological computer simulation". Journal of Research in Science Teaching, 25(5), pag. 335–360.
14. Minton, S. & Zweben (1993), "Learning, Planning and Scheduling: An Overview". Machine Learning Methods for Planning. Minton (Ed.) Morgan Kaufmann.
15. Paper, S. (1980), "Mindstorms: Children, Computer and Powerful Ideas". Basic Books Inc., New York.
16. Paper, S. (1987), "Computers in Education:Conceptual Issues". Saphiro, S., Encyclopaedia of Artificial Intelligence, Edit. Willey, New York.
17. Rivers, R.H. & Vockell, E. (1987), "Computer simulations to stimulate scientific problem solving". Journal of Research in Science Teaching, 24, 403–415.
18. Schank, R. Clearcy, C., (1994), "Engines for Education". Lawrence Erlbaaum Associates, Hillsdale, New Jersey. http:// www.ils.nwu.edu/~e_for_e
19. Schank, R., Kass, A., "A Goal-Based Scenario for Higher School Students". Comm. of the ACM, 39(4), 28 (April-1996).
20. Shute, V.J. (1990), "A comparison of inductive and deductive learning environments: Which is better for whon and why?". Paper presented at the American Educational Research Association (AERA) Annual Meeting, Boston. USA.
21. Soloway, E. (1986), " Learning to Program = Learning to Construct Mechanisms and Explanations". Communications of the ACM.
22. Wason, P.C. (1966), "Reasoning". In Foss, B.M. (Ed.). Nes Horizons in Psycology. Harmondsworth, England: Penguin.
23. Wasson, B. (1990), "Determining de Focus if Instruction: Content Planning for Intelligent Tutoring System" Doctoral Thesis, Dep. Computational Science, University of Saskatchewan.

Organizing Problem Solving Activities for Synchronous Collaborative Learning of Design Domains

Crescencio Bravo, Miguel A. Redondo, Manuel Ortega, and José Bravo

Departamento de Informática. Universidad de Castilla - La Mancha
Paseo de la Universidad, 4. 13071 Ciudad Real (Spain)
{Crescencio.Bravo,Miguel.Redondo,Manuel.Ortega,
Jose.Bravo}@uclm.es

Abstract. Scientific community is showing a growing interest in Collaborative Systems, although most of developed systems deal with specific applications. This, together with the effort that implies the construction of complete environments, leads us to explore the application of specification techniques to model some entities of CSCL/CSCW systems, such as the approached domain or the problems to solve. In this work this task is carried out starting from DomoSim-TPC, a web-based CSCL environment for distance education of domotical design. First, its positions are generalized, and next, a specification that will allow users to generate software systems that approach other design domains is defined.

1 Introduction

Nowadays, the CSCW and CSCL paradigms attract the attention of many researchers. However, most of developed collaborative systems approach specific applications and are not flexible nor adaptable to different situations and purposes, especially in the area of the CSCL and of the systems for real time collaboration. One of the directions for future research in the field of CSCW –and of the CSCL– should be to build generic models for collaborative work, by means of architectures or formal languages, allowing us to describe properties and conditions of the systems [1], and to develop tools that can generate software systems starting from these descriptions.

We are interested particularly in CSCL systems for the learning of design tasks. These systems follow instructional methods as Problem Based Learning (PBL) or Project Based Learning, as these methods reinforce the commitment among the learner and the activity he/she carries out. Particular types of problems are the ones concerned with design. Most of them are complex, requiring the designer to use domain knowledge to build an artefact or to carry out a process under certain conditions. The cognitive strategies of problem solving are domain specific [2], and it is necessary to model the domain in order to model the problem solving.

In this work we deal with the modelling of domains and generic problems of design in the context of a collaborative learning environment. Thus, the DomoSim-TPC environment will be described first, which is taken as a reference to generalize its approach.

J.M. Cueva Lovelle et al. (Eds.): ICWE 2003, LNCS 2722, pp. 108–111, 2003.
© Springer-Verlag Berlin Heidelberg 2003

2 The DomoSim-TPC System

We have developed DomoSim-TPC [3, 4, 5], a collaborative system for the distance learning of domotical design (Home Automation). It includes support for setup, realization, monitoring, analysis, and storage of learning activities. This system has been evaluated following diverse techniques and it is being successfully used in different teaching centers. The DomoSim-TPC system has been developed in Java to allow the execution with a web browser, so that the system can be used at a distance.

We represent the Domotics domain by means of a set of object types and of relationships among them. We call operators to these domain-specific objects. The types of operators we identify are regulation systems, activators, receivers, and other elements (plugs, buses...). The systems are related with the activators and the receivers they regulate. Another type of relationships among operators are, for example, the connections to plugs or data buses. The operators are classified in five management areas: thermal comfort, luminosity comfort, energetic control, accident security, and intrusion security.

The process of problem solving is structured in two stages:

- Planning of the Design Strategy [5]: The learners decide the steps that determine the strategy to follow to build the model they consider satisfy the problem objectives, first individually and then in group.
- Detailed Design and Simulation in group [4]: The learners build a model and simulate it by means of successive refinements, checking if this model solves the problem.

In this work we focus on the second stage, a synchronous task, which facilitates the generation of spontaneous ideas, brings in personal experience, increases motivation, and encourages a content focus.

3 Activities Organization and Collaborative Problem Solving

The users of the DomoSim-TPC system are classified in two profiles: teacher and student. The students are arranged in groups coordinated by one or more teachers. The access to the tools is regulated according to the user's profile. The teachers use management tools, for the definition of the activities and participants, and authoring tools, to create the problems.

The students work actively in groups on problems extracted from the real practice (PBL). Each problem describes the requirements of the model that the students have to build. In this situation the student plays the role of a professional designer. This collection of problems is organized in three levels of complexity: low, medium, and high. Thus, the teacher can propose problems with a certain complexity level according to the knowledge level of the group. The *activity* abstraction allows proposing a concrete problem to a concrete group of students. From the organizational point of view, a problem is a learning object that can be reused. The activity help level, together with the complexity level of the problem, allows teachers to use scaffolding techniques [6]. This way, the problem solving can be considered with different levels of help (reinforcement), depending on the previous knowledge of the participants and in a process of successive integration of knowledge.

The process of detailed solving of problems is framed in the Design and Simulation subsystem. This subsystem is materialized by means of the shared workspace metaphor. There are five workspaces available: Design, Task Distribution, Parameterization, Cases and Hypothesis, and Simulation. The navigation along these workspaces is defined by means of a Collaboration Protocol that synchronizes the joint access of the students belonging to the group. The Design workspace is the first one accessed when the group starts the resolution of a problem. From this, the Work Distribution, Parameterization, and Cases and Hypothesis workspaces can be accessed; from here it is possible to come back to the Design. The Simulation workspace is accessed from the Cases and Hypothesis workspace. All these subspaces integrate different mechanisms of direct manipulation, support for communication and coordination, and awareness techniques [7].

4   Generalization to Generic Design Domains

To carry out this generalization we propose the use of XML to build a language that allows specifying the characteristics of the design domain (DDL, Domain Definition Language) as well as of the problems (PDL, Problem Definition Language). Other authors also use specifications in XML to represent interactions in CSCL systems [8], to describe learning activities (users, tasks, tools...) [9], and to implement an Educational Modelling Language, which allows users to define Units of Study [10]. The choice of the XML notation is because of its feature of standard language and its interoperability. We aim that this specification language of domains and problems has certain degree of formalization, that can be processed automatically and be compatible with standards, allowing the reusability of the learning objects (problems, plans...). For example, XML would allow, by means of XSLT transformations, the generation of XHTML pages with a description of the domain or the problem visualizable on a browser.

The domain and problem models are defined by means of a DTD (Document Type Definition) that describes the valid syntax of the XML documents. So, four files make up the specification: DTD files for the domain and the problem, and the domain itself and problem definition by means of XML (see table 1).

Table 1. A schematic example of specification in DDL and PDL.

Domain specification	Problem specification

`<domain name="dom1" ...>`
`<graphics>...</graphics>`
`<operators>...</operators>`
`<relationships>...</relationships>`
`<variables>...</variables>`
`</domain>`
	`<problem id="p1" domain="dom1" ...>`
	`<description>...</description>`
	`<comments>...</comments>`
	`<behavior>...</behavior>`
	`<variables>...</variables>`
	`<requirements>...</requirements>`
	`<constraints>...</constraints>`
	`<cases>...</cases>`
	`<hypotheses>...</hypotheses>`
	`</problem>`

5   Summary and Future Work

We propose the use of XML for the modelling and specification of the domain and of the problems in collaborative design systems. This way, we have built a Domain Definition Language (DDL) and a Problem Definition Language (PDL) on this domain. These languages would also facilitate the automatic generation of problems as well as the elaboration and verification of solutions for them.

The following objective is to build a tool that automatically processes these languages and can generate collaborative systems to approach the learning of design in different domains.

Acknowledgements. This work was partially supported by the Junta de Comunidades de Castilla – La Mancha and the Ministerio de Ciencia y Tecnología in the Projects PBI-02-026 and TIC2002-01387.

References

1.   Chang, C.K., Zhang, J. & Jiang, T.M.: *Formalization of Computer Supported Cooperative Work Applications.* Proceedings of the Eighth IEEE Workshop on Future Trends of Distributed Computing Systems (FTDCS'01) (2001)3.
2.   Mayer, R.E.: *Thinking, problem solving, cognition* (2nd ed.). New York: Freeman (1992)
3.   DomoSim-TPC Tutorial: http://chico.inf-cr.uclm.es/domosim
4.   Bravo, C.: *Un Sistema de Soporte al Aprendizaje Colaborativo del Diseño Domótico Mediante Herramientas de Modelado y Simulación.* Doctoral Thesis. Computer Science Department, University of Castilla - La Mancha (Spain) (2002)
5.   Redondo, M.: *Planificación Colaborativa del Diseño en Entornos de Simulación para el Aprendizaje a Distancia.* Doctoral Thesis. Computer Science Department. University of Castilla - La Mancha (Spain) (2002)
6.   Rosson, M.B. & Carroll, J.M.: *Scaffolded Examples for Learning Object-Oriented Design.* Communications of ACM, vol. 39, no. 4 (1996)
7.   Bravo, C., Redondo, M.A., Ortega, M. & Verdejo, M.F.: *Collaborative Discovery Learning of Model Design.* Cerri, S.A., Gourdères, G. & Paraguaçu, F. (Eds.) Intelligent Tutoring Systems, 6th International Conference, pp. 671–680, LNCS, Springer (2002)
8.   Martínez, A., Dimitriadis, Y. & de la Fuente, P.: *Aportaciones al análisis de interacciones para la evaluación formativa en CSCL.* Llamas, M., Fernández, M.J., Anido, L.E. (Eds) Proceedings of 4th International Symposium of Computers and Education, p. 41 (2002)
9.   Verdejo, M.F., Barros, B., Read, T. & Rodríguez-Artacho, M.: *A System for the Specification and Development of an Environment for Distributed CSCL Scenarios.* Cerri, S.A., Gourdères, G. & Paraguaçu, F. (Eds.) Intelligent Tutoring Systems, 6th International Conference, pp. 139–148, LNCS, Springer (2002)
10.   Koper, R.: *Modeling units of study from a pedagogical perspective. The pedagogical meta-model behind EML.* Educational Technology Expertise Centre. Open University of the Netherlands. Draft. http://eml.ou.nl/introduction/docs/ped-metamodel.pdf (2001)

Feijoo.net: An Approach to Personalized E-learning Using Learning Styles

Mª del Puerto Paule Ruiz[1], Sergio Ocio Barriales[2], Juan Ramón Pérez Pérez[1], and Martín González Rodríguez[3]

[1] HCI Group- Labtoo- Dpto. Computer Science
C/Calvo Sotelo S/N Facultad de Ciencias. 33007 Oviedo. Spain
{paule,jrpp}@pinon.ccu.uniovi.es
[2] HCI Group- Labtoo- Dpto. Computer Science
C/Calvo Sotelo S/N Facultad de Ciencias. 33007 Oviedo. Spain
djrekcv@terra.es
[3] HCI Group- Labtoo- Dpto. Computer Science
C/Calvo Sotelo S/N Facultad de Ciencias. 33007 Oviedo. Spain
martin@lsi.uniovi.es

Abstract. This paper proposes a model of adaptation called Feijoo.net. Feijoo.net is a system which adapts contents and the presentation of these contents to the learning style of each student. In this model, contents are separated from their presentation on the Web. Feijoo.net is focused on university students. The main goal is to get an adaptation model of the learning of each student following the directives proposed by the cognitive psychology and pedagogy.

1 FEIJOO.NET

One of the major obstacles in Educational Web Sites is the imitation of the traditional way of teaching based in the master class of a teacher due overcrowding in universities. In these circumstances, the teacher cannot do a full adaptation to the learning style of each student because there are a lot of students in the classroom and it is impossible to do it. So, Internet can be an adequate resource to do this adaptation because it is a mass media and the content of individual dynamic pages can be adapted to each learning style.

Nowadays, the Educational Web Sites do not show different contents and presentations of the contents to be selected by the students. In the design of Educational Web Sites it is very important to have prepared the objectives of learning, the motivations, the previous knowledge and the preferences of each student. It is evidence the first step towards the design of high quality courses is the user classification.

Feijoo.net uses the test of CHAEA [1] to classify the user. This test returns the learning style of the student. The cognitive styles are the way of thinking, processing information, and learning of each individual student.

J.M. Cueva Lovelle et al. (Eds.): ICWE 2003, LNCS 2722, pp. 112–115, 2003.
© Springer-Verlag Berlin Heidelberg 2003

This test returns the preferences of the student at the time of learning. There are four styles in this classification: Theorists, Activists, Reflectors and Pragmatists. Each style has its own characteristics and particularities.

Actually, Feijoo.net is adapting the learning styles : Theorists and Activists, because they are the base of the adaptation for the rest of styles. The goal is to adapt the content and the presentation of these contents in a course to students belonging to the cognitive style : Theorists and Activists. This adaptation will increment the quality and the usability of Educational Web Sites. The usability is a subjective factor and it is difficult to measure it, but when a user is comfortable with the site, the usability will increment [2].

Feijoo.net has three main components: the University Student , the professor and the Adaptation Core is how to link and organize the adapted contents.

In the following sections, we are going to explain the particularities of each agent.

2 University Student

In our model the principal agent is the university student. The Test of CHAEA returns the cognitive style of the student, therefore, preferences contribute to their learning.

The student will be registered in one or several subjects. The first time the students enters the system, FEIJOO.NET will request him to do the test of CHAEA, so, the system will know his/her cognitive style. Following times, the student has not to do the test because his/her cognitive style will be stored in database.

The student will select the subject of the course and the Adaptation Core will get its content and the presentation according to the cognitive style of this individual student.

3 The Professor

The professor has to do a planning of the subject. In fact, the professor has to do a didactic programming. This programming consists of a temporary programming, where he/she has to decide the didactic resources, lessons, duration of the lessons, etc.

Previously the professor had had to think the general learning objectives the student has to reach at the end of the course. This general learning objectives have to match with specific learning objectives the student has to reach in each lesson.

When the professor knows the general and specific learning objectives, he has to create the content of each lesson adapted to each cognitive style.

The student will see the contents when he had registered in one subject. The student will see too another complementary information as the teacher's telephone number, the office's number, email, etc.

4 Adaptation Core

The Adaptation Core is how to link and how to organize the information.

In this part, FEIJOO.NET has three parts:

1. POL: PrOgrammed Learning management (Web Platform)
2. IOWA: Intuitive-use Oriented Webtool for the creation of Adapted contents (in a e-learning environment).
3. VIC: Visualization of Contents.

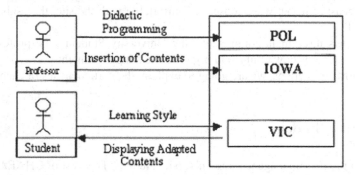

Fig. 1. Relations between agents.

4.1 POL (PrOgrammed Learning Management (Web Platform))

POL will help the teacher to elaborate and organize his work on a Web platform, adjusting contents to a flexible and recognizable structure ,showing the way he should carry out the educational management.

Normally, begging to distribute a subject, the teachers make a planning about how they are going to carry out that work. POL tries to automate this work, so it is made of a more systematic way, rational and reflective.

The teacher is going to do the didactic programming with POL; so, he/she teacher has to decide the general and specific learning objectives of each didactic unit. The general learning objectives will be reached when the specific objectives did .

The system will warn the teacher when general objectives aren't fulfilled or when specific objectives from each didactic unit do not fit into general one.

POL has three types of users: Administrator, Professor and Student. Each kind of user has different privileges, can make different functions and has access to the information in different ways. Each user has a login and a password to access the system.

POL has different benefits and shows different contents according to the type of the user. To get this personalization, the system has XML templates and XSLT Styles sheets.

4.2 IOWA Intuitive-Use Oriented Webtool for the Creation of Adapted Contents (in a E-learning Environment)

When the teacher finishes inserting the didactic programming, then he will add the contents of the didactic unit or lesson.

IOWA, is the part of the system that allows the teacher to add contents adapted to cognitive style of each student content. It is designed with a very intuitive interface. It is thought to be used by a teacher who doesn't know anything about computers or he /she has user-level knowledge .

IOWA has two main functions :

1. Helping the teacher : IOWA guides the teacher in the task of creating adapted to the cognitive style the teacher is working with contents.
2. Contents will be shown according to the type of the individual student. To get this goal, IOWA will have a template editor. We will use templates to define how we want contents to be displayed . The editor will be a wizard-like one, so we can guide the teacher easily through the process. Every Learning Style will have a template associate to it each course.

The information is organized as tree. Feijoo.net uses the concept of "context" proposed in the methodology OOHDM[3]. The traversing of the tree depends on the learning style.

4.3 VIC (Visualization of Contents)

The main functions of VIC are:

1. Knowing the learning style of the student with the test of CHAEA.
2. Showing the user the adapted content according to her/his cognitive style.

With the first function, VIC implements the test of CHAEA.. The student has to answer all of them. VIC uses a subsystem that uses fuzzy logic to know the cognitive style. With the second function, VIC gets the learning style of the student from the database and the core of the VIC shows the adapted content .

5 Conclusions

In this paper we presented an Adaptive System Hypermedia. The adaptation is cognitive. This adaptation will increment the usability of Educational Web Sites, because, the Web Site adapts itself to the student , not, the opposite way.

Actually, there is not any Web Tool [4] that it had the characteristics of Feijoo.net.

References

1. Alonso Catalina M., Gallego Domingo, J., Honey Peter, "Los estilos de aprendizaje: procedimientos de diagnóstico y mejora". 5a ed. Bilbao, Mensajero, ISBN: 8427119143, 2002
2. "Designing Web Usability". Jakob Nielsen. http://www.useit.com.
3. Rossi, Gustavo. Gustavo Rossi's Home Page. http://www-lifia.info.unlp.edu.ar/~gustavo/oohdm.html
4. "Multi-model, Metadata Driven Approach to Adaptive Hypermedia Services for Personalized eLearning". Owen Conlan, Vicent Wade, Catherine Bruen and Mark Gargan. Adaptive Hypermedia and Adaptive Web-Based Systems. Springer Verlag. ISBN 0302-9743. 2002

A Collaborative E-learning Component for the IDEFIX Project

T. Hernán Sagástegui Ch., José E. Labra G., Juan M. Cueva L.,
José M. Morales G., María E. Alva O., Eduardo Valdés, and Cecilia García

University of Oviedo, Department of Computer Science, Calvo Sotelo S/N,
33007 Oviedo, Spain
{thsagas, jmmoral, malva360}@correo.uniovi.es,
{labra, cueva}@lsi.uniovi.es
eduardovr@telecable.es, cgpelayo27@hotmail.com

Abstract. This paper presents the design and architecture of a collaborative learning model based on the Web as an experience that it is being done at the University of Oviedo, giving support to the students of a logic course, in the collaborative achievement of exercises by means of e-meetings and in the training of the achievement of exams by means of a virtual reality game. This model is developed like a component of the project IDEFIX and it uses Web services.

1 Introduction

The IDEFIX project (Integrated Development Environment Frameworks based on Internet and eXtensible technologies) is based on the development of e-learning tools based on the use XML and related technologies [1]. IDEFIX can extend its domain to the teaching for Internet of any course at the School of Computer Science Engineering at Oviedo (EUITIO), as well as to the shared teaching of free election courses through Internet in the AulaNet project [2] of other universities. In this context, this article shows an extension component of the IDEFIX project. This component is referred to the design and architecture of collaborative learning model of the logic course through the Web.

At this moment most of the students attend the course in the classroom and it has a didactic guide of the classes and a notebook that gathers the exams carried out in the convocations of previous years that are used as exercises as pedagogic material of support.

The goal is that the students can access the notebook of exercises by Internet and that they can solve these exercises in a collaborative way, and that they can also fill their exams by means of a virtual reality game through the web.

2 Background

Computer supported collaborative learning (CSCL) supports group work in a common task and provides a shared interface for groups to work with [3], [4],[12], by means of a net of computers, supporting the coordination, and the application of the

J.M. Cueva Lovelle et al. (Eds.): ICWE 2003, LNCS 2722, pp. 116–119, 2003.
© Springer-Verlag Berlin Heidelberg 2003

knowledge in certain domains [5], [6]. CSCL is used in the educational environment and it serves from support to the students in the learning, facilitating the group working process and group dynamics in ways that are not achievable by face-to-face learning [12].

There are numerous commercial collaborative applications that support: problems resolutions, tutorials, simulations [9], debates, modeling and CourseWare (Blackboard: Virginia Commonwealth University, LearningSpace: Lotus & IBM [11], WebCT: University British Columbia, TopClass: WBT Systems [10], etc), while for the learning of the logic there is projects like JAPE [7], [8]. Collaborative application inside an outline of group working has the following characteristic: group memory, roles, collaboration protocol, perception and interface [3], [5].

3   Model of Collaborative Learning

The model of collaborative learning for the logic course is based on the group and on the e-meetings of the group, in a distributed environment, being able to design a cycle of life of the e-meetings [3],[4],[5],[6]. The elementary components of the model are:

Group Memory: it is formed by the database of the university (with links to courses and professors), the base of exercises/exams and the games.

Roles: the professor, the student that develops exercises the student that solves the exam and the invited user.

Collaboration Protocols: rules settled down by the professor, rules for the achievement of exercises and exams, rules for the invited users and rules for the administrator.

Perception: it is the information generated in the achievement of assignments and exams; which members of the group are connected, which exercises are developed, obtained results, generation of ideas, taking of decisions, using the chat as main tool.

Interface: It allows the user to interact with the group memory and with the generated knowledge, and to select the work (Collaborative development of the exercises of the exercises notebook, and to carry out training exams).

4   Architecture of the Model

The architecture for the implementation of this model is based on a 3 layer client/server design presented in Figure 1. It is implemented as a component of the IDEFIX project on Microsoft .NET platform.

4.1   Presentation Layer

This layer presents the user interface and takes charge of the visualization of the clients and the data entry. Once the client makes its petitions from the navigator, the Web server takes the petition to an ASP page.

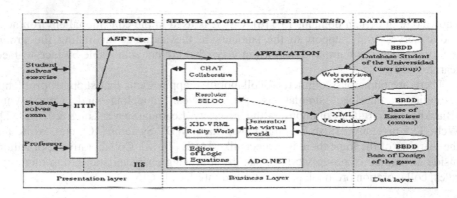

Fig. 1. This graph shows the architecture of design of the application web, corresponding to a structure client-server, where the application layer or business layer it shows the support that will give to the collaborative component for the process of collaborative learning.

4.2 Business Layer

This layer is in charge of the logic of the application and the access to the data. It is formed by:

Logic equations editor: Similar to that of Microsoft Word, it facilitates the creation of logic equations storing the results in an XML specific vocabulary.

Collaborative CHAT: query chat and feedback chat.

SELOG Solver: It allows the collaborative development of logic exercises. It presents an interface and carries out: selection of exercises, solution, consults and evaluation of the difficulty and comments. Chat is mainly used for group work.

Virtual Reality World: It is designed as support to the students in the training and achievement of exams. The micro-world of logic - Logical world - is a world formed by spheres that describe the different levels of the game. At this moment, to pass from one sphere to another, it is necessary to approve all the phases of the corresponding level.

Starting from an XML document and common data from the database a program written in C# generates the virtual world in X3D, which can automatically be converted to VRML.

4.3 Data Layer

This layer stores data of the students, all the exercises/exams and the games and data that the generator of the virtual world needs.

5 Conclusions

This work contributes to the development of collaborative e-learning applications for secondary and higher education [13] that satisfy the communicative requirements and pedagogic features of these educational levels. It also supports the development of e-learning collaborative applications. Although the collaborative application is in development and the prototypes have an autonomous functionality; it is designed to become a components of the IDEFIX project in its scalable development. Future research will be managed to implement the e-learning collaborative application in other courses at the School of Computer Science Engineering of Oviedo.

References

1. Labra, J., Morales, J., Fernandez, A., Sagástegui, H.: A Generic e-Learning Multiparadigm Programming Language System: IDEFIX Project. SIGCSE'03 USA (2003)
2. Pérez, R., López, A.: Aulanet, una Experiencia de Aula Virtual Spain (2000)
3. Ellis, C., Gibbs, S., Rein, G.: Groupware some issues y experiences, Comm. of the ACM, Vol. 34 No. 1 (1991) 38–58
4. Conklin, J.: Capturing Organizational Memory. Readings in Groupware and Computer-Supported Cooperative Work. Morgan Kaufmann Publishers CA (1993) 561–565
5. Guerrero, L. Fuller, D.: CLASS: A Computer Platform for the Development of Education's Collaborative Applications. Proceeddings of CRIWG'97, 3rd International Workshop on Groupware Spain (1997) 1–3
6. Gokhale, A.: Collaborative Learning Enhances Critical Thinking. Journal of Technology Education, Vol. 7, Nº 1, Fall 1995, University Libraries Virginia (1996)
7. Aczel, J.: The Evaluation of a Computer Program for Learning Logic: The Role of Students' Formal Reasoning Strategies in Visualising Proofs. CALRG Technical Report (2000) 192
8. The Jape Visualisation Project
    http://iet.open.ac.uk/pp/j.c.aczel/Jape/index.html
9. LEGO Mindstorms
    http://mindstorms.lego.com/eng/default.asp
10. TopClass e-Learning Suite™
    http://www.wbtsystems.com/products
11. IBM Lotus Software
    http://www.lotus.com/home.nsf/tabs/learnspace
12. Lin, W.: CSCL Theories. Texas University. USA (1996)
    http://www.edb.utexas.edu/csclstudent/Dhsiao/theories.html
13. Computer-Supported Intentional Learning Environments
    http://www.ed.gov/pubs/EdReformStudies/EdTech/csile.html

Engineering a Future for Web-Based Learning Objects

Permanand Mohan[1] and Christopher Brooks[2]

[1] Department of Mathematics and Computer Science, The University of the West Indies,
St. Augustine, Trinidad and Tobago
{pmohan@tstt.net.tt}
[2] ARIES Lab, Department of Computer Science, University of Saskatchewan,
Saskatoon, Canada
{cab938@mail.usask.ca}

Abstract. This paper takes a critical look at current development efforts with learning objects for Web-based e-learning. It points out the limitations of these efforts and argues that they are still a long way off from realizing the potential of learning objects on the Web. The paper then proposes the notion of object-oriented learning objects to address several of the problems identified.

1   Introduction

One aspect of e-learning currently receiving considerable attention is the *learning object* — an entity of learning capable of being reused in different instructional situations. Learning objects now seem poised to fill the ever-increasing need to quickly develop cost-effective training materials for e-learning. Recently, a number of standardization efforts have resulted in several specifications for e-learning and learning objects. These efforts are being spearheaded by groups such as the Learning Technology Standards Committee of the Institute of Electrical and Electronics Engineers (IEEE LTSC) [ltsc.ieee.org] and the IMS Global Learning Consortium [www.imsglobal.org]. These groups have developed specifications to aid in the discovery, management, and exchange of learning objects.

The IEEE 1484.12.1-2002 Standard for Learning Object Metadata (LOM) is the first accredited standard for learning technology. It is essentially a cataloging scheme for learning objects and uses nine categories of metadata elements to describe a learning object. Two important specifications from the IMS are Content Packaging and Simple Sequencing. The former allows learning objects for an individual course or collection of courses to be packaged into interoperable packages, while the latter allows the sequencing of learning objects within a content package.

Different types of repositories are also being developed to allow users to discover, obtain rights to, and use learning objects on the Web. These include global repositories that are based on the client/server approach, repositories employing a brokerage model, and local repositories that provide peer-to-peer access to local repositories of learning objects.

J.M. Cueva Lovelle et al. (Eds.): ICWE 2003, LNCS 2722, pp. 120–123, 2003.
© Springer-Verlag Berlin Heidelberg 2003

2   Limitations of Current Efforts with Learning Objects

LOM metadata allows searching for learning objects based on keywords and other basic pedagogic metadata such as *LearningResourceType*, *TypicalAgeRange*, or *Language*. To determine the suitability of a learning object, an instructional designer must carefully examine each learning object. This can be very time consuming, given that many learning objects may satisfy the query and each one must be examined individually. The Digital Repositories Interoperability (DRI) Specification from the IMS makes it easier for computers to query on-line repositories for learning objects. However, the problem still remains, since the metadata is the same and computers cannot perform the level of filtering required.

Making instructionally principled decisions with learning objects requires deep pedagogic information in the metadata. Current learning object metadata say nothing about how to combine learning objects with others, and indeed, whether such a combination is useful in the first place. Metadata also say nothing about the types of learners for which a learning object is best suited and the kinds of teaching and learning strategies it employs. Worse yet, metadata do not even identify the learning outcome(s) that will be achieved if the content in a learning object was successfully learned [1]. Putting together content packages based on reusable learning objects is a very difficult problem. However, this problem must be solved otherwise it will severely limit the usefulness of the numerous repositories of learning objects that are being developed.

In addition to the problem of locating the 'right' learning objects, the full set of 86 elements in the IMS Metadata Specification is not suited to direct implementation since it entails a huge classification effort [2]. Also, widely varying interpretations of the utility, scope and purpose of individual elements threaten to cause considerable interoperability problems, which the specification was designed to solve in the first place. Thus, even if the metadata specifications were very useful in automatically generating content packages (and they are not), creating the metadata itself entails a huge effort.

We therefore contend that the future of learning objects is at stake. Current development efforts do not address the really important issues associated with using learning objects for e-learning. There is much excitement about metadata, the Semantic Web, RDF, ontologies, and other technology that promise a bright future for locating information on the Web. These technologies are poised to profoundly influence the way in information is used in the future Web. However, they do not address many of the problems related to successfully using learning objects in an instructionally meaningful manner.

3   Nature of Learning Objects

It is often suggested that learning objects are really like the objects of object-oriented software [e.g., 3, 4]. We now examine this claim. Consider audio-visual media files and files of other formats (e.g., GIF, JPEG, PowerPoint Presentations, etc.) which are simply collections of bits. These files are not software, much less software objects. So, it is clear that not every learning object is software. However, files such as HTML files containing markup and code written in scripting languages such as JavaScript and Java applets may be considered software. However, HTML files do not support object-oriented concepts, so are not object-oriented. Java applets are certainly software. From the perspective of its developers, a Java applet may be considered object-oriented. From the perspective of an instructional designer or other programmer wishing to use the applet (without access to the source code), the applet is just like another piece of software, and indeed, its object-oriented features are irrelevant.

Thus, despite the claims being made, a cursory examination reveals that most learning objects today are not truly object-oriented from the computer science perspective. However, from an instructional designer's point of view, there is no real benefit in viewing learning objects as object-oriented and it is best to look at learning objects in terms of their content, context of use, and relationship with other learning objects. To require one to understand object-oriented theory to put together meaningful content packages is perhaps akin to asking a good carpenter to understand the internal structures of the materials that are used to fabricate furniture.

From a computer science perspective, there is much to gain by treating learning objects as object-oriented software artifacts. Object-oriented technology can be used to take learning objects out of their current static form and imbue them with behaviours that allow them to contribute more meaningfully to an instructional situation. Object-oriented learning objects are capable of overcoming several of the limitations mentioned in the previous section. Moreover, instructional designers and other users do not have to be aware of this technology, much like users of Microsoft Office are not aware of the agent-like technology underlying the Office Assistant.

4   The Object-Oriented Learning Object

In this section, we propose the idea of an object-oriented learning object. There is one naturally occurring class of learning objects, *LearningObject*, which is the superclass of all learning objects. Every learning object is an instance of this class. *LearningObject* has properties such as a collection of references to metadata instances (e.g., Dublin Core, CanCore, or LOM). *LearningObject* also contains a set of different *Version* objects that refer to different versions of the learning resources that make up the learning object. An important property is a *Context* object that contains various types of contextual information such as the types of learners for which the learning object is appropriate and the teaching and learning strategies employed by the learning object. Another property is a *Combination* object, which contains information about the characteristics of the learning object that allows it to be combined with other learning objects. *LearningObject* also contains one or more concept maps, describing how the learning object is positioned in the conceptual structure of a domain, and the instructional objectives that will be achieved if the content is successfully learned.

LearningObject provides several useful methods. Query methods accept a *Context* object as well as one or more *Metadata* objects and determine if the learning object is appropriate. Version control [5] is achieved by means of various methods operating on the list of *Version* objects. Since a learning object can contain several learning resources or even aggregate other learning objects, *LearningObject* has methods to enable the easy insertion, deletion, and rearrangement of learning resources within a learning object. This gives content producers (and others) the flexibility to easily make changes to a learning object from time to time. Methods can also be written to render the learning object in different formats, e.g., HTML, text, PDF, XML, etc. In essence, *LearningObject* has meaningful data for reasoning about instruction, and methods to support the reasoning process and the increased complexity of the object-oriented learning object.

Since learning objects are independent chunks of content, it is difficult for them to have *using* relationships with other learning objects. *Using* relationships introduce undesirable coupling between learning objects, preventing them from standing on their own, and decreasing the possibility of reusability. However, *aggregation* relationships allow hierarchies of learning objects to be created out of simpler ones. *Inheritance* is also very useful since it is possible to inherit metadata and other attributes of a learning object when producing similar learning objects. This reduces considerably the data entry required for entering metadata and other information.

We believe that the object-oriented approach can go a long way towards achieving the vision currently being promoted for learning objects. Learning objects with object-oriented features provide a solid foundation for the effective reuse of learning resources on the Web.

References

1. Mohan, P., and Greer, J. (2003). E-Learning Specifications in the Context of Instructional Planning. Accepted for the International Conference on Artificial Intelligence and Education, Sydney, Australia, July 2003.
2. Richards, G. R., McGreal, R., and Freisen, N. (2002). Learning Object Repository Technologies for TeleLearning: The evolution of POOL and CanCore. Proceedings of the Informing Science + IT Education Conference, Cork, Ireland, June 19–21, 2002, p. 1333–1341.
3. Downes, S. (2001). Learning objects: resources for distance education worldwide. *International Review of Research in Open and Distance Learning*, 2 (1).
4. Robson, R. (1999). Object-oriented Instructional Design and Applications to the Web. World Conference on Educational Multimedia, Hypermedia and Telecommunications, Seattle, Washington, USA, June 19–24, 698–702.
5. Brooks, C., Cooke, J., and Vassileva, J. (2003). Versioning of Learning Objects. Accepted for the International Conference on Advanced Learning Technologies, Athens, Greece, July 2003.

Adaptation and Generation in a Web-Based Tutor for Linear Programming

E. Millán, E. García-Hervás, E. Guzmán, A. Rueda, and J.L. Pérez-de-la-Cruz

Departamento de Lenguajes y Ciencias de la Computación. ETSI Informática.
Universidad de Málaga. SPAIN.
eva@lcc.uma.es

Abstract. We present TAPLI, an adaptive web-based learning environment for Linear Programming. TAPLI is a set of adaptive tools offered in a web-based learning environment: a) an adaptive hypermedia component, that is responsible of presenting the learning contents; b) a testing component, based on Item Response Theory and c) *a drill-and-practice component*, which adaptively generates exercises and coaches the student while solving them.

1   Introduction

The development of adaptive web-based educational systems (AWES) can be of great help in the teaching and learning process, providing world-wide accessibility and timeless availability. Along these lines, the main goal in the research work presented here was to use the web and adaptive technologies to create TAPLI (*Tutorial Adaptativo de Programación Lineal* -Adaptive Tutorial for Linear Programming, in Spanish) .The system is available at http://www.lcc.uma.es/tapli.

TAPLI is built upon previous work developed by our team for systems like EPLAR [4] (a problem solver for simplex problems), ILESA [3] (a system capable of generating problems at the right level of difficulty based on the student model and also of coaching students while solving a problem) and SIETTE [2] (a web-based testing tool available at http://www.lcc.uma.es/siette), that can be used by teachers to edit tests for any subject domain and by students to assess themselves on line).

This paper is structured as follows: in the next section we briefly present an overview of the system. In section 3 we focus on the web issues of TAPLI. The paper finishes with some conclusions and future research directions.

2   The TAPLI System

The TAPLI system (Figure 1) is in fact a set of components that have been integrated in a single learning environment: a) a*n adaptive hypermedia component*, that is responsible of presenting the theoretical concepts and examples; b) *a testing component*, that evaluates the student knowledge on each of the topics in which the

J.M. Cueva Lovelle et al. (Eds.): ICWE 2003, LNCS 2722, pp. 124–127, 2003.
© Springer-Verlag Berlin Heidelberg 2003

domain has been decomposed, and c) *a drill-and practice component*, where students can solve problems (automatically generated and adapted to student's knowledge level) while being coached by the system. Together, all these tools constitute a complete web-based environment for learning Linear Programming. They are coordinated by an *instructional planner*, which is responsible of selecting the next component that will be used by the student in his learning process, by using the information provided by the corresponding *student model*.

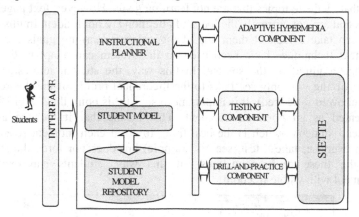

Fig. 1.   The architecture of TAPLI.

The testing component can be used at any time during the interaction with the system. The action *Take a test* is also recommended by the system whenever it is advisable. For example, for new students (to check their state of knowledge), when the student reads a page (to infer if the knowledge presented has been acquired), or when the student enters the drill-and-practice environment (to be able to generate problems at the required level of difficulty for student's level of knowledge). Different tests have been defined for each of the six topics the subject has been divided into. After each topic is evaluated, a global grade is computed as a weighted average.

To use the SIETTE system to allow coached problem solving in a drill-and-practice environment, we have made use of the possibility to define questions by means of Java Applets. Generation of problems for web systems is an interesting issue that has already been discussed in [1]. The problem-solving procedure has been decomposed in TAPLI into *basic skills* and *types of problems* and different applets have been defined for each of the basic skills.

3   The Adaptive Hypermedia Component

This component has been designed so students that cannot attend lessons are able to learn the main concepts and techniques for Linear Programming. TAPLI is *adaptable* (some characteristics are adapted according to information provided by the student) and *adaptive* (some others are adapted based on information gathered by the system during student's interactions):

- *Adaptable characteristics*. When the student connects to TAPLI, she has to provide some information (name and password) so the system can create her student model. Also some personal learning characteristics are included in the model like topics of interest (learning goals), and type of knowledge that she wants to acquire (practical vs. theoretical-practical). According to this characteristics, the system will adapt to the student. Learning goals are used to adapt the suggested navigation structure (*i.e.*, the recommendations provided by the system), and also to hide links to tests that evaluate topics that are not learning goals. However, text pages related to topics that are not currently the focus of attention are not hidden. In this way, the student can take a look at them and change his/her learning goals accordingly. Stretch-text techniques have been used so the system can adapt to the type of knowledge required by the student. In this way, the student interested only in problem solving will only see links to the theoretical proofs of the theorems (that can be followed if desired). It is important to say at this point that TAPLI has been implemented as an open environment. This means that it has the ability to recommend students which is the best thing to do at each moment (read a page, solve an exercise, take a test, see an example) but does not force the student to follow the these recommendations. In this way, students can explore the environment with whole freedom.

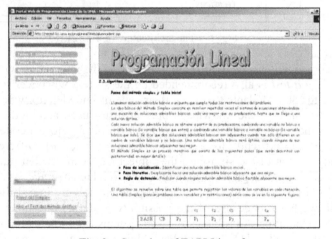

Fig. 2.   Snapshot of TAPLI interface

- *Adaptive characteristics*. Some features are adapted according to relevant information inferred by the system, as the list of visited pages and student's knowledge level. The list of visited pages is used to suggest which page the student should see next. Student's knowledge level is estimated by the SIETTE system after the student takes a test or solves a coached exercise, and kept in the student model. It is used to suggest which kind of action the student should take next (take a test/solve an exercise). Once the student has visited all the pages, the next page to be visited is selected according to the information contained in the student model.

As an example, we show in Figure 2 a snapshot of TAPLI interface during a session. The interface is divided into two different parts: on the right there is a frame that presents; the curriculum structure, a window for recommendations and two informative buttons: *Tu conocimiento*, that allows students to inspect their student model and change his/her learning goals; and *Mapa del web*, which shows a statistics of visited pages. For this particular student, the system offers two recommendations: what to *read* next (*Pasos del Simplex*, i.e. Simplex steps), which is based on the visited pages; and what to *do* next (*Test del método gráfico*, i.e., take a test about the graphic method), which is based on the current estimation of student's knowledge level. On the left side, the learning contents of the selected topic of the curriculum are shown.

The communication of this component with SIETTE is accomplished through a pre-established protocol, based on URL calls from one system to the other with the proper parameters. The testing component sends to SIETTE the set of topics to be assessed, the current estimation of the student's knowledge, the URL to which the results will be returned and some additional parameters. Once the evaluation has finished, SIETTE will invoke to the URL indicated, passing the new estimated knowledge levels of the student.

4   Conclusions and Future Work

In this paper we have presented an adaptive web-based learning environment for Linear Programming. This system has three different educative components: an adaptive hypermedia component, a testing component, and a drill-and-practice component. The TAPLI system presents different kinds of adaptation: adaptive navigation by direct guidance (recommendations) and by link hiding, adaptive presentation by hiding parts of the text, adaptive testing and finally adaptive problem generation and personalized assistance. A fully working version of TAPLI is currently available at http://www.lcc.uma.es/tapli. However, further work is needed in two different directions: first, we would like to increase the range of adaptive techniques. Second, we plan to make a formative evaluation with students in order to see if TAPLI does indeed increase the rate of effective learning.

References

[1]. Belmonte, M. V., Guzmán, E., Mandow, L., Millán, E., & Pérez de la Cruz, J. L. (2002). Automatic generation of problems in web-based tutors. In R. J. a. J. L. C. Howlet *Virtual Environments for Teaching and Learning* (pp. 237–277). World Scientific.
[2]. Conejo, R., Guzmán, E., Millán, E., Pérez, J. L., & Trella, M. (To appear). SIETTE: A WebBased Tool for Adaptive Testing. *International Journal of Artificial Intelligence in Education.*
[3]. López, J. M., Millán, E., Pérez J.L., & Triguero F. (1998). ILESA: A web-based Intelligent Learning Environment for the Simplex Algorithm. *Proceedings CALISCE'98.*
[4]. Millán, E., Mandow, L., & Rey, L. (1999). EPLAR: Un entorno para la enseñanza de la Programación Lineal. En *Desarrollo profesional y docencia universitaria: Proyecto de innovación en la Universidad de Málaga.* Servicio de Publicaciones de la Universidad de Málaga.

A "Development Web Environment" for Learning Programming Languages

Juan Ramón Pérez Pérez, Mª del Puerto Paule Ruiz, and
Martín González Rodríguez

HCI Research Group – LabTOO – Department of Computer Science. University of Oviedo
C/ Calvo Sotelo s/n Facultad de Ciencias. 33007 Oviedo. Spain
{ jrpp, paule, martin}@pinon.ccu.uniovi.es

Abstract. This paper proposes an environment for the teaching of program languages in a web environment. We consider that the student has to do exercises when he is learning a programming language; these tasks cause extra difficulties in conventional web environments. To remove these difficulties we propose an application that we have called DWE (Development Web Environment); the core is a language compiler integrated in the web application. Along with this compiler there are other modules to help the student while he's developing the programs; to obtain this we try to facilitate the communication teacher – student and student – student and we try to use the experience from all users in a group.

1 Introduction

The learning of paradigm of programming and its application in a specific language is not a trivial task. There are many authors that approach the cognitive difficulties that the learning of new paradigm or the change from other paradigms presents [4].

The assimilation and setting in practice of concepts that involves a paradigm of programming implies an important effort to achieve its assimilation by students. On the other hand, for a correct understanding it is essential to combine the work of theoretical concepts with the practical tasks utilizing a programming language. It helps the student to strengthen those things learned in theory and to improve his level of knowledge. If we notice the taxonomy of Bloom's knowledge, is when the student is practicing when he uses more objectives of application and analysis and where he can discover errors of understanding.

All this implies a constant interaction between student – teacher that will provide the student a suitable knowledge of this programming language and of the tool of compilation, and that will permit the student to apply techniques to avoid errors and to solve them if they happen. In a classic learning environment where the teacher is present, this interaction is produced automatically. It is even necessary to take into account the factor of communication student – student. This model of programming learning is hardly transferable to the classical virtual learning environments. These environments are not enough when the student is doing practices of programming languages, because expressing the difficulties that he has with a fragment of code turns out to be difficult for the student. This make difficult the solution of problems.

J.M. Cueva Lovelle et al. (Eds.): ICWE 2003, LNCS 2722, pp. 128–129, 2003.
© Springer-Verlag Berlin Heidelberg 2003

At present, there are tools that allow the automatic correction [1,2] and proposals [3] are being developed so that these tools may make the student receive information about the type of errors that he has committed and the concepts he has to review. But there aren't tools that allow to advise the student while is accomplishing the practices of programming and before the student obtains the final result.

2   Overview of DWE and Conclusions

DWE allows the users to write, compile and correct errors of their programs written on java. The interface of compilation allows the user to go to the principal functions of the manager of files. It has an area of edition of the source files. When the user compiles one file, the system captures errors that are produced and it gives the user information about the errors and he keeps the information in a database (Fig. 1).

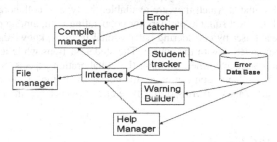

Fig. 1. Modules that constitute DWE

We have designed and developed an environment for the teaching of programming languages that provided several new things on other now existent environments: The compiler integrated in a web environment, avoids the installation and configuration by the user of environment and permits the centralization of maintenance. Help contribution for the user while he's writing the code, not only when errors happen. The user can make good use of the experience of others in the solution of happening errors. The teacher can do a students' tracking individually looking up the errors that the student has committed.

References

1. Dawson-Howe, K.M. Automatic submission of programming assignments. SIGCSE Bulletin 27, 4 (1995) 51–53.
2. Huizinga, Dorota M. Identifying Topics for Instructional Improvement Through On-line Tracking of Programming Assignments. SIGCSE Bulletin 33, 3 (Sep. 2001) 129–132.
3. Marco Galindo, Ma Jesús; Prieto Blázquez, Joseph Necesidades específicas para la docencias de programación en un entorno virtual. Actas JENUI 2002, 5–12.
4. Whitelaw, M. and Weckert, J. The Humannness of Object-Oriented Programming. I Cognitive Technology Conference. Hong Kong (1995).

Adaptive Collaborative Web-Based Courses

Rosa M. Carro[1,2], Alvaro Ortigosa[1,2], and Johann Schlichter[1]

[1] Institute for Informatics, Technical University of Munich
85748 Munich, Germany
schlichter@in.tum.de
[2] Escuela Politecnica Superior, Universidad Autonoma de Madrid
28049 Madrid, Spain
{rosa.carro, alvaro.ortigosa}@ii.uam.es

Abstract. In this paper we present the way adaptation techniques and collaboration capabilities have been seamlessly integrated to dynamically generate adaptive collaborative Web-based courses. In these courses collaborative and non-collaborative tasks are dynamically proposed. The most appropriate tasks to be performed, the time at which they are available, the type of collaboration tools provided and the most suitable partners for cooperating with, among others, are decided for each user by considering her personal features, knowledge and behavior while interacting with the course. The student actions while learning individually are considered when deciding the collaboration aspects. Student actions during the collaboration can affect the course evolution. A system to support the generation and delivering of this type of courses is being implemented.

1 Motivation and Goals

Adaptive hypermedia has proved to be effective for the development of adaptive Web-based courses. In these courses students are guided during the learning process. Each course is adapted by selecting the most suitable topics to be presented at any particular moment, their structure and organization, the navigational options available at each step, the help offered and the multimedia contents for page generation, taking into account the student features, preferences and actions [1]. The main goal is for every student to learn in the most efficient way. Each student can interact with an adaptive course, usually alone, in her own time frame, and learn at her own pace.

In addition, the use of collaboration tools in distance learning allows the users to communicate among each other, to share their knowledge, to work together on the resolution of problems and to discuss topics or doubts, among others. It reduces student isolation and facilitates the development of reasoning skills such as making ideas explicit, arguing, interacting with others to build a common solution, etc. [2].

Remarkable works concerning adaptive teaching can be found in the literature (see [1] for a survey on existing systems and tools). Interesting works on collaborative learning [3] have also been developed, some of them focusing on the interaction protocols [2] or on the support of teacher-student cooperation [4].

---

[1] This work is being partially supported by the German Academic Exchange Service (DAAD) and the Spanish CICYT, projects TIC2001-0685-C02-01 and TIC2002-01948.

J.M. Cueva Lovelle et al. (Eds.): ICWE 2003, LNCS 2722, pp. 130–133, 2003.
© Springer-Verlag Berlin Heidelberg 2003

Our approach deals with the integration of collaboration capabilities in Web-based adaptive courses and with the use of adaptation methods and techniques for the personalization of not only the course contents but also of the collaboration aspects. It consists not just of putting adaptive courses and collaborative tools together, but of integrating adaptation and collaboration in a seamless way. Therefore, the users can benefit not only from both of them separately, but also from a combination of the two.

With this purpose, we are extending the TANGOW system [6], which has been used during the last years for dynamic generation of adaptive Web-based courses, to create a system for the generation of collaborative adaptive Web-based courses. In this new system, the progress of the student while learning topics, solving exercises individually, navigating through the course, etc. is taken into consideration for decisions about collaborative aspects such as the presence or absence of collaborative tasks or the group formation, among others. In a similar way, the student's actions while performing collaborative tasks can affect the remaining course evolution.

2 Adaptive Collaborative Courses

While interacting with an adaptive collaborative course the students will be: i) guided individually through the course contents, ii) invited to cooperate with other students in the resolution of certain problems at specific points of the course and iii) able to share ideas, contact other students, and ask/answer questions about the course. Concerning the cooperative activities, aspects such as the particular collaborative exercises proposed, the time at which they are presented, the collaboration tools available, the type of collaboration, and the partners who a student will interact with, among others, are decided by taking into account each user's personal features, knowledge and behavior while taking the course. Some of these adaptation capabilities are explained next.

Collaborative Tasks Proposed. The time at which certain collaborative tasks are presented can differ depending on the user taking the course. Besides, collaboration can be available after the student has performed certain tasks or at any time. Sometimes it can be convenient to present different collaborative tasks, related or not to the same subject, to different students. Moreover, it can be considered inconvenient to propose collaborative tasks to certain types of students. The presence or absence of collaborative tasks, as well as the time at which they are presented, is described by means of *course structure rules*, in which collaborative tasks are included in the same way as the non-collaborative ones [5].

Group Formation. The main criterion used in this direction is the automatic grouping of students who have reached certain milestones while taking the course. The groups are formed, at a first stage, by considering the user's personal features and preferences (including aspects such as the learning style and background, among others), and their interaction style (frequency of interactions, bandwidth, etc.). Secondly, the knowledge acquired (topics visited, results while performing exercises, etc.) is considered. For each collaborative task, as soon as it is available to more than one user belonging to the same group, subgroups start to be formed, so that users can start performing the task. During the student sub-grouping, their opinions and preferences based on previous collaboration experiences are also considered (for example, other users they do not wish to interact with again, etc.). Finally, other default rules can also be specified (i.e., the maximum size of a group is three persons).

Problem Statement. In this work, a collaborative task is defined as "a task to check the comprehension of a particular topic, to put into practice the knowledge acquired related to a particular subject or to develop certain skills, that is performed collaboratively". The specific problem itself can be different for distinct students, although related to the same subject. When a pool of statements is provided for a particular collaborative task, the most suitable one for each group is selected depending on the problem characteristics and also on the group features and achievements while learning the involved subjects.

Collaboration Tools. Generally, students with a textual learning style prefer to propose solutions and discuss by writing texts, while those with a visual learning style usually prefer to create diagrams and draw their proposals and bases for discussion. The collaboration interface is adapted so that the most suitable tools for each group of students are presented in the main interface. The other tools will also be available. The adaptation of collaboration tools and problem statements is expressed by means of *collaborative-workspace rules* and *collaborative-tool rules*. The activation of these rules gives rise to specific collaborative workspaces, with a particular problem to be solved and a set of tools to support the cooperation [5].

Type of Collaboration. Since distance-learning systems allow the users to interact with them at any time, it is probable for the users to mainly collaborate in an asynchronous way. This communication can become synchronous when the users involved are online. The students are continuously informed which users from their group, if any, are connected, and the access to synchronous tools, if present, will be enabled so that they can go on solving their collaborative task synchronously.

Additional Support during Collaborative Task Execution. When a high degree of interaction has existed among the users in a group and yet no solution has been obtained, clues about the subjects that would be convenient for them to review may be given. It is also possible to inform them about other groups that have solved the problem (when agreed upon by these groups) for consultation purposes.

In order to reach these goals, adaptive collaborative courses are described by:

- A set of tasks to be performed, representing theoretical explanations to be studied, examples to be observed, or exercises to be solved individually or collaboratively.
- Relationships among these tasks, including *decomposition*, *sequencing* (if any) and possible *dependances*.
- Collaboration tools to be used for general purpose (email, forum, chat).
- Descriptions of collaborative workspaces, including the statements of the problems to be proposed and the sets of tools that will be available for each type of student.
- Adaptation rules, which determine the way in which the previous components are adapted to each student.
- Rules for student grouping.

The course designer must provide the multimedia contents that will be used for page generation (texts, images, etc.). In order to facilitate the description of adaptive collaborative courses, an *authoring tool* will be developed, starting from the one used for the development of Web-based adaptive courses in TANGOW [6]. In this tool, collaborative graphical editors, forums, chats, file sharing and e-mail programs will be available, so that the course designers can select the ones that will be accessible in each case. It would be possible to include specific-purpose collaborative editors, if necessary. Concerning the *student features* to be considered for adaptation, the course designers will be able to select among those proposed in the authoring tool (user experience, age, learning style, etc.). They will also be able to establish other features considered as relevant for the course adaptation. All the user features and actions while interacting with the course are stored to be used with adaptation purposes.

3 Conclusions and Current Work

In this paper we have focused on the way adaptation and collaboration methods and techniques have been seamlessly integrated for the dynamic generation of adaptive collaborative Web-based courses. This approach is being implemented starting from the previous work done in the TANGOW system. The formalism for describing courses has been extended [5]. New modules are being developed to manage the collaboration aspects and will be integrated in the system soon. Existing adaptive courses will be turned into adaptive collaborative ones, so that this approach can be evaluated.

References

1. Brusilovsky, P.: Adaptive hypermedia. In: Kobsa, A. (ed.): User Modeling and User-Adapted Interaction, 11. Kluwer Academic Publishers (2001) 87–110
2. Barros, B., Verdejo, M.F.: Designing Workspaces to support collaborative learning. In: Pobil, A.P., Mira, J., Moonis, A. (eds.): Tasks and Methods in Applied Artificial Intelligence. LNAI, Vol. 1416. Springer-Verlag, Berlin (1998) 668–677
3. Dillembourg , P.: Collaborative learning: cognitive an computational approaches. Elsevier, Oxford (1999)
4. Schlichter, J.: Lecture 2000: More than a course across wires. Teleconference – The Business Communications Magazine. (1997) 18–21
5. Carro, R.M., Ortigosa, A., Schlichter, J.: A Rule-based Formalism for Describing Collaborative Adaptive Courses. In: Palade, V., Howlett, R., Jai, L. (eds.): KES2003. LNAI. Springer-Verlag (2003). In press.
6. Carro, R.M., Pulido, E., Rodríguez, P.: Developing and Accessing Adaptive Internet-based Courses. In: Jain, L.C., Howlett, R.J., Ichalkaranje, N.S., Tonfoni, G. (eds.): Virtual Environments for Teaching and Learning. World Scientific Publishing Company (2002) 111–149

An Educational Component Based Framework for Web ITS Development

Mónica Trella, Ricardo Conejo, Eduardo Guzmán, and David Bueno

Departamento de Lenguajes y Ciencias de la Computación.
E. T. S. I. Informática. Universidad de Málaga. Apdo. 4114, 29080 Málaga. SPAIN
{trella, conejo, guzman, bueno}@lcc.uma.es

Abstract. This paper presents a framework for the integration of web-based educational systems. It is part of a research project, MEDEA[1], whose final goal is to develop a general framework to build open Intelligent Tutoring Systems (ITS). We understand "open system" as a set of autonomous educational modules which communicate between themselves, following high-level pre-established protocols. Each module can be an intelligent component with its own instruction strategies, or other components like support tools, web pages, etc. In the second case, the adaptive capabilities are left to the ITS instructor core. The architecture opens up the possibility to include new web-based components.

1 Introduction

The structure of the Internet is distributed, and in most cases it is used just as a huge repository of unorganized information. When teachers use the Internet for tutorial purposes, they can construct courses either collecting different URLs to give their students links where they can find lecture notes, exercises, etc. about the subject that they are studying; or using web-based systems to hold up their tutorial contents.

In the first approach, if not fixed courses are wanted, an intelligent behavior is required. In order to do that, teacher must redirect students to those systems that are more appropriate according to the student profile, and supervise their progress. For instance, he should suggest students to skip some parts, conduct them through pages with exercises, simulators, etc., *i.e.* he should adapt the contents to each student. Although generally the web systems used are non-adaptive, if they have some kind of intelligent behavior, it should be advisable to take advantage of these features [1].

Web Intelligent Tutoring Systems (ITS) might be constructed by gathering pages or systems, like *building blocks* in the sense of Chandrasekaran [2]. Some of them might be new, and some others reused from existing material. Most technologies used for Web ITS development are designed for small systems, and they do not have the necessary resources to guarantee a high-level conceptual organization. This kind of problems has been traditionally treated with software engineering techniques, and more recently with knowledge engineering techniques, following the Newell's *knowledge level* paradigm [3]. Using this idea, high-level methodologies and tools for the intelligent systems development have been proposed as KADS [4], PROTÉGÉ [5], KSM [6], etc.

---

[1] This project has been partially financed by Spanish CICYT/FEDER, with number IFD97-1286.

J.M. Cueva Lovelle et al. (Eds.): ICWE 2003, LNCS 2722, pp. 134–143, 2003.
© Springer-Verlag Berlin Heidelberg 2003

In this regard, MEDEA system (a Spanish acronym of *Methodology and Tools for the Development of Intelligent Environments of Teaching and Learning*) is not a new ITS authoring tool, but a general framework for the development and integration of open intelligent tutoring systems [7] [8]. We understand "open system" as a set of autonomous educational components that communicate between themselves following high-level pre-established protocols. In the case of web-based open tutorial systems, this protocol is the well known HTTP. MEDEA also adds a new higher level layer to communicate intelligent tutoring components.

The components used in MEDEA can be intelligent, with its own instruction strategies. In other case, the adaptive capabilities are left to the ITS instructor core. The architecture opens up the possibility to include general-purpose components which are able to interact with the general framework. MEDEA offers to educators a generic environment to develop Web ITS, without the limitations of a close set of utilities, like in the most of the authoring systems [9].

2   MEDEA Architecture

The elements that compose MEDEA architecture can be classified in three main groups: those that contain knowledge (*knowledge modules*), those that use this knowledge for making adequate decisions along the instruction (*functional modules*), and those that are used to access and configure the system (*tools*). The base of MEDEA architecture is a core that plans the instruction, based on a set of external tutorial components.

It could be said, comparing the MEDEA architecture and the traditional ITS architecture, that *what* (knowledge about the learning subject) is explicitly represented by the domain model, *who* (knowledge about the student) is given by the student models (knowledge and attitudes) and *how* (teaching knowledge) is divided between the instructional planner, tutorial components and domain model. All knowledge models are represented in XML for computational use. Fig. 1 shows the structure of MEDEA modules:

Knowledge modules:

- **Conceptual Knowledge Domain Model**. It contains the knowledge about the subject to be taught. Both domain concepts and relationships among them are represented. It will be approached in section 4.

- **Student model**. It is decomposed into the *Student Knowledge Model* and the *Student Attitude Model*. It will be described in section 5.

Functional modules:

- **Instructional planner**. This module provides to the students the necessary guidance during the learning process. It decides at each moment the most adequate task to be performed by the student. It uses the conceptual domain knowledge, the student's state of knowledge, the student's profile and the tutorial components definitions.

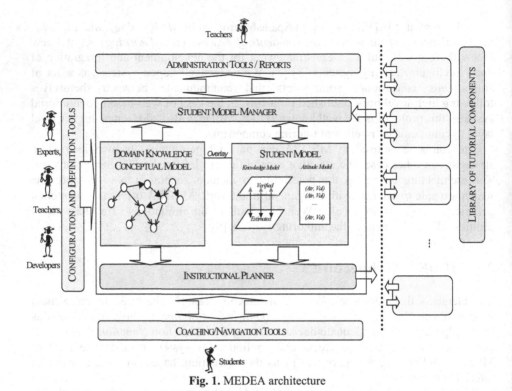

Fig. 1. MEDEA architecture

The tutoring systems generated by this tool, allow students to freely navigate. The system only recommends but does not impose the next student's action. The planner will also have the capability of justifying the recommended actions, so the student has the necessary information before deciding to accept the suggestions made by the system.

- **Student Model Manager**. It creates and updates the student model. It is updated after the execution of a tutorial component. Some components can evaluate the student knowledge about some domain concepts. The information provided by them, goes to the *Student Verified Knowledge Model*. MEDEA assumes the existence of other components which are not able to determine exactly the variations of the student knowledge level. For instance, a component which displays a text to be read. In these cases, MEDEA is just informed that the student has visited these components. This information is used to update the *Estimated Student Knowledge Model*.

- **The library of tutorial components**. They are external educational tools which make a concrete task (electronic books, simulation tools, exercises, making tests, etc.). From MEDEA point of view, the architecture of a component (Fig.2) is composed by a *partial domain model*; a *development interface* to introduce contents; a *student interface*; a *student temporal model*; a *component functional description*, where the functions of the teaching component and the way of communicating with MEDEA planner are defined; and a *control*, that is the execution engine of the component.

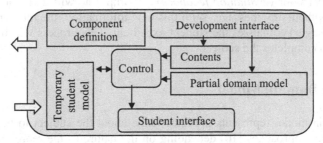

Fig. 2. Tutorial component architecture

Tools (Interfaces):

- **Configuration and definition tools**. They are used by domain experts, teachers and designers. They allow to introduce the contents, define and configure the data and knowledge modules using specific interfaces.

- **Administration tools**. They are used by teachers to monitor the evolution of their students. They show the progress of each student, statistics about the use, the average of the student's performances, and other management and administrative tasks.

- **Navigation tools**. They are used by students to support their navigation and the interaction with the whole system. It can be conceptualized as an advisor during the learning. It is currently implemented as an additional frame of the web browser.

3   The Behavior of MEDEA

To describe the behavior of MEDEA the simile of a school personal tutor can be used. Suppose that a student asks for help to his personal tutor (*instructional planner*), to study a subject (*domain model*). The tutor examines his academic expedient (*student model*) and takes into account other student's features (*student attitude model*). He selects the best topic and style of teaching for the student. After that, he consults the school staff (*tutorial components library*) and chooses the best teacher for that specific topic, according to the student's current profile. The tutor must know the teaching methods of all the available teachers (*i.e.* this usually does a lot of exercises, that prefers to explain theory, this wants the students to make exercises on the blackboard, etc.). The tutor sends the student to the selected teacher (*tutorial component*) with a message (*communication protocol*) indicating the concept which the student must study, and maybe, other information (*e.g.* this is the third time this student tries this concept, he has low learning rate,...). This teacher will apply his effort and expertise to improve the student knowledge in the concept proposed (*intelligent component*); or for instance, he may just give the student a proper text to read (*non-intelligent component*), without controlling what he is doing. When the teacher ends the class, he will send back a message to the tutor explaining the student's behavior (*evaluation feedback*), or simply he will give back the control to the tutor without any message. With this new information, the tutor (now *the student model manager*) actualizes the student expedient. This process will be repeated until the student completes the subject.

4   The Domain Model

The domain model represents the knowledge about the subject to be learned. There are different approaches [10] depending on the nature of the represented domain. In MEDEA, declarative domains representation are used. The most extended models for representing this kind of domains are the semantic networks of knowledge units. They have been used in systems like DGC [11], Eon [12] and IRIS [13].

From a conceptual point of view, the domain is defined by *a)* a semantic network of concepts and relations between them, and *b)* pedagogical knowledge required for the instruction.

From the implementation point of view, the basic elements of MEDEA domain model are:

a) *Concepts*. They are the basic pieces in which the subject is divided. During the task of modeling a knowledge area for an ITS, the pedagogical purpose of the system should be taken into account. First of all, the net granularity is chosen, *i.e.* the decomposition of the units in other simpler ones. As Anderson says [10], sometimes to model accurately a domain, a computational charge is required. From the tutorial point of view, that is not necessary. Second, it is necessary to include pedagogical knowledge in the domain model, to guide the student through the knowledge units [8]. This pedagogical information is included as attributes associated to the concepts.

b) A set of binary *relations* between the concepts. They are used by MEDEA to describe the domain. These relations are: *prerequisite, part of, is a, belongs to, is useful to understand, is similar to* and *is opposite to*. Each relation should define an acyclic graph of concepts which is used by the functional modules to guide the instruction (*the instructional planner*), and to make inferences about the student's knowledge (*the student model manager*). The current semantic of the relation is very fixed in the functional modules. However, MEDEA includes an informal description about the semantic of the relations to guide authors in the creation process of these graphs. Currently, the domain model supports all these relations, but only *prerequisite*, and *part of*, are used by the *instructional planer*. Other relations can be defined by the authors course and stored for future use. The *student model manager* is still under development.

c) *Evaluation types*. The student knowledge model is based on the overlay technique. Each concept has a magnitude associated which represents the student's degree of knowledge. The *evaluation types* in MEDEA are the types of those magnitudes. They are not fixed, but they are defined, when the course is created between a set of *internal types* supported by the architecture. These types are: *enumerated* (*i.e.* the knowledge level of a concept can be A, B, C or D), *real* (a real number) and *distribution* (*i.e.* the knowledge level can be {A/0.2, B/0.3, C/0.4,

D/0.1}, indicating the probability of that the student's knowledge level in concept A is 0.2 and so on). MEDEA is a general framework which can use different components for its instructional purposes. Each of these components can have its own internal representation of the student's knowledge. Implicit conversion between internal types has been defined to support compatibility between different components.

```
<!DOCTYPE DOMAIN_MODEL SYSTEM "http://sirius.lcc.uma.es/medea/dtd/DOMAIN_MODEL.dtd">
<DOMAIN_MODEL id="domain_model01" name="Logic of proposals">
    <EVALUATION_TYPES>
        <EVALENUM id="EvalEnum" default_minimum_mark="Passed">
            <ENUMERATED id="Passed"/>
            <ENUMERATED id="Failed"/>
        </EVALENUM>
        <EVALREAL id="EvalReal" lower_boundary="0" upper_boundary="10"default_minimum_mark="5"/>
    </EVALUATION_TYPES>

    <CONCEPTS>
        <CONCEPT id="t1" idref_evaluation="EvalEnum" name="Introduction" difficulty="Low"/>
        <CONCEPT id="t2" idref_evaluation="EvalEnum" name="Formal sintax" difficulty="Low"/>
        <CONCEPT id="t3" idref_evaluation="EvalEnum" name="Semantic" difficulty="Low"/>
        [...]
        <CONCEPT id="c32" idref_evaluation="EvalReal" name="CDN" difficulty="High"/>
    </CONCEPTS>

    <RELATIONS>
        <RELATION id="r1" id_origin_concept="c21" id_destiny_concept="c1" type="prerequisite"/>
        <RELATION id="r4" id_origin_concept="c4" id_destiny_concept="c2" type="is_a "/>
        [...]
        <RELATION id="r73" id_origin_concept="c31" id_destiny_concept="t6" type="belongs_to"/>
        <RELATION id="r74" id_origin_concept="c32" id_destiny_concept="t6" type="belongs_to "/>
    </RELATIONS>
</DOMAIN_MODEL>
```

Fig. 3. Representation of the domain model

Fig. 3 shows a fragment of an XML file, which contains the domain model of a course of Logic. At the beginning, the types used to evaluate each domain concept are defined. The second part is a list of concepts which includes some pedagogical information required for the instruction, like the difficulty level of each concept. At the end, there is a list with the relations between concepts.

5   The Student Model

The *Student Model* in MEDEA is divided into two main subcomponent. The *Student Knowledge Model* and the *Student Attitude Model*. The first represents what the student knows about the subject. The second represents other features of the student.

The *Student Knowledge Model* is an overlay model divided into two levels: *the estimated model* and *the verified model*. Each level is a list of *concept/mark* pairs. This multilayer approach has already been used by other authors like Brusilovsky, in the last versions of ELM-ART-II [14]. He uses different layer for concepts visited, evaluated, inferred, etc. At this moment, we have only proposed two layer, grouping in the estimated layer, all the uncertain information and inferences.

Fig. 4 shows an example of the student knowledge model expressed in XML. Each concept has associated a value according to the evaluation type defined in the domain model. The last concept that has been taught is stored too.

```
<!DOCTYPE STUDENT_MODEL SYSTEM "http://sirius.lcc.uma.es/medea/dtd/STUDENT_MODEL.dtd">
<STUDENT_MODEL courseid="d03" lastconcept="c5" studentid="s432">
  <ESTIMATED_STUDENT_MODEL>
      <CONCEPT id="c1" value="VERY WELL"/>
      <CONCEPT id="c2" value="VERY BAD"/>
      [...]
      <CONCEPT id="c5" value="WELL"/>
      <CONCEPT id="c6" value="VERY BAD"/>
  </ESTIMATED_STUDENT_MODEL>
  <CHECKED_STUDENT_MODEL>
      <CONCEPT id="c1" value="VERY BAD"/>
      <CONCEPT id="c3" value="REGULAR"/>
      <CONCEPT id="c5" value="REGULAR"/>
      <CONCEPT id="c6" value="VERY BAD"/>
  </CHECKED_STUDENT_MODEL>
</STUDENT_MODEL>
```

Fig. 4. Representation of the student knowledge model

There are also some relevant student's features which are important for the learning process. In MEDEA, some of them has been included in the *Student Attitude Model*: cognitive development (formalization and abstract concepts understanding skills), motivation, learning style, time dedicated to the subject study (*i.e.* the student effort degree to pass the subject), progress (the student's learning speed), experience with computers, Internet connection speed, etc.

This model is used by teachers or course designers to establish relations between a concrete student profile and some instruction parameters. For example, a teacher can specify in the course definition that, when a student with *low motivation* level makes a test, he should see the right response after he answers to each question, instead of at the end of the test.

6   The Instructional Planner

This is the core of MEDEA architecture. It is the module which puts in sequence the domain and adapts the instruction process to each student. Usually a teacher takes decisions in several levels. First, he decides the instruction goals (concept to be taught) and then, he takes other decisions like the topics content, material to be used, the pedagogical strategy to be used, etc.

There are several examples in the ITS literature in which the planner task is divided into subtasks: some oriented to concept selection, and others to decide how to teach the selected concept [13] [15] [16].

The MEDEA planner takes three main decisions: 1) Does the student need to be evaluated?, 2) if YES: about which topic will he be evaluated?, if NO: which concept should the student learn now?, and 3) How will he be evaluated or taught better? The knowledge needed to answer these questions is in the domain model, the student models and the pedagogical elements of the system (domain model pedagogical contents and tutorial components).

The modular structure of the MEDEA architecture and the separation between knowledge representation and knowledge use, allow that this module could be easily changed. The final goal of this project is to have a planner library in the system. For the first prototype, a heuristic planner has been implemented. It carried out the task of selecting a concept to be evaluated or learned in two phases: first, it selects an ordered set of candidate concepts. This selection takes into account the relations *prerequisite* and *part of*, and the current student model state. Second, the planner selects the first concept from the candidates set. The criteria to decide if a concept is candidate are: a) The student has not reached at the minimum required by the teacher to pass the concept. b) The concept is *prerequisite* of any other concept that cannot be learned because the student has not passed this one. c) The concept is *part of* any other concept that cannot be learned because the student has not passed this one.

A weight is assigned to each candidate. The most weighted are those that are selected by the criterion 2.

The implemented planner takes this decision using the teacher's criterion. That is, when a teacher designs a course, he links each tutorial component registered in the system, to a student's profile. The planner only has to consult the *student attitude model* and to assign him the most adequate tutorial component according to the teacher.

7   Tutorial Components

The pedagogical knowledge in MEDEA system is distributed between several modules: the domain model, the instructional planner and the tutorial components. Anyway, it is not strictly necessary for the instructional process that a component provides any knowledge. Most of the instruction tasks fall on the pedagogical system core composed by the domain model and the planner. A tutorial component can complement this task providing its tutorial strategies and a more exhaustive control over the student's actions.

MEDEA classifies the educational components as *evaluation components* or *information components*. The difference is that components of the former type are able to evaluate the student's knowledge level about a concept.

The problem of the components integration can be approached as the communication between two web-based systems. This communication can be established through URLs. Therefore, the planner needs from the component, some low-level knowledge about its performance (call format, parameters, etc.), and some high-level knowledge about its pedagogical offer (tutorial strategies, options, user options, etc.). Also, this communication can be established through two different interfaces: from teacher's interface for the creation of courses, and from student's interface for the execution of instruction session.

A web-based tutoring system can be constructed by developing specific components, which are also called *general-purpose components*. Currently, MEDEA uses the following components: HERMES, which is an authoring tool to create web-based electronic books; SIGUE [17], which is a system that allows the construction of web courses by collecting the references to existing web pages; and SIETTE [18], which is an adaptive test-based assessment system.

These components work in MEDEA as plug-ins. They are invoked from the MEDEA core. The authoring tools of these components are linked to the development tools of MEDEA; the administration tools are linked to the administration tools of MEDEA, and the course presentation is linked to the student interface.

8   Conclusions

As a consequence of the increasing importance of the distance education, and the advance of this field due to the new information technologies, many researchers have realized the necessity of applying intelligent techniques of existing educational systems to the Web.

MEDEA is a proposal of an open architecture for Web ITS development. It is an open system that contains the traditional modules of an ITS architecture. It has been designed to allow the integration and reutilization of educational tools, and teaching material already developed. The main idea is that any teacher could develop a course, reusing other material and software. After a tutorial session in a component, if this returns any kind of feedback information, it will have to implement the protocol defined. The difficulty degree of this integration depends on the information required and provided by the component. Some other attempts have been made to integrate preexisting web-based adaptive systems (see for instance [19]).

Other advantage of MEDEA is that this is a web based system, and therefore the requirements to be accessed are minimum: only a web navigator tool is required. Also, even though this system can recommend the student which is the best step to accomplish, the final decision is taken by him. At last, its inference machine is upgradable, since planners with new instructional strategies can be added.

MEDEA is still under development. Although some courses have been added, the current instructional planner is only a first attempt, and must be tested. Besides, although a first version of the communication protocol between the core and the library of components is being used, a new enhanced version is being implemented.

References

1.   Eklund, J. & Brusilovsky, P. The Value of Adaptivity in Hypermedia Learning Environments: A Short Review of Empirical Evidence. In *Proceedings of the Second Workshop on Adaptive Hypertext and Hypermedia at Ninth ACM International Hypertext Conference, Hypertext'98*. (1998).
2.   Chandrasekaran, B. Generic Task in Knowledge Based Reasoning: High level building blocks for expert systems design. *IEEE Expert*, 1, (1986) 23–29. Re-printed in Buchanan, B.G. y Wilkins, D. C. (eds.) *Reading in Knowledge acquisition and learning*. Morgan Kaufmann. San Mateo. CA. (1993) 170–177
3.   Newell, A. The Knowledge level. *Artificial Intelligence*. (1982); 18.

4. Wielinga, B.J., Schreiber, A.T. & Breuker, J.A. KADS: a modeling approach to knowledge engineering. *Knowledge Acquisition* 4, (1992).
5. Musen, M. A. Automated Support for Building and Extending Expert Models. *Machine Learning.* (1989); 4:347–375.
6. Cuena, J. & Molina, M. KSM: An Environment for Knowledge Oriented Design of Applications Using Structured Knowledge Architectures. *Applications and impacts. IFIP'94*; (1994).
7. Self, J. Open Sesame?: Fifteen Variations on the Theme of Openness in Learning Environments. Keynote speaker at AI-ED'99. Abstract published in Lajoie, S. & Vivet, M. (eds.) *Artificial Intelligent in Education*: IOS Press (1999).
8. Murray, T. A Model for Distributes Curriculum on the World Wide Web. In *Journal of Interactive Media in Education.* (1998),5
9. Murray, T. Authoring Intelligent Tutoring Systems: an analysis of the state of the art. In *International Journal of Artificial Intelligence in Education.* (1999), 10, 98–129
10. Anderson, J. R. The Expert Module. In Polson, M.C. & Richardson, J.J. (eds.) *Foundations of Intelligent Tutoring Sytems.* Lawrence Elrbaum; (1988).
11. Vassileva, J. Dynamic Course Generation on the WWW. In Brusilovsky, P., Nakabayashi, K. & Ritter, S. (eds.) *Proceedings of the Workshop 'Intelligent Educational Systems on the World Wide Web' at AI-ED'97.* (1997).
12. Murray, T. Authoring Knowledge-Based Tutors: Tools for Content, Instructional Strategy, Student Model, and Interface Design. In *Journal of Learning Sciences.* V. 7, N.1, pp. 5–64
13. Arruarte, A., Fernández-de-Castro, I., Ferrero, B. & Greer, J. (1997), The IRIS shell: How to build ITSs from pedagogical and design requisites. In *International Journal of Artificial Intelligence in Education.* V. 8, N.3‑4, pp. 341–381
14. Weber, G. & Specht, M. User modeling and adaptive navigation support in WWW-based tutoring systems. In Jameson, A., Paris, C. & Tasso, C. (eds.) *User Modeling*, Springer-Verlag, Wien (1997) 289–300
15. Woo, C. W. *Instructional Planning in an Intelligent Tutoring System: combining global lesson plans with local discourse control.* Illinois Institute of Technology, PhD. Thesis. (1991).
16. Woolf, B. & McDonald, D. Context-Dependent Transition in Tutoring Discourse. In *Proceedings of AAAI.* (1987).
17. Carmona, C., Bueno, D., Guzmán, E. & Conejo, R.: SIGUE: Making Web Courses Adaptive In De Bra, P., Brusilovsky P. & Conejo, R. (eds.) *Proceedings of the AH2002*, Springer-Verlag LNCS 2347 (2002).
18. Conejo, R., Guzmán, E., Millán, E., Pérez-de-la-Cruz, J. L. & Trella, M. SIETTE: A web-based tool for adaptive testing. In *International Journal of Artificial Intelligence in Education.* (to appear).
19. Brusilovsky, P., Ritter, S. & Schwarz, E. Distributed intelligent tutoring on the Web. In Brusilovsky, P., Nakabayashi, K. & Ritter, S. (eds.) *Proceedings of the Workshop 'Intelligent Educational Systems on the World Wide Web' at AI-ED'97*, (1997).

Adaptive Interaction Multi-agent Systems in E-learning/E-teaching on the Web

Antonio Fernández-Caballero, Victor López-Jaquero, Francisco Montero, and Pascual González

Laboratory on User Interaction & Software Engineering (LoUISE)
University of Castilla-La Mancha, 02071 Albacete, Spain
{caballer, victor, fmontero, pgonzalez}@info-ab.uclm.es

Abstract. In this paper we propose to include two up-to-date separate concepts, namely social computing and usability metrics, in intelligent interaction agents to enhance a user-centred, adaptive human-computer interaction (HCI) on the Web. Social computing refers to the application of sociological understanding to the design of interactive systems. Usability metrics are software quality metrics with a long history of successful application in software engineering. We introduce preference metrics, which quantify the subjective evaluations and preferences of users, and performance metrics, which measure the actual use of working software, as suggested parameters that enable user interface adaptation. From all terms, a new user-centred and adaptive interaction multi-agent model and architecture is proposed in e-learning/e-teaching on the Web.

1 Introduction

Human-computer interaction (HCI) in traditional application development is focused on the interaction between a task and a single user interface designed for a single kind of user. Application user mass is treated as a single entity, making no distinction between the different user stereotypes included in that user mass (figure 1a).

A logical evolution should lead interaction to a development model where these stereotypes are taken into account. There are different kinds of users, and that is a fact we cannot ignore. Human society is full of diversity and that must be reflected in human-computer interaction design (figure 1b). However, one step forward in interaction design is required in order to translate this diversity into application development. Adding support for different user profiles is, of course, more accurate than developing for a single kind of user. But the real thing is that users are all a little bit different. This user may match a user profile, but with his own particularities, leading to the concept of specialization (figure 1c). Thus, we need to engage users in a new kind of interaction concept where user interfaces are tailored-made for each user and where the user interfaces are intelligent and adaptive [18] [19].

J.M. Cueva Lovelle et al. (Eds.): ICWE 2003, LNCS 2722, pp. 144–153, 2003.
© Springer-Verlag Berlin Heidelberg 2003

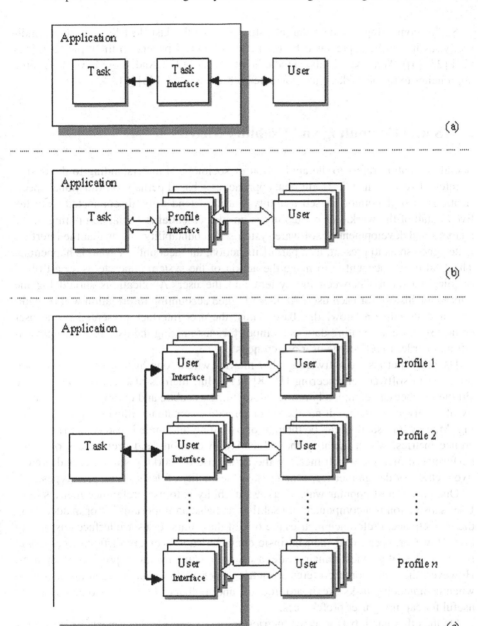

Fig. 1. (a) Unity, (b) diversity, and (c) specialization in computer interaction.

In this paper we propose to include two up-to-date separate concepts, namely, social computing and usability metrics, in intelligent interaction agents to enhance user-centred, adaptive e-learning / e-teaching applications on the Web. As already clearly stated [25], "people should not have to change radically to 'fit in the system'; the system should be designed to match their requirements".

Social computing has been largely studied over the last decade, directly or indirectly, as it may be appreciated by the great amount of papers on the topic (e.g. [12] [22] [23] [4]). Adaptivity is also a today's hit [2] [26] [27]. And, there have been some approaches to fit these ideas into concrete architectures [26] [5] [8].

2   Social Computing and Usability Metrics

Social computing refers to the application of sociological understanding to the design of interactive systems [7]. Traditional approaches – based perhaps on functional specifications or on laboratory-based usability studies – tend to be disconnected from the lived detail of the work. Accountability is an idea essential to social computing in the analysis and development of software systems. Accountability means that the interface is designed so as to present, as a part of its action, an "account" of what is happening. The goal of the account is to make the action of the system concrete as a part of an ongoing interaction between the system and the user. Applications should log the interaction history for each user. All these logged accounting information will be gathered and stored in a knowledge base. Thus, the user interface presented to the user could use those accounting data as an input for customizing the user interface presentation, in order to reflect the user preferences.

Usability metrics are software quality metrics with a long history of successful application in software engineering [1] [8] [11]. But, metrics also carry risks [3]. No simple number can completely represent anything as subtle and complex as the usability of a software system, but numbers can sometimes create the illusion of understanding. Metrics for usability can be thought of as falling into three broad categories: preference metrics, which quantify the subjective evaluations and preferences of users, performance metrics, which measure the actual use of working software, and predictive metrics, or design metrics, which assess the quality of designs and prototypes.

One of the most popular ways to assess usability is to use preference metrics [24]. User satisfaction is a component of usability and also an important factor in success in the marketplace. Preference metrics are one of the pillars for user interface customization. However, because of their intrinsic characteristics, they are difficult to assess at run time. Usually, questionnaires are used for evaluating these preference metrics. However, there are some preference metrics, such as the manipulation artefact used when commanding tasks (keyboard, menus, and toolbars) that can become especially useful for capturing user preferences.

On the other hand, performance metrics are indices of various aspects of how users perform during actual or simulated work. User performance is almost always measured by having a group of test users perform a predefined set of test tasks while collecting time and error data [21]. Typical quantifiable usability measurements include: the time users take to complete a task; the number of tasks of various kinds that can be completed within a given time limit; the ratio between successful interactions and errors; the time spent recovering from errors; the number of user errors; and so on [21]. Of course, only a subset of these measurements would be collected during any particular study. Performance metrics are especially useful for assessing overall usability. One important point for this kind of metrics is that most of them can be evaluated at run time in a simple manner. Performance metrics are one more input parameter to advance towards interfaces adapted to the user. Our proposal is to forget user interfaces where the user must adapt to a given and fixed interface.

A central goal in software metrics is the prediction of software characteristics based on other metrics of the software or its production process. In [29], Rosenberg addresses this problem by providing a simple methodology for the predictive evaluation of metrics, one which reflects what most statisticians would recommend in general terms. Predictive metrics are estimators or predictors of some one or more aspects of the actual performance that can be expected once a system has been implemented and put into use.

3   An Interaction Multi-agent System

To build a system that enhances the user's motivation in Web based applications [6] [10], it would require nearly constant surveillance of the user, and at least strong artificial intelligence – knowledge, intelligence, memory, insight, and reasoning ability equivalent to that possessed by an intelligent being. A quite recent study [15] integrates that the person feeling frustrated suddenly has diminished abilities for attention [16], memory retention [14], learning [17], thinking creatively [13], and polite social interaction [9], among other things – as well as a penchant for getting more frustrated in the immediate future. Our proposal is to design and build interaction multi-agent systems that significantly help users in their relationship to the WWW. Humans are much more than information processors. Humans are affective beings, motivated to action by a complex system of emotions, drives, needs, and environmental conditioning [20].

The ultimate goal for HCI must be the creation of user interfaces based on each individual user preferences. Those preferences can be captured initially, to a certain extent, in analysis development stages. By using those captured data, user profiles can be created in accordance with the identified user stereotypes. However, user advances, and his preferences change. One rookie user will become an average user, and finally an expert user, as he gets more familiar with the system. Thus, the environment should reflect these changes in both user skills and preferences. Intelligent agents with the ability to capture those changes are required.

Figure 2 illustrates the user-centred interaction multi-agent architecture proposed for the adaptivity on the Web. The Multi-Agent System (MAS) monitors the interaction between the user and the user interface, and captures two different parameters. On one hand, the MAS logs the interaction history in an accounting process. On the other hand, the agent assesses preference metrics, such as the preferred interaction artefact for each action (keyboard, menu, toolbar, etc).

Besides the described parameters, the user-centred adaptive interactive MAS assesses some behavioural systems issues (performance metrics), the error ratio regarding the number of correct interaction actions, or the time spent performing a task or recovering from an error. All these data are processed and stored in a knowledge base that the agent uses to decide the actions required in order to achieve its goals; to find out the possible changes applicable to the user interface to get it closer to what the user is expecting. Thus, a new user interface is created tailor-made in accordance with the skills, experience and preferences the user shows.

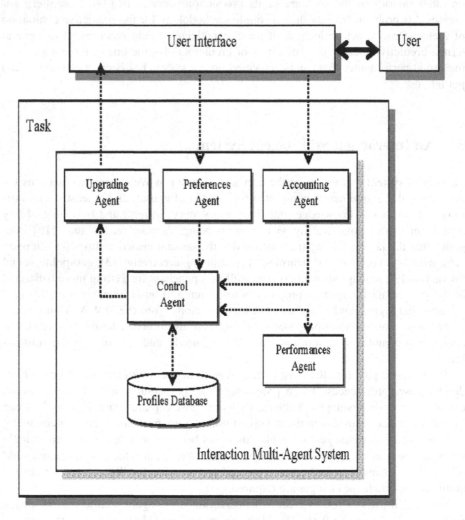

Fig. 2. The interaction MAS architecture.

4   Adaptive E-learning and E-teaching on the Web

The architecture proposed so far is being tested in an on-line Web-based e-learning system as an intelligent tutoring system (ITS) for an Engineering course taught at the Polytechnic Superior School of Albacete, University of Castilla-La Mancha.

One of the main goals is that the alumni learn more and better, that is to say, to be able to structure learning matter in such a way to facilitate the learning facilities. One characteristic to take into account in learning is the rhythm the student is able to learn. Thus, a ITS has to adapt the rhythm it introduces the concepts to the learning rhythm of each student (for instance, to show more or less exercises, to show more or less tests, etc.). Another aspect widely considered in learning theory is reinforcement by rewarding a correct answer and punishing a failure. Rewarding and punishment can be carried out by means of messages, sounds, etc. Another goal in our environment is to enhance teaching as well as learning. One of the main problems a professor faces when teaching is that he does not know the skills of his students. Our proposal leads to conclusions that "teach how to teach".

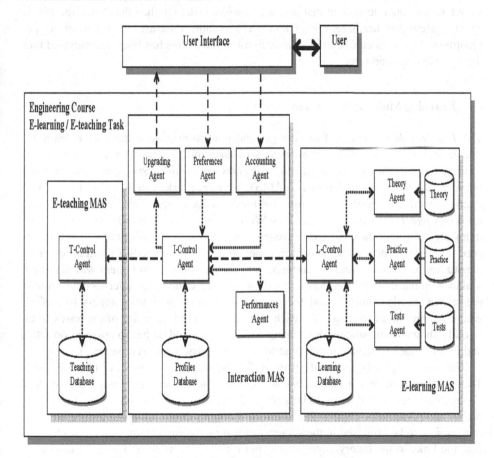

Fig. 3. The adaptive Engineering course task architecture.

In our learning system on the Web (figure 3) we have introduced three MAS: (1) The *Interaction MAS*, which captures the user preferences by means of some usability metrics (affect, efficiency, helpfulness, control and learnability). The contents shown to the user are created in accordance to the captured preferences and behaviours. (2)

The *Learning MAS* composes the contents for the user in accordance to the information collected by the *Interaction MAS*. (3) The *Teaching MAS* is one of the most important contributions in our experience. It offers recommendations of how to enhance the layout of the Engineering course.

The user (the student) is in front of the user interface. From the interaction of both entities, modelled by the *Interaction MAS*, different metrics that are stored in a *Profiles Knowledge Database (KDB)* are collected. This database contains the different profiles as a result of the use of the system by different students, with different aptitudes, motivations, etc.

The multi-agent system for the learning (*Learning MAS*), gets data obtained from the profiles (analysis of the distinct metrics captured) and adequates the contents shown to the concrete student that accesses the Web site. On the other hand, the multi-agent system for teaching (*Teaching MAS*) obtains measures that permit to get recommendations to enhance the course. Finally, the course has been decomposed into theory, exercises and tests.

4.1   Learning Multi-agent System

The *Learning MAS* appears from the general goal to maximize the course learning. The *learning control agent* communicates bi-directionally (asks for and receives information) with the *theory agent*, the *exercises agent*, the *tests agent* and with the *interaction control agent* (*Interaction MAS*). This agent asks for/receives Theory Web Pages to/from the *theory agent*, asks for/receives Exercises Web Pages to/from the *exercises agent*, asks for/receives Tests Web Pages to/from the *tests agent* and communicates (through the *interaction control agent*) with the *performance agent* to record the performance of the student in order to decide if he needs a reinforcement. If the student needs some kind of reinforcement the *learning control agent* will elaborate a plan with the material that has to be shown to the student. In order to determine if the student needs reinforcement the *performance agent* will have access to a *KDB* where the minimum requisites for each subject are stored (quantity of exercises to be initially shown to the student, how many exercises the student has to answer correctly, and in how much time, maximum time to correctly answer an exercise, etc.).

The *theory agent* is constantly waiting for the *learning control agent* to ask for a Theory Web Page. When this occurs, it looks for the proper theory page and sends it to the *learning control agent*. The *exercises agent* is autonomous as it controls its proper actions in some degree. The agent by its own means (pro-active) selects the set of exercises to be proposed in the subject studied by the student and adds to each exercise the links to the theory pages that explain the concepts related to the exercise. It sends to the *learning control agent* a Web page containing the exercises proposed. The *tests agent* is continuously listening to the *learning control agent* until it is asked for Tests Web Pages. The agent by its own means (pro-active) goes on designing a set of tests for the subject the student is engaged in. These tests will be shown to the student in form of a Web.

4.2 Teaching Multi-agent System

The *Teaching MAS* is the result of the second general goal fixed, namely, to maximize the teaching capacity of the course. The *Teaching MAS* will be collecting the goodness or badness of the parameters defined for the learning system. The *Teaching MAS* is pro-active in the sense that it will be providing recommendations to the teacher on those parameters.

4.3 Interaction Multi-agent System

The *Interaction MAS* has been conceived to facilitate the adaptive communication between the system and the user. The *interaction control agent* tells the *upgrading agent* what the user preferences are, as obtained by the *preference agent*, and which has to be the next Web page to be shown (*learning control agent* of *Learning MAS*). When speaking about the preferences of the student, we mean the type of letter, the colour, the icons, etc., the user prefers. The information collected is stored in the *Profiles KDB*. All information concerning time-related parameters and some of the user's behaviours are obtained through the *performance agent* and the *accounting agent*.

The *preference agent* perceives the interaction of the user with the user interface and acts when the user changes his tastes. The *preference agent* is continually running to know the student's preferences at any time.

The *performance agent* calculates the performance metrics when the student leaves the system (at the end of a working session) y goes evaluating everything the student does in order to know if he needs reinforcement. It is autonomous and pro-active; as it may calculate metrics at the same time the student performs other tasks. Some of the metrics the *performance agent* handles are: for each Theory Web Page, the mean time alumni spend there; for each exercise Web page, the mean punctuation obtained by the alumni, as well as the time spent to get the correct answer; for each Tests Web Page, the mean time spent to answer all questions, and the mean punctuation obtained in the tests.

The *accounting agent* perceives the interaction between the student and the user interface and acts (gets information) when the student changes to another Web page, scrolls up and/or down, performs an exercise or a test, etc.

Finally, the *upgrading agent* is constantly waiting for the *interaction control agent* to ask to update the user interface with the new information to be shown to the student (to show another Web page or to show the same Web page but changed to the new tastes of the student).

5 Conclusions

User interface generation on the Web has become a software engineering branch of increasing interest. This is probably due to the great amount of money, time and effort spent to develop user interfaces, and the increasing level of exigency of user requirements for usability [21] and accessibility [28] compliances. Besides it, users engaged in HCI are becoming more and more heterogeneous, and that is a fact we cannot ignore.

In this paper we have proposed an architecture that considers the high diversity of users' skills and preferences: a user-centred and adaptive interaction multi-agent system. Our model proposed has been applied to e-learning / e-teaching of an Engineering course. This architecture is inspired in social computing and usability metrics. In our learning system on the Web we have introduced three MAS: (1) The *Interaction MAS*, which captures the user preferences by means of some usability metrics (affect, efficiency, helpfulness, control and learnability). The contents shown to the user are created in accordance to the captured preferences and behaviours. (2) The *Learning MAS* composes the contents for the user in accordance to the information collected by the *Interaction MAS*. (3) The *Teaching MAS* is one of the most important contributions in our experience. It offers recommendations of how to enhance the layout of the Engineering course.

Acknowledgements. This work is supported in part by the Spanish CICYT TIC 2000-1673-C06-06 and CICYT TIC 2000-1106-C02-02 grants.

References

[1]   Card, D., Glass, R., 1990. *Measuring Software Design Quality.* Prentice-Hall.
[2]   Cardon, A., Lesage, F., 1998. Toward adaptive information systems: considering concern and intentionality. *Proceedings of the Eleventh Workshop on Knowledge Acquisition, Modeling and Management, KAW'98* .
[3]   Constantine.L.L., Lockwood L.A.D., 1999. *Software for Use: A Practical Guide to the Models and Methods of Usage-Centered Design.* Addison-Wesley.
[4]   d'Inverno, M., Luck, M., 2000. Sociological agents for effective social action. *Proc. of the 4th International Conference on Multi-Agent Systems*, IEEE Computer Society, 379–380.
[5]   Eisenstein, J., Rich, C., 2002. Agents and GUIs from task models. *International Conference on Intelligent User Interfaces.* ACM Press, 47–54.
[6]   Fernández-Caballero, A., López-Jaquero, V., González, P., Lozano, M.D., 2002. A game editor for Virtual-Prismaker learning environment to improve teaching and learning in classroom. *Proceedings of ED-MEDIA 2002*, 505–506.
[7]   Garfinkel, H., 1967. *Studies in Ethnomethodology.* Polity Press.
[8]   Gilb,T., 1977. *Software Metrics.* Winthrop Publishers, Inc., Cambridge MA.
[9]   Goleman, D., 1995. *Emotional Intelligence.* Bantam Books.
[10]   González, P., Montero, F., López-Jaquero, V., Fernández-Caballero, A., Montañés, J., Sánchez, T., 2001. A Virtual Learning Environment for Short Age Children. *Proceedings of the IEEE International Conference on Advanced Learning Technologies, ICALT2001*, IEEE Computer Society, 283–284.
[11]   Henderson-Sellers, B., 1996. O-O Metrics: Measures of Complexity. Prentice-Hall.
[12]   Horovitz, E., 1999. Uncertainty, action, and interaction: In pursuit of mixed-initiative computing. *Intelligent Systems.* Computer IEEE Society. September / October, 17–20.
[13]   Isen, A.M., Daubman, K.A., Nowicki, G.P., 1987. Positive affect facilitates creative problem solving. *Journal of Personality and Social Psychology,* Vol. 52, No. 6, 1122–1131.

[14] Kahneman, D., 1973. *Attention and Effort*. Prentice Hall.
[15] Klein, J.T., 1999. *Computer Response to User Frustration*. MIT.
[16] Kitayama, S., Niedenthal, P.M., 1994. Heart's Eye: Emotional Influences in Perception and Attention. Academic Press.
[17] Lewis V.E., Williams, R.N., 1989. Mood-congruent vs. mood-state-dependent learning: Implications for a view of emotion. In Kruiken, D. (ed.) Mood and Memory: Theory, Research, and Applications (vol. 4) of Special Issue of the *Journal of Social Behavior and Personality*, Vol. 2, 157–171.
[18] López-Jaquero, V., Montero, F., Fernández-Caballero, A., Lozano, M.D., 2003. Towards adaptive user interfaces generation: One step closer to people. *Proceedings of ICEIS 2003*.
[19] López-Jaquero, V., Montero, F., Fernández-Caballero, A., Lozano, M.D., 2003. Usability metrics in adaptive agent-based tutoring systems. *Proceedings of HCI International 2003*.
[20] Myers, D.G., 1989. *Psychology*. Worth Publishers.
[21] Nielsen, J., 1993. *Usability Engineering*. Academic Press.
[22] Oliveira, E., 2001. Agent's advanced features for negotiation and coordination. *Multi-Agent Systems and Applications*. LNAI, Vol. 2086. Springer, 173–186.
[23] Petta, P. Trappl, R., 2001. Emotions and agents. *Multi-Agent Systems and Applications*. Lecture Notes in Artificial Intelligence, Vol. 2086. Springer, 301–316.
[24] Porteous, M., Kirakowski, J., Corbett, M., 1993. *SUMI User Handbook*. University College Cork, Ireland.
[25] Preece, J., Rogers, Y., Sharp, H., Benyon, D., Holland, S., Carey, T., 1994. *Human-Computer Interaction*. Addison-Wesley.
[26] Sycara, K.P., 1998. Levels of adaptivity in systems of coordinating information systems. *Cooperative Information Agents II*. LNAI, Vol. 1435. Springer , 172–189.
[27] Suzuki, J., Tashiro G., Abe, Y., Yamamoti, Y., 1998. Persona: a framework to provide adaptive presentation for web documents. *Proceedings of the IPSJ Summer Programming Symposium, IPSJ Prosym '98*, 101–108.
[28] W3C, 2002. http://www.w3.org/WAI/
[29] Rosenberg, J., 1998. A methodology for Evaluating Predictive Metrics. *Proceedings of the 5th International Symposium on Software Metrics*. Maryland. USA, 181.

Platform of Virtual Training for Work

José N. Pérez[1], Edward P. Guillén[1], Nubia X. Sepúlveda[1], and Carlos O. Ramos[2]

[1] Universidad Distrital "Francisco José de Caldas", Bogotá, D. C, Colombia
http://www.udistrital.edu.co
[2] Servicio Nacional de Aprendizaje "SENA", Bogotá, Colombia
http://sena.edu.co
nelsonp@udistrital.edu.co
{cramos,eguillen}@ieee.org
nxsepulveda@alcaldiabogota.gov.co

Abstract. The Colombian state function of training skilled workers is assigned to SENA (National Apprenticeship Service), which, in order to cope with the companies' needs related to qualified work, has been interested on using the current informatics network infrastructure. The existing pedagogical model as well as a pedagogical model applied to the virtual training will be described in this paper. Based on this, an infrastructure of technical resources is proposed to implement a National Virtual Training. The suggested solution implies making the existing national training Centers suitable for this kind of virtual program, using appropriate informatics network technologies to favor learning and skills development.

1   Introduction

A description of pedagogic model given in a technical training institution is made in this paper. Section two presents the current process for a person that wants to become an apprentice in a vocational occupation that is needed by the productive sector. In section three an appropriate solution is presented to cover the territory thoroughly, keeping in mind the telematic network, human and existent didactic resources and adding new technology to this, like virtual reality, instead of investing in a variety of real equipment and tools for qualifying. An instructional model for doing this, is exposed here. In section four the necessary tools to interconnect the whole territory are presented, having the current net and the new technologies.

2   Current Pedagogical Model

A person enters SENA in order to develop some skills which allow him/her to get a job. The future worker is guided by an expert team of instructors through a process that includes theoretical, technical and ethical background to enlarge their acting range (polivalency) [1], [2].

J.M. Cueva Lovelle et al. (Eds.): ICWE 2003, LNCS 2722, pp. 154–157, 2003.
© Springer-Verlag Berlin Heidelberg 2003

The current SENA's infrastructure only covers 15% of the training needs at the whole Colombian territory, according to the national law [3]. The remaining 85% is covered by private institutions[1].

The apprentice, at the beginning, receives theoretical concepts and then receives a guided training in technological skills in a true workshop. This process is completed in the company that needs his/her working profile in a competitive environment [4].

3 The Proposed Pedagogical Model

The proposed pedagogical model includes: a curriculum that aims to some training goals of in agreement with the labor necessities; an appropriate virtual training teaching method, supported in physical infrastructure, appropriate to the whole national territory and modern equipment with hypermedial structuring [5] of the courses.

The logical sequence of virtual training is presented in the Fig. 1, where the center of the process is the apprentice who interacts with other apprentices to share information and to carry out consultations with the tutor, in a same way, he/she takes part in the modules of the content, as well as the virtual laboratories and the evaluation that is checked by the tutor for a later feedback. With the self-evaluation, the apprentice can verify his/her advance in the training [6].

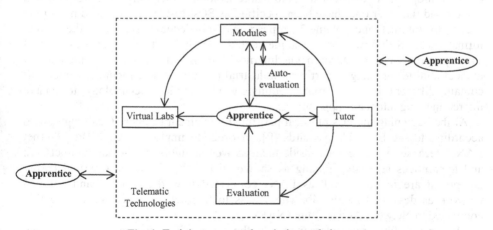

Fig. 1. Training process description and elements

The contents of a specialty using virtual training, have as a goal to accomplish the same skills and abilities like in the traditional formation [7].

The formation Centers will be located in the whole national territory endowed with telematic resources, in flexible schedules where the apprentice can choose the place and the time to receive his training. The virtual training at technical level should be carried out from Primary Centers (PCs) where conferences will be managed toward

---

[1] Obtained data from one of the Sectorial Tables that gather SENA with the companies.

Secondary Centers (SCs) located in different regions around the country; these SCs will have the necessary network infrastructure for the connection with the PCs.

The PCs would have tutors that will lead and evaluate the apprentice's progress, in order to observe the development of abilities and minimum skills a specific work in the labor field. A typical SENA's apprentice does not have resources for acceding Interenet, that is why he/she needs to go to a PC or SC.

The fact of training the apprentices in manual abilities, implies that they should manipulate current equipment in the industry, but due to the impossibility of endowing Centers with all type of equipment in the whole country and, in order to increase the coverage, it is necessary to apply technologies of virtual reality.

The peripherical technologies to use, consist on the group of necessary hardware for interaction; this equipment includes helmets of stereoscopic vision or *Head Mounted Displays (HMDs), scanners*, and *gloves.*

The software programming will be carried out based on Virtual Reality Modeling Language (VRML) [8], that allows the interaction of the virtual environments to be used in Internet or in a broadband public network of different characteristics.

4 The Proposed Technological Model

The virtual training will demand the presence of the apprentices in the SCs. From 110 Centers in operation, distributed in the whole Colombian territory, five are proposed as PCs and the other ones have been specified as SCs. Inside the proposed model the access to Internet and Internet2, appears as knowledge base, since the virtual formation for SENA will not be implemented over Internet, but it is possible that some programs can be diffused via Internet, if it is not required development of manual abilities or using in particular industrial equipment. Each training center will contain different kinds of rooms equipped with modern technology to enable interconnecting tutors and apprentices.

At the beginning the PCs physical part must implement category 6 cabling system according to the EIA/TIA standards [9], in order to implement Giga Bit Ethernet LANs, because the servers are inside them as well as tutors for the national network and apprentices receiving training as shown in Fig. 2a. In the SCs virtual reality equipment are found as well as LANs connected toward the broadband national network as described in Fig. 4b. The access to Internet is carried out by the PCs connected to Network Access Point (NAP).

The optical fiber ring interconnecting the cities where the centers are located, through the ATM network, allows the flexibility of increasing the bandwidths to the required values of 10 Mbps for the PCs and of 2 Mbps for the SCs. The last mile solutions for each one of the Centers will be implemented with Asymmetric DSL (ADSL) connections in the SCs and High Data bit Rate DSL (HDSL) connections for the PCs without direct access to the ATM ring. For the different connections toward Internet, the IP networks belonging to SENA will implement Multi Protocol Label Switching (MPLS) [10], as solution of a quick interconnection that allows the use of virtual circuits emulated on the IP networks increasing the routing speeds and so of convergence in the connections.

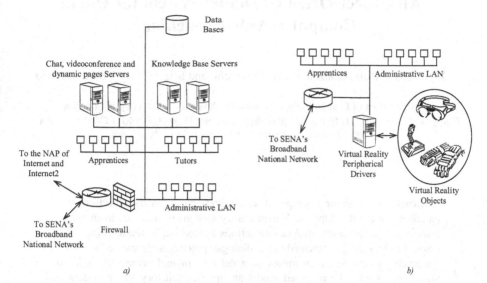

Fig. 2. *a)* Primary Centers (PCs) infrastructure *b)* Secundary Centers (SCs) infrastructure

IPv6 is going to be used with all the improvements that this network represents [11]. In Colombia the network access is done by four nodes. Internet2 will be implemented as knowledge base.

References

1. Monteiro L., E.: El Rescate de la Calificación.Cinterfor - SENA. Bogotá (1997) 87–101
2. de Moura C., Claudio.: La Capacitación en Oklahoma: parece que la están haciendo bien. Cinterfor - SENA. Bogotá (1997) 51–85
3. Ministerio de Trabajo y Seguridad Social: Ley 119, febrero 9 de 1994. Bogotá (1994)
4. Weimberg, P. D.: Tendencias de la formación profesional en américa Latina - Seminario Formación Profesional: Fundamentos para la Productividad y Competitividad en el Nuevo Milenio (memorias). SENA - Ministerio de Trabajo y Seguridad Social. Bogotá (2000) 80–142
5. Gutiérrez, A.: Educación Multimedial y Nuevas Tecnologías. Ediciones La Torre, Madrid (1997) 50–81
6. Silvio, J.: La Virtualización en la Educación Superior: Significación, Posibilidades y Alcance. IESAL/UNESCO, Caracas (2000) 211–276
7. Rosenberg, M.: E-Learning: Strategies for Delivering Knowledge in the Digital Age. McGraw-Hill, New York (2000)
8. Ashdown, N.: The Virtual Reality Modelling Language in Art & Design Higher Education. SIMA Report Series, Advisory Group on Computer Graphics, No 17, 1st Edition (1996)
9. Groth, D., et al: Cabling: The Complete Guide to Network Wiring, second edition. Sybex, (2001)
10. Guichard, J. Pepelnjak, I.: MPLS and VPN Architectures. Cisco Press, Indianapolis (2001)
11. Naugle, M.: Network Protocols. Signature edition.McGraw-Hill, New York (1999) 477–518

An Object-Oriented Dialog System for Use in Computer-Aided Teaching

Irene Luque Ruiz, Gonzalo Cerruela García, and Miguel Ángel Gómez-Nieto

Department of Computing and Numerical Analysis. University of Córdoba.
Campus Universitario de Rabanales, Building Einstein, Plant-3. E-14071 Córdoba (SPAIN)
{mallurui, gcerruela, mangel}@uco.es

Abstract. In this paper is proposed an ontology based on the object-oriented paradigm for the development of explanatory systems to simulate, in an appropriate way, the professor-student interactions carried out in the teaching processes. The knowledge explained in the dialogue process is represented at different levels of complexity by means of a network of multi-connected units of knowledge. Under the proposed model an open explanatory dialog system is built and incorporated into the Virtual Chemistry Laboratory, a virtual system for practical chemistry learning, developed by the authors.

1   Introduction

The teaching process is changing in the last years thanks to the use of computers and the development of intelligent tutorial systems. These systems are widely used in fields such as chemistry, where numerous tutorial and learning systems have been developed [1-4]. Nowadays, advances in computing and resources have allowed the development of systems that aim to place the student in a virtual world — the closest thing to a real chemistry lab — in order to carry out experiments that are either considered too dangerous or expensive, or when there is simply a lack of laboratory resources and/or time for large numbers of students [5, 6].

The definitive installation of these systems will suppose a drastic change in the current paradigm teaching-learning, although for that is necessary of a technological advance in the communications and software development based on teaching models that simulate, in an appropriate way, the present teaching to the use of the information technologies.

Usefull software that simulates the process of real teaching should keep in mind that professor-student interactions cannot be restricted to the mere presentation of information to the student through help options included in these systems, the access to documents or pages and addresses Web. The professor-student interactions are based, mainly, for doubts or questions that in fact arise to the student when the student tries to assimilate the contents of these kinds of documents, needing to solve some doubts for a correct assimilation of this information.

J.M. Cueva Lovelle et al. (Eds.): ICWE 2003, LNCS 2722, pp. 158–166, 2003.
© Springer-Verlag Berlin Heidelberg 2003

Therefore, the teaching-aided systems should have the necessary functionality to allow the student to ask questions, and the system (that simulates the professor) can respond them in an appropriate way, that is to say, depending on the level of the student's knowledge, which is the foundation of the dialog or explanatory systems.

The development of the explanatory systems is very complex. In the first place, it is necessary to define an ontology on which the teaching process is based on the context of the professor-student communication [7-8]. On basis of this ontology, it is necessary to model the knowledge that will be transmitted to the student, and to develop a series of components in order to perform the professor-student communication process, allowing the student to ask questions, and that the professor (the explanatory system) transmits the explanation with a form and content appropriate to the student's knowledge.

In the last decade have been developed a great number of explanatory systems oriented to specific fields of the sciences, engineering and humanities. Mainly, the systems are ad-hoc systems that hardly can be adapted to be used in other areas or educational environments, because are based in an ontology and knowledge model restricted to the educational problem for which its were built. The challenge in next years is the construction of open explanatory systems that can be integrated, with few or any adaptations, in any intelligent tutorial system.

In the present study is proposed an ontology for the development of explanatory systems and a model for the representation of the knowledge that is transmitted in the professor-student interactions. Under this model an open explanatory dialog system has been developed and incorporated into the Virtual Chemistry Laboratory [5], a model previously proposed by the authors. The proposed theoretical model and its development under the object-oriented paradigm are presented, alongside its application to the building of an explanatory system for use in the help feature of a chemistry laboratory teaching application [5].

2   A Dialog System for the Building of Explanations

Virtual Chemistry Lab (*VCL*) [5] is multimedia teaching software aimed at simulating a working environment (in this case a chemistry lab) where students can work in a virtual environment in a similar way to they would in a real practice lab at any teaching center. The help system included in *VCL*, based on a web tutorial, could not be classed as an interactive virtual teacher, rather as a complete textbook available at any moment. With this in mind, development of an interactive dialog system to allow the student to ask questions about any aspect of the lab (materials, working methods, etc.) as well as inquire about theory and/or technique for chemistry experiments would complete the teaching model of the system.

Creation of the dialog system should provide complete representation of the real teaching model; in other words, all the elements of the real educational process involved in the teaching of practical chemistry technique will have their virtual equivalent, as shown in Table 1.

Table 1. Correspondences between the real world and the *VCL* virtual world

VCL Virtual World	↔	Real World
3D Virtual environment	↔	Chemistry lab
On line help system	↔	Text / Reference book
Interactive dialog system	↔	Lab practice teacher

The first objective of the present study was to propose an ontology for the dialog process between the user and the *VCL*, which could be integrated into the $E(V)=M + m$ (Virtual Experiment is represented by means of Materials and a method), paradigm on which it is based [5]. This approach has to take into account the adaptation for the student of the explanatory dialog with respect to how the dialog process is fairing (e.g. using more generic explanations if the student displays, through his questions, a significant lack of knowledge about the topic).

Creation of an interactive dialog system incurs the need to model a complete knowledge network composed of multi-connected nodes, such that it may be browsed using the functions connecting the different network nodes [8, 9, 10, 11].

The proposed model is based on the formulation of suitable paradigms for the representation of the knowledge to be taught, the student model, the content planner (teaching component) and the dialog planner (interface), in line with existing proposals concerning ITS components [12, 13].

Figure 1 shows the architecture of the proposed model in a component diagram [14]. Student and knowledge models are represented by a *Knowledge Base* that stores the concepts to be taught and their relationships, together with the belief of the student's knowledge of the concepts. The dialog generator is represented by three components: the *Dialog Planner*, which takes on the role of teacher and handles communication with the student, extracting explanations from the knowledge base to display them in an order determined by the *Organizer*, whose *Content Planner* presents the concepts to be explained, based on the knowledge extracted from the knowledge base.

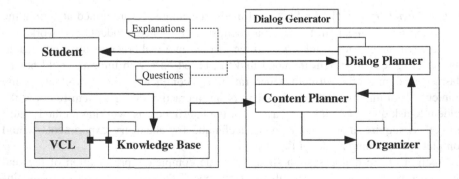

Fig. 1. Component diagram of the proposed model

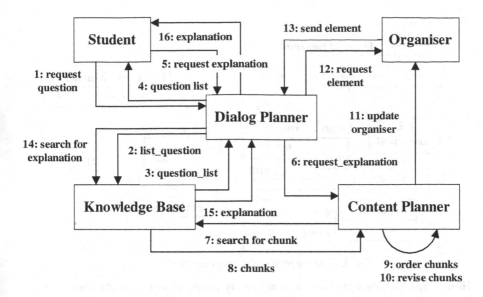

Fig. 2. Explanatory process in the dialog system

As shown in Figure 1, the *dialog generator* has been integrated with the components of the *VCL* [5], thus allowing the creation of explanations for any element of the *VCL* and the incorporation of the explanatory system in its virtual interface.

2.1 Generating Explanations

The proposed discourse model is student-dominated [15, 16], where student initiative is limited to asking questions, and is based on the use of explanatory transactions whose aim is to simulate the real-world interaction between students and their lab teacher and allows the dialog flow shown in the collaboration diagram [14] in Figure 2.

A hierarchical model of a dialog structure may produce a useful basis for modeling the organization of interactions, and as an explanation may be expressed as a plan, then a higher level rule for planning transactions will describe an application and will consist of an opening delimiting exchange, a sequence of pedagogical exchanges and a closing delimiting exchange.

In the proposed model, student initiative is limited to asking questions about any material or conceptual element appearing in the experiment to be performed, while the system has the initiative when deciding on the form and content of the explanation.

When an explanation has not been fully understood by the student, the student can either ask the system for clarification or ask new questions. Clarifications on a topic are dealt with thus: (a) Revision of the prerequisites and explanation of the subobjectives which were not explained, (b) The use of another explanatory paradigm, different from its predecessor; or (c) Asking the student questions to reappraise his knowledge level, making a global evaluation of the student through a test examination.

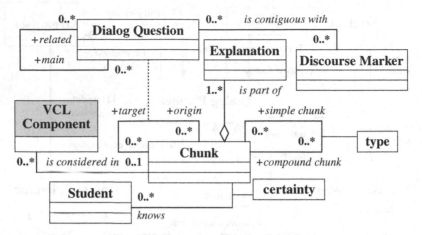

Fig. 3. Class diagram of the proposed model

However, sometimes the student is not really aware of not understanding what is being explained, and it is up to the system to identify the problem and attempt to correct this situation. This happens when the student does not correctly answer the questions posed by the system, and it is more effective to somehow show the student why the answer was wrong instead of simply supplying the correct answer.

To find out where the student was going wrong, the system places in the discourse model the assumptions about the user's knowledge level that had been used to plan the explanation. If the system has assumed that the user had a good knowledge of certain information, but this has proved to be untrue, it may presume that the root of the problem is that the information was unknown to the user (*case a*), and propose an explanation.

If the system is unable to find a reason for the confusion, it will try to explain the information in another way (*case b*). In order to achieve this, when there is more than one possible way of explaining something, the discourse model includes links to other forms of explanation.

These clarification subdialogs, which appear as a result of a lack of understanding on the student's part, are dealt with as interruptions and not as part of the prior discourse, so the planned discourse will continue when clarification has been attained.

To add coherence to these clarification subdialogs, there is an interruptions transaction rule responsible for planning appropriate opening and closing sentences for the dialog, which includes the use of discourse markers (Figure 3) that point to the beginning and end of an interruption (e.g. "Anyway" or "Getting back to where we were...".

2.2   Management Knowledge to Be Taught

Teaching-aided systems require knowledge to be explained must be represented as related portions for be used depending of the pedagogical features required for each instance [9].

Under an object-oriented paradigm (used in this work) the use of frames – represented as classes – allows faithful representation of these related portions of knowledge. Thus, given a discourse domain corresponding to the topic to be taught, the knowledge elements (and their relationships) of which it is comprised may be structured in the form of a network and represented as classes and class associations, as shown in the class diagram [14] in Figure 3.

Knowledge elements have been named *chunks*, such that a node in the knowledge network may be defined by a name that relates the *chunk* to its teaching material (*explanation*).

The relationships (edges between nodes or *chunks* of the knowledge network) have a specific meaning, an address, and may join pairs of nodes; different types of relationships are allowed, characterized by the *Type* attribute (Figure 3). This attribute permits represent prelations or prerequisites between *chunks* (the root node must be known for the target node to be taught), as well as, aggregation or composition relationships between *chunks* (the root node is a subset of the knowledge in the target node).

Thus, taking a node (knowledge *chunk*) as a learning objective, all *prerequisite* relationships arriving at that node may be analyzed, and a check can be made to ensure the student knows each and every node. In this way, if one of the nodes is unknown, it can be marked as a learning objective.

Explanations should be related to the *chunk* network so that it can be presented to the student when working with the *chunk* in question. The class diagram in Figure 3 shows how a *chunk* may contain zero (composite *chunks*) or several explanations, each of which has a series of distinguishing features and may contain text or graphical information.

Figure 3 also shows a reflexive association of the *chunk* class, which allows the representation of the directional knowledge (the prerequisites). Additionally, this association is characterized by the *Dialog Question* class, which in turn maintains a reflexive association with the relationships that exist between specific frames of the knowledge domain.

Representation of student knowledge is based on the knowledge on *chunks*. Given a certain object from the model (e.g. the titration of 0.1 N HCl with 0.1 N NaOH), the user-modeling component works out whether or not the student knows the element.

The extent of the student's awareness of the knowledge elements is represented by certainty measurements, defined by the labels "*known*", "*perhaps known*", and "*unknown*", which characterize the association between the student and the *chunk*, as shown in Figure 3. These labels provide a simple representation of the degree of belief assigned to the student's knowledge of a concept.

Since the system requires information about the student in order to produce a personalized dialog, the student model is based on examination of the *Student* class in which contains, among others: a base level of the student knowledge (following the stereotype model [16]), which is update in terms of the history of student-system interaction, and the session level or evaluation of the student performance during a specific session.

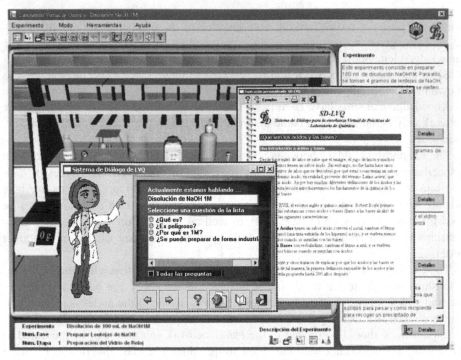

Fig. 4. A sample of the dialog system integrated in the Virtual Chemistry Lab

The initial user model is set up according to the user's experience and a series of indirect inferences based on the relationships between concepts or *chunks* held in the knowledge network, and the model is updated according to feedback from user interaction. Moreover, the student model also plays a part in the choice of dialog actions. The system uses the model to offer an explanation of a concept to the student, or perhaps to carry out a test.

Discussion

In this paper an ontology for the explanatory dialog generation is proposed. The representation of the knowledge to be explained is represented by a network of multi-connected *chunks*, where each *chunk* can be further specialized in specific knowledge frames, may contain associated explanations of varying degree of complexity and with different explanatory models, and can be associated with one or a set of questions the student might ask. Student model is represented through the belief of user's knowledge on *chunks* and throughout the learning process by the use of both stereotypes and direct or indirect inference, enabling the explanation to be adapted to the requirements of each student.

The solution developed considers a student-dominated dialog in which the (virtual) teacher answers any pertinent questions posed by the student, providing a fair representation of the real teaching processes.

Based on the proposed model and employing the Java language [17] in conjunction with the Oracle 9i DBMS [18] for knowledge-base management, a system was developed to build the knowledge network. The teacher can define all the elements appearing in the dialog (*chunks*, questions, etc.) and interconnect them. These elements and their relationships are manipulated by the system through a drop-down hierarchical menu, enabling the student to easily browse the knowledge network.

While the predefined questions for each *chunk* are simple text sentences, explanations may be constructed as .html or .xml files (also stored in the nucleus of the database), thus allowing inclusion of multimedia content (text, graphics, images, and so on).

The system is flexible and may be incorporated into any other object-based teaching aid. This is achieved by importing the classes for which knowledge-explanation items are required and linking those classes to the knowledge (*chunks*, dialog questions, etc.), as we have carried out with Virtual Chemistry Laboratory [5] (see Figure 4).

References

1. Cartwright, H.M., Valentine, K. A Spectrometer in the Bedroom. The Development and Potential of Internet-Based Experiments. *Computers & Education*. **2002**, 38, 53–64.
2. Colwell, C., Scanlon, E., Cooper, M. Using Remote Laboratories to Extend Access to Science and Engineering. *Computers & Education*, **2002**, 38, 65–76.
3. Rzepa, H.S., Tonge, A.P., VchemLab: A Virtual Chemistry Laboratory. The Storage, Retrieval and Display of Chemical Information Using Standard Internet Tools, *J. Chem. Inf. Comp. Sci.*, 1998, 36(6), 1048–1053.
4. (a) *www.modelscience.com/products.html*, (b) *www2.acdlabs.com/ilabs*,
    (c) *www. chemsw.com/10202.htm*, (d) *www.compuchem.com/dldref/formdem.htm*,
    (e) *www.ir.chem.cmu.edu /irProject/applets/virtuallab/applet_wPI.asp*,
    (f) *chem.lapeer.org/Chem1Docs/ Index.html*, (g) *chem-www.mps.ohio-state.edu/~lars/ moviemol.html*
5. Luque Ruiz, I. López Espinosa, E., Cerruela García, G. Gómez-Nieto, M.A. Design and Development of Computer-Aided Chemical Systems: Virtual Labs for Teaching Chemical Experiments in Undergraduate and Graduate Courses. *J. Chem. Inf. Comput. Sci.*, 2001, 41(4), 1072–1082.
6. Crosier, J., Cobb, S., Wilson, J.R. Key Lessons for the Design and Integration of Virtual Environments in Secondary Science. *Computers & Education*, **2002**, 38, 77–94.
7. Moore, J.D. Participating in Explanatory Dialogues. MIT Pres, Cambridge, Massachusetts, 1995.
8. Cawsey, A.J. *Explanation and Interaction: the Computer Generation of Explanatory Dialogues*. MIT Pres, Cambridge, Massachusetts, 1992.
9. Sinclair J. McH., Coulthard R.M. *Towards an Analysis of Discourse: The English Used by Teachers and Pupils*. Londres. Oxford University Press. 1975.

10. Nussbaum, M., Rosas, R., Peirano, I., Cárdenas, F. Development of Intelligent Tutoring Systems using Knowledge Structures. *Computers & Education.* **2001**, 36, 15–32.
11. Fernández-Castro, Y., Díaz Harraza, A., Verdejo, F. Architectural and Planning Issues in Intelligent Tutoring Systems. *Journal of Artificial Intelligence and Education.* **1993**, 4 (4), 357–395.
12. Angelo C. Restificar, Syed S. Ali and Susan W. McRoy, ARGUER: Using Argument Schemas for Argument Detection and Rebuttal in Dialogs, *In Proceedings of the Seventh International Conference on User Modelling* (UM-99), Banff, Canada, June 20–24, 1999.
13. Soller, A. Computational Analysis of Knowledge Sharing in Collaborative Distance Learning Doctoral Dissertation. University of Pittsburgh, 2002.
14. Rumbaugh, J., Jacobson, I., Booch, G., *The Unified Modeling Language. Reference Manual,* Addison-Wesley Longman Inc, USA, 1999.
15. Ishizaki, M., Crocker, M., Mellish, C. Exploring Mixed-Initiative Dialogue using Computer Dialogue Simulation. *User Modelling and User Interaction,* **1999**, 9(1), 79–91.
16. Rich, E. User Modeling Via Stereotypes. *Cognitive Science*, 1979, 3,339–354.
17. Campione, M. The Java Tutorial Third Edition. McGraw-Hill. 2002 (http://java.sun.com)
18. Loney, K., Koch, G.. *Oracle 9i The Complete Reference.* Oracle Press. 2002.

Adaptable Contents Visualization (VIC)

Raúl Fernández González, Mª del Puerto Paule Ruiz, Juan Ramón Pérez Pérez,
Martín González Rodríguez, and Marcos González Gallego

² HCI Group- Labtoo- Dpto. Computer Science
C/Calvo Sotelo S/N Facultad de Ciencias. 33007 Oviedo. Spain
raulFG79@hotmail.com, {paule,martin, jrpp}@pinon.ccu.uniovi.es,
mgg@telecable.es

Abstract. VIC is the item inside the e-learning tool PWGD which is addressed
to the student, it interacts with him or her, as well. Currently available tools are
mainly focussed on teachers, helping them whereas the student can only watch
the contents provided by the teacher and in the same way the teacher arranged
them. This application aims to make learning easier, in order to do that subject
contents will be shaped according to the learning habits of the student. The
application follows the pattern Model-View-Ruler, which allows splitting
contents and shape, so contents will be adapted to different shapes.

1 Introduction

There are a lot of e-learning tools on the market, but none is focussed on the student.
They all tend to assist the teacher to introduce and arrange the subject. These tools
always show the contents in the same way which will limit the learning as students
will have to adapt themselves to the tool (its functions, the way information is
introduced ...), before they actually start learning the matter they are concerned with.

VIC is created to solve this problem, it is the item inside PWGD e-learning tools
which adapts the contents of subjects to the learning habits of students [1]. These will
be defined by Chae´s Test [2] and aterwards thanks to XSL patterns, Adaptative
Presentation and Navigation [3] the contens will be adapted to the learning techniques
of the user is asking for them. By means of VIC the student feels more comfortable
using an e-learning tool and is able to learn easily and naturally.

2 Building of the System

The application follows the conceptual pattern " Model – View – Ruler " [4].

2.1 Model

Inside the model we will use a web service to make communication with data base
easy.

J.M. Cueva Lovelle et al. (Eds.): ICWE 2003, LNCS 2722, pp. 167–170, 2003.
© Springer-Verlag Berlin Heidelberg 2003

2.2 View

The application provides several views depending on the data it is displaying and the user who asks for it. All the views are dynamically generated to suit the requests of the user at once. Among these views we can find the following:

Subjects
When students enter the application they are shown the subjects they are registered on. In case students stand up in more than one learning technique, a link to Chae's Test should be included so that they can choose a pattern.

Chaea's Test
In order to carry out its two tasks it is given two views. If a student is not assigned a learning method, it will show the test so that he or she takes it. If a student stands up in several methods, he or she will be shown all the suitable methods for him or her to select one.

Development of the Student
This view will display a short description of the subject or the development of the student showing him or her the latest unit they studied. The information varies whether it is the first time they enter the subject or not.

Contest of the Unit
The contents of a subject are shown adapted to the learning techniques of the student using the tool.

Help
This view displays the help provided by the application. The other views should show a link to this one.

2.3 The Ruler

In the application, one ruler is in charge of watching any possible performance and of addressing one user or another to carry it out.

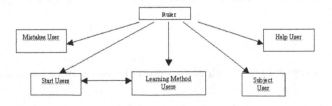

Fig. 1. Ruler Components

The different users a ruler can call for are:

Mistakes User
It manages any mistake that may arise when using the application.

Start Users
In this group we will find the users which identify the student, assign him or her a learning method and show him or her the subjects they are registered for.

Subject User
It arranges the surfing along the subject (current node, previous, following, related nodes ...). The display of all the contents will vary acccording to the learning technique of the student. This user gives support to the Adaptable Navigation.

The user can be separated into two parts:
- Subject Contents: It determines the contents requested.
- Subject Patterns: It chooses a pattern for each learning method.

Subjects Contents
It selects the information about the subject which has to be displayed. Contents are arranged in two ways, the common information which should be provided to all students and some other information regarding the different learning methods (we use Fragment Conditioned Introduction for that). The nodes related to the current one should be checked, too, and the position of the node in the sequence path, ...

Besides to reinforce this adaptation the Rearrangement of Information should be helped, that is, contents do not have to be dispayed in the same order using different learning methos, sometimes they can follow the same order and some others cannot. This application not only accepts it but also favours it.

Adaptable Navigation is used as well, in order to shape contents to learning methods, it leads the student along a subject he must study but in the way he likes studying.

Subject Patern
To achieve the adaptation of contents we need some patterns, the XSL patterns which will show information shaped by the learning technique of the users.

The Subject User chooses the information required and the Pattern, then the Pattern adapts the information to the learning ways of the student and the User sends all the data to the view which will then show it.

Learning Method Users
The user in charge of Chaea's Test is included in this group, its assistant; Analyser Test which interprets the answers to Chaea's test. And another who enables the student to change the method if he or she has stood up in more than one.

Help User
It provides the students with help whenever they ask for it. It will show how the application works.

3 Contents Adaptation

The only aim of this application is the shaping of information according to the student.

So as to succeed the application gives support to Adaptable Presentation using Content Conditioned Introduction and Information Rearrangement, it also supports Adaptable Navigation and uses Direct Leading, Links Arrangement, Links Concealing, ... XML and XSL patterns are used as well.

Consequently, every piece of information will only be shown adapted to the learning habits of the student who is asking for them.

4 Conclusion and What Is New about VIC

On the one hand we think that adapting contents to the learning habits of students would highly improve their learning itself as it would help the understanding of the matter.

On the other this concern is completely new; none of the already existing didactic applications are adapted to students, at least as regards contents and learning habits. VIC aims had never been achieved before.

References

1. Alonso Catalina M., Gallego Domingo, J., Money Peter, "Los estilos de aprendizaje: procedimientos de diagnóstico y mejora". 5a ed. Bilbao, Mensajero, ISBN: 8427119143, 2002
2. CHAEA's test. Deusto University. http://www.ice.deusto.es/guia/test0.htm
3. Brusilovsky, Peter. Peter Brusilovsky's Home Page. http://www.sis.pitt.edu/~peterb/
4. Buschmann, F., Meunier, R., Rohnert, H,, Sommerlad, P., Stal, M. "Pattern Oriented Software Architecture: A System of Patterns". JohnWiley & Sons, 1996.

XbotML: A Markup Language for Human Computer Interaction via Chatterbots

André M.M. Neves and Flávia A. Barros

Centro de Informática & VIRTUS – Laboratório de Hipermídia, Universidade Federal de
Pernambuco, Caixa Postal 7851 CEP 50732-970 – Recife (PE) – Brazil
{ammn, fab}@cin.ufpe.br

Abstract. Since 1995, we have been watching the emergence of a new
paradigm for the construction of chatterbots based on markup languages. The
most prominent of these languages is AIML. Despite its success, XML
chatterbots have drawbacks in what concerns the level of fluency in dialogues.
We present here XbotML, a new language for the construction of chatterbots
based on principles of the Conversational Analysis theory. Following this
theory, XbotML structures dialogues between user and chatterbot in adjacency
pairs, each pair bearing one associated intention. As proof of concept, we
constructed a chatterbot that has reached fluency level around 75% in dialogues
with people. This is an original work that contributes to raise the fluency level
of XML chatterbots by: providing a linguistically grounded model for
chatterbots' markup languages bases; providing a modular model for these
bases; and allowing the extension of existing bases to different domains and
applications.

1 Introduction

The dissemination of the Web stimulated the revival and faster growing of systems
that communicate with users in natural language. These systems, currently known as
chatterbots [1], have being used in the Internet for the most varied tasks (e.g., to take
part on chat rooms and RPG, to sell products, to represent companies, to give
technical support, to answer FAQs, to accompany students in distance-learning
environments, among others). In this scenario, the aim of chatterbots is to facilitate
human computer interaction, since the Web counts on millions of users with different
computer literacy levels.

In our research work, we identified three generations of chatterbots (section 2).
The first generation was strongly based on pattern-matching techniques, whereas the
second generation used Artificial Intelligence techniques. Since 1995, we have been
watching the emergence of a third generation of chatterbots, based on the use of
markup languages [2]. AIML (*Artificial Intelligence Markup Language*) [3], the first
of these languages, was used in the construction of ALICE[1], the owner of two recent
Loebner prizes[2]. Despite its success, the robots developed using AIML still present

---

[1] http://www.alicebot.org
[2] http://www.loebner.net/Prizef/loebner-prize.html

J.M. Cueva Lovelle et al. (Eds.): ICWE 2003, LNCS 2722, pp. 171–181, 2003.
© Springer-Verlag Berlin Heidelberg 2003

problems with *fluency* in dialogues with humans (reaching levels up to 65%), which, according to Rooijmans [4], is a central point in the chatterbots development.

Our research work verified two main factors that may cause loss of fluency in this kind of dialogues: (1) the chatterbot does not have domain information about the theme chosen by the user; and (2) the chatterbot is not able to recognize the user sentences' intentions in the dialogue. Clearly, a gap exists in the available markup languages, which should be tackled in order to improve the performance of these robots.

We present here XbotML, a new language for the construction of chatterbots based on principles of the Conversational Analysis theory [5]. Following this theory, XbotML structures dialogues between user and chatterbot in *adjacency pairs* (stimulus-and-response pairs), each pair bearing one associated intention. For that, XbotML organizes chatterbots' knowledge bases into three different XML patterns (section 3.3). We focused our work on the solution of the second factor mentioned above as contributing to the loss of fluency in dialogues. We believe that the first factor (lack of domain information) is easier to treat, since it can be solved simply by the creation of large bases of pairs (such as in ALICE, which counts on a base of 42.000 categories). As proof of concept, we constructed a chatterbot which has reached fluency level around 75% in dialogues with people of different ages and interests.

This is an original work that contributes to raise the fluency level of XML chatterbots by: (1) providing a linguistically grounded model for chatterbots' markup languages bases; (2) providing a modular model for these bases; and (3) allowing the extension of existing bases to different domains and applications. This way, our research work aims at contributing to the emergence of a new approach in the construction of chatterbots, raising the markup languages' level of abstraction in order to reach dialogues' fluency rates around 90%.

In section 2 we give a brief description of chatterbots state-of-the-art. In section 3 we present XbotML in detail, and in section 4 we show the experiments results. Section 5 brings conclusions and future work.

2   Chatterbots in the Cyberspace

The idea of communicating with machines in natural language dates from 1950, when Turing proposed what was later known as the *Imitation Game* [6]. Since then, we can identify several attempts of creating such system, from Eliza [7], a landmark in the area, to ALICE, the owner of two recent Loebner Prizes.

After a careful analysis of the area, we identified three main "generations" of chatterbots that differ in what concerns the technological paradigm within which the system was designed and implemented. The first generation can be characterized by the use of pattern-matching techniques of question-answer pairs and grammatical rules. Eliza is, for sure, the most successful system under this paradigm. Some other examples are PC Therapist [8] and FRED [9].

The second generation deploys Artificial Intelligence techniques, such as production rules and neural networks, in the construction of chatterbots. Julia [10], which is based on production rules, is probably its most prominent representative. Although this generation used more sophisticated techniques, the obtained results (regarding dialogue fluency) were not superior to the levels obtained in the previous generation. This fact becomes more evident when we observe the results of the Loebner prizes.

The third generation is based on the use of markup languages for the construction of chatterbots' knowledge bases. The proponent of this new paradigm is Dr. Richard Wallace [3], who developed AIML (*Artificial Intelligence Markup Language*). An AIML knowledge base consists of "categories" of question-answers pairs (see an example of AIML category in figure 1). Due to its relatively simple syntax, AIML is contributing to the popularization of chatterbots in websites[3].

```
<category>
    <pattern> BYE </pattern>
    <template> See you later. </template>
</category>
```

Fig. 1. Example of AIML category

AIML was used in the construction of ALICE (*Artificial Linguistic Internet Computer Entity*), the owner of the Loebner Prize in 2000 and 2001. Currently, ALICE counts on a base of approximately 42.000 AIML categories. Its interpreter deploys a technique very similar to the traditional pattern matching used in Eliza (question-answer pairs). Despite its good results in the Loebner Prize, ALICE showed some drawbacks in a thorough analysis undergone during the development of our research. Even with its huge categories base, ALICE reached fluency level no higher than 65%. Besides that, its base is flat and therefore very difficult to read and update.

The following section presents XbotML, which tries to overcome these drawbacks, aiming to reach fluency levels of 90%, as well as to improve the readability and extensibility of chatterbots bases.

3   The XbotML Framework

In this section, we present XbotML, a new framework for the construction of chatterbots based on principles of the Conversational Analysis theory [5]. XbotML structures dialogues in adjacency pairs, each pair bearing one associated intention. Our main goal is to improve the fluency level in dialogue sessions between users and chatterbots.

This work was initially motivated by the aim of building a chatterbot for the Portuguese language to be used in a distance-learning environment running at VIRTUS (UFPE's Laboratory of Hypermedia) [4]. This research was developed in the context of a larger project, FIACI [11][12], sponsored by Protem-CC/CNPq Brazilian Research Council.

---

[3] See ALICE's Website for details - http://www.alicebot.org
[4] http://www.virtus.ufpe.br

In what follows, we present an overview of our research work (section 3.1), the linguistic concepts underlying this proposal (section 3.2), as well a description of XbotML language (section 3.3). Finally, we show the architecture of the developed processor for XbotML (section 3.4). The practical benefits of this work are illustrated in section 4, where we present experiments results.

3.1 Research Development

The primary aim of our research work is to provide a framework for the construction of chatterbots capable of leading dialogues with high fluency levels (around 90%). We opted to work within the third generation of chatterbots, which is centered around the use of markup languages for the construction of chatterbots' knowledge bases, due to the clear advantages offered by this paradigm: extensibility, modularity, adequacy to Web applications, among others.

In the quest for a solution to fluency problems in dialogues between chatterbots and users, our research investigated three different approaches to build these systems.

Starting from the state-of-the-art AIML solution, we initially used the AIML processor available for download in ALICE's Website to build a chatterbot for the Portuguese language. As in the original AIML language, the chatterbot's base was formed by a list of AIML categories [11][12]. The implemented chatterbot showed a very low fluency level in dialogues (around 25%), what motivated us to search for a more appropriate solution (see section 4.1 for details).

A thorough analysis of this initial work revealed that, as in natural conversations, dialogues could be seen as structured according to participants' intentions. We then envisioned the Speech Acts theory [13] as a possibility to structure AIML categories into classes according to their intentions. We extended the syntax of the original AIML language and its processor to cope with classes of intentions, and organized our original categories into 14 classes. The extended language was named as AIML-Plus [14]. The new chatterbot implemented based on these ideas presented much better results - around 50% in dialogues' fluency level (see section 4.2). After several attempts to improve this rate, a serious drawback was revealed by a deep qualitative analysis: Speech Acts account solely for the intention of the speaker, not considering the hearer's response in one go. This finding put forth the need to review our choices.

Building on that, our next step was to search for a linguistic theory which could account for intentions covering dialogues' basic units, the stimulus-and-response pairs [15], also known as *adjacency pairs*. This sociolinguistic concept has already been deployed in the field of agents communication (in particular, to model conversational agents) [16]. A careful bibliographic investigation naturally led us to adopt the Conversational Analysis Theory [5] (section 3.2) as the conceptual model upon which to build our chatterbot systems. A new markup language, XbotML (section 3.3), was devised and a new processor was developed (section 3.4) to account for the particularities of this new approach. The previous knowledge base was completely revised according to this new paradigm, resulting on a chatterbot that has reached fluency level around 75% in dialogues with people of different ages and interests (section 4.3). The obtained fluency rate so far is considered very satisfactory, since not even in dialogues between two humans the fluency always reaches 100%.

3.2 Conversational Analysis Theory

This section briefly presents the Conversational Analysis theory [5], used as the basis for a consistent structuring of chatterbots' bases. Marcuschi [5] proposed that the analysis of conversations (dialogues) should be empiric, starting from single occurrences, aiming to reach general rules that account for different situations. Besides, he treats dialogues in two levels: local and global.

In what concerns the dialogues' local organization, Marcuschi highlights two essential concepts: (1) *turn*, which represents each contribution of the dialogue's participants while talking; and (2) *adjacency pair*, a term used "to refer to a single stimulus-plus-response sequence by the participants" [17] in the dialogue. In this approach, speaker and hearer exchange roles as the dialogue unfolds. As such, each participant will play the role of speaker in one turn of the adjacency pair. Each adjacency pair has an intention associated to it, such as invitation-acceptance/refuse, question-answer, etc. The pair's intention may be identified via stereotyped terms (words or expressions) named *markers* (e.g., what, who, how much). In short, adjacency pairs are sequences of two turns which co-occur and are complementary in an ordered way. The notion of fluency here is guided by the intention associated to the initial contribution.

When analyzing Marcuschi's proposed model, we noticed that the identification of the initial contribution's intention is essential for selection of an adequate response, which could minor fluency problems found in dialogues between humans and chatterbots. However, it was still necessary to identify the adjacency pairs that occur in dialogues between a user and a chatterbot, since they differ from a natural conversation between two humans (see section 4.3 for details).

The dialogues' global organization is view by Marcuschi as a structure which may be divided into several parts. Among them, he highlights three parts that are most usually found in ordinary conversations: (1) the opening session, where the participants in the dialogue introduce themselves and/or greet each other; (2) the development, which focuses on one or more topics; and (3) the closing session, where the participants say goodbye to each other.

Concerning our work, the undergone experiments revealed that dialogues with chatterbot are more similar to conversation over the telephone than to face-to-face dialogues. In the opening session, the user identifies himself/herself to the chatterbot (such as in dialogues over the phone). In the development session, it is also the user who defines the first dialogue's topic, and in the closing session, the user says goodbye first, like in telephone calls (where the one who called usually finishes off the dialogue) [5].

3.3 XbotML Structure

We present here the structure of XbotML, a chatterbots markup language based on principles of the Conversational Analysis theory. We centered the language's design around the two major concepts of this theory: turn and conversational pair.

XbotML consists of four different XML patterns[5]: (1) the *input pattern*, consisting of classes of markers which guide the identification of the user's sentence intention, the first contribution of the adjacency pair; (2) the *strategy pattern*, consisting of classes of if-then rules used to determine the intention of the chatterbot's response, according to the user's sentence intention and to the log records; (3) the *output pattern*, with classes of chatterbot's response templates, the second contribution in the adjacency pair; and (4) the *log pattern*, which registers every adjacency pair in the dialogue together with its input and output associated intentions. In contrast to AIML, XbotML structure is not guided by categories, but rather by classes of intentions which aggregate *markers* in the input pattern, *rules* in the strategy pattern and *response templates* in the output pattern.

To illustrate our proposal, we present below examples of XbotML elements for each of the patterns seen above. Initially, figure 2 presents a class in the input pattern that has as intention *"say goodbye to the chatterbot"*. If the user types the sentence "Good bye, I'm too tired", for instance, the system will match this input to the marker "good bye", and the intention of this class will be selected and associated to the input sentence. Similarly, if the user types the sentence "Bye, it's late", the same class will be selected by the system. It illustrates how XbotML deals with several different (but equivalent) input sentences, always selecting the same input class. Clearly, the user's intention in both cases was the same: *say goodbye to the chatterbot*. The algorithm deployed in the intention's selection process is presented in section 3.4.

```
<class>
<intention> say goodbye to the chatterbot </intention>
<marker> bye </marker>
<marker> bye now </marker>
<marker> good bye </marker>
<marker> so long </marker>
...
</class>
```

Fig. 2. Example of an XbotML class in the input pattern

The corresponding class in the strategy pattern to the above example is shown in figure 3. The use of the strategy rules is explained in section 3.4 below.

```
<class>
<intention> say goodbye to the chatterbot </intention>
    <if last_class = current_class output_pattern = say goodbye to the user>
        <else output_pattern = convince the user to carry on with the dialogue></else>
    </if>
</class>
```

Fig. 3. Example of an XbotML class in the strategy pattern

The corresponding classes in the output pattern to the above example are shown in figure 4. As seen, these classes contain output templates that may have slots to be filled in (in the case below, the username, indicated by the </username> element).

---

[5] The XbotML DTD is available at http://150.161.183.220/pixel/xbotml

```
<class>
<intention> say goodbye to the user </intention>
<response> good bye </username></response>
...
</class>
```

Fig. 4. Example of an XbotML class in the output pattern

3.4   XbotML Processor

We present here the general architecture of chatterbots based on XbotML, as well as some implementation details. The XbotML processor counts on the four patterns presented in the above section plus one dictionary of common words abbreviations, and six processing modules, each one with a different functionality.

The *Botmaster Interface* is used by the chatterbot's manager to create and update the Input, Strategy and Output blocks, as well as to consult the log records. This module is not accessible to end users.

The *User Interface* receives the user's input and presents the chatterbot's response, this way simulating a chat room. It keeps the full dialogue on the screen, so that the user can always read past contributions. This module is implemented in HTML and can be accessed via any available browser.

The *Input Pre-processor* translates the user's sentence into a format compatible with the XbotML input markers. Every token in the input string is verified with the help of the system's dictionary, and the recognized abbreviations are replaced by the corresponding full word (for example, "vc" is replaced by "voce" – "you" in Portuguese). Besides, the existing accents are suppressed (e.g., "você" is replaced by "voce") and upper case letters are replaced by lower case. The aim here is to facilitate the matching process.

This internal representation is passed onto the *Intentions Classifier* module, which is responsible for identifying the input sentence's intention from among the ones available in the Input block. The structure of XbotML patterns is fixed (section 3.3), however, the content of the Input, Strategy, and Output blocks may vary from one chatterbot to another. The decision about what intentions will be included in each block is at the Botmaster's hands.

The identification of the input sentence's intention is based on a pattern matching algorithm specially built for the XbotML processor. This algorithm has three major steps:

(1) first, the algorithm selects all markers in the Input block which perfectly match or include the input sentence (e.g., for the input sentence "bye" the algorithm selects "bye" and "bye now" markers in the example of figure 2); (2) following, the algorithm selects all markers in the Input block included in the input sentence (e.g., for the input sentence "good bye, I'm too tired", the algorithm selects "bye" and "good bye" markers in the example of figure 2); (3) finally, it computes the words in common between every selected marker and the input sentence, and the marker with higher number of words in common to the input sentence is selected (only if the matching rate is above a limit defined by the Botmaster).

When no match is obtained, this module associates the intention "not recognized" to the input sentence.

Our strategy differs from the one deployed by the AIML interpreter, which always selects the longer category pattern that includes the input sentence. We point out two problems here: (1) the longer category pattern may not always be the most precise match; and, (2) in case no available category includes the input sentence, there will be no possible partial match with a pattern included in the input sentence (which might very well represent its intention).

The *Decision Making* module receives the input sentence's internal representation together with its associated intention, and determines the class of the response to be built by the Response Composer module. This process is guided by the rules available in the Strategies block (see an example of the system in use below).

The *Response Composer* receives the input sentence's internal representation and the response's class, and builds the most appropriate reply based on that class' templates available in the Output block. Finally, this module returns the chatterbot's output to the user via the User Interface.

The *Log records* are created with information provided by the Input Pre-processor (user ID and name, date and input sentence), by the Intentions Classifier module (input class) and by the Response Composer (chatterbot's response and associated class).

The running version of this processor is implemented in PERL[6], due to the language offered facilities to deal with text matching and Internet applications.

4   Experiments Results

This section describes three major experiments undergone within our work. We implemented three chatterbots for Portuguese language, each one corresponding to one of the approaches described in section 3.1 (Research Development). These experiments were central for the evolution of our research, since they pointed out the drawbacks of each adopted solution.

In what follows, we present details of each implemented chatterbot, together with experiments results. The current version, based on the XbotML, is a standalone application running at VIRTUS Laboratory of Hypermedia[7]. It is worth to point that the dialogues' fluency level of our chatterbots improved from 25% (in the first version) to 75% (in the current version).

4.1   Experiment 01 – An AIML Chatterbot for Portuguese

The first version of our chatterbot, released in June 2001, bore the same structuring as any other chatterbot in AIML. Its base consisted of a flat list of 2.000 AIML categories for the Portuguese language. Some of these categories were simple translations of standard AIML categories from English to Portuguese, and some were

---

[6] http://www.perl.com
[7] http://www.virtus.ufpe.br/pixelbot

based on log files of dialogues among users of VIRTUS Website chat rooms[8]. The processor used in this experiment was adapted from the available AIML free Java code to cope with particularities of the Portuguese language (e.g., the use of possessive pronouns and prepositions in verb phrases).

In order to access the system's performance, dialogues between the chatterbot and 143 individual users were analyzed during 30 consecutive days. Regarding quantitative results, we verified that our chatterbot was able to respond with fluency only 25% of the users' contributions, and that approximately 45% of the contributions were classified as "ignored", in which case the chatterbot returned generic responses such as "would you like to change subject?".

On the other hand, a qualitative analysis of the log files of this experiment revealed that the users' contributions could be grouped into classes, according to their intentions. This analysis identified 14 different users' intentions when communicating with our chatterbot (see section 4.2). This finding was the main motivation for the creation of AIML-Plus (section 3.1).

4.2   Experiment 02 – An AIML-Plus Chatterbot for Portuguese

As said above, a thorough analysis of the log files obtained during experiment 01 revealed that the users' contributions were not random, but rather they could be grouped according to their intentions. We identified 14 different intentions among the users' contributions, as following: to start a dialogue with the robot, to thank the robot, to compliment the robot, to insult the robot, to ask how the robot is feeling, to claim something, to ask a general question to the robot, to ask the robot to define a specific issue, to ask who is a specific person, to affirm that he/she understands the robot, to affirm that he/she is charmed by the robot, to ask personal questions to the chatterbot (e.g., where it lives, where it works, where it was born, who created it etc), to ask how it is codified, and to say good-bye to the robot.

Based on this analysis, and inspired by the Speech Acts theory [13], we grouped the original AIML categories into classes according to their intentions. The initial 2.000 categories were then classified into the 14 intentions identified during our analysis. In order to implement this new approach, it was necessary to extend the original AIML language such that it could cope with some structuring on its categories base. This extension was named AIML-Plus [14]. The main modifications to the original AIML format were: (1) the creation of a new element, <class>, to aggregate categories with the same intention; and (2) the inclusion of different, however equivalent, input patterns in each category, to improve fluency. The previous processor had to be modified to deal with the implemented extensions.

The AIML-Plus version was released in September 2001 in VIRTUS Website. This experiment ran during 12 months, having in average 200 users a day. The recorded dialogues formed a corpus for analysis of approximately 3.000 sentences daily.

Qualitative and quantitative analyses of this data revealed a fluency level around 50% in dialogues between chatterbot and users. This chatterbot presented much better

---

[8] http://www.virtusclass.org

results than its predecessor. However, despite several efforts, this rate could not be improved. As seen in section 3.1, we verified that a new linguistic model was necessary to overcome this problem.

4.3 Experiment 03 – An XbotML Chatterbot for Portuguese

Following our new research directions, another chatterbot was created based on XbotML. The chatterbot's base is now organized within three different blocks (Input, Strategy and Output), which substitute the previous class-categories base. The processor had to be rewritten, since the previous base structure had to be radically modified (section 3.4). The available log files were analyzed and 45 adjacency pair classes of intentions were identified as the most usual ones in dialogues between chatterbots and users. This version is available at VIRTUS Website. The XbotML chatterbot is still under test, and has reached fluency level superior to 75% so far.

5   Conclusion and Future Work

We presented here XbotML, a new language for the construction of chatterbots. This is an original work whose main aim is to raise the fluency of XML chatterbots to levels around 90%. For that, we adopted a linguistically grounded model for XbotML bases (based on principles of the Conversational Analysis theory), favoring the modularity and extensibility of these bases. The results obtained with our experiments clearly show that we are in the right track. Currently, the available XbotML base for Portuguese is being augmented, and we expect to reach higher levels of fluency (around 85%) within the next six month.

As future work, we can point out several simultaneous extensions to XbotML. At the moment, we are working on four different subprojects: (1) the development of a tool for the semi-automatic learning of new markers (to augment the current XbotML input block); (2) the construction of a chatterbot capable of communicating in several languages at the same time (e.g., English and Portuguese) to be used as an interpreter in chat rooms with speakers of different languages; (3) the incorporation of new XbotML elements which provide for chatterbots with personality and mood; and (4) the construction of a chatterbot that serves as a natural language interface to a system which recommends films to its users based on profiles. In this application, the chatterbot is also responsible for automatically acquiring the user's profile from the undergone dialogues.

References

1.   Laven, S.: Online at http://www.simonlaven.com
2.   W3schools: Online at http://www.w3schools.com/xml
3.   Wallace, R. S.: Don't read me – A.L.I.C.E. and AIML documentation. Online at http://www.alicebot.com/dont.html

4. Rooijmans, B:. Believable Agents. Master's thesis at Faculty of Science, University of Amsterdam, 2000
5. Marcuschi, L.A.: Análise da Conversação. Editora Ática, São Paulo, 1986
6. Turing, A. M.: Computing machinery and intelligence. Mind, vol. 59 n. 236:433–460.
7. Weizenbaum, J. ELIZA: A computer program for the study of Natural Language Communication between man and machine. In Communications of ACM, vol. 9, n.1, 1966.
8. Weintraub, J.: History of the PC Therapist Online at
    http://www.loebner.net/Prizef/weintraub-bio.html
9. Garner, G.R.: Generation5, 2000. Online at http://www.generation5.org/garner.shtml
10. Foner, L. N.: What's an agent, anyway? A sociological case study. Online at http://foner.www.media.mit.edu/people/foner/Julia/Julia.html.
11. Barros, F.A., Neves, A.M.M., Costa, F.P.D. & Cavalcante, P.S.: FIACI: A Methodology for the Constructions of Intelligent Tools for Cooperative Learning in the Internet. In Prugner, N, Costa, C.D. & Lima, P.M. (eds.) Proceedings of ProTem-CC Projects Evaluation Workshop - Informatics in Education. Pp 161–175. October 1–3, Rio de Janeiro (RJ), Brasil. 2001.
12. Neves, A.M.M, Paraguaçu, F., Barros, F., Cavalcante, P.S. & Barros, S.G. Projeto FIACI: Concepção de Ferramentas Inteligentes para Aprendizagem Cooperativa na Internet. In Anais do XII Simpósio Brasileiro de Informática na Educação. Vitória (ES) Brasil. Nov/2001.
13. Searle J. R.: Expression and Meaning. Cambridge University Press. 1979
14. Neves, A. M. M., Diniz, I., Barros, F. A.: Natural Language Communication via AIML Plus Chatterbots In: V Symposium on Human Factors in Computer Systems (IHC 2002), 2002, Fortaleza - CE. Proc. of the IHC 2002 – V Symposium on Human Factors in Computer Systems 2002. , 2002. p.387
15. Schegolof, Emanuel E.: Sequencing in Conversational Openings, New York 1972
16. Zacharski, R.: Conversational Agents for Language Learning. in Innovative Applications of Artificial Intelligence Conference 2002, New Mexico.
17. Crystal, D. A.: Dictionary of Linguistics and Phonetics. 3rd edition. Basil Blackwell Ltda. 1991.

Modelling Interacting Web Usability Criteria through Fuzzy Measures

Miguel-Angel Sicilia[1] and Elena García[2]

[1] DEI Laboratory, Computer Science Department, Carlos III University
Avda. de la Universidad, 30, 28911 Leganés, Madrid, Spain
msicilia@inf.uc3m.es
[2] Computer Science Department, Alcalá University
Ctra. Barcelona km. 33.600, 28871 Alcalá de Henares, Madrid, Spain
elena.garciab@uah.es

Abstract. Usability is a multifaceted concept that is usually evaluated in terms of a number of aspects or attributes that are not independent but interacting, due to their correlation or to concrete, context-specific design interests. In consequence, the aggregation of partial scores should be carried out by devices that are able of taking into account these interactions in the resulting overall score. In this paper, we describe how fuzzy measures can be used and evaluated as models of a number of the interactions between usability aspects in evaluation processes. It is also described how they can be subsequently used to obtain more realistic final scores by using aggregation operators that are based on that measures, like the Choquet integral.

1 Introduction

Usability is a multifaceted concept [11] that encompasses several attributes regarding the interaction of humans with software systems, which are in many cases summarized in three generic interdependent aspects named efficiency, effectiveness and satisfaction. Many usability evaluation processes include an aggregation stage in which partial scores regarding different attributes or measures need to be summarized in an overall score (which is specially important for automated tools [6]). Examples include the aggregation of the results of different factors in the WAMMI questionnaire [7] and other models [3] and analysis tools. These specific aggregation processes are usually carried out by using (weighted or not) arithmetic means — like in WAMMI and some usability metrics [1] —, which are not appropriate for cases in which the aggregated criteria interact in some way. Thus, other forms of aggregation are required if meaningful final scores are desired. In addition, it should be noted that the results of evaluation processes are inherently imprecise or uncertain due to the subjectiveness involved in the process — e.g., in heuristic evaluation [9] — or to the limitations of the measurement instrument — e.g., in the case of questionnaires — so that aggregation operators that are based on fuzziness [4] are good candidates for the task.

In this paper, we describe how fuzzy measures can be used to model interactions between diverse usability criteria, resulting in more realistic summarization

J.M. Cueva Lovelle et al. (Eds.): ICWE 2003, LNCS 2722, pp. 182–185, 2003.
© Springer-Verlag Berlin Heidelberg 2003

processes (a related approach is used in WebQM [10]). These measures are able of considering empirical research results about the correlations existent between usability aspects, but also expert or designer considerations about their relative importance in each specific evaluation setting.

2   Fuzzy Measures as Models for Interacting Usability Criteria

Several types of interactions between usability attributes [11] can be modelled by fuzzy measures. Among them, we have known relationships in the form of correlations and designer-established interactions. The latter include substitutiveness and complementarity between criteria and preferential dependencies as described in [8]. A fuzzy measure on a set X is a monotonic (i.e. $v(S) \leq v(T)$ whenever $S \subseteq T$) set function $v : 2^X \rightarrow [0 \dots 1]$.

To illustrate the modelling approach, the following fuzzy measure can be used to describe a concrete evaluation case in which four well-known usability attributes are used as criteria: efficiency (e), memorability (m), satisfaction (s) and learnability (l). Two interactions between criteria are considered. First, a positive correlation is assumed between efficiency and satisfaction (cited in [5], although it's validity depends on the application context). Second, memorability and learnability are considered as substitutive by the experts, so that the presence of both of them is not strictly additive. Table 2 shows one of the possible fuzzy measures modelling the just described interactions between criteria.

Table 1. Case Study fuzzy measure $v(X)$

n = 1	n = 2	n = 3	n = 4
$\{e\} \rightarrow 0.4$	$\{e, s\} \rightarrow 0.5$	$\{e, m, s\} \rightarrow 0.6$	$\{e, m, s, l\} \rightarrow 1$
$\{m\} \rightarrow 0.15$	$\{e, m\} \rightarrow 0.55$	$\{e, s, l\} \rightarrow 0.65$	
$\{s\} \rightarrow 0.3$	$\{e, l\} \rightarrow 0.55$	$\{e, l, m\} \rightarrow 0.6$	
$\{l\} \rightarrow 0.15$	$\{m, s\} \rightarrow 0.45$	$\{m, l, s\} \rightarrow 0.5$	
	$\{s, l\} \rightarrow 0.45$		
	$\{l, m\} \rightarrow 0.2$		

Note that in Table 2 the values are heuristically selected to model the interaction between criteria. For example, the weight of $\{e, m\}$ is only slightly augmented when the substitutive criterion l is added to the set, and the set of correlated criteria $\{e, s\}$ has a weight of 0.5, which represents a difference of 0.2 from absolute additivity. In more complex cases, mathematical functions are required to model those relationships. The requirement for two correlated criteria i and j is that they are not completely additive, i.e., that $v(\{i, j\}) < v(\{i\}) + v(\{i\})$. Two substitutive criteria are required to satisfy the relationship expressed in 1, so that the addition of a substitutive criterion have a small effect in the fuzzy measure (having no effect if the criterion are completely interchangeable).

$$v(T) < \left\{ \begin{matrix} v(T \cup i) \\ v(T \bigcup j) \end{matrix} \right\} \approx v(T \bigcup \{i,j\}) \quad T \subseteq X - \{i,j\} \tag{1}$$

The discrete Choquet integral introduced can be used as a generalization of the weighted arithmetic mean that accounts for interacting criteria [8]. The general expression of the integral given in 2 is a specific instance of the general form of a discrete aggregation operator on the real domain: $M_v : \mathbb{R}^n \to \mathbb{R}$, which takes as input a vector $x = (x_1, x_2, \ldots, x_n)$ and yields a single real value.

$$\mathcal{C}_v(x) = \sum_{i=1}^{n} x_{(i)} [v(\{j|x_j \geq x_{(i)}\}) - v(\{j|x_j \geq x_{(i+1)}\})] \tag{2}$$

In expression 2 we have that $x' = (x_{(1)}, x_{(2)}, \ldots, x_{(n)})$ is a non-decreasing permutation of the input n-tuple x, where $x'_{n+1} = \emptyset$ by convention. The integral is expressed in terms of a fuzzy measure (or Choquet capacity) v.

The results of the Choquet integral for the measure in Table 2 can be compared with those of a simple weighted mean $(\mathcal{W})$ to appreciate the differences (both expressed in a zero to three scale). For example, $\mathcal{C}(3,3,0,2) = 1.45$, while $\mathcal{W}(3,3,0,2) = 2.4$, showing how the second values overweights the correlated criteria (in addition, $\mathcal{C}(3,2,0,2) = 1.4$, so having a consistent small increment of 0.05, while the weighted mean delta is 0.3). In cases in which the participating criteria are independent, like $(0,2,2,0)$, $\mathcal{C}$ and $\mathcal{W}$ yield the same value. A thorough analysis lead to concluding that weighted means are not always appropriate overall usability scores.

3   On Evaluating Fuzzy Measure Design

Designer-dependant decision on the form of fuzzy measures must be empirically evaluated for adjustment. This entails asking about the degree to which the resulting aggregations are considered as (approximately) realistic to domain experts (in our case, usability experts) with regards to the established correlations and criteria. A procedure to accomplish this task can be that of eliciting a membership function describing the *appropriateness* of the aggregation. Existing membership evaluation techniques can be used for this purpose [2]. A modified pooling technique can be used to validate the aggregation. The technique proceeds by taking a evenly distributed sample of input vectors, and asking each evaluation participant, for each input value, the question "is the output value appropriate for the design at hand?" — after informing him/her about concrete the design considerations embodied in the fuzzy measure —, and whenever the answer is negative, a gradation of appropriateness in the [0..100] interval is asked for. A weighted mean using the weights $v(x)$ for each individual criterion is used as a clue to help experts in assessing the quality of the aggregation with respect to it. The resulting n-dimensional function can be analyzed to help in detecting potential pitfalls in the fuzzy measure (this graphical inspection approach will be subject of future analysis in the search of heuristics for the task itself).

4   Conclusions and Future Work

The use of fuzzy measures to model different interactions between usability attributes used as criteria has been described. The Choquet integral can be used to use these measures for the aggregation of partial scores in global ones that reflect a summarized usability analysis estimation. Techniques for membership elicitation have been proposed as evaluation procedures for the adequacy of the design of those fuzzy measures.

Future work should address a systematic analysis of the properties and validity of the approach with regards to current usability definitions and empirical evidence.

References

1. Babiker, E. M., Fujihara, H. and Boyle, C.D.B.: A metric for hypertext usability. A metric for hypertext usability. In: Proceedings of the 9th annual international conference on Systems documentation (1991):95–104
2. Bilgiç, T. and Türksen, T.: Measurement of Membership Functions: Theoretical and Empirical Work. In: D. Dubois and H. Prade (eds.) Handbook of Fuzzy Sets and Systems Vol. 1, Chapter 3, Fundamentals of Fuzzy Sets, Kluwer (1999):195–232
3. Drajnik, J.: Towards valid quality models for websites. In Proc. of 7th Human Factors and the Web Conference, Madison, Wisconsin June 2001.
4. Calvo, T., Kolesárová, A., Komorníková, M. and Mesiar, R. : Aggregation Operators: Basic Concepts, Issues and Properties. In Calvo, T., Mayor, G. and Mesiar, R. (eds). Aggregation Operators: New Trends and Applications. Studies in Fuzziness and Soft Computing, 97 (2002):3–106
5. Frøkjær, E., Hertzum, M. and Hornbæk, K.: Measuring Usability: are effectiveness, efficiency and satisfaction really correlated?. In: Proc. of Human Factors in Computing Systems (2000):345–352
6. Ivory, M.Y. and Hearst, M.A.: The State of the Art in Automated Usability Evaluation of User Interfaces. ACM Computing Surveys, 33(4) (2001):1–47
7. Kirakowski, J., Cierlik, B. Measuring the usability of web sites. Human Factors and Ergonomics Society Annual Conference (1998)
8. Marichal, J.L.: An axiomatic approach of the discrete Choquet integral as a tool to aggregate interacting criteria, IEEE Transactions on Fuzzy Systems 8 (6) (2000):800–807
9. Nielsen, J.: Heuristic evaluation. In Nielsen, J., and Mack, R.L. (eds.): Usability Inspection Methods, John Wiley and Sons, New York (1994):25–61
10. Olsina, L. and Rossi, G.: Measuring Web Application Quality with WebQEM. IEEE Multimedia Magazine 9(4) (2002):20–29
11. Van Welie, M., van der Veer, G.C. and Eliëns, A. (1999), Breaking down usability. In: Proc. of Interact'99 (1999):613–620

A Concept-Based Approach for the Design of Web Usability Evaluation Questionnaires

Elena García[1], Miguel A. Sicilia[2], León A. González[1], and José R. Hilera[1]

[1] Computer Science Department. Polytechnic School.
University of Alcalá. Ctra. Barcelona km. 33.6. 28871. Alcalá de Henares. Spain
{elena.garciab, leon.gonzalez, jose.hilera}@uah.es
[2] Computer Science Department. Polytechnic School.
Carlos III University. Av. de la Universidad, 30. 28911. Leganés. Spain
msicilia@inf.uc3m.es

Abstract. Questionnaires are widely used instruments for usability evaluation, but their correct construction is often a complex task since several previous administrations are required to obtain a fine-tuned version of the questionnaire. In this work, we describe a novel approach to design questionnaires that is based on a knowledge representation of the concepts involved in questionnaire-based usability evaluation. As a proof of concept of the model, a prototype has also been constructed, aimed at supplying a guided questionnaire development process especially useful for novel Web designers.

1 Introduction

Nowadays, the usability of Web interfaces is being considered a factor of increasing importance in application development and, therefore, it should be taken into account in all phases of the development life cycle [3], including evaluation in different process stages. In this work we focus on the use of questionnaires [5] in usability evaluation, which are commonly used in this process.

There exist some tools that allow for the construction of generic questionnaires, but there are very few ones focused on usability questionnaires, like Perlman's user interface questionnaire page[1], however, this artifact is exclusively based on predefined standard questionnaires, and it is no possible to guide the evaluators in the definition of the tasks that participants have to perform to carry out the evaluation. In this paper we sketch how the construction of questionnaires can be facilitated using an ontological questionnaire model which allows the development of guided design applications. In contrast with database information storage approaches, the use of ontologies provides flexibility and enables the sharing of own and external model entities instances and also reasoning on them. All these features can give rise to a useful approach for novice Web architects who need a questionnaire to evaluate and to improve the usability of a concrete Web application.

---

[1] Perlman, G.: Web-Based User Interface Evaluation with Questionnaires. Available at http://www.acm.org/ perlman/question.html

J.M. Cueva Lovelle et al. (Eds.): ICWE 2003, LNCS 2722, pp. 186–189, 2003.
© Springer-Verlag Berlin Heidelberg 2003

2   A Questionnaire Model for Usability Evaluation

The model must hold all the entities that take part in the evaluation, and also it must be rich enough to enable some reasoning activities that allows for the construction of a solid questionnaire suitable for the application that the tester wants to evaluate. Focusing on the aim of this paper, the following main model entities must describe: the questionnaire and the questions it includes, the usability attributes, the different functionalities that the application holds, which depend on the kind of Web application and the tasks that are required to be carried out by the participant in the course of the evaluation. The model also includes other terms, some of they described in [2], that enable the representation of all the knowledge needed to carry out a usability evaluation using attitude questions along with opinion or factual-type ones. Figure 1 depicts a conceptual UML diagram that shows the core model entities used in this paper. The <<ontology-term>> stereotype is used to denote elements in a richer logic-based conceptualization.

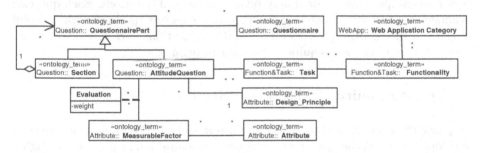

Fig. 1. Core classes of the usability questionnaire model

As we are aimed to design close-ended attitude questionnaires, we represent here exclusively the knowledge about the questions that enable the collection of the user opinion according to his/her personal experience. It would be possible that evaluation participants had never used the application before, so that providing them with a collection of concrete tasks is useful to guide their evaluation process. Each task is aimed at evaluating a specific functionality of the application, and in addition, we have considered that usually each kind of Web application contains a minimum well-defined set of functionalities. Questions are formulated to the user according to the task that he/she has to carry out, so it's possible to adjust the statement text with the performed task.

Another important model section is about the attributes that can be evaluated using the questionnaire. Taking into account the terminology used in [4], a usability attribute can be defined as a system feature that contributes to make the system more easy-to-use. As we have previously exposed, the questionnaires we are modelling are attitude questionnaires, so they enable the acquisition of the user satisfaction measure about the application, and we can't consider that the results directly reflect a usability attribute but rather they obtain the perception the users have about the attributes. Then we have defined as measurable factor the system feature measure that can be obtained using an attitude questionnaire. These factors can have different impact level on different usability attributes. Only the satisfaction attribute can be directly obtained taking into account the overall questionnaire results. Normally, different questions relate to different measurable factors, and each factor is composed of weighted contributions from the ratings received for its statements.

The model elements are divided in four interrelated ontologies: The *Web applications ontology*, that represents the knowledge about the different kinds of applications available through the Web, the *functionalities and tasks ontology*, that models both the main Web application (or section of the application) elements that enable the more typical functionalities and the task/s that lead the participant to accomplish them, the *attributes ontology*, that represents the knowledge about the usability attributes and the different factors that can be measured using a questionnaire and the *questionnaires ontology*, that models close-ended questionnaire items that can contain different sections — which in turn contain questions — or simply be a sequences of questions. Each question is aimed to contribute in one or more measurable factors (perhaps with different weight) or dialog principles, and it's usual that sections correspond to specific tasks, if more of one are required, or dialog principles.

3   Questionnaire Design Case Study

To prove the usefulness of the questionnaire model based on ontologies we have developed a prototype that guides the questionnaire design process through a number of sequential steps (a "wizard"). The information requested in the different phases of the design process doesn't require a thorough knowledge about usability evaluation, so, this approach can be considered a tool specially useful for novice information architects and Web designers. In order to determine the tasks that the test respondents have to complete, the first step is the specification of the application type. The Web application ontology supports this process. It allows the questionnaire designer to navigate in the ontology to find the most appropriate, until no more subclasses of selected terms are found.

Once the application type is specified, the wizard shows the elements that this kind of systems usually include to support their more typical functionalities. The tool retrieves the elements using the semantic relationships defined among terms of Web application ontology and functionality and task ontology, such as the displayed elements are associated with the selected application type or its ancestors and are subsumed by high-level `functionality-element` term defined in the functionality and task ontology.

In the basis of the previously selected elements, tasks that guide the participants are retrieved using the relationships among the terms of the functionality and task ontology. In the third step of the construction process the designer is required to introduce such specific items as the tasks require using other ontology terms, in order to complete meaningfully their statement. The use of a knowledge representation like the functionality and task ontology also enables some other reasoned behaviors like the establishment of pre-required tasks, in addition to the ones derived from other ontology features like the subsumption.

Using the questionnaire ontology and before tasks are confirmed, the questionnaire is displayed and the designer can make used of it. The attribute ontology is built so that a generic default attribute list that covers the other ones exists, and both the questions and evaluation are selected and carried out according to it.

4 Conclusions and Future Work

In this work we have described a new approach to design usability attitude questionnaires. The approach is based on a knowledge representation of a questionnaire which includes four different ontologies: questionnaire, attribute, functionality and task and Web application.

The use of a well-defined ontological model enables the development of different applications like a guided construction of questionnaires and also the shallow reasoning on the model and its instances, which is applicable in our current case study in the selection of the task and the presentation/performance order in which they have to be carried out. An another important advantage derived from the questionnaire model definition is that of enabling the representation and storage of all necessary data to subsequently apply artificial intelligence techniques that optimize and enhance several process in the usability evaluation, like those described in [1].

Further evaluation would be needed for a detailed account of the benefits of the proposed tool. In addition, the Web application taxonomy should be extended to obtain a more comprehensive coverage of the current variety of Web applications.

References

1. García, E., Sicilia, M.A., Hilera, J.R., Gutiérrez, J.A.: Extracting knowledge from usability evaluation databases. Proc. of the Intl. Conf. on Human Computer Interaction INTERACT01 (2001) 713–715.
2. García, E., Sicilia, M.A., Hilera, J.R., Gutierrez, J.A.: Computer-aided usability evaluation: A questionnaire case study. Advances in Human Computer Interaction. Typorama (2001) 85–91.
3. Mayhew, D.: The Usability Engineering Lifecycle. Morgan Kaufmann (1999).
4. Nielsen, J.: Usability Engineering. Morgan-Kaufmann (1993).
5. Oppenheim A. N.: Questionnaire Design, Interviewing and Attitude Measurement. Printer Pub Ltd (1992).

Adaptive Interactive Dialogs through the Web: Addressing User's Interaction Requirements Dynamically

Martín González Rodríguez, María del Puerto Paule Ruiz,
Juan Ramón Pérez Pérez, Aitor de la Puente Salan, and
María del Carmen Suárez Torrente

Laboratory of Object Oriented Technologies (OOTLab), Department of Computing Science,
University of Oviedo, c/Calvo Sotelo s/n, 33007 Oviedo, Asturies, Spain
{martinc, paule, jrpp}@pinon.ccu.uniovi.es,
aitor@petra.euitio.uniovi.es, macamen@correo.uniovi.es

Abstract. Addressing the interaction requirements of the users of a web site at its the design stage seems to be an impossibly task as there are too many cognitive, perceptive and motive factors involved. If a web site pretends to be usable for dozens or even hundreds kinds of different users, it must be generated dynamically, depending on the interaction requirements of the current user.

1 Introduction

Traditional design of user centered interfaces is based on the identification and definition of the target audience for the application under development. Some design guidelines include the identification and understanding of the target audience as the most important steps to start the design of a product. The idea is that once the target audience has been defined; an interface that effectively satisfies their needs can be designed.

However, the quest for the typical user is opposite to the individuality and diversity that makes up some much of our identity. If the design of the interaction mechanisms of an application aims to make interfaces accessible and appealing to all users, it shouldn't rely on an abstract generalization [4]. In the design of applications targeted to a wide range of users, it is almost impossible to determine the typical user without falling in serious misconceptions. Maybe is it possible to describe the typical user of generic applications such Microsoft Explorer?

2 Guidelines versus Human Diversity

The uncertainty about the interaction requirements of the real user of an interface makes any decision taken at design stage completely useless. To show this, we would

J.M. Cueva Lovelle et al. (Eds.): ICWE 2003, LNCS 2722, pp. 190–193, 2003.
© Springer-Verlag Berlin Heidelberg 2003

like to analyze an everyday task in web engineering: the design of the navigation bar (table of contents) for a web portal. We are going to consider the design of the syntactical level for the user interface of the navigation bar, that is, the location and appearance of the bar.

If the designers decide to include buttons in the navigation bar, they will get in trouble simply defining the size of these widgets. Small buttons will be difficult to be used by elderly users or by people with visual disabilities (short-sighted people, for example), while big buttons will look ugly for people with good perceptive systems.

Another pending question that designers must solve is where the navigation bar should be included.

When the World Wide Web became a profitable business and a massive corporate presence was a reality in the net, many graphic designers coming from the printed medium, translated their knowledge to the electronic one, porting many of their design guidelines and principles. One of them, was the relevance that the left side of the visual space of a publication has on a user of a Roman writing system. Notice for example that the headlines included in the covers of western magazines are consider as eye-catching section, acting as a real advert to promote the magazine's content [1].

When the headlines of printed magazines were ported to the web, they were grouped together in a bigger visual object which acted as a table of contents for the site (the navigation bar). Although the navigation bars can be found in any side of a web site, the left side location is still the most popular for graphic designers, as it is supposed to act as attraction pole for –western– readers.

If the designers of our example are working on a web portal for western readers, this guideline will solve the dilemma. However, the solution is not as simple as it seems, as this guideline miss and important feature of the electronic medium that isn't present in the printed one.

Some years ago, we conducted an experiment to corroborate the relevance of the left side of a visual space over the right side [2]. The experiment consisted in a web site from which the volunteers had to obtain certain information. The only way to obtain that information was by mean of the navigation bar. However, the web site had two identical navigation bars, one at each side of the visual space (left and right side).

As both bars were identical in appearance and both conduced to same information, the selection of the preferred bar wasn't performed in terms of cognition but on the relevance of location the bar.

Obviously, the selection of the users was registered by data-gathering agents embedded inside the web pages. The results obtained were amazing, as they didn't showed a clear preference for the left side bar as it was expected. In fact, only 179 users out of 342 selected the left side bar (52,9%). It is a quite relevant fact that 47,5% of the users selected the right side bar.

The experiment was repeated again with similar results, but this time, once users got the information they were looking for, they were asked to indicate whether they were left or right handed. The results obtained probed a clear correlation between right handed users and selections of the right side bar. This was the feature missed by graphic designers when they ported their general design principle to the electronic medium. In the printed medium, readers are attracted through their perceptive system only (visual attraction). However, in the electronic medium, the motive system of the users also plays a crucial in the scoring of the relevance of an objet, as users must select the object by mean of a mechanical action which depends on their laterality.

As the user interface of any application should be usable and accessible by any kind of users (independently of their perceptive system or their laterality), each design decision should be taken at execution time, once that the interaction requirements of the real user have been finally detected. As designers are not present at execution time, the application should be able to emulate the human designer, creating the user interface on the fly.

Following this design principle, we have developed GADEA, a User Interface Management Expert System (UIMES) able to generate dynamic versions of the syntactical level of the interactive dialogs of a user interface at execution time.

3 The Architecture of GADEA

The UIMES GADEA tries to emulate the behavior of a human expert in Human-Computer Interaction (HCI) who is in charge of the design of an interactive dialog for a specific user, employing multimodal communication channels [5] (visual and auditory communication channels). The emulated expert will select the most suitable interaction style available for the target platform (the web or a standalone applications), accordingly with the unique cognitive, perceptive and motive requirements of the target user, adapting the appearance, contents and access mode of every widget included in the dialog.

The internal architecture of GADEA relies on three independent components who has been specially designed to cope with the problems derived of the three most important features of the system. Those components are DEVA, ANTS and CodeX (see Figure 1).

The CodeX (Code eXplorer) module represents the interface between GADEA and the client applications of this UIMES. This module must convert the user interaction requests into calls to specific methods inside the application's domain workspace. To reach this objective, this module automatically inspects the binary code of every client application at execution time, looking for any user process defined by the programmers during the design time. CodeX consider a 'user process' as those methods designed to satisfy a specific user's interaction request and will represent them as options or commands in the respective application user interface. This module is also in charge update every single piece information displayed by the user interface, keeping track of possible changes in the value of public variables and data structures associated to the interface by the application at both execution and design time. All this information is obtained automatically inspecting the client application's code by mean of the structural reflection mechanism of the Java platform.

The information collected by CodeX is sent periodically to DEVA (Dialog Expert Valuator for Adaptation) which represent the agent software in charge of the simulation of the behaviour of human expert in Human-Computer Interaction (HCI). This module converts the application's and user's interaction requests into adaptive interactive dialogs. Based on the general knowledge and guidelines provided by the HCI discipline as well as by specific knowledge stored about the current user model of the client application, DEVA uses its fuzzy inference engine to evaluate, to select and to adapt the best interactive dialog available for the current user. The dynamic creation of the user tailored interactive dialog will depend on the current user's cognitive, perceptive and motor skills, which might fluctuate over the time.

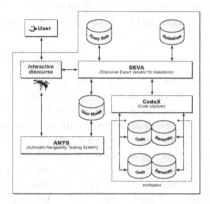

Fig. 1. General Architecture of GADEA, composed by three modules: DEVA, ANTS and CodeX.

Finally, the ANTS module will be the agent responsible for keeping the information about the users of any client application of GADEA updated. This component makes use of different kinds of automatic remote agents designed to observe the user behavior in any of the interactive dialogs designed by DEVA. Those agents obtain crucial information about the specific user's skills, which is stored in specific distributed user model.

References

1. Gordon, Druce; Designing Covers, Mac Format, Future Publishing, Bath, England. Issue: January. 1994.
2. González Rodríguez, Martín; ANTS: An Automatic Navigability Testing Tool for Hypermedia. Correia Nuno; Chambel, Teresa; DAVENPORT Glorianna; (Eds.) Multimedia'99. Springer-Verlag. ISBN 3-211-83437-0. 2000.
3. Nielsen, J.; Alertbox. http://www.useit.com/alertbox/. 2002.
4. Reynolds, C.; A Critical Examination of Separable User Interface Management Systems: Constructs for Individualization. ACM SIGCHI. 29(3). 1997.
5. Wahlster, Wolfang; User and Dialog Models for Multimodal Communication. Sullivan, Joseph W.; Tyler, W. Sherman (Eds.) Intelligent User Interfaces. Frontier Series. ACM Press. 1991.

Dialog Model Clustering for User Interface Adaptation

Guido Menkhaus and Sebastian Fischmeister

Software Research Lab, Department of Computer Science
University of Salzburg A-5020 Salzburg, Austria
{lastname}@SoftwareResearch.net

Abstract. In recent years, the dramatic growth of the PDA and mobile phone market demonstrates that users are willing to be constrained to small displays, limited storage and battery life, slow CPU speeds and data transfer, in the hope of achieving truly portable access to electronic data. Most of the limitations that users experience with current devices will disappear in future generations. These changes will not have an effect on the primary user interface constraint: the display size. The actual screen size will not change, since users demand devices that can be easily carried around and held in one hand. The article presents a hybrid approach to the generation of adaptive UIs based on a linking strategy of hierarchies of graphs. The nodes of this graph consist of clustered UI elements.

1 Introduction

From the increasing miniaturization of hardware arose a broad spectrum of mobile computers, which extend from mobile phones, computerized notepads, and PDAs to notebooks. This created a heterogeneity of computing platforms that stands in contrast to the past homogeneity of the desktop computer paradigm. This diversity often makes a transfer of knowledge difficult on how to build user interfaces (UI) between the platforms. The application of specific techniques for user interfaces, which are suitable for a desktop PC graphic user interface, to a miniaturized version fails. The objective is to develop UIs for the same application only once and not for each particular class of computing device.

There are research projects looking into new generation UIs that no longer consist of a conventional display. These UIs, although small in physical size, will no longer have size constraints concerning the UI. However, user acceptance seems to be low [1]. We think that traditional user interfaces still have a strong potential for improvement and that this technology will prevail in the near future on the consumer market [2].

The article presents an approach to UI adaptation. It is based on an abstract UI description, which is shared among different platforms. The adaptation technique tailors the UI description to minimize the mismatch between its presentation and the platform's capability to present it.

J.M. Cueva Lovelle et al. (Eds.): ICWE 2003, LNCS 2722, pp. 194–203, 2003.
© Springer-Verlag Berlin Heidelberg 2003

The remaining of the article is organized as follows: The following section presents a short overview of UI architecture. Section 3 introduces the concept of adaptation mechanisms. A special adaptation technique is discussed in Section 3.2 along with related work in Section 3.1. Results are presented in Section 4 and Section 5 closes the article with concluding remarks.

2   User Interface Architecture

Model-based UI software development has introduced concepts and techniques that assist in the process of UI development [3,4]. These concepts give developers a better understanding of the field of UI design. There are three phases in the process of UI design [5]: The *semantic level design* describes the tasks users should be able to perform using the application for which the UI provides the interaction means. The *syntactic level design* describes the structure and the interaction behavior of the UI. The *lexical level design* consists of the detailed description of the visual part of the UI. The semantic design level consists of the task model. The dialog model presents the syntactic design level. The lexical design level describes the platform and the presentation model [6]:

1. **Task Model.** The task model is a formal description of the service the user accesses. It is hierarchically organized and contains information regarding the trigger of a task, its precondition, postcondition, and the action of the task itself.
2. **Dialog Model.** The dialog model describes the syntactic sequence of human-computer interaction through UI elements and determines the ordering of the set of tasks and actions. Since the task model is hierarchically organized, so is the dialog model. It is usually implemented as a sequence of windows consisting of a set of UI elements and a set of transitions that allows navigation from one window to the next.
3. **Presentation Model.** The presentation model accounts for the different devices from which a user may access a service. It maps conceptual elements of the dialog model onto platform specific elements.
4. **Platform Model.** The platform model contains information about the capabilities, restriction, and limitations of the target platform. This model is usually exploited dynamically at run-time.

The main obstacle to single authoring is the growing number of networking enabled devices with a wide variety of UI capability. One of the main differences they share is different screen size. How to enable content to be adapted to various screen sizes? The same content may require varying numbers of windows to display and a different navigational structure, depending on the platform. For example, content fitting on one PC window may require 3 windows on a mobile phone. Yet, all these windows originate from the same, single authored UI. The platform model delivers information about the limitations and restrictions of the target platform. The adaptation process exploits this information for adapting the content and the navigational structure.

The challenge is to remodel the UI elements into a composition which allows the user to adequately interact with the application and that respects the dialog model independent of the target device.

2.1   Short Overview of Adaptation Mechanisms

Until recently, UI software has been designed with a specific environment in mind, resulting in ideal properties in this environment. Any other environment entails an adaptation of the system resulting in an output having properties less optimal than the ideal properties. An ideal adaptable software maintains the same ideal properties under all environments. However, in practice it is impossible to maintain the ideal properties under a varying environment. Therefore, the goal of the adaptable software system is to result in an output having properties close to the ideal properties. Following the notation of [7]: Let s be a software system. E is the space of environments hosting all possible environments. $e_i \in E$ is one environment having a set of properties $p_i \in P$. Let $I \subset E$ be the input space, and $i_i \subset e_i$ provides the inputs of the environment e_i. $O \subset E$ is the output space, and $o_i \subset e_i$ the output space of the system s under the environment e_i. A computation of the system s produces the results o_i with properties p_i in an environment e_i: $s(i_i) \rightarrow o_i : o_i \models p_i, p_i \in P, i_i, o_i \in e_i$ The equation states that s guarantees the properties p_i under the environment e_i. An ideal adaptable system maintains the same properties under all environments. Since there is no such ideal system, the objective of the adaptable software system is to aim at an output with properties close to the ideal properties. The adaptation process adaptation can be regarded as an energy minimization problem, with the energy function:

$$E(e_i) = \frac{1}{n} \sum_{j=1}^{n} d(p_{i,j}, p_{i,ideal})^2$$

with $p_{i,j} \in p_i$, $j = 1, \ldots, n$ being specific properties of the environment e_i and $d(\cdot, \cdot)$ being a distance measure between properties. The energy is minimal, when the ideal properties are met after the process of adaptation.

3   Dialog Model Adaptation

In this article a dialog of the dialog model will be represented by a two-dimensional discrete function $UIelement(x, y)$, which is digitized both in spatial coordinates and feature value: $dialog = [UIelement(x, y)]_{P \times Q}$ where $P \times Q$ is the size of the dialog, (x, y) denotes the spatial coordinate and $UIelement(x, y) \in UIE$ the type of UI element from the set of available abstract UI elements UIE. Without loss of generality we consider only the case, where $Q = 1$.

Grouping UI elements that implement the dialog model into a hierarchical structure of windows is the essential step our adaptation process that leads to single authoring. For this, the dialog model adaptation process partitions the UI elements implementing the dialog model into non-intersecting regions, such that each region satisfies a homogeneity predicate and the resulting hierarchical structure of windows minimizes an energy function.

Formally, the process of adaptation of the dialog model can be defined as follows: If a dialog model consists of a set of UI elements and P is a homogeneity predicate, then the adaptation of the dialog model is a partitioning of UI elements into a set of connected regions $(r_1, r_2, \ldots, r_n)$, which will eventually be converted into a hierarchical navigationable structure of windows, such that:

$$dialog = \cup_{i=1}^{n}(r_i \backslash navigationUIelements(r_i))$$
$$r_i \cap r_j = \emptyset, i \neq j$$
$$r_i \text{ is a connected set of regions}$$
$$P(r_i) = \text{true}, i = 1, \ldots, n$$
$$P(r_i \cup r_j) = \text{false, if } r_i \text{ is adjacent to } r_j$$

The adaptation of the dialog model partitions a dialog into regions of non-intersecting UI elements complying with a homogeneity predicate. A user accessing a service supported by a dialog model needs to navigate from one region to the next region. However, not all navigation elements are in the original dialog. Thus, they have to be integrated into the regions, resulting from the adaptation process. The set of all UI elements in the regions equals the UI elements in the original dialog plus the integrated new UI elements dedicated to the navigation between the regions, the $navigationUIelements(r_i)$.

3.1 Related Work

The above definition of the process of adaptation is very similar to image segmentation as defined in [8]. Analogous to segmentation and clustering processes, the more context and domain information is known beforehand and integrated into the process, the better the process' results. Approaches exploring dialog model adaptation can broadly be divided into two categories. Processes of the first category do not consider context knowledge such as screen size during design time. They work bottom-up and rely uniquely on dynamic adaptation of the dialog model. The other category explicitly uses top-level domain and task model knowledge during design time. The processes are configured with a priori known target contexts.

Adaptation without Context Knowledge. One of the key features of the Microsoft Mobile Internet Toolkit (MMIT) is the ability to transcode content of a Web form to the screen size of the target device. This process is called paginating and chunking [9]. Pagination is similar to the fragmentation process in IBM's Websphere [10]. The places where the process of pagination cuts a Web forms into two different pages depends on the device screen's size requirements, but not on semantic dependencies between controls. For example, textual information explaining the use of a button and the button itself are modeled as two distinct controls. If these two UI elements were grouped into two different regions after the adaptation process, the adapted dialog model had low usability. In MMIT, this process may be controlled by inserting *Panel* controls, which avoid page breaks between controls. The result is a set of regions, which can be navigated in a linear, sequential way only. To access the last control of a dialog, each new window (region) has to be linearly traversed.

Adaptation with Context Knowledge. Approaches of this category allow the designer to submit to the adaptation process specific configuration information concerning possible target device types [11]. The designer creates the appropriate configuration for each class of device. On the one hand, these configurations are best adapted to the requirements of the underlying service. On the other hand, a single modification of the requirements of the service entails the modification of each configuration.

The quality of the latter approach depends on the configuration and the type of content that is presented. The first approach has the drawback of working only on syntactic information. We propose a hybrid approach that combines the advantages of the first bottom-up working approach (fast design, non need to produce sophistic configuration data) and the latter top-down approach (integration of semantic information).

3.2   Dialog Model Adaptation Using UI Element Clustering

The two main challenges of the hybrid approach to dialog model adaptation are:

1. How to incorporate low-level semantic information into the dialog model?
2. How to adapt the dialog model respecting the semantic information?

No current approach to UI software development implements a clear separation of presentation, dialog and task model, nor does any current markup language supports the feature of integrating adaptation configuration that could guide any adaptation process. We have developed the Multi UI Single Application (MUSA) model and Event Handler Graph XML. MUSA implements a clear separation of task, dialog, presentation and platform model. The Event Graph Handler XML representing the dialog model is a markup language that allows adding information to each element stating the semantic relation to its neighboring elements. For more information on MUSA and Event Handler Graph XML, refer to [12,13]. In the next section, we introduce the dialog model adaptation process.

Dialog Model Clustering. The adaptation technique is based on a linking strategy of two hierarchies of graphs [14,15]. The first hierarchy of graphs forms a syntactic based and static structure that guarantees that the resulting regions are connected. The second hierarchy is dynamically built up respecting the low-level semantic information integrated into the dialog model at design time. The two hierarchies of graphs implement the dialog model adaptation process.

The elements of the dialog model are placed as abstract UI elements into a stack of regular grids, as illustrated in Figure 1. In the lowest level of the stack, each cell of the grid corresponds to a single UI element. Each cell of level $i + 1$ represents a group of cells of level i. The adaption algorithm always forms linear structures of 3×1 cells. The cells overlap in such a way that the outer cells on level i belong to two cells of level $i+1$. The cells in a group of level i, represented by a cell of level $i + 1$, are called the subcells or the children of this cell. The

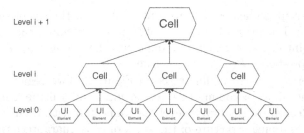

Fig. 1. Stack of a regular grid of cells that places a structure on a set of UI elements. Three UI elements form a cell on the lowest level. Cells on a lower level are candidates for cells on a higher level.

representing cell is called the parent of its children. The clustering of a set of UI elements into a set of regions is done within the boundaries of the induced stack of cells and is of primary interest. To come to the final set of regions, we dynamically build up a stack of regions. A UI element corresponds to a region on the lowest level. Adaptation of a window is performed by clustering regions of level i into regions of level $i+1$. However, regions can only be grouped within the boundaries of a cell in which they reside, as illustrated in Figure 2, and if they satisfy the homogeneity predicate. This guarantees that we cluster only connected regions.

A hierarchy of regions is built up by applying a clustering process to each cell while moving up the stack of cells. The clustering process stops at the boundary of each cell and the cell overlap is responsible some regions taking part in two cell-based clustering processes. The receptive field RF [15] of a region $r \in R_i$, with R_i being the set of regions of level i, is defined as the set of all regions on the lowest level, which represent the region r. The semantic information σ integrated into the dialog model is assigned to each region r. $\sigma(r)$ is the average value of the semantic information of each region's receptive field.

The adaptation process adapts dynamically the dialog model by composing and decomposing UI elements of the dialog model into a set of regions, which results finally into a hierarchical structure of linked windows. The process consists of the following four phases:

- **Bottom-up Clustering.** Regions of level i are grouped into regions of level $i+1$ within the boundaries of their cell and satisfying a predicate P.
- **Top-down Separating.** Regions that fail to group on level i are separated recursively down to level 0.
- **Horizontal Separation.** Large-sized regions of level i, especially when they contain a single UI element, are split into smaller regions of level i.
- **Relinking.** The user should be able to navigate from one region to the next region. To ensure usability, regions are relinked by integrating additional navigation UI element.

Bottom-up Clustering. The clustering process determines the set of connected regions of level i of a specific cell and groups them. In order to form a new region

r_{i+1} (the subscript indicates the level) in a cell c_{i+2}, the set of subcells of c_{i+2} are determined. Each subcell has a set of regions associated that are candidates for clustering into r_{i+1}. A region s_i groups into the region r_{i+1}, if it satisfies the homogeneity predicate $P(r_{i+1} \cup s_i) = $ true.

The clustering process is illustrated in Figure 2. Two regions s_i, t_i are connected i.e., they have a common subregion u_{i-1} and will be grouped into the region r_{i+1}. Regions of the lowest level are connected with their neighboring regions. The overlapping structure of the stack of cells guarantees that the grouping process considers only those regions, which are connected or have a path of connected regions on the lowest level, the UI element level. The homogeneity

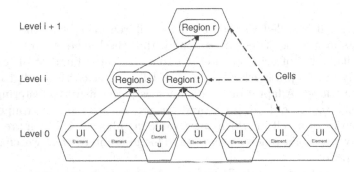

Fig. 2. Grouping process. Regions are grouped within the boundary of a cell.

predicate decides if regions are clustered or not. The predicate consists of two parts, which both need to evaluate to true; $P(r) = Size(r) \wedge Context(r), r \in R_i$.

- **Size.** On different platforms a dialog is displayed with a varying number and size of UI elements. If the size of a region and its parent region is lower than a predefined threshold (e.g., three times of the screen size) the regions are clustered, otherwise they are separated, either horizontally or top-down. The size of a region is the size of its receptive field.
- **Context.** The designer of the original dialog model integrates in it semantic information. The information deals with the semantic relation of a UI element with its neighboring UI elements. A region s_i and its tentative parent region r_{i+1} are grouped if their semantic intent does not exceed a predefined threshold $d(\sigma(s_i), \sigma(r_{i+1})) < \Theta$. In the current version of the adaptation process, we simply assign integer values to UI elements, to indicate semantic similarity. $d(\cdot, \cdot)$ is a distance measure like the Euclidian distance.

Top-down Separating. If the grouping process fails, because a region s_i does not satisfy the homogeneity predicate P, the region need to be separated from its connected region t_i. The region need to be separated since they have a common subregion u_{i-1}, which needs to be assigned to a single parent region (Figure 2).

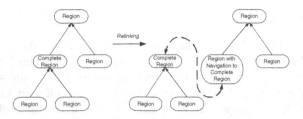

Fig. 3. A region containing a single navigation UI element will replace a *complete* region. The new region takes part in the building phase on behalf of the *complete* region.

The separation process assigns the common subregion to the region, whose semantic value is the most similar. This means that u_{i-1} is removed from the set of subregions of the other region. The process is recursively applied down to the lowest level. For level $i - 1$ in Figure 2 it would be applied to u_{i-1}, the common subregion of s_i and t_i, and to those subregions of regions of level i, which have a common subregion with u_{i-1}.

The process of bottom-up clustering and top-down separating can be seen as an energy minimization problem. The energy is defined as follows:

$$E = \sum_{i, r_j \in R_i} \frac{\sum_{u_{j-1} \in \kappa(r_j)} \left\| RF(u_{j-1}) \right\| d(\sigma(u_{j-1}), \sigma(r_j))^2}{\sum_{u_{j-1} \in \kappa(r_j)} \left\| RF(u_{i-1}) \right\|}$$

with κ being the mapping that assigns to a region r its subregions. Two regions are top-down separated such that the energy of the resulting regions in the hierarchy of graphs is minimal with respect to the size requirements of the homogeneity predicate.

Horizontal Separation. If the size of a region r_i prevents it from clustering with other regions although it could from the context part of the homogeneity predicate's point of view, it is split into a sequence of n smaller, mutually linked regions $r_{0,i}, r_{1,i}, \ldots, r_{n,i}$. E.g., a lengthy text message is split into a sequence of regions containing each a part of the text message. Only the head of the sequence continues to take part in the grouping process.

Relinking. A region that cannot further be clustered with other regions into a region of a higher level is called *complete*. A *complete* region that has reached the threshold of maximal allowed size or that cannot further be clustered from a semantic context point of view does not drop out of the grouping process. Instead, a new region is created containing a single navigation UI element pointing to the *complete* region. The new region takes the place of the *complete* region and continues the grouping process on behalf of it. The process is illustrated in Figure 3. The set of regions resulting from the adaptation process are transformed applying the presentation model into a hierarchical structure of windows containing concrete UI elements.

4   Results

To illustrate the adaptation technique of a dialog model we have implemented a
location-based message board [12]. The message board contains location specific
information and users can read and store messages on the message board. A
mobile user moving from location to location accesses different message boards
depending on the geographical position. Different users use different devices
to access the message board such as laptops, PDAs, or mobile phones. The
dialog model that results in the graphical UI on a HTML browser is shown in
Figure 4(a). The same dialog model but this time adapted to the small screen
of a mobile phone is shown in Figure 4(b). There are two things to note. Firstly,

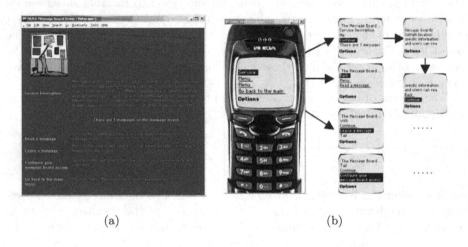

(a)   (b)

Fig. 4. (a) HTML browser showing the Message Board "Main Menu". (b) WML
browser showing the Message Board "Main Menu".

the menu is hierarchically structured into a two level menu, with a main menu
containing links to each menu item, which are presented on their distinct screen.
The main menu is created during the relinking process of the adaptation and
is not present in the original dialog model. The grouping process groups the
newly created navigation UI elements together, which results in the main menu.
Second, the service descriptions, which are lengthy text messages, are split into
a series of screens, which are linked with each other. The user navigates with the
"Continue" and "Back" links from one screen containing part of the description
to the next screen.

5   Concluding Remarks

The article has presented a new approach to dynamic UI adaptation. The adaptation process is based on bottom-up clustering and top-down separation using

low-level semantic context information. It results in a hierarchical structure of windows by clustering, separating, and relinking regions. The process is guided by low-level semantic information that is provided by the designer of the dialog model at design time. The adaptation process remodels dynamically a presentation of the dialog model to better fit it to the current platform model.

The presented experiments with the dialog model adaptation technique are promising and show that the concept is sound. The use of the hierarchy of graph has been proven flexible and is a viable concept for future UI development.

In our future work, we will elaborate the adaption algorithm to include user specific settings such as window size of the running application or user-preferred font size.

References

1. Alpert, M.: Machine Chic. Sci.Am (2002)
2. Marcus, A., Chen, E.: Designing the PDA of the Future. Interactions **9** (2002) 34–44
3. Pinheiro da Silva, P.: User Interface Declarative Models and Development Environments: A Survey. In Palanque, P., Paternò, F., eds.: Proceedings of DSV-IS2000. Volume 1946 of LNCS., Ireland, Springer-Verlag (2000) 207–226
4. Szekely, P.: Retrospective and Challenges for Model-Based Interface Development. In Bodart, F., Vanderdonckt, J., eds.: Design, Specification and Verification of Interactive Systems '96, Wien, Springer-Verlag (1996) 1–27
5. Schlungbaum, E.: Model-based User Interface Software Tools – Current state of declarative models. Technical Report 96–30, Graphics, Visualization and Usability Center, Georgia Institute of Technology, Atlanta (1996)
6. Puerta, A.: A Model-Based Interface Development Environment. IEEE Software **14** (1997) 41–47
7. Seng, A.R.: An Adaptability Framework for Mobile Applications (1999) http://citeseer.nj.nec.com/290640.html.
8. R.Pal, N., K.Pal, S.: A Review on Image Segmentation Techniques. Pattern Recognition **26** (1993) 1277–1294
9. Microsoft: Mobile Internet Toolkit – QuickStart Tutorial (2002)
10. Britton, K., R.Case, A.Citron, Floyed, R., Li, Y., Seekamp, C., Topol, B., Tracey, K.: Transcoding. Extending e-business to new environments. IBM Systems Journal **40** (2001) 153–178
11. Mandyam, S., Vedati, K., Kuo, C., Wang, W.: User Interface Adaptations: Indispensable for Single Authoring. In: W3C Workshop on Device Independent Authoring Techniques, SAP University, Germany, W3C (2002)
12. Fischmeister, S., Menkhaus, G., Pree, W.: MUSA-Shadow: A Location-Based Service Supporting Multiple Devices. In: Proceedings of Pacific TOOLS, Sydney, Australia (2002) 71–79
13. Menkhaus, G.: An Architecture for Supporting Multi-Device, Client-Adaptive Services. Special Volume of the Annals of Software Engineering Journal on OO Web-based Software Engineering (2002)
14. Nacken, P.: Image Segmentation By Connectivity Preserving Relinking in Hierarchical Graph Structures. Pattern Recognition **28** (1995) 907–920
15. Hartmann, G.: Recognition of Hierarchically Encoded Images by Technical and Biological Systems. Biological Cybernetics **57** (1987) 73–84

AVE – Method for 3D Visualization of Search Results

Wojciech Wiza, Krzysztof Walczak, and Wojciech Cellary

Department of Information Technologies, Poznan University of Economics
Mansfelda 4, 60-854 Poznan, Poland
{wiza,walczak,cellary}@kti.ae.poznan.pl

Abstract. A novel approach to three-dimensional visualization of search results is presented. In the proposed method a search result is progressively visualized by a sequence of customizable 3D interfaces. The interface applied at each visualization stage is selected with regards to properties of the search result and user interactions. A user may also change mapping of search result properties to visual attributes of the interfaces.

1 Introduction

With the creation of the World Wide Web service, which caused the Internet to grow exponentially, the question: "IS the information accessible" is often replaced by: "WHERE the information can be found". The answer to this question comes with search engines – specialized systems that store data about WHAT and WHERE information is kept.

To provide better search capabilities, numerous research initiatives focus on either invention of new technologies for Internet search (like P2P systems) or improving existing search systems. While the first solution brings many uncertainties and is in general difficult to implement, the later can be realized on many different stages of information indexing and retrieval. Examples include use of more and more sophisticated crawlers, improvements in data retrieval by the use of new indexing techniques and query languages, and new methods of information visualization. The later seems to be a little neglected, even though it is a promising method of enhancing search systems.

A natural way to enhance visualization capabilities of search engines is the use of graphical interfaces. In the recent years there were several attempts to create graphical search interfaces. Many of them used two-dimensional graphics (e.g. Antarctica [1], InXight [2]), but there were also several attempts to apply three-dimensional visualization, e.g. 3D cards [3], Antarctica 3D, VR-VIBE [4][5], Cat-a-Cone [6], Nirve [7], or ViOS system [8]. The tendency to use 3D visualization techniques increases with the advances in 3D technology. Current standardization efforts in this field and availability of cheap and powerful 3D graphic accelerators allow to anticipate wider use of 3D interfaces in the future.

Most of the 3D visualization interfaces proposed up to now share similar drawbacks: data visualization is performed in a single universal 3D environment, which in many cases causes improper presentation of information and thus decreases user perception; lack of presentation of aggregated data first, and then – in response to user interaction – more specific data; the interfaces either require installation of dedicated software or have limited interaction capabilities due to the use of purely standard-based 3D browsers.

J.M. Cueva Lovelle et al. (Eds.): ICWE 2003, LNCS 2722, pp. 204–207, 2003.
© Springer-Verlag Berlin Heidelberg 2003

2 The AVE Method

To solve the above problems a new approach to 3D visualization of search results, called AVE (Adaptive Visualization Environments), has been developed. The fundamental concept of the AVE method is the creation of an interface that permits visualization of the entire search result. Such an interface presents a global view of retrieved search result instead of the first dozens of most relevant documents. Data presented using the AVE method are not divided into a sequence of chunks or pages. This permits a user not only to browse through the information but also to understand its nature. Appropriately constructed and applied interface permits a user to perceive trends in data faster and with bigger precision through differences in color, shape, connectedness, continuity, symmetry, etc. Use of 3D environments enhances the number of available visualization dimensions in a natural way and gives a user a multi-criterion overview of the retrieved data. A 3D environment permits a user to change a viewpoint within the scene, therefore allows to exploit the entire data set from the best perspective.

In the AVE method, depending on the search result volume, the visualization system may present data in detailed view or classify data using one or more classification criteria (cf. Fig. 1). The classification criteria may be selected automatically by the system based on search result properties, can be pre-selected by a user, or both.

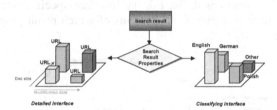

Fig. 1. Selection of the interface based on search result properties

While the search results may differ significantly in the number of documents and other properties (e.g., number of domains, hosts, document types), it is impossible to find a single universal interface that would reflect all possible search results in a readable way. Therefore, in the proposed AVE method, a number of automatically or manually selected interfaces are used. The interfaces differ in their visualization capabilities. Selection of the best-fitted interface may be performed automatically by the visualization system, manually by a user, or both methods may be combined. An automatic selection of the interface is based on properties of the search result, like number of retrieved URLs, number of languages and semantic relationships between documents. In the manual mode a user may select an interface, which in his/her opinion shows the result in the most appropriate way. Therefore, main factors, which influence manual selection of the interface are user preferences and experience. Joining these two methods of interface selection, a user may choose an interface from a set of interfaces pre-selected by a system, or the system may choose the best environment from the list of interfaces selected by the user.

A user explores the search result in a number of subsequent steps (cf. Fig. 2). Using different levels of abstraction and applying the most appropriate 3D environment at each step, the proposed method permits to navigate from a classified, aggregated view of the entire search result, through aggregated views of sub-results, up to precise visualization of particular documents of user interest.

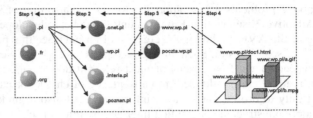

Fig. 2. Exploration of the search result from general to detailed view

In the proposed method, a user may apply a number of different environments to the same search result. This permits to visualize retrieved data in different ways to better understand the information displayed and to detect trends and patterns.

Another technique that improves perception of the visualized data in the AVE method, is flexible assignment of search result properties to visual attributes of the interfaces (cf. Fig. 3). A user may decide which characteristic of the retrieved data should be visualized by a particular dimension in the 3D environment, e.g. the size of a document can be reflected in the size of an object. Possible mapping choices are described by mapping functions defined in the interface specification. These functions guarantee proper transformation from domains of search result properties to domains of visual attributes.

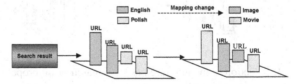

Fig. 3. Selection of the mapping for search result attributes

The AVE method is independent of the search engine database, therefore it can be applied to virtually every commercial (like Altavista or Google) or non-commercial search engine. For testing purposes a search system, implementing the proposed method, has been built. This system, called *Periscope* [9], uses a simple database (loaded with data gathered by a web crawler) and a set of interfaces (cf. Fig. 4). More information about the interfaces in Periscope system can be found in [10].

3   Conclusions

First trials with end-users show that the AVE method implemented in the *Periscope* system can be efficiently used for Web searching. Although, the system response time is sometimes higher than in case of popular search engines (like Altavista or Google) reaching up to 15 seconds for complex queries, end-users felt that the accuracy of the information retrieved was higher, especially in the case of vague initial information requirements. Current tests focus on the ergonomics and user perception of different

3D interfaces. Future works include improvement of interface models based on results of system evaluation performed by end-users.

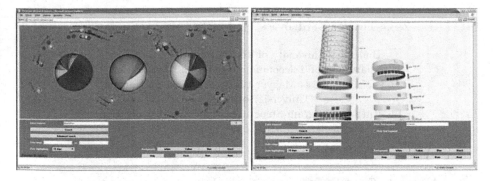

Fig. 4. Example interfaces used in the *Periscope* system

References

1. Antarctica homepage: http://www.antarcti.ca/
2. InXight homepage: http://www.inxight.com/map/
3. Mukherjea, S., Y. Hara: Visualizing World-Wide Web Search Engine Results, ICIV International Conference, July 14–16, 1999 London, England
4. Benford, B., D. Snowdon, C. Greenhalgh, R. Ingram, I. Knox, C. Brown: VR-VIBE: A Virtual Environment for Co-operative Information Retrieval, Eurographics'95, 30th August – 1st September, Maastricht, The Netherlands, pp 349–360.
5. VR-VIBE homepage: http://www.emptiness.org/vr/vrvibe.html
6. Cat-A-Cone project homepage: http://www.sims.berkeley.edu/~hearst/cac-overview.html
7. NIRVE project homepage: http://www.itl.nist.gov/iaui/vvrg/cugini/uicd/nirve-home.html
8. ViOS – how does it works?: http://www.howstuffworks.com/vios.htm
9. Periscope project homepage: http://periscope.kti.ae.poznan.pl/periscope/
10. Wiza, W., K. Walczak, W. Cellary: Adaptive 3D Interfaces for Search Result Visualization IADIS International Conference e-Society, 3–6 June 2003, Lisbon, Portugal

Ubiquitous Access to Deep Content via Web Services

Zsolt Tivadar Kardkovács[1] and Gábor Mihály Surányi[2]

[1] Budapest University of Technology and Economics,
Department of Telecommunications and Telematics,
H-1117, Budapest, Magyar tudósok körútja 2., Hungary
[2] University of Karlsruhe,
Institute for Program Structures and Data Organization,
Am Fasanengarten 5, D-76128 Karlsruhe, Germany

Abstract. Current research activities in the computer science area focus on integration of systems with diverse purposes and architecture. They include the usage of mobile devices just like any immobile computer and the efficient, combined presentation and utilisation of contents from multiple providers together on the web. Even though these two tasks are naturally tackled in different ways, in this paper we propose a single solution to both problems based on logic, which, furthermore, makes their seamless integration possible. That is, without scrapping the well known models that have proven good, we offer a scalable architecture that supports wireless access to the most valuable pieces of the Internet keeping parts of the existing infrastructure and with no duplication of functionality.

1 Introduction

They provide long-distance and in-motion communications, however, mobile phones have raised novel problems for the technical experts since there is a natural demand to be able to make use of the everyday services anywhere and at any time. At the same time the Internet and its main application, the World Wide Web gained increasing popularity and support as an inexhaustible knowledge store.

Nowadays the technology of connecting a mobile device to the Internet is fully elaborated. The mobile device is always linked to a base station. It is the proxy of the mobile service provider, that requests web pages on behalf of the customer and forwards them to the base station. Data can be sent to the cell phone via two different software protocols. One of them is the native language of the Web, the HTTP. The other one is the WSP, which has been specially developed for mobile devices. Although theoretically the original HTTP content is delivered to the mobile devices, in practice it is not. The main reason is that most of the mobile devices have limited capabilities compared to a usual computer (eg. they have smaller display, they do not run Java applets). After all, it is noticeable that web servers present the same content in two different formats for mobile and

J.M. Cueva Lovelle et al. (Eds.): ICWE 2003, LNCS 2722, pp. 208–211, 2003.
© Springer-Verlag Berlin Heidelberg 2003

immobile clients. It results in unnecessary duplication, which makes the system less manageable. To solve this problem, gateways are built between protocols and languages. It can not be a permanent solution, however, because those protocols and languages are evolving as well. In the near future we can not even expect that mobile devices become capable of displaying most web pages for the protocols adaptable to bandwidth and display environment are still missing.

The increase of data and information surrounding us has changed the operation of the Web qualitatively. There have been content providing databases installed behind the web servers [1]. Databases only manage the data, which are formatted by the web servers on the fly in response to client queries. This architecture is not only unsuitable for mobile access because of the restricted capabilities we mentioned before, but it is also difficult to integrate the knowledge of systems about different subjects due to the human-oriented, look-centric interface.

According to researches there are two ways to (at least) virtually consolidate the data sources on the web. One of them is more technical and invents web services, which have proven good in proprietary systems. The protocols and languages of web services (XML, WSDL, SOAP, UDDI etc.) are standardised but have different views of modelling so each service is unusable beyond its direct purpose. The other idea attaches further data to all data on the web so that computers can also understand them, that is the Semantic Web. A convergence between the two approaches is emerging [2], we are going to amplify it.

An unprecedented mathematical formalism F-logic[3] was published in 1995. Its creators' aim was to unify the object-oriented paradigm, the so-called frames of artificial intelligence and the precise logical entailment systems. Further researches revealed that F-logic is suitable to model not only well structured (eg. object-oriented) but also semi-structured information, such as that found in web pages [4].

2 Architecture

To get an overview easily, we present our solution by a concrete problem. The example, along with the implementation, serves also as a proof-of-concept.

Imagine that you are going to give a birthday present to a friend of you called Jim. You realise on Tuesday driving home after a hard day that the birthday party will be on Saturday and you have nothing to present him with. Fortunately, you know Jim has a new hobby: the contemporary English. But a problem arises: if you order a book tonight, you probably will not receive it in time. Therefore you have to personally go to a bookshop *nearby, open after usual working hours,* offering *high quality books on that topic at reasonable prices.* Is it possible to find such a shop easily now? Our proposal is a step towards it.

Obviously, we need the appropriate data sources and a mobile phone to deal with this problem. It is worth supposing two other components as it is on Fig. 1. To the databeses there are applications connected. Their task is to make the data available to other software operating in the same domain providing simplified functions, access control etc. The lion's share of the work is done by the agents. They mesh the pieces of information from the content providers and represent them in a uniform way. Agents serve as fat servers for the clients. The only job of the clients is to ask the agents. This is also adequate for current, immobile access. Since agents, not the clients at individuals, have the intelligence, this architecture is quite easy to manage.

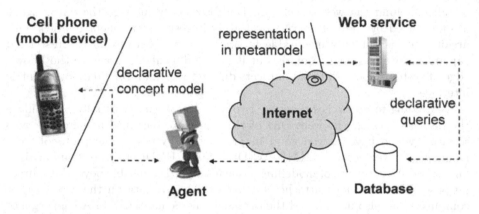

Fig. 1. Architecture for mobile access of deep web services

The architecture comprises three tiers if databases and the components that represent them, the web services are regarded as one unit. The only requirement for the databases is to answer schema queries as well as ordinary data queries. Based on this schema information the web service forms its *single, general* interface to the agents. F-logic can be successfully applied to this task because it makes no distinction between schema and data instances, it always treats schema as data and it allows the usage of object-oriented methodologies resulting in improved efficiency of development. In our example, the web service tells when each shop is open, provides geographical information and book records: their topic and price. But all these concepts are meaningful only for software designed for this subject. In general, a third party application is needed.

Web services are joined together via agents. That is why a single, self-descriptive interface is beneficial. The agents' world is made up of numerous pieces by means of information-retrieval methods. It is represented via well known semantic methods, eg. ontologies. In ontologies DAML+OIL is often used, which is based on description logic. Although expressive parts of DAML+OIL are undecidable[5,6], Description Frame Logic (DFL), an F-logic integrated with description logic is not[7], fortunately. Therefore, the application of F-logic turns out practical. In our example, the agent interprets the concepts *nearby, opening hours, usual working hours, high quality, reasonable price, topic* taking data from other databases and systems into consideration. Furthermore, if there is no proper book to buy, it can suggest another one based on less strict conditions. Note, F-logic and its roots in artificial intelligence can be good support for that.

Despite being thin, logic-based mobile clients have some benefit. On one hand, agents respond only to F-logic queries, which are easier to formulate by logic-based applications. On the other hand, the agents' world changes from time to time. To make use of that world, the model of the client software has to change, as well. It means that an application written in an interpreted language is necessary. Java, the most popular object-oriented language nowadays, falls into that category. So do object-oriented Prolog languages, in which, due to their higher abstraction level, problem solving requires much less lines of source code. That means eventually better debuggability, transparency and manageability.

We are currently implementing a system based on the introduced theory. We chose XSB Prolog as programming language for every component. XSB Prolog has an Oracle interface to declaratively communicate with the lowest elements of the architecture. A built-in implementation of F-logic, called FLORA, is also available. Unfortunately, there are no XSB Prolog interpreters on cell phones. So we use immobile computers instead of mobile devices but everything else is ready and works properly.

3 Conclusion

In this paper we addressed the problem of integrating content providers of the Web without duplication of functionality. We proposed a mobile architecture in which all components are logic-based. It incorporates the recent results and technology of object-oriented modelling, web services and the Semantic Web. The fact that the models of the components are closely related to each other not only requires less transformation at each interface but also simplifies the process. That has a favourable impact on productivity and cost-effective operation.

References

1. Michael K. Bergman: The Deep Web: Surfacing Hidden Value. Bright Planet White Paper (2001)
2. Hendler, J.: Agents and Semantic Web. IEEE Intelligent Systems **16(2)** (2001) 30–37
3. Kifer, Michael, Lausen, Georg, Wu, James: Logical Foundations of Object-Oriented and Frame-Based Languages. Journal of the ACM **42(4)** (1995) 741–843
4. Ludäscher, B., Himmeröder, R., Lausen, G., May, W., Schlepphorst, C.: Managing Semistructured Data with FLORID: A Deductive Object-Oriented Perspective. Elsevier-Pergamon Information Systems **23(8)** (1998) 1–25
5. Baader F., Calvanese, D., McGuinness, D., Nardi D., Patel-Schneider, P. (eds): The Description Logic Handbook: Theory, Implementation and Applications. Cambridge University Press (2003)
6. Horrocks, I.: Logical Foundations for the Semantic Web. Reasoning with Expressive Description Logics: Theory and Practice CADE-18 Invited Talk (2002)
7. Balaban, M.: The F-logic Approach for Description Languages. Annals of Mathematics and Artificial Intelligence **15(1)** (1995) 19–60

NDT-Tool: A Case Tool to Deal with Requirements in Web Information Systems

M.J. Escalona, J. Torres, M. Mejías, and A. Reina

Department of Computer Languages and Systems
University of Seville
{escalona, jtorres, risoto, reinaqu}@lsi.us.es

Abstract. Internet progress and the rising interest for developing systems in web environment has given way to several methodological proposals which have been proposed to be a suitable reference in the development process. However, there is a gap in case tool[3][4][6]. This work presents a case tool named NDT-Tool that allows to apply algorithms and techniques proposed in NDT (Navigational Development Techniques) [2], which is a methodological proposition to specify, analyze and design web information systems.

1 Introduction

In the last years, several methodological proposals have been developed by the research community: OOHDM[7], UWE[5], WebML[1] or, UWA project[8] are only some examples. However, after studying them and analyzing several comparative studies [4][6], we can deduce most of them are mainly focused on the design and implementation phases. They often do not offer a guide to deal with web requirements and, they often propose use cases and only some of them, like UWE, propose techniques to describe or validate requirements. This paper offers a global vision of NDT, a web methodological proposal that is focused on the first phases of the life cycle and it presents a case tool, NDT-Tool, which guides in NDT application.

2 NDT (Navigational Development Technique)

The first phase in NDT, requirements treatment, starts capturing requirements and studying the environment. NDT proposes to use some requirements capture techniques like interviews and brainstorming. After this phase, the objectives must be captured and described. The process continues based on these objectives and proposes to define the system requirements. NDT classifies requirements into storage information, actor, functional, interaction and non-functional requirements. Each kind of them is described using a pattern. After that, and starting with these patterns three design models can be obtained systematically: the conceptual model, that expresses the static aspect of the system; the navigational model, that describes how the user can navigate in the system; and the abstract interface model, that expresses interface.

3 NDT-Tool

NDT-Tool is a case tool, which allows to apply NDT algorithms and techniques and to generate results, documents and models automatically. Nowadays, only require-

J.M. Cueva Lovelle et al. (Eds.): ICWE 2003, LNCS 2722, pp. 212–213, 2003.
© Springer-Verlag Berlin Heidelberg 2003

ments phase is completely codified, but some algorithms and models of the next phases are already implemented. The first form in NDT offers a global menu with several options: management project, requirements treatment, conceptual model, navigational model, interface model and prototypes generation option. Models in the conceptual model, the navigational model and the abstract interface model can be obtained automatically and visualized in Rational Rose environment. Nowadays, algorithms which generate these models are implemented but we are still working in the connection with the Rational Rose tool.

a   b   c

Fig. 1. Some screens of NDT

In the figure 1, some screens of NDT are shown. In a, the graphical option to work with actors and roles in requirements definition is offered. In b, the matrix of trazability which makes possible to evaluate if all the objectives have been covered in the specification is presented and in c, a example of a requirements pattern is shown. Data in this screen has been obtained from a real system developed with NDT and NDT-Tool. NDT has been applied to several real problems giving very good results. Now, we are applying our proposal of NDT-Tool to these examples to evaluated it.

References

1   Ceri, S. Fraternai, P., Bongio, A. *Web Modelling Language (WebML): A Modelling Language for Designing Web Sites.* Proc. of WWW9/Computer Networks 33 2000

2   Escalona, M.J.,Mejías, M., Torres, J. Reina.A. *NDT: Una técnica para el desarrollo de la navegación.* Congreso IDEAS 2002. Cuba. Abril 2002

3   Escalona, M.J., Koch, N. *Ingeniería de Requisitos en Aplicaciones para la Web- Un estudio comparativo.* Technical report. Dep. Language and Computer Science. Seville. 2002.

4   Koch, N. *A comparative study of methods for Hypermedia Development.* Technical Report 9905. Ludwig-Maximilian-University, Munich, Germany. 1999.

5   Koch, N. *Software Engineering for Adaptative Hypermedia Applications.* Ph. Thesis, FAST Reihe Softwaretechnik Vol(12), Uni-Druck Publishing Company, Munich. Germany. 2001.

6   Retschitzegger, W. & Schwinger, W. *Towards Modeling of Data Web Applications - A Requirement´s Perspective.* American Conference on Informatin Systems AMCIS 2000,

7   G. Rossi An Object Oriented Method for Designing Hipermedia Applications. PHD Thesis, Departamento de Informática, PUC-Rio, Brazil, 1996

8   UWA Consortium, UWA Requirements Elicitation: Model, Notation, and Tool Architecture.

A Design Toolkit for Hypermedia Applications

Susana Montero, Paloma Díaz, and Ignacio Aedo

Laboratorio DEI. Dpto. de Informática
Universidad Carlos III de Madrid
Avda. de la Universidad 30. 28911 Leganés, Spain
{smontero,pdp}@inf.uc3m.es aedo@ia.uc3m.es

Abstract. The development process of hypermedia applications involves a variety of users with different levels of knowledge and skills. In order to get a good communication among participants, a graphical toolkit based on a method facilitates this work. In this paper, we present a design environment, AriadneTool, that allows a designer to model a hypermedia application, to validate such a design and to generate dynamically XML + SMIL implementation templates. This environment is based upon the Ariadne Method which offers a set of integrated activities to model hypermedia applications in a systematic and iterative way.

1 Introduction

Hypermedia systems, and in particular web applications, have been extremely demanded in different areas in a very short period of time. This situation has led most developers to skip the conceptual design and directly go to the implementation, producing applications of poor quality, usability and maintainability. The majority of these implementations have been made with tools such as NetObjects' Fusion or DreamWeaver which allow an automated implementation by contents and an easy set up, but do not pay attention to intrinsic features of hypermedia systems such as sophisticated navigational structures, interactive behaviours and multimedia compositions. Several hypermedia methods and theirs CASE tools have been proposed including Autoweb [4], WebML [1] and OO-H [5]. However, these methods have the following weak points (more details can be found in [6,7]):

- **Validation and integrity rules** to test the correctness, completeness and integrity of the design.
- **Contents modeling** to organize and harmonize multimedia contents both in their temporal and spatial dimension.
- **User modeling** to model different types of application users and to apply personalization as well as security constraints.
- **Security modeling** to model which contents should be delivered to which users, who can modify or personalize items and which constraints have to be applied.
- **Evaluation stage** to collect information about the potential usability of a system to improve features and functionality of application interface.

In this paper, we present a software environment, AriadneTool, to support the hypermedia application development from conceptual modeling to dynamic generation of XML+SMIL templates. The Ariadne Method [2] is aimed at dealing with the above described problems and provides the methodological foundations for AriadneTool.

J.M. Cueva Lovelle et al. (Eds.): ICWE 2003, LNCS 2722, pp. 214–217, 2003.
© Springer-Verlag Berlin Heidelberg 2003

2   The Ariadne Method in a Nutshell

In order to cover modeling process of a hypermedia application, Ariadne proposes the process illustrated in figure 1. The first phase, Conceptual Design, allows us to specify the system structure and function from an abstract point of view, for next performing a Detailed Design where the elements defined in the previous phase are specified in a more detailed way. Moreover, the Evaluation phase can be performed in parallel, what allows the method to be more iterative and generate a feedback to improve the design in the earlier phases. Validation and Integrity Rules are not considered a phase, but a way to guarantee the completeness and integrity of the design. For more information about the method see [2].

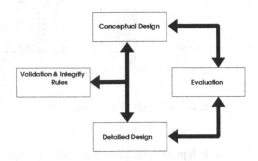

Fig. 1. The development process of Ariadne

3   AriadneTool

AriadneTool is an environment devoted to the development of hypermedia applications based upon the above design process. The main components to support such mechanisms are (see figure 2): (1) the Front-End that provides a perfect environment for elaborating the Ariadne Method products, which will be mentioned below, in a graphical way; (2) the Validation and Verification Module that holds the rules to validate and verify the completeness and correctness of the design, notifying any mistake or warning to the designer; (3) the Dynamic Repository that holds the components of the front-end in dynamic memory, so that access is faster; and (4) the Central Repository that holds the components in a persistent way.

The development environment is implemented using JDK1.4 what allows us to obtain an independent operation platform. The Validation and Verification Module is represented by DTD documents in which the rules defining well-formed design products are specified. Elements designed in the different products of the method are stored in the Central Repository by JAXB1.1 which allows an automatic two-way mapping between Java objects stored in the Dynamic Repository and final XML documents. We have built a module to translate our synchronization operations to SMIL specifications.

The main functionalities that supports AriadneTool are:

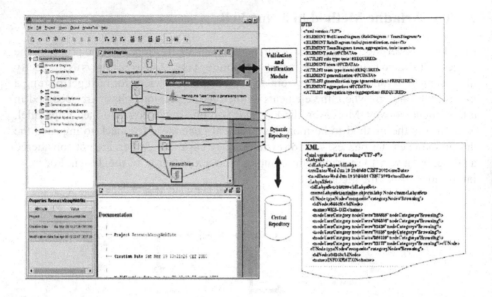

Fig. 2. The AriadneTool architecture

– The *Structural Diagram*. It depicts the logical structure of the application by means of nodes (simple or composite) and connect them through two abstraction mechanisms: generalization and aggregation.

– The *Navigation Diagram*. It specifies the navigation structure by means of tagged links and navigation tools.

– The *Attributes Catalogue*. It is a repository where properties of elements are defined by a name/default-value pair.

– The *Events Catalogue*. It is a repository where actions that take place at runtime when a condition is fulfilled can be defined and reused in different scenarios.

– The *Internal Diagram*. It collects multimedia contents, attributes and events, as well as anchors of a node. The Internal Diagram is made up of a Spatial and Timeline Diagram.

  The *Spatial Diagram* lets specify logically the appearance of a node by placing contents and space-based relationships among them. The *Timeline Diagram* allows us to represent how the node evolves throughout a time interval. Time-based relationships can be defined among contents to specify delays in the beginning/end of the target content.

– The *Users Diagram*. It represents the kinds of users in a hierarchical way using two abstractions: roles and teams. A role is a responsibility or job function but no an individual user meanwhile a team represents a group of roles which join together to work.

– The *Categorization Catalogue*. It holds the security category assigned to each node or content to determine the most permissive operation that can be performed over it by a user. These categories are no access, browsing, personalizing and editing.

- The *Access Table*. It allows us to define the security policy of the system assigning a manipulation category to each role for each node and content. Thus the actions that users can perform are controlled. More details on the security model for hypermedia applications applied in this method can be found in [3].
- The validation and verification of the above products to check completeness and consistency of the model.
- The automatic documentation generation about the made design.
- The assignment of data to multimedia contents in order to generate dynamically XML+SMIL templates from which, for example using XSLT stylesheets, the web application can be set up.

4   Conclusions

In this paper, we present an environment, AriadneTool, to support the design and development of hypermedia applications following the Ariadne Method, which pays special attention to products to model users structures, interactive behaviours, multimedia compositions and security policies. Moreover, we have evaluated AriadneTool by collecting feedback from the students in a course on Hypermedia Design. This feedback has been very positive, and a large majority believed that the tool supported well the method tasks and made much easier to use the Ariadne Method.

Acknowledgements. We'd like to thank Jose Ángel Cruz for his cooperation in the development of AriadneTool. This toolkit is part of the Ariadne project funded by "Dirección General de Investigación del Ministerio de Ciencia y Tecnología" (TIC2000-0402)".

References

1. S. Ceri, P. Fraternali, and A. Bongio. Web modeling language (WebML): a modeling language for designing web sites. *WWW9 / Computer Networks*, 33(1-6):137–157, 2000.
2. P. Díaz, I. Aedo, and S. Montero. Ariadne, a development method for hypermedia. In *proceedings of Dexa 2001*, volume 2113 of *LNCS*, pages 764–774, 2001.
3. P. Díaz, I. Aedo, and F. Panetsos. Modelling security policies in hypermedia and web-based applications. In *Web Engineering: Managing diversity and complexity of web application development*, pages 90–104, 2001.
4. P. Fraternali and P. Paolini. Model-driven development of web applications: the autoweb system. *ACM Transactions on Office Information Systems*, 18(4):323–282, 2000.
5. J. Gómez, C. Cachero, and O. Pastor. Conceptual modeling of device-independent web applications. *IEEE MultiMedia*, 8(2):26–39, 2001.
6. S. Montero, P. Díaz, and I. Aedo. Requirements for hypermedia development methods: A survey of outstanding method. In *Proc. of Advanced Information Systems Engineering, 14th International Conference, CAiSE*, pages 747–751, 2002.
7. S. Montero, P. Díaz, and I. Aedo. A framework for the analysis and comparison of hypermedia design methods. In *Proc. of The IASTED International Conference on Software Engineering (SE'2003)*, 2003.

WebML+ for Communication of Information Flows: An Empirical Study

David Lowe and Rachatrin Tongrungrojana

University of Technology, Sydney
PO Box 123 Broadway NSW 2007, Australia
{david.lowe, rachatrin.tongrungrojana}@uts.edu.au

1 Introduction

A key element in supporting the development of Web systems is suitable Web modelling languages. Most existing work on Web modelling (such as WebML [1]) has focussed on understanding the structure of the information space and how this relates to the underlying content.These approaches however have rarely addressed the connection between detailed design aspects and the broader information environment, particularly in terms of the flow of information between the system, the organisation, and external entities.Work on information architectures [2] address these issues to a limited extent, especially when incorporating an understanding of user interactions and engagement with a site [3]. However these models are rarely consistent with those used for lower level information modeling. Our work to date has focused on the development of a notation (based on extending WebML to incorporate abstract information flows and referred to as WebML+) that addresses these limitations and bridges the gap between business models and information design [4,5]. This characteristic is crucial in Web-development where the systems under development often lead to fundamental changes in business operations. In this paper we present the results of an empirical evaluation of whether or not WebML+ provides more rapid and consistent communication of information flows within Web system design processes.

2 WebML+

WebML+ enables developers to express the core information features of a system at an abstract level without committing to detailed designs. It can be considered as an extension to WebML (see [1] and www.webml.org). The purpose of WebML+ modeling is to define the internal and the external information flows within a Web system. As with WebML, we have defined both a graphical notation and an XML-based formal notation for representing WebML+ models (though we do not show the formal XML DTD here).

Figure 1 shows an example WebML+ model: FreeMail is a provider of Web-based e-mail that allows users to send and receive messages through a Web interface. The system (shown as a dashed geometrical polygon) encloses a set of information units which represent coherent and cohesive domains of information that are managed by, or necessary for utilising, the system. We also have both

J.M. Cueva Lovelle et al. (Eds.): ICWE 2003, LNCS 2722, pp. 218–221, 2003.
© Springer-Verlag Berlin Heidelberg 2003

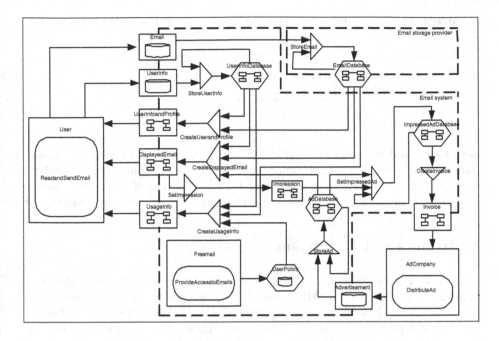

Fig. 1. Typical Web System represented using WebML+

external actors (e.g. users) and internal actors (e.g. the FreeMail organisation) who supply and consume information units. Some information units are provided directly by actors (e.g. the advertisements) whilst others are derived from other units. These derivations (shown as triangles with incoming and outgoing arrows) capture the inter-relationships between the information units.

3   Experimental Design

Our intention was to investigate whether the WebML+ modelling technique could (when contrasted with purely textual descriptions) provide more rapid and consistent communication of information flows. An experiment was carried out where we investigated the ability of two groups of participants (one having access to textual descriptions, and the other to WebML+ models) to answer questions about information flows within the Web system. In order to minimise the likelihood of the results being biased by the specific construction of the two descriptions (WebML+ and textual), they were authored by different people. Each of the two authors was able to provide half the questions to be asked of the participants, and then to design their descriptions in light of the full set of questions. Further, we developed two different Web system scenarios (a Web-based Email service and an online-auction system) and provided the textual and WebML+ models of both. The participants were randomly allocated to one of the scenarios, and one of the descriptions. The participants were then asked to answer a series of questions about the system described. The answers

Table 1. The averaged number of correct answers for each group of participants

	MEAN	MEDIAN
Of textual description group	6.4	6
Of WebML+ Group	7.4	7.5

were timed and recorded automatically. Steps were taken to address possible confounding factors such as the experience of the modeller and reader, and the type of scenario. This was counteracted by the adoption of multiple scenarios and through the way in which the descriptions and questions were constructed.

4   Results and Discussion

Table 1 shows the descriptive statistics for the two groups. We note that participants who read the WebML+ model had, on average, a greater number of correct answers than those who had read the textual description. Further, we took the Independent Samples T-Test to determine whether this difference was statistically significant. Whilst space prohibits inclusion of the details, we carried out an independent samples T-Test of the null hypothesis that the difference was not statistically significant. The results indicates that the null hypothesis can be rejected (i.e. the difference between the means of the two groups was statistically significant) at an 80% confidence level, but not at a 95% confidence level. Further data (beyond the 20 participants in the experiment) would be required to provide stronger power within the test.

Figure 2 shows the relationship between time spent on questions and the number of correct answers - i.e. how quickly participants could develop an understanding of the system. Figure 2a shows our expectations prior to commencing the experiment. We had expected that the WebML+ participants would be able to more rapidly answer questions initially due to the graphical notation inherent in WebML+ and also expected that the participants who had the textual description would eventually be able to answer questions more correctly given that the text was not constrained by the limitations of a graphical notation.

Figure 2b shows the actual experiment results. We find that both curves have similar characteristics. The deviation from our expected results may be caused by two possible factors. Firstly, the WebML+ participants did not have a significant prior degree of exposure to WebML+ concepts, leading to the need for greater time to understand the WebML+ models. To investigate this we conducted a sub-test with a small number of researchers who were more familiar with WebML+. Whilst not statistically rigourous, this subsequent result was much closer to that which we expected (i.e. Figure 2a). Secondly, there was an unexpected confounding factor related to the participants use of the "search" facility in the browser find information when reading the textual descriptions - leading to an ability to answer the specific questions more rapidly without having to develop a broader understanding of the system.

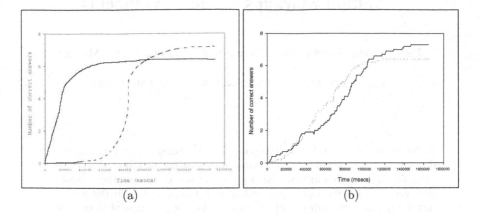

(a)   (b)

Fig. 2. Relationship between times spent on question and number of correct answers (solid line = WebML+, dotted line = textual description)

5   Conclusion and Future Work

In this paper, we have presented an empirical evaluation of WebML+, a high-level specification language for defining Web system information flows. The results provided an initial indication that WebML+ was indeed a useful tool. In brief, we found that participants could answer questions about information flows more correctly when they read the WebML+ model as compared to participants who read a textual description of the system. This led to our conclusion that users are able to understand a system based on a WebML+ model more consistently than when based on a textual description.

References

1. Ceri, S., Fraternali, P., Bongio, A.: Web modeling language (WebML): a modeling language for designing web sites. In: Procs of WWW9 Conf, Amsterdam (2000)
2. Rosenfeld, L., Morville, P.: Information Architecture for the World Wide Web. O'Reilly (1998)
3. Haverty, M.: Information architecture without internal theory: An inductive design process. Journal of the American Society for Information Science & Technology **53** (2002) 839
4. Tongrungrojana, R., Lowe, D.: WebML+: A web modeling language for modelling architectural-level information flows. Int J of Web Engineering and Technologies (2003-pending)
5. Lowe, D., Tongrungrojana, R.: WebML+ in a nutshell: Modelling architectural-level information flows. In: WWW2003: 12th International World Wide Web Conference, Budapest, Hungary (2003)

Multiple Markups in XML Documents

Luis Arévalo, Antonio Polo, Miryam Salas, and Juan Carlos Manzano

Department of Computer Science. University of Extremadura[1]
{ ljarevalo, polo, juancman,miryam }@unex.es

Abstract. The nesting rule for markup tags in XML brings about, on occasions, that different interpretations of the same text may not be represented in the same document. This situation leads to a duplication of the text into different files, each one with the appropriate markup to that interpretation. In this work, a technique, which we will regard as *meta-markup*, is put forward in order to solve this problem. The technique consists in storing the information of each mark -either beginning tags or end tags- in a single element. The mechanisms to integrate all the markups in a single file are shown, and also how to get -from it- each independent markup through XSL transformations. This solution allows an integration of multiple knowledge of the document that may be applied in problems either as versioning or as evolution.

1 Introduction

The standard XML[1] has consolidated as a tool for information exchange and representation due to its flexibility. The specification for XML documents needs a correct nesting for tags. On occasions, such nesting might not be fulfilled, for example, when different interpretations of the same text are to be represented within the same document. If each interpretation is reflected through a specific markup, the combination of different markups in the same document may bring about incorrect tag nesting.

This work starts by showing an example illustrating the problem and the current solutions. Then, we introduce a technique that allows the transformation of a XML document into an equivalent one, called meta-markup. Fourthly, it is shown that, through this technique, multiple markups for a text may be carried out by complying with the XML specification. Finally, the conclusions and future works are introduced.

2 Motivation

Let's imagine that we want to carry out a film adaptation of Shakespeare's play *Hamlet*. We have an adaptation of the dialogues of the play in XML format[2]. This dialogue must be completed with new information (for example with text and the camera shots) in the document so that its contents not be affected. The problem we face is synchronising the text with the shots to be shown at each moment. This problem

[1] This work has been financed by the Spanish CICYT project "TIC2002-04586-C04-02"

© Springer-Verlag Berlin Heidelberg 2003

might be solved through the labelling of the original document with shot markups. However, the labeling in fig.1 results in a XML document, which is not well formed, because of its incorrect tag nesting. A possible solution for this problem might be to duplicate the text into different files, each one with the appropriate markup for each interpretation but this solution does not allow a single representation integrating all the different markups in the same document.

```
........
<SPEECH>
    <SHOT id="shot10-g1" description="general overview">
    <SPEAKER>RODERIGO</SPEAKER>
    <LINE>Tush! never tell me; I take it much unkindly</LINE>
    <LINE>That thou, Iago, who hast had my purse</LINE>
    <LINE>As if the strings were thine, shouldst know of this.</LINE>
</SPEECH>
<SPEECH>
    <SPEAKER>IAGO</SPEAKER>
    <LINE>'Sblood, but you will not hear me:</LINE>
    </SHOT>
    <SHOT id="shot24" description="Iago movement">
    ......
</SPEECH>
.........
```

Fig. 1. XML document with multiple markups.

The need to store different markups for a text within the same document has been studied by the Metalanguage Working Group of the Text Encoding Initiative (TEI) [3]. Different research works have been also carried out in [4, 5, 6, 7]. Many of these solutions have been developed mainly for research activity in linguistic fields, where it is necessary to define different interpretations based on the physical and logical characteristics of the text and their relationship. Our proposal is a generic solution based on empty elements [3].

3   Meta-markup Technique

Our solution allows us to transform any XML document into another equivalent one, through the substitution of each opening or ending tag by an element standing for it, that we will refer to as *metamark*. The meta-markup function, M (1), is defined as:

$$M: \chi \to \chi' = M(\chi) \subseteq \chi \qquad (1)$$
$$\forall D \in \chi, D = E + T \to M(D) = D' = E' + T$$

Where:
- χ is the type of every XML document well formed, and χ' is the type of every metamarked XML document.
- D is any well formed XML document that we will express as D=E+T, being T an initial text to which a set of E tags are added, in conformity with the XML specification and that represents an interpretation of the initial text T.

- D' is the metamarked D document, in which each E tag has been substituted for its corresponding metamark, so that D'=E'+T, being E' the set of metamarks obtained from this transformation process.

Every metamarked document D' follows the definition of an XML-Schema that we will call *basic schema*. In order to obtain the D' document, each opening or closing tag is substituted for the element MM:oe (MM:ce). For each element MM:oe or MM:ce it is only necessary to store the name of the mark (attribute nm) completing the information of an opening or closing tag. These metamarks are defined as empty elements in the document, except when an opening tag has attributes; in this case the element "MM:oe" may include several elements "MM:at", each one including the information of one attribute used in the original opening mark, with its name (nm attribute) and corresponding value (attribute value). The location of each metamark in the document must be the same as the one of the tag from the original document for which it stands. The original document can be obtained from the metamarked document through the definition of an inverse function M^{-1}(2).

$$M^{-1} : \chi' \to \chi \tag{2}$$

$$\forall D' \in \chi' \to M^{-1}(D') = E' + T = D$$

4 Definition of Multiple Markups or Dimensions in a Document

The previous technique can be used to combine, in a single file, different interpretations D on the same text T, represented by different markups E in the form D=T+E. In order to do so, we apply the meta-markup function to each interpretation and combine all the metamarks in a single document, obtaining a document D' represented as D'=E'+T. N interpretations of T would be (3):

$$T \begin{cases} D_1 = T + E_1 \\ D_2 = T + E_2 \\ \\ D_n = T + E_n \end{cases} \xrightarrow{M} \begin{cases} T + E'_1 = D'_1 \\ T + E'_2 = D'_2 \\ \\ T + E'_n = D'_n \end{cases} \quad T + \bigcup_{1 \le i \le n} E'_i = T + E' = D' \xrightarrow{M^{-1}/dim_i} T + E_i = D_i \tag{3}$$

Through the *join* function ($\cup$), we obtain a meta-markup document D' with the metamarks E'_i resulting from each interpretation D_i. Each D_i, will be distinguished by an identifier we will call *dimension*. Accordingly, in order to store the information from the different markups it is necessary to modify the basic schema. A new attribute, "dim", has been added to the three meta-tags we put forward before (oe, ce, at). This attribute will represent for which dimension or dimensions a tag is valid. Besides, we will add a new metamark called "mm:dim" to store the information from each dimension defined over the text.

The validation of a metamarked document will consist, on the one hand, in checking whether it is valid regarding the basic schema, and, on the other hand, in checking whether it is well formed and valid for each dimension regarding the original schema.

An example of transformation of an XML into a metamarked document with two dimensions is shown in fig. 2.

5 Conclusions and Future Works

In this work it has been put forward a technique that might be applied in those situations in which one may wish to store multiple interpretations within a single document or to solve tag nesting problems. The advantages of meta-markup technique are: *1)* it is only necessary to define an XSL transformation sheet to retrieve the different markups in the document and *2)* all the XML documents in the system can be easily turned into metamarked documents using an XSL transformation sheet. The next research steps will be to measure the performance of this technique; to study queries based on the relationships among two or more interpretations and to apply this technique to the development of a system of XML documents versioning.

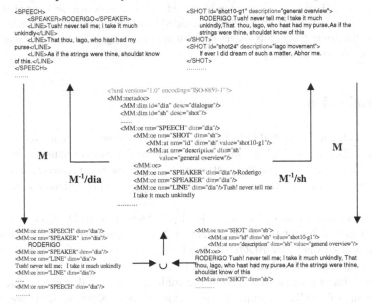

Fig. 2. Validation and retrieval of a metamarked document.

References

1. XML. Available in http://www.w3.org
2. Shakespeare's Plays in XML Format. v2.00. J.Bosak.
3. TEI. Multiple Hierarchies. http://www.tei-c.org/P4X/NH.html
4. Markup Languages and (Non-) Hierarchies. Technology Reports. Cover Pages (Oasis). http://xml.coverpages.org/hierarchies.html. September 2002.
5. TexMECS. An experimental markup meta-language for complex documents. Claus Huitfeldt, Sperberg-McQueen, M. C. 2001
6. Concurrent markup for XML documents. Patrick Durusau, Matthew Brook O'Donnell. XML Europe 2002.
7. The Layered Markup and Annotation Language (LMNL). Tennison, Piez, Wendell. Extreme Markup Language 2002.

BDOviedo3: Data XML Storage and Management

Ana Belén Martínez, Darío Álvarez, Francisco Ortín, Juan Manuel Cueva,
and Mª Ángeles Díaz

Dept. Informatics. University of Oviedo. Calvo Sotelo s/n 33007, Oviedo, Spain
{belen,darioa,ortin,cueva,fondon}@lsi.uniovi.es

Abstract. OOBDMS provide a good solution for the management of XML documents. This article shows the different approach (specific and generic) of coupling an object model with XML and emphasizes the possibilities offered by BDOviedo3 system. It is an object-oriented database built over an integral object-oriented system. The flexibility provided by its object-oriented construction and the extensibility of its mechanisms (such as indexing) can transform it into a XML document manager.

1 Introduction

The XML language (eXtensible Markup Language) is now a standard for information interchange. Due to the high amount of data involved, aspects related to the management of XML documents, such as efficient storage, indexing, queries, transactions, data integrity, multi-user access, etc., traditionally provided by databases, have special relevance.

This paper presents the options provided by Object-Oriented Database Management Systems (OODBMS) for the management of XML documents, with an emphasis on the possibilities offered by BDOviedo3 [9]. BDOviedo3 is an OODBMS built on a persistent object-oriented abstract machine [2].

Section 2 introduces an overview of the main alternatives that can be used for the management of XML documents using OODBMS. Next section presents the BDOviedo3 system. Finally, in section 4, a number of extensions of BDOviedo3 system for the storage and management of XML documents are discussed.

2 Object-Oriented Database Systems and XML

The potential of OODBMS for the management of XML documents is well known [6]. Besides, they have a number of advantages when compared with other models, such as the relational model [1].

The goal of coupling an object model with XML has two main approaches: *specific* and *generic* [5]. *Specific approach* is very adequate for XML documents where data is what is really interesting. Describes a new class for each new kind of information. It models the data in the XML document as a tree of objects that are specific to the data in the document. There are already a number of products implementing XML data

J.M. Cueva Lovelle et al. (Eds.): ICWE 2003, LNCS 2722, pp. 226–229, 2003.
© Springer-Verlag Berlin Heidelberg 2003

binding [3,7] and even many of these can transfer data between the objects and the database as well. *Generic approach* is appropriate in general for *document-centric* applications. The Document Object Model (DOM) uses such as approach. Generic approach considers all document information (tags, attributes, etc.) as objects of pre-defined classes, interconnected between each other with links that preserve XML structure. This approach is used by several model-based native XML databases [10,16]. A model-based native XML is a database that stores a binary model of the document (DOM or a variant) in an existing or custom data store.

3   BDOviedo3

BDOviedo3 is an OODBMS built over an integral object-oriented (OO) system [9], which provides direct support for the OO paradigm [2]. This integral system is supported by an OO abstract machine that provides a set of minimal capabilities (persistence, concurrency, security and distribution), and an OO operating system that extends them. The abstract machine provides a common object model shared for the other system elements.

The main element of the architecture of the BDOviedo3 OODBMS is the engine [11], that provides the basic functionality of the OODBMS. It is structured into eight managers (extensions, schemas, integrity, queries, indexes, transactions, authorization, and distribution). As an example of the facilities provided by the integral system, the extensibility [14] of the indexing mechanism can be mentioned. This mechanism easily allows the incorporation of new indexing techniques. These techniques are implemented as object sets with a particular interface. Every new indexing technique added to the system, by using inheritance, will have that interface. These classes can be used and extended by any user, thus reusing the OODBMS code itself. The initial set of indexing techniques coded are Single Class, CH-Tree and Path Index [15].

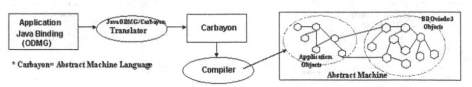

Fig. 1. Architecture of BDOviedo3

The languages selected [9] for the manipulation and querying of the database are the ones proposed by the ODMG standard [4]: Definition Language (ODL), Management Language (OML), and Query Language (OQL) in its Java binding incarnation. However, the addition of new languages to the OODBMS just involves the coding of a translator of the language into the bytecode of the abstract machine using the already present functionalities of the objects of the database engine.

4   Possibilities for the Management of XML Offered by BDOviedo3

BDOviedo3, as mentioned before, is an OODBMS. As such, it can host the management of XML documents. Nevertheless, the special features of the system offer a big number of possibilities. Some of them are discussed below.

The first one is along the lines proposed in [8], for instance. It is based on extending the ODMG standard to support structured and semi-structured data. This implies the existence of a model to represent semi-structured data (OEM in the case of Ozone [8]). The extension of the OQL language to support queries on hybrid data is also required. The solution in BDOviedo3 will need the addition of a new layer to deal with these extensions. First, a new schema manager is needed. This schema manager will add new types representing semi-structured data to the ODMG class declarations. Then a new preprocessor translating extended OQL queries into plain OQL should also be added.

In order to achieve a *generic* management of XML documents, a solution will be the developing of a persistent DOM (PDOM style [5]). However, in BDOviedo3, the implementation will be very easy, as all the aspects related to the synchronization of objects between main memory and hard disk, object lifecycle control, etc. are transparent to the programmer of the persistent DOM. A module for making XML specific queries (XQuery for instance) can also be easily added. The extensibility of the indexing mechanism allows to introduce without effort new indexing techniques that prove to be better [12,13] for searches involving these documents.

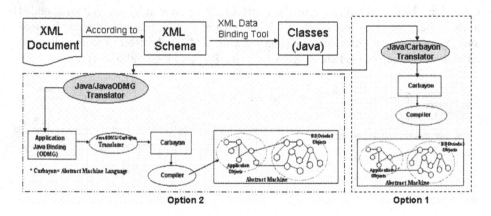

Fig. 2. Alternatives to add specific XML document management to BDOviedo3

Finally, in order to achieve a *specific* management of XML documents there are a number of possibilities. The BDOviedo3 languages are ODMG standard (Java binding), so any of the Java language tools implementing the XML data binding (such as [3,7]) can be directly used to translate between the database schema and the XML document schema. Then we have two options (Fig.2). The first one is to translate the Java source generated by the tool to the language of the abstract machine. Then the schema is now persistent (thanks to the persistence of the machine), and data in main memory is synchronized with data stored in the database. The other option is to translate into a language understood by the ODBMS (the ODMG extended Java), which then in turn is translated to machine bytecode by an already existing tool in the ODMS. An extra step is taken but the translator is simpler.

5 Conclusions

Object-Oriented databases are a feasible and adequate option for the storage and management of XML documents. The BDOviedo3 OODBMS offers different possibilities for the storage and management of XML documents, for data-centric and document-centric applications as well. The flexibility provided by its object-oriented construction over a persistent OO abstract machine, and the extensibility of its managers and mechanisms (such as the indexing mechanism) can easily transform BDOviedo3 into a XML document manager.

References

1. Abiteboul, S., Buneman, P., Suciu, D. Data on the Web. From Relations to Semistructured Data and XML. Morgan Kaufmann Publishers (2000)
2. Álvarez D. et al. An Object-Oriented Abstract Machine as the Substrate for an Object-Oriented Operating System. 11th ECOOP'97. Finland (1997)
3. Castor. http://www.castor.org/. January (2003)
4. Cattell, R., Barry, D., Berler, M. et al. The Object Data Standard: ODMG 3.0. Morgan Kaufmann Publishers (1999)
5. Chaudhri, A. and Zicari, R. Succeding with Object Databases. John Wiley & Sons (2001)
6. Futtersack, P., C. Espert, and Bolf, D. Good Performances for an SGML Object Database System. Proceedings of the SGML 97 Conference. Boston (1997)
7. Java Architecture for XML Binding (JAXB). Proposed Final V.0.90. (December 2002) http://java.sun.com/xml/jaxb/
8. Lahiri, T., Abiteboul, S. and Widom, J. Ozone: Integrating Structured and Semistructured Data. 7th Workshop on Database Programming Languages, Scotland (1999)
9. Martínez, A.B. Un Sistema de Gestión de Bases de Datos Orientadas a Objetos sobre una Máquina Abstracta Persistente. PhD thesis.University of Oviedo, ISBN 84-8317-277-1 (2002)
10. MindSuite 2.0 XDB. http://xdb.wiredminds.com/ (2003)
11. Ortín, F., Martínez, A.B.et al. A Reflective Pesistence Middleware over an Object Oriented Database Engine. 14th Brazilian Symposium on Databases. Brasil (1999)
12. Rizzolo, F. and Mendelzon, A. Indexing XML Data with ToXin. 4th International Workshop on the Web and Databases (with ACM SIGMOD). Santa Barbara (2001)
13. Sacks-Davis et al. Indexing Documents for Queries on Structure, Content and Attributes. International Symposium on Digital Media Information Base, Nara, Japan (1997)
14. Stonebraker, M.R. Inclusion of New Types in Relational Data Bases Systems. Proc. 2nd IEEE Data Engineering Conf. Los Angeles (1986)
15. Yu, C. and Meng, W. Principles of Database Query Processing for Advanced Applications. Morgan Kaufmann (1998)
16. 4Suite. http://4suite.org/index.xhtml (2003)

Building Applications with Domain-Specific Markup Languages: A Systematic Approach to the Development of XML-Based Software[1]

José L. Sierra, Alfredo Fernández-Valmayor, Baltasar Fernández-Manjón, and Antonio Navarro

Dpto. Sistemas Informáticos y Programación. Fac. Informática. Universidad Complutense.
C/ Juan del Rosal n° 8. 28040. Madrid. Spain
{jlsierra,alfredo,balta,anavarro}@sip.ucm.es

Abstract. This paper presents ADDS, a systematic approach to sofware development using Domain-Specific Languages (DSLs) and markup technologies. XML is used as a common descriptive framework for DSLs formulation, obtaining Domain Specific Markup Languages (DSMLs). According to ADDS, the construction of applications in a domain starts with the provision of suitable DSMLs. Then, the applications in such a domain are described by means of sets of structured documents conforming these DSMLs. Finally, the application is produced by processing this documentation according to an operationalization model called OADDS. Hence ADDS provides a systematic approach to software development based on the processing of XML documentation that can be used in a great variety of domains.

1 Introduction

XML [26] has acquired a great relevance in the construction of web applications and in many other areas of software development. XML inherits from its predecessor SGML [13] a linguistic approach in the development of applications. Indeed, developing a SGML/XML application is equivalent to using SGML/XML in devising a special-purpose markup language. Previously, this linguistic approach was successfully applied to the electronic publishing domain but, with the advent of new SGML applications and, specially XML, this initial domain was quickly broadened. Now, XML is usually considered as a standard framework for information interchange between heterogeneous systems despite its origins as a document markup (meta)language. Nevertheless, the new application domains should not change the initial linguistic conception: in order to develop an XML application the focus must be put on devising a markup language for describing the informational structure of the application domain. Once this language is available, one (or several) processor(s) must be provided, depending on the task to be solved using the marked up documents.

---

[1] The Spanish Commitee of Science and Technology (TIC2000-0737-C03-01, TIC2001-1462 and TIC2002-04067-C03-02) has supported this work.

J.M. Cueva Lovelle et al. (Eds.): ICWE 2003, LNCS 2722, pp. 230–240, 2003.
© Springer-Verlag Berlin Heidelberg 2003

This paper presents our approach to software development called ADDS (Approach to Document-based Development of Software). This approach is the outcome of our previous experience using markup technologies in the educational domain [6][7], in the prototyping of model-driven hypermedia applications [15], and in the development of component-based software [19]. ADDS put the stress on the linguistic potentiality of XML, instead on its data oriented features. ADDS can actually be considered as a specific case of the paradigm of software construction based on Domain-Specific Languages (DSLs) [22] that uses XML as a common descriptive framework for DSLs formulation. Because ADDS conceives DSLs as XML applications, our approach provides new insight into the systematic development of these kinds of applications.

The structure of the paper is as follows. Section 2 gives a general overview of the ADDS approach. Section 3 describes the operationalization model of ADDS (i.e how executable applications are produced from documents describing them). Finally, section 4 describes related work and section 5 outlines the conclusions and future work. To illustrate the different aspects described in the paper, a case study application domain is used: the Subway Networks Route Search (SNRS) domain. Each SNRS application allows the search for paths from origin to destination stations in the subway network of a city.

2 The ADDS Approach

The ADDS approach is outlined in Fig.1. This approach comprises the following three activities: (i) the *provision of DSMLs*, oriented to provide the Domain-Specific Markup Languages (DSMLs), (ii) the *authorship of documents*, oriented to produce the documentation describing the application, and (iii) the *operationalization* activity, oriented to produce the application from the documentation. The following subsections detail these activities.

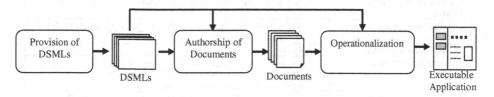

Fig. 1. Main activities and products involved in ADDS.

2.1 Provision of DSMLs

The goal of this activity is to produce DSMLs that will be used to markup the documents that describe the application and the data needed by the application in a given domain. In ADDS, each DSML comes with a set of software components which represent the primitive operations in the domain and that will be used for assembling processors for documents conforming the DSML. There might be different components used to validate, or to edit documents, to perform domain-dependent tasks, etc.

Fig. 2 gives a top-level categorization of DSML types. There are (i) *problem* DSMLs, languages for marking up the relevant data and information about the domain of the problem to be solved by the application, and (ii) *application* DSMLs, languages for marking up documents describing high-level aspects of the application. Documents conforming problem DSMLs are called *problem domain* documents, while those conforming application DSMLs are called *application* documents.

Problem DSMLs can integrate two different sublanguages: (i) a *use-independent problem* DSML for the description of information independent of any particular use imposed by the application, and (ii) a *use-enabling problem* DSML for giving additional information not describable with the use-independent problem DSML. Moreover, to lower the cost of developing new DSMLs, more complex application DSMLs can be obtained by combining simpler ones.

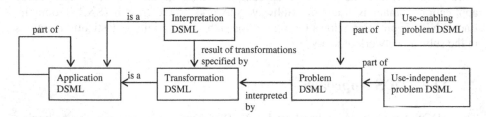

Fig. 2. An initial ADDS linguistic framework.

Table 1. DSMLs used in the SNRS domain.

Problem DSMLs	
Use-independent problem DSMLs	– Subway Network Markup Language (SNML)
Use enabling problem DSMLs	– Subway Network Geometry and Styling Markup Language (SNGSML)
Application DSMLs	
Transformation DSMLs	– XSLT
Interpretation DSMLs	– Weighted Directed Graph Markup Language (WDGML)
	– Simple Diagram Description Markup Language (SDDML)
	– Simple Terminological Mapping Language (STML)
Other Application DSMLs	– Subway Network Route Searching Markup Language (SNRSML)

By maximizing the independence between problem and application DSMLs, we can improve the reusability of the DSMLs and of the documentation. Indeed, in some cases, application documents can be used with different problem domain documents, and problem domain documents can be used in different applications. To facilitate the relative independence between both types of languages, the application DSML must abstract the problem domain. The problem of coupling and decoupling these more specific and abstract languages used to describe the domain is solved in ADDS using *transformation* and *interpretation* DSMLs. *Transformation* DSMLs are used to specify document transformations, which, by taking problem documents as input, produce *interpretation documents* as output. Therefore, transformation DSMLs are the link between application DSMLs and problem DSMLs. Furthermore, interpretation documents are compliant with *interpretation* DSMLs. These DSMLs are not directly used in the description of the application. Instead, they are used as the target languages for the transformation DSMLs

Table. 1 enumerates the different DSMLs used in the SNRS domain. The problem DSMLs include a use-independent problem DSML, SNML, for describing the structure and the schedules of subway networks, and a use enabling language, SNGSML, for the description of the geometry (eg. coordinates of the stations) and other stylistic aspects (eg. line colors) of subway networks. The application DSMLs include standard XSLT [26] as transformation language, and SNRSML for describing the variabilities of the application. The following interpretation DSMLs are also included: (i) WDGML for representing the weighted graph used in the search, (ii) SDDML for giving a visual representation of the subway network, and (iii) STML, used to relate the names of the stations in the SDDML diagram with the names of the nodes in the WDGML graph. These languages will be the target languages for the transformations.

2.2 Authorship of Documents

Domain experts can provide descriptions of applications as collections of marked up documents using the appropriate DSMLs. This is done during the *authorship of documents* activity.

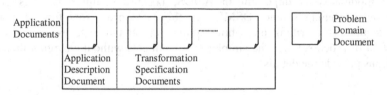

Fig. 3. Documentation associated with a typical application description in ADDS.

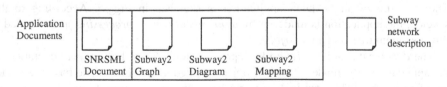

Fig. 4. Documentation associated with an SNRS application.

Fig. 3 sketches the documentation associated with a typical application description in ADDS. There is only one problem domain document. There are also several application documents: (i) an *application description* document describing the variabilities of the application, some of which are given as transformations of the problem domain information, and (ii) a set of *transformation specification* documents describing how to carry out these transformations.

Fig. 4 sketches the documentation associated with an application in the SNRS domain. The problem domain document includes a SNML description of the subway network. This also includes a SNGSML description of the geometry and style of the network. The application description document conforms to SNRSML. Finally, there are three XSLT transformations: (i) a first one (Subway2Graph) for generating a WDGML graph from the subway network description document, (ii) a second (Subway2Diagram) for generating a SDDML diagram, and (iii) a third (Subway2Mapping) for generating a STML mapping.

2.3   Operationalization

The operationalization activity produces an application from the marked up documents that describe it. This activity is detailed in the next section.

3   Operationalization in ADDS

The operationalization activity follows an operationalization model called OADDS (Operationalization in ADDS). It is based on the well-known techniques of syntax-directed translation [1] and attribute grammars [11][16] used in the construction of language processors. In addition, the model provides for *semantic modularity* [10]. Accordingly, processors can be built using reusable language-processor components. Semantic modularity is important in ADDS, because complex DSMLs can be obtained by combining simpler DSMLs. In this way, processors for the resulting markup document describing the whole application should arise as an appropriate combination of processors for the simpler subdocuments without changing them. The next sections provide the details.

3.1   OADDS Applications

The structure of an OADDS application is sketched in Fig. 5. According to this scketch, the application is made up by a *document tree*, a *processing graph* added to this document tree, and an *interface*.

The *document tree* is a *grove*-like representation [17] of the *top-level* document of the application. It is made of a set of objects, called *nodes*. Each node has an assigned set of *properties*. This tree includes properties for representing the markup structure (*primitive* properties), but also properties for representing other information (*semantic* properties). Each property is represented as an object that has an associated *value*, and an associated set of *observers*. The value of a property can be either a list of nodes or an object of another type (including a node from a different document tree). Each observer is a *processing object* which can be notified when the property value changes.

The *processing graph* is a graph with properties and processing objects as nodes. The only arcs allowed are (i) from properties to processing objects, indicating that the process carried out by the processing object depends on the property value, and (ii) from processing objects to properties, indicating that the source processing object updates the target property. Actually, the processing graph is added to the document tree registering processing objects as observers. In turn, each processing object can be asked for the properties that it updates. In terms of attribute grammars, this graph can be understood as a *dynamic* version of the *dependency graph* associated with an attributed parse tree, together with the *semantic functions* used to compute the values of the attributes.

Interface   Document   Processing   Application
             Tree   Graphs

Fig. 5. Structure of an OADDS application.

The *interface* mediates between the application and its environment. Usually, this environment will be populated by the *users* of the application (either people or other programs). In this way, the concept of *interface* in OADDS is a very abstract one. For instance, in the case of a batch application it could be a black-box, in the case of an interactive application (such as those used in the SNRS domain), it could be a graphical user interface. It could even be a SOAP [26] mediator for applications conceived as web services. In addition, the application description can also describe certain aspects of the interface. Such aspects will usually be eminently pragmatic (eg. in a GUI, label names, colors, etc.).

This structure induces a natural execution model based on the *propagation* of the properties values. Hence, computation of attribute values in the attribute grammar context has a counterpart on the behaviour induced by the network of observables/observers. Indeed, the propagation of a property value means that its observers should be notified about the availability of this value. In this way, the execution starts with the propagation of the values of the primitive properties. Next, the interface takes control. This interface can update other semantic properties in the tree in order to finish the propagation process. Finally, execution is guided by user interaction. When the user interacts with the interface, the appropriate semantic properties are updated and re-propagated. As a consequence, other semantic properties are established and their values are used to update the state of the interface.

3.2   The OADDS Model

The activities and products involved in the OADDS model are shown in Fig.6.

OADDS uses two types of *software* componentes to produce applications from structured documents: (i) (tree) *analyzers* that validate and set up the document tree to ensure that it can be properly operationalized, and (ii) *operationalizers* that enlarge the document tree by adding the processing graph. These components are provided during the *provision of software components* activity. While analyzers abstract the productions of a context-free grammar, operationalizers provide an implementation of the semantic equations associated with each one of these productions.

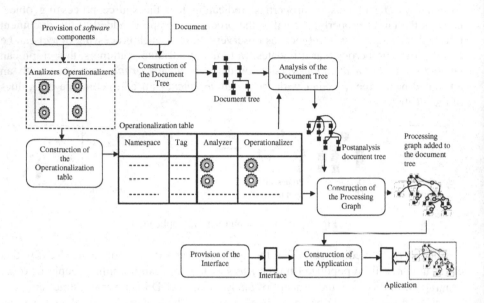

Fig. 6. Products and activities in OADDS.

The operationalization of a DSML is performed by assigning an analyzer and an operationalizer to each tag. The resulting structure is called an *operationalization table*, and it is provided during the *construction of the operationalization table* activity. Therefore, this table can be thought as an abstraction of an attribute grammar/syntax-directed translation schema. Because DSMLs can be produced by combining simpler DSMLs, the operationalization table uses XML namespaces [26] to avoid name conflicts. In addition, both the analyzer and the operationalizer associated with a given tag can be obtained by *composing* different analyzers/operationalizers. This is the main OADDS mechanism for achieving semantic modularity.

The operationalization of a particular document begins with the construction of its document tree, during the *construction of the document tree* activity. This document is subsequently analyzed during the *analysis of the document tree* activity. This activity is carried out using the analyzers referred to in the operationalization table. The tags associated with element nodes in the document tree are used to index the appropriate analyzers in the table, which are applied to the corresponding nodes. To facilitate the actuation of subsequent components, analyzers can add new properties (*postanalysis* properties) to the document tree. The resulting tree is called a *postanalysis* document tree.

The addition of the processing graph to the (postanalysis) document tree is carried out during the *construction of the processing graph* activity. Here element tags are used to index operationalizers in the operationalization table. Then, the recovered operationalizers are applied to the corresponding nodes. When applied to a node, an operationalizer adds part of the processing graph by registering processing objects as observers of node properties. Finally, the application is produced by putting together the interface (obtained during the *provision of the interface* activity) with the document tree and the added processing graph. This is performed during the *construction of the application* activity.

Currently, we have developed an experimental Java object-oriented framework for supporting OADDS. The framework provides facilities to connect either with DOM [26] or SAX [3] compliant software for the construction of the document tree.

4   Related Work

A pioneering work in the use of SGML/XML for the description of DSMLs is [8]. In [25], some relations between markup languages and the DSL approach are highlighted. Although these works recognize the value of markup metalanguages as a vehicle to define DSLs, they largerly use SGML/XML as abstract syntax representation formalisms rather than as descriptive markup (meta)languages.

The key idea behind Jargons [14] is similar to ADDS. In Jargons, DSMLs are directly formulated, and even operationalized (using a script language), by domain experts. While we agree with this *author centered* conception of DSL development, we think that to assign language design and operationalization responsabilities to domain experts is not realistic. In ADDS, operationalization is separated from DSL provision. Therefore, operationalization can be carried out by software development experts while DSMLs can evolve according to the markup needs of domain experts. A third category of experts in ADDS can mediate between domain and software development experts, taking the responsability for maintaining the DSMLs. Semantic modularity (not comtemplated in Jargons) is essential in order to accomodate operationalization to this evolution of DSMLs.

DSLX [13] is another example of a framework to operationalize DSLMs. Although this framework enables DSL composability, it does not provide any special mechanism to ensure semantic modularity.

A well-known approach to semantic modularity in the development of DSLs is that based on *monads* and *monad transformers* [10] in the functional programming community. Because control in OADDS is imposed by the processing model itself, modularity is oriented to adaptation of the information flow between the document tree nodes, instead of control adaptations. This solution is weaker, but also more usable than monadic approaches. Another well-known approach, this time in the object-oriented arena, is based on the use of *mix-ins* [4]. Composition of analyzers/operationalizers in OADDS can be resorted into a single mix-in composition, where the execution of mix-ins do not interfere.

There are several works describing the application of syntax directed translation techniques and attribute grammars to markup languages [5][12][18]. Actually, OADDS can be considered an abstraction of these approaches, where the grammatical specification is reduced to the operationalization table. Because of this, all these approaches are feasible in OADDS. In particular, the facilities provided by higher-order attribute grammars [24], where the value of an attribute can be another attributed tree, can be easily achieved. This enables OADDS to deal with interpretation documents. In addition, some usual techniques used to obtain semantic modularity in the context of attribute grammars can also be easily achieved [23].

Existing technologies for building XML-based software fit in well with our approach. Therefore, the *construction of the document tree* OADDS activity can be built on top of basic document processor technologies, such as DOM or SAX. On the other hand, data-binding proposals [2] (i.e. compilation of document grammars into object oriented representations of documents conforming these grammars) can be understood as a particular case of OADDS. In addition, Knuth's principle, which states that attribute grammars are as powerful as any other semantic specification formalism [11], can be applied here, because, at the limit, processing objects can be applied to entire document (sub)trees. This facilitates the integration of pre-existing processors (eg. standard XSLT transformers).

The work described here relies on our previous work on the DTC (structured Documents, document Transformations and software Components) approach [19][21][20]. ADDS abstracts the key idea under DTC: the use of DSMLs. In addition, the treatment of document transformations exposed here (closer to the idea of *overmarkup* exposed in [15]), where the application of transformations is a part of the application description, is more flexible than in DTC. In DTC transformations were applied for the content (problem domain) documents to obtain a pre-established set of document entities integrated into the application documents.

5   Conclusions and Future Work

ADDS is a systematic approach to sofware development founded on DSLs and markup technologies. It is based on a comprehensive linguistic view of the application development that deals with the description of the applications and the problem domains by means of marked up documents, and also with the operationalization of these descriptions. Therefore, by using the markup documents (produced according to suitable DSMLs) and a related group of software components, the executable application is obtained.

Recently we have realized that the use of descriptive markup, together with the modular nature of OADDS, enables the conception of ADDS as a pragmatic, authorship-driven, particular case of the DSL approach. Consequently, we are refining ADDS in that direction. In addition, we are working on the recursive application of ADDS to ADDS itself, either for the production of specialized editors for domain experts, and for the supporting of *meta* DSMLs to give higher-level descriptions of OADDS processors. Next step in the project is to give a precise characterization of the application domains where the ADDS particular use of the DSL approach could be competitive.

References

1.   Aho, A. Sethi, R. Ullman, J. D. Compilers: Principles, Techniques and Tools. Adisson-Wesley. 1986
2.   Birbeck,M et al. XML Data Binding. Professional XML 2nd Edition. WROX Press. 2001.
3.   Brownell, D. SAX2. O'Relly. 2002

4. Duggan, D. A Mixin-Based Semantic-Based Approach to Reusing Domain-Specific Programming Languages. 14th European Conference on Object-Oriented Programming ECOOP'2000. Cannes. France. June12–16 2000

5. Feng, A.Wakayama, A. SIMON: A Grammar-based Transformation System for Structured Documents. Electronic Publishing. 6(4). 1993

6. Fernández Manjón, B. Fernández-Valmayor, A. Improving World Wide Web educational uses promoting hypertext and standard general markup language content-based features. Education and Information Technologies, vol 2, no 3, pp. 193–206. 1997.

7. Fernández-Valmayor, A.; López Alonso, C. Sèrè A. Fernández-Manjón,B. Integrating an Interactive Learning Paradigm for Foreign Language Text Comprehension into a Flexible Hypermedia system. *IFIP WG3.2-WG3.6* Conference Building University Electronic Educational Environments. University of California Irvine, California, USA August. 4–6 1999

8. Fuchs, M. Domain Specific Languages for *ad hoc* Distributed Applications. First Conference on Domain Specific Languages. USENIX. Sta. Barbara. CA. October 17–17. 1997

9. Goldfard, C. F. The SGML Handbook. Oxford University Press. 1990

10. Hudak,P. Domain-Specific Languages. Handbook of Programming Languages V. III: Little Languages. And Tools. Macmillan Tech. Publishing. 1998

11. Knuth;D.E. Semantics of Context-free Languages. Math. Systems Theory. 2:127–145. 1968

12. Kuikka, E.Pentonnen, M. Transformation of Structured Documents with the Use of Grammars.Electronic Publishing. 6(4). 1993

13. Morrow,P. Alexander,M. Domain Specific Languages – Tools for Better Programming. PCAI Magazine. Vol 13. Issue 1. Jan/Feb 1999

14. Nakatani,L.H. Ardis,M.A. Olsen,R.G. Pontrelli,P.M. Jargons for Domain Engineering. Second Conference for Domain Specific Languages. USENIX. Austin. Texas. October 3–6. 1999

15. Navarro, A., Fernández-Manjón, B., Fernández-Valmayor, A., Sierra, J.L. Formal-Driven Conceptualization and Prototyping of Hypermedia Applications. Fundamental Approaches to Software Engineering FASE 2002. ETAPS 2002. Grenoble. France. April 8–12. 2002

16. Paakki,J. Attribute Grammar Paradigms - A High-Level Methodology in Language Implementation. ACM Computing Surveys 27(2): 196–255. 1995

17. Prescod,P. Addressing the Enterprise: Why the Web needs Groves. ISOGEN White Paper. 1999

18. Psaila, G.Crespi-Reghizzi, S. Adding Semantics to XML. Second Workshop on Attribute Grammars and their Applications. WAGA'99. Amsterdam. The Netherlands. March 26. 1999

19. Sierra, J. L. Fernández-Manjón, B. Fernández-Valmayor, A. Navarro, A. Integration of Markup Languages, Document Transformations and Software Components in the Development of Applications: the DTC Approach. International Conference on Software ICS 2000. 16th IFIP World Computer Congress. Beijing - China. August 21–25. 2000

20. Sierra, J. L. Fernández-Manjón, B. Fernández-Valmayor, A. Navarro, A. An Extensible and Modular Processing Model for Document Trees. Extreme Markup Languages 2002. Montreal. Canada. August 4–8. 2002.

21. Sierra, J. L. Fernández-Valmayor, A. Fernández-Manjón, B. Navarro, A. Operationalizing Application Descriptions with DTC: Building Applications with Generalized Markup Technologies. 13th International Conference on Software Engineering & Knowledge Engineering SEKE'01. Buenos Aires. Argentina. June 13–15. 2001.

22. Van Deursen, A. Klint, P.Visser, J. Domain-Specific Languages: An Annotated Bibliography. ACM SIGPLAN Notices. 35(6). 2000.
23. Van Wyk,E. de Moor, O. Backhouse, K. Kwiatkowski,P. Forwarding in Attribute Grammars for Modular Language Design. Compiler Construction CC 2002. ETAPS 2002. Grenoble France. April 8–12. 2002
24. Vogt, H, H. Swierstra, S, D. Kuiper, M, F. Higher-Order Attribute Grammars. Proceedings of the ACM SIGPLAN'89 Conference on Programming Language Design and Implementation. 1989
25. Wadler,P. The next 700 markup languages. Invited Talk of the Second USENIX Conference on Domain Specific Languages. USENIX. Austin. Texas. 1999
26. www.w3.org/TR

An XML-Based Approach for Fast Prototyping of Web Applications

Antonio Navarro, Baltasar Fernandez-Manjon, Alfredo Fernandez-Valmayor, and Jose Luis Sierra

Departamento de Sistemas Informaticos y Programacion, Facultad de Informatica, C/ Juan del Rosal 8, 28040, Madrid, Spain
{anavarro, balta, alfredo, jlsierra}@sip.ucm.es

Abstract. This paper presents an XML-based approach for the fast prototyping of Web applications. Two XML Document Type Definitions (DTDs) are used to rationalize the development of these prototypes and a Java engine processes the instances of both DTDs to automatically obtain a running prototype of the application.

1   Introduction

The use of markup technologies to develop hypermedia applications, and more specifically to develop Web hypermedia applications has been from the beginning at the core of the Web. The basic language for the development of Web applications has been the *HyperText Markup Language* (HTML) [1], an SGML [2] based language. Other significant efforts have been the *Hypermedia/Time-based Structuring Language* (HyTime) [3], a very powerful SGML-based standard for the characterization of hypermedia applications, and the *Synchronized Multimedia Integration Language* (SMIL) [1], a markup language mainly centered on the multimedia domain. More recently the *Web Modeling Language* (WebML) [4] has become one of the most successful languages for Web development.

Our approach tries to gather the key benefits of the previous markup technologies while avoiding some of their shortcomings, and it is strictly centered at the prototyping stage.

In this short paper we introduce our general approach for the development of hypermedia applications. Then we present the process model that manages the use of our XML-based approach in the prototyping of Web applications. Finally, we present the conclusions and future work.

2   Plumbing, Pipe, and PlumbingXJ

The use of Software Engineering techniques is a must during the development of hypermedia applications [5]. In our approach we have defined the *Plumbing* process

J.M. Cueva Lovelle et al. (Eds.): ICWE 2003, LNCS 2722, pp. 241–244, 2003.
© Springer-Verlag Berlin Heidelberg 2003

model [6] (which is an specialization of Fraternali's process model [7]). Plumbing has two loops. The first loop is centered on the conceptualization-prototyping phase, and the second on the design-development phase. We have focused our work at the conceptualization-prototyping stage, preferring an open solution (like the one presented in [8]) for the design-development stage. In our approach, the conceptualization-prototyping loop is guided by the *Pipe Hypermedia Model* [6], a model that characterizes a hypermedia application using three components: (i) the Pipe *contents graph* that characterizes the structure of the informational content of the application and its navigational relationships; (ii) the Pipe *navigational schema* that characterizes the elements of the graphical user interface and their relationships; (iii) and finally the Pipe *canalization functions* that relate both aspects of the hypermedia application. The Pipe model also has a default browsing semantics that describes the behavior of the application after an anchor selection.

The conceptualization stage is focused on obtaining a Pipe representation of the hypermedia application. Then, at the prototyping stage we need different formalisms to represent the Pipe characterization of the application in such a way that it can be processed by a tool that automatically builds the prototype. The selected mechanisms for representing the Pipe structures during the prototyping stage must be tuned with the technologies used at the design-development stage, or it must be flexible enough to permit a smooth transition from prototyping to development.

PlumbingXJ [6] is a specialization of Plumbing where XML is the selected mechanism for describing the structure of the contents graph and the navigational schema of the application, and where a Java tool generates the prototypes automatically processing the XML documents (hence the *XJ*). In PlumbingXJ the only changes appear at the prototyping stage, and as in Plumbing, PlumbingXJ is mainly centered at the conceptualization and prototyping stage. There are two reasons for choosing XML for describing the application at the conceptualization stage: today XML is accepted as a universal interchange format [9], and it provides a great structuring capacity [10]. Both characteristics make XML a perfect choice for the characterization of hypermedia applications [11].

3   Content DTD and Application DTD. Overmarkup

In PlumbingXJ the *content DTD* defines the markup language that structures the informational contents and links of the hypermedia application (and therefore it structures the Pipe contents graph). Due to the heterogeneous structure of the contents that can appear in a hypermedia application it is specific for every case. The *content document* is an instance of the content DTD and represents the contents and links of the hypermedia application (i.e. codifies the Pipe contents graph).

In PlumbingXJ the *application DTD* defines the language that structures the graphical user interface of the hypermedia applications (and therefore it structures the Pipe navigational schema). It is unique for every application and uses a closer GUI terminology instead of the Pipe vocabulary. The *application document* is an instance of this DTD and not only provides the elements of the GUI and their navigational relationships, but also codifies the canalization functions that relate this GUI with the contents of the hypermedia application (i.e. it represents the Pipe navigational schema and the Pipe canalization functions). The overmarkup technique and some element attributes in the DTD are responsible for this canalization.

The key idea behind *overmarkup* is quite simple and extremely useful. The actual contents of the XML elements of the application document are XPath [1] references to the content document. These references select the contents that must appear in every pane. The Java application *Automatic Prototypes Generator*, APG, processes the application and content documents and produces the desired prototype. The navigational schema of the application is generated by the APG from the application document. This schema is a Java Swing skeleton that supports the GUI of the application. The contents that appear in this Java Swing skeleton are HTML pages generated by the APG from the content document and the XPath expressions that appear in the application document. An XSLT transformation [1] produces the transition from XML to HTML. This transformation is always the same and uses the hypermedia structure codified in the content document via some selected attributes. In this way the content document can be structured in any desired way because the XSLT transformation only needs a few attributes to produce the HTML pages.

The separation of layers (as in the Dexter model [12]) allows for a fast generation of prototypes where changes in the navigational schema have no effect at the content level, or changes in the content level (maintaining the structure referenced by XPath expressions) have no effect on the navigational schema.

The construction of the navigational schema and its relationships with the contents can be done manually, or via a CASE tool. At the last stage, the customers evaluate the prototype, and when the hypermedia structure is stable enough, the design stage begins. The use of XML in the structuring of the document offers an easy transition to HTML (or another format) using XSLT transformations. This approach is preferable to the direct use of HTML in prototyping due to the flexibility and structuring power provided by XML [1].

4   Conclusions and Future Work

The presence of a process model assures a systematic way for application development, while the design of the Pipe hypermedia model allows for the changes in one of the two main aspects of hypermedia applications (contents or GUI) without affecting the other.

Moreover, the utilization of XML at the prototyping stage adds legibility and produces a high-level language appropriated for the prototyping of Web applications. Note that all the markup technologies referenced in this paper increase the abstraction level in the development of Web applications, constraining the flexibility of direct coding using a general purpose programming language (e.g. Java), and our approach is not an exception. Finally, XML and Java provide valuable platform independence.

At present, we are working on the APG finalization in order to deal with the full expressive power of Pipe. The APG is the kernel of the *PlumbingMatic* application, a CASE tool that integrates the Pipe structures and the automatic generation of prototypes. This tool will help us in the application of PlumbingXJ to the development of several applications that we are creating.

Finally, we plan to extensively apply PlumbingXJ to confirm the viability of using our techniques of conceptualization and prototyping in the design and development phases.

Acknowledgements. The Spanish Committee of Science and Technology (TIC2000-0737-C03-01, TIC2001-1462 and TIC2002-04067-C03-02) has supported this work.

References

1. World Wide Web Consortium. http://www.w3.org/
2. International Standards Organization: Standard Generalized Markup Language (SGML), ISO/IEC IS 8879 (1986)
3. International Standards Organization: Hypermedia/Time-based Structuring Language (HyTime), ISO/IEC IS 11744.1992 (1992)
4. Ceri, S., Fraternali, P., Bongio. A.: Web Modeling Language (WebML): a Modeling Language for Designing Web Sites. In Proc. www9 Conference, Amsterdam (2000).
5. Garzotto, F., Paolini, P., Schwabe, D.: HDM: A model-based approach to hypertext application design. ACM Transactions on Information Systems 1 (1993) 1–26.
6. Navarro, A., Fernandez-Manjon, B., Fernandez-Valmayor, A., Sierra, J.L.: Formal-Driven Conceptualization and Prototyping of Hypermedia Applications. In: Kutsche, R.D., Weber, H. (eds.): Fundamentals Approaches to Software Engineering 2002, Proc. European joint conferences on Theory and Practice of Software 2002, Lecture Notes in Computer Science, Vol. 2306. Springer-Verlag, Berlin Heidelberg New York (2002) 308–322.
7. Fraternali, P.: Tools and Approaches for Developing Data-Intensive Web Applications: A Survey. ACM Computing Surveys 3 (1999) 227–263.
8. Rossi, G., Schwabe, D., Lyardet, F.: Designing Hypermedia Applications with Objects and Patterns. International Journal of Software Engineering and Knowledge Engineering 7 (1999) 745–766
9. Bryan, M.: Guidelines for using XML for Electronic Data Interchange. http://www.xmledi-group.org/xmledigroup/guide.htm (1998).
10. Sperberg-McQueen, C. M., Goldstein, C.M.: HTML to the Max A Manifesto for Adding SGML Intelligence to the World-Wide Web. In Proc. 2nd World Wide Web Conference '94: Mosaic and the Web, Chicago (1994).
11. Navarro, A., Fernandez-Valmayor, A., Fernandez-Manjon, B., Sierra, J.L.: Using Analysis, Design and Development of Hypermedia Applications in the Educational Domain. In Ortega, M., Bravo, J. (eds.): Computers and Education: Towards an Interconnected Society. Kluwer Academic Publisher, The Netherlands (2001) 251–260.
12. Halasz, F., Schwartz, M.: The Dexter Hypertext Reference Model. Communications of the ACM 2 (1994) 30–39

X-SHAAD: An XML Implementation for Hypermedia Systems Modeling through SHAAD

David Mérida, Ramón Fabregat, Carlos Arteaga, and Anna Urra

Institut d'Informàtica i Aplicacions (IIiA)
Universitat de Girona (UdG)
17071 Girona, SPAIN
{david.merida, ramon.fabregat, carlos.arteaga,
anna.urra}@udg.es

Abstract. In this paper we present an implementation using XML and Java (X-SHAAD) based on a modular architecture of SHAAD to support a web-based Adaptive Hypermedia System. This architecture considers the hypermedia adaptation along three different "adaptivity dimensions": user characteristics, technology (the network and the user's terminal), and user interaction. At present, web content delivery from server to clients is carried out without taking into account such heterogeneous and diverse characteristics as user preferences, the different capacities of the clients' devices, the different types of access, the state of the network and the current load on the server, all of which directly affect the behavior of web services. The growing use of multimedia objects in the design of web contents further complicates the issue, greatly affecting appropriate contents delivery. Thus, the objective of the system we present here is a treatment of web pages that takes into account such heterogeneity and adapts content with the aim of improving web performance.

1 Introduction

At present, the enormous heterogeneity in terms of types and capacities of access devices, network bandwidth and the needs or preferences of users is not taken into account by a server when providing web content that is rich in images, audio or video. The server will deliver the document requested even if the terminal being used (WebTV, PDAs or mobile telephones) cannot access this content due to various limitations (e.g. display, storage capacity, processing or network access) The page is also provided independently of users' preferences. In addition, the interaction between users in different environments (i.e. commercial, educational, etc.) modifies the requirements made on a requested web page.

To tackle this problem, different alternatives have been developed that allow universal access to any type of material while taking into account certain aspects of this heterogeneity. For example, user preferences [1][2][3]; the capacity of client devices [4][5], access types [6][7], the state of the network [8], or/and current load on the server [9][10], and/or the interaction of users[11].

J.M. Cueva Lovelle et al. (Eds.): ICWE 2003, LNCS 2722, pp. 245–254, 2003.
© Springer-Verlag Berlin Heidelberg 2003

We consider that adaptation can be made along three different adaptivity dimensions (Fig.1):

– *User characteristics*: preferences, background knowledge, navigation activity, etc.
– *Technology*: network state, client's device characteristics, bandwidth, etc.
– *User interaction*: collaborative, cooperative, etc.

One point in this space represents the adaptation to be made for one user, the state of their technology and their interaction with other users. In other words, it represents the adaptation as a function of three dimensions.

$$adaptation = f(user, technological, interaction)$$

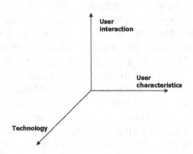

Fig. 1. Adaptativity dimensions

Cannataro in [12] and [13] proposes an architecture where the Application Domain is modeled along three different orthogonal adaptivity dimensions: *User's behavior* (browsing activity, preference, etc.), *Technology* (kind of network, bandwidth, Quality of Service, user's terminal, etc.), and *External environment* (times-spatial location, language, socio-political issues, etc.). The *External environment* dimension differs from the *User interaction* dimension of the SHAAD model. *User interaction* reflects the existing interaction between users which depends on the working environment, i.e. educational hypermedia, on-line information systems, hypermedia for information retrieval, etc. it also reflects the collaborative or cooperative aspects of this interaction.

In [14], SHAAD[1] is defined as a system that takes into account the problem of heterogeneity and tries to adapt the available information dynamically or statically and to deliver it in the most efficient way. It incorporates concepts of adaptability, adaptivity and dynamism summarized from work carried out by Brusilovsky [1] [15], and De Bra [2] [16] [17]. SHAAD represents, through its nested structure, a simple model that takes into account these concepts for hypermedia systems and reflects the necessary mechanisms for an appropriate content delivery.

---

[1] SHAAD is the Spanish acronym for "Adaptable, Adaptive and Dynamic Hypermedia System"

The latest modification of the system takes into account adaptivity dimensions, and is made up of 4 modules (Fig. 2):

– *Mechanisms for characterization of adaptation variables.*
– *Content repository*: data can be provided by different sources.
– *Decision Engine*: the kernel of the system and the place in which the adaptation variables and the available content are evaluated. This module reflects through three decision types the three different "adaptivity dimensions": *user characteristics*, *technology*, and *user interaction*.
– *Content Generator*: includes the adaptation mechanisms decided upon by the Decision Engine

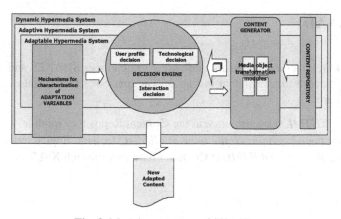

Fig. 2. Modular structure of SHAAD

The SHAAD modular structure allows an independent development of the parts it is made up of. The function of the *Content Generator* is to deliver the requested content, either through a dynamic generation (from the unit elements that make up the web page - on-line generation), or by selection from the various different static versions of this content (previously generated - off-line generation). This generator includes the media object transformation module that will make the necessary transformations of media objects.

In the present work we describe the X-SHAAD, an XML-SHAAD approach dedicated to the analysis, regeneration and adaptation of HTML content, which takes into account some of the variables of the *technological* dimension (the characteristics of the client's device and the current state of the net).

In our research, we are also developing two implementations that consider:

– the *User characteristics* dimension through MAS-PLANG (MultiAgent System PLANG[2])[3]. This is a multiagent system developed to transform the virtual

---

[2] This is a Broadband Communications and Distributed System (BCDS) group project of Girona University for the "Implementation and study of a new generation telematics platform to support open distance learning.

educational environment of USD[3] into an Adaptive Hypermedia System, AHS, which takes into account the student learning style; and
- the *User interaction* dimension through an Adaptive Collaborative Learning Hypermedia System [11] that relates the individual learning and the collaborative learning through an adaptive model.

This paper is organized as follows: In Section 2, we describe the implementation and processes of X-SHAAD. In Section 3, we describe how requested pages are readdressed to X-SHAAD. In Section 4 we show some adaptation examples of the system. Finally, in Section 5 we give some conclusions and describe future work.

2   X-SHAAD

X-SHAAD architecture represents one way to implement SHAAD, and the different modules defined by it are shown in Fig. 3. The processes to take into account in the X-SHAAD are:

- *HTML to XHTML transformation* at the Content Repository module.
- *Obtaining the adaptation profile to be applied* at Decision Engine module.
- *Obtaining the Adapted HTML* at Content Generator through XSLT parser.

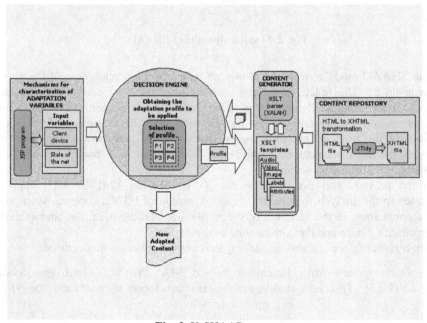

Fig. 3. X-SHAAD structure

---

[3] USD is Spanish acronym of "Teaching Support Unit"

We used XML [18] and XSL for the implementation of X-SHAAD. XSL (eXtensible Stylesheet Language) uses XML notation and is a language for expressing stylesheets. An XSL stylesheet specifies the presentation of a class of XML documents by describing how an instance of the class is transformed into an XML document that uses the formatting vocabulary.

XSL consists of three parts: *XSL Transformations (XSLT)* [19], a language for transforming XML documents; *XML Path Language (XPath)*, an expression language used by XSLT to access or refer to parts of an XML document; and *XSL Formatting Objects (XSL-FO)*, an XML vocabulary for specifying formatting semantics.

2.1 HTML to XHTML Transformation

Currently different browser technologies exist. Some browsers run internet on computers, and some browsers run internet on mobile phones and hand held devices. Each of these handle "bad" marked up HTML documents in a different way. For example, the following HTML could present a problem for them:

```
<html>
<head>
<title> Bad HTML code </title>
<body>
<h1>Bad HTML
</body>
```

Transforming HTML to XHTML solves problems that arise from mal-formed HTML files. XHTML [20] consists of all elements in HTML 4.01 combined with the syntax of XML. HTML was designed to display data and XML was designed to describe data. XML is a markup language where everything has to be marked up correctly, which results in "well-formed" documents

Some of the most important characteristics of XHTML are as follows: XHTML elements must be properly nested, XHTML documents must be well-formed, tag names must be in lowercase, all XHTML elements must be closed and attribute values must be quoted.

In X-SHAAD, for one time only, HTML to XHTML transformation is carried out beforehand through JTidy [21]. It is an open source code program that allows HTML files to be analyzed and to obtain a well formed XHTML. Then, we can apply XSL and its tools to make the transformation.

2.2 Obtaining the Adaptation Profile to Apply

In order to check the operation of the X-SHAAD, the user specifies values of input variables by means of a web interface. The assignment is carried out through a given values list. Table 1 shows the variables considered in this implementation and the set of possible values for each variable. X-SHAAD's Decision Engine infers the adequate profile for each situation and determines a set of adaptation mechanisms will be applied to the requested web page in the Content Generator. Table 2 shows various adaptation mechanisms to be applied to each media object.

In the current implementation, different static versions of each multimedia object exist in the server to simulate the adaptation mechanisms. When a profile is applied, the directory that contains the elements to send is determined. Table 3 shows two system application examples with the corresponding adaptation mechanisms to be applied.

Table 1. Variables considered and possible value

Variable considered	Possible value
Screen area	High
	Medium (640x480)
	Low (PDA)
Color	Color
	Gray Scale
Video	Yes
	No
Sound	Yes
	No
State of the network	Free
	Semi-busy
	Busy

Table 2. Adaptation mechanisms to be applied to each media object.

Media object	Adaptation mechanism
Image (*)	Image in original size
	Reduced size image to 1/2
	Reduced size image to 1/4
	No image
Video (*)	Original video
	Sequence of 10 images
	Sequence of 5 images
	No video
Sound	Audio file is sent
	Audio file is not sent

(*) Both of these take the values that are indicated in Table 1.

Table 3. Application examples of X-SHAAD operation

Screen Area	Color	Video	Sound	State of Network	Adaptation Mechanism to be applied
High	Color	Yes	Yes	Semi-busy	Image: Reduced image to 1/2 Video: Sequence of 10 images Sound: Audio file is sent
Low	Grayscale	Yes	No	Free	Image: Reduced image to 1/4 Video: Sequence of 5 images Sound: Audio file is not sent

2.3 Obtaining the Adapted HTML

The adaptation of requested HTML files is carried out through the XSLT templates that are applied on obtained XHTML files (section 2.1)

From these XHTML files and using XSL / XSLT, transformations can be implemented in two ways:

- Defining, on a unique XSLT template, all profiles that can be applied to the XHTML document. This template will include as many conditional branches as there are profiles. In order to consider a new profile, a new branch in this template must be introduced.
- Defining individual templates, one for each media object and considering profiles inside these templates. Taking a new profile into account means modifying each

template individually. Considering a new media object implies generating the corresponding XSLT template. This treatment, carried out on individual templates, allows for easier maintenance. It has been selected for our proposal.

Now, to apply an XSLT template to an XHTML file and to introduce parameters, a stylesheet processor should be used, for example SAXON[22] or XALAN[23]. This processor is used to check that the document is well formed and validates against the corresponding DTD and it is in charge of applying the stylesheet XSL, etc.

SAXON, is a processor written in Java with its own parser, although it can use an external one. XALAN, from the Apache XML project, is a free tool written in Java that needs a Java virtual machine (JVM) and an XML parser to work. Xerces is the parser used and the corresponding file (xerces.jar) is included in the distribution.

Since we use an Apache server, we have used XALAN to implement our analyzer.

3 Readdressing of Requested Pages

The X-SHAAD execution is carried out on-line. When receiving the petition, the requested page is analyzed. If the petition is an HTML file, X-SHAAD is executed and the page obtained is adapted to the particular profile.

The module *mod_rewrite* of Apache server is used [24] to do this. It provides virtually all of the functions required to manipulate URLs, and works in most situations. Consequently, *mod_rewrite* can be used to solve all sorts of URL-based problems. We considered two directives of this module:

- *RewriteEngine*. This directive enables or disables the runtime rewriting engine. If it is set to off, then *mod_rewrite* does no runtime processing
- *RewriteRule*. This directive allows us to write the rules that will readdress the requested URLs. The basic syntax of this directive is:

RewriteRule url-pattern url-new

The *url-pattern* is a regular expression that is applied to the current URL. The current URL may not be the URL requested originally, because any number of rules could have already matched and altered it. The *url-new* argument is the string that is substituted for the original URL matched by the url-pattern.

The module activation *mod_rewrite* of the Apache is carried out through the file httpd.conf. The code below shows part of this file, in which the *mod_rewrite* module is activated, including the rules to apply with the *RewriteRule* directive:

```
<IfModule mod_rewrite.c>
RewriteEngine On
    RewriteRule /adaptador/web/([^\.]+)/([^/\.]+)\.(html|htm)
    /adaptador/jsp/adaptar.jsp?&PATH=$1&XML=$2 [R]
</IfModule>
```

Where:
  [^\ ]   : any text that doesn't contain point + /
  PATH   : requested URL address, without the name of the HTML / HTM file
  XML   : name of requested page –HTML / HTM

If the requested page coincides with some of rules specified through the *RewriteRule*, a JSP program is executed that will trigger the processor of style sheets to carry out the adaptation (Xalan). The following command shows the sentence of Xalan execution.

```
java org.apache.xalan.xslt.Process -IN prova.xml -XSL
prova.xsl -OUT prova.out  -PARAM perfil 2
```

4 Adaptation Examples

In this section we describe some adaptations. For this experiment, a web site was designed with the purpose of showing how X-SHAAD operates. Table 4 shows the different input variable values considered and the resulting web page.

Table 4. Application examples of X-SHAAD operation

Screen Area	Color	Video	Sound	State of Network	Adaptation Mechanism to be applied
High	Color	No	No	Free	Figure 4a
Medium	Grayscale	Yes	No	Free	Figure 4b
Low	Color	Yes	No	Semi-busy	Figure 4c
Medium	Color	Yes	Yes	Busy	Figure 4d

5 Conclusion

We believe that adaptation can be made in three different "adaptivity dimensions": *technology, user characteristics* and *user interaction*. In this paper, we considered a particular implementation that takes into account the *technological* dimension.

X-SHAAD shows the feasibility of adapting the requested web page according to a series of input variables. The main advantage of the proposed approach is its simplicity. At the same time, it represents a way of implementing SHAAD architecture.

In this way, the final objective is to use SHAAD to obtain an integral system that represents the Adaptive Hypermedia System, and completely takes into account the problem of heterogeneity and independent technologies used to implement it. In this case, XML and Java are a simple way to implement and maintain X-SHAAD.

Further work in the future will include more elaborated profiles for X-SHAAD in order to obtain an integrated support for adapted content delivery. Furthermore, the different "adaptivity dimensions" have so far been considered separately, and the results of these studies must be integrated into one system.

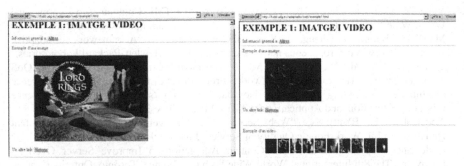

Fig. 4a.   Fig. 4b.

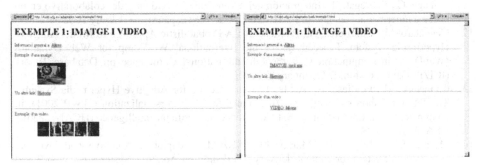

Fig. 4c.   Fig. 4d.

Fig. 4. Web page examples

Acknowledgments. This work has been partially financed by CICYT TEL-99-0976 and Galecia project (UE-SOCRATES-MINERVA).

References

1. Brusilovsky, P.: Adaptive Hypermedia. User Modelling and User-Adapted Interaction 11: 87–110, Kluwer Academic Publishers, Netherlands, 2001.
2. De Bra, P.: Design Issues in Adaptive Web-Site Development. Proceedings of the 2nd Workshop on Adaptive Systems and User Modelling on the WWW, Canada, 1999.
3. Peña, C.I., Marzo, J.L., de la Rosa, J.L.: Intelligent Agents in a Teaching and Learning Environment on the Web. 2nd IEEE International Conference on Advanced Learning Technologies (ICALT2002), Kazan (Russia), September 9–12, 2002, ISBN 0-473-08801-0.
4. Perkis, A.: "UMA Project – Universal Multimedia Access from wired or wireless systems". NTNU – Department of Telecommunications
5. Campadello, S., Helin, H., Koskimies, O., Misikangas, P., Mäkelä, M., Raatikainen, K.: Using Mobile and Intelligent Agents to Support Nomadic Users. 6th International Conference on Intelligence in Networks (ICIN2000), Bordeaux, France, 2000.

6.   Yang, Y., Chen, J., Zhang, H.: Adaptive Delivery of HTML Contents. 9th International World Wide Web Conference – The Web: The Next Generation, Amsterdam, 2000.
7.   Ma, W-Y., Bedner, I., Chang, G., Kuchinsky, A., Zhang, H.: "A framework for adaptive content delivery in heterogeneous network environments". Hewlett-Packard Laboratories.
8.   Shaha, N., Dessai, N., Parashar, M. : Multimedia Content Adaptation for QoS Management over Heterogeneous Networks. Proceedings of the International Conference on Internet Computing (IC 2001), Nevada, USA, pp 642–648, Computer Science Research, Education, and Applications (CSREA) Press, June 2001.
9.   Abdelzaher, T., Bhatti, N.: "Web Server QoS Management by Adaptive Content Delivery". In Int. Workshop on Quality of Service, June 1999
10. Abdelzaher, T., Bhatti, N.: "Web Content Adaptation to Improve Server Overload Behavior". The 8th International World Wide Web Conference, Toronto, Ontario, Canada, 1999
11. Arteaga, C., Fabregat, R.: Integración del aprendizaje individual y del colaborativo en un sistema hipermedia adaptativo. JENUI 2002. Cáceres (España), 10–12 july 2002
12. Cannataro, M., Cuzzocrea, A., Pugliese, A.: A Probabilistic Approach to Model Adaptive Hypermedia System. Proceedings of the International Workshop for Web Dynamics (WebDyn), in conjunction with the 8th International Conference on Database Theory (ICDT 2001), London, UK, January 3, 2001.
13. Cannataro, M., Pugliese, A.: A Flexible Architecture for Adaptive Hypermedia Systems. The Int. Workshop on Intelligent Techniques for Web Personalization (ITWP 2001), in conjunction with International Joint Conference on Artificial Intelligence (IJCAI), Seattle, USA, 2001.
14. Mérida, D., Fabregat, R., Marzo, J.L.: SHAAD: Adaptable, Adaptive and Dynamic Hypermedia System for content delivery. Workshop on Adaptive Systems for Web Based Education (WASWE2002), Málaga (España), 28 may 2002.
15. Brusilovsky, P.: Methods and Techniques of Adaptive Hypermedia. User Modeling and User-Adapted Interaction, Vol. 6, pp. 87–129, Kluwer academic publishers, 1996.
16. De Bra, P., Calvi, L.: Towards a Generic Adaptive Hypermedia System. Proc. 2nd Workshop on Adaptive Hypertext and Hypermedia, Pittsburgh, pp. 5–11, 1998.
17. De Bra, P., Houben, G.J., Wu., H.: AHAM: A Dexter-based Reference Model for Adaptive Hypermedia. Proceedings of ACM Hypertext' 99, Darmstadt, pp. 147–156, 1999.
18. Bray, T., Paoli, J., Sperberg-McQueen, C. M., Maler, E.: Extensible Markup Language (XML) 1.0 (Second Edition). W3C Recommendation, 6 October 2000. http://www.w3.org/TR/2000/REC-xml-20001006
19. Clark, J.: XSL Transformations (XSLT) Version 1.0. W3C Recommendation, 1999. http://www.w3.org/TR/xslt
20. Pemberton, S., et al.: XHTML 1.0: The Extensible HyperText Markup Language. W3C Recommendation, 26 January 2000. http://www.w3.org/TR/2000/REC-xhtml1-20000126
21. Tidy - http://www.w3.org/People/Raggett/tidy
22. Saxon Version 6.3 - http://users.iclway.co.uk/mhkay/saxon/saxon6.3/index.html#Scope
23. Xalan-Java Version 2.3.1 - http://xml.apache.org/xalan-j/index.html
24. Apache HTTP Server Version 1.3, mod_rewrite Module Information. http://httpd.apache.org/docs/mod/mod_rewrite.html

Semi-automatic Assessment Process in a Ubiquitous Environment for Language Learning

M. Paredes[1], M. Ortega[2], P.P. Sánchez-Villalón[2], M.A. Redondo[2], C. Bravo[2], and J. Bravo[2]

[1] Escuela Superior de Ciencias Experimentales y Tecnología,
Universidad Rey Juan Carlos
28933 Móstoles, Madrid
m.paredes@escet.urjc.es
[2] Escuela Superior de Informática, Paseo de la Universidad s/n,
Universidad de Castilla La Mancha
13071 Ciudad Real
Manuel.Ortega@uclm.es

Abstract. This work presents a research on the methods and mechanisms necessary to bring the Information and Communication Technologies in the traditional classroom. This will be achieved by putting collaborative and Ubiquitous Computing paradigms together to integrate both fields into the educational environment. As a study case we have developed a system for language learning, in particular English as a Foreign Language (EFL), through a composition writing activity in group.

1 AULA: A Ubiquitous Computation Environment for the Collaborative Composition of Documents

At present, ubiquitous applications and systems applied in the environment of the classroom are scarce and they provide little collaborative work in group support. The existing applications or systems [1-5] satisfy some scenario needs that we suggest, but not all. These applications do not satisfy our domain's needs because of two reasons: the application is not sensitive to the user context and the collaborative tools do not support the proposals discussion process.

The AULA system is composed of: a projection whiteboard and other edition whiteboard, a data base server, the Localization Manager (providing context-aware to the system), the Session Coordinator and the mobile devices (PDA) (each student has his own PDA). The communication technologies used are: a wireless network (RF), ultrasonic and infrared communications. The system architecture is described with more detail in [6]. When the class starts, the teacher indicates the main subject of the document and other characteristics or properties that he considers appropriate to the students. After this first phase, a brainstorming process about the composition subject starts. Now the student can make use of collaborative tools (see Figure 1 and 2). The system structures all the information resulting from the brainstorming process into the

J.M. Cueva Lovelle et al. (Eds.): ICWE 2003, LNCS 2722, pp. 255–258, 2003.
© Springer-Verlag Berlin Heidelberg 2003

aspects, which are broken down into several ideas. The process of discussion finishes when the group of students get to an agreement, accepting some aspects and ideas suggested and refusing others, through a polling process provided by the system.

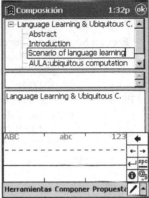

Fig. 1. Electronic mail tool.   **Fig. 2.** Inserting & proposing an Aspect.

2   Assessment Tools for the Teacher

AULA system offers help for the teacher with some tools accessible through a desktop PC. These tools help the teacher to do several tasks, such as: defining parameters about the type of composition, carrying out a follow-up study of the construction process and evaluating the students and the group. The collaborative activity closer to composition writing we can think of in a typical class of English is one based on writing projects in groups. Here, the teacher carries out the evaluation through a postproduction process, consisting of the teachers establishing a dialogue with the students or just analyzing the results. The teacher evaluates the activity marking two aspects: the resulting document(s) provided by the group of students and the teacher's memory and ability to infer about every student's performance in the project development process. This system of evaluation is really complex for the teacher.

In the composition processes, this evaluation phase is one of the hardest due to the emotional implication. Evidently, in this situation teachers wonder about this type of questions: Who has suggested this particular idea? Has this student taken part in the process of discussion actively? To what extent? Did such a student contribute proposals with aspects and ideas to the group?. We should keep in mind the indicators of effective collaborative learning as shown in Soller [7]. AULA system traces and records the students' actions and through a synthesis process it can provide answers to such questions. This way, the teacher will receive help to analyze questions such as: the progress of each student in their language development (globally as well as in particular areas), the student's reaction to errors made by other members of the group or the history participation of a student in previous activities.

This synthesis process generates some conclusions about the working process and solution provided by the group (see Figure 3). The system infers these conclusions based on two types of information: the traces (the actions carried out by the students) and the information about the quality of the solution. This last information is provided by the teacher. The teacher analyzes the document suggested by the group and gives his/her opinion about aspects such as the grammatical accuracy or the communication ability. The inference system consists in linking attributes isolated from the user with processes of action. These processes of action are blocks of information, which define communicative characteristics of the user and of the group in the activity of writing compositions.

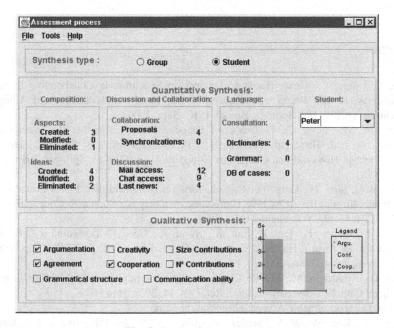

Fig. 3. Synthesis process result.

The process of synthesis is composed of two subprocesses: quantitative synthesis and qualitative synthesis as a way in which other systems have developed the assessment process [8]. On the one hand, the subprocess of quantitative synthesis shows information about the times that a student has performed some actions, such as the number of proposals (aspects or ideas) sent, modified or erased by a student, the number of times that a student has accessed the email facility, etc. On the other hand, the subprocess of qualitative synthesis informs about the characteristics of a student's profile, such as whether the student was active and decisive during the composition activity, or on the contrary, if the student was passive and hesitant in their proposals, whether the student took part in the processes of discussion and put proposals forward and succeeded, or else, if the student did not take part in the group discussions. We can make the process of synthesis (quantitative as well as qualitative) for each student or for the group.

In order to carry out this individual and group synthesis process, we need to establish a mechanism which structures all the information generated throughout the composition process. The actions carried out by the user about the written composition and use of tools (collaborative as well as language tools) are structured in user's traces. Therefore, every time the student executes an action, in the database of the system an entry is created and the student's trace is written. Finally, the teacher chats with the group about the conclusions and the corrections of the composition.

Acknowledgements. This work was partially supported by the Junta de Comunidades de Castilla – La Mancha and the Ministerio de Ciencia y Tecnología in the Projects PBI-02-026 and TIC2002-01387.

References

1. Roth, J., Unger, C.; Using Handheld Devices in Synchronous Collaborative Scenarios., Proceedings of the Second International Symposium on Handheld and Ubiquitous Computing, pp.187–199, Springer. Bristol, U.K., Sept. 2000.
2. Baldonado, M., Steve, C., Gwizdka, J., Paepcke, A.; Notable: At the Intersection of Annotations and Handheld Technology., Proceedings of the Second International Symposium on Handheld and Ubiquitous Computing, pp.100–113, Springer. Bristol, U.K., Sept. 2000.
3. Myres, B.A., Stiel, H., Gargiulo, R.; Collaboration Using Multiple PDAs Connected to a PC., Proceedings of the ACM 1998 conference on Computer Supported Cooperative Work, pp. 285–294, Seattle, Washington, USA, 1998.
4. Danesh, A., Inkpen, K., Lau, F., Shu, K., Booth K.; Geney™: Designing a Collaborative Activity for the Palm™ Handheld Computer., Proceedings of the SIGCHI'01, pp. 388–395, Seattle, Washington, USA, 2001.
5. Zurita, G., Nussbaum, M.; Mobile CSCL Applications Supported by Mobile Computing., Pontificial Catholic University of Chile, Ret. Feb. 14, 2002 from http://julita.usask.ca/mable/Accepted.htm#Submission6
6. Ortega, M., Redondo, M.A, Paredes, M, Sánchez-Villalón, P.P., Bravo, C., Bravo, J.; Ubiquitous Computing and Collaboration: New paradigms in the classroom of the 21st Century., Computers and Education: Towards an Interconnected Society, M. Ortega and J. Bravo (Eds.), Kluwer Academic Publishers (2001), pp. 261–273.
7. Soller A.L.; Supporting Social Interaction in an Intelligent Collaborative Learning System, International Journal of Artificial Intelligence in Education, Volume 12, pp. 40–62 (2001).
8. Barros, B., and Verdejo, M.F.; An approach to analyse collaboration when shared structured workspaces are used for carrying out group learning processes., Proceedings of Artificial Intelligence in Education. IOS Press, S. Lajoie and M. Vivet (Eds.), pp. 449–456. (1999).

Mobile EC Service Applications by Privacy Management

Whe Dar Lin

The Overseas Chinese Institute of Technology
Dept of Information Management,
No. 100, Chiao Kwang Road Taichung 40721, Taiwan

Abstract. In this article, we shall propose an efficient privacy management for mobile EC service applications. The EC service applications embrace the problem of both privacy and authentication. We consider the mobile station on the broad contest of networking, from the wireless devices through which network communication occur to the EC service application being communicated. The privacy problem is concerned with the task of preventing an opponent from extracting message information from the communication channel on EC service applications. On the other hand, mobile station requests EC service applications on visit network authentication deals with preventing the injection of false data into channel. We can avoid employing public key cryptography in the using privacy EC service applications phase since to keep the computation cost down.

1 Introduction

A mobile EC service applications system comprises the wireless network that closely link very aspect of EC service applications and security issues. Basic operation such as authentication, access control, plus privacy management use for mobile station. The privacy managements using in confidentiality of the identity, privacy of the certificate user the state necessity of management when the situation is using the dining cryptographer problem for unconditional sender and recipient untraceability, electronic voting scheme, anonymous group discussions, untraceable electronic mail, untraceable mobile agent. [1, 2, 6, 8, 9, 11]

When mobile user roams between different visit network uses the different random name, so mobile user can keep location privacy. The structure of our paper is organized as follows: In section 2, based on the wireless communication system architecture, we shall propose our privacy management and authentication scheme. In section 3, the security issue shall be considered are proposed. Section 4, we addresses the conclusion on performance.

2 The Proposed an Efficient Privacy Management

Let M denote a mobile station MS, V denote the visit network VN of MS, H denote the home network HN of MS, and X->Y : Z denote the event that a sender X sends a message Z to a receiver Y. Let $k_{h,v}$ be the secret key shared by H and V, HD represents home identification number. Let $k_{h,i}$ be the secret key shared by H and $M(ID_i)$, $\{m\}_{eh}$

J.M. Cueva Lovelle et al. (Eds.): ICWE 2003, LNCS 2722, pp. 259–262, 2003.
© Springer-Verlag Berlin Heidelberg 2003

denotes the ciphertext for m encrypted by some public key cryptosystem using a public key e_h, and $(m)_k$ denotes the ciphertext for m encrypted using the secret key k of some secure symmetrical cryptosystem. Let f_1 be a secret one-way function known only to H and M. Let f_2 be a secret one-way function for use in a privacy EC service applications area known only to V and M.

The request message for privacy EC service applications protocol is as follows:

Step 1: M->V: HD, N_1, $\{ID_i, T, T_{expire}, Cert_i\}_{e_h}$

Step 2: V->H: N_1, $\{ID_i, T, T_{expire}, Cert_i\}_{e_h}$

Step 3: H->V: $(d_M, T_{expire}, D_M)_{k_{h,v}}$, N_1, $(C, T_{expire}, E_M)_{k_{h,i}}$

Step 4: V->M: N_1, $(C, T_{expire}, E_M)_{k_{h,i}}$

In step 1, M sets the time stamp T, An expiration time T_{expire}, and the certificate $Cert_i = (ID_i, T, T_{expire})_{K_{h,i}}$

In step 2, V transfers a nonce word N_1 and the received encrypted message sent to H.

In step 3, H computes

$$d_M = f_1(k_{h,i}*V), \quad E_M = x_h * f_1(k_{h,i}*T_{expire}) + cC \bmod Q \tag{1}$$

$$D_M = g^{x_h*f_1(k_{h,i}*T_{expire})+f_1(k_{h,i}*V)}C^C \bmod P \tag{2}$$

In step 4, M can check the EC service request message and see if the following equation holds or not.

$$g^{E_M} = y_h^{f_1(k_{h,i}*T_{expire})}C^C \bmod P \tag{3}$$

$$where \ g^{E_M} = g^{x_h*f_1(K_{h,i}*T_{expire})+cC}$$

$$= (g^{x_h})^{f_1(K_{h,i}*T_{expire})}(g^c)^C = y_h^{f_1(K_{h,i}*T_{expire})}C^C$$

The using privacy EC service applications protocol is following:

Step 1:M->V: NEW-ID, T

Step 2:V->M: R

Step 3:M->V: B, J

In step 1, M computes NEW-ID as follows:

$$NEW\text{-}ID = f_2(f_1(k_{h,i}*V)) \tag{4}$$

In step 2, V sends R (R= $g^r \bmod P$) to M where the challenge R is used for freshness.

In step 3, M computes B= $g^b \bmod P$, $k_s = R^b \bmod P$, and

$$J=E_M+f_1(k_{h,i}*V)+b* f_2(f_1(k_{h,i}*V)*T_{expire})*T*R \bmod Q, \tag{5}$$

Upon receiving the message, V uses d_M to compute $f_2(d_M)$ and gets D_M to verify B and L according to the equation

$$g^J = D_M * B^{f_2(d_M*T_{expire})*T*R} \bmod P \tag{6}$$

If the above equation holds, then the mobile station (M) can use the privacy EC service applications on the visit domain V.

3 Security Considerations

Proposition: The visit network can authenticate the mobile station and support the privacy management on mobile EC service applications.

Proof:

The visit network can check the privacy EC service request holder to see if the following equation holds or not.

$$g^J = D_M * B^{f_2(d_M * T_{expire}) * T * R} \bmod P \, , where \tag{7}$$

$$g^J = g^{E_M + f_1(k_{h,i} * V) + b * f_2(f_1(k_{h,i} * V) * T_{expire}) * T * R}$$

$$= D_M * g^{b * f_2(d_M * T_{expire}) * T * R} = D_M * (B)^{f_2(d_M * T_{expire}) * T * R}$$

Even if some forger can generate (B', J') by getting the random number r as a challenge but the forger still needs to solve the equation $g^{J'} = D_M * B'^{f_2(d_M * T_{expire}) * T * R} \bmod P$. However, the difficulty of solving this problem is as hard as the discrete logarithm problem even the attacker has D_M. Therefore, (B, J) cannot be forged, the authentication of the NEW-ID is well established. The intruder could give (D'$_M$, E'$_M$, d'$_M$, C') to forge a valid anonymous channel verification data (D_M, E_M, d_M, C). If the anonymous channel verification data is forged (D'$_M$, E'$_M$, d'$_M$, C') and satisfies $D'_M = g^{x_h * f_1(k_{h,i} * T_{expire}) + d'_M} C'^{C'} \bmod P$ then the forged anonymous channel verification data is valid. This is exactly the discrete logarithm problem so the intruder will fail. The computations will run in exponential time.

In using privacy EC service applications protocol, when MS visits VN nodes $(V_1, V_2, ..., V_n)$, HN deducts a fixed amount of money from MS's account, then the HN broadcasts $(d_{M,1}, T_{expire}, D_{M,1})_{Kh,v1}$, $(d_{M,2}, T_{expire}, D_{M,2})_{Kh,v2}$, ..., $(d_{M,n}, T_{expire}, D_{M,n})_{Kh,vn}$ to the VN nodes $(V_1, V_2, ..., V_n)$, where $d_{M,j} = f_1(K_{h,i} * V_j)$, $D_{M,j} = g^{x_h * f_1(A' * k_{h,i} * T_{expire}) + d_{M,j}} C^C \bmod P$, $K_{h,i}$ is the secret key shared with ID_i and the home domain, V_j is the visit domain ID number and f_1 is the secret one way function.

When the VN nodes $(V_1, V_2, ..., V_n)$ receive the message $(d_{M,j}, T_{expire}, D_{M,j})_{Kh,vj}$, V_j computes the NEW-ID$_j$ = $f_2(d_{M,j})$ and stores (NEW-ID$_j$, T_{expire}, $D_{M,j}$) in the V_j user database.

The V_j user database stores (NEW-ID$_j$, T_{expire}, $D_{M,j}$). There is no information about the user ID_i.

    1: NEW-ID$_j$=$f_2(d_{M,j})$
    2: $d_{M,j} = f_1(k_{h,i} * V_j)$

There is no information about the user ID_i, the secret key $k_{h,i}$ is only known to HN and user ID_i. No attacker can get $k_{h,i}$ from $d_{M,j}$ because the hash function f(x) is assumed secure since it is infeasible to determine x such that f(x)=y for a given y. Moreover, f_1 is a one-way hash function known only to HN and the mobile station (MS). The attackers do not know the hash function $f_1(x)$. In fact, in our proposed scheme, the user ID_i is kept unknown to any attacker and V_j.

Therefore, the MS (ID_i) can use NEW-ID$_j$ to roam VN(V_j). The different IDs used in different VNs maintain the anonymity of location service.

This is exactly the discrete logarithm problem so the intruder fails. It will run in exponential time. As mentioned above |P| >= 512, that this attack is not successful in terms of execution time.

4 Conclusion

In this article, we propose an efficient privacy management for mobile EC service applications to consider several security characteristics of wireless network. The most important feature of our proposed protocol is its untraceability issue. In our proposed method, the possible wireless network vulnerabilities that have been protected privacy management and EC service application of authorized mobile user.

Mobile station only computes addition, multiplication and hashing implement in hardware, which can satisfy the requirement of low computational, and communication cost due to the limited power of handset application. We can avoid employing public key cryptography since we regard the computation requirements as low. Our method satisfies the requirement for EC service applications contain privacy, secure, reliable, transparent and scalable for mobile stations.

References

[1] B. Pfitzmann. Breaking an efficient privacy management, Advances in Cryptology: Proc. EuroCrypt'94, Lecture Notes in Computer Science, 950, springer, Berlin, 1995,pp. 332–340.
[2] C. Park, K. Itoh, and K. Kurosawa, Efficient privacy management and all /nothing election scheme, Advances in Cryptology : Proc. EuroCrypt'93 , Lecture Notes in Computer Science, 765, Springer, Berlin, 1993, pp.248–259.
[3] D. Chaum, Untraceable electronic mail, return address, and digital pseudonyms, Commun. ACM 24 (2) (1981) 84–88.
[4] D. Chaum, The dining cryptographers problem: unconditional sender and recipient untraceability, J. Cryptology 1 (1988) 65–75.
[5] D. Naccache, and D. M. Raihi, Cryptographic Smart Cards, IEEE Micro, June 1996, pp. 14–25.
[6] D . Samfat, R Molva, N, Asokan, Untraceability in mobile net works, in: Proc. First ACM Int. Conf. On Mobile Computing and Network , November 1995, pp. 26–36
[7] ETSI: GSM recommendations: GSM 01.02-12.21, February, 1993, Release 92.
[8] L. Jianwei, W. Yumin, A user authentication protocol for digital mobile communication network, in : IEEE International Symposium on Personal , Indoor and Mobile Radio Communications, 1995, pp. 608–612.
[9] M. Beller, Y.Yacobi, Fully-fledged two-way public key authentication and key agreement for low-cost terminals, Electronic Letters 29(11)(1993) 999–1101.
[10] Whe Dar Lin, "EC Transactions Use Different Web-based Platforms," Lecture Notes in Computer Science, 2003'
[11] W. S. Juang, C. L. Lei, C.Y. Chang, Privacy management and authentication in mobile EC service applications, Computer communications, 22(1999), pp. 1502–1511.

User Interfaces: A Proposal for Automatic Adaptation

Montserrat Sendín[1], Jesús Lorés[1], Francisco Montero[2], Víctor López[2], and
Pascual González[2]

[1] Computer Science and Industrial Engineering Department, University of Lleida, Spain
{msendin, jesus}@eup.udl.es
[2] Higher Polytechnic School of Albacete, University of Castilla-La Mancha, Spain
{fmontero, victor}@info-ab.uclm.es

Abstract. In previous works we have been developing a tourism support prototype that offers a proven solution for aspects of multi-platform, personalisation and spatial-awareness. The aim of this paper is to analyse its drawbacks and limitations, and to propose an architecture that solves these problems relying on the principle of abstraction. It consists of a reflexive architecture based on models, and component-oriented, that allows specifying the user interface independently of the rest of the implementation. Thus, developers only have to focus on modelling the functionality of the application –which resides at a base level-, leaving the interface to a meta level, constructing thereby *applications without apparent interface*. The generation of the UI is not carried out until run-time, applying an automatic translation from abstract interaction components to concrete ones according to the device and the user's features and current state.

1 Introduction

Mobile computing offers the possibility of dramatically expanding the versatility of computers, by bringing them off the desktop and into new and unique contexts. As it grows, it offers a wider variety of devices suitable for multiple and varied *contexts of use*[1]. However, to take advantage of all these new possibilities, UI designers are forced to accommodate a growing variety of devices and contexts of use, as well as to solve any contextual or environmental changes, while preserving usability. Only that way it will be possible to create UIs that get together all of the demanded features: adaptivity, context-awareness, device independence and usability.

In this line, what we intend is to exploit the possibilities of mobile computing in the tourism sector. Our specific aim is to develop a generic tourism support tool that gets together all of the previously mentioned features, applicable to any tourist enclave. Nevertheless, our experimentation laboratory has been until now the mountainous zone of Montsec. It is an area of outstanding natural and cultural wealth, situated in the western sector of the Catalan Pre-Pyrenees (province of Lleida).

The previous prototype we developed –tested and published in [1] -, already solved the adaptation to the device and to the user's profile, by providing a specific template

---

[1] It includes a set of environment parameters that describe a particular context in which a determined user is realizing a concrete task.

J.M. Cueva Lovelle et al. (Eds.): ICWE 2003, LNCS 2722, pp. 263–266, 2003.
© Springer-Verlag Berlin Heidelberg 2003

in XSL (eXtensible Style Language), adapted to each context of use. However, that solution had strong limitations. On one hand, it is a method notably inflexible and difficult to maintain. On the other hand, it is necessary to diversify and extend the offer of pre-designed templates for each new demand, turning this task into a repetitive, complex and hard process that makes it difficult to preserve the consistency between the different interfaces. This approach could only be appropriate if the set of devices or of adaptation possibilities to different profiles taken into consideration was quite restricted. However, if we do not want it to fall quickly into disuse, we cannot ignore the increasing availability of diverse devices. It is accordingly necessary to make the accommodation to different platforms easier and more flexible, and thereby the generation of suitable UIs.

We think that many of the portability problems in UI development are caused by the low abstraction level at which design decisions are made, resulting in lack of overview in the design process. The abstraction level is the key, and also the base of programming paradigms, such as the *component-oriented paradigm* [2]. This paradigm proposes implementing systems by means of the incorporation of components adaptable to different contexts and formalised through *models*, as in a *model-based technique* -see [3] to look up a complete overview of some of the best-known model-based techniques. This is the design and implementation base that is proposed in this paper: the provision of as many concrete components of interface as necessary, which will be automatically selected according to the user's technology (device) and preferences. The rest of the application will work making use of the abstract interface components, obtaining therefore *generic UIs*[2], and accordingly reusable in other applications. The translation of abstract to concrete components, and also the relation between functionality and interface are situated at a meta level corresponding to a typical *reflexive architecture*.

2 Our Proposal

2.1 Environment Recognition

As a tourism support tool, our system also has to solve all kind of spatial consultations, thus providing the *spatial-awareness* property. In order to offer environment recognition, a detailed spatial model from the real world is required, which has to be built and integrated into the architecture.

The modelling is being solved using an object-oriented approach - this makes the adaptation to each particular case easier, following the concept of ontology-, in an XML-based language. Henceforth, we will name this model Augmented World model (AW-m). It provides an integrated and homogeneous view of the data.

The automatic extraction of the objects in the model that may interest the user – according to his profile, state and current circumstances- with regard to position, is going to be delegated to a spatial data managing module: the *Nexus platform* [4]. We can define this as a global and open infrastructure, sufficiently versatile to contact to any spatial-awareness application –independently of its functionality-, provided that

---

[2] UI whose aspects can vary in different devices, while its functionality prevails in all of them.

the application works with XML-based languages to define the AW-m, and also with XML-based query languages to formulate the queries.

The essential components of the AW-m are the static geographical objects (in the Montsec case: castles, towers, monasteries, rural areas, churches, etc), the location information of mobile objects (the zone visitors), and also virtual objects which provide additional information or services to Nexus users. The answer to a query consists of a list of matching objects in a particular zone. For example, a list of the nearest restaurants with their respective attributes –address and menu-, if it is lunchtime, or a list of the castles that can be visited in the zone, according to attributes such as historical period and visiting timetable. This would be suitable if our user had a certain preference for History. Other parameters that also take part in the adaptation are, for example, the information level required by the user, if he already knows a term related to the information -such as the features of the Romanesque style of a church-, the number of similar visits already realised, etc.

The Nexus platform is currently being developed at the University of Stuttgart [4]. For more details about it or how to join our prototype, consult [1].

2.2 The Reflexive Architecture

Under an object-oriented reflexive architecture view [5], [6], a system is considered to be integrated by two parts: the application part and the reflexive part, which reside at two different levels: the base level and the meta level, respectively. The application is represented at the base level and is manipulated by the meta level. Both levels are connected causally, so that changes in the base level are reflected in the meta level.

Our objective consists of developing a system where the part destined to contemplate the interface and the part destined to the functionality are independent. At the base level, following the abstraction principle, there is no conception of interface. The interface will be taken on in the meta level, at run-time, fixing which concrete interface components will represent the functionality described by the abstract ones, depending on the device and the user's profile. Other responsibilities of the meta level will be the interaction validation, the aid to the user in his actions, etc, in a transparent way for the user. Following the *component-oriented programming approach* [2], the base level can be formed, independently of its functionality, by a control structure similar to a *states machine*, where each state is associated with a dialogue, identified in the design phase. Fig. 1 represents the whole idea.

With respect to the required models, the ones that we consider relevant for applying the proposed architecture to tourism, are the next ones: user model, task model, dialogue model, presentation model and platform model. The AW-m described previously corresponds to the domain model.

In device-based UIs the connections between the platform model and the presentation model acquire crucial importance, because they tell us how the constraints posed by the various platforms will influence the UI visual appearance. In short, they determine the transition from abstract components to concrete ones, decision that depends in a great deal on the final device to interact with.

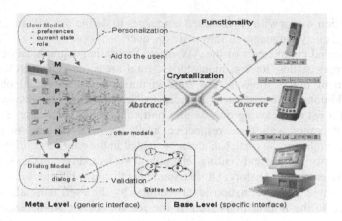

Fig. 1. Reflexive architecture and distribution of responsibilities

3   Conclusions

This paper proposes the construction of an *application without apparent interface*. As happens in the hardware elaboration, we can dispose of concrete interface components available for selection, leaving the interface generation at run-time. At this moment the suitable crystallization from abstract to concrete components occurs, making use of a reflexive architecture. One of the advantages of this mechanism is that the developer only has to focus on modelling the functionality of the application, leaving the interface to a meta level. This will be, for definition, reusable.

The use of abstract models to describe the UI makes the development of usable UIs to mobile devices substantially easier, providing an automated support that allows designers to overcome the challenges posed by mobile computing.

References

1. Sendín, M., Lorés, J., Solà, J.: Making our Multi-device Architecture Applied to he Montsec Area Heritage Adaptive and Anticipating. Proc. Workshop on HCI in Mobile Tourism Support (Mobile HCI 2002) Pisa, Italy (2002) 51-56
2. Szyperski, C.: Component Software-Beyond Object-Oriented Programming. Addison-Wesley. ACM Press. ISBN: 0-201-17888-5 (1998)
3. Pinheiro, P.: The Unified Modelling Language for Interactive Applications. (2002) http://www.cs.man.ac.uk/img/umli/links.html
4. Grossmann, M., Leonhardi, A., Mitschang, B., Rothermel, K.: A World Model for Location-Aware Systems. Published on behalf of CEPIS by Novática and Informatik/Informatique http://www.upgrade-cepis.org., Vol. II, Issue, 5. Ubiquitous Computing (2001) 32-35
5. Maes, P.: Concepts and Experiments in Computational Reflection. Proc. of the 2nd OOPSLA'87 (1987) 147-156
6. Zimmerman, C.: Advances in Object-Oriented Metalevel Architectures and Reflection. CRC Press, Inc., Boca Raton, Florida 33431 (1996)

Moving Vehicle Tracking for the Web Camera

Seongah Chin and Moonwon Choo

#147-2, anyang-8 Dong, Manan-Gu, Anyang-City, Kyunggi-Do, Korea
Division of Multimedia, Sungkyul University
{solideo,mchoo}@sungkyul.edu

Abstract. In this paper, color invariant co-occurrence features for moving vehicle tracking in a known environment is proposed. It extracts moving areas shaped on objects in Web video sequences captured by the Web camera and detects tracks of moving objects. Color invariant co-occurrence matrices are exploited to extract the plausible object blocks and the correspondences between adjacent video frames. The measures of class separability derived from the features of co-occurrence matrices are used to improve the performance of tracking. The experimental results are presented.

1 Introduction

Tracking the motion of objects in video sequences captured by the Web camera is becoming important as related hardware and software technology gets more mature and the needs for applications where the activity of objects should be analyzed and monitored are increasing [1]. In such applications lots of information can be obtained from trajectories that give the spatio-temporal coordinates of each object in the environment. Information that can be obtained from such trajectories includes a dynamic count of the number of object within the monitored area, time spent by objects in an area and traffic flow patterns in an environment [2][3][4][5]. The tracking of moving object is challenging in any cases, since image formations in video stream is very sensitive to changes of conditions of environment such as illumination, moving speed and, directions, the number and sizes of objects, and background. Color image can be assumed to contain richer information for image processing than its corresponding gray level image. Obviously three color channels composing color images give richer information than gray level counterparts. Invariance and discriminative power of the color invariants is experimentally investigated here as the dimensions of co-occurrence matrix and the derived features for finding correspondences of objects. William [7] suggests motion tracking by deriving velocity vectors from point-to-point correspondence relations. Relaxation and optical flow are very attractive methodologies to detect the trajectories of objects [8]. Those researches are based on the analysis of velocity vectors of each pixel or group of pixels between two neighboring frames. This approach requires heavy computation for calculating optical flow vectors. Another method infers the moving information by computing the difference images and

J.M. Cueva Lovelle et al. (Eds.): ICWE 2003, LNCS 2722, pp. 267–270, 2003.
© Springer-Verlag Berlin Heidelberg 2003

edge features for complementary information to estimate plausible moving tracks [4][9]. This method may be very sensitive to illumination and noise imposed on video stream.

2 Methodology

Many block detection methods assume that the lighting in the scene considered would be constant. The accuracy of these methods decreases significantly when they are applied to real scenes because of constantly changing illumination conditioned on background and the moving objects. Kubelka-Munk theory models the reflected spectrum of a colored body based on a material-dependent scattering and absorption function, under assumption that light is isotropically scattered within the material [12][13]. H is an object reflectance property independent of viewpoint, surface orientation, illumination direction, illumination intensity and Fresnel reflectance coefficient. These color invariants may show more discriminative power than gray levels, so can be used

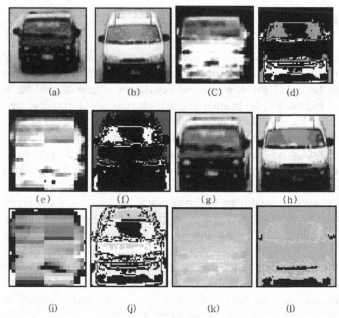

Fig. 1. (a) (b) Two original color images (truck and van), (c)(d) *C_invariant*, (e)(f) *E_variant*, (g)(h) *Intensity* (i)(j) *Hue*, and (k)(l) *Saturation*. The intensities are rescaled for viewing.

for detection of the trajectories of objects reliably. To get these spectral differential quotients, the following implementation of Gaussian color model in RGB terms is used (for details, see [12]). Figure 1 shows the original color images and the results after computing the color invariance maps. Since the object detected with its bounding

rectangular block in current frame should be uniquely associated with the corresponding block in neighboring frame, each block should have local block features possess-
ing proper discriminating power. There are many researches done in this area [8][9].
The co-occurrence matrix is a well-known statistical tool for extracting second-order
texture information from images. Entropy is a measure of randomness and takes low
values for smooth images. Inverse Difference Moment (IDM) takes high values for
low-contrast images due to the inverse $(i - j)^2$ dependence. Correlation is a measure of
image linearity, that is, linear directionality structures in a certain direction result in
large correlation values in this direction. Energy or angular second moment is a measure of image homogeneity-the more homogeneous the image, the large the value. The
optimal features and other related conditions for class separability should be determined from the implementation reasons,. In this paper, a set of simpler criteria built
upon information related to the way feature vector samples are scattered in the l-
dimensional space is adopted. The goal of object tracking is to determine the 3-D
positions and the motion parameters of objects recognized by the local block detection
phase at every time instant. The first requirement for this task is to determine the correspondence of each object detected from adjacent image frames. To establish the
correspondence relations of blocks between sequential frames, the selected feature
values of local blocks at time t are compared with those of blocks detected at time $t+1$.

$$(x', y') = \arg \min_{k} D_{\lambda} (D_t^k (x, y), D_{t+1}^k (x', y')) \qquad (1)$$

where (x,y) is the central position of D_t^k, which is the kth detected blocks in D_t. The
function D_{λ} is defined by computing the weighted L_2 error of the transformed data
using a combination of feature value difference and Euclidean distance C_t^k between
the central positions of D_t^k and D_{t+1}^k.

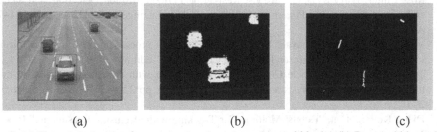

(a)   (b)   (c)

Fig. 2. (a) The original video frame tested and resultant detected blocks, (b) Detected blocks by
color invariant features and (c) The detected tracks of three objects given in (a)

Figure 2 shows the detected tracks of three vehicles. In this experiment, d=1, and
correlation feature is used.

3 Conclusions and Future Research

A system for tracking objects for a Web camera using color invariance features is presented. The system outputs tracks that give spatio-temporal coordinates of objects as they move within the field of view of a camera. We try to solve the occluded objects problem, which may be ignored in many researches intentionally by utilizing radial cumulative similarity measures imposed on color invariance features and projection. But the projection scheme presented here is too primitive to solve this problem. But this system is very fast to be used in real time applications and to eliminate noise, which may be very difficult when using gray level intensity only. Future research needs to address these kinds of issues and tracking objects across moving Web cameras.

References

1. Ismail Haritaoglu, "Real time Surveillance of people and their activities", IEEE Trans. on pattern analysis and machine intelligence, Vol. 22, No. 8, Aug. 2000
2. D. Beymer and K. Konolige, " Real-Time Tracking of Multiple People using Stereo, " Proc. IEEE Frame Rate Workshop, 1999
3. Gian Luca Foresti, et. al,"Vehicle Recognition and Tracking from Road Image Sequences," IEEE Trans. On Vehicular Tech., vol. 48, NO. 1, Jan. 1999.
4. Rita Cucchira, Massimo Piccardi, Paola Mello "Image analysis and rule based reasoning for a traffic monitoring system" IEEE, Intelligent transportation system, pp119-pp130VOL.1, No.2, June 2000
5. Robert M, Haralick, Linda G, Shapario "Computer and Robot vision Vol I ", Addision-wesley, USA pp 318–321, 1992
6. Jakub Segen and Sarma Pingali, "A Camera-Based System for Tracking People in Real Time," IEEE Proceedings of ICPR '96, 1996
7. Ross Culter, Larry S. Davis "Robust Real-Time Periodic Motion Detection, and analysis and Application ", IEEE Pattern analysis and machine Intelligence Vol22 No 8, pp781–795 August 2000
8. Milan Sonka, Vaclav Hiavac, Rogger Boyle " Image processing Analysis and machine vision," International Thomson Publishing Co., 1999, 2nd edition
9. Trevor Darrell and Michele Covel " Correspondence with cumulative similiarity transforms" IEEE pattern analysis and machine intelligence, pp 222–227 Vol.23 No2 February 2001
10. Dieter Koller, et. al, "Robust Multiple Car Tracking with Occlusion Reasoining," Proc. 3rd European Confer. On Computer Vision, May 2–6, 1994
11. Gerhard Rigoll, et. al, "Person Tracking in Real-World Scenarios Using Statistical Methods," IEEE Inter. Confer. On Automatic Face and Gesture Recognition, Grenoble France, March, 2000
12. Jan-Mak G., et. al, "Color Invariance,"IEEE Trans. On PAMI, vol.23, no. 12, Dec. 2001
13. Kristen Hoffman, "Applications of the Kubelka-Munk Color Model to Xerographic Images,"www.cis.rit.edu/research/thesis/bs/1998 / hoffman

Measuring End-to-End Quality of a News-on-Demand Web Service

J.R. Arias, F.J. Suárez, D.F. García, and J.I. Marín

Departamento de Informática, Universidad de Oviedo, Spain
{arias,fran,daniel,nacho}@atc.uniovi.es

Abstract. A key issue in any system for distribution of continuous media-on-demand is the capacity of the system with regard to quality of the service specifications, that is, the number of simultaneous streams the system can provide until degradation of quality of reproduction and interactivity perceived by the users. This work presents the evaluation of a web based interactive video-on-demand system, with special attention to limitations caused by the video server. The evaluation is based on the measurement of the end-to-end quality of the service. A set of metrics has been designed to determine the number of streams the video server can support under specific quality requirements. To validate the utility of these metrics, a prototype of a news-on-demand web service has been built and the load for this kind of systems has been characterised. In addition, a load generator which emulates the concurrent access of several users to the system has been built. The evaluation establishes the relationship between the video server limitations and the quality of the service perceived by the users.

1 Introduction

Examples of commercial video-on-demand services are movies-on-demand and news-on-demand, where the user can interact with the streams through the typical fast-forward, rewind, pause and stop functions. There are two main factors that define the capacity of this kind of system: the service capacity or number of simultaneous streams the system can serve, and the quality of the service perceived by users, both at reproduction of streams and interactivity levels. The greater the number of streams the system can serve, and the higher the quality of reproduction and short response times to interactive functions, the more economically feasible it becomes. The principle elements of the system that limit its capacity are the video server and the communication network. In this work, the influence of the video server, which provides news-on-demand service, is studied, considering the communication network to be ideal. The work focuses on the end-to-end quality of the service, that is, the quality perceived by users in each interaction, from the initial request to the end of the reception of the corresponding stream. The main goal is to design a set of metrics to measure and relate the video server capacity and the end-to-end quality of the service. These metrics will help in dimensioning server capacity in function of the required quality of the service.

J.M. Cueva Lovelle et al. (Eds.): ICWE 2003, LNCS 2722, pp. 271–274, 2003.
© Springer-Verlag Berlin Heidelberg 2003

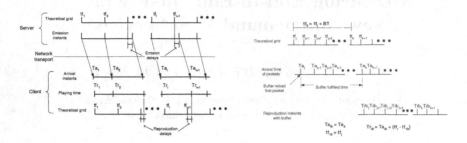

Fig. 1. Multimedia stream reproduction   **Fig. 2.** Stream reproduction with *buffer*

2   Prototype of Service

News-on-demand is one of the most popular on-demand services. To built a prototype representative of real systems the BBC Audio/Video News has been selected as a reference. The synthetic prototype implemented emulates a daily service to which 50 news items are incorporated each day. The prototype contains news for one week. The news items are classified according to their length: a) Short (30 sec.-1 min., 6% of total), b) Medium (1min. -3:30 min., 84% of total) or c) Long (3:30 min.-1 hour, 10% of total). News is available at three transmission speeds: a) Low (28 kbps. maximum), b) Medium (28-56 kbps.) and c) High (more than 56 kbps.). Frame size is always 176x144, so transmission speed relates directly to frame speed (8-30 fps). For all the news, the video server stores streams coded for the three possible transmission speeds.

3   Quality of the Service Metrics

The metrics used to measure quality of the service are based on two fields carried with each packet of the stream transmitted: the sequence number and the timestamp. The sequence number marks the order in which the packet was emitted from the video server. The timestamp places each packet in its temporal position in the stream. These positions form the *temporal theoretical grid* of emission or playing of the stream. The more the emission/playing of the stream conforms to the theoretical temporal grid, the better the quality of the service obtained. The temporal position of the $i th$ packet in the stream is denoted with tf_i and is calculated using the timestamp of each packet and the stream sampling frequency.

3.1   Metrics of Quality of Reproduction

Using the value of tf_i of the $i th$ packet, the arrival time, Ta_i, of this packet, and the calculated playing time of the $i th$ packet(see Fig. 1), $Tr_i = Ta_1 + (tf_i - tf_1)$, several metrics of quality of reproduction of the stream can be defined.
Percentage of delayed packets: This shows how well the stream received conforms to the theoretical temporal grid. For each packet the delay is calculated

with $D_i = Tr_i - Ta_i$. When $D_i < 0$ there are discontinuities in the stream. If N_D is the number of packets delayed, it is possible to calculate the total percentage of delayed packets, D, using the total number of packets received, N_r as $D = \frac{N_D}{N_r} * 100$

Mean packet delay: This is the arithmetic mean of the delays: $\bar{R} = \frac{\sum D_i}{N_r}$

Percentage of packets lost: If N_e is the number of packets emitted, this metric is obtained with $L = \frac{N_e - N_r}{N_e} * 100$

Total amount of bytes received: If L_{ij} is the number of bytes carried in the ith packet received by the jth client, we can calculate the total amount of bytes received by the clients as $L = \sum_{j=1}^{n} \sum_{i=1}^{m} L_{ij}$, where n is the number of clients connected and m the number of packets received by each client.

Number of client buffer reloads: The client buffer tries to compensate for the transmission delays suffered by the packets. When delays are too long, the packet to play can not be in the buffer. In this case, there is a *buffer failure* and it must be reloaded completely. The greater the number of reloads, the worse the quality of reproduction of the stream. When the client has a buffer, the new playing time of each packet is $Tr_{ib} = Ta_{lb} + (tf_i - tf_{1b})$, where Ta_{lb} is the arrival time of the packet which fills the buffer in the last complete reload, and tf_{1b} is the temporal position of the first packet to arrive at the buffer in the last reload (see Fig. 2). To determine when a buffer failure is taking place, the arrival time of each packet must be checked: $bf_i = Tr_{ib} - Ta_i$. When $bf_i < 0$ there is a buffer failure and the buffer must be reloaded. The total number of a client buffer failures is calculated as $BF = \sum bf_i$.

Buffer reloads frecuency: If T is the time spent by a client requesting multimedia streams to the server, the metric value is $FR = \frac{BF}{T}$.

Buffer Reload Mean Time: When a buffer failure is detected a reload must be started. If the time spended by the client awaiting for the complete fullfil of the buffer is too long, clients will be leads to abandon the service. We measure this parameter with this metric.

3.2   Metrics of Quality of Interactivity

Mean start response time: quantifies waiting time between a request for the start of a stream and confirmation of the transmission from the server.

Mean interaction response time: measures the waiting time between client interaction and response from the server.

3.3   Metrics of Server Capacity

These metrics relate server load with the number of client requests.

Throughput metrics	Resource utilization metrics
Streams served	**CPU utilization**
Total number of bits served	**Hard disk utilization**
Mean number of concurrent connections	**Network utilization**
Total number of bits served per connection	

4   Workload Characterization and Experimental Procedure

In the service model proposed in this paper the user can request as much news as he wants. The choice of news is made randomly among all available news. The access probability to each piece of news is driven by the Zipf law [3]. According to [2], half of the requests are abandoned before completion due to lack of interest on the part of the user. Each one of the client states and the thinking time before the selection of a new stream has a length which follows constant statistical distributions. These distributions are based on the work presented in [2].

The experimental procedure was carried out with two computers, one of them working as the news server and the other playing the role of multiple clients by running a specific emulation tool. The computers were linked by a dedicated 100 Mb/s Fast-Ethernet. Measurements were taken in both computers: in the server using the sar system utility and in the client using the specific tool built.

5   Current Results

A preliminary analysis of the prototype, without considering the use of buffers in the clients, has been carried out. The analysis is based on the value of the metrics as a function of the number of users simultaneously connected to the server. As a result, can be concluded that the server application (Darwin [1] server in this work) does not go beyond a certain level of throughput, even if the hardware resources do not reach saturation levels. Just before reaching the maximum throughput, as the throughput (load level) of the server increases, the server application discards more and more packets with the goal of maintaining the average delay of packets at a minimum. This behaviour of server application is reflected in the metrics as a progressive increase in lost packets, while the average delay of packets remains stationary with low values. Once the point of maximum throughput has been reached, the loss of packets stabilizes.

In the experimental framework of this work, the prototype of the news-on-demand service used has capacity for: a) 120 users for high speed, b) 200 users for medium speed, and c) 260 users for low speed, while maintaining an acceptable quality of the service. With these numbers of supported users using economical personal computers as servers, the economic feasibility of interactive video-on-demand services is evident.

References

1. Apple Computer Inc. Open source streaming server, 2002.
   http://www.publicsource.apple.com/projects/streaming/.
2. S. Jin and A. Bestavros. A generator of internet streaming media objects and workloads. Technical report, Boston University. Computer Science Department, October 2001. http://citeseer.nj.nec.com/jin01generator.html.
3. G.K. Zipf. *The human behaviour and the principle of least effort*. Addison Wesley, 1949.

Continuous Media Streams Service Based on the Adaptive Buffer Sharing Policy

Yong Woon Park[1] and Si Woong Jang[2]

[1]Department of Computer Science, Dong-eui Institute of Technology, san72, Yangjung Dong, Pusanjin Ku, Pusan, Rep. of Korea
ywpark@dit.ac.kr

[2]Department of Computer Science, Dong-eui University, san24, Kaya Dong, Pusanjin Ku, Pusan, Rep. of Korea
swjang@hyomin.dongeui.ac.kr

Abstract. In this paper, a stream service strategy based on the adaptive buffer sharing and prefetching policy for the continuous media stream service is proposed. In the proposed caching policy, a stream is given one of the three service modes- *direct*, *shared* or *object*- with its requested object's access patterns and frequency. With *direct* mode, a stream is serviced directly from disk using its own read-ahead buffer, which is necessary to buffer the speed discrepancy between disk's transfer rate and user's playback rate for the requested stream. In *shared* mode, the interval between two consecutive streams accessing the same object is cached whereas in *object* mode, which could be set when the access frequency of the requested object exceeds a given threshold; an object is cached in its entirety. The service mode of each object could be changed dynamically with its access frequency.

1 Introduction

Traditionally, caching has been studied in the literature to reduce the cost of the internal device I/O by caching the frequently reused objects in the buffer memory. However, traditional caching policies employed for non-multimedia applications are not appropriate for multimedia applications[3]. So, in this paper, we propose a stream service strategy based on the adaptive caching policy where each stream is given one of the following three service modes - *direct*, *shared* or *object* - based on the access patterns and frequency of its requested object. In *shared* mode, the interval formed with the preceding stream accessing the same object is cached while in *object* mode, which could be set when the access frequency of the requested object exceeds a given threshold; an object is cached in its entirety. The processing mode of the object could be changed dynamically with its access frequency. Other streams that are not permitted to share buffer cache are run in *direct* mode; a stream is serviced directly from disk using its own read-ahead buffer, which is necessary to buffer the speed discrepancy between disk's transfer rate and user's playback rate for the requested stream.

J.M. Cueva Lovelle et al. (Eds.): ICWE 2003, LNCS 2722, pp. 275–278, 2003.
© Springer-Verlag Berlin Heidelberg 2003

2   Related Research

Earlier works in multimedia buffer management have studied the buffer requirement for various disk-scheduling algorithms[1, 4, 6, 7]. In these works, the video data block is discarded once it has been transmitted to the clients and is not retained for subsequent reuse by other clients. In continuous media data caching policies in the literatures[8, 9], the buffer space is allocated to the interval between two consecutive streams of the same object. In this policy, a stream is cached as a function of the interval length and the size of the buffer cache. In this approach, the buffer blocks held by existing intervals are passed to the new interval formed by the new request if there is not so much free memory as the length of the newly formed interval. However, in this policy, in most cases, the succeeding streams must access the initial portion of the requested object from disks since those blocks are not guaranteed to be found in the buffer cache even if all subsequent accesses are serviced from the cache.

3   Stream Service Strategy and Caching Policy

3.1   Data Retrieval in Direct Mode

For streams requesting the rarely requested objects, their requested objects are serviced directly from disk and then delivered to the users(we call this type of data retrieval *direct* mode) with their own read ahead buffer. The very thing we must bear in mind is that as the number of disk streams increases, the aggregate disk bandwidth utilization increases and what is worse is that the amount of buffer memory increases extremely high as the disk utilization reaches 100%. For more detailed information, how much read-ahead buffer is required with different numbers of concurrent streams, see [5, 10].

3.2   Data Retrieval in Shared Mode

For some streams accessing the same object, the data blocks existing between two streams are cached such that the following stream could avoid disk access until the end of the delivery(*shared* mode). In data retrieval in shared mode, when there is not so much free buffer space as new interval, interval changing occurs. In the existing interval caching algorithm[9], interval changing is made based only on the interval length of the new and existing intervals. But in our proposed caching scheme, the interval changing occurs only if the result of the interval changing reuires less buffer memory .

3.3   Data Retrieval in Object Mode

In the existing interval caching or buffer sharing policy, even if an object is rarely accessed, its interval between two consecutive streams will be cached provided that their interval is short enough to be cached.   On the other hand, even if an object is accessed frequently, its interval between two consecutive streams will not be cached once their interval is too long to be cached.   This means the existing interval caching policy does not consider the access patterns of the objects; it only considers the temporal locality in terms of request arrival. Therefore, in most cases, the buffered blocks are reused only once by the succeeding stream because not every object is requested so constantly such that all of their intervals are cached.   So, if all blocks of some objects with high access frequency are cached entirely, its all blocks are cached as one logical interval.

4   Experimental Results

We assume that users' access patterns follow a *Zipf* distribution and all of the media objects are assumed to be MPEG II compressed with a playback rate of 8 Mbps. We also assumed that the size of media objects used in this simulation ranges from 10 to 30 minutes in terms of playback time.

The experiment is done only to check cache performance that the network resources are not taken into consideration. The *proposed* in the graphs means the proposed adaptive caching policy where two caching modes – *shared* and *object* – are applied together and *eff* is the caching policy, to which *object* mode is not applied to check the efficiency of *shared* mode caching. Finally, *int* is the existing caching policy proposed by [9]. As the experiment, *buffer user ratio* of three algorithms are checked and evaluated, with different arrival rates and buffer capacity. By buffer user ratio, it means how many streams out of all requested streams are serviced in the buffer cache, not by *direct* mode. As shown in Figure 3 and 4, the proposed algorithm shows higher buffer user ratio than other two algorithms except some cases; when the buffer cache is relatively small(600 MB) or the number of archived objects is large(1200). As the size of the buffer cache is large(2000 MB) and the streams' inter-arrival time is relatively long(say, 1.7 sec), three algorithms show not so much difference as in the case of short inter-arrival time(0.43 or 0.56). This is because, when the buffer size is large and the inter-arrival time is long, the buffer cache replacement does not occur so frequently that it is highly possible that once the object is cached, it could remain in the buffer cache as long as it could.   The *buffer user ratio* also depends on the number of objects archived in the disks that as the number of objects archived gets larger, the buffer user ratio gets lower.

5   Conclusion

In this paper, we proposed a stream service strategy using the adaptive buffer sharing policy based on each object's access pattern. With the proposed policy, a steam is serviced one of three modes: *direct*, *shared* and *object*. The streams accessing rarely accessed objects are serviced directly from disks while active streams accessing the same object are serviced in *shared* mode where the interval between two streams is cached. Finally some objects accessed frequently are cached fully so as to fully avoid disk access.   As a result of simulation, the proposed caching scheme is known to be more effective than other caching policies.   This is because with the proposed algorithm, objects with less likely to be accessed are filtered as a function of its caching effectiveness by checking the requirement of read-ahead buffer memory and access frequency of objects archived. Moreover, some highly accessed objects are prefetched in their entirety so that unnecessary buffer replacement could be reduced.

278   Y.W. Park and S.W. Jang

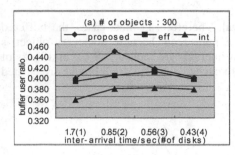
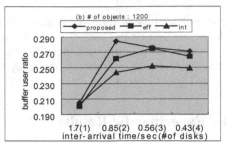

Fig. 1. Buffer user ratios when the buffer cache size is 600 MB

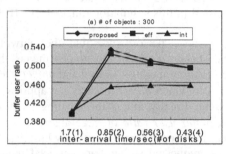
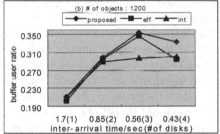

Fig. 2. Buffer user ratios when the buffer cache size is 2000 MB

References

1. Anderson D. P, Y. Osawa, and R. Govindan, "A File System for Continuous Media", ACM Transactions on Computing Systems, Vol. 10, No. 4 pp. 311–337, Nov. 1992
2. A. Dan, D. Sitaram, and P. Shahabuddin , "Dynamic batching policies for an on-demand video server", Multimedia Systems, 4(3):112–121, Jun 1996.
3. A. Dan and D. Sitaram. "Multimedia Caching Strategy for Heterogeneous Application and Server Environments", IBM Research Report, RC 20670, Yorktown Heights, NY, 1996
4. Mon-Song Chen, Dilip D. Kandlur, P. Yu, "Optimization of the Grouped Sweeping Scheme(GSS) with Heterogeneous Multimedia Streams", Proc. ACM Multimedia 92 pp. 235–242, Anaheim CA, Aug, 1993
5. Kenchammana-Hosekote DR, Srivastava, "Scheduling Continuous media on a Video on Demand Server", In Proceedings of ACM Multimedia Computing and Systems, May 1994, Boston, Mass
6. Rangan P. V., H. M. Vin, and S. Ramanathan, "Designing an On-Demand Multimedia Service", IEEE Communication Magazine pp. 56–65, Vol. 30 Jul. 1992
7. F. Tobagi, J. Pang, R. Baird, and M. Gang, "Streaming RAID – a disk array management system for video files", ACM Multimedia , pp 393–400, Aug. 1993
8. W. Shi and S. Ghandeharizade, "Trading Memory for Disk Bandwidth in Video On Demand Servers", In Proceeding of International Conference on Multimedia Computing and Systems, pp172-180, Jun 1998
9. R. Tewari, A. Dan, etal, "Buffering and Caching in Large-Scale Video Servers", In Proceedings of IEEE CompCon, 1995, pp. 217–224
10. Youjip Won, Jaideep Srivastava. "Minimizing Buffer Requirement for Continuous Media Servers, Multimedia Systems 8 (2000) 2, 105–117

New WAKE Key Recovery Protocol on M-commerce

Yong-ho Lee[1], Im-yeong Lee[2], and Hyung-woo Lee[3]

[1]S/W Quality Evaluation Center, Telecommunications Technology Association, Korea
abysskey@tta.or.kr
[2]Division of Information Technology Engineering, Soonchunhyang University, Korea
imylee@sch.ac.kr
[3]Dept. of Software, Hanshin University, Korea
hwlee@hanshin.ac.kr

Abstract. The ASPeCT project first tried to support the key recovery in wireless authentication and key establishment protocol Since then, a variety of protocols have been proposed. In this thesis, problems of conventional protocols are analyzed and new protocol is suggested to solve those problems.

Keywords: M-Commerce, Authentication, Key Establishment, Key Recovery

1 Introduction

The WAKE(Wireless Authentication and Key Establishment) Key Recovery protocol, which added the key recovery function to the WAKE protocol, was started by ASPeCT and is now in use for various security scenarios. In this thesis, methodologies introduced in existing researches are analyzed, the requirements of the WAKE Key Recovery protocol are derived based on the analysis, and finally, a new protocol is proposed to address the requirements.

Here, the three studies proposed so far are explained. First study, R-M WAKE Key Recovery protocol[1], proposed by Rantos and Mitchell in 1999 is hereby introduced. This is not satisfies requirements that Masquerade Attack Prevention, Public Verification of Key Recovery, Domain Extension, and Illegal Key Recovery Prevention. Second study, N-P-B-E WAKE Key Recovery protocol[2], proposed to solve problems as Masquerade Attack Prevention and Public Verification of Key Recovery of first study. Third study, K-L WAKE Key Recovery protocol[3], proposed to solve problems as Domain Extension of second study. But all conventional study is not satisfies Illegal Key Recovery Prevention.

2 Contribution

In this chapter, we propose a new wireless authentication and key establishment protocol supporting key recovery. The proposed method solves the problems of the existing wireless authentication and key establishment protocol and promotes efficiency and security, while supporting the key recovery function with a minimum level of overhead. This is consists of a total of three stages: initialization, wireless authentication and key establishment, and a key recovery stage in case of an emergency. New protocol has distinguishing mark about conventional protocols.

J.M. Cueva Lovelle et al. (Eds.): ICWE 2003, LNCS 2722, pp. 279–280, 2003.
© Springer-Verlag Berlin Heidelberg 2003

In this proposed protocol, masquerade attack is not possible, unless all information on the user possessed by the key recovery agency and the escrow agency is disclosed. Masquerade attack is possible only when all secret information on the user, divided among the key recovery agency and the escrow agency and possessed by each other, is disclosed.

The existing protocols implement all public verification and key recovery functions by generating and using key recovery information. The new protocol is constructed, however, so that the process for public verification of key recovery is implemented separately. A unique feature of this is that to implement public verification of key recovery, it utilizes all the information that the key recovery agency, the escrow agency, and the user make public individually.

This proposed protocol assumes two users belonging to the same domain. When a domain is extended into multiple domains, additional information is used to solve any problem.

In this proposed protocol, each of two key recovery informations is put in escrow by the key recovery agency and the escrow agency. Illegal key recovery is thus prevented, unless the two agencies illegally confer with each other. To prevent this occurrence, a number of escrow agencies may be considered. The key recovery information is divided into two in this thesis in order to emphasize the different roles of the key recovery agency and the escrow agency.

Table 1. Compare among protocols

	R-M protocol	N-P-B-E protocol	K-L protocol	Proposal protocol
Public Verification of Key Recovery	X	O	O	O
Masquerade Attack Prevention	X	O	O	O
Domain Extension	X	X	O	O
Illegal Key Recovery Prevention	X	X	X	O

3 Conclusion

In this thesis, we consider that problems and requirement of WAKE Key Recovery protocol. The proposed protocol is proven to be much better in security and efficiency than existing protocols.

References

[1]   K. Rantos and C. Mitchell, Key Recovery in ASPeCT Authentication and Initialization of Payment protocol, ACTS Mobile Summit, 1999
[2]   J. Nieto, D. Park, C. Boyd, and E. Dawson, Key Recovery in Third Generation Wireless Communication System, PKC2000, Springer-Verlag, pp.223–237, 2000
[3]   ChongHee Kim and PilJoong Lee, New Key Recovery in WAKE Protocol, PKC2001, Springer-Verlag, pp.325–338, 2001

An Improvement of VeriSign's Key Roaming Service Protocol

Jeeyeon Kim[1], Hyunjo Kwon[1], Haeryong Park[1], Seungjoo Kim[1], and
Dongho Won[2]

[1] KISA (Korea Information Security Agency),
78, Garak-Dong, Songpa-Gu, Seoul 138-803, Korea
{jykim, hckwon, hrpark, skim}@kisa.or.kr
[2] Sungkyunkwan University,
300 Chunchun-Dong, Suwon, Kyunggi-Do, 440-746, Korea
dhwon@dosan.skku.ac.kr
http://dosan.skku.ac.kr

Abstract. In the past two or three years, most major Public Key Infrastructure(PKI) vendors have released products which allow users to roam from one machine to another without having to manually manage the export and import of their credentials such as private keys and corresponding certificates onto temporary media like diskettes. In this paper, we survey three popular key roaming products of Baltimore's, Entrust's and VeriSign's. We also propose key roaming system which improves VeriSign's roaming service and analyze its security.

1   Introduction

In PKI systems, user's credentials are often stored in the client system's hard disk. Credentials may consist of public/private key pairs, X.509 public key certificates and/or other private user data. These PKI systems are vulnerable to various attacks where the private key may be stolen or substituted, usually without user's even being aware of it. Furthermore the use of hard disk does not satisfy the needs of the roaming user, who accesses the Internet from different client terminals.

So far, there are two basic approaches to provide a secure roaming service.

– portable hardware key storage such as smartcards
– password-only mechanisms

While smartcards are commonly understood to be the best medium in which to store, carry and utilize the credentials, it is not currently practical because of the low level of penetration of smartcard readers into the general PC environment. Given the cost and availability problems of hardware storage devices today, more sophisticated approach is to use the password-only mechanisms. In this approach, a roaming users store their credentials at a central server and download temporary copies when needed to their local machine.

J.M. Cueva Lovelle et al. (Eds.): ICWE 2003, LNCS 2722, pp. 281–288, 2003.
© Springer-Verlag Berlin Heidelberg 2003

In the past two or three years most major PKI vendors have used this password-only methods to release products which allow users to roam from one machine to another without having to manually manage the export and import of their credentials onto temporary media like diskettes.

Generally, key roaming systems consist of the following components.

- User : a roaming user or client.
- CA(Certification Authority) : a server to issue and manage certificates for encryption or authentication.
- RS(Roaming Server) : a server to provide a roaming user with an information needed to obtain user's credential.
- CS(Credential Server) : a server to store and manage a roaming user's credentials.

Note that RS and CS can be operated on the same server.

Generally, key roaming systems are vulnerable to exhaustive password guessing attack at server. Ford and Kaliski presented the key roaming protocol which overcomes this deficiency[8] and is used to VeriSign's roaming service. Ford and Kaliski's methods use multiple servers to further prevent guessing attacks by an enemy that compromises all but one server. However, their method which relies on techniques like server-authenticated Secure Sockets Layer(SSL) which is known to be vulnerable to web-server spoofing attacks[4],[7].

In this paper, we survey three popular key roaming products of Baltimore's, Entrust's and VeriSign's. We propose key roaming protocol which does not need a prior sever-authenticated channel such as SSL and analyze its security.

2   Existing Commercial Key Roaming Systems

In this section, we briefly survey the existing commercial key roaming systems of Baltimore's[1], Entrust's[6],[16] and VeriSign's[3], [8], [14], [15].

[Notations]
We use the following common notations throughout our paper.

- Alice : honest user.
- A : Alice's roaming client software.
- $ID(A)$: an identity of Alice.
- PWD : a password memorized by Alice.
- PRI and PUB : private and public key pair of Alice.
- E_X : a symmetric or public encryption with cryptographic key X.
- H : a cryptographic hash function.
- p : a prime, $p = 2q + 1$, where q is a large prime.

2.1 Baltimore's UniCert Roaming Service

[User Registration Process]

1. A → CA : A sends the request for registration to CA.
2. CA : CA generates A's password, PWD, key pair (PRI, PUB) and certificate, $Cert(A)$, and CA stores $Cert(A)$ in the repository.
3. CA → CS : CA forms A's .p12 file, such as .p12 = $(E_{PWD}(PRI), Cert(A))$ and sends it to CS, called "UniCERT Roaming Server Administrator and UniCERT Roaming Server" in [1].
4. CS : CS generates A's roaming authentication key, RAK, such as $RAK = H(PWD)$ and roaming encryption key, REK. CS computes $E_{REK}(.p12)$ and $E_{PUB(RS)}(RAK, REK)$, where $PUB(RS)$ is a public key of RS, called "UniCERT Roaming Protection Encryption Key Server" in [1]. And then CS stores $ID(A)$, $E_{REK}(.p12)$ and $E_{PUB(RS)}(RAK, REK)$ in the repository.
5. CA → A : CA securely sends PWD to A.

[Roaming Process]

1. A → CS : A prompts Alice to enter her ID and password. When Alice has done this, A sends a roaming request to the CS.
2. CS : After receiving and verifying the request, CS generates a protected access request number, ARN. Then CS retrieves A's $E_{PUB(RS)}(RAK, REK)$ and $E_{REK}(.p12)$ from the repository and gets RS's certificate, $Cert(RS)$ and Internet address.
3. CS → A : CS sends $E_{PUB(RS)}(RAK, REK)$, $E_{REK}(.p12)$ and ARN to A with RS's URL and certificate, $Cert(RS)$.
4. A → RS : A computes $E_{PUB(RS)}(OSK)$, where OSK is an one-time local session key, and sends it to RS with $E_{PUB(RS)}(RAK, REK)$, $E_{REK}(.p12)$, ARN and $H(PWD)$.
5. RS → A : RS checks ARN to its database of recent request number's received. If ARN exists within the database, the request is rejected. Otherwise RS decrypts $E_{PUB(RS)}(RAK, REK)$ using its private key corresponding to $PUB(RS)$, verifies $H(PWD)$ using RAK, and decrypts $E_{REK}(.p12)$ using REK to obtain .p12. Then RS computes $E_{OSK}(.p12)$ and sends it to A.
6. A : A decrypts $E_{OSK}(.p12)$ using OSK to get .p12 file.

[Security analysis]

If $H(PWD)$ is sent to CS without the security protocol such as SSL, Baltimore Unicert Roaming can be vulnerable to password guessing attack. Furthermore, CS's or RS's operator or attacker who compromises RS to obtain RS's private key can always mount an exhaustive search attack on a user's password.

2.2 Entrust's Authority Roaming Service

[Registration Process]

When creating/recovering a roaming user, Entrust/Session can be used to secure communications between RS/CS, called Entrust/Profile Server in [6], and A.

1. A → CA : A requests CA to register and issue its credential, $E_{PWD}(PRI)$ and $Cert(A)$.
2. CA → A : CA issues and sends the credential to A.
3. A → RS/CS : A calculates $H(PWD)$ and sends its credential and $H(PWD)$ to RS/CS.
4. RS/CS : RS/CS generates a symmetric key, K and encrypts A's credential with K. Then RS/CS computes $E_{RSK}(H(PWD), K)$, where RSK is a key of RS/CS, and stores it in the repository with $E_K(E_{PWD}(PRI), Cert(A))$.

[Roaming Process]

On roaming login, prior to decrypting the credential, SPEKE(Simple Password Exponential Key Exchange)[10] replaces Entrust/ Session as the mechanism used to secure communications between RS/CS and A.

1. Alice : Alice enter $ID(A)$ and PWD to login.
2. A : A retrieves $E_K(E_{PWD}(PRI), Cert(A))$ and $E_{RSK}(H(PWD), K)$ from the repository. Then A calculate $H(PWD)^x \bmod p$, where x is a random number.
3. A → RS/CS : A sends $E_{RSK}(H(PWD), K)$ to RS/CS with $ID(A)$ and $H(PWD)^x \bmod p$.
4. RS/CS : RS/CS decrypts $E_{RSK}(H(PWD), K)$ to get $H(PWD)$ and K, and then computes a session key $S1 = H(PWD)^{xy} \bmod p$, where y is a random number.
5. RS/CS → A : RS/CS computes $E_{S1}(K)$ and $H(PWD)^y \bmod p$, and sends them to A.
6. A : A also computes $S1 = H(PWD)^{xy} \bmod p$ and decrypts $E_{S1}(K)$ using $S1$ and $E_K(E_{PWD}(PRI), Cert(A))$ to obtain its credential.

[Security analysis]

Entrust's Authority Roaming system uses SPEKE[10] to provide strong password authentication for mobile users. Like Baltimore's Roaming, it also has the same problem that RS/CS's operator or attacker who compromises RS/CS to obtain a private key of RS/CS can always mount an exhaustive search attack on a user's password. Furthermore partition attack and subgroup confinement attack on SPEKE were discussed in [10] and [11].

2.3   VeriSign's Roaming Service

[Notation]

- f : a function that maps passwords to elements of multiplicative order q in Z_p^*
- KDF : a function that computes K by combining K_i
- OWF : an one way hash function

[User Registration Process]

VeriSign's Roaming Service should preferably be implemented in such a way that the integrity of the exchange is protected. For instance, the user might protect the exchange with SSL and trust the server to perform the computation correctly.

1. A : A, called "Personal Trust Agent(PTA)" in [14], generates Alice's key pair, (PRI, PUB).
2. A $\rightarrow$ CA : A sends the request of issuing a certificate and roaming registration to CA.
3. CA $\rightarrow$ A : CA issues and sends $Cert(A)$ to A.
4. Alice : Alice enters $ID(A)$ and PWD to A.
5. A $\rightarrow$ RS$_i$: A generates a random number a for $1 \leq a \leq q-1$, and computes $w = f(PWD)$ and $r = w^a \bmod p$. Then A sends $ID(A)$ and r to RS$_i$ for $i = 1, 2$.
6. RS$_i$ $\rightarrow$ A : RS$_i$ ($i = 1, 2$) selects a secret exponent d_i between 1 and $q-1$ for A, computes $s_i = r^{d_i} \bmod p$, and returns it to A. Then RS$_i$ stores $ID(A)$ and d_i ($i = 1, 2$) in its database.
7. A : A computes $K_i = s_i^{1/a} \bmod p$ ($i = 1, 2$) and $K = KDF(K_1, K_2)$ [1], where $1/a$ is the inverse of a mod q. Then A computes $EPD = E_K(PRI, Cert(A))$.
8. A $\rightarrow$ RS$_i$: A computes and sends $v_i = OWF(K, ID(RS_i))$ for $i = 1, 2$ to RS$_i$, where $ID(RS_i)$ is the identity of RS$_i$. RS$_i$ stores $(v_i, ID(A))$ in its database.
9. A $\rightarrow$ RS$_2$: A securely sends EPD to $RS2$ through secure communications channel such as SSL, and destroys K. RS$_2$ stores EPD in its DB.

[Roaming Process]

1. Alice : Alice enters $ID(A)$ and PWD to it's client software, A.
2. A $\rightarrow$ RS$_i$: A computes $w = f(PWD)$ and $r = w^a \bmod p$, where a is a random number, and sends $ID(A)$ and r to RS$_i$ for $i = 1, 2$.
3. RS$_i$ $\rightarrow$ A : RS$_i$ ($i = 1, 2$) retrieves d_i corresponding to the received $ID(A)$, computes $s_i = r^{d_i} \bmod p$, and returns it to A.
4. A : A computes $K_i = s_i^{1/a}$, where $1/a$ is the inverse of a mod q, and regenerate $K = KDF(K_1, K_2)$.
5. A $\rightarrow$ RS$_i$: A computes $v_i' = OWF(K, ID(RS_i))$ for $i = 1, 2$ and sends it to RS$_i$. To authenticate Alice, RS$_i$ ($i = 1, 2$) compares v_i' with v_i stored in its database.
6. A $\leftrightarrow$ RS$_2$: If successfully authenticated, A requests EPD to RS$_2$. RS$_2$ retrieves EPD and securely returns through secure communication channel, such as SSL.
7. A : A decrypts EPD with K to gain its credential, PRI and $Cert(A)$. After using its credential, A destroys K and its credential.

---

[1] For combining secret components K_i, t-out-of-N threshold secret sharing methods may be applied [3].

[Security analysis]

VeriSign's roaming service with SSL can trick the user into using "valid" SSL connections to malicious RSs. In this case, malicious RSs use bogus secret data, d_i^* for $i = 1, 2$ to mount a password guessing attack on user's password. Each malicious RS, RS_i^*, computes $s_i^* = r^{d_i^*} \bmod p$ for $i = 1, 2$ and returns it to A in the step 3 of the roaming process. Receiving s_i^*, A computes $K^* = KDF(K_1^*, K_2^*)$ and $v_i'^* = OWF(K^*, ID(RS_i))$ and returns $v_i'^*$ in the step 5 of the roaming process. Malicious RSs checks whether $v_i'^*$ received is equal to $OWF(KDF(f(PWD')^{d_1^*}, f(PWD')^{d_2^*}), ID(RS_i))$, where PWD' is a candidate of PWD. This match indicates a correct guess of the password. Therefore, VeriSign's roaming service is vulnerable to the password guessing attack in server spoofing attacks.

3   Our Proposed System

We propose a modified system to solve the problem mentioned in VeriSign's roaming service.

[Notations]

- g : a generator of G_q, where G_q is the unique subgroup of Z_p^* of order q
- x_i : a private key of RS_i for $i = 1, \cdots, n$.
- y : a group pubic key of RSs. It is generated as follows[5],[12],[13][2] : (1) Each RS_i $(i = 1, \cdots, n)$ chooses $r_i \in_R Z_q$ and makes $y_i = g^{r_i} \bmod p$ public. (2) Each RS_i selects a random polynomial $f_i \in_R Z_q[x]$ of degree $t - 1$ such that $f_i(0) = r_i$. Let $f_i(x) = r_i + a_{i,1}x + a_{i,2}x^2 + \cdots + a_{i,t-1}x^{t-1} \bmod q$, where $a_{i,1}, a_{i,2}, \cdots, a_{i,t-1} \in_R Z_q$. RS_i computes $f_i(j) \bmod q$ $(\forall j \neq i, 1 \leq j \leq n)$ and sends it to RS_j securely. And each RS_i computes $g^{a_{i,1}} \bmod p, g^{a_{i,2}} \bmod p, \cdots, g^{a_{i,t-1}} \bmod p$ and makes them public. (3) Using received $f_j(i)$ $(\forall j \neq i, 1 \leq j \leq n)$, each RS_i verifies that $g^{f_j(i)} \overset{?}{=} y_j \cdot (g^{a_{j,1}})^{i^1} \cdot \cdots \cdot (g^{a_{j,t-1}})^{i^{t-1}} \bmod p$. (4) Define H as the set $\{RS_i | RS_i$ is an honest RS satisfying the step (3)$\}$. Each RS_i computes its private key $x_i = \sum_{j \in H} f_j(i)$ and keeps it secure. (5) RSs compute and publish their group public key $y = \prod_{j \in H} y_j$.

[User Registration Process]

- A : A generates PWD and random number, z. Then A computes w and S, such as $w = f(PWD)$ and $S = g^z w \bmod p$, where f is a function that maps passwords to elements of multiplicative order q in Z_p^*.
- A → RS_i : A sends $(ID(A), S)$ to RS_i for $i = 1, \cdots, n$.
- RS_i → A : RS_i $(i = 1, \cdots, n)$ computes $B_i = S^{x_i} \bmod p$ and sends it to A. Then KS_i stores $ID(A)$ in its repository.

---

[2]   In [9], Gennaro et al. proved that one of the requirements in [12] is not guaranteed : more precisely, the property that the key is uniformly distributed in the key space. So far several solutions have been discovered, but for the practicality, we use Pedersen's scheme.

- A $\rightarrow$ CS : A computes $K = KDF((\prod_{1 \le i \le t} B_i^{\prod_{1 \le i \le t, j \ne i} j/(j-i)})/y^z \bmod p)$ and $K_1 = OWF(K, 1)$. Then A sends $(ID(A), K_1, E_{K_1}(PRI))$ to CS.
- CS : CS stores $(ID(A), K_1, E_{K_1}(PRI))$ in its database.

[Roaming Process]

- A : A generates a random number, z. Then A computes $w = f(PWD)$ and $S = g^z w \bmod p$ using PWD and z.
- A $\rightarrow$ RS$_i$: A sends $(ID(A), S)$ to RS$_i$ for $i = 1, \cdots, n$.
- RS$_i$ $\rightarrow$ A : RS$_i$ $(i = 1, \cdots, n)$ checks where A is the registered user. If $ID(A)$ exists within the repository, RS$_i$ $(i = 1, \cdots, n)$ computes $B_i = S^{x_i} \bmod p$ and then sends it to A.
- A $\rightarrow$ CS : A computes $K = KDF((\prod_{1 \le i \le t} B_i^{\prod_{1 \le i \le t, j \ne i} j/(j-i)})/y^z \bmod p)$ and $K_1 = OWF(K, 1)$. Then A sends a roaming request to CS.
- CS $\rightarrow$ A: CS generates c $(1 \le c \le q - 1)$ and sends it to A.
- A $\rightarrow$ CS : A computes $r = OWF(K_1, c)$ and sends r to CS.
- CS $\rightarrow$ A : CS retrieves K_1 from its database, computes $OWF(K_1, c)$, and then checks whether it is equal to r. If it is equal to r, CS sends $E_{K_1}(PRI)$ to A.
- A : A gets PRI by decrypting $E_{K_1}(PRI)$ with K_1.

[Security analysis]

Since our system is designed to store only registered user's identity, attacker accessing to RSs' repository cannot obtain any information about user's password. Unlike VeriSign's roaming service, Alice's key, K, is generated using RSs' private keys and attacker without RSs' private keys cannot masquerade RSs in the roaming process. Therefore, our system is secure against server's spoofing attack without additional security protocol such as SSL. While VeriSign's roaming service requires (n+1) times of exponent calculation, our proposed system requires only two exponent calculations and $(n + 1)$ multiplications, where n is the number of RSs. Therefore it can efficiently compute K even if the number of RSs is increased.

4 Conclusion

We survey three popular key roaming products of Baltimore's, Entrust's and VeriSign's. We also propose key roaming system which retrieves user's credential from multiple related RS and CS, without exposing the password to off-line guessing unless all servers are compromised, and without relying on additional secure channels in roaming process.

References

1. Baltimore: Baltimore Roaming. Private Communications (2001)
2. Bellovin S., Merrit M.: Encrypted key exchange: password based protocols secure against dictionary attacks. In Proceedings of the Symposium on Security and Privacy (1992) 72–84
3. Burton S. , Kaliski JR.: Server-Assisted Regeneration of a Strong Secret From a Weak Secret. US Patent, US Patent Number 09/804,460 (2000)
4. Cohen F.: 50 Ways to Attack Your World Wide Web System. Computer Security Institute Annual Conference, Washington DC (1995)
5. Desmedt Y., Frankel Y.: Threshold cryptosystems. Advanced in Cryptology – Crypto'89, Springer-Verlag, LNCS 435 (1990) 307–315
6. Entrust : The Entrust Roaming Solution. Private Communications (2000)
7. Felton E., Balfanz D., Dean D., Wallach D.: Web Spoofing : An Internet Con Game. 20th National Information Systems Security Conference, Balimore Maryland (1997) available at http://www.cs.princeton.edu/sip/pub/spoofing.html
8. Ford W., Burton S., Kaliski JR.: Server-Assisted Generation of a Strong Secret from a Password. Proceedings of the IEEE 9th International Workshops on Enabling Technologies: Infrastructure for Collaborative Enterprises, NIST, Gaithersburg MD (2000)
9. Gennaro R., Jarecki S., Krawczyk H., Rabin T.: Secure distributed key generation for discrete-log cryptosystems. Advanced in Cryptology – Eurocrypt'99, Springer-Verlag, LNCS 1592 (1999) 295–310
10. Jablon D.: Strong password-only authenticated exchange. ACM Computer Communications Review, vol 26, No.5 (1996)
11. Oorschot P., Wiener M.J.: On Diffie-Hellman Key Agreement with Short Exponents. EUROCRYPT'96, Spriger-Verlag, LNCS 1070 (1996)
12. Pedersen T.P. : A threshold cryptosystem without a trusted party. Advanced in Cryptology – Eurocrypt'91, Springer-Verlag, LNCS 547 (1991) 522–526
13. Pedersen T.P. : Distributed provers with applications to undeniable signatures. Advanced in Cryptology – Eurocrypt'91, Springer-Verlag, LNCS 547 (1991) 221–238
14. VeriSign Inc.: Roaming Service Administrator's Guide. (2002) available at http://www.verisign.com
15. VeriSign Inc.: Roaming Service. (2002) available at http://www.verisign.com/products/roaming/
16. Wiener M. J.: Secure Roaming with Software Tokens. PKI TWG Meeting (2000) available at http://csrc.nist.gov/pki/twg/y2000/presentations/twg-00-32.pdf

Host Revocation Authority: A Way of Protecting Mobile Agents from Malicious Hosts

Oscar Esparza, Miguel Soriano, Jose L. Muñoz, and Jordi Forné

Technical University of Catalonia C/ Jordi Girona 1 i 3, Campus Nord, Mod C3,
UPC 08034, Barcelona (Spain)
{oscar.esparza, soriano, jose.munoz, jforne}@entel.upc.es

Abstract. Mobile agents are software entities that consist of code, data
and state, and that can migrate autonomously from host to host executing their code. Despite its benefits, security issues restrict the use of code
mobility. The approach that is presented here aids to solve the problem
of malicious hosts by using a Trusted Third Party, the Host Revocation
Authority. The HoRA controls which are the hosts that acted maliciously
in the past. The agent sender must consult the HoRA before sending an
agent in order to remove from the agent's itinerary all the revoked hosts.
The HoRA can also revoke a malicious host if the agent sender detects
and proves that this malicious host did not act honestly.

1 Introduction

Mobile agents can migrate from host to host performing actions autonomously on
behalf of a user. Despite their benefits, massive use of mobile agents is restricted
by security issues. This paper introduces a new approach that aids to solve the
problem of malicious hosts by using a Host Revocation Authority. The HoRA
must be considered an independent Trusted Third Party (TTP) in a mobile agent
system. The HoRA stores the revoked host identifiers, i.e. the identifiers of those
hosts that have proven to be malicious. Before sending an agent, origin hosts
must ask to the HoRA if the hosts in the agent's itinerary have been revoked.
All those revoked hosts must be deleted from the agent's itinerary. An origin
host can also try to revoke a host by demonstrating to the HoRA that it acted
maliciously. In this sense, detection and proving of attacks are needed [5,1].

The rest of the paper is organized as follows: Section 2 presents some published approaches to solve the problem of the malicious hosts; Section 3 details
how the HoRA works and finally, some conclusions can be found in Section 4.

2 Malicious Hosts

The problem of malicious hosts is by far the most difficult to solve regarding
mobile agent security. Malicious hosts could try to get some profit of the agent
modifying the code, the data, the communications or even the results due to
their complete control on the execution. Current approaches can be divided in
two categories: attack detection and attack avoidance.

J.M. Cueva Lovelle et al. (Eds.): ICWE 2003, LNCS 2722, pp. 289–292, 2003.
© Springer-Verlag Berlin Heidelberg 2003

2.1 Attack Detection Approaches

This approaches need a TTP to punish malicious hosts in case of detection. This paper tries to solve this lack by adding the HoRA to the mobile agent system.

In [5], Vigna introduces the idea of cryptographic traces. The running agent takes traces of instructions that alter the agent's state due to external variables. If the agent owner wants to verify execution, it asks for the traces and executes the agent again. If new execution does not agree with the traces, the host is cheating. This approach has various drawbacks: (1) Verification is only performed in case of suspicion, but the way in which a host becomes suspicious is not explained; (2) Each host must store the traces for an indefinite period of time because the origin host can ask for them.

In [1] the authors present a protocol for detecting suspicious hosts by limiting the execution time of the agent. Each host saves the agent's arrival and leaving time. When the agent reaches the origin host, a set of time checks verifies if each host in the agent's itinerary spent more time than expected executing the agent. If so, the host is considered suspicious of malicious behavior.

2.2 Attack Avoidance Approaches

Detection techniques are not useful for services where benefits for tampering a mobile agent are greater than the possible punishment in case of detection, so attack avoidance techniques might be used. Unfortunately, there are no approaches that avoid attacks completely.

The environmental key generation [3] makes the agent's code impossible to decipher until the proper conditions happen on the environment, so previous analysis from hosts is avoided. The main drawback of this proposal is that hosts can perform a dictionary attack lying about the environment.

The Time Limited Blackbox [2] uses obfuscation as a way to hide the mobile agent's code and data to a malicious host. Protection is only assured for a period of time that depends on the computation capacity of the host. The scheme also needs a great amount of resources as the obfuscated code length is substantially greater than plain code.

The use of encrypted programs [4] is proposed as the only way to give privacy and integrity to mobile code. Hosts execute the encrypted code directly. Results are decrypted when the agent reaches the origin host. The difficulty here is to find functions that can be executed in an encrypted way.

3 Host Revocation Authority

This paper introduces a new entity in the mobile agent system, the Host Revocation Authority. The HoRA controls which hosts have been revoked in the mobile agent system, i.e. host that have proven to be malicious. The HoRA must be considered an independent TTP like the Certification Authority is considered in the PKI. The approach that is presented here can be considered neither a detection approach nor an avoidance approach, but a combination of them. First attack performed by a host cannot be avoided, but if the agent sender can prove that the host acted maliciously, this host can be revoked. Therefore, any other attack from this malicious host can be avoided.

The rest of the section explains the tasks that the HoRA must perform:

3.1   Keeping the Revocation Information

The aim of host revocation is to distinguish the malicious hosts from the honest ones. Unfortunately, it is not possible to know if a honest host can turn into malicious behavior just in the current transaction. However, it is possible to know if a host acted maliciously in the past. The HoRA knows which hosts have been revoked by saving their host identifiers in a list. Host identifiers must be unique in the mobile agent system, for instance IP addresses or DNS names can be used.

3.2   Revoking Malicious Hosts

Before an origin host starts a host revocation process, one of any existing detection and proving approaches must be used. For instance, the cryptographic traces approach [5] is widely known, but it has two major drawbacks: (1) How a host becomes suspicious and; (2) Each host must store the traces for an indefinite period of time. These drawbacks can be solved by using suspicious detection techniques [1]. Using jointly both mechanisms it is possible to detect suspicious hosts and to ask for the traces just when the agent returns to the origin host.

If there is a way to have proofs that demonstrate that a host did not execute an agent properly, the origin host can start the revocation process by sending to the HoRA this proofs. The HoRA receives the proofs and verifies the execution integrity. If finally the proofs are considered valid, the HoRA adds the malicious host's identifier in the list of revoked hosts.

The rest of the tasks depends on the revocation policy. Assuming that the HoRA works in a similar way as the Certification Authority regarding certificate revocation, two possible revocation policies can be followed.

3.3   Offline Revocation Policy: Generating the HRL

The off-line revocation policy is based on the distribution of revocation information using a Host Revocation List (HRL), i.e. a list of revoked host identifiers signed by the HoRA. Origin hosts must download a copy of the HRL in order to consult it before executing an agent. Origin hosts must also update the list periodically to take into account new malicious hosts. Generating the HRL is as easy as signing the list that the HoRA has internally. As it is a signed list, it can also be downloaded from non trusted repositories. In this sense, the HRL works in a similar way as the Certificate Revocation List in the PKI.

3.4   Online Revocation Policy: Receiving and Replying to Requests

The on-line revocation policy is based on asking the revocation information to the HoRA directly. Before sending a mobile agent, each origin host sends a request to the HoRA asking for the status of the hosts in the agent's itinerary. The HoRA consults if these hosts are included in its internal list, and it sends a signed response to the origin host pointing out which hosts in the agent's itinerary have been revoked. This mechanism works in a similar way as the Online Certificate Status Protocol used in the PKI.

3.5   Improvements

The following improvements can be achieved in the HoRA:

– The list that the HoRA has internally grows in an indefinite way. This problem can be solved by using an Agent Execution Certificate, i.e. a certificate issued by the HoRA that permits the hosts to execute agents during a validity period. In this case, the HoRA does not revoke the host identifier, but the certificate.
– The HoRA must be accessible for all hosts. An alternative topology based on repositories and a replication policy between entities must be thought.

4   Conclusions

The approach that is presented here aids to solve the problem of malicious hosts by using a TTP, the Host Revocation Authority. The HoRA controls which are the hosts that acted maliciously in the past. Each agent sender must consult the HoRA before sending a mobile agent in order to remove from the agent's itinerary all the revoked hosts. The HoRA can also revoke a malicious host if the agent sender proves that this malicious host did not act honestly.

Acknowledgments. This work is supported by the Spanish Research Council under the project DISQET CICYT TIC2002-00818.

References

1. O. Esparza, M. Soriano, J.L. Muñoz, and J. Forné. Limiting the execution time in a host: a way of protecting mobile agents. In *IEEE Sarnoff Symposium "Advances in Wired and Wireless Communications"*, 2003.
2. F. Hohl. Time Limited Blackbox Security: Protecting Mobile Agents From Malicious Hosts. In *Mobile Agents and Security*, volume 1419 of *LNCS*. Springer-Verlag, 1998.
3. J. Riordan and B. Schneier. Environmental Key Generation Towards Clueless Agents. In *Mobile Agents and Security*, volume 1419 of *LNCS*. Springer-Verlag, 1998.
4. T. Sander and C.F. Tschudin. Protecting mobile agents against malicious hosts. In *Mobile Agents and Security*, volume 1419 of *LNCS*. Springer-Verlag, 1998.
5. G. Vigna. Cryptographic traces for mobile agents. In *Mobile Agents and Security*, volume 1419 of *LNCS*. Springer-Verlag, 1998.

Enabling Secure Multicast Using a New Java LKH Rekeying Tool

Josep Pegueroles and Francisco Rico-Novella

Departamento de Ingeniería Telemática. Universitat Politècnica de Catalunya.
Jordi Girona 1 y 3. Campus Nord, Mod C3, UPC. 08034 Barcelona. Spain
{josep.pegueroles, telfrn}@entel.upc.es

Abstract. The most promising protocols for multicast key management
are those based on multilevel logical binary trees of Key Encryption
Keys (KEKs). One of these protocols, Logical Key Hierarchy (LKH) has
become a standard de facto today. This work presents an open implementation of LKH protocol for Java applications that enables the use of
Multicast Security in web applications.

1 Introduction

When multicast applications pretend to be commercial, security services become
essential. Confidentiality in such environment need a common secret shared by
all members. This provides group secrecy and source authentication. The shared
key must be updated every time a member joins or leaves the group [1]. In this
scenario, where session keys are continuously changing, Key Management (KM)
has an important role. The most promising multicast KM protocols are those
based on binary trees of Key Encryption Keys (KEK) [2,3]. This approach results
in a quite efficient key update mechanism in which the number of multicast
messages needed for membership update is not proportional to the number of
members in the group but to the tree depth. If KEK tree is balanced, depth
of the tree is logarithmic in the size of the secure multicast group O(logN),
same behavior shows the number of multicast messages needed for key update.
Logical Key Hierarchy algorithm (LKH) has become the most accepted one.
Neither applications nor libraries allowing secure multicast rekeying are known
prior to this work.

2 JavaLKH Rekeying Tool

According to that, the Information Security Group [4]of the Technical University
of Catalonia has developed a Java tool enabling secure multicast rekeying for
multicast networks by means of LKH algorithm. All the efforts were focused on
the reuse of code for future implementations of other algorithms. The tool takes
advantage of the encryption utilities of JCE [5] and uses the provider-architecture
in order to have algorithm and implementation independence.

J.M. Cueva Lovelle et al. (Eds.): ICWE 2003, LNCS 2722, pp. 293–294, 2003.
© Springer-Verlag Berlin Heidelberg 2003

JavaLKH has 4 main parts. The core classes for the easy management of key tree. The proper classes in order to implement the LKH itself. The class tree programmed for the generation of valid packet formats in GDOI (Group Domain of Interpretation) IETF standard proposal [6]. And two standalone applications (one for the client, and one for the key server) that help the testing of the programmed classes.The developed modules can be downloaded for test purposes from [7]. In this site can also be found the javaDoc class documentation, an easy HOWTO for newbies and a page with snapshots and examples of use.

The core package can be included in java applications in order to add key management functionality to new programs. Apart from that, the standalone Server and Client programs are very useful for educational and demonstrative purposes. These allow a Key Server to stablish secure communications within a multicast group, maintaining the logical key tree and sending valid rekeying messages to the remaining group members every time a joining or a leaving is requested. The same way the client can easily join or leave the group and update the Key Session when needed.

3   Future Work

As future works for our research and development are pointed out the improvement of performance by the programming of more efficient algorithms for managing trees. After that, the extension of the capabilities of package to other rekeying algorithms such as OFC [3] or Balanced Batch Rekeying [8] and inclusion of them in a provider structure are also expected to be achieved in the near future.

Acknowledgments. This work is supported by the Spanish research council under projects DISQET (CICYT TIC2002-818) and CREDO (CICYT - TIC2002-00249)

References

1. Wallner, Harder, Agee. Key Management for Multicast: Issues and Architectures. RFC2627
2. Harney, Harder. Logical Key Hierarchy Protocol (LKH). Mar 99. I-D Harney-sparta-lkhp-sec-00. Work in progress
3. Canetti, Malkin, Nissim. Efficient Communication Storage Tradeoffs for Multicast Encryption. Eurocrypt99 pp 456–470 1999
4. UPC's Information Security Group web page http://isg.upc.es
5. Pistoia. Java 2. Network Security. Prentice Hall PTR. 1999.
6. Baugher, Hardjono, Harney, Weis. The Group Domain of Interpretation. I-D draft-ietf-msec-gdoi-07. Work in progress
7. Download Site for Secure multicast application. http://isg.upc.es/gsec/download.
8. Pegueroles, Rico-Novella. Balanced Batch LKH: New Proposal, Implementation and Performance Evaluation IEEE Symposium on Computers and Communications – 2003

A Taxonomy of Web Attacks

Gonzalo Álvarez and Slobodan Petrović

Instituto de Física Aplicada, C.S.I.C., Serrano 144, 28006 Madrid, Spain,
{gonzalo,slobodan}@iec.csic.es,
http://www.iec.csic.es/

Abstract. A new taxonomy of web attacks is proposed in this paper, with the objective of obtaining a useful security reference framework. Possible applications are described, which might benefit from this taxonomy, such as intrusion detection systems and application firewalls.

1 Introduction

By *web attacks*, we understand attacks exclusively using the HTTP/HTTPS protocol. When the web attacks recorded through the years are analyzed, it is observed that most of them are recurrent attacks. In fact, they correspond to a limited number of types of attacks. Thus, it is generally agreed that classification can help designers, programmers, and security analysts to better understand attacks and build more secure applications.

In an effort to create a common reference language for security analysts, a number of taxonomies of computer attacks and vulnerabilities have appeared in recent years [1,2,3,4,5]. The shortcoming of such taxonomies is that they often include categories unsuitable for the classification of web attacks. Even when their categories can be used in a web context, they fail to cover all the subtleties of web attacks. For example, entry point, target, HTTP Verb, and HTTP Header are web-specific categories that we consider important for a more accurate classification of web attacks, and these are not covered by general taxonomies. In addition, some categories that can also be met in general taxonomies, such as vulnerability, need to take web-specific values (e.g. Code injection, HTML manipulation).

In this paper we propose a taxonomy of web attacks, taking into account a number of important features of each attack category. The role of these features as well as their importance for each of the attack categories is discussed. The ideas about the applications that might benefit from this taxonomy are also presented.

2 Web Attack Properties

A *taxonomy* is a classification scheme that partitions a body of knowledge and defines the relationship of the objects. *Classification* is the process of using a tax-

J.M. Cueva Lovelle et al. (Eds.): ICWE 2003, LNCS 2722, pp. 295–298, 2003.
© Springer-Verlag Berlin Heidelberg 2003

onomy for separating and ordering [2]. Satisfactory taxonomies have classification categories with the following characteristics: mutually exclusive, exhaustive, unambiguous, repeatable, accepted, and useful.

First, we introduce a novel model of web attacks based on the concept of *attack life cycle*. By attack life cycle we understand a succession of steps followed by an attacker to carry out some malicious activity on the web server, as depicted in Figure 1. The attacker gets through an entry point, searching for a vulnerability in the web server or web application, which might be exploited to defeat some security service. The vulnerability is realized by an action, using some HTTP verb and headers of certain length, directed against a given target and with a given scope. The attacker might obtain some privileges that depend on the type of attack. Our taxonomy of web attacks is based on the attack life cycle defined in this way.

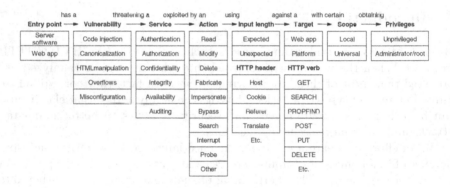

Fig. 1. Taxonomy of web attacks

At every stage of the life cycle we define the following classification criteria or classifiers:

1. Entry point: where the attack gets through. We distinguish between *web server software* attacks and *web application* attacks. The former are due to errors in the server software and, thus, they are shared by all web applications running on top. The origin of the latter depends on the web application. Those may be errors in HTML forms, client-side scripts, server-side scripts (.asp, .jsp, .php, .pl, etc.), business logic objects (COM, COM+, CORBA, etc.), SQL sentences processing, etc.
2. Vulnerability: a weakness in a system allowing unauthorized action. We define the following vulnerabilities in web applications: code injection (script, SQL, or XPath injection), canonicalization, HTML manipulation (often accomplished through URL query strings, form fields, or cookies), overflows, and misconfiguration.

3. Service (under threat): security service threatened by the attack. We distinguish between attacks against the following services: authentication, authorization, confidentiality, integrity, availability, and auditing.

4. Action: actual attack realizing the threat against the web server exploiting the vulnerability. We distinguish among actions aimed at three different objectives: server data, user authentication, and web server. Actions directed against data include *read*, *modify*, *delete*, and *fabricate*. Actions directed against authentication include *impersonate*, *bypass*, and *search*. Actions directed against the web server include *interrupt*, *probe*, and *other*.

5. Length: the length of the arguments passed to the HTTP request. We distinguish between *common-length* and *unusually long* attacks.

6. HTTP Verb: Verbs needed to perform the attack: GET, POST, HEAD, etc.

7. HTTP Header: Headers needed to perform the attack: Host, Cookie, Referer, etc.

8. Target: the aim of the attack. We distinguish between *application* attacks and *platform* attacks. In application attacks, only the application data and functionality is affected, but not the operating system resources. These attacks are typically aimed at web pages, web users, and web data. In platform attacks, the attacker usually seeks after arbitrary command execution, manipulation of machine accounts, tampering with the host's services, obtaining network information, etc.

9. Scope: impact of the attack on the web server. We distinguish between *local* (only one user or a small group of users is affected) and *universal* attacks (all users are affected).

10. Privileges: privileges obtained by the attacker after the successful completion of the attack. We distinguish between *unprivileged* and *administrative* attacks.

3   Possible Applications

This taxonomy is useful in a number of applications, especially in intrusion detection systems and in application-level firewalls.

3.1   Intrusion Detection Systems (IDS)

An intrusion detection system (IDS) detects and reports attempts to misuse or break into networked computer systems in real time [6]. One of the biggest problems faced by these systems is the huge amount of alerts that might be generated in a heavily-attacked environment in a matter of hours. It is impossible for a human operator to analyze so many reports and decide on the severity of the detected attacks to determine the action to take. This taxonomy can be used in the following way: first, the attacks are encoded into vectors using an accepted encoding scheme. Next, these vectors are processed using pattern recognition or information extraction techniques (clustering algorithms, supervised learning, etc.) in order to pinpoint the most dangerous attacks, and analyze attack trends throughout time.

3.2   Application Level Firewalls

Another approach to detect and prevent web attacks consists of using application level firewalls or, more specifically, web application firewalls. Application level firewalls are capable of processing data at the application level as well as decrypting SSL connections. An application-layer solution works within the application that it is protecting, inspecting requests as they come in from the network level. If at any point a possible attack is detected, it can take over and prevent unauthorized access and/or damage to the web server.

Classifying the attacks once they have been blocked by the firewall and deciding on their severity is crucial for a prompt and effective response. This taxonomy helps in this task, providing an exhaustive group of mutually exclusive categories under which the attacks can be unambiguously classified. Afterwards, a decision system can determine the priority of various attacks.

4   Conclusion

In this paper, a taxonomy of web attacks is proposed that intends to represent a forward step towards a more precise reference framework. An attack life cycle is defined as its base, to make it structured and logical. The properties of the most common web attacks are enumerated. Possible applications are described, which might benefit from this taxonomy, such as intrusion detection systems and application firewalls. We are working on the automated encoding of web attacks using different-length vectors and determining their priority using edit distance clustering.

Acknowledgements. This research was supported by Ministerio de Ciencia y Tecnología, Proyecto TIC2001-0586.

References

1. Cohen, F.B.: Information system attacks: A preliminary classification scheme. Computers and Security **16** (1997) 29–46
2. Howard, J.D., Longstaff, T.A.: A common language for computer security incidents. Technical Report SAND98-8667. Sandia National Laboratories (1998)
3. Lindqvist, U., Jonsson, E.: How to systematically classify computer security intrusions. Proceedings of the 1997 IEEE Symposium on Security & Privacy (1997) 154–163
4. Lough, D.L.: A Taxonomy of Computer Attacks with Applications to Wireless Networks. PhD thesis. Virginia Polytechnic Institute and State University (2001)
5. Richardson, T.W.: The Development of a Database Taxonomy of Vulnerabilities to Support the Study of Denial of Service Attacks. PhD thesis. Iowa State University (2001)
6. Northcutt, S.: Network Intrusion Detection, Third Edition. New Riders Publishing (2002)

A Pseudorandom Bit Generator Based on Block Upper Triangular Matrices

Rafael Álvarez, Joan–Josep Climent, Leandro Tortosa, and Antonio Zamora

Departament de Ciència de la Computació i Intel·ligència Artificial. Universitat d'Alacant, Campus de Sant Vicent, Ap.Correus 99, E–03080, Alacant, Spain.
afa@afaland.com   {jcliment,tortosa,zamora}@dccia.ua.es

Abstract. The popularity of the Web has created a great marketplace for businesses to sell and showcase their products increasing the need for secure Web services such as SSL, TLS or SET. We propose a pseudorandom bit generator that can be used to create a stream cipher directly applicable to these secure systems; it is based on the powers of a block upper triangular matrix achieving great statistical results and efficiency.

1 Introduction

A pseudorandom generator [4] is a deterministic algorithm that takes a random sequence of bits of length k, called seed, and generates a sequence of bits of length l, the pseudorandom sequence, being l very large compared to k. The output sequence is not really random, it is simply generated in such a way that it cannot be distinguished from a real random sequence. The size of the seed must be such that 2_k is big enough to prevent successful exhaustive key space search attacks. Also, the period of the sequence must be larger than l; otherwise, the sequence would repeat, not appearing as random anymore. Our proposal is a new pseudorandom bit generator that can be used as a stream cipher directly (a Vernam cipher), which could then be the private key cryptosystem of any Web security system such as SSL, TLS or SET; or be the base to create more sophisticated cryptographic algorithms.

2 Description of the Pseudorandom Bit Generator

Our generator is based on the powers of block upper triangular matrices defined over $\mathbb{Z}_p$, with p prime. Consider matrix M defined as

$$M = \begin{bmatrix} A & X \\ O & B \end{bmatrix}, \tag{1}$$

where A is an r × r matrix, B is an s × s matrix, X is an r × s matrix and O denotes the s × r zero matrix.

The following result is the base of the pseudorandom generator.

J.M. Cueva Lovelle et al. (Eds.): ICWE 2003, LNCS 2722, pp. 299–300, 2003.
© Springer-Verlag Berlin Heidelberg 2003

Table 1. Statistical test results

Length	Monobit	Serial	Poker	Runs	Autocorrelation	Linear Complexity
$2 \cdot 10^4$	0.012	1.579	243.1	8.441	0.800	10001
$2 \cdot 10^5$	1.095	1.451	239.1	26.550	0.789	100000
$2 \cdot 10^6$	0.814	3.313	207.2	37.590	0.807	1000000

Theorem 1. *Let M be the matrix given in equation (1). Taking h as a nonnegative integer and if $0 \le t \le h$ then*

$$M^h = \begin{bmatrix} A^h & X^{(h)} \\ O & B^h \end{bmatrix}, \quad X^{(h)} = \begin{cases} 0 & \text{if } h = 0 \\ A^t X^{(h-t)} + X^{(t)} B^{h-t} & \text{if } h \ge 0 \end{cases}$$

To obtain the pseudorandom bit sequence, we build A and B using primitive polynomials (see [5]) and choose randomly X, the seed of the sequence. From theorem 1 we have a succession of matrices $X^{(h)}$, for $h = 2, 3, \ldots$, adding all elements of each matrix we compute a new element $x^{(h)}$, for $h = 2, 3, \ldots$, in $\mathbb{Z}_p$, from which we take the least significant bit to conform the output sequence. The period of the sequence is determined by the least common multiple of the periods of A and B (see [5]).

3   Results

The algorithm has been checked with five different statistics: monobit, serial, poker, runs, and autocorrelation (see [4]); and with the computation of the linear complexity [1, 3]. In table 1 we can see that the results are particularly good.

4   Conclusions

Using primitive polynomials to generate the diagonal blocks and, taking very small primes as well as small matrix sizes, we can produce very efficiently bit sequences with very high periods, great statistical properties and high linear complexities.

References

1. Berlekamp, E. R.: Algebraic Coding Theory. McGraw Hill, New York (1968)
2. Freier, A. O., Karlton, P., Kocher, P. C.: The SSL Protocol, Version 3.0. Internet Draft, Netscape, March (1996)
3. Massey, J. L.: Shift-Register Synthesis and BCH Decoding. IEEE Transactions on Information Theory, 15 (1969) 122–127
4. Menezes, A., van Oorschot, P., Vanstone, S.: Handbook of Applied Cryptography. CRC Press, Boca Raton, FL,(2001)
5. Odoni, R. W. K., Varadharajan, V., Sanders, P. W.: Public Key Distribution in Matrix Rings. Electronic Letters, 20 (1984) 386–387

Retrofitting Security into a Web-Based Information System

David Bettencourt da Cruz, Bernhard Rumpe, and Guido Wimmel

Software & Systems Engineering, Technische Universität München
85748 Munich/Garching, Germany

This paper reports on an incremental method that allows adding security mechanisms to an existing, but insecure system, such as a prototype or a legacy system. The incremental method is presented and as a showcase its application is demonstrated at the example of a Web-based information system.

1 Introduction

Security is an extremely important issue in the development of distributed systems. This applies in particular to Web-based systems, which communicate over an open network. Failures of security mechanisms may cause very high damage with financial and legal implications. Security concerns, both on the part of enterprises and consumers, are one of the major reasons why new technologies such as E-commerce or E-government are used very reluctantly.

Developing security-critical systems is very difficult. Security is a complex non-functional requirement affecting all parts of a system at all levels of detail. To secure a system, merely adding mechanisms such as cryptography in some places is not sufficient. Whether a system is secure depends crucially on the complex interplay of its components and the assumptions about its environment. A single weakness can compromise the security of the entire system.

Furthermore, many systems are developed initially without security in mind. Reasons for that are that they were designed for a secure environment such as a local network, that existing legacy systems are to be adapted, or because they were first developed as a functional prototype. Retrofitting security into an existing system is generally believed to be extremely hard to achieve, and it is in effect often advised against doing so at all. In this article we report on the experiences of a Java project where exactly this retrofitting was done after developing initial prototypes.

The RAC system is an Internet information system based on the "push" principle: information is presented to the user on a client application ("pushlet") and updated when necessary, without the user having to explicitly check for such updates. The server regularly or on demand contacts the client for updates. The RAC system was initially developed as a prototype without security functionality as its focus was targeting to be production companies' internal information systems.

In this paper, we describe a method to carry out a security analysis of an existing system and to introduce appropriate mechanisms to achieve high trustworthiness. Our method is demonstrated at the example of the RAC system. It is based on a combina-

J.M. Cueva Lovelle et al. (Eds.): ICWE 2003, LNCS 2722, pp. 301–305, 2003.
© Springer-Verlag Berlin Heidelberg 2003

tion of an evolutionary approach and method suggested in [1]. We comment on experiences and difficulties in adding security to an existing system, in particular in the context of Web-based Java applications.

Related Work. The consideration of additional or changed requirements within the lifetime of a system is one of the main aims of iterative processes, such as Boehm's Spiral Model [4]. Few works are available on the integration of security aspects into the development process. In [1], Eckert suggests a top-down approach, which we used as a basis for our work. A mapping of ITSEC security requirements to development activities in the German V-Model 97 is given in [5]. [3] describes a lifecycle process based on the Evaluation Assurance Requirements of the Common Criteria for Security Evaluation, at the example of a payment system. These processes are mainly tailored to the development of new systems. Security aspects of distributed Java applications are covered in detail in [6], but methodical guidance is missing there.

2   The Web-Based Information System RAC

The RAC system is an experimental prototype serving a variety of issues. It is a Web-based information retrieval system that updates its information automatically by pushing new information to its clients. Therefore the presented information is always up to date no matter whether the information changes within seconds (such as in stock information systems) or within minutes or hours (such as e.g. temperature values). Another pleasant effect of the pushing mechanism is that the system has a very efficient communication (no polling needed), which can even be used over low-bandwidth communication lines. For more information about the RAC system, see [9].

3   Method for Introducing Security Features

Early in the development, it was decided that the RAC system is to be developed in increments. Also based on our experiences in building similar systems it was decided to build an efficient feasibility prototype without any security mechanisms. Instead, any security considerations should be retrofitted into the existing system in a later increment. We were well aware that this might make it necessary to refactor parts of the code.

The method used for adding security to the RAC system was based on existing methodologies for developing new security-critical systems ([1], [3]). The main steps taken here and the differences and difficulties found upon retrofitting them into an existing system are sketched in the rest of the section.

Threat Analysis. During the threat analysis each and every possible threat to the system has to be documented (threats are situations or events that may lead to unauthorized access, destruction, disclosure or modification of data, or to denial of service). Obviously, only threats that have been identified at this stage can later on be considered to be countered. Therefore, it is important that the threat analysis is as complete as possible. Hence it is crucial to use a systematic approach to identify the threats. In case of the RAC-System, threat trees [7] were used. The root of a threat tree consists of all possible threats to a system. Its successor nodes correspond to more fine-grained threat classes (which together make up all possible threats), and the leafs consist of single threats or very small related groups of threats. There is some degree of freedom in how the threats are decomposed, as long as no threats are lost during the process.

Threat Classification. After having completed the search for the threats, the resulting threats are classified (1) by an estimate of the potential *damage* caused if the threat can be realized, and (2) by an estimate of the *effort* it would take an attacker to realize the threat. To allow for a systematic risk analysis, damage and effort are measured in a quantitative metrics, depending on the use of the program. In programs with a commercial use, money is mostly a good scale to choose. Other appropriate metrics are necessary time, hardware or knowledge, which can in turn again be represented by money.

In case of the RAC system both, the threat analysis and the threat classification, were greatly facilitated by the available increments. The necessary work for the threat analysis could be reduced from finding threats that might appear in future to finding threats that could actually be encountered in the running version. The classification of identified threats was also easier, since the available components immediately gave an idea of the values for potential damage and effort and if they didn't it was possible to simply try out and check the results.

Finding Countermeasures. The next step to take is to find countermeasures against each of the identified threats independently of how they have been classified. Fortunately, quite a number of standard security techniques, patterns and concepts [1,2] that provide countermeasures against most of the major threats already exist. At this step the countermeasures found against the threats do not yet have to be worked out in great detail. Providing a basic idea is usually enough to be able to classify them in the next step.

Classification of the Countermeasures. The classification of the countermeasures is carried out in a way similar to the way used in threat analysis. For this classification, the effort needed to realize a countermeasure is estimated. Again the classification is based on a metrics and thus allows comparison. Ideally the metrics used is the same as the one used for threat classification, since that would ease the following combination of all classifications.

When retrofitting security into a system, specifying and assessing countermeasures is more difficult, as the design of the existing system must be taken into account. If the countermeasure against a threat cannot be assigned to a small, modular or easily separable part of the program, it becomes much harder to retrofit. Therefore it is very important to classify the countermeasures with great care in order to implement the correct security features in the next increment.

Combining the Classifications. Finally the results from all the classifications are combined to identify which threats should be dealt with. This largely depends on the available budget and the level of security that must be reached. This procedure will result in the functional security requirements, which then can be used as if they were traditional requirements and implemented. As a specialty, we found that these so called "requirements" usually go deep into design activities and thus combine analysis and design phase. In this respect, we deviate from the strictly sequential approach suggested in [1]. Postponing the decision which threats should be countered to the point after the assessment of corresponding countermeasures adds a little overhead. But it is easier in our case as there is already an implemented system available and it leads to a more effective selection of security measures within the given time/budget.

More detailed information on how this approach was applied to the RAC system can be found in [9].

4 Discussion

In our approach, the choice of the countermeasures that should be implemented is based on both an assessment of the threats and of the countermeasures. This was only possible with reasonable time and effort because an implementation and automated tests were already available. Based on this information, the most effective security functions given particular time/budget constraints for their implementation can be selected. The existing tests could be re-used to verify that the program's functionality has not been affected, and additional tests for the security functionality could be added. Finally, it is important that the existing software is well documented. Otherwise the threat analysis becomes hard to carry out.

We believe that Java is to date the most appropriate architecture for information systems where security might become important after some iterations, because of its built-in security features. However, there are also problems. Firstly, the Java Sandbox does not implement the principle of complete mediation [8]. It usually only checks for correct access when a protected object is created. Further use of the object works independently of the Sandbox, thus enabling attackers to gain access to the object through the program. Secondly, if the program is not strictly modularized, the Sandbox becomes much harder to introduce, and restructuring might become necessary to be able to use the access modifiers (private, protected, public).

If these points are considered, a certain level of security can be actually retrofitted into existing software without great overhead.

References

[1]   C. Eckert. IT-Sicherheit (in German). Oldenbourg Verlag, 2001.
[2]   R. Anderson: Security Engineering: A Guide to Building Dependable Distributed Systems. Wiley, 2001.
[3]   M. Vetterling, G. Wimmel, A. Wißpeintner. Secure Systems Development Based on the Common Criteria. 10th International Symposium on the Foundations of Software Engineering (FSE-10), 2002.
[4]   B. Boehm. A Spiral Model of Software Development and Enhancement. IEEE Computer, Vol. 21, #5, May 1988.

[5]   IABG. SEC: Using the V-Model and the ITSEC. In: Part 3 of the IABG V-Model 97, 1999. URL: http://www.v-modell.iabg.de/

[6]   Li Gong. Inside Java 2 Platform Security: Architecture, API Design, and Implementation. Addison-Wesley, 1999.

[7]   E. G. Amoroso. Fundamentals of Computer Security Technology. Prentice Hall, 1994.

[8]   J.H. Saltzer, M.D. Schroeder. The Protection of Information in Computer Systems. Proceedings of the IEEE 63, 9, 1975.

[9]   D. Cruz, B. Rumpe, G. Wimmel. Retrofitting Security into a Web-based Information System. Technical report, available from: http://www4.in.tum.de/~wimmel/.

A Quantitative Analysis of eCRM Tools in the Austrian Pharmaceutical Industry

Arno Scharl[1] and Horst Treiblmaier[2]

[1] University of Western Australia, Information Mgmt & Marketing Department;
Graduate School of Management; 35 Stirling Highway, Crawley, WA 6009, Australia
Arno.Scharl@uwa.edu.au
[2] Vienna University of Economics and Business Administration,
Information Systems Department; Augasse 2-6, A-1090 Vienna, Austria
Horst.Treiblmaier@wu-wien.ac.at

Abstract. Electronic Customer Relationship Management (cCRM) integrates the potential of Web-based interactivity with traditional marketing tools. It supports companies by improving their overall Web appearance and offering customized services. The pharmaceutical industry in particular benefits from Internet technologies due to legal restrictions that often inhibit a direct relationship with the customer. This paper analyzes how pharmaceutical companies leverage eCRM tools in order to enhance their quality of service. We used an automated tool that parsed the source code and integrated this information with results from a traditional survey based on expert judgments. The profiles of 33 Web sites were categorized and used to evaluate eCRM functionality.

1 Introduction and Methodology

Steadily increasing demands of customers and the availability of new technologies have led to profound changes in marketing. Attention has shifted from the product to the consumer. Mass marketing concepts in the 1950s were followed by direct marketing in the 70s and 80s. In recent years the relationship between vendors and customers has been the focus of a variety of different approaches that come under the umbrella term *Customer Relationship Management (CRM)*. Most definitions of this term concentrate on the processes of acquiring customers and keeping them loyal to a company's products and services [1, 2]. To reflect the increasing importance of electronic media, the concept subsequently evolved to *electronic Customer Relationship Management*, or *eCRM* [3]. Several authors classified eCRM tools according to the information needs of the customer and the company's control over the content [4, 5]. Personalization and customization strategies facilitate addressing single customers individually and enable tailored approaches such as one-to-one marketing [6].

In order to categorize and evaluate the different ways companies are utilizing eCRM we pursued a two-fold strategy. We manually analyzed 33 Austrian Web sites of the pharmaceutical industry with respect to various communication features. Subsequently, an automated tool extracted information directly from the published documents and parsed the available source code including markup tags and scripts [7, 8]. The site metrics from both sources were combined and grouped into different catego-

J.M. Cueva Lovelle et al. (Eds.): ICWE 2003, LNCS 2722, pp. 306–309, 2003.
© Springer-Verlag Berlin Heidelberg 2003

ries. Our results reveal that, despite the fact that the Internet represents an established marketing medium, many companies only partially utilize the potential of eCRM. To keep our findings comparable, we concentrated on the pharmaceutical sector, which is an industry that can utilize eCRM tools for a broad spectrum of tasks. First of all, information is an important product component, provided not only to end consumers but also to pharmacies, physicians and hospitals that require comprehensive product information. In addition to that, legal regulations in many countries restrict the way pharmaceutical companies can conduct offline marketing campaigns. Therefore a strong electronic brand (supported by eCRM) can help establish a direct relationship to new customer segments.

Automatic gathering and extracting information assures scalability, speed, consistency, rigorous structure, and abundance of data. While data mining is quite common in the pharmaceutical industry at the point-of-sale [9], Web-based knowledge discovery and competitive intelligence remain an active area of research.

In the *data gathering phase* of our research, Web sites are mirrored in regular intervals while respecting the wishes of site owners with regards to where robots may search as stipulated in the *robots.txt* file. The algorithm, which ignores graphical data and multimedia files, follows a site's hierarchical structure until reaching a limit of ten megabytes. Only textual information is considered, which includes both visible (raw text including headings, menus, or link descriptions) and invisible text (embedded markup tags, scripting elements, and so forth). These limitations help compare systems of heterogeneous size, and manage available local storage space. Specialized information found in hierarchical levels below that limit does not belong to the primary user interface and thus can be disregarded for most analytical objectives.

In the *data extraction phase*, actionable knowledge is derived from processing the mirrored data. The computation of ratios, means and variances reduces data redundancy and provides aggregated parameters that are easier to convey and interpret. Statistical methods can then be applied on the preprocessed output. Automated coding removes subjective interpretations and many of the questionable aspects of manual coding from the analytical process. It renders the problems of time-consuming and expensive coder training or intra- and intercoder reliability obsolete [10], as the process does not involve human coders who could disagree on attribute values. The nature of the object to be analyzed – i.e., Web-based information systems that are publicly available – does not require interviewing members of the organization or privileged access to the computing resources of third parties beyond those available to regular Web users.

2   Analysis of the Austrian Pharmaceutical Market

Prescriptions by medical practitioners dominate the Austrian pharmaceutical market. Pharmacies may only sell non-prescription products over the counter. In 1999 this market segment accounted for merely 12% of the total market, which is due to a relatively restrictive legal situation in Austria. Nevertheless, more and more consumers actively search for product information and demand specific pharmaceuticals.

Web-based information systems can support this decision-making process and help establish a direct customer relationship. Figure 1 compares the percentage of Austrian pharmaceutical companies that provide certain eCRM core functionalities.

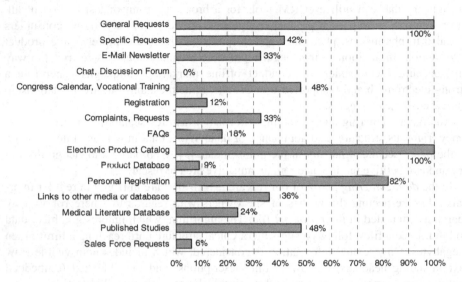

Fig. 1. eCRM features of Austrian pharmaceutical sites (n = 33)

The subsequent competitive Web analysis used 21 criteria grouped into 6 categories: product information, asynchronous communication, virtual community, personal registration, specific medical services, and overall interactivity.

Product Information – Basic product information represents a common feature. However, only a few companies provide FAQ sections (18%) or product databases (9%). This comes as a surprise, since many products and their applications are complex and thus require detailed information.

Asynchronous Communication | Electronic Mail – Not surprisingly, all of the analyzed sites offer an email address for general requests. But less than half of the companies (42%) encourage specific requests by offering the possibility to contact experts directly. On average, the sites comprise links to 19.6 email addresses. One third of the companies (33%) publish an electronic newsletter that enables them to keep in contact with their stakeholders (although not on a one-to-one basis).

Virtual Community – None of the Austrian pharmaceutical companies offers synchronous online communication (e.g., online chats) or a discussion forum, which is partly due to legal issues regarding product information. 48% offer congress calendars or information about vocational training, whereas only 12% allow for online registration. One third (33%) encourage comments or general feedback.

Personal Registration – 82% of the companies enable personal registration, which allows them to gather user-specific data.

Specific Medical Services – About a third of the Web sites (36%) link to other medical media or databases, while only 24% offer an online database. On a per document basis, there are 12.9 (sd = 11.7) internal and 2.3 (sd = 2.3) external hyperlinks.

The number of internal broken links is rather heterogeneous, with an average of 14.0 (min = 0; max = 238; sd = 44.7). Nearly half of the sites (48%) publish scientific studies. The low percentage of sites that allow for sales force requests (8%) suggests that many business partners still prefer to use traditional communication channels.

Interactivity – As far as interactive features are concerned, a number of variables were used to compare the sites. The provision of email addresses and differences in the hyperlink structure have already been discussed above. On average, the sites comprise 1.5 (sd = 2.9) inline scripts, and 16.3 (sd = 39.9) distinct forms with 8.7 (sd = 7.4) fields/form. Among the sites contained in the sample, 17% use Java applets.

3   Discussion and Further Research

This paper introduces a methodology for analyzing Web-based eCRM tools. Integrating an automated tool and manual evaluation, we concentrated on the pharmaceutical sector and analyzed 33 Austrian Web sites. All of them offer features such as general feedback and basic electronic product catalogs, whereas no chat or discussion forum could be identified. Direct sales force requests (6%) and comprehensive product databases (9%) are still neglected by a majority of companies. By applying our scheme to other industries and extending the survey by longitudinal aspects, we expect important insights into the industry-specific application of Web-based eCRM tools.

References

1. Sheth, J., Parvatiyar, A.: The Domain and Conceptual Foundations of Relationship Marketing. In: J. Sheth and A. Parvatiyar, (eds.): Handbook of Relationship Marketing. Sage (2000) 680
2. Gummeson, E.: Total Relationship Marketing. Butterworth-Heinemann, Oxford (2002)
3. Cap Gemini, E. Y. (2003) Stetig wachsende Kundenanprüche und und anhaltende Verbreitung neuer Technologien verändern erfolgreiche Marketingansätze.[Online]. Available: http://www.at.cgey.com/edit/obtree/ecompass/archiv/ecrm.htm
4. Fassot, G.: eCRM-Instrumente: Ein beziehungsorientierter Überblick. In: A. Eggert and G. Fassot, (eds.): eCRM - Electronic Customer Relationship Management: Management der Kundenbeziehung im Internet-Zeitalter. Schäffer-Poeschel (2001)
5. Stauss, B.: Using New Media for Customer Interaction. In: T. Henning-Thurau, (ed.) Relationship Marketing: Gaining Competitive Advantage through Customer Satisfaction and Customer Retention. Springer, London (2000)
6. Peppers, D., Rogers, M.: The One to One Future: Building Relationships One Customer at a Time. Currency/Doubleday (1997)
7. Scharl, A.: Evolutionary Web Development. Springer, London (2000)
8. Bauer, C., Scharl, A.: Quantitative Evaluation of Web Site Content and Structure. Internet Research: Networking Applications and Policy 10 (2000) 31–43
9. Hamuro, Y., Katoh, N., Matsuda, Y., Yada, K.: Mining Pharmacy Data Helps to Make Profits. Data Mining and Knowledge Discovery 2 (1998) 391–298
10. Krippendorf, K.: Content Analysis: An Introduction to Its Methodology. Sage, Beverly Hills (1980)

A Browser Compatibility Testing Method Based on Combinatorial Testing[*]

Lei Xu[1,3], Baowen Xu[1,2,3], Changhai Nie[1,3], Huowang Chen[2,3], and Hongji Yang[4]

[1] Department of Computer Sci. & Eng., Southeast University, Nanjing 210096, China
[2] Computer School, National University of Defense Technology, Changsha 410073, China
[3] Jiangsu Institute of Software Quality, Nanjing 210096, China
[4] School of Computing, De Montfort University, England
bwxu@seu.edu.cn

Abstract. For ensuring the displaying effects of Web applications, it is important to perform compatibility testing for browsers under the different configurations and it is a hard task to test all. So this paper focused on the improvements for browser compatibility testing. Firstly, we introduced the related work. Then we analysed the functional speciality of the current popular browsers, and provided the preconditions to simplify problems. Next we gave an instance and brought forward the single factor covering method and the pair-wise covering design to gain testing suits. Finally, we introduced the assistant tools we have developed and the future work.

1 Introduction

In recently years, Web applications are attracting more and more users with their important characters of universality, interchangeability and usability [11]. Browser compatibility testing is needed to guarantee the displaying functions of Applets, ActiveX Controls, JavaScript, CSS, HTML, etc in all kinds of system configurations. This job is quite fussy, so we demand some test cases to cover the huge combinations.

At present, people start researching web testing and propose some elementary methods [3,4,6,7,8]. This paper focuses on how to improve browser compatibility testing. Section 2 presents the related work. Section 3 provides two methods to obtain the suits of test cases. Section 4 is concerned with the tools and the conclusions.

2 Related Work

At present, the browser is constitutive of HTML Render, Java VM, JavaScript, Plug-in Handler, etc. Browsers take charge of parsing and showing the Web page elements. By now, there are many types of browsers, such as NN, IE, AOL, etc. Each type of browser

[*] This work was supported in part by the National Natural Science Foundation of China (NSFC) (60073012), National Grand Fundamental Research 973 Program of China (2002CB312000), National Research Foundation for the Doctoral Program of Higher Education of China, Opening Foundation of Jiangsu Key Laboratory of Computer Information Processing Technology in Soochow University, and SEU–NARI Foundation.

J.M. Cueva Lovelle et al. (Eds.): ICWE 2003, LNCS 2722, pp. 310–313, 2003.
© Springer-Verlag Berlin Heidelberg 2003

has different versions, and they can be applied on the platforms of Windows, Macintosh, UNIX, Linux, etc. Different browsers may have different functions, parsing results and fault-tolerances; different type of computers may have different font types and sizes. So it is urgent to test the displaying of applications in different browser environments.

Presently, the combinatorial testing is used in many software-testing fields, and the research focuses on the generation of test cases. David M. Cohen put forward a heuristic generating method based on pair-wise coverage [1,5]. Y. Lei proposed a gradually expanding generation method for pair-wise covering test cases based on parameter sequence [10]. Noritaka Kobayashi brought forward a kind of algebra method to generate cases, which was better than heuristic method [9]. Our study emphasizes on how to use these methods to the Web compatibility testing.

3   The Methods for Browser Compatibility Testing

3.1   Preliminary Methods

Firstly, it is needed to make clear of the related configuration requirements. Next, we should confirm that all the relative equipments are useable. Further more, we should find out the popular equipments and compress the kinds into a controlled range. Then, we can generate test cases based on different algorithms and execute the compatibility testing. Suppose we need to test n kinds of equipments after the pre-process, named $d_1, d_2, ..., d_n$, and d_1 has a_1 values, ..., d_n has a_n values. It needs $m = \max_{1 \le i \le n} a_i$ test cases to cover all the values of every parameter at least, $m = \max_{1 \le i \ne j \le n} a_i * a_j$ test cases to cover all the pair-wise combinations of every parameter at least... and so on. With the increase of parameters, the number of test cases increases quickly.

The relationships between the Web page elements and the relative parsing equipments are direct, thus they have little interacting influences among themselves. So pair-wise coverage is enough, and sometimes the single factor coverage is suitable.

3.2   Browser Compatibility Testing Based on Single Factor Coverage

Now we give an example of compatibility testing under the popular configurations. Supposing the software under testing (SUT) is a network game, we only consider five equipments for simplify, and d_1=video, d_2=audio, d_3=printer, d_4=browser, and d_5=operating system, $a_1 = a_2 = a_3 = a_4 = a_5 = 2$, shown in Table 1.

Table 1. The Equipments Types for Web Compatibility Testing

Video	Audio	Printer	Browser	Operating System
A1	B1	C1	D1	E1
A2	B2	C2	D2	E2

If we consider all the possible combinations, we need 32 test cases ($2^5 = 32$). The single factor covering method changes the value of one factor once a time and keeps the typical values of other factors. In our example, we designate the typical values of all the equipments, and when one changes its value, others keep their typical values. Through this method, we obtain the testing suits as follows:

(1) A1, B1, C1, D1, E1   (4) A1, B1, C2, D1, E1
(2) A2, B1, C1, D1, E1   (5) A1, B1, C1, D2, E1
(3) A1, B2, C1, D1, E1   (6) A1, B1, C1, D1, E2

As a result, we gain the six test cases to replace the thirty-two ones. In the view of combinatorics, there are five parameters in the SUT and each parameter has two values, then the number of arbitrary two parameters is 40 ($C_5^2 \times 2^2 = 40$), while this method only cover 10 ($C_5^1 \times 2^1 = 10$). This method is easy to accomplish and suits for the situation that every factor does not interfere with others, but when the SUT has many factors and each factor has many values, this method is not practical.

3.3 Browser Compatibility Testing Based on Pair-Wise Coverage

In order to make sure the possible influences between the arbitrary two factors, we should have the testing based on pair-wise coverage.

Definition 1 Suppose $A = (a_{i,j})_{n \times m}$. The j-th column represents the j-th parameter, and the elements of the j-th column are from the finite symbol set T_j (j=1, 2,..., m), i.e. $a_{ij} \in T_j, i = 1,2,...,n$. If the arbitrary two columns of A satisfy these conditions: the total symbol combination of T_i and T_j are occurred in the pair-wise which consists of the i-th and j-th columns, we call A the *pair-wise covering table*.

The row number, n, of matrix A is the number of test cases. If the number is the least positive integer to ensure the conditions, we call A the least pair-wise covering table, and each row of A is a test case [2,12]. Now we give the testing suits based on *pair-wise covering table*:

(1) A1, B1, C1, D2, E1   (4) A2, B1, C2, D1, E2
(2) A1, B1, C2, D1, E2   (5) A2, B2, C1, D2, E2
(3) A1, B2, C1, D1, E1   (6) A2, B2, C2, D2, E1

The above six test cases cover all the pair-wise covering situations, so it has better quality than the former six cases which are based on single factor coverage.

3.4 Testing Steps

After generating the test cases, we can perform the browser compatibility testing. Firstly, select the related equipments and prepare for the testing. Next, build a matrix for testing information, in which, each row represents one kind of configuration, each column for one displaying page element. Then work in the respective configure environment. We should check the showing functions and impressions of every Web page element in detail, compared with the specifications. Finally, after obtaining the full matrix, we can analyse the testing status and draw some conclusions such as wanting parsers, hardware conflicts, element's functional errors, etc.

4 Conclusion Remarks

Presently, there are multiple kinds of assistant tools for Web browser compatibility testing in practice. They take effective actions in reducing the testing tasks and improving efficiency. But due to the limitation of the algorithms, these tools only fit for some special cases and do not have general properties.

We have done much research in the test cases generation and selection. Our algorithms concluded the idea of single factor coverage, pair-wise coverage, orthogonal array experimental design, uniformity design, etc, and we made progress in the construction of coverage tables. At present, we have developed the related testing assistant tools based on the above algorithms. As a consequence of these research, we can obtain the most appropriate algorithms and test cases in different situations when we testing a system with multi-factor and multi-level.

The work of browser compatibility testing is very burdensome. In most cases, it is impossible to cover all the possible combinations during software testing. In this study, we analysed the characters of Web applications and the function speciality of current popular browsers, and simplified the problems greatly. Then we provided two methods, i.e. single factor coverage and pair-wise coverage to obtain the suits of compatibility test cases. At last, we presented the assistant tools we developed for the test cases generation. Future work includes algorithm optimisation and generalisation.

References

1 Williams, A.W. and Probert, R. L.: A Practical Strategy for Testing Pair-wise Coverage of Network Interfaces. Proc. of 7th Int. Symp. Software Reliability Engineering (1997): 246–254.

2 Nie, C. and Xu., B.: An Algorithm for Automatically Generating Black-box Test Cases Based Interface Parameters. Chinese Journal of Computer (in Chinese), to appear in 2003.

3 Kallepalli, C. and Tian., J.: Measuring and Modeling Usage and Reliability for Statistical Web Testing. IEEE Trans. Software Engineering, 2001, 27(11): 1023–1036.

4 Kung, D.C., Liu, C.H. and Hsia, P.: An Object-Oriented Web Test Model for Testing Web Applications. Proc. of 1st Asia-Pacific Conf. on Quality Software (APAQS) (2000): 111–121.

5 Cohen, D. M., Fredman, M. L.: New Techniques for Designing Qualitatively Independent Systems. Journal of Combinational Designs, 1998, 6(6): 411–416.

6 Ricca, F. and Tonella, P.: Web Site Analysis: Structure and Evolution. Proc. of Int. Conf. on Software Maintenance (ICSM) (2000): 76–86.

7 Xu, L., Xu, B. and Chen, Z.: Survey of Web Testing. Computer Science (in Chinese), 2003, 30(3): 100–104.

8 Xu, L., Xu, B. and Chen, Z.: A Scheme of Web Testing Approach. Journal of Nanjing University (in Chinese), 2002, 38(11): 182–186.

9 Kobayashi, N., Tsuchiya, T. and Kikuno, T.: A New Method for Constructing Pair-wise Covering Designs for Software Testing. Information Processing Letters, 2002, 81(2): 85–91.

10 Mandl, R.: Orthogonal Latin Squares: An Application of Experimental Design to Compiler Testing. Communications of the ACM, 1985, 28(10): 1054–1058.

11 Zhang, W., Xu, B., Zhou, X., Li, D. and Xu, L.: Meta Search Engine Survey. Computer Science (in Chinese), 2001, 28(8): 36–41.

12 Xu, B., Nie, C., Shi, Q. and Lu, H.: An Algorithm for Automatically Generating Black-Box Test Cases, Journal of Electronics, 2003, 20(1): 74–77.

Analyzing Errors and Referral Pairs to Characterize Common Problems and Improve Web Reliability*

Li Ma and Jeff Tian

Southern Methodist University, Dept. of Computer Science and Engineering
Dallas, Texas 75275, USA
{lima, tian}@engr.smu.edu

Abstract. In this paper, we analyze web server error logs and the corresponding referral pairs from web access logs to identify and characterize common web errors. We identify missing files as the primary type of web errors and classify them according to their incoming referral links into internal, external, and user errors. We also identify major missing file types within each error category. Based on these analysis results, we recommend different quality assurance initiatives to deal with different types of web problems for the effective improvement to web reliability.

Keywords: Web problems, quality and reliability, web server logs (error and access logs), referral pairs, defect analysis and classification.

1 Introduction

As a direct consequence of people's reliance on the World Wide Web for information and service, quality assurance for the web has gained unprecedented importance. Reliability, usability, and security are the three dominant quality attributes for the web [9]. The primary determinant of reliability is the number of internal defects or faults (or web errors for web applications) and how often they are triggered by specific usages to manifest into problems experienced by users [7]. In this paper, we analyze web errors and related triggers through referral pair analysis to identify and characterize common problems, and recommend appropriate quality assurance actions to deal with the identified problems.

For web applications, various logs, such as the commonly used access logs and error logs, are routinely kept at web servers. In this paper, we extend our previous study on statistical web testing and reliability analysis in [6] to extract information from these logs to support our analyses. We analyze the web logs from www.seas.smu.edu, the official web site for the School of Engineering at Southern Methodist University (SMU/SEAS), to demonstrate the viability and effectiveness of our analyses. This web site utilizes Apache Web Server [2], a

---

* This work is supported in part by NSF grants 9733588 and 0204345, THECB/ATP grants 003613-0030-1999 and 003613-0030-2001, and Nortel Networks.

J.M. Cueva Lovelle et al. (Eds.): ICWE 2003, LNCS 2722, pp. 314–323, 2003.
© Springer-Verlag Berlin Heidelberg 2003

popular choice among many web hosts, and shares many common characteristics of web sites for educational institutions. These features make our observations and results meaningful to many application environments.

The rest of the paper is organized as follows: Section 2 analyzes the web reliability problems, and examines the contents of web logs and applicable analyses. Section 3 presents our analyses of web errors and the corresponding referral pairs, and recommends different quality assurance activities to deal with different types of problems identified by our analyses. Conclusions and future directions are discussed in Section 4.

2   Web Problems, Logs, and Analyses

We next examine the general characteristics of web problems, the information concerning web usage and errors recorded in the web server logs, and possible analyses that can be applied to assess these problems. Some preliminary analysis results from our previous work is also presented as the starting point for the analyses to be performed in this paper.

2.1   Characterizing Web Reliability Problems

We can adapt the standard definition of software reliability to define the *reliability for web applications* as the probability of failure-free web operation completions [7]. Acceptable reliability can be achieved via prevention of web failures or reduction of chances for such failures by detecting and removing the related internal defects or faults. We define *web failures* as the inability to obtain and deliver information, such as documents or computational results, requested by web users. This definition conforms to the standard definition of failures being the behavioral deviations from user expectations [5]. Based on this definition, we can consider the following failure sources:

- *Host, network, or browser failures*: These failures are similar to regular system, network, or software failures, which can be analyzed by existing techniques. Therefore, they are not the focus of our study.
- *Source or content failures*: These failures possess various characteristics unique to the web environment [9]. We will examine the unique characteristics of web sources and analyze these web failures in this study.
- *User errors* may also cause problems, which can be addresses through user education, better usability design, etc. Although these failures are not the focus of this paper because they are beyond the control of web contents providers, we will encounter some related problems in Section 3.

The number of observed failures can be normalized by the time interval, usage instances, or other appropriate measurements, to obtain the failure rate, which also characterizes the *reliability* for the software [7]. For web applications, the number of user requests or *hits* provides a good characterization of overall usage, and therefore can be used to measure failure rates and reliability for a given web site [6]. For example, if n is the number of hits for a web site, which results in f failure observations, then the failure rate r is given by $r = f/n$. The reliability R is related to r by the equation $R = 1 - r$ in the Nelson model [8], one of the earliest and most widely used input domain reliability models. Therefore, we directly use failure rate in this paper to characterize web reliability.

2.2   Web Logs and Their Contents

Two types of logs are commonly used by web servers: individual web accesses, or hits, are recorded in *access logs*, and related problems are recorded in *error logs*. Sample entries from such logs for the www.seas.smu.edu web site are given in Figure 1.

```
129.119.4.17 - - [16/Aug/1999:00:00:11 -0500] "GET /img/XredSeal.gif
HTTP/1.1" 301 328 "http://www.seas.smu.edu/" "Mozilla/4.0 (compatible;
MSIE 4.01; Windows NT)"
```

```
[Mon Aug 16 00:00:56 1999] [client 129.119.4.17] File does not exist:
/users/csegrad2/srinivas/public_html/Image10.jpg
```

Fig. 1. Sample entries in an access log (top) and in an error log (bottom)

A "hit" is registered in the access log if a file corresponding to an HTML page, a document, or other web content is explicitly requested, or if some embedded content is implicitly requested or activated. Most web servers record relevant information about individual accesses in their access logs. Of particular interests to this study is the referring URL, or the web page that the user visited just before she "hits" the requested page. This information can be used to analyze and classify web errors.

Although access logs also record common HTML errors, separate error logs are typically used by web servers to record details about the problems encountered. The format of these error logs is simple: a timestamp followed by the error message, such as in Figure 1 (bottom figure). Common error types are listed in Table 1. Notice that most of these error types conform closely to the source or content failures we defined in Section 2.1. We refer to such failures as *errors* in subsequent discussions to conform to the commonly used terminology in the web community. Questions about error occurrences, distribution, etc., can be answered by analyzing error logs and access logs.

2.3   Error Analysis for the Web Using ODC

Our strategy for error analyses in this paper is influenced by orthogonal defect classification (ODC) [3]. ODC is a general framework for software defect

Table 1. Common error types and error distribution for www.seas.smu.edu

Error type	Description	Number of errors
A	permission denied	2079
B	no such file or directory	14
C	stale NFS file handle	4
D	client denied by server configuration	2
E	file does not exist	28631
F	invalid method in request	0
G	invalid URL in request connection	1
H	mod_mime_magic	1
I	request failed	1
J	script not found or unable to start	27
K	connection reset by peer	0
all types		30760

analysis and classification that has been successfully used in various industrial applications to improve overall software product quality. Among the various ODC attributes, we focus on the following:

- Defect *impact*, or failure type, which indicates what kind of problems (or failures) are caused by certain defects. For the web environment, this attribute corresponds to web error type listed in Table 1, which indicates what kind of problems was experienced by web users. It can be analyzed directly based on information extracted from the error logs, such as we did in [6] and summarized in Table 1.
- Defect *trigger*, or what facilitated the software fault to surface and result in a failure. For the web environment, this attribute corresponds to specific usage sequences or referrals that lead to problems recorded in the error logs. It can be analyzed by examining the referral pair information that can be extracted from the access logs, as discussed in Section 3.
- Defect *source*, or the type of code that is corrected (or to be corrected) to fix the observed failures. For the web environment, this attribute corresponds to specific files or file types that need to be changed, added, or removed to fix problems recorded in the error logs. It can be analyzed by examining both the errors and referral pairs, as discussed in Section 3.

2.4   Web Logs from www.seas.smu.edu and Preliminary Analyses

In this paper, server log data covering 26 consecutive days recently for the web site www.seas.smu.edu were analyzed. The access log is about 130 megabytes in size, and contains more than 760,000 records. The error log is about 13.5 megabytes in size, and contains more than 30,000 records. These data are large enough for our study to avoid random variations that may lead to severely biased results. On the other hand, because of the nature of constantly evolving web contents, data covering longer periods call for different analyses that take change into consideration, different from the analyses we performed in this study. We also extended utility programs we implemented in Perl for our previous study in [6] to support additional information extraction and analyses.

For the 26 days covered by our web server logs, a total of 30760 errors were recorded in our error log. The distribution of these errors by error types was obtained by us in [6] and summarized in Table 1. The most dominant error type is type E, "file does not exist", which accounts for 93.08% of all the errors recorded. This type of errors is also called "404 errors" because of their error code in the web logs. Type A errors, "permission denied", account for 6.76% of the total errors. All the rest 9 error types account for only 0.16%, a truly negligible share, of the total. Type A errors are more closely related to security problems instead of reliability problems we focus on in this study, and further analyses of these errors may involve the complicated authentication process. Therefore, further analyses using referral pair information in this study focus on type E or 404 errors, the most dominant type of recorded errors.

3   Referral Pair Analyses, Error Classification, and Web Quality Assurance

A referral pair consists of two web pages, 1) a referred page or currently requested page by a web user, and 2) a referring (or referral) page, or simply called the *referrer*, which is the web page that the user visited just before she "hits" the requested page. Analysis of referral pairs can provide useful information for us to identify, understand, and classify common problems experienced by web users, as well as to recommend appropriate quality assurance initiatives to deal with the identified problems.

3.1   Error Classification by Referral Pairs — A Qualitative Analysis

Some type E ("file does not exist") or 404 errors may be true problems caused by internal faults at a web site, while others may well be user typos or external problems beyond the control of the local web site, as analyzed below:

— *Internal referrer*, or the referrer has an internal URL. In our case, the URL starts with "http://www.seas.smu.edu/". This case includes two scenarios:
  • When a page in the SMU/SEAS web site is visited through an explicit link contained in another page in the same web site.
  • When components such as graphs or Java classes embedded in a page are loaded to the client machine or activated while the page is visited. This case can be viewed as if there are implicit links to these embedded web contents contained in the page, and those links are activated automatically when the page is visited.

  404 errors resulted from both these types of internal referrers should be considered as actual web failures, because they are triggered by the use of defective web contents and/or links at the local web site. These problems

can be corrected easily by the local webmaster or page owners by correcting the corresponding links or by including the requested pages or files. Consequently, these errors should be the primary focus of any local quality assurance activities for the web.

- *External referrer*, which happens when a page or a file of the web site is accessed through a link provided by a page from other web sites, an external index page, or a page containing results produced by a search engine. This situation represents the case when the local web site is accessed indirectly via other web sites.

  Although 404 errors resulted from such external referrers also lead to problems from a user's view, they are not the responsibilities of the local web site and can not be fixed by the local webmaster or page owners. They are more of a "global" problem, i.e., they represent problems for the web as a whole. Different quality assurance activities, such as concerted effort involving multiple web sites, are needed to deal with such problems.

- *Empty referrer*, which is represented by a "−" for the referring page URL field in the logs. There are several distinct cases in this situation:

  - A web robot (or a web spider, or a web crawler) is visiting the page.
  - A user directly types in the URL or requests the file directly.
  - A bookmarked URL is used.
  - A web browser may request some file directly from the web site without involving the user. For example, IE5 requests the "`favicon.ico`" file whenever user bookmarks a page.

  These cases can be distinguished by other information recorded in the access logs, such as client name or IP address, agent type, etc.

  Among the above cases, the web robot case is similar to the external referrer situation, because these web robots are typically associated with some special web sites external to the local web site. In the case where a web browser automatically requests a file without user involvement, the related problem can be treated as a browser compatibility problem instead of a web source problem. The wrongly typed or bookmarked URL cases above all involve the user directly as the responsible party to fix the problem. Such user-originated requests should be treated as user errors, not web service problems.

As a consequence of the above analysis and classification, different quality assurance activities can be carried out to deal with these different categories of problems. However, before doing that, we need to evaluate the scope and severity of the problems, so that appropriate resources can be allocated to carry out these different quality assurance activities.

3.2   Error Distribution by Referral Pairs — An Quantitative Analysis

Based on the classification above, we can analyze the error log as well as the access log for our SMU/SEAS web site, and obtain the error distribution by individual classes. Because the error rate gives us a direct measure of the reliability, or the likelihood for a user to experience a problem, we also calculated the error rates for these individual classes (See Section 2.1). The results are presented in Table 2. Notice that the total 404 errors is slightly different from that in Table 1 because of minor inconsistencies between the access log used here and the error log used before.

Table 2. Error distribution and error rates for different error categories

referrer type and sub-type		number of hits	number of errors	error rate
internal		578757	17544	3.03%
external		63478	1233	1.94%
empty	user originated	93917	7744	8.25%
	robot originated	25697	1268	4.93%
	browser originated	849	849	100%
all types		763119	28638	3.75%

The internal referrer category accounts for 75.84% of all the hits and 61.26% of all the 404 errors, resulting in an error rate of 3.03%, which is slightly lower than the average error rate of 3.75%. This category command a lion's share of both the hits and errors. Therefore, fixing the local problems related to such references will significantly improve the web site reliability and user's overall experience using the web site. Further analysis in Section 3.4 identifies major error sources for focused reliability improvement.

The 404 error rate for the web robot originated hits is slightly worse but still comparable to that for internal referrer category. This can probably be explained by the attempt to "cover" the entire web site by the web robots. Therefore, all (or almost all) links related to 404 errors will be exposed, resulting in comparable 404 error rate. On the other hand, frequently used internal references are less likely to contain 404 errors, because they are more likely to be observed and fixed because of their high visibility resulted from their high usage frequency. This difference probably explains the lower error rate for internal referrers than that for web robots originated hits. Further studies are needed to conclusively validate this observation.

The external referrer category has the lowest 404 error rate. Further examination of the referral pairs reveals that about half of them come from the results of search engines. The lower error rate of this category may be caused by the relative stability of the SMU/SEAS web site and periodic updates of search engines' databases to keep their links up to date. Another important contributing factor is the use of web robots by many Internet search engines: Once a 404 error has been observed by the web robot, the search engine's database would be updated, resulting in no more such 404 errors. As a result, we can probably conclude that the relatively higher 404 error rate for web robots contributes to the relatively lower 404 error rate for web search engines.

The user-originated empty referrer category has a significantly higher error rate than the above categories. It accounts for only 12.31% of all the hits, but 26.85% of all the 404 errors. When the URL is typed in by a user, the higher failure rate can be explained by the frequent mistakes of misspelling, mistyping, and memory lapses. Some users may not perform timely update to their bookmarks, also leading to 404 errors when such out-of-date pages are requested.

Browser originated requests and errors constitute a special case, which is analyzed in Section 3.4 in connection with our analysis of error sources.

3.3   Discussions and Other Uses of Referral Pair Analysis

As seen from the above classification and assessment, different quality assurance activities can be carried out to address different categories of 404 errors in order to improve the reliability for the whole web in general and for the local web site in particular. Although some of the errors, such as user errors, are unavoidable, concerted quality assurance effort for individual web sites and for the Internet as a whole could lead to significant reduction of 404 errors.

One interesting observation from the above assessment of error rates for different categories is the combination of relatively higher error rate for web robots and relative lower error rate for search engines. This fact points to a possible strategy for web testing and quality assurance using web robots, in much the same way that search engines update their internal databases. Of course, the error correction or defect fixing activities would still be much more complicated, involving fixing links and files, instead of simply deleting or updating database entries as in the case for search engines.

With the shifting focus to usage patterns and frequencies by target users for web applications [4], statistical testing based on actual usage scenarios will play a more important role for web quality assurance [6]. The referral pair analyses will help the implementation of this strategy in many ways:

- A quantification of relevant referral pairs will provide automated information extraction to assess state transition probabilities used in building such usage-based testing models.
- Both the empty referrer and external referrer categories also provide information about the entry points to the models.
- The overall referral pairs ranked by usage frequency can be used to test commonly used referral pairs, much like the testing of frequently used call pairs in [1].

Consequently, our overall statistical testing strategies that use existing web checkers for individual pages [10] and server log analysis for overall usage patterns [6] can benefit from these analysis results, and can be augmented with the use of web robots and other automated support tools, to fulfill our general goal of effective web testing and quality assurance.

3.4   Error Source Analysis in Connection with Referral Pair Analysis

Another important attribute for 404 errors is the error source information, or the type of files that were missing. For our web site, there are more than 100 different file types, as indicated by their different file extensions, with most of them accounting for very few 404 errors. We sorted these file types by their corresponding 404 errors, and found that the top 10 file types accounts for more than 99% of the overall 404 errors. In fact, only the top four file types, ".gif", ".class", directories, and ".html", represent about 90% of all the errors, with each type accounts for 44%, 17%, 16%, and 13% of the total respectively.

On the other hand, ".gif", directories, and ".html" files are also associated with high numbers of hits. Their error rates do not deviate far away from the average error rate. In fact, only ".class" and ".ico" files stand out in this analysis, with error rates of 49% (4913 errors out of 10055 hits) and 100% (849 hits all resulted in errors) respectively. Consequently, fixing these problematic file types would improve the overall web site reliability.

However, when we analyze the above results in connection with the error classification by referrer types (or defect triggers in the ODC terminology [3]), we get a quite different picture. None of the ".ico" errors are from internal referrers, and only a negligible few for ".class" (2 errors from 6 hits, out of a total of 4913 errors and 10055 hits) are from internal referrers.

For the internal referrer category, ".html" files have slightly higher error rate than other major file types. Consequently, we should focus a little more on this file type, but with due attention to other file types too, in our quality assurance effort. As stated before, this category should be our primary focus because problems related to external or empty referrers represents user errors, browser compatibility problems, or problems of external web sites, which are beyond local control.

Because of the significantly higher error rates and quality impact of the ".class" and ".ico" files, further analysis is needed to locate the major external sources for these errors, and to identify primary users who requested these files. Once this is done, these identified external web sites and users can be alerted and constructive information can be provided to help them fix their web sites and usage problems. In fact, ".ico" file type represents a special case in our study: All the 849 ".ico" requests involve a single file, "favicon.ico". All of them originated by the web browser, because IE5 automatically requests this file when a user bookmarks a page. This analysis points out a browser compatibility problem that urgently needs to be resolved.

4   Conclusions and Perspectives

In this paper, we have developed an approach for identifying and characterizing web errors and for initiating appropriate quality assurance and improvement activities, based on analyzing referral pairs and other information extracted from existing web logs. Using our referral pair analysis, we can classify web errors into internal ones, user errors, and external ones, and recommend different quality assurance activities specifically suited for different error categories. By focusing our attention on the internal errors, we can apply local actions and drive effectively improvement to the overall web site reliability.

Two other important error attributes we analyzed in this paper are error impact (or type of problems experienced by web users) and error source (or type of files that caused these problems). Error distributions for both these attributes are highly uneven, with a few problem types or file types representing a dominant share of all the problems. Referral pair analysis was also used in connection with these analyses to identify problematic areas within individual error categories. The identification of such problematic areas can help us focus our quality assurance effort. Consequently, our analysis results can help web site owners to prioritize their web site maintenance and quality assurance effort, which would lead to better web service and user satisfaction due to the improved web site reliability.

The primary limitation of our study is the fact that the web site used in this study, the official web site for the School of Engineering at Southern Methodist University, may not be a representative one for many non-academic web sites. Most of our web pages are static ones, with the HTML documents and embedded graphics dominating other types of pages, while in e-commerce and various other business applications, dynamic pages and context-sensitive contents play a much more important role. To overcome these limitations, we plan to analyze some public domain web logs, such as from the Internet Traffic Archive at `ita.ee.lbl.gov` or the W3C Web Characterization Repository at `repository.cs.vt.edu`, to cross-validate our general results.

References

1. A. Avritzer and E. J. Weyuker. The automatic generation of load test suites and the assessment of the resulting software. *IEEE Trans. on Software Engineering*, 21(9):705–716, Sept. 1995.
2. B. Behlandorf. *Running a Perfect Web Site with Apache, 2nd Ed.* MacMillan Computer Publishing, New York, 1996.
3. R. Chillarege, I. Bhandari, J. Chaar, M. Halliday, D. Moebus, B. Ray, and M.-Y. Wong. Orthogonal defect classification — a concept for in-process measurements. *IEEE Trans. on Software Engineering*, 18(11):943–956, Nov. 1992.
4. L. L. Constantine and L. A. D. Lockwood. Usage-centered engineering for web applications. *IEEE Software*, 19(2):42–50, Mar. 2002.
5. IEEE. *IEEE Standard Glossary of Software Engineering Terminology.* Number STD 610.12-1990. IEEE, 1990.
6. C. Kallepalli and J. Tian. Measuring and modeling usage and reliability for statistical web testing. *IEEE Trans. on Software Engineering*, 27(11):1023–1036, Nov. 2001.
7. M. R. Lyu, editor. *Handbook of Software Reliability Engineering.* McGraw-Hill, New York, 1995.
8. E. Nelson. Estimating software reliability from test data. *Microelectronics and Reliability*, 17(1):67–73, 1978.
9. J. Offutt. Quality attributes of web applications. *IEEE Software*, 19(2):25–32, Mar. 2002.
10. J. Tian and A. Nguyen. Statistical web testing and reliability analysis. In *Proc. 9th Int. Conf. on Software Quality*, pages 263–274, Cambridge, MA, Oct. 1999.

Towards the Design of a Metrics Cataloging System by Exploiting Conceptual and Semantic Web Approaches

L. Olsina[1], Mª A. Martin[1], J. Fons[2], S. Abrahao[2], and O. Pastor[2]

[1]GIDIS, Department of Informatics, Engineering School at UNLPam
Calle 9 y 110, (6360) General Pico, La Pampa. Argentina
{olsinal, martinma}@ing.unlpam.edu.ar
[2] Department of Informatics Systems and Computing at UPV,
Camino de la Vera s/n. Aptd. 22.012. E-46071 Valencia. Spain
{jjfons, sabrahao, opastor}@dsic.upv.es

Abstract. In this article we thoroughly discuss conceptual and navigational modeling and query issues for repositories of metrics and their cataloging system by exploiting as well the power of the semantic web approach. This environment can finally allow tools, evaluators and other stakeholders to have service and consultation mechanisms starting from a sound specification of the entity type, the attribute definition and motivation, the metric definition as well as the measure type, unit, scale type, data collection instruments, protocols, among other metadata.

Keywords: Metrics, Semantic Web, OOWS, Cataloging Tool.

1 Introduction

As we know, quality assurance is one of the challenging processes both to the Software Engineering (SE) and to the Web Engineering (WE) –as a new discipline [2]. A common building block shared for many assessment methods and techniques that give support to the quality assurance process is the specification of nonfunctional requirements stemmed from a sound definition and documentation of attributes and metrics for entities. In fact, huge volumes of information about attributes and metrics for different purposes and domains have been published in diverse fora and media. However, observing the rapid and caothic growth and heterogeneity of information sources related to metrics, it urges to provide mechanisms for consensuating, structuring, and retrieving that information in order to be useful to diverse quality assurance activities. For this end, repositories of metrics and cataloging environments will basically provide to different stakeholders consultation, retrieval and reuse mechanisms starting from a sound and consensuated specification of the entity type, the attribute and metric definition, the counting rules, among other metadata.

Some initial efforts have been recently made to classify metrics for some entity type as for example metrics for software products. It is worthy of mention the initiative of the ISO 9126 standard [4] in the 2 and 3 draft documents. However, the paper-based template of information used to describe those metrics is not sufficiently complete, and is not intended to be automated by retrieval tools. Furthermore, it is also remarkable the effort carried out by Kitchenham *et al.* [6] in the definition of a

J.M. Cueva Lovelle et al. (Eds.): ICWE 2003, LNCS 2722, pp. 324–333, 2003.
© Springer-Verlag Berlin Heidelberg 2003

conceptual framework and infrastructure (based on the Entity-Relationship model) to specify entities, attributes and relationships for measuring and instantiating software projects, with the purpose of analysing metrics and datasets in a consistent way.

This last framework served as a starting point for our proposal [9], which we are trying to strengthen not only from the conceptual modeling point of view (using O-O approaches), but also from the cataloging technologies and offered services. The contribution of this paper stems from a thorough analysis of conceptual and navigational design to the metrics cataloging system by using the OOWS (*Object-Oriented Web Solutions* [11]) approach, and the discussion of query issues for repositories of metrics by exploiting the power of semantic web models and technologies [1]. The semantic web approach bridge the gap between the enormous amount of semi-structured and heterogeneous data available in the Net and the ability to cope with all this with machine-processable semantics.

The rest of this article proceeds as follows. In Section 2, we outline a high-level view of the architecture for the Metrics Cataloging Web System (MCWS). In Section 3, we specify the conceptual model for the metrics domain, and we present a mapping between the object model and RDF (*Resource Description Framework*) Schemas. In the next section we specify navigational models for a registered user of the system using the OOWS approach; in addition, we give some examples of semantic queries to the repository of metrics by means of RQL (*RDF Query Language*). Finally, concluding remarks and future works are drawn.

2 Architecture for the Metrics Cataloging Web System

2.1 System's Users Overview

The metrics cataloging system will provide a Web-based collaborative mechanism for discussing, agreeing, and adding approved metrics to the repository on one hand, and a Web-based robust query functionality (based on Semantic Web principles) for consultation and reuse, on the other hand. These subsystems are outlined in Fig. 1.

From the MCWS design of users' point of view, five user's role types with different responsibilities and access privileges were considered, namely: *Administrators, Moderators, Reviewers, Registered Users* and *Tools/Agents*. The user's role types were discussed in [9].

2.2 The Architectural Design

In order to design the MCWS architecture, we wanted to use *semantic web* principles to define queries to repositories and documents, and *web services* to facilitate to reach the system functionality through the web.

To put these ideas into practice, we have chosen a *multi-level* architectural style or, the so-called *n-tier* architecture (see Fig. 1). The defined tiers are the following:
1. The *user interface* tier provides a personalized access to the system for "humans", i.e. administrators, reviewers, moderators and registered users. This tier redirects the incoming functionality requests to the lower level tiers.

2. The *business logic* tier specifies the system functionality using a web service approach to publicize it.

3. The *data logic access* tier is made up of a set of software components that isolates upper tiers for accessing to the stored data and documents.

4. The *persistency* tier stores the cataloged data and documents. This tier must be capable of resolving semantic web queries and of providing storage support for the metrics reviewing process.

To simplify the system structure, it has been divided into two subsystems: the *Metrics Catalog Review System*, and the *Metrics Semantic Query System*.

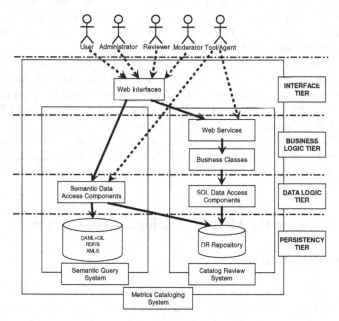

Fig. 1. An Architectural view of the Metrics Cataloging Web System.

2.2.1 The Catalog Review System for Metrics

This system is the responsible for the management and manipulation of the metrics catalog. It provides the functionality to perform the metrics reviewing process through the web and to extract data about metrics. It is mainly made up of the following tiers:

1. *Business logic* tier. It defines the functionality required by *Administrators*, *Reviewers* and *Moderators* for the metrics reviewing process and the functionality to extract data for the *Tools/Agents*. It is compound of: *a)* the *Web Services* interface; i.e. a set of services that publicize the system functionality using standard technology (e.g. SOAP/HTTP, WSDL/XML and UDDI [8]). They rely on the *business classes* to resolve the incoming requests. And b) *Business Classes* that implement the catalog review policies and provide the functionality to be used by the system users.

2. *Data logic* tier. It provides a set of SQL-based software components to facilitate and isolate data accesses (to the persistency layer).
3. *Persistency* tier. It is a relational database that stores the metric items and additional information for its management.

2.2.2 Semantic Query System for Metrics

This system is the responsible for the publication of cataloged metrics, making use of the semantic web principles. It does not implement any management functionality; however, it must be capable of querying on-line semantic documents and repositories. It is made up of two core tiers:

1. *Data logic* tier. It contains a set of components to accede for example to different on-line repositories and documents using RQL-based semantic queries [5] (see Section 4.2 for details). It can be used by the interface layer and by other software applications (represented by *Tools/Agents*).
2. *Persistency* tier. A set of web pages and documents with semantic information about metrics (specified in DAML+OIL, RDF/RDFS and XML/XMLS).

3 Conceptual Modeling for the Metrics Domain

The conceptual model specifies the main classes and relationships for the metrics domain useful to define and exploit all the information for cataloging purposes. This conceptual model is not intended to store and process instances of metric values for different entities' attributes in particular software or Web projects. An ongoing research is being carried out for this enhanced model.

3.1 The Conceptual Model

Fig. 2 shows the UML-based conceptual model for metrics (this model is called Object Model in OOWS [11]). Classes such as *Entity*, *Attribute*, *Factor*, *Metric*, *Protocol*, *ScaleType*, *MeasurementTool*, among others, and their relationships can be observed (see also [9] for details).

From the measurement process viewpoint, in the empirical domain we have mainly *Entity*, *Attribute* and *Factor* classes. The *Entity* class represents tangible or intangible objects we observe in the empirical (real) world. Types of entities of interest to SE and WE are: Project, Product, Product in Use, Process, and Resource. An entity can be hierarchically broken down into sub-entities. The *Attribute* class represents a measurable property of an entity. For a given attribute, there is always at least an empirical relationship of interest that can be captured and represented in the formal domain (by means of a *Metric*), enabling us to explore the relationship mathematically. Attribute is an object at the lowest level of abstraction that can be quantified directly or indirectly by a metric, meanwhile a *Factor* class represents objects at the highest level of abstraction such as Quality, Effort or Cost. A factor can be modeled by a *FactorModel* (e.g. the ISO 9126-1 specifies a quality model to both software product and product in use entities. In turn, the quality model is specified in terms of *Characteristics* and *Subcharacteristics* [4]).

The *Metric* class represents the specific mapping of an empirical attribute (that belongs to an entity) to the formal world, in addition to the specific criteria and procedures to measure it. The metric concept can't be fairly understood if we don't consider also other related concepts such as Measure, Unit, Scale Type, Protocol, Equation and Measurement Tool and their relationships.

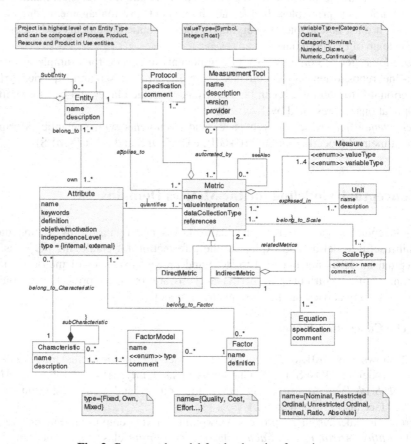

Fig. 2. Conceptual model for the domain of metrics.

The *Measure* class is part of the metric class. It has field members such as the value and variable types (we don't include the value field itself because we store just metadata for cataloging purposes, not instances of metric values). In Fig. 2, the types of values and variables can be observed in the UML-comment element. The *Protocol* class specifies the counting rules and procedures to be applied to the respective metric. On the other hand, a measure of a metric can be expressed in one or more *Units* (e.g. the *Size of Visible Text* metric applied to a *Webpage* entity can be measure in number of bytes or number of word units). Furthermore, the *Scale Type* of a metric affects the sort of arithmetical and statistical operations that can be applied to a measured value. A scale type is defined by admissible transformations. Ultimately, all the information observed in the conceptual model is necessary in order to have a sound specification of attributes and metrics for cataloging and consultation purposes.

3.2 Mapping between the Object Model and RDF Schemas

For the conceptual model of metrics previously discussed, we present here the definition of one layer of the semantic approach [1], [3]. We used RDF Schemas in order to build the model of resources and their relationships. RDF schema is about making machine-processable semantic statements.

As shown in the graph of Fig. 3, we map a RDF class for each class of the conceptual model (a more thorough and robust mapping will be presented in a follow-up work). In addition we define a property for each relationship (the *subClassOf* and *seeAlso* properties are defined beforehand in the de facto W3C standard [12]). Notice that in Fig 3 we show the main resource classes and relationships of the model in a RDF-graph format for readability and space reasons; the reader can access the full RDFS specification in http://gidis.ing.unlpam.edu.ar/rdf/RDF-Metricas1.

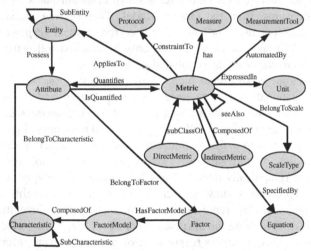

Fig. 3. A representation in RDF-graph format for the metrics domain.

The main resource type is the Metric class, which conceptualize all the available information for a particular metric by interlinking other resources as well, namely: the *Entity* type to which applies to; the *Attribute* that quantifies; the *Protocol* to which is constraint to; the *Unit* which is expressed in, among other relationships.

4 Designing the Navigational Model

We argue that the conceptual modeling process is necessary in order to document and develop correct web applications. In addition, navigational requirements are a critical feature. In this section we analize the navigational model introduced by the OOWS

[11] approach to specify navigational requirements at conceptual level. Next subsections present the navigational modeling of the MCWS for the *Registered User* in addition to the use of a semantic query language to retrieve semantic information.

4.1   The Navigational Model for the Registered User

OOWS is a conceptual modeling method that uses a *Navigational Model* to properly capture the navigation semantics of a web application by providing a set of conceptual constructors to define navigation capabilities (structure, *"navigability"*, etc.).

The navigational model is made up of a set of navigational maps, one for each type of user of the system. This *Navigational Map* (see Fig. 4) represents the view that each kind of user has over the system, defining how users would access system information and functionality. It is represented by means of a directed graph where nodes represent user interaction units (navigational contexts), and arcs (navigational links) represent node reachability (defining valid navigational paths). A *navigational context* is a graph node (depicted as UML packages stereotyped with the «context» reserved word) and represents a view over a set of class attributes and services, and also class relationships, from the Object Model. There exist contexts that can be reached at any moment independently of the current context (*exploration contexts,* labeled with an "E") and contexts that can only be reached following a predefined navigational path (*sequence contexts,* labeled with an "S").

Fig. 4 presents the navigational map for the Registered User (see Section 2.1). It defines six navigational contexts: Factors, Entities, Metrics and Tools (exploration contexts that have a dashed arrow starting from the user), Characteristics and Attributes (sequence contexts, only reachable following predefined navigational paths).

The following step is to define with detail each context. A navigational context is made up of a set of *navigational classes* and *navigational relationships*. A *navigational class* (graphically depicted as UML classes stereotyped with the «view» reserved word) represents a view of a class over a subset of visible attributes and services. A navigational class represents a graphical query to retrieve all the instances of the related class, specifying the attributes to retrieve. Fig. 5 shows the definition of the Metrics context. This context is responsible of provide relevant information about metrics for the Registered User. This context has thirteen navigational classes (Metric, Attribute, ..) with its attributes (name, ...). All navigational classes must be related by a unidirectional binary relationship, called *navigational relationship* (depicted as an

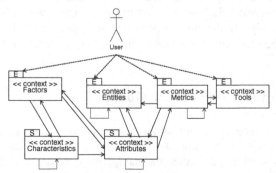

Fig. 4. Navigational Map for the *Registered User* of the MCWS

arrow). It is defined over an existing aggregation/association/composition or specialization relationship and specifies a retrieval of all the instances of the target navigational class related to the origin class. For instance, all the related (quality) Attributes (name and keywords), Entities (name), Protocols (specification and comment), etc... for each retrieved Metric will be shown.

There exist navigational relationships of two types: (1) *context dependency relationships* (depicted as dashed arrows) and (2) *context relationships* (depicted as solid arrows). The former only defines a population retrieval. The latter also defines a navigation to a *[target context]* using as the *anchor* an attribute of the target class. For instance, when retrieving all the MeasurementTools for a given Metric, it will be possible to navigate to the target context [Tools] by selecting one of them using the name of that measurement tool as the anchor.

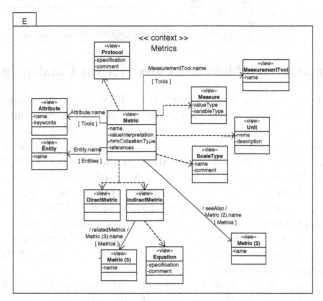

Fig. 5. *Metrics* context for the *Registered User*

4.2 Using a Semantic Query Language

We are using a semantic query language as RQL [5] in order to retrieve the semantic information from the cataloging system. RQL is a typed declarative query language, which is based on the evaluation of path expressions on RDF graphs, featuring variables on labels for both nodes (i.e., classes) and edges (i.e., properties). One of the main RQL features that distinguishes from some other RDF query languages is its capability of querying both RDF schemas and descriptions (i.e., instances). For the MCWS this is a powerful feature for exploiting semantic documents and repositories of metrics, by allowing us not only to retrieve metrics data and its relations but also descriptive information (metadata) of available resources and services in the web, without human-processing intervention. Moreover, RQL has inference capabilities on hierarchies of classes and properties. This feature allows us exploiting additional information, even information that is not explicitly modeled in schemas. In Table 1, we specify a set of queries for the metrics cataloging system in order to illustrate some RQL features and powerness.

Table 1. RQL query examples for the metrics RDF schemas and descriptions.

Description	Query Example
1) Retrieves all instances of attributes and metrics for a subentity (named Webpage)	Select X, Y, Z from http://gidis.ing.unlpam.edu.ar/rdf/RDF-Metricas1#Entity{X}. http://gidis.ing.unlpam.edu.ar/rdf/RDF-Metricas1#Possess{Y}. http://gidis.ing.unlpam.edu.ar/rdf/RDF-Metricas1#IsQuantified{Z} Where X="Webpage"
2) Retrieves all instances of metrics, supported by the Bobby Measurement Tool	Select X, Y from http://gidis.ing.unlpam.edu.ar/rdf/RDF-Metricas1#Metric{X}. http://gidis.ing.unlpam.edu.ar/rdf/RDF-Metricas1#AutomatedBy{Y} Where Y="Bobby"
3) Retrieves all properties names and their ranges to the Metric class	Select @P, range(@P) from [$C]@P Where $C ="http://gidis.ing.unlpam.edu.ar/rdf/RDF-Metricas1#Metric"

5 The Semantic Web Modeling Power for the Cataloging System

In this section we briefly address the power of the semantic web approach focusing us particularly on queries for the metrics cataloging system and some used OOWS modeling primitives. In order to model the metrics cataloging system, in this work, we proposed the use of the OOWS Object Model for conceptual modeling, in addition to the use of semantic statements specified in the form of RDF Schemas (and DAML+OIL). This is possible due to the feature of reification that allows define classes and relationships of the conceptual model as semantic statements. Furthermore, we modeled the navigational aspects of the MCWS using Navigational Maps, and Navigational Contexts. These OOWS navigational primitives, particularly, Navigational Contexts depend on query specifications of different expressive power. Even if we have index access structure and filter capabilities in the OOWS primitives, the power of semantic queries are far beyond.

In order to illustrate the power of semantic queries, we describe some of them exemplified in Table 1. In the first example, the RQL query acts only on RDF descriptions (instances) without the need of schemas. In the second case we just use a property (the *AutomatedBy property* -see the graph of Fig. 3) in order to recover all instances of the *Metric* class starting from the *MeasurementTool* class, without the need of defining either the inverse property (*Automates*) or a new index access structure in the navigational model. Lastly, in the third case the query retrieves all the properties information related to the *Metric* class, i.e. the labels of all edges.

6 Concluding Remarks and Future Work

In order to contribute to the comprehension and selection process whether metrics can be useful, easy to collect and understand, a sound metric specification, flexible documentation, consultation and retrieval mechanisms are needed. For this end, we argued that a well-designed repository of metrics and a powerful cataloging system can be efficiently used to support quality assurance processes such as nonfunctional requirement definition and specification, metrics understanding and selection, quality testing definition, amongst others.

Unfortunately, in the recent research initiatives of the SE and WE communities, sound metrics specifications and cataloging environments as technological support for quality assurance processes have often been neglected. As a way to contribute to fill this gap, our current research concern is manifold. Firstly, regarding the designed cataloging system we are, on the one side, building a virtual community mechanism that basically will provide a Web-based synchronous and asynchronous collaborative facilities for discussing, agreeing, and adding approved metrics to the repository. On the other side, we are implementing the cataloging application with a Web-based browse and query functionalities for consultation and reuse based on semantic web capabilities. One key factor for the repository is getting consensus between researchers and practicioners about the terminology in the metrics domain in order to have a robust ontology: We are in the first steps of discussions and agreements. Secondly, we are exploring the inclusion of OOWS-centered modeling primitives (similar to the initiative reported in [7]) that embrace the power of the semantic web principles and models: This concern is in the start-up stage. Thirdly, we are designing the web services in order to allow the WebQEM_Tool be able to use the metric repository services to retrieve protocol and formula specifications, amongst other items. WebQEM_Tool is the supporting tool for the WebQEM [10] methodology.

References

1. Berners-Lee, T.; Hendler, J.; Lassila, O., 2001, *The Semantic Web.* Scientific American, http://www.scientificamerican.com/2001/0501issue/0501berners-lee.html.
2. Deshpande, Y.; Murugesan, S., et al., 2002, Web Engineering, *Journal of Web Engineering*, Rinton Press, US, 1(1), pp. 61–73.
3. Fensel D., 2002, Ontology-Based Knowledge Management, *IEEE Computer*, 35(11), pp.56–59
4. ISO 9126-1: 2001 Int'l Sdr, Software Engineering, Product Quality, Part 1: Quality Model.
5. Karvounarakis, G.; Alexaki, S.; et al, 2002, RQL: A Declarative Query Language for RDF. *In Procced. of 11th WWW12*, Honolulu, Hawaii, US.
6. Kitchenham B.A., Hughes R.T., Linkman S.G., 2001, Modeling Software Measurement Data. *IEEE Transactions on Software Engineering*, 27(9), pp. 788–804.
7. Lima F.; Schwabe D., 2002, Exploring Semantic Web Modeling Approaches for Web Application Design. *In Proc. of the 2nd Int'l Workshop on Web-Oriented Software Technology" (IWWOST)*, in the framework of ECOOP 2002, pp. 120–133, Malaga, Spain.
8. Newcomer, E.; 2002, *Understanding Web services: XML, WSDL, SOAP, and UDDI.* Addison-Wesley, Boston, MA.
9. Olsina, L.; Lafuente, G. Pastor, O., 2002, Towards a Reusable Repository of Web Metrics, *Journal of Web Engineering*, Rinton Press, US, 1(1), pp. 61–73.
10. Olsina L., Rossi G., 2002, Measuring Web Application Quality with WebQEM, *IEEE Multimedia*, 9(4), pp. 20–29.
11. Pastor, O.; Abrahão, S. M.; Fons, J. J., 2001, Object-Oriented Approach to Automate Web Applications Development, *2nd EC-Web'01*, Munich, Germany, Springer Verlag, 16–28.
12. W3C, WWW Consortium, 2002, *RDF Primer*, W3C Working Draft 19 March 2002 http://www.w3.org/TR/2002/WD-rdf-primer-20020319/

Choosing the "Rightweight" Model for Web Site Quality Evaluation[1]

Luisa Mich[1], Mariangela Franch[2], Pierluigi Novi Inverardi[2], and Pietro Marzani[2]

[1]Department of Computer and Telecommunication Technology
University of Trento, Via Sommarive 14, I 38050 Trento (I)
Tel. +39-0461-882087 – Fax +39-0461-882093
mich@dit.unitn.it
[2]Department of Computer and Management Sciences
University of Trento, Via Inama 5, 38100 Trento (I)
Tel. +39-0461-882150 – Fax +39-0461-882124
{franch, pnoviinv, pmarzani}@cs.unitn.it

Abstract. One of the most critical decisions in a quality evaluation project is to establish the level at which to analyse the characteristics of the Web sites. This choice should be driven by the underlying goals of the evaluation. Scalability and flexibility are thus desiderable features of the models used to evaluate the quality of a Web site. In this paper we describe two separate studies of Regional Tourist Boards in the Alps that were conducted using the meta-model 2QCV3Q. Specifically, we will show that the results of the first study - based on a lightweight model - are consistent with those obtained with the more detailed heavyweight model in the second study.

1 Introduction

To use a frequently cited metaphor in methodologies for software systems development, this paper aims to deal with the problem of choosing a "weight" for the model to be used to evaluate the quality of a Web site. In the software engineering field this implies comparing and choosing between lightweight (often called "agile") and heavyweight methods [2]. The right question is not so much which of the two approaches is the better, but rather which method has the "right" weight for a given project. Several models and frameworks for evaluating the quality of Web sites currently exist.[2] Nonetheless, it would be useful to have a theoretical reference framework or meta-model to serve as a conceptual schema for the quality criteria used in an evaluation project. This framework must therefore be (a) scalable, to allow for an evaluation at varying degrees of detail, based on the "evaluation purpose", the sponsor's requirements and the user's needs (see for example [7]); (b) domain

---

[1] This paper has been produced within the scope of the eTourism project financed by the Fondazione Cassa di Risparmio di Trento e Rovereto.
[2] An extensive bibliography is available at http://www.cs.unitn.it/WebSiteQuality.

J.M. Cueva Lovelle et al. (Eds.): ICWE 2003, LNCS 2722, pp. 334–337, 2003.
© Springer-Verlag Berlin Heidelberg 2003

independent, applicable in diverse sectors, from the tourist sector to non-profit organizations, from service companies to the public administration; (c) general purpose, whether corporate or individual, educational or for electronic commerce (B2B, B2C, etc); and (d) user-friendly, to facilitate its comprehension and application by people with different skills. In studying the need for and possibility of having a common conceptual base for the evaluation of quality in Web sites, we will refer to the 2QCV3Q framework, which we developed using classical rhetorical principles [4] and which can be seen as a meta-model for classification of diverse criteria for Web site quality. The results of the evaluation projects realised thus far have shown that it indeed satisfies the requirements listed above. More recently, we have used the 2QCV3Q meta-model to carry out two studies of the quality of the Web sites of Regional Tourist Boards (RTB) in the Alps, having different objectives and the sites included in the first group were a sub-group of the second.

2 Evaluating the Quality of Web Sites of the Regional Tourist Boards (RTB) in the Alps

In our Web site evaluation projects we refer to an original framework, or meta-model called 2QCV3Q (in Latin V stands for U), which takes its name from the initials of the Ciceronian loci of classical rhetoric that it is based on [1], [6] (table 1). Using the Ciceronian loci made it possible to identify the fundamental dimensions of a Web site, resulting in a general framework of the "quality models", which is independent of the sites under analysis. For purposes of this paper, the most important activity is the "instantiation" or calibration of the 2QCV3Q meta-model (also called 7Loci), which gives as output the specifications of the characteristics for each *locum* and determines the level of detail at which each dimension must be analysed. From a project management point of view, the "weight" of the resulting model determines the resources (time and financial) necessary for the evaluation project. For this reason it is very important to adapt the evaluation method to the different projects, tailoring it to their goals.

Table 1. Dimensions of the 2QCV3Q (7Loci) meta-model

QVIS? (Who?)	Identity
QVID? (What?)	Content
CVR? (Why?)	Services
VBI? (Where?)	Location
QVANDO? (When?)	Maintenance
QVOMODO? (How?)	Usability
QVIBUS AVXILIIS? (With what means?)	Feasibility

To evaluate the quality of the Web site of the (public) tourist boards is the principal objective of one line of study of a triennial research project on tourism in the Alps (www.cs.unitn.it/etourism/). In this context we realised two different projects evaluating Web site quality; in short, the aims for each project were, respectively:

1. to compare the principal Web sites of the alpine regions, to identify possible benchmarks [3];
2. to identify guidelines and recommendations for the design or re-design of the Web site for a tourist destination [5].

Both the projects were carried out with a consideration that the tourism offering in the Alps is based on the activity of hundreds of small- and medium-sized enterprises (SMEs) and focusing on the importance of the "do it yourself" tourist. In such a context, we focused on the Regional Tourist Boards (RTB). Scouting the official alpine RTBs' sites we identified 26 Web sites distributed as follows: 7 in Italy, 8 in Austria, 6 in Switzerland, 3 in France, 1 in Slovenia (the national Tourist Board site was considered, given that there are no RTBs) and 1 in Germany.

Starting from a consideration of the role of the RTBs, the general aim of the first quality evaluation project can be formulated as follows: "to analyze the diffusion and practical application of DMSs in the alpine tourist regions in order to identify the best RTB Web sites, taking into account both organizational and technological aspects". Considering the purpose of the evaluation and the results of a preliminary survey of the RTBs, for the first evaluation project we used a standard model that instantiated the 7Loci meta-model as a table with 24 questions, from 3 to 6 for each dimension (excluding in this phase the last dimension – feasibility). The table was adapted from one used in projects with similar objectives and constraints. In addition, each question was assigned a weight that reflected its importance. We focused on ten RTB sites (Tirol, Ticino, Valais, Zentralschweiz, Freiburgerland,[3] Piemonte, Valle d'Aosta, Trentino, Alto Adige, Veneto). As regards the evaluators, we involved four experts in the tourism sector, two of whom were also expert in marketing, one in statistics and one in quality evaluation.

Given the aim of the second evaluation project - to identify guidelines and recommendations for the design or re-design of the Web site for a tourist destination – in the first part of the research we gathered more information on the needs of the "do-it-yourself" tourist and those of other categories of users (local operators and tourists, as well as the professionals and technicians involved in designing and maintaining the Web site). We then analysed and classified - following an iterative approach - the requirements on the basis of the first six dimensions of the 7Loci meta-model. Then we reformulated them as Boolean questions, resulting in a detailed model to support the assessment of the quality of the Web sites of these organisations. The end result was a table with about one hundred "elementary" questions for the dimensions of the 7Loci framework and as such it represents a "heavyweight" model in respect to that used in the project described above.

---

[3] A deeper analysis of tourism data for Freiburgerland showed that the alpine sector played only a secondary role, and was therefore not included in subsequent studies.

3 Comparing the Results of the Light-Heavyweight Models

Both evaluation projects revealed that the quality of the RTB Web sites is vastly different from one region to another. The nature of the evaluation tables used in the two projects differs greatly. However, in the comparison of the nine sites examined in both projects, the difference in scores using the two models were modest, with only one site shifting two positions while the others change only one or remain unchanged (table 2). Also more accurate comparisons showed that the two models divide the sites in a largely coherent and homogeneous manner (comparison results are given in [6]). The results obtained with the standard/lightweight version of the model in the first study are consistent with those obtained with the more detailed heavyweight model in the second study.

Table 2. Ranking of the sites

	Average scores for the dimensions		Ranking		Delta ranking
	2002	2001	2002	2001	
Canton Ticino	0,81	0,76	1	2	1
Tirol	0,80	0,86	2	1	1
Trentino	0,73	0,75	3	3	0
Alto Adige	0,70	0,68	4	6	2
Valais	0,70	0,74	5	4	1
Valle d'Aosta	0,66	0,72	6	5	1
Zentralschweiz	0,56	0,63	7	7	0
Piemonte	0,52	0,44	8	9	1
Veneto	0,46	0,57	9	8	1

Acknowledgements. We would like to thank the members of the eTourism group and all the experts that cooperated to the development and validation of the models.

References

1. Cicero M.T., "De Inventione", 58 BC, in De Inventione, De Optimo Genere Oratorum, Topica, Vol. 2, Rhetorical Treatises E.H. Warmington (ed.), Harvard University Press
2. Fowler M., "The New Methodology", SW development, Dec 2002, www.martinfowler.com/articles/newMethodology.html
3. Franch M., Martini U., Mich L., "The quality of promotional strategies on the Web: the case of Alpine Regional Destination", in Proc. TQM, VR, I, 25–27 Jun 2002, 2: 643–652.
4. Mich L., Franch M., Gaio L., "Evaluating and Designing the Quality of Web Sites", IEEE Multimedia, Jan-Mar 2003, pp. 34–43
5. Mich L., Franch M., Cilione G., Marzani P., Tourist Destinations and the Quality of Web Sites: a Study of Regional Tourist Boards in the Alps, in Proc. Enter2003, Helsinki, F
6. Mich L., Franch M., Novi Inverardi P., Marzani P., Web site quality evaluation: Lightweight or Heavyweight Models?, Tech. Rep. DIT-03-015, http://www.dit.unitn.it
7. Olsina L., Rossi G., "Measuring Web Application Quality with WebQEM", IEEE Multimedia, October-December 2002, pp. 20–29.

WLGauge – A Web Link Gauge to Measure the Quality of External WWW Links

Omar Garcia, Srivalli Vilapakkam Nagarajan, and Peter Croll

Centre for Dependable Software Engineering and Training (CDSET)
School of IT and Computer Science (SITACS)
University of Wollongong Australia
{omar, svn95, croll}@uow.edu.au

Abstract. External Broken links have a negative impact on any web page user. However, little or no information is provided in advance to advise the user of the quality of the available links before they hit them. Our contributions in this paper are: (1) To present our arguments to suggest that the external link quality is not binary (broken or available) but instead it is a continuous value from low reliability to high reliability (2) To emphasise the need for the web designers to provide some information in advance to the user suggesting the quality of the link. This approach is very similar to having the image size next to a potential loading image giving the user a broad idea about the resources needed to download that image. (3) To present a new tool called WLGauge that can measure some quality attributes of the external links in a web page. WLGauge is an open framelet that can be easily plugged on to any web site development toolbox. WLGauge has been designed with an intention to help the web designer and web maintenance teams to understand as well as improve the quality of their web pages.

Keywords: *Website, open framelets, external link quality, website quality and automatic testing.*

1 Introduction

Websites attracts audience from all corners of the world. Web users are increasingly annoyed by the poor quality and performance of some web sites. Poor web site quality, performance or accessibility is potentially dangerous to business operations in today's competitive market. Because of this reason, Web Engineering has attracted more attention in recent years than ever before. Nowadays, much of the effort is put into producing websites that are not only good in quality but also are reliable at all times. Therefore, reliability (or accessibility) and quality have been the two main factors in deciding the web user's satisfaction. Link rot is one of the many challenges facing the web community. Link rot is a situation in which the decay of the www links occurs as the sites they connect to changes or disappears [1]. Link rot has a direct impact on the website usability [2]. The objective of this paper is two fold. Firstly, we emphasise that the link rot problem is not binary but instead falls within a range of

J.M. Cueva Lovelle et al. (Eds.): ICWE 2003, LNCS 2722, pp. 338–348, 2003.
© Springer-Verlag Berlin Heidelberg 2003

quality levels from low to high reliability. Secondly, we suggest that the open framelets is a viable technique to build and test the web software for external broken links.

In section 2 we provide a background to the current situation and identify the problems surrounding the web community. The external broken links problem has been analysed and a solution to handle them has been proposed. Section 3 discusses the related work done by other software companies/developers to handle the broken external links and related problems. Section 4 highlights our contribution on the development of a Web Link Meter called "WLGauge" which is an open framelet capable of measuring the quality of the external links. In section 5 the WLGauge design is described in detail. Section 6 will discuss the work done in the evaluation of the WLGauge and its performance. In section 7 potential areas for future work are identified and our contributions and conclusions are highlighted.

2   Background to the Link Rot Problem

According to GVU [2] slow speed of Internet access (66.1 %) and the proliferation of the broken links (49.90%) are the main problems facing today's Web users. In order to improve the speed of the service, faster links and data compression algorithms are widely used. The broken link problem is seen as a manifestation of a more general problem known as link rot. As mentioned earlier, link rot can be defined as the decay of World Wide Web links since the sites that they connect to change or disappear. This is a huge problem, as it cannot be easily brought under control in any way. The web designer does not have control over these links. On top of all this, link rot now seems to be a fairly common problem. It has been recently reported in [3] that at least about 30% of all the web pages experience link rot.

Professors Brooks and Markwell, from the University of Nebraska-Lincoln, compared the rate of link rot to the type of "extinction equation" commonly used to describe natural processes such as radioactive decay [4]. According to them, the hyperlinks in their study had an expected "half-life" of 55 months. Also, the extinction rate was dependant on the domain. For example, '.edu' has the biggest loss of all the domains.

The World Wide Web is constantly changing. While dynamicity is a certainty in web the lesson to learn from link rot is to regularly check the status of all the links used in your websites. It is even more important with online education (e-learning) to make sure that all the links work properly. This should be the norm in preparing any course that relies on Internet resources beyond our control [5]. The advice is to detect and correct the rotten links before they destroy you.

2.1 A Closer Look at the Problem and a Proposed Solution

The problem of link rot is not binary (broken or not broken). There may be many reasons why some of the links are not available at a particular time. Some of the common reasons are - server down, links down and faulty router. It is worth noting that not all websites work 24 hours a day. However, in order to give a sensible measure of the link quality, frequent testing and recording of the response time(s) as well as the behaviour of the external links in a web site must be stored in a test profile. This profile will provide information to generate a quality measure of the link. Sampling can be done on a timely basis. The user can make a decision on when and how often sampling should be done.

External links are those WWW links over which we have no control. Some external links are not available all the time. Few others are always available. Therefore there is a range here with always available on one end and not available at all at the other end. It will be extremely helpful if the quality of the link can be measured and then used to determine where the link falls in the range. The clients can then be informed about the information on the quality of the link before they hit the link. The following measures will provide web users with valuable information on the quality of the link:

- *Percentage of success versus failure:* It is a measure to find out the percentage of time when the link's accessibility works (or is successful) or not. This measure will provide an indication of the reliability and accessibility of the websites.

- *Average time to respond*: This is the average time required to retrieve the information from an external link. This measure will give an indication of the speed and performance of the website after hitting the link. Response time and latency parameters will help to understand end-to-end response time as well as to check if there are parts of a site that are very slow in comparison to the other parts.

- *Date of last successful hit*: It becomes easy to look at the history and tell if the link has been accessed in the recent past. This information will help the user know about the status of the link.

In the current world, developing tools to automatically measure and to collect the above information for the web users has become a crucial matter in meeting the user's needs. Therefore, an open framelet called "WLGauge" was developed to help the webmasters, web application developers and the web site quality assurance managers to collect the above useful data so that quality related information can be provided to their clients. WLGauge is capable of measuring the quality of the external links and generating a profile of it, which in turn can be used to either provide a report that can be forwarded automatically to the clients in a simple manner or be able to dynamically update the web page to show a visual clue of the link quality.

3   Related Work

A variety of products are available to alleviate the link rot problem and they can be classified in to two groups:

- Tools that are able to test a link or group of links and generate a report with the status of the link among other things. Example: Tetranet LinkBot [6] and NetMechanics toolbox [7]; also freeware or shareware like CheckBot [8] and Xenu's Link Sleuth [9]
- A service provider (a company) that on a timely basis checks the client's website and informs them if the website has problem like broken links and others. Example: Link Alarm [10] and LinkWalker [11] belong to this group.

Table 1 lists a few of the products available and their characteristics.

Table 1. Software to check broken links

Product Name	Features
Link Walker	• Verifies the external links for access • Scans sites daily to check for broken links • Lets the client know when an inbound link is broken
Xenu's Link Sleuth	• Link verification covers all the links, images, frames, plug-ins, backgrounds; local image maps scripts and java applets. • Displays a updated list of URLs • Free and has a simple user interface
Checkbot	• Link verification on a set of HTML pages • Can check for single or more documents on one or more server • Creates a report which summarises all the links with errors
Link Alarm	• Online web service that checks every link on every page of the client's site • Confidential reports are sent about any problems • Link failure is classified according to the type of defect • LinkAlarm rating for each check is generated

Difference between the other products and WLGauge: First, as stated before, all these product/services consider the link rot problem as binary and therefore do not provide a history of tests whereas WLGauge is able to provide a history of the test results. Secondly, the current tools and services do not provide any automatic ways to fix the problem or to provide a graph or textual clue of the quality of the link to the web user. It is up to the web manager to feed this information on his web site.

4 WLGauge – An Open Framelet

4.1 Framelets

Pree and Koskimies first introduced the word framelet in [12] and later reinforced in [13], where they defined framelets as mini frameworks) that have the following characteristics:

- They are small in size (less than 10 classes);
- They do not assume main control of an application;
- They have a clearly defined interface

A framework is a design of a reusable application or a part of an application represented by a group of classes in such a way that they collaborate with each other.

4.2 Open Source

One of the ongoing impediments to increase software reuse has been the concern experienced by the developers when the source code is not available to them. Even when the developers do not need to modify the source code, there appears to be a psychological problem whenever the source code is not available. The lack of source code is perceived as a potential threat that hinders the reuse of somebody else's code. We are aware that software developers may face potential economic threats by delivering open source products, but we still embrace the open source movement because the benefits to the development community must prevail over the benefits to individual component developers. For a more detailed discussion on open community see [14,15]. We consider WLGauge as an open framelet because it is both a mini framework (satisfying the definition of framelets) and is free software for anyone to use.

5 WLGauge Design

One of the goals of the WLGauge design is to make the system as automated as possible. This means reduced human interaction and reduced amount of work to be done due to the use of automatic testing tools [16].

Figure 1 shows the operations involved in the usage of WLGauge. The main processes involved in the design of WLGauge are:

1. URLCollector: Collecting the external url from the web page and storing them in a file. This process can be done manually or automatically. A simple program to achieve this comes with the framelet.

2. URLChecker: This process will run basically an http request to the external link and collect the data in a file or database. It basically checks all links in the file generated in the previous step. It does only one test on the link and appends the information to the test profile records or create a new test profile if it does not exist.

3. WebPageMechanic: This process will transform the http pages in a java servlet page by adding graph or textual information next to the external links. The following is a java scriptlet that will be inserted in a web page and will show the success ratio of an external link.

<%= new WLGauge ("www.uow.edu.au").getSuccessRatio(). %>

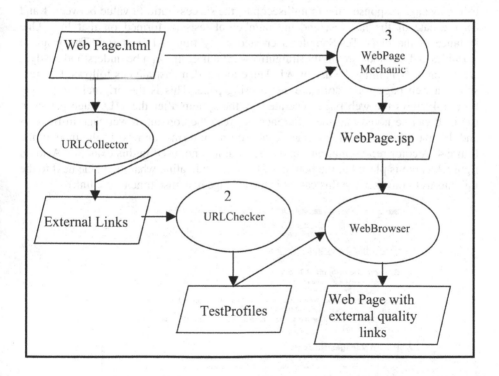

Fig. 1. WLGauge Operation

The class diagram for WLGauge framelet is shown in figure 2.

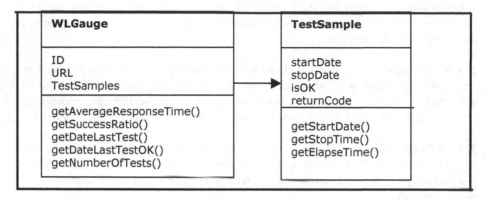

WLGauge	TestSample
ID URL TestSamples	startDate stopDate isOK returnCode
getAverageResponseTime() getSuccessRatio() getDateLastTest() getDateLastTestOK() getNumberOfTests()	getStartDate() getStopTime() getElapseTime()

Fig. 2. WLGauge Class Diagram

Basically, the instance variables for the class WLGauge are the URL for the external link, an internal ID for control purpose and the set of test samples. The methods give us the average response time in milliseconds, the success ratio (a value between 1 and 0), the date of the last test and the number of tests performed on that link. One instance of the class TestSample is created every time a test is run. The instance variables and methods are pretty straightforward things that can be understood easily.

An example explaining the use of WLGauge tool is demonstrated as follows. Figure 3 shows a web page for a software engineering page. This is the original html page. Figure 4 shows the web page generated by the system after the WLGauge has been used. It can be noted that the difference between the content in webpage in figure 3 and 4 is the addition of the average response time information next to the links in the figure 4. A color representation can be used but it is not used in this example. Also, in figure 4 a note is placed at the bottom of the page indicating what the value next to the link means to the user (in this case it is the average response time to the link).

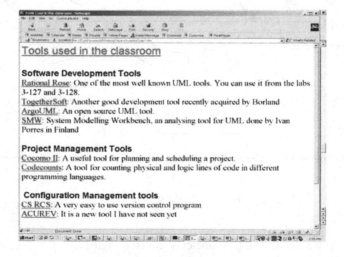

Fig. 3. An original html page

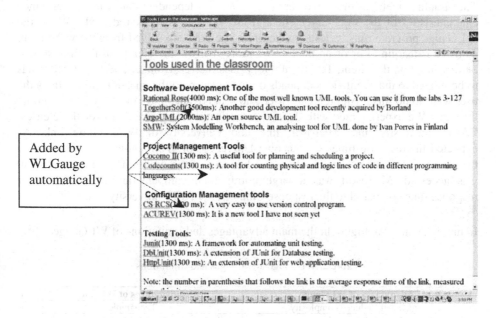

Fig. 4. A modified web page generated with the use of WLGauge

The WLGauge software is available at www.uow.edu.au/~omar/WLGauge.

6   Evaluation Work Done on WLGauge

In this section an evaluation of the tool developed is provided. WLGauge has a very limited functionality, for example it has only the skeletal framework and the tester/user has to provide the code for testing for the sampling scheme (information like when the test has to be carried out, test dates, timings etc have to be supplied to the existing framework).

The main question is how to report the quality of the link measured?
- A graphical representation based on different colours like green, yellow or red.
- A textual value, for example: the average time to access the link, the ratio of success.
- A hover over the link that will display some information about the quality of the link.
- A sound, which conveys some sort of guiding information about the quality of the link.

To provide the above functionalities one must devote thousands of programming hours. This means increasing costs for the product and fattening the software [17]. However the reality is that a typical user will not choose all these features. Therefore, framelets provide a blueprint where additional features are easily plugged when they are really needed.

The quality metrics measured are very much dependent on the performance characteristics of the web server client from where it is measured [18]. When the WLGauge program runs its tests on the links, the links are solved from the web client, so there is margin of error on this. To be more realistic the quality of the link should be measured on the client. Technically it is possible, TestRunner and PageUpdate has to be moved to the client. This depends on the answers to the questions like – does the user want to do this? And does the user know in advance the links they will be going through? We experimented with the tool to collect the response times for three cases: EAFIT university link, Microsoft link and University of Wollongong link. As expected the response times for our own University of Wollongong link was quicker than the response times for the other two because of the proximity of the server that was accessed. Microsoft was a large commercial company and they had better response time compared to the response time of the EAFIT university link.

In table 2, below we highlight the main advantages and limitations of WLGauge.

Table 2. WLGauge advantages and limitations

Advantages of WLGauge	Disadvantages of WLGauge
Small and Reduced complexity	Too simple
Easy to learn and use Easy to plug onto the wed designer/manager's tools	It does not support some additional features available in other products
Open framelet	Not much support offered
It uses Java as the language for implementation (Java offers platform-independence, designed for internetworking, portability and security)	It uses Java as the language for implementation (interpreted Java programs runs slower than the compiled programs)

7   Future Work and Conclusions

7.1 Future Work to Be Done

WLGauge can be made slimmer by not using the HttpUnit framework [20] and by directly using java.net, we have not done this yet mainly because it will increase the development time. HttpUnit is another popular framework for testing based on Junit [21] with the purpose of testing web applications, specifically, to simulate certain functionalities of the browser with the purpose of examining the result of a web page. It is important not to add complexity to the existing framework by adding unwanted features and clearly draw the difference between indispensable and luxurious features.

WLGauge has to be used extensively before its usefulness can be completely understood. Therefore it will have to be tested in the field for a long term before determining how easy it is to work with.

In the future, to move the URLChecker to the client (instead of the server) will be explored. A similar idea will be to rewrite the WLGauge system as a browser plug in.

More effort must be put into finding answers for some of the following questions: Is it worth the cost of tracing the links? And what are the challenges in doing so ? (privacy, ethical, etc).

Based on the results of our experimentation and the feedback collected from the user experiences, the WLGauge framelet will be continuously improved. A multithreaded version of WLGauge will also be explored. A multi-threaded option can be useful where more than one link is checked at the same time. This idea was not incorporated in the first version because of one important user behaviour – very often, users will go one link at a time and the test will reflect the way users operate.

7.2 Conclusions

Our contribution to this paper includes identification of the link rot problem as non binary problem and that the quality of the external links should be measured so that the quality of the web sites can be understood. WLGauge was specifically developed to let users know the crucial information on the quality of the external links on their websites. According to [22] automated website quality testing is both an opportunity and a challenge.

Watchfire [23] tell us that 58% of the consumers said that if the site failed on their first visit, they would never return to it. Jakob Nielsen [24] says that broken links annoy the users and deprive them of the value they would have gotten from the site. In our opinion simple framelets like WLGauge have a huge potential to perform very well for small-scale web applications and we certainly believe that in the years to come everyone will realise how crucial such simple tools are in meeting the web user's expectations.

Acknowledgment. We appreciate the comments and value suggestions of my friends and colleagues Lourdes de Miguel Garcia and Khin Than Win.

References

[1] The Jargon Dictionary at http://info.astrian.net/jargon/ dated 19/01/2003
[2] Graphic, Visualization, & Usability Center's (GVU) 7th WWW User Survey at http://www.cc.gatech.edu/gvu/user_surveys/survey-1997-04/ dated 19/01/2003
[3] Evans, M P. Furnell, S M., "The Resource Locator service: Fixing a law in the web", The International Journal of Distributed Informatique, v 37 n3-4 Nov 5 2001, Computer NetWorks.
[4] Markwell, J. Brooks, D.W. "Broken links: The ephemeral nature of educational WWW hyperlinks", Journal of Science Education and Technology, June 2002
[5] Rumsey, M. "Runaway Train: Problems of Permanence, Accessibility, and Stability in the Use of Web Sources in law Review Citations", Law Library Journal vol 94:1
[6] Link Bot at http://www.watchfire.com/ dated 20/01/2003
[7] Toolbox at http://www.netmechanic.com/ dated 19/01/2003
[8] Checkbot at http://degraaff.org/checkbot/ dated 19/01/2003

[9]   Xenu at http://home.snafu.de/tilman/xenulink.html dated 20/01/2003
[10] Link Alarm at http://www.linkalarm.com/ dated 20/01/2003
[11] Link Walker at http://www.seventwentyfour.com/ dated 19/01/2003
[12] Pree, W. Koskimies, K. "Rearchitecturing Legacy Systems—Concepts & Case Study",
       First Working IFIP Conference on Software Architecture (WICSA), San Antonio, Texas,
       February 1999
[13] Pree, W. Koskimies, K. "Framelets small is beautiful", in Building Application Frame-
       works: Object-Oriented Foundations of Framework Design, Wiley & Sons, New York
       City, 2000
[14] Newman, N. "The Origins and Future of Open Source Software", at
       http://www.netaction.org/opensrc/future/oss-whole.html
[15] Gabriel, R. "The Feyerabend Project", at http://www.dreamsongs.com/Projects.html, dated
       20/01/2003
[16] Garcia, O. "Automatic Software Testing in O.O. Languages", Proceedings of SigSoft
       2001, Encuentro Iberoamericano, Universidad Distrital, August 29-31, 2001 Bogota,
       Colombia.
[17] Shin, D. Koh, K. Won, Y. "Measurement and Analysis of Web Server Response Time",
       Proc. of APCC 2000(Asia Pacific Conference on Communications), Seoul, Korea, Oct.
       2000.
[18] Wirth, N. "A plea for lean software", IEEE Computer, Volume: 28 Issue: 2, Feb 1995 pp:
       64–68
[19] http://www.wired.com/news/business/0,1367,10251,00.html dated 18/01/2003
[20] HttpUnit at http://sourceforge/ dated 19/01/2003
[21] JUnit at http://junit.org/ dated 19/01/2003
[22] The WebSite Quality Challenge, at
       http://www.soft.com/eValid/Technology/White.Papers/ dated 19/01/2003
[23] WebSite Quality Matters, at http://www.watchfire.com/solutions/quality.asp dated 18/01/
       2003
[24] Jakob Nielsen, "Fighting linkrot ", at http://www.useit.com/alertbox/, dated 18/01/

Hyperlinks Analysis of Dynamic Web Applications

Angle Hsieh and Dowming Yeh

National Kaoshiung Normal University
Kaoshiung, Taiwan 802, Republic of China
AngleHsieh@ttnt.com.tw, dmyeh@nknucc.nknu.edu.tw

Abstract. There are several approaches available to implement complex and adaptive Web Application. One of the most favorite approaches is dynamic Web page technique. Many structural problems such as void links and broken links may be hidden in a web site with dynamic pages. Thus, techniques to aid in understanding and restructuring of a Web site can help Web masters significantly. This work proposes a set of structural analysis methods for diagnosis of some common problems to meet real maintenance needs. Systemized analyses are employed to gather key attributes of the structure in a Web site, and the structural information gathered can be utilized to analyze the quality of the site structure easily.

1 Introduction

Maintaining a Web-based application is not easier than a traditional application. Numerous arts, page layouts and hyperlink designs are used and slacked in designing Web-based application, aside from database connection and program code. There are several approaches available to implement complex and adaptive Web Application. One of the most favorite approaches is to produce Web pages dynamically using server-side script languages such as ASP. This gives developers flexibility and adaptability to construct more powerful Web applications. A Web page produced by the script is a dynamic Web page. Web sites or Web applications with dynamic pages are thus called dynamic Web sites or applications.

There are few studies addressing the issues of Web site understanding and restructuring [1]. Ricca and Tonella completely tendered a method for structure readjusting and implemented tools, *ReWeb* and *TestWeb*, for modeling and understanding Web sites [4] [5]. These tools can analyze Web sites, and display the outcome of structural analyses. However, they only can analyze sites consisted of static pages with frames.

Di Lucca et. al. also present a tool for reverse engineering Web applications into UML diagrams [2]. They extract the attributes of Web pages into an Intermediate Representation Form, and then translate this Form into a relational database. The class diagrams can be produced directly from the database. Other diagrams such as use case diagram and sequence diagram may be constructed after performing some queries on the database. There is little discussion regarding dynamic page issues in these works.

J.M. Cueva Lovelle et al. (Eds.): ICWE 2003, LNCS 2722, pp. 349–352, 2003.
© Springer-Verlag Berlin Heidelberg 2003

2 Algorithms for Gathering Hyperlinks

The *StruGatherer* algorithm processes all Web pages in a target site, and the results are represented in the form of page objects and link objects. A page object may own many link objects, but a link object can only belong to one page object. A page object $P<p, lo, d)>$ has attributes "page name", "page location", "page type". The page name p with page location lo attributes can identify a unique page in the site. In the following discussion, the Active Server Page (ASP) will be used to explain the concept of our methods and how it works.

A page object may own zero to n link objects, $L<q, llo, lvn, lvp>$. A link object has attributes "target page name", "target page location", "identification number", and "variable location". The attribute lvn is an identification number to identify links that are created from the same hyperlink through variable assignments. The name of the page containing the link will be saved in lvp. Each link object will be conjoined with its containing page object upon creation.

The pseudo-code of the algorithm is shown in Figure 1. *PageInfo* creates a new page object $P(v)$ corresponding to the page v. The *DecomposePage* procedure separates the dynamic blocks B^D from the static blocks [3]. Similar to *PageInfo*, *LinkInfo* extracts the essential information from a hyperlink and creates a link object. Then the target page name is examined to determine whether it is a regular link. If it is a variable, the link object $L(l)$ becomes a *virtual* link object by setting its identification number lvn to i. The number i is a unique number beginning with zero and increases progressively when new variables are processed. This number is to identify that different virtual link objects are in fact assigned with the same hyperlink.

Algorithm StruGatherer (D)
Input: D = {all pages in home directory, sub-directory, virtual directory}
```
1.     i ← 1
2.     for each pages v in D do   //visit all of pages
3.              P(v) ← PageInfo(v)
4.              B^D (v)← DecomposePage(v)
5.              for each link l in B^D(v) do
6.                       P(v).L(l) ← LinkInfo(l)
7.                       if P(v).L(l).q is not a regular link // variable
8.                                P(v). lvn ← i
9.                                Call GatherLinkVariable (D, P, v, P(v).L(l).q, l)
10.                               i ← i + 1
11.                      end if
12.             loop
13.    loop
14.    return P     // Return the set of page objects
```

Fig. 1. The *StruGatherer* algorithm

The pseudo-code of algorithm *GatherLinkVariable* is divided into three segments depending on the kind of the variable under analysis: dynamic and static local variable, inquiry variable, and global variable. We do not consider database objects since for a database field object, all possible links can be determined from the database field.

Algorithm GatherLinkVariable (D, P, v, b, l)
Input: D = { all pages in home directory, sub-directory, virtual directory}, the page
object set P, current page v, the variable name b, the link l
1.   *select case type(b)*
2.   *case local variable*
3.   *fv ← open(v)*
4.   *while not fv.EOF and **MatchLHS**(b) do*
5.   *r ← **FetchRHS**() //right hand side of "b="*
6.   *if r is a variable then Call **GatherLinkVariable**(D, P, v, r, l)*
7.   *if r is a page then Call **CreateActualLinkObject**(r, P(v).L(l))*
8.   *loop*
9.   *case inquiry variable*
10.   *for each pages cp in D do*
11.   *fcp ← open(fcp)*
12.   *while not fcp.EOF and **MatchLHS**(**FetchArg**(b)) do*
13.   *if **SamePageName**(cp, P(v).p))*
14.   *r ← **FetchRHS**()*
15.   *if r is a variable then Call **GatherLinkVariable**(D, P, v, r, l)*
16.   *if r is a page then   Call **CreateActualLinkObject**(r, P(v).L(l))*
17.   *end if*
18.   *loop*
19.   *loop*
20.   *case global variable*
21.   *for each pages cp in D do*
22.   *similar procedure to local variable*
23.   *loop*
24.   *end select*

Fig. 2. The *GatherLinkVariable* algorithm

The scope of a local variable is the containing page. Therefore, all possible link
values can be extracted from v. In the loop, all tokens at the left hand side of an assignment statement and matching the variable b are successively discovered and the
value at the right hand side of the assignment statement is extracted. If an actual page
is found, a new link object will be created by *CreateActualLinkObject* and added into
the page object $P(v)$. This algorithm may be called recursively since variable may be
assigned values by the other variables.

Inquiry variables act like parameter passing for conventional programs and appear
as parameters for a *request* method in the target page. According to the transmission
principle of inquiry variable, the source of an inquiry variable could be any page.
Therefore, the outer loop processes every page including itself and the link objects are
extracted in the inner loop. The inquiry variable must be extracted by *FetchArg* for-
asmuch it is an argument in a *request* method. An important point is to ascertain that
the target page of the submitted value is the same as the current page $P(v).p$ when the
variable name is found. This is accomplished by the *SamePageName* procedure.

Global variables are visible to all pages in a site so that a page can communicate
with any other page without passing arguments. In the case of ASP, the lifetime of
global variables can exist in a user session or the lifetime of the application.

Many structural problems, such as broken link, long-distance path, different root, etc., may be hidden in a dynamic Web site. If a hyperlink is composed of a variable, but the variable is not given any page name or the target of a regular link is not specified, it is called a void link. A void link involving variables is represented by a virtual link object without corresponding link objects with actual target page. Recalls that any link objects created by *GatherLinkVariable* must correspond to a virtual link object with the same ID number in attribute *lvn*. Therefore, by examining the attribute *lvn* of virtual link objects, if a ID number appears only once, it is a void link. Algorithms to detect void link and broken link errors in a Web site are described in [3]. Broken links result from unavailable target pages.

3 Conclusions

A real running Web site is studied to test the feasibility of our methods. The site under study contains a total of 85 pages, and more than 80 percent of them are dynamic pages. The main scripting languages are ASP and JavaScript. There are a total of 325 hyperlinks in this site. Most are dynamic links. After analysis, two hyperlinks are found void. There are five broken links, three dynamic links and two static links. The analysis result gives Web master some helpful suggestions to improve the site.

Dynamic pages are becoming more popular because pages can reflect most updated information and can be customized much easier than a static page. However, the maintenance issue of a dynamic Web site has presented new challenges to the research community. Our contribution to Web site maintenance is in defining a set of structural analysis methods for diagnosis of some common problems to meet real maintenance needs. In the future, we plan to implement these algorithms to be able to gather and analyze dynamic Web sites automatically.

References

1. S. Chung and Y. S. Lee, "Reverse software engineering with uml for web site maintenance", in *Proceedings of the 1st International Conference on Web Information Systems Engineering*, Hong-Kong, China, June 2001.
2. G. A. Di Lucca, A. R. Fasolino, F. Pace, P. Tramontana, U. De Carlini, "WARE: a tool for the Reverse Engineering of Web Applications", in *Proceedings of the Sixth European Conference on Software Maintenance and Reengineering,* Budapest, Hungary, 2002.
3. A. Hsieh, "StruWeb: A Mehthod for Understanding and Restructuring Dynamic Web Sites", *Master Thesis*, MIS Dept. National Pingtung University of Science and Technology, July 2002.
4. F. Ricca and P. Tonella, "Understanding and Restructuring Web Sites with ReWeb", IEEE *MultiMedia*, April-June 2001.
5. F. Ricca and P. Tonella, "Analysis and Testing of Web Applications", in *Proceedings of the 23rd IEEE International Conference on Software Engineering*, Toronto, Ontario, Canada, May 12–19, 2001.

Why Not RSVP over DTM ?

Cláudia J. Barenco Abbas[1] and L. Javier García Villalba[2]

[1] Dept. Electrical Engineering, University of Brasilia, Brazil
barenco@redes.unb.br
[2] Dept. Computer Systems and Programming, Complutense University of Madrid, Spain
javiergv@sip.ucm.es

Abstract. This paper suggests the use of the DTM technology as a solution to the transmission of applications with strict need of bandwidth, instead of the use of the traditional ATM technology. The DTM is a broadband network architecture based on synchronous fast circuit switching solution with a constant delay, perfect to the telephony network which is optimized for the characteristics of voice communication, that is, fixed-sized channels and provision of QoS real-time guarantees. Furthermore, the users require access to new services like audio, video and data which is discussed in this paper by proposing the IETF IntServ and the DTM integration supporting dynamic allocation of resources in a circuit switching network. An overview of the integration of the IntServ guaranteed service/RSVP protocol with the DTM technology on the signalling, reservation and management of the allocated bandwidth before the DTM channel establishment is presented.

1 Introduction

Since its first publication in 1988 the ATM technology has been seen as a good cell switching solution. Moreover it has the support of different categories of QoS (*Quality of Service*) services (CBR, rt-VBR, nrt-VBR, ABR). Actually it has been asked if the facilities offered by this technology continue to bring great advantages as a solution for real-time applications with strict needs of throughput, delay, jitter, etc. The inefficiency of the 5 bytes of cell overhead and 4 bytes of the AAL3/4 overhead (SN/MID parameters) results in a maximum use of 91% for ATM when the traffic is not varied. Furthermore, many solutions for attribution, management and control of QoS were designed in the network level, where the applications can have easier and more specific use of the QoS facilities than with the direct use of ATM QoS solution. Others problems are: (1) the cells are small and have fixed size, so ATM is more oriented to the packet switching solution. This means that many of the deficiencies of the packet switching technology are in the cell-switching technology, particularly about the guarantees of QoS. As a consequence, many mechanisms have to be implemented: admission control, shaping, scheduling and resynchronization in the receptor, all at a good effective cost; (2) problems of the CDV (Cell Delay Variation) occur frequently in ATM, as the cells from many transmitters have to be multiplexed in the switch, multiplexer or in other intermediary system. Accumulated delay can be critical if the application doesn't tolerate delays (e.g., video and audio); (3) the lack of

J.M. Cueva Lovelle et al. (Eds.): ICWE 2003, LNCS 2722, pp. 353–363, 2003.
© Springer-Verlag Berlin Heidelberg 2003

applications that use directly the ATM classes of service with distinct QoS; (4) high operational cost.

Nowadays some solutions, like the DTM (Dynamic Synchronous Transfer Mode) technology [1], are bringing up the use of antique switching solutions, more simple and with reasonable performance to real-time applications with QoS constraints.

The DTM is an architecture based on the high-speed circuit switching architecture with dynamic resources reallocation. It provides multicast services, channels with varied bit-rates and low circuit configuration time.

As any other circuit switching solution, the DTM isolates the traffics in each circuit, which means that the activities in one circuit do not disturb the activities in the other one. This brings the possibility of the transmission with guaranteed quality, with a constant delay. This architecture can be extended to include a large number of buses using the switching on the nodes. The switching is synchronous, so the delay caused by the switching is constant on each channel.

The channels in DTM are multirate so each channel can have a arbitrary number of data slots and the capacity of each channel is a multiple of 512 Kbps until the maximum capacity of the bus.

The DTM is constructed with fast-circuit switching technology and dynamic resource reallocation. So, if a specific channel does not have sufficient resources for the transmission, it can ask for resources (slots) from the neighbor nodes. Each node maintains a status table that contains information about free slots in another nodes so when it needs more slots, it consults the table to decide where to ask for resources. This approach is the distributed control of the slots. The manager only have to transfer the control of the slots involved from one node to another, if we have the central control of slots, which is the proposed solution here.

As everyone knows the Internet protocols are widely deployed in network architectures, so we can't ignore that there's a enormous number of applications that use them. If we want a wide spread solution, the IP (Internet Protocol) has to be the network layer protocol.

For guaranteed resources the applications need to reserve them, so it's necessary to have mechanisms to provide this. In the Internet, there's a lot of resource reservation signalling solutions: (1) CoS (Class of Service), (2) CBQ (Class-Based Queuing), (3) ST-II (Revised Internet Stream Protocol), (4) IntServ/RSVP (Resource reservation Protocol) and recently, Differentiated Service (DiffServ). The IntServ[2]/RSVP protocol[3] seams to be the most appropriate solution to work with DTM as it provides a strict specification of the bandwidth. This parameter requires reserving slots in the DTM technology and in many others aspects they are compatible. On next section they will be indicated. Others solutions like DiffServ are appropriate if you want to classify a provider's customers group and define the QoS level that will be offered to this group. Moreover there is not a better protection against complex QoS solution and there isn't any suggestion about properly dimensioning of the network solution for this. The ST-II has some overhead in their control mechanisms, so it doesn't have good performance. The CoS doesn't have a flexible QoS specification in their classes of services and the CBQ is static in the reservation of resources.

There are many interoperability problems between the ATM technology and the RSVP protocol: (1) the renegotiation of the QoS parameters during the lifetime of the connection is forbidden; the ATM Forum TM-4.0 specifies the ability of the renegotiation of some specific data rate bits, but no one knows if this is enough to provide the requirements of the RSVP protocol; (2) dynamic participation of the members of a multicast group causes serious problem in VC (Virtual Circuit) control; (3) the ATM technology is oriented to the sender and the RSVP protocol to the receiver. The ATM Forum UNI 4.0 proposal defined the LIJ (Leaf Initiated Joint), which is a technique trying to minimize this problem; (4) the ATM signalling Q.2931 is so complex; (5) there's a need of some policy to prevent the resources abuse; (6) the lifetime of the ATM VCs is controlled by inactivity and the RSVP protocol has a soft-state or a timeout control; (7) how to send the RSVP messages in a best-effort VC? (8) the dynamic reservations of RSVP bring a great problem to VC management.

The DTM can be integrated perfectly with the RSVP protocol, as many of the capabilities of RSVP is easy to be supported in the DTM architecture: (1) dynamic reservation: the DTM uses a dynamic reallocation of slots; (2) like as in RSVP, the reservation in DTM can be done by the receptor; (3) in DTM the access medium is shared, so it inherently supports the multicast transmission; (4) guaranteed reservation: the DTM uses a strict scheme of reservation; if there isn't enough resources, it can't establish the channel; (5) in DTM there isn't any specification of the lifetime of the channel; it has to be controlled by the application and the RSVP with its soft-state characteristic can adapt perfectly; (6) the signalling scheme of the DTM is simple; (7) there isn't a need to prevent abuse of resource use because DTM has a token control to the use of the data and control slots; (8) the RSVP messages can be transported in the control slots.

Below there's a table with the principal characteristics of the RSVP protocol and the solution to provide them in both the ATM and DTM technologies.

Table 1. Confrontation between ATM and DTM in the Support of the RSVP Protocol.

Characteristic	ATM	DTM
Dynamic Reservations	There's only a theoretical suggestion	Dynamic reallocation of slots
Orientation	Sender	Sender/receiver
Multicast	Complex members control	Inherent multicast support
Lifetime of reservation	Controlled by the inactivity of ATM VCs	Controlled by RSVP protocol
Styles of reservation	The suggestion is to use a unique VC to the support of each RSVP reservation [4]	Slot sharing (SE or WF styles), slot exclusive (FF style)
Policy Control	Need policy control from abusive use of resources	Token slot owner control

2   Requirements and Objectives

In this section we describe the functions and facilities related to the admission control, reservation and administration of bandwidth in a RSVP/DTM environment, that are supported in this proposal.

   a. Resource reservation: the capacity of resource reservation in a unique segment or multiple segments.

   b. Admission control: estimation of resource availability.

   c. Soft-state: dynamic and automatic lifetime control of the reservations by the soft-state characteristic of the RSVP protocol.

d. Central control of resources: the switch DTM in each segment is the resources controller and administrator, which is not a completely centralized approach of DTM slot management but gives a better interaction with the functionality of the RSVP protocol.
e. Scalability: the scalability problem of the RSVP protocol is greatly decreased in this proposal. Since the reservation is not done on each IP node but on a unique switch that controls the segment that the data have to pass through, only the switch DTM has to control the reservation state.
f. Interaction with the resource control mechanism: the RSVP protocol has interaction with the resource administration control mechanism of the DTM.
g. Support of different styles of filters: the support of FF (Fixed Filter), SE (Shared Explicit) and WF (Wildcard Filter) filters [3].
h. Controlled channel management: DTM channels are created and managed by the higher layers, in this case the RSVP protocol.
i. The routing and addressing take place at the IP layer.
j. At the DTM layer, the network performs the switching, the interaction with the fiber medium and the access control.

As explained above, in the DTM technology has constant delay of around 125 μs in each hop which leaves as the only parameter to be measured and controlled. This is represented by the 'R' parameter of the Integrated Service Guaranteed Service (GS) [5]. Here we call the "DTM cloud" to the region of the network that has the DTM technology implemented. Every node in this cloud that wants to participate in the resource reservation and admission control, using the RSVP protocol, has to implement this protocol. The RSVP protocol is transparent to no-RSVP nodes but we strongly recommend that in this environment of study every node has to be RSVP-like, in order to avoid breaking RSVP signalling in the establishment of DTM channels. The parameters assigned in the IntServ GS are: Tspec, flow specification and Rspec, reservation specification. Inside the "DTM Cloud" the only Tspec parameter that is interesting is 'M', maximum packet length to assembly and reassembly functions. There isn't traffic control in the DTM switches. About Rspec, 'R' is the only parameter. 'S' may be interesting to buffer control in end-systems, but it's out of this document's scope.

3   Basic Architecture

In this section we describe the components and mechanisms necessaries for the interaction of the RSVP protocol and DTM architecture. This proposal concerns reservation, control admission and management of bandwidth. We describe the interaction of the RSVP protocol and the DTM technology in a switch DTM node as it is the responsible for the control admission and management of resources. In sections 4 and 5 we discuss how this is provided.

Before entering in the "DTM Cloud" the IP packets have to pass through a classifier, that decides if the packet will be routed hop-by-hop or it will be switched at DTM layer. To avoid the overhead of establishing and tearing down frequently the DTM channels, short lived flows may be routed hop-by-hop and the long ones (e.g., internet telephony) switched in the DTM layer. The network performance depends greatly on this decision, since with the IP switching technology where the IP Switcher Controller decides if the flow is going to be sent hop-a-hop or to be switched. Here we suggest the use of the Logical Interface Handle (LIH) of the PATH messages to indicate if the referenced packet has to be switched in the "DTM Cloud".

Label binding is not necessary in this proposal. The binding of the slots with respective owners will happen intrinsically in the DTM protocols.

In this proposal we are interested in the study of the packets that will be switched in the DTM layer. In this case each IP packet has to be assigned to a DTM channel that has previously been established using the RSVP protocol. In this proposal, each IP flow (IP address + port) has a dedicated DTM channel, which works like a RSVP protocol that assigns a reservation per each IP flow. We can spend a lot of resources without the multiplexing of various IP traffic in a unique channel, but we are discussing here about guaranteed services, which need strict QoS facilities. There's a necessity of a priority police to manage the queue of packets of each channel. A kind of shaper for bursty traffic can be implemented too in case of buffer overflow, for example using the RED (Random Early Detection).

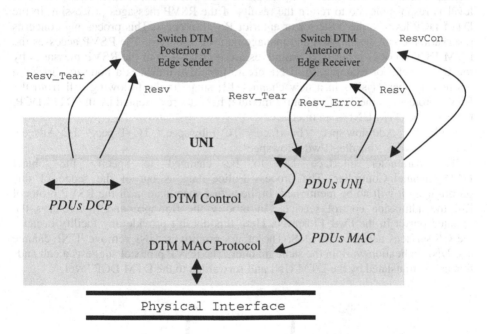

Fig. 1. Upstream Interaction of RSVP/DTM in a Switch DTM in the Reservation and Admission Control of Resources.

The switch DTM architecture proposed here is very simple. It doesn't have any function about IP routing nor RSVP controls. It only has a mechanism to detect the RSVP PATH and Resv messages, send them to DTM UNI level and forward them to the next/prior switch DTM or IP node. For the interaction of RSVP protocol with DTM architecture, the RSVP Resv message has to have a new object that is called DTM_Channel_Controller. This object defines the node that has initiated the establishment of the channel, the edge receiver of the "DTM Cloud". We have to remind that in DTM technology the node that establishes the channel is the transmitter, here the edge transmitter of the "DTM Cloud". The RSVP messages

ResvTear, ResvErr and ResvConf formats have the same format as the specification of the RSVP protocol [3]. About the Error_spec object of the ResvErr message, the important error here is the code error 01, "Failure in the admission control" [3].

The DTM UNI level. One of the functions of this level is to provide a interface between the applications or the protocols in higher level (RSVP, STII, SNMP, etc.) and the DTM Control Protocol (DCP). To start a reservation the application or protocol has to send the following parameters: the desired service (guaranteed or controlled load), description of the traffic (Tspec) and the quantity of resources (Rspec). Here we are only interested in the IntServ GS service. The DTM technology only specifies a strict and deterministic resource reservation, which means that if there isn't enough resources, the admission control fails. This is very compatible with the QoS strict necessity of QoS of the GS services. Moreover, in this proposal the DTM Level UNI has the function of the object translation of RSVP messages to an adequate format, which is to the others components of the switch DTM model. The DTM UNI level is responsible too to return the results of the RSVP messages processing in the DTM DCP level to the posterior or anterior RSVP process. This processing concerns reservation, control admission and management of resources. The RSVP accesses the DTM DCP services using UNI primitives are translated from the RSVP messages by the UNI level. For example, the UNI_create primitive indicates a node to allocate a defined number of slots in a new channel. [3] suggests the following call from the RSVP protocol to the Traffic Control module; here it's represented by the DTM DCP, that uses the DTM UNI as an interface.

Call: TC_AddFlowSpec (Interface, TC_Flowspec, TC_Tspec, TC_Adspec, Police_Flags) -> Rhandle, [Fwd_Flowspec].

The parameter interface has to be changed to specify the object DTM_Channel_Controller. The process Police_flags is out of the scope of this proposal, so it will no be mentioned. In the actual specification of the RSVP protocol [3], the admission control service can modify the flowspec and this returns the updated object in the Fwd_Flospwec. Here this doesn't provide any facility because the GS services need a strict QoS. The others primitives: UNI_remove, UNI_change and UNI_indication work in the same manner. The RSVP protocol suggests a call and this call is translated by the DTM UNI and forwarded to the DTM DCP level.

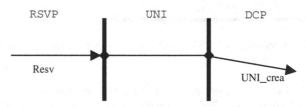

Fig. 2. UNI_create Primitive.

The DTM Control Protocol (DCP) level. This protocol has four responsibilities: (1) allocation of slots; (2) mapping from slot to channel; (3) transmitter/receiver synchronization and (4) management functions. It provides services to user through the UNI level and communicates with others nodes through DTM PDUs (Protocol Data Units). On this proposal, the DCP will respond for the admission control, reservation and management slots. Applications using the RSVP protocol can ask for various services (bandwidth, change of reservation, information about available resources, etc.). These petitions are processed by the DCP.

The DTM MAC level. The DTM MAC (Medium Access Control) defines the access to the medium, in our case the fiber. In the DTM technology the nodes access the medium using the TDM Multiplexing (Time Division Multiplexing). There are three primitives defined to this function: slot_request, slot and slot_indication.

4 Resource Management Function

In this section we describe the resources management function in DTM, that consists of two basic principles: resources allocation between nodes in the network and the resource reservation in the channels.

Allocation of resources. As resources allocation we prefer the central approach, because it brings a good conformance with the RSVP protocol. Moreover, (1) the clients become simpler as they only contain the information about their own channels; (2) it is easier to have admission control and fairness; (3) the fragmentation of the free slots in the controller is very modest.

The slot controller will be the DTM switch on each physical segment that takes part in a transmission. It has the responsibilities to create and terminate a channel on the reception of RSVP Resv and Resv_Tear messages and the resource management. Each time a user request arrives to a node, it first requests tokens from the slot controller. The delay in finding and allocating free slots is around 100 μs [7]. In this approach the slot controller has to have more signalling capacity, that means that it will have access to a large number of control slots. The main advantage of the distributed approach is that it doesn't depend on the round-trip time on the bus; but in [7] was proven that the central approach performs close to the ideal protocol and is relatively simple. A study [8] demonstrated that in situations of low load (70%), the probability of asking for slots from others nodes is 55%, which is high and means drawback to algorithms like KTH and KTHLR (KTH Ring), since even in situations of normal load nodes need to request slots frequently. There's another algorithm called BCA (Background Channel Allocation) that intents to minimize this problem.

Resource Reservation. The RSVP protocol is responsible for the indication of the amount of resources that a host wants using its reservation soft-state characteristic. It also establishes the channel duration. At the starting of the network, the DTM guarantees to each node a certain number of slots in each fiber. If we have m nodes, listed $v = 0, 1, ..., m\text{-}1$, the number of slots to each node in each fiber 0 and 1 is [9]

$$N_{vo} = (2 N / m) * [v / (m - 1)]$$

$$N_{v1} = (2 N / m) * [1 - v / (m - 1)]$$

being N the number of slots in each cycle defined as $N = B * T / (n + c)$ where B is the bandwidth, T the time cycles length, n the number of data bits in each cycle and c the number of control bits in each cycle.

The DTM uses a strict resource reservation scheme, where a new channel is admitted only if there is enough free slots. The main point in DTM resource reservation is that a host gets a bandwidth in direct proportion to the number of slots [10]. The DTM supports dynamic reallocation of slots between nodes. This means that the network can adapt to traffic variations. Dynamic priorities in resource reservation can be used between the nodes of the same fiber segment. The proposal is using GS service Tspec parameters and the 'D' parameter of the Adspec to infer the traffic characteristics, to assign or modify node's access priority. A future study will describe this suggestion. In DTM a node has to explicitly indicate if it wants to share the use of its channel. From this possibility we can map the three types of filters defined in the RSVP protocol by channels sharing possibilities. For FF filter, DTM doesn't share channels and for SE and WF filters nodes share channels.

5 Admission Control Function

In this section we describe the admission control function that takes place before the connection establishment phase. As the DTM needs strict resources reservation, the RSVP protocol interacts with it in the signalling of the bandwidth necessary for the transmission of a certain flow. If there is enough resources, RSVP will alert the application and automatically the reservations established before for this flow will be turned down.

RSVP-based Admission Control over DTM. Here we describe generically a signalling method and procedures for RSVP-based admission control over DTM. This study is based on the SBM (Subnet Bandwidth Manager) specification of IEEE 802-style LANs [11]. The IntServ and RSVP definitions do not depend on the underlying network technologies; so it is necessary to map these specifications onto specific subnetwork technologies, in our case the DTM technology. In section 3 we give a example of how the RSVP message Resv is mapped to UNI_create primitive of DTM.

In this proposal the switches DTM (L2 devices) only implement the link-layer functionality. As was mentioned, these devices only have a simple mechanism to detect, capture and forward RSVP messages, without requiring the L2 device to snoop for RSVP messages. The L3 devices are the IP routers that use the network layer and the RSVP protocol. Here every physical segment is managed, which means that they have implemented the protocol DBM (DTM Bandwidth Manager) on their DTM switches. The EDBM (Entity of DTM Bandwidth Manager) is the protocol entity responsible for managing resources on an L2 segment. Here this entity will be always present in the DTM switch. An extended segment includes members of the same IP subnet but interconnected by a switch DTM. The DBM clients are the IP routers that require resource reservation and support some features of the DBM protocol.

Similar to the SBM algorithm in the procedure of admission control using RSVP in switched Ethernet [11], we present the DBM algorithm:

1.   DBM Initialization: The EDBM obtains information of the bandwidth available on each of the managed segment under its control. As we suggested the central control approach, each DTM switch has the information of the free slots in the

segment under its control. A static configuration has to be done to specify the amount of bandwidth that can be reserved.

2. DBM Client Initialization: The DBM client has to communicate with the DTM switch that controls its segment for admission control purposes.

3. DBM Admission Control: To request the reservation of bandwidth the DBM client follows 3 steps:

a) The DBM client sends/forwards a PATH message to the next IP router only to update the switch DTM with the link layer address and network address of the next IP router for which it will have to send the PATH message and to map the switches DTM that are along the path. The IP routers along the route don't participate in the transmission of the Resv messages. For this purpose, the IP router sends this message using a reserved IP Multicast address called EDBMLogicalAddress (224.0.0.16). The EDBM doesn't have implemented the IP protocol, so it doesn't know how to forward the PATH message. As in [11] a new RSVP object has to be introduced, called DTM_NHOP. When a DBM client sends out a PATH message to the EDBM, it must include in the DTM_NHOP the address of the next IP router or the destination address. When the EDBM receives a PATH message, it can now look at the address in the DTM_NHOP object. We can have a problem if the next IP router is reached through another EDBM. In this case the PATH message is sent to it using a reserved IP multicast address called AllDBMAddress (224.0.0.17) and the DTM_HOP has to follow untouched. The DSBM forwards the PATH message towards the RSVP receiver and puts its L2 and L3 addresses in the PHOP object, with this procedure it inserts itself as an intermediary node between the sender and the receiver. The DTM switch is not expected to have ARP capability to determine the MAC address, therefore the DTM_HOP address has to include both the IP address and the MAC address.

b) When an application whishes to make a reservation for the RSVP session established, it follows the normal RSVP message processing rules and sends a RSVP Resv to the EDBM of its segment obtained from the PHOP object defined in the PATH message. If there's enough resources and the reservation is granted, the EDBM forwards the Resv message to the next hop based on the PHOP object of the PATH message. If not, it has to send a ResvErr message to the receiver.

c) If the "DTM Cloud" has more than one physical segment, the PATH message will be propagated through many EDBMs. The Resv message will be propagated hop-by-hop in a reverse direction and will reach the "channel creator" (the edge transmitter of the "DTM Cloud") if the admission control at all EDBMs succeeds.

The Control Slots in the Transmission of the RSVP Messages. In DTM the signalling capacity of a node is determined by the number of control slots it has. It's possible to change the signalling capacity of a node during the operation of the network by changing the number of control slots, which is called dynamic signalling.

In the DTM specification each node has at least one control slot per cycle and there's a problem if the segment has many nodes. To prevent a signalling overhead, [12] advises the use of a Basic Signalling Channel (BSC). Each node has at least one control slot in the base frame. The first 'n' nodes share one control slot and so on. This means that a node can get access to a control slot in every nth cycle. This kind of signalling is not useful to Path messages because of the dynamism of the route changes in the IP environment. The Resv messages could decrease the dynamism of the resource allocation of the DTM technology.

As the channels in the DTM environment are unidirectional, we have to specify how the RSVP Resv and Path messages have to be signalled. They can use the virtual network signalling concept [12]. A node creates a virtual network by signalling to the nodes with which it wants to communicate using the BSC signalling, described before. It specifies which data slots that will be used for signalling within the virtual network. This signalling can be used not only by RSVP Resv messages, but by any kind of control messages to be sent in a multicast group. This concept has similarities with the metasignalling virtual channel (MSVC) of the ATM technology.

6   Conclusion and Future Works

Compared to ATM and SONET/SDH, DTM offers a higher network utilization rate and provides the support of advanced integrated services at a much lower cost. The IntServ/RSVP approach has been seen as the solution for applications with quantitative strict QoS needs. The DTM provides a interface with IP layer and the DTM admission control concerns about bandwidth allocation. So the integration of these technologies in the signalling, reservation and management for guaranteed services is perfect. To analyze how strongly the admission control function effects call setup times is necessary. Here, the focus was the analysis of the additional delay imposed by the use of the RSVP protocol as the QoS signalling mechanism. A fair central control slot allocation algorithm using dynamic priorities and based on the traffic characteristics has to be defined. Today the algorithms proposed (KTH-S, KTH-CF, KTH-LR and KTH-RA) are based only on the number of slots available, the closest neighbor or per broadcast.

Acknowledgements. Javier García's work is supported by the Spanish Ministry of Science and Technology under Projects TIC2000-0735 and TIC2002-04516-C03-03. This author would like to express his appreciation to the Programa Complutense del Amo for providing him a grant to stay at IBM Research Division. Part of this work was done while he was with the Information Storage Group at the IBM Almaden Research Center (San Jose, California, USA).

References

1.   C. Bohm et al. *Fast Circuit Switching for the Next Generation of High Performance Networks*. IEEE Journal on Selected Areas in Communications, Vol. 14 (2), Feb. 1996.
2.   R. Braden, D. Clark and S. Shenker. *Integrated Services in the Internet Architecture: an Overview*. RFC1633. June 1994.
3.   R. Braden et al. *Resource Reservation Protocol (RSVP) - Version 1 Functional Specification*. RFC2205. September 1997.
4.   L. Berger. *RSVP over ATM - Implementation Guidelines*. RFC2379. August 1998.
5.   S. Shenker et al. *Specification of Guaranteed Quality of Service*. RFC 2212. Sept. 1997.

6. B. Davie et al. *Use of Label Switching with RSVP*. Draft-ietf-switching-rsvp-00.txt. March 1998.
7. L. H. Ramfelt. *Performance Analysis of Slot Management in DTM Networks*. Technical Report TRITA-IT. Dept. of Teleinformatics, KTH, Stockholm. January 1996.
8. C. Antal. *Performance Study of Distributed Channel Allocation Techniques for a Fast Circuit Switched Network*. Computer Communications, Vol. 21. April 1998.
9. L. Gauffin et al. *Multi-Gigabit Networking Based on DTM. A TDM Medium Access Technique with Dynamic Bandwidth-Allocation*. Computer Networks and ISDN Systems, Vol. 24 (119–130), 1992.
10. C. Bohm et al. *Resource Reservation in DTM*. Proc. First IEEE Symposium on Global Networking. December 1993.
11. R. Yavatkar et al. *SBM (Subnet Bandwidth Manager)*. Draft-ietf-issll-is802-sbm-08.txt. May 1999.
12. P. Lindgren. *A Multi-Channel Network Architecture Based on Fast Circuit Switching*. Ph.D. Thesis at Royal Institute of Technology. May 1996.

Scalable QoS Approach in a Core Internet Network

Cláudia J. Barenco Abbas[1] and L. Javier García Villalba[2]

[1] Dept. Electric Engineering, University of Brasilia, Brazil
barenco@redes.unb.br
[2] Dept. Computer Systems and Programming, Complutense University of Madrid, Spain
javiergv@sip.ucm.es

Abstract. A special attention about scalability has to be paid to QoS solutions for Core Internet Networks as they deal with a lot of flows and demand many resources. This paper analyses and proposes integrated solutions from the physical layer (SDH/SONET and DTM) to the IP layer (IntServ and DiffServ), concentrating not only on scalability, but also QoS guarantees.

1 Introduction

The QoS (*Quality of Service*) concept can be interpreted as a method to give a preferential treatment to some traffic, according to their QoS requirements as opposed to the Best-Effort treatment. The QoS solutions in a Core Network are different from those used in the Access Network, as the former has a higher cost of bandwidth and deals with a large number of flows. Consequently, scalability is an important aspect in this case. It motivated us to analyse the Core Internet environment from the transport solutions (SDH and DTM) to the IP QoS models (DiffServ and IntServ), highlighting the scalability view and proposing scalable QoS integrated architectures.

The paper is organised as follows. Section 2 analyses the SDH/SONET and DTM as transport solutions, in relation to scalability aspect. Section 3 describes a comparative study of IP/ATM and IP/DTM in aspects of multicast support, throughput, delay, jitters and losses. It also presents a study of maximum throughput of IP/SDH. Section 4 proposes architectures to integrating DiffServ/MPLS/ATM and DiffServ/DTM. Section 5 describes a study of the bandwidth demand of aggregated RSVP reservations, reaffirming that the IntServ model is not appropriate in a Core environment. Finally in section 6 we have the conclusion.

2 Network Transport Solutions – A Scalability Study

As the Internet is dynamic and grows rapidly, the increase of the number of access networks connected to a Core Network can bring some scalability problems principally in a full-mesh scenario. This section analyses the well-known SDH/SONET and the new DTM in this kind of topology. The SDH/SONET has been used as a transport solution and it showed to be very simple and with low overhead.

J.M. Cueva Lovelle et al. (Eds.): ICWE 2003, LNCS 2722, pp. 364–373, 2003.
© Springer-Verlag Berlin Heidelberg 2003

Another transport solution, DTM (*Dynamic Synchronous Transfer Mode*) [1], is fundamentally similar to SONET/SDH in terms of low complexity and low overhead. But, to increase the flexibility and avoid the hierarchical structure of SONET/SDH, DTM includes signalling and switching.

SDH. This technology doesn't support multichannel interface. So if we want a full-mesh environment, we need to provide a complete combination of physical connections, which make it not scalable. To solve this is necessary to build a topology where we have to pass through a number of routers from one side of the network to the other. This introduces delay and jitter, a problem for QoS sensitive traffic.

DTM. It is an architecture based on high-speed circuit switching architecture, with dynamic resource reallocations which don't appear in the traditional solutions of circuit switching. It provides multicast services, channels with varied bit-rates (from 512 Kbps until the specific media capacity) and low circuit configuration time (few milliseconds). It can be used as an end-to-end solution or as a transport protocol like ATM and IP, which is our focus here. The folded bus and ring topologies are unsuitable for large geographical distances. If a receiving node is located on the "wrong" side, the delay propagation can be large. Two rings can be established to avoid it, one in each direction. So the information is transmitted on both rings, but this scheme requires more bandwidth. With a dual-bus topology the average distance between nodes is minimized. The bus can support full duplex communication. Moreover, two-dimensional mesh is significantly higher than the capacity of a linear topology with the same number of nodes [2]. Here we will study only one direction bus, as we can have the same conclusions about the other direction. We assume a bus topology of 'M' x 'N' where not every router (node) is active (figure 1).

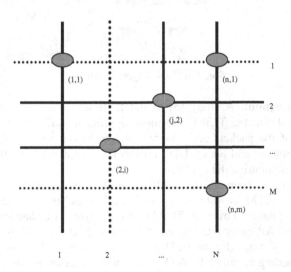

Fig. 1. Full-mesh Topology.

The inactive buses are on dotted lines and the buses necessaries to the full interconnection between the active nodes (painted nodes) are on highlight black lines.

Suppose each router has a geometric address (x_j, y_i) with $1 \leq j \leq M$ and $1 \leq i \leq N$. Being NB(R) the set of buses seen by router 'R' and B the total set of buses, a sufficient condition for the best connectivity is NB(R) > B/2.

As we can see, the scalability doesn't depend on the number of nodes but on the number of buses and its distribution. In figure 1, each active node (red node) can see at least 3 buses, so they have the best full interconnection.

3   IP/Link Layer QoS Solutions

In figure 2 we can see some solutions for the integration of IP with the link and physical layers. It is not necessary to say that we are walking to have the IP level directly over a dynamic physical layer, like IP over SDH. In this section we compare some features of IP/ATM, IP/DTM and IP/SDH like throughput, delay and so on. The MPLS does not introduce any QoS service, but it provides a better forwarding of IP packets and is a good "tunnelling" solution. It will be our discussion on next section.

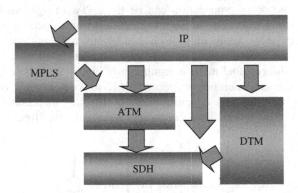

Fig. 2. IP/Link Layers Solutions.

Maximum Throughput. A study [3] of the IP flows characteristics in an Internet Backbone showed that the TCP is the most significant traffic (95% or more of the bytes, 85-95% of the packets and 75-85% of the flows), so the following study is based on TCP protocol and not on UDP protocol, even though the latter is being used more frequently by multimedia applications.

A TCP maximum segment size (MSS) used is 512 bytes. The TCP data is encapsulated over ATM as follows: a set of headers and trailers are added to every TCP segment. We have 20 bytes of TCP header, 20 bytes of IP header, 8 bytes for the RFC1577 LLC/SNAP encapsulation and 8 bytes of AAL5 (*ATM Adaptation Layer*), that is, a total of 56 bytes (figure 3). Hence, every 512 bytes become 568 bytes. This payload with padding requires 12 ATM cells of 48 data bytes each. The maximum throughput of TCP over ATM is (512 bytes/(12 cells x 53 bytes/cell))=80.5%.

DTM has several proposals for the frame format to be used to multiplex packets on top of DTM channels. But the usual implemented environment uses a 64 bits trailer after each TCP/IP packet. With a 512 bytes MSS 520 bytes will be transported on the medium (65 slots), where 472 bytes are data (59 slots) and 6 slots are overhead (figure 4). So we have 90% of maximum throughput. Moreover in DTM there's a overhead of control messages (e.g., having 40 nodes attached to a bus of 622 Mbps, with one control slot each, the overhead is 3.3% and a final maximum throughput of 86.7%). Obviously, the overhead of control messages depends on the number of nodes per bus, the capacity of the bus and the number of control slots per node.

20 bytes TCP Header	20 bytes IP Header	8 bytes LLC/SNAP	8 bytes AAL5

Fig. 3. TCP/IP Encapsulation over AAL5 ATM.

20 bytes TCP Header	20 bytes IP Header	472 bytes DATA	8 bytes DTM Trailer

Fig. 4. TCP/IP Encapsulation over DTM.

The SONET framing includes a 7 bytes per packet PPP (*Point-to-Point*) header and additional SONET framing overhead of 90 bytes per 2340 bytes of payload. So for IP over SONET, the bit-efficiency is 94% [3]. It has however a static hierarchical structure, if it comes with some flexible protocol, such as ATM

Delay and Jitter. The recommendation of ITU-T I.356 [4] gives the worst guess case for a 27500 km connection, passing 29 ATM systems. Here we are only interested in ITU-T QoS Class 1, which is appropriate for real time services and demands strict QoS performance.

Table 1. ATM QoS Classes according to I.356 [4].

QoS Class	CTD	CDV (2 points)	CLR all cells
Class 1	400 ms	3 ms	3.0 E -7

In DTM the most representative delay is the access delay, since the transfer delay is constant and depends only on the number of hops along the path.

Access delay depends mainly on the load on the control slots, and on how many control messages that need to be sent to establish a channel. The access delay is typically a summation of several delays (and typical values): (a) node controller processing delay (5 µs); (b) delay in finding and allocating free tokens, which depends on the kind of slot control (on average 100 µs. Distributed control requires also time for sending and receiving slot requests. Central control requires 10 µs before the message hits the medium, physical distance 10 µs, 10 µs before the replay hits the fiber and 10 µs more to the physical distance); (c) waiting for the first available control slot to pass (50 µs); (d) waiting for the first allocated data slot to be filled with user data (62.5 µs) and finally, (e) waiting in the queue at the input to node controllers, that for high priority traffic is zero. If one message is generated at each cycle time, the total average access delay is 0.217 ms. Average delay on each hop is around 125 μs, but the fundamental delay on each hop is the time between an incoming slot and the scheduled outgoing slot, which is on average 62.5 μs, since there is not processing nor queuing on DTM switches.

Having 29 DTM hops along the path, as on the table 1, we have around 3.625 ms of transfer delay, considering that we are using a fiber medium with propagation delay irrelevant. We have a total of slot transfer delay around 3.842 ms. Here we are not considering the worst case, but the average in case of a normal load in the network. So total slot delay is extremely lower than it is an ATM environment with 29 systems (400 ms). The jitter is almost non-existent because there isn't congestion on the hops, and DTM isolates one channel from another.

Losses. In DTM looses are controlled on the queues in the transmitters, so it is only necessary to implement the correct buffer management algorithm. For high priority it is not expected to have losses, if the controller node has capacity to efficiently handle traffic flows and the channel capacity is adequate. In ATM CBR (*Constant Bit Rate*) and rt-VBR (*Real-Time Variable Bit-Rate*) the losses are guaranteed and low as can be seen on the table 1.

Multicast. As DTM uses a shared medium multicast transmission is easily supported. The number of multicast channels for a full-mesh scenario does not depend on the number of nodes of the multicast group, since various senders can share the same channel. So it is only necessary to establish a unique multicast tree per multicast group. Considering the multicast service on ATM, the number of possible multicast trees in a full-mesh of VCs (*Virtual Circuit*) is

$$\sum_{m=2}^{n} \frac{n!}{(n-m)!\, m!} \quad n \geq 2$$

being n the number of border routers and m the number of members of a multicast group (unicast is a special case of multicast (m=2)).

4   Interaction of IETF DiffServ Model with Link Layers QoS

The IP over ATM has limited scalability due to the "n-squared" problem when a full mesh of VCs is provided. This section suggests an IP/MPLS/ATM architecture as it is more appropriate for large networks, like Core Internet, in terms of flexibility, scalability and manageability. Another architecture discussed is IP/DTM. As DTM automatically performs the rapid forwarding of packets by the time-switching slots, the MPLS does not have any functionality on this architecture. The Traffic Engineering feature provided by the MPLS may be performed by IP QoS protocols, since routing on this architecture depends on the IP routing decision. The DiffServ (*Differentiated Service*) [6] recently proposed by IETF provides simple guarantees of QoS that, in majority, are 'qualitative' because it is based on that some applications don't need an explicit guarantee of QoS. So adequate traffic engineering and classification of flows by priority suffice for the necessary functionality. Due to these characteristics DiffServ model seems more scalable than IntServ model.

DiffServ/MPLS/ATM. MPLS [7] provides an overhead of 4 bytes (figure 5) but the packet path is completely determined by the label. In terms of header overhead, it is more efficient than other tunnelling solutions (e.g. RSVP TE extensions [8]).

20 bits Label	3 bits CoS	1 bit Label Stack Indicator	8 bits TTL

Fig. 5. MPLS Overhead.

Using MPLS to have a full-mesh of LSPs (*Label Switched Paths*) between `n´ border routers, we can establish a maximum of 'n' "sink trees" in DiffServ. So this architecture is scalable. Figure 6 shows a proposed architecture for the interaction of DiffServ, MPLS and ATM technologies.

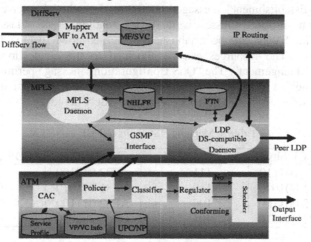

Fig. 6. DiffServ/MPLS/ATM Architecture.

The functional elements are:

(i) **Mapper MF to ATM SVC.** Responsible for the mapping of a DiffServ MF (Multi Field) filter. For example: DSCP bits, source/destination address, ingress/egress routers, etc., to an ATM SVC. The capacity of the SVC can be defined by static provisioning or by signalling (e.g. RSVP protocol). The QoS class of the SVC inside the ATM Switch can be mapped from the LDP CoS TLV.

For the EF (*Expedited Forwarding*) mapping of the DSCP bits to the 3-bit LDP CoS TLV may be CoS TLV = `111´and BE (*Best-Effort*) = `000´.

In ATM we only have two CLPs (*Cell Loss Priority*). As [9] show that more than 2 priorities is not better than 2 priorities, we only define two classes of Drop Priority inside each EF Class (table 3).

New MPLS FEC (DSCP/Border Addresses TLV) is proposed here, which is compatible with the MF Filter (table 2).

Table 2. DSCP/Border Addresses TLV.

FEC Element Name	Type	Value
DSCP/Border Addresses	0x04	MF Field

The "Value" field could be for example: (a) DSCP bits (6 bits), (b) Ingress Address Length (8 bits), (c) Ingress Address (32 bits), (d) Egress Address Length (8 bits), (e) Egress Address (32 bits), (f) MPLS Daemon (the Core of the MPLS protocol), (g) LDP Daemon (Responsible for the label binding. Here it has extensions to transport the MF attributes on its LDP PDUs as the FEC DSCP/Border Addresses TLV described before), (h) GSMP Interface [10] (Before asking for the establishment of a new SVC, it is necessary to define the QoS capacities of the ATM Switch ports and group the VCs on QoS classes, allocating resources for QoS classes. The DiffServ QoS classes can be mapped directly to the QoS classes inside the switch. To do this we use the "Quality of Service" message, which is sent to the ATM switch. "Scheduler Establishment" messages configure the scheduler on each output port. Configuration of QoS Classes is made by sending "QoS Class Establishment" message. The SVCs can be established or turned-down using "QoS Connection Management". The resources can be allocated to the connections through "QoS Connection Management". The "QoS Configuration" message permits to discover the QoS capacities of each port of the ATM Switch). We will not detail the Traffic Control functions of an ATM Switch since it is widely deployed.

Table 3. Mapping DSCP bits to LDP CoS TLV.

DSCP bits	LDP Cos TLV	DSCP bits	LDP Cos TLV
EF 101110	111	AF22 010100	010
AF11 001010	110	AF31 011010	011
AF12 001100	100	AF32 011100	001
AF21 010010	101	BE 000000	000

(ii) The MF/SVC database stores the relation of the DiffServ MF filter used to group the flows to the output configured SVC ATM. For example

Table 4. Mapping FEC/SVC.

FEC			SVC		
DSCP bits	Ingress Router	Egress Router	Port	VPI	VCI

(iii) Like the MF/SVC, the FTN and NHLFE databases have also to be extended to support the MF DiffServ filter.

DiffServ/DTM. In this architecture (figure 7), the DiffServ MF filter defines the flows aggregation to an specific DTM channel. As DTM supports the dynamic reallocation of bandwidth, it supports dynamic signalling of the amount of bandwidth (e.g. RSVP protocol) to be allocated on the channel. But it is out of scope of this paper.

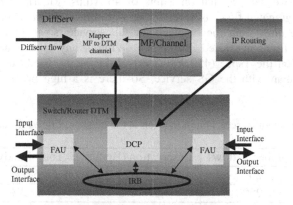

Fig. 7. DiffServ/DTM Architecture.

5   IETF IntServ Model Aggregated Reservations

The IETF IntServ model [11] demands a lot of processing and memory on the routers along the path (source-destination), because it is a per flow policing, scheduling, classification and reservation method. The aggregation of reservations [12] simplifies the classification and scheduling meanwhile it maintains less reservation states. It diminishes the bandwidth reservation demand too.

The guaranteed service (GS) [13] specified by this model guarantees bandwidth and delay but wastes a lot of resources, especially for low bandwidth (characteristic of the actual Internet traffics [3]) and short delay (necessity of real-time applications), even though the reservations are aggregated. We confirm this by calculating the bandwidth aggregated reservation needs for GS service in some links of the UUNET Europe Internet Backbone (figure 8) with arbitrary number of flows [3] [13] [14].

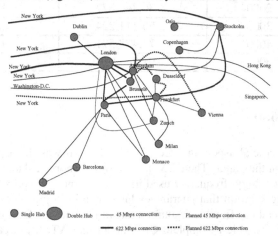

Fig. 8. European Internet Backbone (UUNET).

In table 5 we can see that on a link of 45 Mbps (Madrid-Paris) the maximum number of aggregated flows is around 300, with almost 100% of bandwidth use. In a real case, we must limit the resource for GS service, so in this example we may consider 200 flows agregated reservation. Without any QoS guarantees, these 200 flows, based on the Tspec (450,900) used in this study, need 90,000 Bps, which is 41,77 lower than with the GS service. So there is a high price to pay for the GS guarantees.

Table 5. Bandwidth reservation in function of the number of flows (Link Madrid-Paris).

Number of flows	Reservation (Bps)	% Total Bandwidth
200	3,759,375	6.6%
250	4,696,875	82.2%
300	5,634,375	100%
350	6,571,875	
400	7,509,375	
500	9,384,375	

In the link London-New York (622 Mbps), obviously we can support more aggregated reservation. For example, (table 6) to have a limit of 23.63% of the total bandwidth used by GS service, it can support 1000 RSVP aggregated flows. With this study we reaffirm that the IntServ/RSVP model is not adequate for a large network, because apart from the scalability problem, it wastes a lot of resources.

Table 6. Bandwidth reservation in function of the number of flows (Link London-New York).

Number of flows	Reservation (Bps)	% Total Bandwidth
900	16,539793	21.22%
1000	18,376,530	23.63%
2000	36,743,877	47.10%
3000	55,111,224	70.73%
4000	73,478,571	94.37%
5000	91,845,918	

6   Conclusion

Scalability is a crucial aspect in a Core Network, so it was the aspect that was given more attention in the paper. The DTM technology is more scalable than SDH/SONET in a full-mesh topology, frequently used in Core Internet networks. The DTM is a fast circuit switching solution that guarantees latency, a little jitter, constant little transfer delay, traffic isolation, flexible resource reservation and has less overhead than ATM [15]. It does not provide a complete QoS model like ATM, but can be a simple and cost effective solution when it becomes a standard specification.

Meanwhile, an evolution of the ATM environment already existent can be provided with the MPLS technology, as a good tunnelling solution, which is scalable, as an improvement to forward IP packets. Based on the architectures presented, the scalable DiffServ model can be the aggregator and differentiator of QoS flows.

Finally, we conclude that the cost to provide a guaranteed QoS in the IntServ model can be high, as it wastes a lot of bandwidth, even though traffic is aggregated. So this is not the appropriate model in a Core Network where a great number of flows share the same resource. With this the use of the DiffServ model on the proposed architectures is ratified.

Acknowledgements. Javier García's work is supported by the Spanish Ministry of Science and Technology under Projects TIC2000-0735 and TIC2002-04516-C03-03. This author would like to express his appreciation to the Programa Complutense del Amo for providing him a grant to stay at IBM Research Division. Part of this work was done while he was with the Information Storage Group at the IBM Almaden Research Center (San Jose, California, USA).

References

1. C. Bohm et al. *Fast Circuit Switching for the Next Generation of High Performance Networks*. IEEE Journal on Selected Areas in Communications, Vol. 14 (2), February 1996.
2. A. Girard. *Routing and Dimensioning Circuit-Switched Networks*. Addison-Wesley Publishing Company. 1990
3. K. Thompson et al. *Wide Area Internet Traffic Patterns and Characteristics*. IEEE Network. November/December 1997.
4. ITU-T Recommendation I.356. *B-ISDN ATM Layer Cell Transfer Performance*. 1996.
5. L. H. Ramfelt. *Performance Analysis of Slot Management in DTM Networks*. Technical Report TRITA-T. Dept. of Teleinformatics, KTH, Stockholm. January 1996.
6. S. Blake et al. *An Architecture for Differentiated Services*. IETF RFC2475. December 1998.
7. E. C. Rosen. *Multiprotocol Label Switching Architecture*. Draft-ietf-mpls-arch-04.txt. February 1999.
8. D. Awduche et al. *Extensions to RSVP for Traffic Engineering*. Draft-ietf-mpls-rsvp-lsp-tunnel-02.txt. March 1999.
9. P. Goyal et al. *Effect of Number of Drop Precedences in Assured Forwarding*. Globecom´99. March 1999.
10. P. Newman et al. *Ipsilon´s General Switch Management Protocol Specification Version 2.0*. RFC2297. March 1998.
11. R. Brader, D. Clark and S. Shenker. *Integrated Services in the Internet Architecture: an Overview*. RFC1633. June 1994.
12. F. Baker et al. *Aggregation of RSVP for IPv4 and IPv6 Reservations*. Draft-baker-rsvp-aggregation-01.txt. February 1999.
13. S. Shenker, C. Partridge and R. Guerin. *Specification of Guaranteed Quality of Service*. RFC2212. September 1997.
14. J. Schmitt et al. *Aggregation of Guaranteed Service Flows*. IWQoS'99. May/June 1999.
15. C. J. Barenco, J. I. Moreno and A. Azcorra. *An architecture of QoS services for Core Internet Network over DTM*. IEEE ECUMN´2000. Colmar, France. October 2000.

Accessibility Metrics of Web Pages for Blind End-Users[1]

Julia González, Mercedes Macías, Roberto Rodríguez, and Fernando Sánchez

Escuela Politécnica. University of Extremadura
Avd. Universidad s/n, 10071, Cáceres, Spain
{juliagon, mmaciasg, rre, fernando}@unex.es

Abstract. The Internet offers new possibilities to the access of information, but sometimes the design of web pages obstructs the contents making them inaccessible to everybody, especially for those people with visual disabilities. Accessibility of web pages is an area that is gaining more and more interest. Not only do we have technique recommendations from the World Wide Web Consortium but also legal policies following these recommendations in several countries. In order to measure the fulfilment of these guidelines, different tools have been designed. These tools are useful mainly from the point of view of designers. However, they do not offer a global indicator of accessibility to end-users at the moment of surfing the net. For visually handicapped people, especially blind people, not only is a way necessary to know the degree of accessibility of web pages when being visited (not only the page as a whole, but also the different parts of the page). In the context of the project KAI (Kit for the Accessibility to the Internet), an accessibility measurement module has been developed, able to give a global indicator of accessibility at the moment of surfing the net. Moreover, the degree to which accessibility can be obtained in an independent way for each element belonging to the web page. This paper presents the main ideas behind this module.

1 Introduction

Since its creation the Internet has offered new branch of possibilities to the access of information. Through this media, published data are available in the entire world at the same time. But sometimes the design of pages and web applications are not accessible for everybody. People with disabilities often find difficulties when retrieving information from the net. Some interfaces have replaced the functionality and simplicity with aesthetics and attractiveness; this obstructs the access to the contents, especially for people whose physical disabilities make them unable to enjoy with the design, blind people.

Accessibility of web pages and applications has been recently considered. On the contrary to other fields, technical recommendations have been defined before legal policies. The most important recommendation has been made by the World Wide Web Consortium, W3C [1]. In 1995 the W3C formed a workgroup devoted to accessibility issues, called Web Accessibility Initiative, WAI [2]. Four years later, in 1999, the Web Content Accessibility Guidelines 1.0 [3] were published.

---

[1] This work has been developed with the support of CICYT under project TIC2002-04309-C02-01 and Junta de Extremadura under project 2PR01A023

J.M. Cueva Lovelle et al. (Eds.): ICWE 2003, LNCS 2722, pp. 374–383, 2003.
© Springer-Verlag Berlin Heidelberg 2003

On the other hand, some countries have recently established policies of accessibilities. The USA, in 2000, defined the standards of Section 508, Rehabilitation Act [4]. This norm establishes that all software products sold to Federal Agencies should accomplish this section. Paragraph 1194.22 is related to Web-based intranet and Internet information and applications and its points are based on the WAI guidelines. In Europe, the action plan *eEurope 2005* [5] has been approved. This plan indicates that WAI guidelines must be taken into account, but they are not mandatory.

All the policies have taken WAI guidelines as a foundation, because these guidelines provide technical criteria to code a site in the right way, obtaining, according to accessibility, correct structure and functionality. In this document fourteen guidelines are defined, each one having different checkpoints classified into three categories, according to their relevance:

- Priority 1, mandatory
- Priority 2, strongly desirable
- Priority 3, simply desirable

Different techniques of implementation have been defined and tools such as Bobby [6] or Taw [7] have been designed to validate the fulfillment of these guidelines. These tools analyze each element on a page verifying automatically many checkpoints and pointing out those checkpoints that should be verified by hand. As such, it is necessary to be an evaluator to know whether a page is accessible or not. These tools are useful for designers. But, what happens with end-users? How do they know the degree of accessibility of the web page being visited? How do they know the degree of accessibility of the different parts of the web page? How can a blind user decide if he or she must leave the web page because of its inaccessibility? To our knowledge there is no tool integrated in a web browser or search engine able to give a global indicator of web accessibility for blind users.

So, our position is that it is important for an end user to know clearly if a page is accessible or not. For a user with visual handicaps it is essential to know which pages are accessible in order to choose the most suitable for his/her needs. Not always is the page with more accurate information about the searched topic, the best for him/her. It is surely better to recover a page less accurate but more accessible.

In this paper we present a module for web accessibility measurement. This module has been integrated in KAI, a Kit for the Accessibility to the Internet for blind people. In section 2, an overview of KAI is shown; section 3 presents the different metrics to measure accessibility and, finally, section 4 shows conclusions and future work.

2 Overview of KAI

KAI [8] tries to make navigation easier for blind people. It relies on two different parts: software and hardware components. Its software component is based on BML (Blind Markup Language) a new language developed following the specifications of XML. This language has been designed to build accessible web pages. One can write code directly in BML or one can translate existing HTML code to BML. In this second case, the page is filtered, repaired, and restructured according to the user needs. Once the page has been improved it can be shown in whatever browser (translating the page again into HTML) or it can be shown in WebTouch [9], which is the hardware component of KAI. WebTouch is a multimodal web browser. It gives the user the possibility to access the information using tactile or/and auditory skills. The input devices are the keyboard, the mouse and a voice recognition system [10]. The output devices are a special mouse (PinMouse), a synthesizer and the screen (for visually unimpaired users).

Taking into account the problems of visually handicapped people, WebTouch offers the possibility of configuring the mode of navigation: visually, by audio, by touch or a combination of them. One of the main advantages of WebTouch is selective reading rather than sequential. For example, one can choose surfing only by way of e-mail addresses. In this way, finding information for blind users is quicker.

Figure 1.a shows an example of a web page in a usual web browser, and in Figure 1.b the same page is shown in WebTouch. All the elements shown on the page, figure 1.b, are icons. There is a special mouse also developed in the context of KAI, Pin-Mouse, with two cells of pins. When the mouse is over an icon the pins raise in such a way that the user can know the kind of element below the mouse. The pins also give information about the accessibility of the element. For example, if the element below the mouse is a table, one can obtain information such as if the table has a summary or a title or appropriate headers.

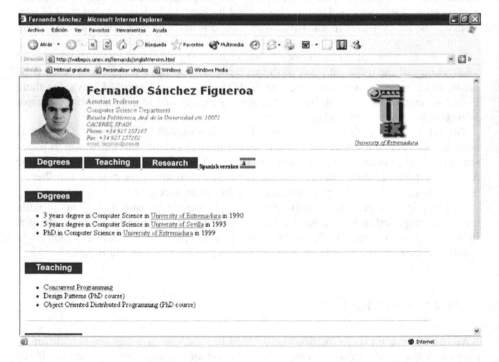

Fig. 1.a. Web page in a usual Web Browser

When the link of a page has been written, and before it is presented, its accessibility is calculated, giving the user the possibility to reject it according to a single value expressed as a percentage. In this process an accessibility data structure of the original web page is obtained. Once the page has been translated into BML, the same process is carried out, getting an accessibility data structure for BML. This structure stores the accessibility information of each BML element.

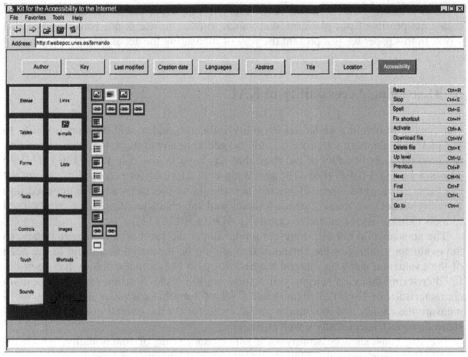

Fig. 1. b. A graphic representation of the previous web page in WebTouch

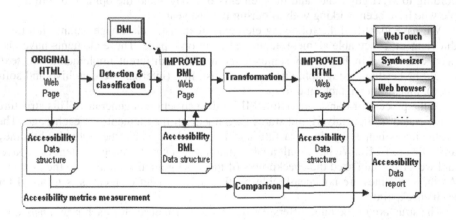

Fig. 2. Architecture of KAI

At the end both values, original and improved pages, can be compared in order to ascertain the achievements of KAI.

All the steps are shown in Figure 2. Although the accessibility module also pretends to measure the satisfaction of the user with different output systems, and establishes the profits of our platform WebTouch, quality in use is not considered in this work. In this paper we just present the way of measuring the accessibility in KAI.

3   Measuring Accessibility in KAI

Our goal is to obtain a global accessibility indicator, and to add this functionality to our platform, although the process could be added to any system. It is also interesting to know the global quality of the page that has been modeled in ISO 9126 [11], ISO 14598-5 [12] and IEEE 1061 [13] as a main characteristic formed by a minimum set of characteristics and "these characteristics should be hierarchically decomposed into a quality model composed of characteristics and sub characteristics which can be used as a checklist of issues related to quality" (ISO/IEC 9126 [11]).

The standards do not elaborate the model under the level of sub characteristics, so the evaluator establishes the attributes that should be measured according to the need of the evaluation using an integral methodology. In [14] a methodology has been defined covering the main activities of a software life cycle. Starting from the six main characteristics of ISO9126, it presents a set of sub characteristics and attributes to measure the quality and to obtain a global indicator for the overall quality of the considered product, specifically a web artifact.

We can consider accessibility as a sub characteristic of functionality, which directly affect overall quality. Metrics for the other characteristics have been developed in some previous papers [15]. We have centered on the metrics of accessibility according to WAI guidelines and the elements of a page, and the opinion of blind people who have been working with us during the last year.

We have identified the following elements: text, list, link, image, sound, multimedia element, executable element, table and form on a page. These elements have also been considered in BML, but some of them with a different implementation: text, (could be heading, paragraph, cite or code), list, link (internal, web, archive and software), image, sound, table and form.

In the process of translating into BML, a data structure is generated. This structure is generated in the analysis and stores data about all the elements on each page. The evaluation is helped by this structure and improved pages can be studied while they are coded in BML. We have built a table that has an entry for each element on a page, and we have established the checkpoints of the WAI guidelines related to the element. As the guidelines are not measurable by themselves, a set of metrics is grouped for each checkpoint.

The structure of the table offers the defined set of metrics for each previously considered element. In the first column, the element is defined; the criteria used to check it is in the second, usually WAI guidelines and their priorities, the relative importance given by a visually handicapped person to that guideline is in the following and the metrics related to the checkpoint is in the last one.

Table 1. Metrics for WAI guidelines

	Criteria		Relative importance	Metrics
	WAI	**Checkpoint**	**portance**	**Metrics**
Image / Priority 1	1.1	Provide a text equivalent for every non-text element	100%	% different visual information % images with descriptive/non descriptive alternative text % images with long descriptive/non descriptive description % different images with descriptive/non descriptive alternative text % different images with long descriptive/non descriptive description % images with descriptive/non descriptive alternative text or long description % different images with descriptive/non descriptive alternative text or long description % descriptive alternative texts % descriptive long descriptions
	2.1	Ensure that all information conveyed with color is also available without color, for example from context or markup	100%	% images seen without colour % different images seen without colour % images with high contrast
	1.2	Provide redundant text links for each active region of a server-side image map	100%	N° maps Average zones/map % zones with links % average of zones with links per map
	9.1	Provide client-side image maps instead of server-side image maps except where the regions cannot be defined with an available geometric shape	%blindness	1.2
Priority 2	2.2	Ensure that foreground and background color combinations provide sufficient contrast when viewed by someone having color deficits or when viewed on a black and white screen.	% (1/blindness)	N° changes in background colour N° changes in foreground colour N° colours used as background N° colours used as foreground N° different matches background/foreground N° matches with high contrast % matches with high contrast The most used background colour The most used foreground colour
	3.1	When an appropriate mark-up language exists, use mark-up rather than images to convey information	%blindness	% images used as marks % different images used as marks N° equivalent marks % images with equivalent mark
Priority 3	1.5.	Until user agents render text equivalents for client-side image map links, provide redundant text links for each active region of a client-side image map		1.2 and 9.1
Others				
		Images used to supply textual information	%blindness	% images containing text

Criteria			Relative importance	Metrics
	WAI	Checkpoint		
Table	Priority 1	1.1	Provide a text equivalent for every non-text element	%blindness	% tables with descriptive/non descriptive alternative text % tables with long descriptive/non descriptive description % different tables with descriptive/non descriptive alternative text % different tables with long descriptive/non descriptive description % tables with descriptive/non descriptive alternative text or long description % different tables with descriptive/non descriptive alternative text or long description % descriptive alternative texts % descriptive long descriptions
		5.1	For data tables, identify row and column headers	%blindness	%tables with identified rows %tables with identified headers %tables with identified rows and identified headers
		5.2	For data tables that have two or more logical levels of row or column headers, use markup to associate data cells and header cells	%blindness	Maximum logical level Minimum logical level %tables with more than one level
	Priority 2	5.3	Do not use tables for layout unless the table makes sense when linearized. Otherwise, if the table does not make sense, provide an alternative equivalent	%blindness	%tables used for layout %layout tables with an linear equivalent Nº different contended elements in a table %cells containing images %cells containing links %cells containing tables %cells containing text %cells containing multimedia element %cells containing executable code
		5.4	If a table is used for layout, do not use any structural markup for the purpose of visual formatting	%blindness	%false row marks %false header marks
	Priority 3	5.5	Provide summaries for tables	%blindness	%tables with summaries %tables with descriptive summaries
		5.6	Provide abbreviations for header labels	%blindness	%headers with abbreviation
			If, after best efforts, you cannot create an accessible page, provide a link to an alternative page that uses W3C technologies, is accessible, has equivalent information (or functionality), and is updated as often as the inaccessible (original) page	%blindness	%alternative links

Some criteria do not match any guideline, and they are considered as *other*. Table 1 shows the entries for image and tables, the guidelines related to them and the metrics considered for each one. Other elements are left out for simplicity.

Images are one of the main reasons because a page is often inaccessible. For example, sometimes images are only used to represent text, avoiding the reading by a synthesizer, and, therefore, making this information inaccessible. The more visually impaired the person is, the more important the criterion is. However, the contrast of images is not useful for a person unable to distinguish it. Then, when the percentage of blindness increases, the importance of this guideline decreases for the user. Equally there are some guidelines that could be considered irrelevant for blind users.

Accessibility report

Evaluator	Julia González	
Date	15/01/2003	
Site	**www.informandote.com**	
Analyzed page	**www.informandote.com/presen.asp**	
Accessibility rate		45 %
▶ **Images**		0 %
Items		1
Guidelines		WAI
1.1		0 %
2.1		100 %
9.1		100 %
2.2		100 %
3.1		100 %
1.5		100 %
Guidelines		KAI
IMG		100 %
▶ **Sounds**		100 %
Items		0
▶ **Multimedia**		100 %
Items		0
▶ **Executable code**		100 %
Items		0
▶ **Tables**		60 %
Items		1
▶ **Forms**		100 %
Items		0
▶ **Lists**		100 %
Items		1
▶ **Texts**		100 %
▶ **Links**		85 %
Items		2

Fig. 3. Example of an accessibility report

Each element is considered individually and can be contended in other, e.g. a table might be accessible, but if an inaccessible image is in it, this will affect the table's accessibility rate. In Figure 3, an example of accessibility report is shown. The user can obtain this report before surfing the page. A blind user can access the report via a synthesizer. The example in the figure is an inaccessible page, because of the structure. The single image on the page does not have an alternative text, so visual information is lost. As there are not any sounds, forms, multimedia elements, or executable code, they are not used in the calculation. One table is used for layout, and also its headers, used to give format to the text. In spite of the table, the text completely accessible and linear, therefore the table is quite accessible. With all this information the end-user decides whether to navigate through the page or not.

Once that all the elements have been measured and we have obtained the accessibility reports, similar to Figure 3, for original and improved pages, they are compared in order to know the process achievements. If the accessibility rate obtained for the improved page is higher than the one obtained for the original one, KAI transformation would have improved the page, offering more accessibility to the end-user. The results obtained until now with simple pages written in HTML are reasonably good.

4   Conclusions and Future Work

With the Internet, barriers such us distance and technology have disappeared in the attempt to access to the information. But not all the barriers have been broken and even new ones have been built. A lot of sites are designed following principles of beauty and attractiveness instead of simplicity and functionality. These characteristics often entail a restrictive, insufficient and inadequate access to the information, especially for users with visual handicaps, such as blind people.

Accessibility has been recently considered, but it is a global goal, supported by technical recommendations, and legal policies. Considering these recommendations we have developed KAI. The aim of this tool is to provide more accessible information to blind users. KAI translates existed web pages into improved ones, more accessible, and also allows navigating through the page with WebTouch, a multimodal web browser, which allows the user to move around the page using his/her voice/audio/tactile skills. This platform also permits the end-user to know the accessibility rate of a web page, before being presented in WebTouch. For this, we consider WAI recommendations and data supplied by blind users.

The accessibility rate is calculated considering that a page is accessible if all of its elements are accessible. Giving the address of a web page it is established the accessibility rate of each element, and a general value for the page is calculated, following WebQEM [14].

The obtained rates of each page can be compared. We are interested in the comparison between an existing web page and its transformed page, in order to know KAI achievements.

The accessibility measurement module is still in progress and more functionality will be included. One of our goals is to know and quantify user satisfaction. Therefore new metrics and process are being designed to achieve this.

References

1.   World Wide Web Consortium . http://www.w3c.org.
2.   Web Accessibility Initiative. W3C. http://www.w3c.org/WAI.
3.   Chisholm W., Vanderheiden G. and Jacobs I., "Web Content Accessibility Guidelines 1.0.", W3C Recommendation, http://www.w3.org/TR/WAI_WEBCONTENT/, 5/5/1999.
4.   "Section 508 Rehabilitation Act". USA. http://www.section508.gov/final_text.html
5.   "eEurope 2005. An information society for all". 28 May 2002.
     http://europa.eu.int/information_society/eeurope/news_library/eeurope2005/index_en.htm
6.   "Bobby". Center for Applied Special Technology. http://www.cast.org/bobby
7.   "TAW". Fondo Formación Asturias. http://www.tawdis.net

8. Macías M., González-Rodríguez J., Sánchez F. ,"On Adaptability of Web Sites for Visually Handicapped People". In Adaptive Hypermedia and Adaptive Web-Based Systems. Ed. Springer-Verlag, LNCS 2347, Málaga, Spain, 2002.
9. Macías M., Sánchez F. "Improving Web Accesibility for visually Handicapped People Using KAI". 3rd International Workshop on Web Site Evolution. IEEE Computer Society. ISBN: 0-7695-1399-9
10. Díaz, J.C.; García, J.J.; Álvarez, J.F.; Espada, P.; Gómez, P.; Rodríguez, J.M., "DIARCA: A Component Approach to Voice Recognition". Eurospeech 2001, 7th European Conference on Speech Communication and Technology, Aalborg, Denmark, 2001.
11. ISO/IEC 9126-1: 2001 (E), International Standard Software Engineering - Product Quality- Part 1: Quality model.
12. ISO/IEC 14598-5:1998 International Standard, Information technology - Software product evaluation - Part 5: Process for evaluators.
13. IEEE Std 1061-1992, IEEE Standard for a Software Quality Metrics Methodology.
14. Olsina L., "Web Engineering: A Quantitative Methodology for Quality Evaluation and Comparison of Web Applications". Doctoral Thesis (in Spanish), Ciencias Exactas School, UNLP, La Plata, Argentina, 2000.
15. Olsina L., González-Rodríguez, J., Lafuente G., Pastor O.; 2002, "Providing automated support to web metrics". 8th Quality European Week, Brussels, Belgium, 2002

A Three Dimensional Web Quality Model[1]

Julián Ruiz, Coral Calero, and Mario Piattini

Computer Science Department. University of Castilla-La Mancha
Paseo de la Universidad, 4
13071, Ciudad Real (Spain)
{Julian.Ruiz, Coral.Calero, Mario.Piattini}@uclm.es

Abstract. We propose a model, whose primary objective is web quality assessment. Furthermore, the model can be used for the classification of web metrics, and the classification of web research works.

1 The Model

The model is based on the work developed by [4]. Figure 1 shows a graphic representation of our model. In this figure, we can observe each model dimension: features, quality characteristics, and life cycle processes. Each dimension must be considered as a hierarchical structure, composed by other more basic elements.

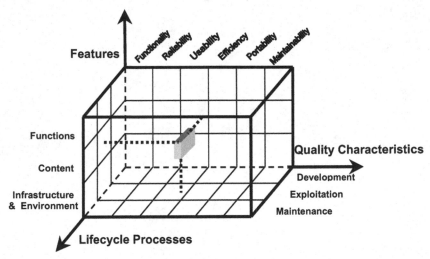

Fig. 1. Graphic representation of the model.

---

[1] This research is part of the TAMANSI project (PCB-02-001) supported by the Consejería de Ciencia y Tecnología of Junta de Comunidades de Castilla-La Mancha (Spain).

J.M. Cueva Lovelle et al. (Eds.): ICWE 2003, LNCS 2722, pp. 384–385, 2003.
© Springer-Verlag Berlin Heidelberg 2003

For the quality characteristic dimension, we use the standard ISO 9126 [1], extended with characteristics of the Quint2 model [3], and for the life cycle processes dimension, we use the standard ISO 12207-1 [2].

2 Applications of the Model

The model can be used for:

1. **Classifying existing metrics**. In this way, we will be able to know, in which cell we have metrics. Once we know this information, we will be able to use the metrics for the correct purpose. As a result of the classification of the existing metrics, we will know which cell has been disregarded, and it will be needed to propose new metrics.

2. **Research works characterization**. To determine the reach and the scope that have the works developed in a subject as multidimensional as the one of the web quality.

3. **Web quality assessment**. The quality of a web site will be represented by a set of indicators that will be obtained for each region of the cube. These indicators will be calculated in function of more elemental metrics, as lincal dependencies or more elaborated functions. In this way, the model provides a flexible framework to the evaluation of a web site, which can be used by system stakeholders from different perspectives, making possible to concentrate in certain aspects, or to detach from them (when we go from subcharacteristics to characteristics). Each of these perspectives or scenarios has its own representation in the model, like a region of the cube.

This is a preliminary version of the model. Therefore, it should be taken as an idea that must be evolutionary. For instance, we keep on working in the revision of quality subcharacteristics for a more appropriate adaptation to the web. And likewise, we consider to include the main processes of acquisition and provision in the life cycle processes dimension.

References

1. ISO/IEC (1995) ISO/IEC 12207. *Information Technology*. Software Life Cycle Processes.
2. ISO/IEC (1999) ISO/IEC 9126. *Software Product Evaluation-Quality Characteristics and Guidelines for their Use*.
3. Niessink, F. (2002) *Software Requirements: Functional & Non-functional Software Requirements*. www.cs.uu.nl/docs/vakken/swa/ Slides/SA-2-Requirements.pdf
4. Ramler, R., Weippl, E., Winterer, M., Shwinger, W., Altmann, J. (2002). *A Quality-Driven Approach to Web Testing*. Iberoamerican Conference on Web Engineering, ICWE'02. Argentina. September. Vol. 1. pp. 81–95.

Comparison of Methods and Existing Tools for the Measurement of Usability in the Web

Maria E. Alva O., Ana B. Martínez P., Juan M. Cueva L.,
T. Hernán Sagástegui Ch., and Benjamín López P.

University of Oviedo, Department of Computer Science, Calvo Sotelo S/N,
33007 Oviedo, Spain
{malva360, thsagas}@correo.uniovi.es
{belen,cueva,benjamin}@lsi.uniovi.es

Abstract. This paper presents the evaluation of a group of methods and tools for the measurement of usability in software products and software artefacts in the web. The evaluation carried out consists on studying the measurement principles and dimensions considered for each one of the methods and tools, with the purpose of comparing the degree of vicinity among them and with the principles enumerated by the ISO 9241-11 standard: efficiency, effectiveness and satisfaction.

1 Introduction

Nowadays, usability is a fundamental factor to consider when designing a web site. According to ISO 9241-11 [14] usability is, "the degree to which a product can be used by specific users to reach specific goals with efficiency, effectiveness and satisfaction in a given use context". It is considered by many as a fundamental part to determine the quality of a software product.

The need to measure the usability of software products or web artefacts is become gradually more relevant. It is not strange, keeping in mind that the existence of a poor user interface (from the point of view of the usability) will reduce user productivity. This produces unacceptable learning times, and high error levels that will frustrate the user. In the end, the system will be rejected. There are different methods and tools aimed to measure the degree of usability of a software product or web site. However, the same measuring procedures are not used by all the methods. Some use questionnaires only, while others include additional tools that facilitate a more precise measuring.

The goal of this paper is to carry out a revision of some of the most relevant methods and tools related with the measurement of the usability of a web site. The purpose is to determine the degree of vicinity among them and with the principles enumerated by the ISO 9241-11 standard. That is, the question is to find how the principles of the standard are taken into account by these methods and tools.

J.M. Cueva Lovelle et al. (Eds.): ICWE 2003, LNCS 2722, pp. 386–389, 2003.
© Springer-Verlag Berlin Heidelberg 2003

2 Methods and Tools for the Measurement of Usability

The methods of evaluation of usabilidad of software products and web site considered in this paper correspond to formative methods, as specified in [17], which are methods applied during the development to improve a design.

a) MUSiC [1], [9], [11], considers that usability can be evaluated through the measurement of the quality in use, measuring three components of usability: *i) Measure of the Task Performance of Users*. It measures the effectiveness, efficiency, productive period, and learning of the system in use, using the DRUM tool [1], [2], *ii) Measure of Satisfaction* It assesses the comfort and acceptability of the product the SUMI questionnaire [1], [10], *iii) Cognitive workload]*. It measures the mental effort required to perform a task subjectively using the SMEQ y TLX [2],[10] questionnaires or objectively way with electrodes connected to a recording system.

b) WAMMI questionnaire [4], [15], it measures user satisfaction with web sites. It is based in five factors: attractiveness, control, efficiency, utility and learning. In [15] information is added: for the assessment of individual differences and web tasks.

c) MAGICA [5], [8], this project has developed a methodology of the measurement of usability, which involves *i) Measurement of user satisfaction.* It makes use the WAMMI questionnaire; *ii) Measurement of task completion time.* It controls the time used to complete a task using the RUE metric (Relative User Effective); *iii) Measurement of cognitive effort.* To know the stress level the user suffers when completing a task, measured with SMEQ [1], [2]; *iv) Measurement of heuristic principles.* It evaluates the adhesion to heuristic principles for the web [10].

d) IsoMetrics [3], [16] it is utilized in comparison of competing products or different releases or prototypes of a software or a system. It is based on the ISO 9241-10 standard and adapted to the principles of the ISO 9241-11 standard: suitability to the task, self-description, controllability, and conformity with user expectations, error tolerance, suitability for individualization and suitability for learning.

e) Web-site QEM [12], [13] is a quantitative methodology for the evaluation of the quality in applications centred on the web. It considers four features: reliability, efficiency, usability and functionality. Concerning usability, it carries out the measurement through a questionnaire that evaluates global understandability of the site, mechanisms of help, aspects of interfaces and miscellaneous items.

f) USE [6], [7] is a questionnaire which measures usability through three dimensions (utility, easiness, and satisfaction), and four domains (hardware, software, documentation, and services). It uses the same dimensions to measure the four domains, with brief and general questions.

3 Principles Supported by the Methods and Tools

According to the ISO 9241-11[14] standard. The evaluation measures to consider when measuring the usability of a web artefact are effectiveness (the accuracy and completeness with which users achieve a goal with the system), efficiency (the resources expended in relation of the goal) and satisfaction (the comfort and acceptability of the user using the system).

Method/Tool	Performance of Users	User Satisfaction	Cognitive Workload	Assessment Individual Differences	Heuristics Principles	Task Time	Summative	Formative	Features of Quality	Useful of Product	Functions and Specific Attributes
MUSiC	X	X	X								
MAGICA		X	X		X	X					
WAMMI		X	X	X							
ISOMETRIC							X	X			
QEM	X								X	X	X
USE	X										

Fig. 1. Shows that measures considered more important when measuring usability (50% of the study methods) are: performance, satisfaction and cognitive workload.

4   Evaluation Dimensions Used in the Methods and Tools

Once the high-priority measures in which the studied tools and methods are based were analysed (Fig. 1). The dimensions of each measure were considered in addition for each one of the methods and tools, with the purpose of establishing the vicinity among them and with the principles stated by the ISO 9241-11 standard. The results obtained can be seen in Fig. 2.

Method/Tool	Effectiveness	Efficiency	Productive Period	Measure of learning	Attractiveness	Useful	Control	Mental Effort	Task Load	Perception satisfaction	Adhesion to principles	Suitable for the task	Self descriptiveness	Error Tolerance	Suitable individualizath	Use easiness	Reliability	Capability
MUSiC	X	X	X	X	X	X	X	X	X	X								
WAMMI	X			X	X	X	X											
MAGICA	X	X		X	X	X	X	X		X	X							
ISOMETRIC				X		X				X		X	X	X	X			
QEM	X															X	X	X
USE				X		X				X						X		

Fig. 2. Shows that the dimensions more considered for the evaluation of usability are: learning (in 83% of methods), followed by efficiency, utility, control and perception of satisfaction of the user (in 66.7%). The efficiency is next (50%), and finally, the effectiveness, the mental effort, and the easiness of use of the product (33%).

Conclusions

To measure the usability of a product software has become an important purpose within the development of a product or web site. It seeks to avoid the redesign that is translated in a more difficult learning and in lost of effectiveness for the realization of the tasks. These causes lack of motivation in the user, and in many occasions the system can be rejected.

With the purpose of measuring the usability of software products at present we have methods and tools that consider the measuring in different aspects (e.g. satisfaction, performance). This allows to obtain different usability measures and therefore more information for diagnostics, and offering tools aimed to measure specific aspects of the usability

In this work some methods and tools related with the measurement of the usability are analysed with the purpose of comparing the vicinity among them and with the principles enumerated by the ISO 9241-11 standard. From the analysis presented in this paper, we conclude that not all the examined elements are based on the principles mentioned in the standard. Thus MUSiC and MAGICA are the most coincident methods with the standard, while WAMMI for example, only defines with clarity the satisfaction and effectiveness principles. Others such as USE and IsoMetrics, although they claim to be based on them do not establish them with clarity.

In the study made it has been determined that the revised methods were designed to measure the usability of traditional software products and/or trade oriented and on-line sale web site. This is an indication of the importance the usability has for a web site, and also outlines the necessity of methods of this type aimed to measure the usability of web site for educational services.

References

1.   Bevan, N., Macleod, M.: Usability Measurement in Context. Behaviour and Information Technology,. (1994) 13, 132,-145
2.   Bevan, N.: Measuring Usability as Quality of Use. Software Quality Journal (1995) 115-150
3.   Gediga, G., Hamborg, K., Duèntsch, I.: The IsoMetrics usability inventory: Behaviour & Information Technology (1999). VOL. 18, NO. 3, 151 ± 1644. Kirakowski, J., Claridge, N., Whitehand, R.: Human Centered Measures of Success in Web Site 4th Conference on Human Factors and the Web Basking Ridge. USA (1998)
5.   Kirakowski, J., Cierlik, B.: Measuring the Usability of Web Sites. HFRG-University College Cork, Ireland. 'Information Engineering' European Long Term Research Project 2069.
6.   Lund, A.: Measuring Usability with the USE Questionnaire. STC Usability SIG NewLetter, Usability Interface (2001)
7.   Lund, A. : USE Questionnaire (2002) http://www.mindspring.com/~alund/USE
8.   MAGICA.: Project Summary (2003). http://arti4.vub.ac.be/previous_projects/magica.
9.   Macleod, M.: Usability: Practical methods for testing and Improvement. Norwegian Computer Society Software Conference. Sandvika, Norway (1994)
10. Macleod, M.: Usability in Context: Improving Quality of Use. DITC, G Bradley and HW Hendricks (Eds.). 4th International Symposium on Human Factors. Holland (1994).
11. MUSiC 5429. Metrics for Usability Standards in Computing. ESPRIT Project 5429.
12. Olsina, L. Rossi, G.: Web Engineering: A Quantitative Methodology for Quality Evaluation and Comparison of Web Applications Thesis Doctoral, Universidad de La Plata, Argentina.
13. Olsina, L., Godoy D.,La Fuente, G., Rossi, G.: Assessing the quality of academic websites: A case study. The New Review of Hipermedia and Multimedia 5 (1999) 81-103
14. Smith, W.: ISO and ANSI- Ergonomic Standard for Computer Products. A Guide to Implementation and Compliance. (eds.), Prentice Hall Saddle, New Jersey (1996)
15. Uttl, B., Newman, C., Pikenton-Taylor C.: DO Web Usability Questionnaires Measure Web Site Usability? The Rocky Mountain Psychological Association, UT (2002.)
16. Willumeit, H., Hamborg, K., Gedica, K.: ISOMETRIC^L. Questionnaire for the evaluation of graphical user interfaces based on ISO 9241/10.
17. Scriven, M.. The methodology of evaluation. In R. Tyler, R. Gagne, & M. Scriven (Eds.), Perspectives of curriculum evaluation (pp. 39–83). Chicago: Rand McNally. (1967)

Automatic Generation of Wrapper for Data Extraction from the Web

Suzhi Zhang [1,2] and Zhengding Lu [1]

[1] College of Computer science and Technology, Huazhong University of Science and technology, Wuhan, Hubei, China, 430074
zhsuzhi@sohu.com
[2] Department of Computer science and Technology, ZhengZhou Institute of Light Industry, Zhengzhou, Henan, China, 450002
zhsuzhi@sina.com

Abstract. With the development of the Internet, the Web has become invaluable information source. In order to use this information for more than human browsing, web pages in HTML must be converted into a format meaningful to software programs. Wrappers have been a useful technique to convert HTML documents into semantically meaningful XML files. In this paper, we propose a data extraction approach based on extracting schema, which generates automatically a wrapper to extract data from an HTML document, and produces an XML document conforming to given DTD. After the user defines extraction data schema in the form of DTD, the wrapper is generated automatically with the induction and leaning algorithm. The experiment indicates that the approach can correctly extract the required data from the source document with high accuracy.

1   Introduction

With the development of the Internet, the Web has become invaluable information source [1,2]. Enterprises publish information and goods price on the Web. To address the issues related to the effective use of information available on the Web, researchers from the database community view the Web as a large distributed database and apply database technologies to search information from the Web. However, HTML is a mark-up language originally designed for platform-independent formatting and displaying. Such Web pages are more suitable for human browsing, rather than consumption by computer programs[1]. How to extract the data on the Web into an integrated system is urgent work for many enterprise applications.

A popular approach to capture HTML information in a format meaningful to software programs is to write wrapper, which encapsulates the access to source and produces more structured data, such as XML[2]. However, developing and maintaining wrapper by hand turn out to be slow, labor-intensive and error prone[2]. In this paper, we propose a data extraction approach based on defined schema that can generates automatically a wrapper to extract data from HTML document, and produces an XML document conforming to given DTD.

J.M. Cueva Lovelle et al. (Eds.): ICWE 2003, LNCS 2722, pp. 390–394, 2003.
© Springer-Verlag Berlin Heidelberg 2003

2   System Architecture

The process of wrapper generation is implemented by a software tool, which takes a URL as input and output is a set of mapping rules between information Blocks of Interest (BOI) on the Web and user defined schema. A wrapper is essentially a set of such rules. Figure 1 shows the system architecture of the software tool, called Awdgs, that is automatic Web data extraction guided by schema. It can convert the HTML document into meaningful XML data conforming to defined schema.

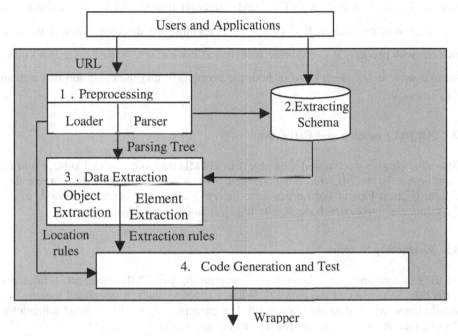

Fig. 1. System Architecture

Preprocessing includes two steps: loader and parser. Loader fetches the web page using the URL given by the user. The fetched HTML source is parsed into an HTML tree. *Extraction Schema* is defined by user based the parsing tree and interested data on the Web page. *Data Extraction* is divided into two steps, (1) Object extraction identifies interested regions in the Web pages, and Element extraction identifies the elements inside of the objects. A data object typically consists of several elements that are separated by a group of element separators., such as <td> in an HTML table. *Code Generation and Test* generates the wrapper program code through extraction roles. The rules of extracting data define the mapping between HTML document structure and defined schema. By such a set of mapping rules, the extracted data can be located in the HTML document.

3   System Realization

3.1   Fetching Web Document and Tree Representation

The HTML document is fetched by its URL, and the given page is transformed into a well-formed document. A well-formed document defined in [2]. It can be modeled as a tag tree.

Define[Minimal Subtree]: Let $T=(V,E)$ be a tag tree of a web document D where $V=V_T \cup V_C$, V_T is a finite set of tag node (internal nodes) and V_C is a finite set of content nodes(leaf nodes); $E \subset (V \times V)$, representing the directed edges. A *minimal subtree* with property p is a subtree anchored at node u, $u \in V$, and there is no other subtree w, $w \in V$, which satisfies both the property P and the condition that u is an ancestor of w.

3.2   Object Location and Extraction

By visual choosing interested data object in HTML tree, the minimal subtree and its location in the HTML tree are generated. We adopt three methods, Largest Tag Count, Highest Fanout and Largest Size Increase, and some heuristic methods to get the minimal subtree, which are similar to [2]. It can achieve higher accuracy.

3.3   Extracting Schema

An HTML tree represents the syntactic structure of an HTML document. It does not reflect the semantics of the data [2]. When extracting data in integrated system, we should know which data are our needed. For example, Figure 2 is defined schema for data extraction from object subtree, and its corresponding schema tree.

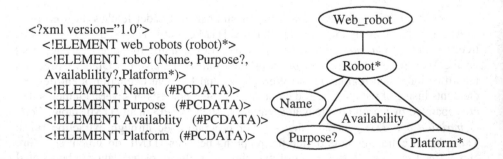

```
<?xml version=”1.0”>
  <!ELEMENT web_robots (robot)*>
  <!ELEMENT robot (Name, Purpose?,
  Availablility?,Platform*)>
  <!ELEMENT Name   (#PCDATA)>
  <!ELEMENT Purpose  (#PCDATA)>
  <!ELEMENT Availablity  (#PCDATA)>
  <!ELEMENT Platform   (#PCDATA)>
```

Fig. 2. Extracting Schema in DTD and Schema Tree

The corresponding extraction rules as follows:

```
Web_robots: Html[0]{
    Robot:  Body[1].Table[4].tr[*] {
    Name:    td[0].a[0]
    Purpose: td[1].table[0].tr[0].td[0].txt;
    Availability: td[1].table[0].tr[1].td[0].txt;
    Platform:td[1].table[0].tr[2].td[0].txt  split(",")
    }
}
```

3.4 Rule Extraction Algorithm

Rule extraction algorithm purposed in this paper belongs to induction learning method. The main process of the wrapper generation consists of two steps: (1) obtaining initial mapping rules; (2) adopting induction learning algorithm in order to get extracting rules.

Foe example, the mapping rule instance is

Web_robots.Robot.Name=Html[0].Body[1].Table[4].table[0].tr[1].td[0].a[0]

When extracting data from HTML document into XML, the element of Name in the XML document can be generated by the rule, formatted as following

        <Name> Acme.Spider </Name>

The induction learning algorithm is based on obtaining initial mapping rules and extracting schema. The algorithm takes a list of initial mapping rules L as input and returns automatically an extraction rules as output for the web page.

4   Experimental Results and Conclusions

The objective of usability test is to evaluate how easy it is to use the system and whether the algorithm is effective. In the experiment, we take three web pages, including Quotes, Web robots and Amazon books, as the test subjects. We use the time-cost by the user and the system as an indicator to show how easy the system can be used. Experimental data are omitted for the limited space reason, but the results indicate the algorithm is effective and correct.

A lot of technologies and systems have been proposed about web data wrapper in recent year, such as WIEN[6], Muslea[4], TSIMMIS[3], XWRAP[1], ARIADEN[5] etc. Our contributions in the paper are (1) With the guidance of extracting schema, the generated wrapper can be more accurate and better reflect user requirements. (2) The generated XML document conforms to the defined schema. (3) Mapping rules will be generated automatically with induction learning Algorithm.

References

1.   L. Liu, C. Pu, W. Han. XWRAP: An XML-enabled wrapper construction system for web information sources. In Proc. The International Conference on Data Engineering (ICDE), San Diego,California,USA,2000

2. W. Han, D. Buttler, C. Pu. Wrapping Web data into XML. SIGMOD Record, Vol. 30, No.3, September 2001.
3. J.Hammer, M. Brenning, H. Garcia-Molina et al. Template-based wrappers in the TSIMMIS system. In Proc. ACM SIGMOD'97. May,1997.
4. I. Muslea, S. Minton, C. Knoblock. A hierarchical approach to wrapper induction. In Proc. The 3rd International Conference on Autonomous Agents (Agents'99). Seattle,WA, USA,1999.
5. C. A. Knoblock, S. Minton, J. L. Ambite et al. Modeling web source for information integration. In Proc. AAAI'98, Madison, WI, 1998.
6. N. Kushmerick, D. Weil, R. Doorenbos. Wrapper induction for information extraction. In proc. Int. Joint Conference on Artificial Intelligence (IJCAI'97), Nagoya, Japan,1997.

Semantic XML Filtering by Ontology Combination

Kyeung Soo Lee, Dong Ik Oh, and Yong Hae Kong

Division of Information Technology Engineering, Soonchunhyang University,
Asan-si, Choongnam, 336-745, Korea
{kslee, dohdoh, yhkong}@sch.ac.kr

Abstract. An XML document search method which expands XML query through conceptual structuring and association on intra/inter-ontology is proposed. The method can filter out semantic information from various XML documents and can be effective for a large application.

1 Introduction

Expanding XML queries based on ontology enables filtering out semantic information from various forms of XML documents: [1],[2]. To do this, complete and elaborate ontology is required: [3]. However, building and accessing such ontology is very hard and inefficient. To be effective and efficient in XML document filtering, combining ontology is attempted in expanding XML query. A query expanding algorithm is first developed through conceptual structuring and concept association for intra-ontology. Then, the algorithm is generalized for inter-ontology structuring and association.

As an application example, ontology 'College-Research-Center' is combined with ontology 'Programming-Skills' and 'College-Courses' shown by dotted lines in Fig. 1. XQL(XML Query Language) is used for query application and the effectiveness of XML filtering is tested by a sample XML document.

2 Query Expansion by Ontology Combination

Expansion by conceptual structuring: Add sub-concepts to XML query. Query '//Person[skill="C"]' is expanded to '//(Person | Professor | Engineer | Student | MasterStudent | PhDStudent)[skill="C"]' in 'College-Research-Center'.

Expansion by concept association: Set an association between concepts A and B if attribute of concept A is concept B and vice versa. In 'College-Research-Center', concepts 'Student' and 'Project' are associated as shown by a solid line in Fig. 1(b). The following is the corresponding rule for query expansion.

FORALL Pers1, Proj1
    Proj1 : Project[member ->> Pers1] <-> Pers1 : Student[project ->> Proj1]

This research was supported by University IT Research Center Project

J.M. Cueva Lovelle et al. (Eds.): ICWE 2003, LNCS 2722, pp. 395–398, 2003.
© Springer-Verlag Berlin Heidelberg 2003

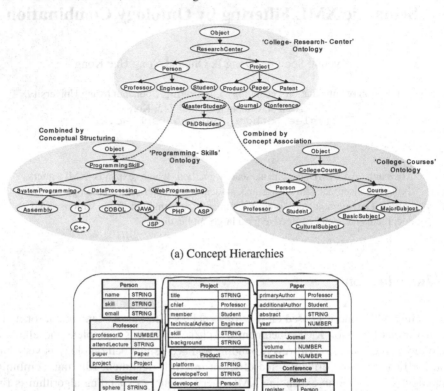

(a) Concept Hierarchies

(b) Attributes of Concepts

Fig. 1. Ontology Combination

Combined expansion by conceptual structuring: Conceptual structuring is generalized to include other ontology. By combining 'College-Research-Center' and 'Programming-Skills' by the following rules, query on attribute 'skill' of concept 'Person' can include skill 'C++'.

FORALL Obj1, Obj2
    Obj1 : C -> Obj2 : Student[skill ->> Obj1]
FORALL Obj1, Obj2
    Obj1 : ProgrammingSkill -> Obj2 : Student[skill ->> Obj1]

Combined expansion by concept association: Concept association is also generalized to include other ontology. By combining 'College-Research-Center' and 'College-Courses' by the rule given below, concepts 'Student' and 'Course' can be associated for inter-ontology query expansion.

FORALL Pers1, Cour1
    Cour1 : Course[student -> Pers1] <-> Pers1 : Student[takesCourse -> Cour1]

3   Semantic XML Filtering Application

Semantic XML filtering effect is tested by the XML document in Table 1. By conceptual structuring and concept association, queries '//Student[name="Kim"]' and '//Student[project]' are expanded to '//(Student | MasterStudent | PhDStudent)[name="Kim"]' and '//Project[member]' respectively.

Table 1. XML Document Example

```
<ResearchCenter>                          <takesLecture>C</takeLecture>
  <Person>                                <project>Home Page Production
    <Professor>                           </project>
      <name>Kong</name>                 </Student>
      <email>yhkong@sch.ac.kr</email>  </Person>
      <attendLecture>Artificial Intelligence   <Project>
      </attendLecture>                    <title>Semantic XML Query</title>
      <project>Laser Slice</project>      <chief>Kong</chief>
      <project>Semantic XML Query         <member>Lee</member>
      </project>                          <skill>Java</skill>
    </Professor>                          <background>XML</background>
    <PhDStudent>                        </Project>
      <name>Kim</name>                   <Project>
      <email>mskim@sch.ac.kr</email>      <title>Home Page Production</title>
      <skill>C++</skill>                  <chief>Kong</chief>
      <skill>Open GL</skill>              <member>Kim</member>
      <takeLecture>Artificial Intelligence  <member>Shin</member>
      </takeLecture>                     </Project>
      <attendLecture>Assembly           </ResearchCenter>
      </attendLecture>
      <project>Laser Slice</project>      <Course>
    </PhDStudent>                         <BasicSubject>
    <MasterStudent>                        <subjecTitle>C</subjectTitle>
      <name>Lee</name>                     <professor>Kong</professor>
      <email>kslee@sch.ac.kr</email>       <student>Shin</student>
      <skill>C</skill>                   </BasicSubject>
      <skill>Java</skill>                 <MajorSubject>
      <takeLecture>Artificial Intelligence   <subjectTitle>Home Page Production
      </takeLecture>                       </subjecTitle>
      <project>Semantic XML Query          <professor>Chun</professor>
      </project>                           <student>Kim</student>
    </MasterStudent>                       <student>Lee</student>
    <Student>                            </MajorSubject>
      <name>Kim</name>                   <Course>
      <skill>ASP</skill>
```

Query '//Student[skill="C"]' is expanded to '//(Student | MasterStudent | PhDStudent)[skill="C", "C++"]' by combining 'Programming-Skills'. And query //Student[takeLecture] is expanded to //(Course | BasicSubject | MajorSubject)[student] by combining 'College-Courses'. As seen in Fig. 2, the expanded queries by ontology combination successfully filter out the necessary XML documents which were not possible to search before the expansion.

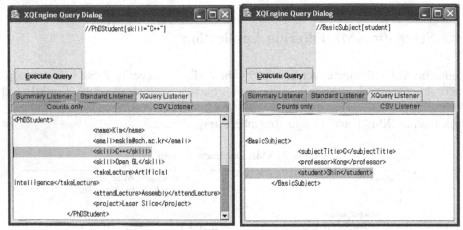

(a) Result of Query //Student[skill="C"]   (b) Result of Query //Student[takeLecutre]

Fig. 2. XML Filtering by Ontology Combination

4 Conclusions

To filter out semantic information from various forms of XML documents and to be effective to a large domain application, a semantic XML filtering method expands XML queries by conceptual structuring and association in inter-ontology as well as inter-ontology. Experimental result showed that the XML filtering method effectively extracts important information which was undetected before.

References

1. Fensel, D., Angele, J., Decker, S., Erdmann, M., Schnurr, H.P., Studer, R., Witt, A.: On2broker: Lessons Learned from Applying AI to the Web. Institute AIFB. International Journal of Cooperative Information Systems, Vol. 9. No. 4 (2000) 361–382
2. Erdmann, M., Studer, R.: Ontologies as Conceptual Models for XML Documents. In: Proceedings of the 12th Workshop for Knowledge Acquisition, Modeling and Management (KAW'99), Banff, Canada (1999)
3. Heflin, J., Hendler, J.: Semantic Interoperability on the Web. In Proceedings of Extreme Markup Languages 2000. Graphic Communications Association (2000) 111–120

Genre and Domain Processing in an Information Retrieval Perspective

Céline Poudat[1] and Guillaume Cleuziou[2]

[1] CORAL, Centre Orléanais de Recherche en Anthropologie et Linguistique
Orléans - FRANCE
celine.poudat@univ-orleans.fr
[2] LIFO, Laboratoire d'Informatique Fondamentale d'Orléans
Orléans - FRANCE
guillaume.cleuziou@lifo.univ-orleans.fr

Abstract. The massive amount of textual data on the Web raises numerous classification problems. Although the notion of domain is widely acknowledged in the IR field, the applicative concept of genre could solve its weaknesses by taking into account the linguistic properties and the document structures of the texts. Two clustering methods are proposed here to illustrate the complementarity of the notions to characterize a closed scientific article corpus. The results are planned to be used in a Web-based application.

1 Introduction

The exponential development of the Web has brought about the massive production of extremely diverse textual data which are very difficult to handle. Among the numerous developed for Machine Learning heuristics, the joint use of two corpora is often tried. The first corpus is closed and serves as a training corpus whereas the second is open.

In the prospect of the construction of a Web Information Retrieval (IR) application, the working out of a training corpus has to be seriously thought out. In that respect, we assume that the notion of domain, widely used in IR, might be associated to that of genre. A comparison of two different methods of document clustering, one based on morphosyntactic variables and the other on words has been led on a French corpus of linguistic scientific research articles.

In this paper, we present the results obtained by the coupling of these two approaches on a corpus of restricted size. The conclusive first results we obtained brought us to consider extending the method on more voluminous data within the framework of a domain and genre-based Web application.

2 Relevance of a Domain and Genre Coupling in IR

Although it is accepted that IR with textual data has to work with texts rather than with sentences or words, the various variables of discourse analysis (domain,

J.M. Cueva Lovelle et al. (Eds.): ICWE 2003, LNCS 2722, pp. 399–402, 2003.
© Springer-Verlag Berlin Heidelberg 2003

genre, register, document typology, document structure, etc.) are regrettably little defined and overlap largely. The common assumption that a set of domains (or discourse fields) describing a particular field of knowledge would exist is often worked out in terms of sub-languages and explains the growing success of ontologies. However, the hypothesis is not really founded because it does not allow to solve polysemy nor does it take into account social conditions surrounding texts nor their structure, the latter being essential for IR.

Even if we do not question the importance of domains as regards the processing of the lexicon, and their importance in IR contexts, the notion has to be refined. The notion of genre, which is more and more common in corpus linguistics, turns out to be quite useful. Among the numerous works trying to connect specific features of language with certain types of writing or styles, few studies aim at distinguishing the level of variation of a genre. Yet genres implement recognizable formal processes and they are by definition part of social practices. Consequently, texts of common genre can be indexed in a very relevant way with a set of linguistic and structural variables, obtained thanks to a socially relevant genre corpus [4].

As genres attest specific structures and regulated linguistic properties, they may be implemented within generic profiles, obtained from a characterization of their specificities. Thanks to the coupling of the applicative concepts of genres and domains, i.e. two possible information classifications, we may certainly obtain more conclusive results than the existing systems.

3   Materials and Method

3.1   The Corpus and Its Constitution

The corpus has been built up according to the domain and genre variables. The choice of the scientific article, considered as a genre, has been determined because of its bureaucratic and structural characteristics, and of its strategic interest in IR and scientific watch applications. The corpus has been reduced to articles belonging to the linguistic field in order to increase domain homogeneity.

247 scientific articles (34 volumes taken from six different French linguistics journals) belonging to the linguistic field have been chosen. As the impact of languages on genres and domains is still little known, the corpus has been restricted to the French language. Texts were all issued between 1994 and 2001 to limit the possibilities of diachronic variations. The notion of sub-domain was not taken into account. Even if we suppose that they will emerge from the soft clustering presented farther, they might emerge from the morphosyntactic-based clustering.

3.2   Methodology

Clustering based on a morphosyntactic labeling of the texts.
The inductive typological methods [3] used by Corpus Linguistics have been used as they demonstrate that local and global variables can be connected [4]

[5]. Thus it becomes possible to validate or invalidate the intuitions we tend to have on the presence or absence of linguistic markers in certain genres of texts.

Following the example of Biber [1], the use of a quantitative approach seems to be heuristically relevant. The application of multidimensional statistics on genres leads to sound results that can constitute the foundations of a further analysis to check predefined typologies[4].

The 247 texts were labeled by the Cordial© tagger with a set of 198 morphosyntactic variables. The labeled results were then processed by the SAS© system. A factorial analysis (Principal Component Analysis) coupled with a hierarchical ascending classification (Ward method) was used to classify the individuals. The number of clusters was incremented by five, from five to fifty.

Concept-based document clustering.
Recent works have demonstrated that using semantic classes of words (concepts) in the conceptual (or thematic) organization process of a document-based corpus leads to a relevant improvement of the group's final quality and homogeneity [6]. Moreover, the method enables to characterize documents in a limited space, as features focus on word groups rather than on words. The process is divided into two major steps: the construction of semantic word classes and the use of a document clustering algorithm.

The semantic word class construction method differs in two main points from the previous studies: (1) the Web as a contextual resource [2] is more efficient than any training corpus or ontology, (2) the definition of a robust clustering algorithm generating non disjoint clusters (a same object can belong to several classes). Let us underline that the use of soft clustering techniques allows to take polysemy and thematic plurality into account.

The frequent terms of the corpus are extracted and the semantic relations between the terms are quantified from their common use in Web documents via the Mutual Information measure. This measure provides a similarity matrix over the words, which is changed into a correlation matrix which constitutes the entry of the clustering algorithm (TAB.1).

Table 1.	Soft-clustering Algorithm
Input:	The matrix of similarities between objects
Initialisation:	Each object is allocated to one cluster
Loop:	Object extraction from a group
or	Object adjunction into a group
Until:	No adjunction nor extraction is possible

This ongoing clustering algorithm offers three main advantages: (1) as mentioned before, it is a soft clustering algorithm, enabling to obtain non disjoint groups; (2) contrary to other classical hierarchical algorithms, the groups can be corrected in order to improve their homogeneity whereas a hierarchical representation of clusters is made possible and (3), contrary to most of the existing algorithms, the algorithm is not defined by any factor and there is no a priori decision on the final number of clusters.

Word or concept classes are finally obtained. The documents are represented under a vectorial form with a component for each extracted concept. The occurrences of the concept words are added to each component. A conceptual similarity matrixof the documents, which will be given to the same clustering algorithm, is then obtained from the correlations between the documents vectors. The conceptual characterization step enables to reduce the documents description space. As with the clustering method a same document can belong to different classes, the hypothesis according to which a document can handle different themes is taken into account.

4   Results and Perspectives

The very first results obtained from the two different classification methods are on the whole different. This could validate our first hypothesis according to which genres and domains are additional notions which could be jointly used in the framework of an IR application.

In fact, thanks to the concept-based clustering document, it is possible to extract cohesive conceptual groups[1] so as to form thematically relevant document clusters[2]. Thus, the singletons deal with very specific research objects. For instance, we found a text containing a high number of theater play extracts, which was pushed aside by both methods. The genre and domain notions are additional and their coupling allows to obtain a fine characterization of the corpus. This may certainly contribute to increase the quality of the results of a scientific text query on the Web.

We presented here the first incomplete results of an ongoing research, which will be extended to other scientific domains. The structural properties of genres will be taken into account. A similar work on English scientific articles is in progress and the results will be assessed on the Web.

References

1. BIBER, D. *Variation across Speech and Writing*. Cambridge University Press, Cambridge, 1988.
2. CLEUZIOU, G., CLAVIER, V. and MARTIN, L., *Organisation conceptuelle de mots pour la Recherche d'Information sur le Web*. Conférence francophone d'Apprentissage CAp'02, 2002.
3. KARLGREN, J. *Text genre recognition using discriminant analysis*. International Conference on Computational Linguistics, 1994.
4. MALRIEU, D. et RASTIER, F. *Genres et Variations morphosyntaxiques* in TAL, Vol. 42, num. 2/2001.
5. POUDAT, C. *Characterization of French linguistic research articles with morphosyntactic variables* in Academic discourse - multidisciplinary approaches, 2003.
6. SLONIM N. and TISHBY N. *The power of word clusters for text classification*. In 23rd European Colloquium on Information Retrieval Research. 2001.

---

[1] Here are some examples of the concepts we obtained: Amphitryon, Molière, Plaute, Sosie/Charcot, schizophrène, etc.

[2] Documents were besides very correlated (0.95 on average).

An Architecture for Semantics-Based Interaction of Spontaneously Connecting Software

Teemu Vaskivuo

VTT Electronics, P.O. Box 1100, 90571 Oulu, Finland
teemu.vaskivuo@vtt.fi

Abstract. Generally, software entities such as components or objects are made to interact with each other according to information that is known at design-time. Spontaneously interacting software elements have to overcome this, as they are not necessarily designed together. This paper presents an approach for connecting software functionality by utilising semantically linked information about the capabilities and features of software entities, instead of utilising their strictly defined software interfaces. The approach is presented through a software architecture for a design that performs suggested kind of functionality.

1 Introduction

Generally, software entities such as components or objects are made to interact with each other according to information that is known at design-time. The design-time information used in connecting software functionality is commonly present in forms of interfaces, class descriptions, or similar information structures. Those structures carry very little information according to which the functionality represented by them could be analysed or categorised. By complementing the presence of software entities with additional, semantically linked information, software interactions can be made understandable on a higher conceptual level. Additional semantic information provides the software entities the means to access the meaning related to the actions that they commit, the events that take place, and the services they provide and use.

In a spontaneous environment, connections and disconnections between software entities take place in an unplanned manner. Such connectivity requires that the software entities are able to extract information about each other's properties. Enabling technologies for spontaneous networking such as Jini, UPnP, and Salutation [3] provide limited capabilities to express the semantic relations between software entities that they connect together. This paper presents a model and an implementation of a software framework that provides spontaneously connecting software entities the ability to utilise knowledge about the semantic connections there are between them and other entities (such as software entities, conceptual entities, or information).

Annotations about the semantic connections between pieces of information should be able to be understood by several individual parties. Such consistency can be achieved by agreeing on certain rules that are used when annotating information. In the computerised world, an ontology is an explicit specification of a conceptualisation [1]. By agreeing upon the used ontology, the information presented about a piece of information can be understood correctly at the specified level of conceptualisation.

J.M. Cueva Lovelle et al. (Eds.): ICWE 2003, LNCS 2722, pp. 403–406, 2003.
© Springer-Verlag Berlin Heidelberg 2003

Different ways to represent [5] and to use conceptual semantic information and ontologies in order to describe content of information plays an important part in research efforts related to agents [2], and the semantic web [4]. Also the presented approach utilises ontologies in specifying the used conceptualisation.

2 Model and Implementation

Spontaneous networking of software that bases on semantically linked information requires a mechanism that helps in representing the semantic relations between information and functionality. With the help of such mechanism, the software can be made to handle generic occurrences, each of which can be defined on a conceptually high level. The conceptual definitions can then be applied to many practical cases.

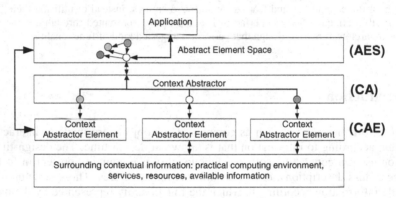

Fig. 1. Conceptual architecture of semantic middleware

Here, "semantic middleware" is proposed to perform the task of creating an abstract representation of the environment. Semantic middleware can be considered as an architectural layer that abstracts the practical functionality of a service environment to a conceptually higher level. Practical tasks of semantic middleware are to:

- Produce a semantically cross-linked *view* of the elements in the surrounding environment (or context) of a software entity.
- Enable efficient queries to explore the content of the produced *view*.
- Provide means to interact with the environment presented in the *view*.

The semantic view can be considered as an automatically updated space that represents the state of the surrounding context with semantically cross-linked elements. Information in the semantic view is then further utilised by applications in various tasks.

Presented semantic middleware comprises a layered architecture. The layers, visible in Figure 1, are *abstract element space, context abstraction, and context sensing*. Abstract Element Space (AES) embodies the semantic view. Applications utilise semantic middleware by interacting with the AES. Context Abstractor (CA) is the layer that produces information to the AES according to ontologies that specify the semantic relations between pieces of information. Context Abstractor Elements (CAEs) sense the context and create an abstracted representation of it. Together several CAEs produce the context-sensing layer. CAEs are add-on components. They can be connected to the CA to sense some specific feature, ability, service, resource, sequence, event, or any other element from the surrounding computing environment.

Some of the CAEs can abstract information that already exists within the AES. Thus it is possible to create a taxonomy where more atomic elements are used in constructing larger conceptual entities within the AES. An example of such operation is visualised by the leftmost CAE in Figure 1. That particular CAE only abstracts information that is already present in the AES.

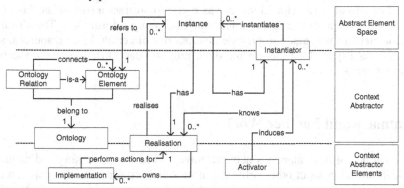

Fig. 2. A diagram representing the most important class relations within the implementation

A demonstration implementation of semantic middleware was created as a part of the presented work. Figure 2 shows the classes that form the core framework of the implemented system. From Figure 2 it can be seen that the CAE layer comprises instances of *Activators* and *Implementations*. *Activators* function when CAE-initiated active operation is required, for example when a CAE senses something. *Implementations* represent the CAE's closest relationship to resources. Each CAE has to embody the ways to interact with the resources it abstracts.

In the CA layer, *Realisations* represent realisable *Instances* of different conceptual entities that are defined within an *Ontology*. *Realisations* are provided by CAEs and used by *Instances* through the CA layer. The CA layer stores representations of *Ontologies*. An *Ontology* comprises (not shown in Figure 2) a certain *BaseOntology*, and special *CAE Specific Ontologies* that accompany each CAE in order to represent the information provided by each particular CAE. Information within the *Ontology* is described with *OntologyElements* that represent the elements within the ontology, and *OntologyRelations* that represent the relations between the interconnected elements.

The AES layer incorporates the actual storage for instantiated elements. The instantiated elements are represented by instances of the *Instance* class. Each *Instance* is connected to a certain *OntologyElement*. Accordingly, the semantic relations of an *Instance* can be examined through the relations its representative *OntologyElement* has within the *Ontology*. An *Instantiator* represents an entity that is in charge of instantiating *Instances*. *Instantiators* control the instantiations and keep count of the elements instantiated by them. For example, CAEs or applications can act as *Instantiators*. Utilisation of the semantic middleware takes place through the AES layer, which provides its users an efficient set of operations for examining and interacting with the contents of the AES.

The demonstration implementation was created with Java and C++. The CAEs in it were limited to a *Bluetooth Abstractor* element, a *Visual Abstraction* element, and a *Primitive Abstractor* element. By utilising these abstractor elements, a test case of context abstraction was carried out. In the test case, a demonstrative and simple text-based communication was made to establish itself between spontaneously connected devices each time the communication ability was available. The Bluetooth abstractor element provided a source of spontaneous connections and disconnections between devices. The Visual Abstractor Element was made to abstract a part of the Java class library in order to produce a generic tool for displaying information. The Primitive Abstractor Element was made to provide abstractions of certain basic resources, such as primitive data types for time, textual data, numeric data, location, and conceptual input/output operations.

3   Summary and Further Work

Software entities of a spontaneous network have a need for expressing and acquiring semantic information about other software entities and resources. In this paper, a conceptual approach of a semantic middleware has been presented for performing the provision of semantic information. Through the experiences brought by the conceptual design and the implementation, the approach has been experienced as feasible in enhancing connectivity between spontaneously connecting software entities.

Despite of the conceptually high-level information structures within semantic middleware, its use does not provide any intelligence to any application per se. Instead, the ability to access the information about the surrounding context and the semantic relations in it as presented, may provide a better basis for such intelligent information processing. The task of further reasoning and intelligent operation is in the case of semantic middleware always left to the applications.

The applicability of the approach is currently limited by the restricted amount of CAEs. A new CAE has to be produced for acquiring the ability to sense a new element from the context. Efficient and simple ways for integrating legacy resources and applications to operate with the presented concept would provide a change to leverage their already developed potential, making it a strong topic for further research work.

References

1. T. R. Gruber, "Toward principles for the design of ontologies used for knowledge sharing", Technical Report KSL 93-04, Stanford University, Stanford, CA, August 1993.
2. Foundation of Intelligent Physical Agents (FIPA), http://www.fipa.org
3. S. Helal, "Standards for Service Discovery and Delivery", IEEE Pervasive Computing, Vol.1, Iss.2, 2002, pp. 95–100.
4. The Semantic Web Initiative, http://www.w3.org/2001/sw/
5. A. Gomez-Perez, O. Corcho, "Ontology languages for the semantic web", IEEE Intelligent Systems. Vol.17, Iss.1, 2002, pp. 54– 60.

Integration of Spatial XML Documents with RDF

J.E. Córcoles, P. González, and V. López Jaquero

LoUISE: Laboratory on User Interface & Software Engineering.
Universidad de Castilla-La Mancha
02071, Albacete (Spain)
{corcoles, pgonzalez}@info-ab.uclm.es

Abstract. The fact that GML is an XML encoding allows it to be queried. In order to query a GML document we have designed a query language over GML/XML enriched with spatial operators. This query language has an underlying data model and algebra that supplies the semantics of the query language. In this paper, we propose an approach for integrating Geospatial data on the Web, stored in GML documents, using our Spatial Query language. This approach has been inspired by Web Portals technology for retrieving Geospatial information. We have used ontologies to solve the semantic heterogeneity between different GML documents.

1 Introduction

Actually, a rich domain that requires special attention is the Semantics of Geospatial Information [1]. The enormous variety of encoding of geospatial semantics makes it particularly challenging to process requests for geospatial information. Work led by the OpenGIS Consortium [2] addressed some basic issues, primarily related to the geometry of geospatial features. The Geography Markup Language (GML) provides a syntactic approach to encoding geospatial information through a language in which symbols need to be interpreted by users, because associated behaviour is not accounted for.

The fact that GML is an XML encoding allows it to be queried. In order to query a GML document we have developed a query language over GML/XML enriched with spatial operators [3]. This query language has an underlying data model and algebra that supplies the semantics of the query language [4].

This preliminary work is the base for developing a Web environment that allows spatial queries over GML on the Web. At this moment, querying spatial XML documents (GML) requires knowledge of the DTD (XMLSchema). In addition, if two GML documents have semantically the same information but are represented by different DTDs, it is necessary to manually make two queries, one for each document. Thus, the user has to make two queries to select the same semantic information, and must know the DTD offered by each GML document. In order to solve this problem, it is necessary to implement some approach that allows querying of the common knowledge and interests that people share within their community. In this way, the user can apply the same query and the same structure to query several GML

J.M. Cueva Lovelle et al. (Eds.): ICWE 2003, LNCS 2722, pp. 407–410, 2003.
© Springer-Verlag Berlin Heidelberg 2003

documents that satisfy, either fully or partially, this general structure. This common knowledge is Ontologies and it is used in this paper for solving the semantic heterogeneity between Spatial XML documents.

In this paper, we propose an approach for integrating Geospatial data (expressed with GML documents) on the Web. We focus this approach in the definition of a mapping between the ontology and the DTD/Schemas. Our Spatial Query language over spatial XML documents is used in this approach like a canonical language that allows: (i) a single query language that the users can express their queries in, and (ii) a single query language for querying each GML document in the same way.

This paper is organized as follows: Section 2 briefly describes the catalog definition to facilitate the mapping between the general query (over de ontology) and concrete query over each GML document. The conclusions and future work are presented in Section 3.

2 Catalog Structure

The Catalog has been defined using the Resource Description Framework (RDF) standard [5][6] proposed by W3C in order to facilitate the creation and exchange of resource descriptions between Community Webs.

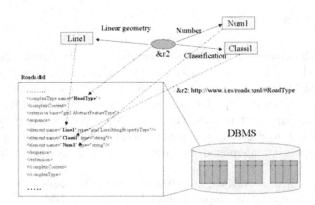

Fig. 1. Relation between ontology and Local Schemas

In the RDF model, the resources are parts of a DTD that contains the schema offered for each site. A simple resource may be a simple element or attribute in a DTD. A complex resource is a complex element in a DTD. The simple resources are represented by Literals in a RDF schema and the complex resources are represented by RDF. The RDF establishes a correspondence between the ontology and parts of the schema in each site (local schemas). With this information, it is possible to translate a query expressed in an ontology into a query expressed in terms of the different schemas.

Figure 1 shows an example. We have used the graphical notation used in [6]. The resource &r2 defines an element *RoadType* offered by the site *http://www.infob.ulm.es/roads.xml*. The properties *LineGeometry, number* and *classification* are related to the elements *Line1, num1* and *Classi1* in the Resource *TypeRoad*. The DTD offered defines, partially or fully, the Schema of the DBMS.

In Figure 2, an example of the Portal Schema and its instances is shown. The example has been obtained from the specification documents of GML by OpenGIS [GML01]. Due to RDF's capability for adding new feature and geometry types in a clear and formal manner [7], this example has been carried out extending the geospatial ontology defined by OpenGIS, where the class (Geometry, LineString, etc) and properties (*coordinates, Polygonmember*, etc) are defined.

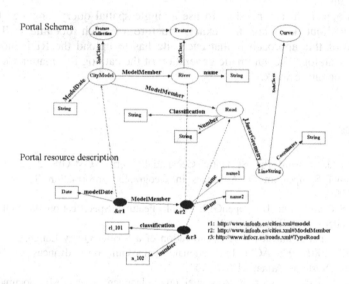

Fig. 2. Example of Catalog

The *cityModel* contains a property *modelDate* and *modelMember* (*River* or *Road*). A *River* is defined by a *name*, and the *Roads* are defined by *Classification, Number* and *LinearGeometry* (string of coordinates). *River* and *Road* are subclasses of the class Feature. *CityModel* and *LineString* are subclasses of the class *FeatureCollection* and *Curve* respectively. These classes are defined in the Geospatial ontology by [7]. In this RDF schema the properties inherited have not been included for the sake of simplicity. Except for the complex elements (*Road, LineString*, etc) the properties have a literal Range. Furthermore, the scope of the declarations is determined by the corresponding *namespace* of each schema, e.g. Ns1 (http://www.opengis.org/gml#). For the sake of simplicity, we will henceforth omit the namespaces prefixing in class and property names. In the Portal resources description the instances of the model are shown.

The translation of the general query expressed in terms of the Portal Schema, into queries expressed in terms of the sites is carried out querying the Portal Catalog using

RQL [8]. RQL is a declarative query language for RDF. It is defined by a set of basic queries and iterators which can be used to build new ones through functional composition.

3 Conclusions and Future Work

In this paper, we have proposed an approach for integrating Geospatial data (expressed with GML documents) on the Web. We focus this approach in the definition of a mapping between the ontology and the DTD/Schemas using RDF(S). Our Spatial Query language over spatial XML documents is used in this approach like a canonical language

With this approach it is possible to use a single spatial query language for GML documents without knowing the exact structure of each document. The main disadvantage of this approach is that each site has to upload the RDF model to be stored in the Catalog. The automatic generation of the catalog is a matter we intend to deal with in our future work.

References

1.   Egenhofer J. Toward the Semantic Geospatial Web. ACM-GIS 2002. 10th ACM International Symposium on Advances in Geographic Information Systems. McLean (USA). 2002.
2.   Open GIS Consortium, Inc. OpenGIS: Simple Features Specification For SQL Revision 1.1 OpenGIS 99-049 Release. 1999.
3.   Córcoles, J. and González P. A Specification of a Spatial Query Language over GML. ACM-GIS 2001. 9th ACM International Symposium on Advances in Geographic Information Systems. Atlanta (USA). 2001
4.   Córcoles, J. and González, P. A spatial query language over XML documents. Fifth IASTED International Conference on Software Engineering and Applications (SEA). Los Angeles, USA. pp.1–6. 2001
5.   Brickley, D. and Guha, R.V. Resource Description Framework (RDF) Schema Speci_cation 1.0, W3C Candidate Recommendation. Technical Report CR-rdf-schema-20000327, W3C, March 2000. Available at http://www.w3.org/TR/rdf-schema.
6.   Lassila O. and Swick, R. Resource Description Framework (RDF) Model and Syntax Specification. W3C Recommendation, February 1999. Available at
     http://www.w3.org/TR/REC-rdf-syntax. 1999
7.   OpenGIS. Geography Markup Language (GML) v2.0. Document Number: 01-029. Http://www.opengis.net/gml/01-029/GML2.html. 2001
8.   Karvounarakis, G., Alexaki, S., Christophides, V., Plexousakis, D., Scholl, M. RQL: A Declarative Query Language for RDF,WWW'02.Hawaii, USA.2002.

Foundations of a New Proposal for Querying Relational Databases and XML Documents

Ana Fermoso García[1], María José Gil Larrea[2], Luis Joyanes Aguilar[1], and
Jesús Luis Díaz Labrador[2]

[1]Facultad de Informática. Universidad Pontificia de Salamanca, Compañía 2, 37002
Salamanca, Spain
afermoso@upsa.es, ljoyanes@fpablovi.org
http://www.upsa.es
[2]Facultad de Ingeniería. Universidad de Deusto, Avda. Universidades 24, 48007 Bilbao,
Spain
{marijose, josuka}@eside.deusto.es
http://www.deusto.es

Abstract. Today, a large amount of information has been stored in XML, which
has become the most useful standard of data interchange in the web and e-
business world. Nonetheless, a large quantity of information remains stored in
Relational Databases.

It is very important to be able to jointly manage these two data formats. One
solution would be an integrated query model that would at the same time allow
the query of a relational database and of XML data. Because of the growing
number of applications that have to work in a web environment, the proposed
system should use a query language based in XML and also return answers in
the same XML format.

After having made a detailed study, in this paper we make comparing different
systems that link both, databases and XML. Besides, we propose a new system
to overcome the limitations found in them.

1   Introduction

This paper tries to center in three aspects. First, a specific kind of database, Relational
databases, because it is one of the most used methods to store and manage data.
Second, the relation between the XML world, because XML has reached the status of
standard of exchange and data representation in the web, and the relational database
one. Finally, to query the two kinds of information at the same time with the same
system and in an efficient way. That is to say, in the end the user makes the query
without knowing what the real data source queried is.

2   A New Database Query System Based on XML

The main aim is to create a system that allows querying relational database and XML
documents using the same query system in an efficient way. Besides, this system
should be XML based, in this way all the environment has the same appearance.

The first step would be to establish the model that allows to rewrite the relational
database structure in a special format XML-accessible, but without any kind of
translation of the data or database records, which was one of the problems of other

J.M. Cueva Lovelle et al. (Eds.): ICWE 2003, LNCS 2722, pp. 411–412, 2003.
© Springer-Verlag Berlin Heidelberg 2003

similar systems. The idea would be to translate the database data model, the relation-entity database model, to a special XML format, but without any change in the database data.

The second important step would be to establish the query XML based language, to access databases in this environment. Then we would define the model to translate the query from this language into SQL, to make the final access to the database using the Management Database System, which will be more efficient.

The query language should have enough power to extract information from XML documents. As XQuery [1] is not yet standardized nor implemented, we assume as a premise that XSL (Extensible Stylesheet Language), could serve us to get the intended goal. This language is defined [2], widely implemented, and nowadays an industry de facto standard.

To translate a database model into an XML model, we would have to map database elements such as tables, relations and fields, into concepts of XML as elements and attributes. The resulting XML document would appear as a XML Schema document.

In the second step we would have to translate the sentences of the query XML language selected, to the SQL language clauses.

Once we have the query in SQL, we can execute it over the database using the Database Management System. Finally, the returned results of the query are translated into XML.

The architecture of the proposed system would be made up of two independent components. The first one translates the data model in the database to a special XML Schema. The second component receives a query in a XML language over the database, which would have already been adapted to the system with the previous component, and gives out the query results in XML. Figure 1 shows this architecture format.

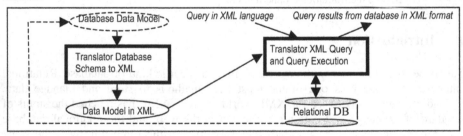

Fig. 1. Architecture of the XML Query System to Relational Databases

In this moment this system is in its final development process and have already been made tests that show it's suitable.

References

1. Scott et all. XQuery 1.0: An XML Query Language. http://www.w3.org/TR/xquery/ (2002)
2. W3C World Wide Web Consortiun The Extensible Stylesheet Language (XSL) http://www.w3.org/Style/XSL/ (2003)

Selection of Ontologies for the Semantic Web*

Adolfo Lozano-Tello[1], Asunción Gómez-Pérez[2], and Encarna Sosa[1]

[1] Escuela Politécnica de Cáceres. Universidad de Extremadura
Avda de la universidad, s/n. 10071 Cáceres. Spain
{alozano, esosa}@unex.es
[2] Facultad de Informática . Universidad Politécnica de Madrid
Campus de Montegancedo, s/n. 28660 Boadilla del Monte. Madrid. Spain
asun@fi.upm.es

Abstract. The development of the Semantic Web has encouraged the creation of ontologies in a great variety of domains. Web users currently looking for ontologies in order to incorporate them into their systems, just use their experience and intuition. This makes it difficult for them to justify their choices. Mainly, this is due to the lack of methods that help the user to measure that the most appropriate ontologies for the new system are. To solve this deficiency, this work proposes a method which allows the users to measure the suitability of the existent ontologies, regarding the requirements of their systems.

1 Ontologies for the Semantic Web

Nowadays, there is a growing interest to transform the huge amount of World Wide Web information in documents with "semantic markup" that can be processable by machines and humans. This new vision was created by Tim Berners-Lee [Ber01] to enable computers and people to work in better cooperation. Ontologies are the key pieces to provide semantic to the Web. In spite of the great increase that the use of ontologies has acquired (in Semantic Web, information search, knowledge management and electronic commerce [Fen01]), nowadays, the knowledge engineers need to look for ontologies disperse in quite a few of web servers. When they find several that can be adapted, they should examine their characteristics attentively and to decide which the best are to incorporate them to their system. Moreover, the ontologies are implemented in a great variety of languages [Cor00], applying several methodologies [Fer99], and using numerous technological platforms related with ontologies [Gol02]. Keeping in mind these dimensions, election procedures usually depend on the experience and the engineer's intuition. If the system is being developed with commercial goals, it will be very difficult for them to justify the taken election.

Although most of the methodologies for building ontologies [Fer99] propose a phase on reusing existent ontologies, there are not works that indicate the users how to choose ontologies for a new project, and there are not methodologies that quantify

---

* This work has been developed with the support of CICYT under contract TIC2002-04309-C02-01 and Junta de Extremadura under project 2PR01A023.

J.M. Cueva Lovelle et al. (Eds.): ICWE 2003, LNCS 2722, pp. 413–416, 2003.
© Springer-Verlag Berlin Heidelberg 2003

the suitability of these ontologies for the system. This election problem would be palliated if it existed a metric that quantified, for each one of the ontologies candidates, how of appropriate they are for a new system. The method that is described in this work (called *ONTOMETRIC*) presents the set of processes that the user should carry out to obtain these measures.

2   *ONTOMETRIC*: A Method to Choose Ontologies

In this section we describe *ONTOMETRIC*, the adaptation of AHP for selection of ontologies. The Analytic Hierarchy Process (AHP) was devised by Thomas L. Saaty in the early seventies [Saa77]. It is a powerful and flexible tool for decision-making in complex multicriteria problems. This method allows people to gather knowledge about a particular problem, to quantify subjective opinions and to force the comparison of alternatives in relation to established criteria.

The *ONTOMETRIC* method is based on a taxonomy of 160 characteristics of ontologies [Loz03], called **multilevel framework of characteristics**, that provides the outline to choose and to compare existent ontologies. The multilevel framework of characteristics has, in the superior level of the taxonomy, five basic aspects on the ontologies that are denominated **dimensions**. These are: the **content** of the ontology and the organization of their contents, the **language** in which is implemented, the **methodology** that has been followed to develop it, the software **tools** used to build and edit the ontology, and the **costs** that the ontology will be necessary in a project. The multilevel framework of characteristics is the base to build an ontology in the ontology domain, call *Reference Ontology* (RO). The conceptual model of this ontology will gather the characteristics of the framework exposed. A direct relationship exists among all the descriptive characteristics identified in the dimensions, and the instance attributes specified in the RO. The development methodology of ontologies METHONTOLOGY [Fer97] and the development environment of ontologies (that follows METHONTOLOGY) WebODE [Cor02] were used to build the RO. A first version of the RO was used in (ONTO)^{2}Agent [Arp98] to search ontologies.

Taking into account the general steps of AHP, we have adapted the method to be used in the reuse of ontologies:

STEP 1: specify the project objectives. The knowledge engineer should know the exact guidelines of their company and available resources in relation to the new business.

STEP 2: build the decision tree from the MTC, so that the objective, "select the most appropriate ontology for a new project", is placed at the rood node; the dimensions (content, language, methodology, tool and costs) are placed at the first level; the factors of each dimension at the second level; and underneath these factors, the sub-trees of specific characteristics of the particular evaluation project. The general characteristics of ontologies should be specialised according to: the particular ontology, the specific target project and the organization that will develop the project.

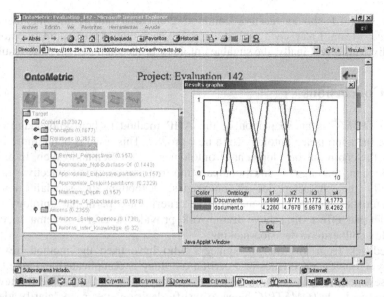

Fig. 1. Comparison of two ontologies (Documents and Document.o) in the factor "taxonomy" using *OntoMetric Tool*.

STEP 3: for each set of brother nodes, make the pairwise comparison matrixes [Saa77] with the criteria of the decision tree. The *eigenvectors* are calculated from these matrixes. These weights represent the relative importance between criteria.

STEP 4: for each alternative ontology, assess its characteristics. These values will (always multiplying by the weights calculated in step 3) ascend up to the superior nodes of the tree, until the node root is calculated. For each one of these characteristics, the user should establish a scale of appropriate ratings.

STEP 4.1: this method assigns linguistic values (non-numbers) to the alternatives because the human beings, in their daily activities, usually make this type of judgement. For example, if users evaluate the "essential relations for the system are defined in the ontology", they can assess this quality using the linguistic scale: (*very_low*, *low*, *medium*, *high* and *very_high*). It is more intuitive than a numeric scale between zero and ten. In this process, it is important that the groups of the linguistic values are precisely defined.

However it is not possible to perform calculations with linguistic values. One possible representation of these linguistic values is fuzzy intervals. Their angular points in a scale from 0 to 10, determine the fuzzy intervals (see graphic in figure 1).

STEP 4.2: with these established linguistic scales for each one of the criteria, the user will proceed to study each one of the ontologies that have been considered as alternatives, and to value them using these scales.

STEP 5: lastly, combine the vectors of weights *W* obtained in step 3 with the values of the alternatives *V* obtained in step 4, using (e.g.) the formula: $\Sigma_n w_i\ v_i$. Figure 1 shows an example with the comparison of two ontologies in the factor "taxonomy".

In large projects, which require a team of analysts, each person can provide their own values, and it will be necessary to reach an agreement. In this case, all the steps up to step 4.1 should reach a common consensus among the members of the evaluation team. Later, each analyst can value each one of the candidate ontologies in an individual way. Finally, the suitable ontology is chosen based on these results.

3   Conclusions

ONTOMETRIC is an adaptation of the AHP method to help knowledge engineers choose the appropriate ontology for a new project. This issue is being more important due to the enormous development of ontologies for the Semantic Web. In order to do this election, the engineer must compare the importance of the objectives, and study carefully the characteristics of ontologies. Although the specialisation of the characteristics and the assessment of the criteria of a particular ontology require a considerable effort, the above framework provides a useful schema to carry out complex multicriteria decision-making.

Feedback from knowledge engineers who have used the method, reveals that specifying the characteristics of a certain ontology is complicated and take time, and its assessment is quite subjective; however, they state that, once the framework has been defined, *ONTOMETRIC* helps to justify decisions taken, to "clarify ideas", and to weigh up the advantages and the risks involved in choosing one ontology from other options. The prototype *OntoMetric Tool* (figure 1) assists the user in applying the method. Shortly, this prototype will be integrated in WebODE platform [Cor02].

References

[Ar98]   Arpírez J., Gómez-Pérez A., Lozano-Tello A., Pinto S.: (Onto)²Agent: An Ontology-Based WWW Broker to Select Ontologies. European Conference of Artificial Intelligence (ECAI'98). Brighton. UK. (1998) 16–24.

[Ber01]   Berners-Lee T., Hendler J., Lassila O.: The Semantic Web. Scientific American, Volume 284, N. 5. May. (2001) 34–43.

[Cor02]   Corcho O, de Vicente O., Fernández-López M., Gómez-Pérez A.: WebODE: an Integrated Workbench for Ontology Representation, Reasoning and Exchange. Proceedings of EKAW'02. Sigüenza, Spain. (2002) 138–153.

[Cor00]   Corcho O., Gómez-Pérez A.: A Roadmap to Ontology Specification Languages. Proceedings of EKAW'00. Jean-Les-Pins. (2000) 80–96.

[Fen01]   Fensel D.: Ontologies: Silver Bullet for Knowledge Management and Electronic Commerce. Springer-Verlag, Berlin (2001).

[Fer97]   Fernández M., Gómez-Pérez A., Juristo N.: METHONTOLOGY: From Ontological Art Toward Ontological Engineering. Spring Symposium Series on Ontological Engineering. (AAAI'97). Stanford. (1997) 33–40.

[Fer99]   Fernández M.: Overview of Methodologies for Building Ontologies. Proceedings of the IJCAI'99. Workshop on Ontologies and PSMs. Stockholm. (1999).

[Gol02]   Golbeck J., Grove M., Parsia B., Kalyanpur A., Hendler J.: New Tools for the Semantic Web. Proceedings of EKAW'02. Sigüenza, Spain. (2002) 392–400.

[Loz03]   Lozano-Tello A. and Gómez-Pérez A. ONTOMETRIC: A Method to Choose the Appropriate Ontology. Journal Of Database Management to be published in (2003).

[Saa77]   Saaty, T.: A Scaling Method for Priorities in Hierarchical Structures. Journal of Mathematical Psychology, Vol.15, (1977) 234–281.

Modeling Applications for the Semantic Web

Fernanda Lima and Daniel Schwabe

Depto de Informática, PUC-RIO, R. Marquês de São Vicente, 225, Gávea,
Rio de Janeiro – RJ – 22453-900 – Brasil
{ferlima, schwabe}@inf.puc-rio.br
http://www-di.inf.puc-rio.br/~schwabe

Abstract. This paper proposes the Semantic Hypermedia Design Method,
SHDM. By extending OOHDM with primitives taken from Semantic Web
languages such as DAML+OIL, we show how a larger, easier to evolve, set of
applications can be specified. Such applications also allow tapping the richness
of resource descriptions that are becoming available with the Semantic Web.

1 Introduction

The Semantic Web is currently an active topic of research and industry efforts, as it is
regarded as the next evolutionary step of the current Web. The main goal of this
future Web is to have a large amount of data available with its metadata, to help
machines and humans find and process useful resources as well as reuse data across
various applications [21].

The major emphasis so far has been in the search for useful resources, and many
interesting proposals for organizing and searching Web data based on the Semantic
Web are being put forward. For most people, though, the Web is important because of
the functionality provided by Web applications, through which they can not only
access, but also process the information stored in the Web itself. Therefore, much of
the Semantic Web's promise can only be delivered if Web applications are able to
fully take advantage of its added (meta) information. Therefore, in addition to
metadata about Web resources, we must also provide metadata about applications.

We have been investigating Web application design models for several years in the
context of Object Oriented Hypermedia Design Method (OOHDM) [9, 8]. Being a
model-driven approach, it stands as a logical candidate to be integrated with the
Semantic Web approach, since its models can be used as metadata describing the
application. Our goal is to provide authoring methods that help designing applications
that can tap on the Semantic Web. In particular, the purpose of this paper is to show
that we can express this information building SHDM - Semantic Hypermedia Design
Method, a new version of the original method. A complementary goal is to evolve
more traditional design methods such as OOHDM by enriching the languages used to
specify its various models with Semantic Web languages such as RDF [16], RDF
Schema (RDFS) [17], DAML+OIL [19], and OWL[22], while keeping the basic
underlying fundamental abstractions.

J.M. Cueva Lovelle et al. (Eds.): ICWE 2003, LNCS 2722, pp. 417–426, 2003.
© Springer-Verlag Berlin Heidelberg 2003

In addition to these general languages, we also enrich navigation modeling by providing primitives to specify Faceted Navigations, where we can express abstractions for faceted access structures and faceted contexts in a concise model. This allows the design of richer access structures, providing the user with more flexible ways to reach the set of objects that are relevant to task at hand. We also offer primitives that allow the Web application designer to describe concisely hierarchical faceted metadata.

This paper is organized as follows. In Section 2, we describe the main concepts of the SHDM method, its main design steps, showing how one can take advantage of more expressive modeling primitives extending the original OOHDM, both for data and navigational models. In this section, we use an Art Ontology as an example to show a summarized example of the method. In Section 3 we conclude and make brief comments about our future work.

2   The SHDM Method

One of the cornerstones of OOHDM is that it explicitly separates conceptual from navigation design, since they address different concerns in Web applications. Whereas conceptual modeling and design must reflect objects and behaviors in the application domain, navigation design is aimed at organizing the hyperspace taking into account users' profiles and tasks. Navigational design is a key activity in the implementation of Web applications and we advocate that it must be explicitly separated from conceptual modeling [8].

The foundations mentioned above are maintained in this new version of the method called SHDM, enriched with several new mechanisms inspired by the languages being proposed for the Semantic Web. The first step is treating "information items" described in described in the Conceptual Model, and in the Navigation Class Model of OOHDM as resources manipulated in Semantic Web languages, such as the W3C Resource Description Framework (RDF), which is used to describe resources and their properties. By generalizing the concept of "Web resource", RDF can be used to represent information about anything that can be identified on the Web. The characterization of resources in SHDM is done using ontology definition languages such as RDF Schema, DAML+OIL and the recent "work in progress" W3C Web Ontology Language (OWL), expressing more advanced features such as constraints (restrictions), enumeration and datatypes according to XML Schema[1].

We would like to stress that, even though we know that the Semantic Web underlying framework (RDF) is not object-oriented (OO), we still find it useful to use some of the OO modeling principles, mainly because it decreases the level of granularity, suppressing details by allowing grouping of descriptions.

---

[1] In our examples we used DAML+OIL only because OWL in still at "W3C Working Draft" status, i.e., not completely specified as a Recommendation. Since OWL is derived from the DAML+OIL we plan to make any adaptations easily as soon as it reaches a more mature status.

In this paper we focus more on the main SHDM novelties; more details can be found in [4]. In the following subsections we will specify two of the activities, namely Conceptual Design and Navigational Design.

2.1 The Conceptual Design

During the SHDM Conceptual Design step we build a model (the Conceptual Model) showing classes and their relationships specifically related to a domain. Classes are described as in object-oriented (OO) UML models [6] with three distinguished details on attributes: they can be multi-typed (representing different perspectives of the same real-world entity), they are described with multiplicity (referring to the number of times the attribute may occur in instances) and they can have explicit enumerations (defining the possible values for that attribute in instances). Relations are described also as in OO UML models, with one additional detail: relations can be specialized creating subrelation hierarchies.

The conceptual model obtained using the UML class diagram can be mapped to a RDF/XML serialization format according to heuristic rules [4] summarized next. In the following subsections we present the notations of the new Conceptual Model primitives, their general semantics and their mapping to one of the Semantic Web languages, DAML+OIL.

When comparing the object-oriented model (OO) with the RDF model it is possible to state that the concepts of classes and subclasses (specialization and generalization relations) can be modeled equivalently. However there is a significant difference in modeling OO attributes and OO association relations in the RDF model. These two OO abstractions are modeled through RDF properties indistinctly, i.e., in RDF models there is no distinction between a property that describes a class (attribute) and a property that describes an association relation with another class. In addition, RDF properties can be specialized through subsumption relation, allowing the creation of subproperties. Our Conceptual Schema takes advantage of these characteristics as shown below; for reasons of space, only the main ones are detailed.

Every class is mapped to a DAML+OIL Class, modeling attributes and relationships as properties. We use DAML+OIL extensions defined as *Datatype* and *ObjectType* Properties to represent attributes and relationships, respectively. Attribute multiplicity is mapped to *minCardinality* and *maxCardinality* on specific properties. Attribute enumerations are mapped to the constructor *one of*, providing a means to define a class by direct enumeration of its members, in such a way that no other individuals can be declared as belonging to the class. Datatypes are defined as in XML Schema.

In addition to defining classes and instances declaratively, DAML+OIL and other Description-Logics languages let us create intensional class definitions using Boolean expressions and specify necessary, or necessary and sufficient, conditions for class membership. These languages rely on inference engines (classifiers) to compute a class hierarchy and to determine class membership of instances based on the properties of classes and instances [5]. SHDM incorporates these Semantic Web languages approaches using Inferred Classes, represented graphically as UML stereotypes (see Fig. 1).

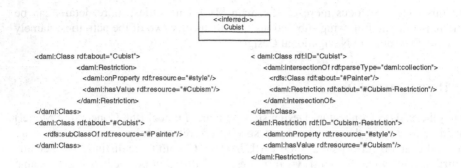

```
                              <<inferred>>
                                 Cubist

<daml:Class rdf:about="Cubist">              < daml:Class rdf:ID="Cubist">
    <daml:Restriction>                           <daml:intersectionOf rdf:parseType="daml:collection">
        <daml:onProperty rdf:resource="#style"/>     <rdfs:Class rdf:about="#Painter"/>
        <daml:hasValue rdf:resource="#Cubism"/>       <daml:Restriction rdf:about="#Cubism-Restriction"/>
    </daml:Restriction>                          </daml:intersectionOf>
</daml:Class>                                 </daml:Class>
<daml:Class rdf:about="#Cubist">             <daml:Restriction rdf:ID="Cubism-Restriction">
  <rdfs:subClassOf rdf:resource="#Painter"/>    <daml:onProperty rdf:resource="#style"/>
</daml:Class>                                    <daml:hasValue rdf:resource="#Cubism"/>
                                             </daml:Restriction>
```

Fig. 1. Inferred Class, with two alternative DAML+OIL equivalent definitions

This simple example states that a "painter" belongs to the "cubist" class if the property value of his/her style is "cubist" or that the "painter" subclass cubist is the intersection of classes "painter" and the set of resources whose "style" property satisfies the condition of having its value equal to "cubist". Since this language relies on inference engines to compute a class hierarchy, we could validate our model using any DAML+OIL inference engine. Other than the inferred classes, we defined in our metamodel another stereotype to represent class hierarchies with arbitrary depth, called "arbitraryClassHierarchy", but due to space restrictions we will not detail it in this article.

2.2 The Navigational Design

During the Navigation Design step we produce a Navigational Model over a conceptual domain, according to user profiles and the tasks that will be supported. As stated in [9, 8], during Navigation Design we are interested in specifying which objects will be reached by the user (the nodes) and the relations between these nodes (the links). We also specify the sets of objects within which the user will navigate (called contexts) and in which way s/he will access these contexts (the access structures). We are also able to specify different contents for the nodes according to the contexts within which they are reached (inContext classes). The basic SHDM navigation primitives are defined at this point, as in OOHDM.

For SHDM, we have identified the need to model some new access structure primitives in order to take advantage of the increased availability in the WWW of taxonomies, which we have named Faceted Access Structures, inspired by the facet concept initially proposed in library and information sciences [7]. Simply put, a facet can be considered as a category. In [12] Taylor defines facets as "clearly defined, mutually exclusive, and collectively exhaustive aspects, properties, or characteristics of a class or specific subject".

In a faceted classification scheme, the facets may be considered to be dimensions in a Cartesian classification space, and the value of a facet is the position of the artifact in that dimension. Within each facet, subfacets or more specific topics are listed. The breakdown continues into subfacets within subfacets. The items in each subfacet, in general, are ordered from more general to more specific, complex or concrete.

We define facet hierarchies based on our navigational attribute types- which are in fact metadata about our Web application. Each hierarchy is defined independently, in order to organize content along a particular dimension. This will be exemplified later on.

Navigational Contexts remains a very important navigational primitive in our approach, since it allows us to describe sets of navigational objects relevant to the user during a task. The novelty lies in the fact that the language used to define contexts is more expressive than the previous one.

Next we show the notations of the new Navigational Model primitives, together with their mapping to a Semantic Web language such as DAML+OIL.

The Navigation Design activity generates two schemas, the Navigational Class schema and the Navigational Context schema. The first defines all navigable objects as views over the application domain. The navigable relations are links between nodes and also the new subrelations that allow a new type of navigation based on subsumption relations between links. The second schema defines navigational contexts (the main structuring primitive for the navigational space), access structures used to reach these contexts and links that connect them.

The representation of navigational classes is graphically identical to OOHDM, using the same innovations introduced for conceptual attribute notations. Navigational classes represent views of conceptual classes, including directly mapped conceptual attributes, derived attributes and also attributes from other conceptual classes. The mappings are specified using an RQL [3] query, exemplified below.

RQL mapping:

RQL query	Description
select y from { Artist } firstName { y }	retrieves the firstName of Artists
select y from {x} creates { y } where x= "parameterA"	retrieves all Artifacts of a specific Artist

As in the conceptual schema, SHDM also allows sub-relations in the navigational class schema.

In addition to using sub-relations defined in the conceptual model, it is possible to use sub-relations in the mapping of the conceptual model into the navigational class model. For example, it is possible to define navigational sub-relations of "creates" by restricting its subclasses, for instance, only those whose counter-domain is a subclass of Painting. In Fig. 2 we illustrate a combination of DAML+OIL and RQL to specify the mapping from the conceptual to the navigational model (identified with namespace shdm).

A context groups objects related to each other by some aspect (e.g., common attributes or being related to a common object) and organizes these objects as sets of nodes, defining in which way they may be accessed (e.g., sequentially).

Navigation contexts may be further specified as groups of contexts, since it is possible to sometimes parameterize their defining property. For example, "Sculpture by Material" is actually a set of sets; each set is a context, determined by one value of the "material" attribute.

```
<daml:ObjectProperty rdf:ID="etches">
        <daml:subPropertyOf rdf:resource="#creates">
        <shdm:rql query:value ="select y  from { x } creates { y : cult:Watercolor" }
        <!-- retrieves all instances according to the description in the text above -->
        <daml:range rdf:resource="#Painter"/>
        <daml:domain rdf:resource="#Watercolor"/>
</daml: ObjectProperty >
```

Fig. 2. Navigational Class attribute mapping using sub-relations

There is an analogous definition for contexts whose property is based on 1-to-n relations, such as "Sculpture by Sculptor".

Access structures are indexes (collections of links) that allow the user to reach navigation objects (within some context). SHDM allows defining both Access Structures and Navigational Contexts using meta-data properties. The <<subClassOf>> stereotype indicates that the corresponding element (access structure of navigational context) is a set of elements, one for each sub-class.

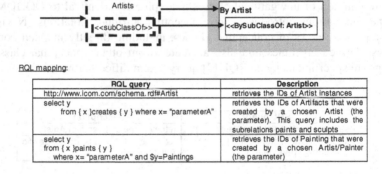

RQL mapping:

RQL query	Description
http://www.icom.com/schema. rdf#Artist	retrieves the IDs of Artist instances
select y from { x }creates { y } where x= "parameterA"	retrieves the IDs of Artifacts that were created by a chosen Artist (the parameter). This query includes the subrelations paints and sculpts

select y
    from { x }paints { y }
    where x= "parameterA" and $y=Paintings
	retrieves the IDs of Painting that were created by a chosen Artist/Painter (the parameter)

Fig. 3. Access Structures and Navigational Contexts defined based on meta-model properties

In Fig. 3 we show the graphical notation, and the RQL statements for an example. In The Artist access structure represents a list of links to all artists (the order is specified in the corresponding card). The inner dashed box represents sub-sets of Artist defined according to its subclass, for example Painter and Sculptor. The context Artifact by Artist that is composed of all artifacts created by a specific artist. This context can be access by choosing an artist as a parameter of selection. The innermost box signifies that the user can also choose any subclass of Artist to group the artifacts.

Faceted Access Structures and Faceted Navigational Contexts are defined using the <<faceted>> and <<ByValidFacetComb>> stereotypes. In Fig. 4 the outside dashed box denotes the valid combinations of facets to reach the Artifact navigational class and three inside dashed boxes that indicate the possibility of choosing just one of the facets. The context Artifact by ValidFacetCombination exemplifies the possibility of accessing Artifacts by any combination of Region or Style. Similarly, Artifact by Style – Faceted stands for all sets of artifacts grouped by Style and by its subclasses.

Faceted elements are detailed in the corresponding specification cards, illustrated in Fig. 5. The designer can use a graphical notation to annotate in the facet hierarchies numbers that represent the invalid combinations. When the designer describes the combinations, he/she does not have to make it extensively; it is enough to only annotate the nodes that are superclasses of the invalid combinations, at any level of the trees. The enumerated combinations can be generated by an algorithm such as proposed by Tzitzikas in [13].

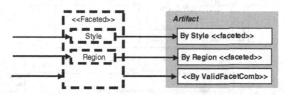

Fig. 4. Faceted Access Structures and Faceted Navigational Contexts

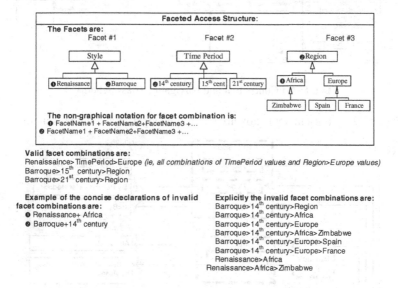

Fig. 5. Navigational Faceted Access Structures Specification Card

We developed an example inspired by a Museum example [2] that we briefly outline, focusing on illustrating the novelties in the navigation schemas.

Fig. 6 presents the Conceptual Model for the example. The superclass Artist has an association relation ("creates") with the superclass Artifact, specialized by: "paints" and "sculpts", meaning that whenever somebody *paints* something, he/she is also *creating* it. It also means that a query for the instances of this model to ask for domain and range of the "creates" relation will also retrieve the union of the subrelations.

Fig. 7 shows the Navigational Class schema. Notice that node Artifact includes attributes that did not belong to the original Conceptual Class, such as *style*.

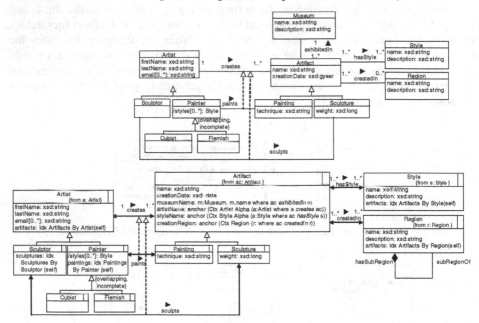

Fig. 6. Art Conceptual and Navigation Class Schema

In Figure 19 we present some novelties in the Navigational Context schema.

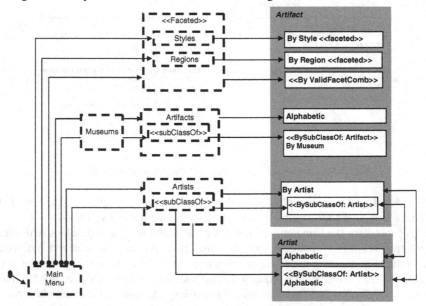

Fig. 7. Art Navigational Context Schema

The abstraction power of the notation proposed is exemplified in several places. The use of compact facet specifications avoids explicit enumeration of all possible combinations, including those not know at design time. The same is true for the use of the <<subclassOf>> stereotype, since it allows definitions of access structures and contexts for an arbitrary class hierarchy. Since we have used RQL, we are able to query both data and metadata. For instance, we can now define a context "Artifact by Style", without knowing ahead of time all possible values (or subclasses) of "Style". If the user later adds a new subclass to "Style", and its corresponding instances, the same application specification still applies. In this sense, SHDM specifications could be regarded as specifying frameworks (as in [10]). Although not shown in here, similar reasoning can be applied to inferred classes.

3 Conclusions

In this paper we have argued that Web application design methods can benefit from modeling language primitives being proposed for the Semantic Web, such as RDF, RDFS, and DAML+OIL. Some approaches, such as HERA [1] propose directly using RDF and RDFS, or slight extensions, as the basic ontology modeling language, equivalent to our conceptual modeling. Others, such as OntoWebber [2], add additional ontologies on top of them, to cover other aspects of application design, such as site structure. In contrast, we have kept the traditional UML-like object model, extending it with a few primitives such as sub-relations, from RDF, and anonymous classes defined through restrictions, from DAML+OIL.

We have followed the original OOHDM approach of defining the Navigational Class model as a mapping of the Conceptual Model, but using RQL as the mapping specification language, which is able to query DAML+OIL models. Another benefit brought by SHDM is the ability to concisely specify faceted navigation structures. It was shown how facet specification is equivalent to very large enumerations of possible navigations paths. With the increasing availability of domain taxonomies, this will allow such taxonomies as part of the navigation structure of applications designed using SHDM. In addition, the resulting applications are able cater to varying user profiles by providing alternative navigation paths better suited to each particular case.

We are now investigating how SHDM can be extended to personalized and adaptable web applications. Additional topics being pursued include integration of interface and interaction models, of application functionalities. In [4] an implementation architecture is outlined, based on the Sesame [11] environment.

References

1.   Frasincar, F., Houben, G-J., Vdovjak, R.: "Specification Framework for Engineering Adaptive Web Applications", In Proceedings of the WWW2002, Honolulu, USA, 2002.
2.   Jin, Y., Decker, S., Wiederhold, G.: "OntoWebber: Building Web Sites Using Semantic Web Technologies", http://www-db.stanford.edu/~yhjin/docs/owedbt.pdf

426   F. Lima and D. Schwabe

3. Karvounarakis, G., Alexaki, S., Christophides, V., Plexousakis, D. and Scholl, M.: "RQL: A Declarative Query Language for RDF", In Proceedings of the 11th International World Wide Web Conference (WWW2002), Honolulu, Hawaii, USA, May 2002, http://139.91.183.30:9090/RDF/RQL/index.html
4. Lima, F.: "Modeling applications for the Semantic Web", PhD Thesis (in preparation), Pontifícia Universidade Católica do Rio de Janeiro, Rio de Janeiro, Brasil, 2003.
5. Noy, N.F., Sintek, M., Decker, S., Crubézy, M., Fergerson, R., Musen, M.A.: "Creating Semantic Web Contents with Protégé-2000", IEEE Intelligent Systems, Vol. 16, No. 2, March/April 2001, special issue on Semantic Web, 60–71.
6. OMG: "Unified Modeling Language Specification version 1.3 (UML 1.3)", June 1999.
7. Ranganathan, S.: "Colon Classification, Basic Classification", 6th ed., New York: Asia Publishing House, 1963.
8. Rossi, G., Schwabe, D. and Lyardet, F.: "Web Application Models Are More than Conceptual Models" In Proceedings of the ER'99, Paris, France, November 1999, Springer, 239–252.
9. Schwabe, D. and Rossi, G.: "An object-oriented approach to Web-based application design" Theory and Practice of Object Systems (TAPOS), October 1998, 207–225.
10. Schwabe, D., Rossi, G., Esmeraldo, L. and Lyardet, F.: "Engineering Web Applications for reuse", IEEE Multimedia 8(1) – Special Issue on Web Engineering, Jan-Mar 2001, 20–31.
11. Sesame.aidministrator bv.: "Sesame: A Generic Architecture for Storing and Querying RDF and RDF-Schema", Technical Report, http://sesame.aidministrator.nl/, 2001.
12. Taylor, A. G.: "Introduction to Cataloging and Classification", 8th ed. Englewood, Colorado: Libraries Unlimited, 1992.
13. Tzitzikas, Y., Spyratos, N., Constantopoulos, P. and Analyti, A.: "Extended Faceted Taxonomies for Web Catalogs", Third International Conference on Web Information Systems Engineering, WISE 2002, Singapore, December, 2002.
14. van Harmelen, F., Horrocks, I. and Patel-Schneider, P.: "Reference Description of the DAML+OIL (March 2001) Ontology Markup Language", http://www.daml.org/2001/03/reference.html
15. W3C1998: "A Discussion of the Relationship Between RDF-Schema and UML", http://www.w3.org/TR/NOTE-rdf-uml/, 1998.
16. W3C1999: "Resource Description Framework (RDF) Model and Syntax Specification", W3C Recommendation 22 February 1999, http://www.w3.org/TR/1999/REC-rdf-syntax-19990222/
17. W3C2000: "Resource Description Framework (RDF) Schema Specification 1.0", W3C, Candidate Recommendation 27 March 2000, http://www.w3.org/TR/2000/CR-rdf-schema-20000327/
18. W3C2001a: "XML Schema Part 2: Datatypes", W3C Recommendation 02 May 2001, http://www.w3.org/TR/xmlschema-2/
19. W3C2001a: "DAML+OIL (March 2001) Reference Description", W3C Note 18 December 2001, http://www.w3.org/TR/daml+oil-reference
20. W3C2002a: "Requirements for a Web Ontology Language", W3C Working Draft 07 March 2002, http://www.w3.org/TR/webont-req/
21. W3C2002c: "Semantic Web Activity Statement", http://www.w3.org/2001/sw/Activity/, retrieved 2002/11/03.
22. W3C2002c: "Web Ontology Language (OWL) Guide Version 1.0", W3C Working Draft 4 November 2002, http://www.w3.org/TR/2002/WD-owl-guide-20021104/

Automatic Derivation of DAML-S Service Specifications from UML Business Models

Darío Franco, Víctor Anaya, and Ángel Ortiz

Research Centre on Production Management and Engineering
Technical University of Valencia
Camino de Vera s/n 46022, VALENCIA
{dfranco,vanaya,aortiz}@cigip.upv.es

Abstract. Today's trend in Web engineering is the automation of Web service interoperation. With this aim, web content is noted with semantic information, using Web Semantic languages. Web Services is becoming the leading technology that provides functionality of an enterprise. This functionality carries out the activities that form a process. Business processes are a set of activities that can be seen as offered business services. Therefore, this article presents a process to derive web services specifications and service composition from business models. The paper considers DAML-S as the web services markup language to represent the description of web services and specify their composition. Rational Unified Process business model is the language used as input. The article shows the set of derivation rules that allows the atomatic generation of DAML-S modules from business models.

1 Introduction

Nowadays, automation of web services interoperation is becoming a key goal in web engineering field. With this aim, web content is noted with semantic information so that it is unambiguously interpretable. To define semantic webs there are a set of languages such as DAML+OIL[1] [5], which is a markup language used to describe ontologies. Ones of the most important web resources to be described are web services. Semantic web services markup languages permit intelligent agents to carry out tasks automatically, such as automatic web service discovery, automatic web service execution or automatic web service composition and interoperation [3].

The goal of this paper is the generation of high level descriptions of services and specifications of their composition from business models. Business models describe enterprise processes that are described by means of workflows. Activities that compose a business process can be seen as high level services carried out by information systems or humans. DAML-S [1] is an ontology of semantic web services expressed with DAML+OIL. Taking into account the extended use of UML as OO-notation, we have considered the Rational Unified Process[2] (RUP) business model as

---

[1] www.daml.org
[2] www.rational.com

J.M. Cueva Lovelle et al. (Eds.): ICWE 2003, LNCS 2722, pp. 427–430, 2003.
© Springer-Verlag Berlin Heidelberg 2003

the enterprise modeling language (EML) used to represent business models. RUP business model is based in a UML profile defined by Rational that extends UML.

With this aim, the paper present a list of derivation rules between constructs of RUP enterprise metamodel and DAML-S metamodel. These rules are used to define a set of well-defined patterns that are used to deduce automatically DAML-S service specifications. In [2], [4] UML is used as a graphical representation to DAML concepts. However, we want to derive DAML-S modules from RUP business models, instead of using them as a graphical representation of DAML-S concepts.

2   From RUP Business to DAML-S Concepts: Derivation Rules

The goal of the article is to define matches between RUP business model constructs and DAML-S constructs. These correspondences are unidirectional, so it is only possible to derive DAML-S modules from business models, but not the opposite. The reason is that the aim is not to use business models as a notation to represent services, but to generate initial DAML-S descriptions of services from them. Some DAML-S services are described to such a low level that generation of process models from DAML-S descriptions by reverse engineering is useless.

The resulting matches can be used to define patterns implemented in a translator. This translator will supply automatically DAML files with service descriptions from business diagrams.

In order to define derivation rules, the semantic of each business and DAML-S concept is taken into account. In this way, a business use case implies interaction with external users and always produces some value to the user. Business use cases are defined by their interactions with clients (business actors). Therefore, a process defined by a business use case can be seen as a DAML-S composite service, but these composite services are independent services (without dependencies of execution order). The description of the business use case is done by means of steps that constitute allowed scenarios (workflows). These activities have an execution order, so they can follow a sequence or be executed in parallel, synchronously or asynchronously. An activity state can be too complex, so it is possible to attach it a nested activity diagram that expresses finer grained functionality. Therefore, we differentiate UML activity states in simple activity states and complex activity states. The former hasn't nested activity diagrams, the later has. In the same way, DAML-S services have an execution order. Simple activity corresponds to an atomic service and complex activity to a composite process.

RUP Enterprise workers can be seen as DAML-S resources (human resources) that are necessary to carry out a process. Business entities represent objects used or produced by a process, so they correspond with inputs and outputs of a service. Object states are states of instances of business entities. The relation of object states with activity states decides if it is an input or an output.

A more detailed list of derivation rules is presented in Table 1 and 2.

Table 1. Derivation rules between RUP Business model constructs and constructs of the Service Process Model of DAML-S

RUP Business Model	Service Process Model (DAML-S Ontology)
Business Entity	Input or output
Attributes	Fine grain inputs (variables)
Methods	Atomic/Composite services
Parameters	Fine grain inputs (variables)
Business Use Case	Composite service
Goal	Simple service's effect
Activity model	
Object Flow State	Input or output parameters
Object Flow	Determine if the object flow state is an input or an output
Complex Activity State	Composite Service
Simple Activity State	Atomic Service
Synchronization bar (branch)	Control Construct (Split)
Synchronization bar (join)	Control Construct (unordered)
Synchronization bar (branch) and Conditional Thread	Control Construct (Choice)
Decision	Control Construct (If-Then-Else)
Transition	Control Construct (Sequence)
Business Worker	Resource

Table 2. Derivation rules between RUP Business model constructs and constructs of the Service Profile of DAML-S

RUP Business Model	Service Profile (DAML-S Ontology)
Business Actor	Actor
Business Use Case	Name of Service
All Inputs and Outputs previously defined in the Service Profile	Inputs, Outputs
Goal of Business Use Case	Effect

The next process can achieve the derivation of DAML-S process model specifications from RUP business models:

1. Each business use case generates an independent composite service (a DAML-S file).
   For each Business Use Case:

   a. Look for activity states in the activity diagrams attached to the business use case. For each simple activity state add an atomic service. For each complex activity state add a composite service.
   b. For each activity state look the incoming and outgoing object state flows that define if the associated object state is an input or an output of the activity, and consequently of the service.

    c.   Inputs of the DAML-S service are decomposed in attributes. With that purpose, sequence diagrams associated with a business use case are explored. Business actors interchange methods with business entities. The parameters of these methods define finer grained inputs.

    d.   Finally, other service's inputs are added. There are inputs that are not provided as object states, because workers or clients supply this information. Looking the outgoing methods of a business worker, remaining inputs can be added.

3 Conclusions

Web services interoperation has motivated the apparition of Web Semantic markup languages used to describe properties and capabilities of web services so they can be computer-interpretable. Use of semantic web services languages will permit intelligent agents to carry out tasks automatically, such as automatic web service discovery, automatic web service execution or automatic web service composition and interoperation [3].

Web Services can be seen as activities that together describe the workflow of a process. Business processes are a set of activities that can be seen as offered services by a business. Therefore, this article has presented a process to derive web services specifications and composition from business models. The paper considers DAML-S as the web services markup language to represent the description of web services. Taking into account the extended use of UML as OO notation, we have considered the Rational Unified Process (RUP) business model as enterprise modeling language.

With this aim, the paper present a list of derivation rules between constructs of RUP enterprise metamodel and DAML-S metamodel. These rules are used to define a set of well define patterns that are used to generate automatically the DAML-S files with the profile and process of the services.

References

[1] Ankolekar, A., et al., DAML-S: Semantic Markup for Web Services, submitted for publication in The Emerging Semantic Web.

[2] Kenneth Baclawski, Mieczyslaw Kokar, Paul Kogut, Lewis Hart, Jeffrey Smith, William Holmes, Jerzy Letkowski, Mike Aronson, Extending UML to Support Ontology Engineering for the Semantic Web at the Fourth International Conference on UML (UML 2001), Toronto, October 1–5, 2001.

[3] McIlraith, S., Son, T.C. and Zeng, H. Semantic Web Services. In IEEE Intelligent Systems. Special Issue on the Semantic }Feb. 16(2):46–53, March/April, 2001.

[4] Paul Kogut, Stephen Cranefield, Lewis Hart, Mark Dutra, Kenneth Baclawski, Mieczyslaw Kokar, Jeffrey Smith, UML for Ontology Development , To appear in Knowledge Engineering Review Journal Special Issue on Ontologies in Agent Systems.

[5] Joint US/EU ad hoc Agent Markup Language Committee. Reference description of the DAML+OIL ontology markup language. http://www.daml.org/2001/03/reference, March 2001.

Swarm Intelligent Surfing in the Web

Jie Wu and Karl Aberer

School of Computer and Communication Sciences
Swiss Federal Institute of Technology (EPF), Lausanne
1015 Lausanne, Switzerland
{jie.wu, karl.aberer}@epfl.ch

Abstract. Traditional ranking models used in Web search engines rely on a static snapshot of the Web graph, basically the link structure of the Web documents. However, visitors' browsing activities indicate the importance of a document. In the traditional static models, the information on document importance conveyed by interactive browsing is neglected. The nowadays Web server/surfer model lacks the ability to take advantage of user interaction for document ranking. We enhance the ordinary Web server/surfer model with a mechanism inspired by swarm intelligence to make it possible for the Web servers to interact with Web surfers and thus obtain a proper local ranking of Web documents. The proof-of-concept implementation of our idea demonstrates the potential of our model. The mechanism can be used directly in deployed Web servers which enable on-the-fly creation of rankings for Web documents local to a Web site. The local rankings can also be used[1] as input for the generation of global Web rankings in a decentralized way.

Keywords: swarm intelligence, information retrieval, search engine, ranking, filtering

1 Introduction

Information seeking is social behavior, and it is shaped by factors that operate at the cognitive, affective, and situational levels [5]. No matter whether the seeking occurs on the Web or in a traditional library, it is always guided by perceptions of information quality, accessibility, conditions and requirements of a particular situation. Ranking according to specific aspects of the documents, e.g. the degree of importance, and the profiles and requirements of the users is thus extremely helpful in the process of seeking information.

1.1 Motivation

Traditional ranking models rely on a static snapshot of the Web graph, basically the link structure among the Web pages. While the ranking models of Web search rely on the static snapshot of the Web graph, including the structure and the

---

[1] Please refer to our companion paper [3] on our Ranking Algebra.

J.M. Cueva Lovelle et al. (Eds.): ICWE 2003, LNCS 2722, pp. 431–440, 2003.
© Springer-Verlag Berlin Heidelberg 2003

document content, the information conveyed in the dynamic interactive browsing activities is simply neglected and wasted. However, the relevance judgements collected at browsing-time by Web surfers should be stronger than those obtained from static Web links authored by single Web authors. Basically, the current research on the Web information seeking has the following problems:

1. Methodology: the relationship among the Web documents is studied in a rather static way. The point is the Web is actually a social system with the clients roaming in it and interacting with the Web servers. Thus browsing as natural relevance feedback is ignored. It should be treated in a dynamic way.

2. Model: given the dynamic nature of the Web social system, the existing static document model does not work for high performance information seeking. Thus the relevance implied by the dynamic surfing sessions is not used to modify the weight of the information contained in a document. A new dynamic and intelligent model has to be developed to describe the dynamic interactions.

3. Technical limitation: the nowadays Web server/surfer model lacks an interaction mechanism between the server and the surfer. The Web server plays no active role in the surfer's decision for choosing highly ranked pages for continuing surfing. Although research was done on customized Web proxies, they mainly deal with the collection of user profiles, accessing patterns, etc.. We expect the Web servers to do more than passively answering file requests in helping surfers identify which links or documents are more important and hence valuable in Web browsing.

Thus, we enhance the ordinary Web server/surfer interaction model with a mechanism inspired by swarm intelligence [1] to make it possible for the Web servers to participate actively in the interactive surfing activities and in obtaining a proper ranking of Web documents according to general importance for them. This is done by adding a swarm intelligent module to the Web server architecture to obtain the necessary information and do corresponding analysis on the fly. Thus our approach not only makes use of the traditional criteria such as link structure but also captures the ranking information provided through the dynamic interactive Web browsing activities of the Web surfers. We believe that it is worthwhile to consider a dynamic server/surfer model instead of one of static links for the following reasons:

1. To verify that the group intelligence in a self-organized system at the collective level is higher than that of any individual.

2. To obtain more precise rankings by exploiting surfer's knowledge embedded in the surfing sessions. In short, we want to infer local ranking information from the interactive surfing activities, which is not possible with current Web server implementation and modern search engines.

We first implemented a little game of *quest for treasure* to show how the idea works in the Web in analogy to the ants' hunting for food. Then we developed a module for the Apache Web server version 2. Preliminary experiments show that it is a very interesting way to get the local document ranking, and this proof-of-concept implementation of our idea demonstrates the potential of our new model which can be extended to a distributed architecture in the future.

1.2 Our Contributions

We particularly study a information seeking problem in the Web, i.e. how to intelligently rank Web documents according to the general importance of them. Here are our main contributions:

1. Raising the idea of using dynamic importance information embedded in the interaction between a Web server and surfing users. We argue that the traditional analysis of static Web links does not satisfy the requirements of precise ranking of ever-changing Web documents;
2. Providing a model inspired by Swarm Intelligence to analyze the emergent behavior of the Web activities. Individual surfing activities can collectively demonstrate some kind of group intelligence that is higher than any single one in a self-organized fashion;
3. Applying the idea in the computation of Web documents ranking for search engines. The emergent result of the interactions may also lead to more recent hence valuable ranking than the results produced by traditional algorithms relying on static link analysis;
4. Having developed a module for the successful Apache Web server to realize our idea. The module can be loaded into the popular Web server after simple configuration. After this module is enabled, the Web server can automatically collect and analyze the dynamic interactions between the server and the surfers and generate on-the-fly document rankings on the Web.

2 Web Surfing and Swarm Intelligence

In many situations human beings are not so different from insects. Some aspects in the analogy are: both the food and information resources are unevenly distributed in the nature or on the Web; the resource procurement is dynamically characterized by all sorts of uncertainty and fluctuation; and both searchers have limited time and chance to explore and exploit the resources. Only those who adopt through learning the strategies that maximize their harvest rates can become winners. Thus, in order to forage information on the Web people may consider making use of the collective intelligence also existing in social insects.

2.1 What's Swarm Intelligence All about?

The social insect metaphor has been studied to solve problems for a long time and in many fields [1]. People find that the approaches are good for dealing with problems distributed, direct or indirect interactions among relatively simple agents, flexibility and robustness. For the purpose of clarification, we include a very short summary of swarm intelligence here. More details of Swarm Intelligence can be found in [1] and the website [2].

The scenario is that some ants are looking for food. Suddenly an obstacle appears and interrupts the ants' moving. Now an important step occurs. The ants choose randomly in front of the obstacle to turn right or left at the beginning, but trails of biological pheromones are left on the road when they move on to the destination or go back to the nest. The more ants pass by a road, the more biological trails are left on it. On the other hand, the higher pheromone density a road has, the higher possibility it is chosen by the ants in the future because these insects instinctively follow the pheromones. With more and more ants' hitting the right spot and successfully getting the food back to the nest, on the shortest path from the nest to the food the pheromones will accumulate with the highest density. Thus the shortest optimal path is found finally, and actually formed without any instructions, in a totally self-organizing way.

Swarm intelligence has been reported to have applications in many fields, such as combinatorial optimization, communication networks, robotics, etc.. As far as we know, nobody else or other research groups have tried to apply this idea for Web surfing to obtain ranking of documents for the purpose of information retrieval.

2.2 Analogies of Insects and Web Servers

Let us make the analogies between our model of Web surfing and the biological society more precise. We call the counterpart of biological pheromone in the Web *Web pheromone*.

Social Insects Society	Web System
Ant	Web client/surfer
Food	information on Web pages
Hunting for food	Web browsing
Biological pheromone trail	recorded Web pheromone maintained by the Web server
Interaction	request from the client and reply from the server
Pheromone density	popularity/importance of a Web page

It is easy to imagine that an important page, which will potentially be ranked by ranking algorithms, needs continuous repeated hits to maintain its level of importance. In a decentralized system, self-organization relies on the following four important components:

1. positive feedback (amplification) recruitment to a food source, high probability that many accesses mean good quality of information;
2. negative feedback (counterbalances positive feedback) food source exhaustion, satiation, crowding at food source;
3. fluctuations, random walks, errors;
4. multiple interactions trail-following events interact with trail-laying actions, moreover individuals should make use of their own activities as well as of others' activities.

With respect to Web surfing we can establish these components as follows:

	Source	Provokes
Positive feedback	Results from search engines link recommendations advertisements ranking system	Frequent visits, long term value exhaustive page exploration recommendations to others crowding, server slowdown
Negative feedback	unreadable content overcrowding, slow server no interest	abandon server relief no recommendations
Fluctuations	curiosity surf for fun individual intelligence	discover new pages discover alternative pages optimized paths
Multiple interactions	collectively used information each click leaves trails follow others	adds to collective knowledge profit of other users feedback give and get at the same time

The Web surfers here are the natural agents in a self-organizing system. Surely surfers are not non-intelligent, but as human have only really limited insight on the Web and most of the time can only follow the hyper links created by someone else without any knowledge of the structure of the Web graph, we can safely take the surfers as the primitive agents that abide by simple operation rules.

Furthermore, the Web server here is not only a passive listener to the requests for Web documents, but also an active participant of the self-organizing system by assuming the role of an arbiter who assures the rules are carried on during the interactive interactions between the requesting visitors and the requested Web documents which form together the ecological environment for the self-organizing system.

3   A Swarm Intelligent Web Server

Surfers with certain intelligence usually lack the knowledge of how to wander efficiently around the Web to satisfy their information needs. In the sense of information foraging, we assume the content of Web pages being the persistent prey that the surfers want to forage and every time a surfer visits a page she leaves some Web pheromone, which is maintained by the environment, i.e. the Web server, to it. Upcoming visits to the same page will enhance the density of its Web pheromone if its content is appreciated by the surfers. If the page is not so useful for the surfers, people will certainly not come back and thus the density of the page's Web pheromone will decrease by means of natural evaporation. By integrating a such dynamic self-organizing mechanism into a Web server, we make the server swarm intelligent. We call a Web server that is equipped with our Swarm Intelligent module a *Swarm Intelligent* Web server.

3.1   Interaction Rules

Interaction is one of the most important features in our dynamic server/surfer model. It is different from the traditional collaborative filtering techniques where a user has to, if not forced to, manually choose or input a feedback value usually in numerical range, e.g. 1 to 10, so as to let the server know how the Web page is evaluated by the visitor. On the contrary, in our model, all the feedbacks are collected automatically without any artificial intervention.

We identify the following feedbacks from the visitors to the server. They are kept in the pheromone data structure.

1. Visitors' evaluation over the general importance of a Web documents. This is maintained through the dynamic change of the density variable *phero* of the Web pheromone tuple after the interactions between the intelligent server and surfers.
2. Time of visit. Visits are made at different arrival time, in different frequencies, from different referrer, with different sojourn length. This information can be inferred from a time stamp variable kept as part of the Web pheromone. All these components of a visit pattern bear information of a visitor's evaluation of the visited page.

Worthy of notice, we do not perform any user tracking. We are not interested in the behavior of individual users, rather in the collective phenomena of this social system which is realized by our dynamic server/surfer model.

We also identify the following feedbacks from the server to the visitors:

1. Content enhancement: colorize (or apply other user interface techniques here) according to the pheromone density of the link. Direct real time feedback inside the Web page helps the surfers to make optimal decisions while looking for specific content.
2. Dynamic page headers can be inserted at the top of each served page on the server, for example, 10 pages of a site that have the highest pheromone density.
3. Dynamic link suggestion: pages with similar amount of pheromone; the pages that visitors who bring much pheromone here also go to; etc.

3.2   Pheromone Representation

The most important attribute of Web pheromone is the density which records the trails, and hence the endorsement of Web surfers on the general importance of a document. As the density is always changing (because of evaporation, accumulation, spreading, etc.), a time stamp of the last access is kept together with it to enable the next round of update computation. Thus we store both the density and the time stamp for each document to keep track of its Web pheromone information. Here is our model:

Given the document set D of a Website, the Web pheromones associated with the documents are defined as:

$$p : D \to V \times T$$

where $V = [0, \infty)$, is the real value representing the density of the Web pheromone; and $T = [0, \infty)$, is the last access time, i.e., the update time of the density variable. For convenience, we will use $p_V(d)$ and $p_T(d)$ to denote respectively the density value and the last access time of the Web pheromone associated with document d.

The rules of pheromone update are as follows:

1. Positive update increasing the density. This may happen due to two kinds of interactions in our model: firstly, a surfer comes to the page and brings more Web pheromone, we call this effect *accumulation*; secondly, the Web pheromone of other Web pages is diffused and arrives here, we call this effect *spreading*.
2. Negative update decreasing the density. This happens due to the natural diffusion of the Web pheromone. We call this effect *evaporation*.

Accordingly, the update strategy is composed of three regulations. Worthy of notice is that variations of the policies are possible, and are subject of further study. However we expect that the results would be quite robust as the situation shown in the study of IR models.

Pheromone Accumulation. The Web pheromone changes when a surfer changes in his surfing session from one document to another by following the link between them. In this case the newly accessed page's Web pheromone is increased.

In the current initial experiments we increase the Web pheromone of a page $d \in D$ accessed at time $p_T(d) := t$ by 1,

$$p_V(d) := p_V(d) + 1$$

We might change the policy of how much to increase in future experiments, e.g. based on the origin of the access (if the referrer is an important Web site to combine the concept of Hub and Authority sites), or the user profile (the weight assigned to a visitor according to her trust records). This leaves space for further study.

Pheromone Evaporation. Evaporation is the mechanism for realizing the negative feedback in the environment.

The evaporation property of pheromone information is very important. The simplest but yet most powerful approach to model it, is the use of a half-life time function. A given half-life time value determines the amount of time during which the pheromone density is halved. These parameters can be set heuristically for example to the mean time gap between two hits to a Web page.

Evaporation leads to the following update of pheromone:

$$p_V(d) := p_V(d) \cdot \left(\frac{1}{2}\right)^{\frac{t - p_T(d)}{\delta}}$$

where $p_T(d) := t$ is the time of access, δ is the half-life time value. This update is done before the accumulation is computed.

For example, suppose the $\delta = 1 \, day = 24 \, hours$ and at the time $p_T(d) = Jan. \, 25, \, 2003, \, 12:40, \, p_V(d) = 14.0452$. If there is no new visitor in the following 30 hours, then at $t = Jan. \, 26, \, 2003, \, 18:40$, the new $p_V(d)$ is diminished drastically to 5.9053.

Pheromone Spreading. As described in Kleinberg's paper on hubs and authorities [8], an important (authoritative) page is usually pointed by many other pages and a directory (hub) page usually points to lots of other pages. This situation fits well the natural spreading of biological pheromone. The Web pheromone is spread across the Web links which mimics the conveyance of importance from one page to another.

Assuming $P_1, \cdots, P_k$ where $|P_i| = N_i, i = 1, \cdots, k$ are the k sets of pages that can be reached from document d by following Web links $i = 1, \cdots, k$ times, then we define the pheromone of the document d with spreading as:

$$p_V(d) := p_V(d) + \sum_{i=1}^{k} \sum_{j=1}^{N_i} P_i(j) \times f^i$$

where $P_i(j)$ is the j'th page in the set P_i; and $f \in [0,1)$ is a fading factor for the pheromone spreading. $p_T(d) := t$ is the time when d is accessed, and the update is done after Pheromone Evaporation but before Accumulation.

Spreading of Web pheromones against the direction of links makes the more relevant documents more "attractive" since it will more likely attract surfers, this also parallels the situation of the natural swarm intelligence where insects return to the net by following and leaving more pheromones on the same path.

We define a maximal spreading radius to avoid cycling. For the purpose of simplicity in our proof-of-concept implementation we set the radius to 1.

Both the fading factor and the spreading radius affect the problem of cycle detection and avoidance. However it is a well studied problem in graph theory and its applications for example the Internet routing algorithms, so we don't further investigate it in our model here.

4   Evaluations

Our evaluations include 2 parts. One is called Quest for Treasure. The idea was to start a quest for a treasure in order to see, if in a self-organised system, changes to the environment will result in a collective optimisation of navigation.

We had 12 rooms where the visitors could navigate through. In two of these rooms were treasure chests, which had to be explored. Above each button were the actual pheromone density of the underlying link and the plain visit counter. Visitors had to use for the navigation the density which was computed and shown by the server module. Red numbers remind people that the pheromone there has very high density. After a certain time we could just follow the red links and we found the treasure. The next morning we removed one of the treasure chests, and we could observe that during the next few hours the colors had changed. On the way to the room where we removed the chest the density of pheromone was decreased and the red links again led now to the one and only chest. So we could observe a very simple form of self-organisation by collectively using the Web pheromone information from the server module.

Hence, we demostrate that the swarm of internet surfers is indeed more intelligent than a single surfer.

The other evaluation we made is the comparison between our method and two other popular approaches in the computation of Web document rankings: plain Web counter and PageRank [7]. We call the ranking of Web documents generated by our *Swarm Intelligent* Web server an *Intelligent Ranking* of the documents. We did a small-scale experiment with a lab Web site which has about 200 Web pages in order to explore this possibility. We pre-computed the static PageRank ranking. We installed the module and requested volunteers to surf the site. Basically the visitors are the professors, assistants and students of the university. The experiment lasted for 2 days (because the module is not quite stable and its crash from time to time influences the Web server's functioning).

The results show that the *Intelligent Ranking* is quite different from the PageRank which shows our dynamic model in the social Web plays an important role in generating potentially more precise and recent Web document rankings.

5 Related Works

Related works have been carried on at different levels. The term *information diet* used earlier in this paper is more at the level of social science. Researchers suggest that [6] the optimal selection of Web pages to satisfy a user's information needs is a kind of optimal information diet problem. Because of these social aspects of the Web information, search engines and information extraction from unstructured sources become extremely important. Two prominent algorithms, HITS [8], and the PageRank [7] are found important. But both of them have their limitations and are not suitable for doing search in a decentralized environment. [3]

At a more technical level, collaborative filtering and relevance feedback techniques are studied. Collaborative filtering is basically a technology for distribution of opinions and ideas in society and facilitating contacts between people with similar interests [4]. It is in fact not directly related to information retrieval, rather a mate of IR, i.e. a way to help people look for information of desire.

Relevance Feedback is tightly related with Collaborative Filtering. Visitors are provided a form to input their evaluation over the Web document in a range of 1 to 10 usually. This sort of system often works as an extension to a Web browser. For example, in the Ant World system [9], which also uses the term pheromone in its Digital Information Pheromones (DIP), when a user starting her quest, she formulates the goals of the quest in a short description, similar to a search engine query, and an optional long description, resembling a TREC query. As the user browses the Web, a small "console window" hovers on top of the screen, soliciting the user's opinion on the usefulness of the pages she visits for the goals of her quest. But this kind of system is quite inconvenient for the end users. It bothers the users to input manually evaluation values or descriptions for every Web page she visits. Its practical significance is limited for this reason. On the other hand our approach does not impose any extra requirements on the surfers in their surfing sessions.

6   Conclusion

In this paper, we propose the idea of using swarm intelligence in the context of learning and mining of the Web. We define a model of users' interaction with a Web server with regard to the accesses to Web documents. We explained the concepts, and the strategies we adopt in the proof-of-concept implementation. We verify our idea in two aspects: one to show that collective intelligence is feasible to obtain and it is better than any single one in a self-organized system; the other to obtain meaningful ranking for Web documents on a Web server. We expect more promising results in the future to demonstrate the significance of social intelligence in the field of Web.

References

1. Eric Bonabeau, Marco Dorigo, Guy Theraulaz, "Swarm Intelligence: From Natural to Artificial Systems", Oxford University Press, 1999.
2. http://iridia.ulb.ac.be/ ants/
3. Karl Aberer, Jie Wu, "A Framework for Decentralized Ranking in Web Information Retrieval", The Fifth Asia Pacific Web Conference, APWeb 2003, Xi'an, China, 23–25 April 2003.
4. Alexander Chislenko, "Automated Collaborative Filtering and Semantic Transports", http://www.lucifer.com/ sasha/articles/ACF.html, 1997.
5. Chun Wei Choo, Brian Detlor, Don Turnbull, "Web Work: Information Seeking and Knowledge Work on the World Wide Web", Kluwer Academic Publishers, 2000.
6. Peter Pirolli, James Pitkow, Ramana Rao, "Silk from a Sow's Ear: Extracting Usable Structures from the Web", Conference on Human Factors in Computing Systems, CHI-96, Vancouver, British Columbia, Canada, 13–18 April 1996.
7. Larry Page, Sergey Brin, Rajeev Motwani, Terry Winograd, "The PageRank Citation Ranking: Bringing Order to the Web", Technical report, Stanford, Jan. 1998.
8. Jon Kleinberg, "Authoritative Sources in a Hyperlinked Environment", in *Proceedings of the ACM-SIAM Symposium on Discrete Algorithms*, 1998.
9. Paul Kantor, Endre Boros, Ben Melamed, Dave Neu, Vladimir Menkov, Qin Shi, Myung-Ho Kim, "Ant World", in *Proceedings of SIGIR'99 (22nd International Conference on Research and Development in Information Retrieval)*, 1999.

The Cooperative Web: A Step towards Web Intelligence

Daniel Gayo-Avello, Darío Álvarez-Gutiérrez, Agustín Cernuda-del-Río,
José Gayo-Avello, Luis Vinuesa-Martínez, and Néstor García-Fernández

Department of Informatics, University of Oviedo, Calvo Sotelo s/n 33007 Oviedo (SPAIN)
{dani, darioa, guti, vinuesa, nestor}@lsi.uniovi.es

Abstract. The Web is mainly processed by humans. The role of the machines is just to transmit and display the contents of the documents, barely being able to do something else. Nowadays there are lots of initiatives trying to change this situation; many of them are related to fields like the Semantic Web or Web Intelligence. This paper describes a new proposal towards Web Intelligence: the Cooperative Web, which would allow us to extract semantics from the Web in an automatic way, without the need of ontological artifacts, with language independence and, besides of this, allowing the usage of browsing experience from individual users to serve the whole community of users.

1   Introduction

Although the Web provides access to a huge amount of information it is not a perfect information retrieval mechanism. Search engines perform a really useful task but we can say that they are toping out since they provide a view of the Web quite poor to get a more powerful use. Besides of this, the current Web shows a problem as serious as its lack of semantics: each time a user browses the Web, he opens a path which could be useful for others and, in the same way, other users can have yet followed such path and have found its worth or its uselessness. However, all that experimental knowledge is lost. Through this paper we will show how we think this situation can be changed in order to provide intelligence and semantics to the Web in an automatic way.

2   The Web as an Information Retrieval System

The main goal of the Web was to avoid the loss of information as well as making the access to it easier. The initial proposal [1] suggested developing the Web starting from a semantic ground showing the drawbacks of keyword-based information retrieval. However, the Web was finally developed in a simpler way, similar to traditional hypertext and with no document retrieval mechanisms.

In 1994 first search engines appeared. They showed that links directories were not enough, albeit they raised two problems: (1) The users had to try their queries with several search engines. (2) Most of the returned documents had little relevance.

J.M. Cueva Lovelle et al. (Eds.): ICWE 2003, LNCS 2722, pp. 441–444, 2003.
© Springer-Verlag Berlin Heidelberg 2003

The main problem of the pair Web + search engines remains in the use of keyword-based queries. It is known that the probability of two users employing the same keyword to refer a unique concept is below 20% [2]. So, if the query keywords are only looked for in the HTML META tags or in the document title the results are quite poor while if the search is performed using free text from the documents the recall is larger but at the expense of a serious lack of precision [3] that lies, mainly, in the ambiguity of the words, even in well defined domains [4].

3   The Semantic Web

In spite of better search engines, the increasing number of documents hinders the precision of the results and keeps the users under a flood of information. In 1998 Tim Berners-Lee started to outline the Semantic Web. The main idea is to mark up the documents on the Web with "semantic tags" that would provide metainformation about the tagged text. In a sense, this idea is quite similar to the use of "concept nodes" described in the original Web proposal [1] and now again the crux of the matter is the way to provide such semantic tags and state the relationships between them. To perform this task ontologies and ontological languages are used.

Other approaches were proposed before the Semantic Web itself and have contributed greatly to it (e.g. SHOE [5], and Ontobroker [6]). Later, a more elaborated version of the Semantic Web [7] was introduced; in this one, ontologies take a leading role similar to the one played in the proposals mentioned above.

The Semantic Web is not widespread enough as to provide search engines comparable to those from traditional Web. However, some solutions have been proposed (e.g. SquishQL [8] or RQL/Sesame [9]). In spite of differences on syntax or architecture, these "search engines" can be seen as a kind of inference engines that accept queries expressed in terms of one or more ontologies and return as results objects belonging to such ontologies. Thus, the Semantic Web depends heavily on ontologies; because of that, many efforts are being made to provide semi-automatic generation of ontologies [10] and automatic semantic markup of documents [11].

We think that the Semantic Web will make the access to information much easier in well-defined environments such as corporate intranets but it would be really difficult to apply the same techniques to the Web as a whole.

4   The Cooperative Web

Traditional keyword-based approaches to fight against information overload are not suitable to help the user in his information searches on the Web. As for the Semantic Web, it will play a vital role in well-defined domains but it is difficult to apply it to the whole Web in an automatic way. Thus, we propose a complementary solution to contribute towards the Web Intelligence, the so-called Cooperative Web:

"The Cooperative Web is a layer on top of the current Web to give it semantics in an automatic, global, transparent and language independent way. It does not require explicit user participation but implicit feedback that would be acquired by software agents. The Cooperative Web relies on the use of concepts and document taxonomies, both of them can be obtained with no human supervision from free text."

Keywords provide poor information retrieval while ontologies can improve precision. However, developing ontologies to support any query on the Web would be really hard. There is a middle point: the use of concepts. A concept would be a more abstract entity than a keyword. It would not require complex artifacts such as ontology languages or inference systems. A concept can be seen as a cluster of words with related meaning in a given scope, ignoring tense, gender, and number. We think that techniques such as Latent Semantic Indexing [12] or concept indexing [13] could serve to automatically generate and process concepts.

So, the Cooperative Web would use the whole text of the document without using any markup as the source for semantic meaning. How could this be done without the need to "understand" the text? A document can be seen as an individual from a population. Among living beings an individual is defined by its genome, which is composed of chromosomes, divided into genes constructed upon genetic bases. Alike, documents are composed of passages, divided into sentences built upon concepts.

Using this analogy, it seems clear that two documents are semantically related if their "genome" is alike. Big differences between genomes mean that the semantic relationship between documents is weak. We think that it is possible to adapt some algorithms used in computational biology to the field of document classification. The important thing about such a classification is that it would provide semantics without requiring the classification process to use any. In fact, it should be able to cluster documents in categories similar to the ones that a person would build.

Besides this, the Cooperative Web intends to employ user browsing experience, extracting useful semantics from it. Each user in the Cooperative Web would have an agent that would learn from its master (building a user profile) and retrieve information for him. Having each user attached to a profile, it is possible to assign to each pair (`profile, document`) a utility level. In order for this utility valuation to be really practical, the utility level should be determined in an implicit way.

The agent would have two ways to perform information retrieval: to retrieve information for a query formulated by the user, or to explore in the background on his behalf to recommend him unknown documents. To perform both tasks we want to employ two well-known techniques: Collaborative Filtering (CF) and Content-Based Recommendation (CBR). If the agent uses CF it would recommend the user documents that have obtained a high utility level from users with similar profiles. If the agent uses CBR it would retrieve documents that would be conceptually related with the user profile, a query or an initial document, without priorizing the utility level.

5   Conclusion

We have described a proposal to provide Web Intelligence: the Cooperative Web. We have compared it with the Semantic Web to avoid information overload in the Internet. In more detail we have describe the information retrieval techniques that the Cooperative Web could provide. If they are compared with modern search engines we think it is clear that our proposal would obtain less but more relevant results since it would employ conceptual taxonomies.

Many researchers involved in the Web Intelligence field share similar views and proposals. Nishida introduces the concept of "virtualized ego" [14], software agents quite similar to the ones proposed for the Cooperative Web. Han and Chang explain the need for automatic building of documents taxonomies [15]. Cercone et al state the relevance of recommender systems and software agents in the Intelligent Web [16].

References

1. Berners-Lee, T.: Information Management: A Proposal
    http://www.w3.org/History/1989/proposal.html (1989)
2. Furnas, G.W., Landauer, T.K., Gómez, L.M., Dumais, S.T.: The vocabulary problem in human-system communication. CACM, Vol. 30, No. 11 (1987) 964–971
3. Pinkerton, B.: Finding what people want: Experiences with the WebCrawler. Proc. of the Second International World Wide Web Conference. Chicago, IL, USA (1994)
4. Krovetz, R., Croft, W.B.: Lexical Ambiguity and Information Retrieval. ACM Transactions on Information Systems, Vol. 10, No. 2 (1992) 115–141
5. Luke, S., Spector, L., Rager, D.: Ontology-Based Knowledge Discovery on the World-Wide Web. Working Notes of the Workshop on Internet-Based Information Systems at the 13th National Conference on Artificial Intelligence (AAAI96) (1996)
6. Fensel, D., Decker, S., Erdmann, M., Studer, R.: Ontobroker: Or How to Enable Intelligent Access to the WWW. Proc. of the 11th Workshop on Knowledge Acquisition, Modeling, and Management. Banff, Canada (1998)
7. Berners-Lee, T., Hendler, J., Lassila, O.: The Semantic Web. Scientific American, 284 (5) (2001) 34–43
8. Brickley, D., Miller, L.: RDF: Extending and Querying RSS channels. ILRT discussion document. http://ilrt.org/discovery/2000/11/rss-query/ (2000)
9. Karvounarakis, G, Christophides, V., Plexousakis, D., Alexaki, S.: Querying RDF Descriptions for Community Web Portals. The French National Conference on Databases. Agadir, Maroc (2001)
10. Maedche, A., Staab, S.: Discovering Conceptual Relations from Text. Technical Report 399". Institute AIFB, Karlsruhe University (2000)
11. Erdmann, M., Maedche, A., Scnurr, H.P., Staab, S.: From Manual to Semi-automatic Semantic Annotation: About Ontology-based Text Annotation Tools. ETAI Journal - Section on Semantic Web (Linköping Electronic Articles in Computer and Information Science), 6 (2001)
12. Foltz, P.W.: Using Latent Semantic Indexing for Information Filtering. Proc. of the ACM Conference on Office Information Systems. Boston, USA (1990) 40–47
13. Karypis, G., Han, E.: Concept indexing: A fast dimensionality reduction algorithm with applications to document retrieval and categorization. Technical Report TR-00-0016. University of Minnesota (2000)
14. Nishida, T.: Social Intelligence Design for the Web. IEEE Computer, IEEE Computer Society, Washington, D.C., 35(11) (2002) 37–41
15. Han, J., Chang, K.C.-C.: Data Mining for Web Intelligence. IEEE Computer, IEEE Computer Society, Washington, D.C., 35(11) (2002) 64–70
16. Cercone, N., Hou, L., Keselj, V., An, A., Naruedomkul, K., Hu, X.: From Computational Intelligence to Web Intelligence. IEEE Computer, IEEE Computer Society, Washington, D.C., 35(11) (2002) 72–76

Partitioning the Navigational Model:
A Component-Driven Approach

Stephen Kerr and Daniel M. German

Department of Computer Science,
University of Victoria,
{skerr,dmgerman}@cs.uvic.ca

Abstract. This paper proposes using a Component Approach to model navigation
in a hypertext application. It proposes Navigational Semantic Units (NSUs), which
are component-oriented units that describe some meaning of navigation from the
user's perspective. The NSUs are an abstraction of a navigational model and are
the basis for a methodology to design hypermedia applications based on the Model
View Controller Architecture.

1 Introduction

Component-oriented software design and implementation is an established school within
the software engineering community. Partitioning of software applications into components is left to the designer who uses experience, domain knowledge, and judgement in
order to define the responsibilities, tasks, and interaction of components within a software
system. Hypermedia applications can benefit from component-oriented techniques to develop, test, and maintain complex systems with greater ease. In models such as OOHDM
and RMM, the hyper-model is generally viewed as a single unit. A large hyper-model
becomes complex as the navigational paths of associative links, structural links, and
navigational design patterns are employed to encompass all possible user navigational
requirements. The relationships between pages must be understood in order for maintenance operations to be successful. Unfortunately, it is difficult to track all the incoming
links to a page. Unless aggressive management is used, the implementation of complex
models diverges from documentation over time. Over time the navigational paths may
change, associative links become invalid, and content become obsolete. Complexity of
model and implementation is an issue of large hyper-media systems. By partitioning a
hyper-model, the partitions can be modelled individually. The internal models are less
complex because the number of inter-related pages (or nodes) is smaller within a partition
than the number of inter-related pages in the whole hyper-model. These characteristics
will make maintenance easier.

2 Partitioning the Hypermedia Navigational Space

A problem with not partitioning the hypermedia model is that the information space of
a hypermedia application in terms of the number of entities, data elements, and data
instances can become very large. A partitioning of the hypermedia system can alleviate

J.M. Cueva Lovelle et al. (Eds.): ICWE 2003, LNCS 2722, pp. 445–448, 2003.
© Springer-Verlag Berlin Heidelberg 2003

the complexity by endorsing the "divide and conquer" philosophy. If we are to introduce a partitioning system, it must still be able to provide associative and referential links between data. The partitioned system will also need to have some navigational structure that will allow the user to traverse the partitions or the areas of important data within an application. Most importantly, the partitioning must allow a designer to create and a coder to implement a large complex system with greater ease than an equivalent system that does not have a partitioning system. The number of components will depend on the scope of the application, its overall size, and the number of natural partitions. It is always possible to partition a given hypermedia application. The partitioning might occur on a site, server, directory, or domain name level. In many design models the notion of a view over the hyper-base can be considered as a partition. OOHDM Abstract Data Views (ADVs), RMM slices or Abstract Design Perspectives (ADP) [1] are groupings, partitions, or collections of data for various different purposes and they enable a designer to deal with conceptual design issues in sections smaller than the entire hypermedia application.

Hypermedia applications are both information presentation applications and functional applications. Many systems employ some sort of dialogue with the user beyond allowing the user to choose navigational paths. Users can also modify, delete, or append information. A partitioning system must be able to encompass both the functions and information presentation needs of the application. The hypermedia space needs to be partitioned into units that are large enough to be useful but not too large to be unwieldy. The elements within a partition need to have some commonality. This commonality can be units of instantiation, units of fault containment, or units of locality.

2.1   Partitioning the Hypermedia Navigational Space Using a Granularity of Abstraction

Using a granularity of abstraction, the hyper-application can be partitioned according to the concept of Navigational Semantic Units (NSU). The NSU is centered on the user's intention when navigating through a hypermedia application. The NSU can be an entity, or represent a task, or be a combination of tasks and entities. How to separate intentions becomes a difficult task. The person who designs the application will have to decide the extent of each component. Cheeseman [2] partitions components by using use case models and business concept models, then separates system services from business services. The business concept model is refined into a business type model, and this is used to develop a set of business interfaces. The components are then implemented to support the interfaces. The "core" business types have independent existence and are characterized as business identifiers that have no mandatory associations except to a categorizing type (i.e. a pointer to another type that is not an aggregation or composition association) [2]. Hypermedia applications can be similarly partitioned, with an emphasis on using Navigational Semantic Units as the level of granularity of a component. The NSUs can be considered as "core" business types. Employing navigational use cases and a Navigational Class Model to initially define the components, similar to the methodology suggested by Cheeseman, greatly increases the likelihood of the designer identifying successful partitions. An NSU represents a user's intention. NSUs themselves, however, can be viewed as abstracted entities. These entities are not necessarily concepts related to the underlying domain information structure [3]. The NSU's are an abstraction of a combination of the elements of the Business Concept Model and elements of the use case model, with a further "intuitive" aspect of user intention. The following are the three main types of components that constitute a hypermedia application:

NSU Components. The majority of the components in a hypermedia application are expected to be NSU components. These components will consist of a session bean that contains all the dynamic data to be displayed, the dynamic links, the actions that constitute the interface, and the views to display the data. The NSU components can provide associative paths to other parts of the same NSU or to specific information in other NSUs.

Structural Components. The Structural Components are those that provide navigational paths between the components. The Structural Components render the menus needed to facilitate the structural navigation. The extensibility of the component framework is dependent upon the navigational structure of the application.

Business Process components. The Business Process Components are those logic components that reside in the presentation layer. These components may have some sort of presentation (views), but are generally used by NSUs or Structural Components in order to affect some aspect of the presentation. Such aspects might be user tracking, user profiling, user configuration, etc. Business Process Components will typically handle user login and authorization, and any other business processing needed that falls outside the NSU components or is applicable to the entire application.

3   A Component-Based Hypermedia Development Model

We propose the following steps for a component-based hypermedia development model:
Step 1. DOM Design–Navigational Model. All the information that is needed in the hyper-application might not be known, but an initial DOM can be built. The designer must determine the data and relationships that exist in the underlying system that are needed in the hypermedia application. The data and relationships can be: 1) a *Class diagram of the underlying application* that describes the information that is needed by the application; 2) *Use Case Diagrams* that describe all the tasks that encompass the Web site; and 3) a *Model Class Diagram* of the DOM that will describe the information that is to be displayed in the Web site. The DOM contains the entities and their operations as viewed from a presentation or user perspective.
Step 2: Conceptual Grouping. The designer must determine the conceptual grouping in the same manner as components are determined. The groupings can consist of Navigational Nodes that are strongly related to each other in terms of the user's intentions or functionality. The Nodes are grouped into NSU units. The NSU can contain information from all the classes in the DOM.
Step 3: Navigation Requirements. Determine navigation needs: 1) Determine structural navigational needs (navigation between NSUs) and create structural components; 2) determine associative needs (calls to information in NSUs, outgoing links to other NSUs); and 3) determine functional needs (within components).
Step 4: Component Requirements. Refine the conceptual boundaries of the component. This will drive the data and display requirements: 1) determine page templates; 2)

for functional processes, determine the HTML forms (use case diagrams of functional processes will give insight about the needed pages /steps); 3) determine navigation within components.

Step 5: Component Interface Design. The interface contains the operation specifications for what the component needs to display. For each page that is meant to be accessible by incoming links, assign an action and determine the parameters needed to gather the information for the view. The interface services calls from within the component and from other components

Step 6: Session Data Design. Determine what data needs to be available for each view in terms of data from the underlying application, titles, and labels. Determine calls or other data retrieval procedures needed to get the required data. Each data element will be represented in a session bean. This includes data structures to hold the results of searches and collections of information.

Step 7: Construction of the Presentation. Construct view frameworks (template pages) to display the data. These would typically be either JSP pages or programs to generate HTML. A framework can be reused to display different data. The view should contain no processing of data, only code to drive the display such as "mode" sensitive branching (i.e. toggle attributes).

Step 8: Displaying the Data. Determine specific display details. A page can be considered as an observed composite that has a set of perspectives. The data can be displayed differently for different users depending on their access to data, their preferences, or even the previously viewed component.

4   Conclusion

This paper proposes a conceptual paradigm for partitioning a hypermedia application. Using a granularity of abstraction based on Navigational Semantic Units, a designer can construct a set of hypermedia components that can be individually constructed and maintained. Three types of components are introduced: the NSU, the Structural Component, and the Business Process component. Each of these components reside in the presentation layer. A methodology to construct the components is suggested. The methodology is similar to a typical component construction methodology. Use case diagrams, component dependency diagrams, and class diagrams are used as examples to guide the specification of the components.

References

1. German, D.: Hadez, a Framework for the Specification and Verification of Hypermedia Applications. PhD thesis, University of Waterloo (2000)
2. Cheeseman, J., Daniels, J.: UML Components: A Simple Process for Specifying Component-Based Software. Addison-Wesley (2001)
3. Cachero, C., Koch, N., Gomez, J., Pastor, O.: Conceptual navigation analysis: a device and platform independent navigation specification. In: 2nd International Workshop on Web Oriented Software Technology. (2002)

A Component-Oriented Framework for the Implementation of Navigational Design Patterns

Mohammed Abul Khayes Akanda and Daniel M. German

Department of Computer Science,
University of Victoria,
{makanda,dmgerman}@uvic.ca

Abstract. In this paper, we describe a framework for the implementation of Web applications based on navigational design patterns. This framework is being implemented as a collection of Java classes that can be easily parameterized or inherited in order to instantiate a given design pattern.

Keywords: Design Patterns, navigational design, reuse, components.

1 Introduction

A design pattern "describes a problem which occurs over and over again and then describes a solution to that problem, in such a way that you can use this solution a million times over, without ever doing it the same way twice" [1]. A design pattern attempts to collect experience from the expert to pass on to other experts or novices in the field, hence avoiding reinvention by others. The navigational structure of a Web application can be improved using navigational design patterns. For example, the pattern *Set-Based Navigation* appears in almost any application. A generalized implementation of this pattern can therefore be instantiated over and over again.

2 A Framework for the Implementation of Navigational Design Patterns

We are in the process of building a framework for the implementation of a set of navigational design patterns in Java, using the Apache Tomcat server. Our framework implements the following design patterns, which we considered to be some of the most commonly used: *Active Reference, Set-Based Navigation, Landmark, News, Shopping Basket, History, Guided Tour, Selectable Search Space* [2]. The architecture of the framework is depicted in figure 1. The three main components are: 1) Client (presentation tier) which is responsible of creating the HTML pages that are sent to the client; 2) Server (middle tier) that processes the request from the client, and it is responsible of calling the corresponding Java class that implements the design pattern; and 3) data tier which contains the application database and the parameterization for the instanstiation of the patterns.

J.M. Cueva Lovelle et al. (Eds.): ICWE 2003, LNCS 2722, pp. 449–450, 2003.
© Springer-Verlag Berlin Heidelberg 2003

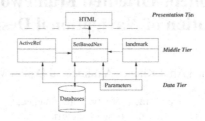

Fig. 1. The architecture of the framework

3 Reuse

The main objective of our framework is to achieve Alexander's goal of using "this solution a million times over, without ever doing it the same way twice" [1]. We do it by using two different approaches: parameterization, and inheritance.

Parameterization. Any design pattern can be parameterized via a two configuration files, one for navigation: *Navigation Parameters*, and another for presentation: *Presentation Parameters*. The *Navigation Parameters* describe the type of navigational object that the pattern is going to be used upon. In its simplest instance, it describes how the pattern instance should retrieve the data from a given database. The *Presentation Parameters* determine how the pattern will look when it is instantiated. For instance, for set-based navigation, it specifies how the table of contents of the set is created and displayed, for each element (e.g. a book) , which of its attributes are shown (title, authors, year of publication) and typeset (e.g. font type, size, color, etc). This parameterization is done via XML documents and XSL and CSS style-sheets.

Inheritance. Further configuration can be achieved by creating a subclass of the design pattern, in order to achieve any special behavior.

4 Current and Further Work

We are actively developing our framework. Our goal is to provide a library of java servlets that is ready to be used, and, if necessary, further extended (using inheritance and parameterization) to implement features not available in our implementation. We are also interested in creating actual Web applications so we can evaluate, first, their effectiveness (how useful they are), and second, their practicality (how easy to implement they are). Patterns are gaining popularity for hypermedia applications and a reusable implementation of those patterns will increase their use.

References

1. Christopher Alexander, Sara Ishakawa, and Murray Silverstein. *A Pattern Language.* Oxford University Press, New York, 1977.
2. D. M. German and D. D. Cowan. Towards a unified catalog of hypermedia design patterns. In *Proceedings of the 33th Hawaii International Conference on System Sciences*, Jan. 2000.

An Internet-Based Collaborative Engineering System

Hwagyoo Park

School of Management, Kyungdong University
San 91-1, Bongpo, Toseong, Goseong, Gangwon-Do, 219-832, Korea
hkpark@k1.ac.kr

Abstract. In the global competition of the 21st century manufacturing industry, collaborative engineering over the Internet is typically defined as the approach to integrating and exchanging manufacturing and design processes to shorten the product development cycle and reduce the cost as well as to provide a product that better meets the customer's expectations. The e-commerce technologies will have a profound impact on the practice and performance of the collaboration in engineering domain. In this paper, we propose an Internet-based collaborative engineering system in which decisions on product design, process design and manufacturing system design are simultaneously made at an initial phase of product development period over the Internet. The system is likely to help improve the engineering product development capability and quality over the Internet.

1 Introduction

As Internet-based collaborative engineering has become a major product development practice of the 21centry in the world class manufacturing, both small and large manufacturers are increasingly adopting the philosophy in designing and developing new products to shorten product development time while maintaining higher product quality, lower manufacturing costs, and satisfying customer's requirements ([2], [10]). Major obstacle to achieving this goal is the nature of distribution in collaboration [8]. There are three main distribution dimensions affecting collaborative work ([3], [4], [7], [10]). One is the geographical dimension, meaning that a project team consists of members from different localities. Another dimension is the disciplinary specialization. That is, team members usually come from diverse disciplines, each with particular expertise and contributing from their relevant areas. The third is the time dimension, implying that different team members participate in the project when available but not necessarily at the same time ([1], [6], [8]). These three issues must be effectively dealt with if the project is to succeed. With this motivation, we propose a framework of the Internet-based collaborative engineering system in which decisions on product design, process design and manufacturing system design are simultaneously made at an initial stage of product development period.

The product design agent develops a prototype of a knowledge-based design decision process using a feature-based solid modeling system. The feature-based product model [9] data are transferred to the process design agent to provide a generative process plan including manufacturing process selection, tool selection,

J.M. Cueva Lovelle et al. (Eds.): ICWE 2003, LNCS 2722, pp. 451–454, 2003.
© Springer-Verlag Berlin Heidelberg 2003

technical parameter determination, and operation sequencing. The system design agent constructs an animated simulation model to establish performance measures, diagnose system performance, detect any bottleneck processes, and eventually propose the optimal system layout. Finally, the central control agent contains a control manager and a blackboard to provide primary controls of redesign processes and resolution of conflicts that may occur in the concurrent design decisions among three major agents.

As depicted in Fig. 1 above, the proposed system consists of four major agents. The system components and their functions are as follows.
- Product design agent to model a redesign process
- Process design agent to generate an automated process plan
- Manufacturing system design agent to provide an optimal manufacturing system layout
- Central control agent to control and coordinate the above three agents

The product design agent, process design agent and manufacturing system design agent individually contain domain knowledge bases and databases needed for solving their own problems, and the central control agent uses control knowledge sources to manage the concurrency and collaboration among three main agents.

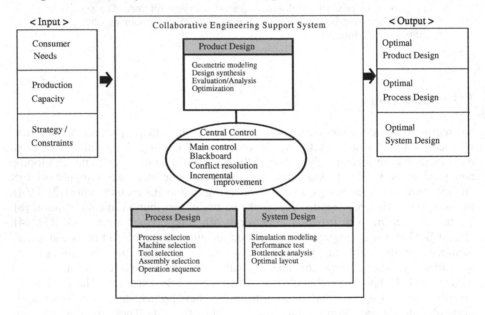

Fig. 1. Schematic Diagram of System Components

2 Implementation Case

The system was constructed as a Web server based on Internet Information Server (IIS) 4.0 for multi-users such as design, manufacturing or system administration expertise. These users can access the system through Web browsers that belong to the client. The Visual Basic script based on DCOM technology [5] was used primarily for implementation. The database was developed with Microsoft SQL Server 6.5.

Implementation of the collaborative engineering system is described by the use of the real-life case for an escalator industry company in South Korea in this section. For the purpose of confidentiality, the company is referred as "H manufacturing company". Fig. 2 shows part design choice processes in the system.

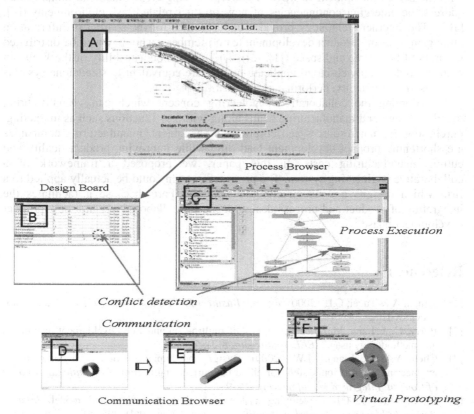

Fig. 2. System Implementation for "H Company"

"A" shows customer's part design specifications to generate design candidates by typing in escalator type and design part selection. The product design agent develops a prototype of a knowledge-based design decision process using a feature-based solid modeling system. The feature-based product model data are transferred to the process design agent to provide the design candidates as shown in "B". "E" shows final design output after checking conflict detection of "C" and "D" to see if selected part specifications are geometrically permitted for the required escalator type.

The representation of design geometry, including ideal geometry and geometric accuracy is generated. The parts relations between design descriptions and geometric descriptions are described as rules. "E" shows the most cost and time effective design for selected parts, gearbox example. It is found out using the optimization search scheme based on classification. Based on these, a virtual prototyping for the gear set is completed. Finally, the most cost and build effective design satisfies the design requirement and requires minimizing production cost, time, and manufacturability.

3 Conclusions

The issue on improving collaborative engineering performance is closely associated with the search for innovative ways of conceptualizing cross-functional linkages that address the emerging contingencies of new product related task environments ([8], [10]). The Internet technology provides opportunities for the sharing of information among engineering product development team members, who may well be distributed in terms of both time and space ([1], [2]). The multimedia capability of the Web can be used to develop web-based applications that are equivalent to standalone systems in terms of functionality, performance and usability.

By adopting the collaborative engineering concept which can virtually bring together design and manufacturing teams along with key functions such as marketing, purchasing, human resources and corporate management, manufacturing companies are shortening product development lead time while improving product quality and cutting manufacturing costs. In this paper, we proposed a framework of a collaborative engineering system. The proposed system could be actually applied to a firm which designs and manufactures mechanical parts because it facilitates the integration of product and process design decisions collaboratively at a new product development phase.

References

[1]   Afuah, A & Tucci, C.L. (2000). *Internet Business Models and Strategies: Text and Cases*. McGraw-Hill.
[2]   Barry, C. & Lang, M. (2001). A survey of multimedia and web development techniques and methodology usage. *IEEE Multimedia*, 8(2), 52–60.
[3]   Chen, Y.M. & Liang, M.W. (2000). Design and implementation of a collaborative engineering information system for allied concurrent engineering. *International Journal of Comput. Integrated Manufacturing, 16*, 9–27.
[4]   Cunliffe, D., (2000). Developing usable web sites: A review and model. *Internet Research: Electronic Networking Applications and Policy*, 10(4), 295–307.
[5]   Eddon, G. & Eddon, H. (1998). *Inside Distributed COM*, Microsoft Press.
[6]   Ginige, A. & Murugesan, S. (2001). Web engineering: an introduction. *IEEE Multimedia*, 8(1), 14–18.
[7]   O'Brien, A., (1998). An intelligent component model for building design, *Second European Conference on Product and Process Modelling in the Building Industry, 19th-21st, Oct.*
[8]   Rosenman, M.A. & Wang, F.J. (1999). CADOM: a Component Agent Model based Design-Oriented Model for Collaborative Design, *Research in Engineering Design II*, 193–205.
[9]   Shah, J. J. (1991). Assessment of Features Technology. *Computer-Aided Design, . 23* (5), 331–343.
[10] Seybold, P.B. (2001). Get inside the lives of your customers. *Harvard Business Review*, May, 81–88.

Data Integration Based WWW with XML and CORBA

Zhengding Lu [1] and Suzhi Zhang [1,2]

[1] College of Computer science and Technology, Huazhong University
of Science and technology, Wuhan, Hubei, China, 430074
zhsuzhi@sohu.com
[2] Department of Computer science and Technology, ZhengZhou Institute
of Light Industry, Zhengzhou, Henan, China, 450002
zhsuzhi@sina.com

Abstract. At the present time, WWW is becoming important and potential resources for delivering and sharing information over the world, and more and more Web applications require querying and integrating the data from multiple, distributed, heterogeneous sources. Web data integration is a challenging research project. In this paper, we propose the architecture of Web data integration with XML and CORBA, which is based on our developing project, *Panorama*. The architecture can integrate the data from multiple data sources, including relational database, object-oriented database, HTML and XML documents, and structured text files. In the architecture, we view Web as a huge database, and take CORBA as object model and XML as mediated data model, and use XML-QL to accomplish data query and integration on the Web. We also elaborate and analyze some implementing methods, such as integrator and wrappers corresponding to various data sources.

1 Introduction

With the increasing of application requirements and development of network technology, more and more users expect to access and manipulate the data from multiple data sources[3][4]. WWW is becoming important and potential resources for delivering and sharing information over the world. The resources on the Web involve not only conventional database, such as relational database and object-oriented database, which have well-form data model, but also unstructured and semi-structured data. It is difficult to store and manage all the Web data with conventional database technology, because of its irregularity and various forms of the web data. How to integrate the data from distributed, heterogeneous, and multiple data sources on the Web into an available whole is a full of challenges and urgent work to many application and enterprises[4][6].

In this paper, we propose our architecture of Web data integration with XML and CORBA, which is based on our developing project, *Panorama*. In the architecture, we view Web as a huge database, and take CORBA as object model, and XML as common data model (CDM), and use XML-QL[3] to accomplish data query and integration on the Web.

J.M. Cueva Lovelle et al. (Eds.): ICWE 2003, LNCS 2722, pp. 455–458, 2003.
© Springer-Verlag Berlin Heidelberg 2003

2 XML Data Management Basis

2.1 Classification of XML Documents

We can look at XML documents in two ways[1]. One is data-centric document, which are regular in structure and homogeneous in content. The other is document-centric document, which is more irregular and data are heterogeneous. Specially, we consider a data-centric document to be a database, called XML database, In which the structured data is called XML data, and its conformed DTD is regarded as schema in this paper[2].

2.2 XML Data Model

XML data are similar to semi-structured data. We can say XML data are semi-structured data on the Web. XML data model is a graph/tree model, and divided into an unordered data model and an ordered data model [3].

2.3 Querying and Transforming XML Data

XML data is fundamentally different from conventional relational and object-oriented data, and therefore, neither SQL nor OQL is appropriate for XML data. XML-QL is a kind of querying language for XML developed by AT&T lab, which can be used for data extraction, transformation and integration.

Due to take XML data model as Common Data Model (CDM) in our architecture, it arose the transformation to XML data model from others. These transformations are implemented by wrappers respectively in our architecture.

3 System Architecture

We proposed our architecture of Web data integration based on the discussion and analysis above, depicted in Fig. 1.

In the architecture, we take XML data model as mediated model and XML-QL as query language to complete data query, schema transformation and data integration against various data sources on the Web. The main program modules involve: *Application and Visual User Interface, XML-QL Querying Processor, XML Data Integrator, Metadata Dictionary* and *Wrappers* corresponding to various data sources.

4 Implementation and Method

4.1 Implementation of Integrator

Integrator is used to combine the multiple mediated results (XML data) which come from the wrappers of local data sources into a whole in the global schema, which is formed a virtual database. Because the inputs of the integrator are all XML data, we can implement integrator by XML-QL. Filter function in integrator is implemented by regular-path expression, join operator in XML-QL.

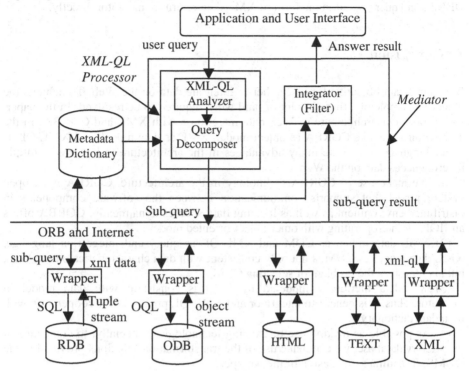

Fig. 1. Architecture of Integrated Web Data

4.2 Metadata Dictionary

Metadata management is important for the data integration of heterogeneous data sources because each source has its own interfaces and attributes. It is necessary to know the interfaces and attributes of local sources when processing a query and collecting query results. In the architecture, metadata dictionary is modeled by the DTD for data representation in order to collaborate with mediator and wrappers.

4.3 Implementation of Wrappers

Wrappers accomplish mainly the transformations from global sub-query (XML-QL) to local data query (such as SQL or OQL), and the transformations from the local query results to mediated data (XML data). There are different wrappers against various data sources, so their implementing methods are also different. (1)XML data source: only need to complete the transformation from XML data to global schema, mainly process the problem of schema integration. (2) HTML data source and structured text are semi-structured and unstructured data sources. The wrapper mainly extracts structured data (XML data) from these files. (3) To speed up the development of RDB and ODB wrappers, it is far more preferable to have the DBMS provider rather than application developer implement data transformation. The wrapper receives XML-QL query and translates it into SQL or OQL in order to query local DBMS, and query result in the form of XML data return to integrator directly.

5 Conclusion

It is significant objective for researcher to integrate data on the Web. To achieve the objective completely, there is a lot of hard work required to be resolved. In the paper, we propose our architecture of Web data integration with XML and CORBA. In the architecture, we take CORBA as object model, XML as data model, and XML-QL as query language. There are many advantages in the architecture to integrate multiple heterogeneous data on the Web.

(1) We make use of CORBA technology in the architecture. CORBA is an open system model that supports communication between the software components in distributed environment as well as locating data sources dynamically. CORBA offers an IIOP for interoperating with other object-oriented model.

(2) XML data model as CDM and XML-QL as query and integration language. XML data model as CDM is not only consistent with data characteristics on the Web, but also resolves the problem of selecting CDM.

(3) Metadata dictionary modeled by DTD is consistent with data model in mediator. Thus, it is benefit to integrator and XML-QL processor for cooperating with metadata dictionary.

(4) As possible as making use of existing technologies. Specially, to conventional proprietary database, we can make use of the transformation functions provided in the DBMS. It facilitates the design of the wrapper.

The architecture is a straightforward and practicable, but there exists still some embarrassment needed to be overcome. We are going for it in order to make it more robust and perfect in *Panorama* project.

References

1. Bertino,E., Catania,B.: Integrating XML and Databases. IEEE Internet Computing. Julu-August(2001) 84–88
2. Salminen,A., Tompa,F. W.: System Desiderata for XML Databases. Proceedings of the 27th VLDB Conference, Roma, Italy(2001)
3. Deutsch, A., Fernandez, M., Florescu, D. et al.: A query language for XML. Computer Networks. 31 (1999) 1155–1169
4. Chang, Y. S., Ho, M. H., Yuan, S. M.: A unified interface for integrating information retrieval. Computer Standards & Interfaces. 23 (2001) 325–340
5. Garcia-Molina, H., Hammer, J. ,Ireland, K.et al.: Integrating and accessing heterogeneous information sources in TSIMMIS. Proceedings of the AAAI Symposium on Information Gathering, Stanford, Galifornia, USA(1995) 61–64
6. Bouguettaya, A., Benatallah, B., Ouzzani, M., Hendra, L.: WEBFINDIT: An Architecture and System for Querying Web Databases. IEEE Internet Computing. July-August(1999) 30–41

Experiences in Web Site Development with Multidisciplinary Teams. From XML to JST

Raúl Izquierdo[1], Aquilino Juan[1], Benjamín López[1], Ricardo Devis[2],
Juan Manuel Cueva[1], and César F. Acebal[1]

[1]Laboratory of Object Oriented Technology. University of Oviedo. Spain
{ric, aquilino, benja, cueva, acebal }@lsi.uniovi.es
[2]Ricardo Devis & Asociados. Madrid, Spain
devis@ieee.org

Abstract. XML and XSLT apparently offer many advantages in Web site development. However after using them in several real projects we have found many disadvantages that results in a development process neither so productive nor easy. We propose a simple development process centered on reducing unnecessary interaction between programmers and graphic designers so they can focus on their fundamental tasks.

1 Introduction

The most usual criticism to technologies like Servlets, PHP or JSP is the lack of separation between data and presentation[1]. Using XML/XSLT programmers generate XML and designers write XSLT style sheets solving the separation problem because they are centered on different tasks.

In *CE B2B2000* (http://www.ceb2b2000.com) we have been using XML in several real projects (from B2B integration to portals like http//www.saunierduval.es, http://www.caloryfrio.com and http://www.conaif.com). Due to the great importance that visual appearance has on the web CE B2B usually works with external graphic design companies. Therefore independence between programmers and graphic designers it's a needed requirement since the development team is composed by people from different companies working in different places.

2 Problems in XSLT Based Web Development

2.1 Complicating Graphical Designer Work

The graphic design team works twice. It is easier for them to work with a WYSIWYG tool than to describe in XSLT text what they want to see. Therefore they usually create first a HTML page with the look & feel they want and they must repeat their work writing the XSLT document. Moreover the synchronization between both versions must be kept during development.

J.M. Cueva Lovelle et al. (Eds.): ICWE 2003, LNCS 2722, pp. 459–462, 2003.
© Springer-Verlag Berlin Heidelberg 2003

Other problem is that designers use to rely heavily on visual composition tools that allows them to focus in the aesthetics details. With XML/XSLT they will have to add more complicated tools (XML and XSLT parsers, test batteries, etc). Therefore now they have a new environment in which the pages must be "*compiled*". Although this doesn't may be perceived as a problem for programmers (because they use this kind of processing tools) designers cannot appreciate the need for a change that doesn't improve their work in the aesthetical area.

2.2   Training Problems for the Designers

When working with XSLT it is difficult to find professional art designers with XML and XSLT knowledge. Time can be dedicated to their training but problems persist:
- Designers never become experts in new technologies. They are not trained to build algorithms so they only grasp trivial transformations.
- XSLT finally must incorporate programming which exceeds the *simplicity* that was promised to designers. They must assume the difficulty of debugging XSLT.
- The project depends on the XSLT trained designers, so teams can't be replaced when the results are not those expected.
The conclusion is that XSLT is easy, but only from the point of view of programmers.

2.3   Complicating the Programmer Work

To apply a XSLT style sheet a source XML document is needed. Suppose the implementation of a shopping site. During a session the server will keep in memory an object model of the ongoing order. In every page transition the object model has to be transformed to XML to be presented in HTML. Obviously this is very inefficient.
Another option is to directly manipulate DOM objects in memory instead of user classes. But this option uses much more memory and requires more code to manipulate the order model. The right class model for this project (order, customer, etc) has to be replaced with DOM classes (Text, Node, etc) loosing the advantages of object oriented modeling.

2.4   Greater Dependency between Programmer and Designer

The designer needs to know the XML tags to transform. This implies that:
- The designer cannot begin to work until the programmer has finished the DTD.
- Whenever a DTD changes, the programmer and the designer must have a meeting. This was the *greatest problem* we found in our projects, since changes in data structures are something inevitable and extremely frequent during development [3].
It's said that XML/XSLT separate presentation and data because they are described in different files. But true independence would mean that designers were not affected by XML structure variations. Therefore *designers have a strong dependency on how programmers model data* (which is something that they even should not know).

3 JST: A Simple Web Site Construction Method

Web usability is focused on finding the user needs and provide them the most direct solution[2]. In the development process programmers and designers are the *users*. It is necessary to analyze their tasks and provide a process *with minimum steps and tools*.
Now we are using a more simple process for web development denominated JST. A JST template is just an HTML file that even can be opened directly from the file system by a browser:

```
<html> <head>
<script>
function p(arg) { document.write(arg) }
</script> </head>
<Data> <script>
name = "Raul"
</script> </Data>
<body>
My name is: <script> p(name) </script>
</body> </html>
```

From the point of view of the designer working with JST just consists of:
1. To isolate the dynamic parts of the page (in this case a person's name) and to assign them a default value in the data tag.
2. The function *p* is used to insert the dynamic data into the static markup.

The *<data>* tag content is known as the *designer's model*. When editing the page the designer simply indicates what he needs independently of what the real data is and where it is located.
Now the work of the programmer begins:
1. The *designers model* in the HTML template shows the dynamic values needed by the page, minimizing communication between designers and programmers.
2. The programmer must implement the code that extracts the real data (from an object model, SGBD, etc) and generate a string with the right dynamic content values.

So if the JST template is opened in a browser directly from the file system the default test data is presented. But if the page is requested through a Web server a simple servlet can change the data tag content on the fly.

3.1 Double Model Pattern

The JST architecture is based on a MVC[5] variation named *double model pattern*. In the MVC architecture a *view* directly use the model methods. So changes in the model interface produces changes in the views. This is just the problem with XML+XSLT: whenever the model changes (XML structure) it is necessary to modify the views (XSLT).
The *double model* pattern is used when modifying views has a high cost. It is based on using two models: the programmer's model and the designer's model. A new component, the *translator*, copies data from the first to the second model. Views only know the designer's model so they become independent of the programmer's model

(which is subject of a continuous refactoring during development). Whenever the programmer changes its model he has to modify the translator to feed the designer's model with the right data.

But when the programmer's model changes, what is the difference between changing the translator and changing the views? The difference is that by using the new pattern only programmers carry out the required changes eliminating communication. Programmers have changed the model and also know how to change the translator. Designers do not need to be aware of the change. The dangerous dissemination of work among different roles has been avoided.

4   Conclusions on JST

The main properties of JST are:
- The processing of the template in the server is trivial and efficient (just a string substitution: the data tag content).
- Language independence. Any programming language can replace the data tag.
- JST *really* separates the view and the model. Independence is so high that views can even work *without a model* (deriving in a prototype which uses the default data tag content).

References

1. Benoit Marchal. Servlet for Programming Teams.
   http://developer.netscape.com/viewsource/marchal_xml.htm
2. Jakob Nielsen. Designing Web Usability. New Raiders Publishing. 2000
3. Kent Beck. Extreme Programming. Addison-Wesley. 2000
4. Wei Meng Lee, Ngee Ann Polytechnic, Singapore. Tailoring Content Using XML and XSL.
   http://www.vbxml.com/wap/articles/wap_xml_xsl/default.asp
5. F. Buschmann, R. Meunier, H. Rohnert, P. Sommerlad, M. Stal. "Pattern-Oriented Software Architecture, Volume 1: A System of Patterns". John Wiley & Son. 1996

The NDT Development Process

M.J. Escalona, M. Mejías, J. Torres, and A. Reina

Department of Computer Languages and Systems
University of Seville
{escalona, risoto, jtorres, reinaqu}@lsi.us.es

Abstract. Web systems are more complex every day. This has produced that the research community poses the neccesity of developing methodological proposals which offer a suitable reference when a web information system is developed. Since the first proposal, HDM, was published [5] a lot of other methodologies have been developed in this environment. This paper presents NDT (Navigational Development Techniques) [3]. This proposal offers a different development process that starts with requirements treatment and allows to get design models using a systematic process.

1 Introduction

The progress of Internet and Communications has given way to a rising interest for developing methodological proposals. However, if these methodologies are analysed, most of them have a similar work process [7][1]. This paper presents a global vision of this classical process and presents some questions. After that, it offers another available vision to develop web information systems and it compares this new possibility with the classical process. In the third section, it presents a new methodological proposal called NDT (Navigational Development Techniques) that uses this new development process. Finally, in the last section some conclusions and future works are offered.

2 The Development Process in Web Methodologies

The number of methods, models and techniques that has appeared in web environment has produced that some comparative studies have been made in order to analyse similarities and differences between them [7][1]. Really, in web environment there is not a consensuos to model systems in the used terminology or in the used development process. Although there are different proposals, the most interesting aspect in our study is to analyse the development process that these methodologies use. The work of these methodologies is focussed on design which is mainly based on the conceptual model. This general characteristic is represented in figure 1. As it is shown, the process starts with the requirements treatment. The group of analysts receive information from the users and customers that allows them to define the system requirements. Some methodologies do not cover this phase. Perhaps OOHDM [9], UWE [8] and UWA[11] are the most interested proposals in requirements treatment. Starting with them, the conceptual model of the system is designed. When this model is developed, other models like navigational model, abstract interface

J.M. Cueva Lovelle et al. (Eds.): ICWE 2003, LNCS 2722, pp. 463–467, 2003.
© Springer-Verlag Berlin Heidelberg 2003

models, etc. are made. These other models are based on the conceptual model. Afterwards, the system implementation is realized using all these models. The user evaluated it and detects errors and bugs. This whole process is repeated until the suitable final system is obtained. However, although this process has been accepted, nowadays, there are some important points which are being questioned:

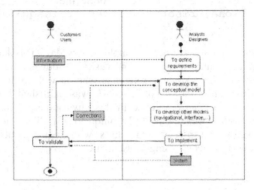

Fig. 1. The general development process in web methodologies

1. Uses cases as a technique to deal with web requirements: in the enumerated methodologies, the conceptual model is the base to define the other system models. Thus, the quality of the result depends on it. To get this model, web methodologies use the obtained information in the requirements treatment phase. This information is usually represented by using the use cases technique proposed in UML. However, several research groups [10][6] have commented that use cases can be a very ambiguous techinique to get the conceptual model easily. For this reason, new proposals are appearing like UIDs in OOHDM [10] or the proposal to refine requirements of UWA. These new proposals are oriented to define a more systematic procedure to get the conceptual model that guarantees its quality.

2. Separating concepts: since OOHDM proposed the division of concepts, the idea of modelling web aspects in an independent way has been hardly accepted [9][8][11]. Modelling these aspects separatelly, the developer can guarantee a cheaper maintenance and more possibilities for the system to be reused. However, this concept separation is being analysed nowadays [2]. There is also a strong dependence between conceptual models and the other ones which is produced directly from the development process (figure 1). To solve this dependence, some authors have classified requirements in different kinds, others propose to treat different requirements in a different way [4]. The question is that when the system is complex, it is not easy to get a conceptual model from the current requirements techniques systematically [4].

3. The communication with users and customers: from the comparative studies [7][1] it can be deduced that most web proposals do not include the user in the process. Web systems need that the development group has a huge knowledge about the system environment and users' neccesities [4]. The problem is how this communication must be done. The class diagram can be very difficult to be understood by some users. Use cases are very easy but they can sometimes be very abstract. The reality is that very few methodologies bear in mind this problem and only some of them offer proposals like reviews [4] or prototypes to make this communication easier.

4. Top-down process vs Bottom-up process: the process studied in the previous section can be defined as a top-down process. Starting with a general requirements definition, mainly made with use cases, a class conceptual model is designed. Opposite to this is the bottom-up process. It is based on doing a very exhaustive study in the first phases and after that, on getting the other models. In table 1, their advantages(+) and disadvantages(-) are enumerated. Obviously, to select one process or another is a development team's decision. Although the most applied tendency is a top-down process [9][8], some new proposals are oriented to a bottom-up process [3][11].

Table 1. Advantages and disadvantages in bottom-up and top-down process

Top-down process	Bottom-up process
+ Requirements definition is often cheaper and easier.	-Requirements definition is often more complex
+ The communication with users is often easier.	- Sometimes, it is difficult to confront all requirements specification since the beginning.
- To get the conceptual model is more complex and it is necessary to interact with users constantly.	+ The conceptual model is made in a more systematic way.
- Other models depend on the conceptual model. The separation of concepts is based on this model.	+ The separation of concepts is made in requirements, so models are more independent.
- Mistakes and errors are detected in late phases	+ Mistakes and errors are detected in the first phases

3   NDT Development Process

According to the previous section, NDT development process can be defined as a bottom-up process. The development process is focused on a very detail requirements definition guided by objectives, which covers three subphases: requirements capture, requirements definition and requirements validation. In figure 2, it is presented.

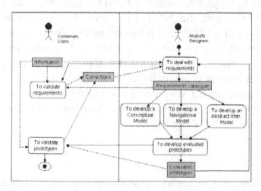

Fig. 2. NDT development process

It is a bottom-up process where models are independent. The process starts by defining objectives. Using a described procedure, requirements are captured and defined. Requirements are classified and dealt with depending on whether they are: information storage requirements, interaction requirements, etc. When requirements are validated, the NDT process continues defining three models: the conceptual model, the navigational model and the abstract interface model. The most important characteristic of the NDT process is that the way from requirements to models is systematic and makes each model independent. It is systematic because NDT offers algorithms which indicate how each model has to be obtained from the requirements definition. And they are independent because, although different models are related between them, because all of them represent an aspect of the same system, each of them can be obtained independently from the requirements. From these models, some evaluated prototypes can be obtained. These prototypes can be evaluated by users and customers. In this section, the NDT process is finished. The main objective of NDT is to offer a systematic process to get models which other accepted web methodologies use as the base to their development process and to guarantee the quality of these models. NDT is not a new web methodological proposal. It is a procedure to get design models from the users' requirements. As it has been indicated, NDT starts with a requirements definition and gets design models from them in a systematic way. The fact that this process can be carried out systematically allows to translate this systematic process in an automatic process using a case tool. Thus, a tool which lets execute the NDT process, apply its techniques and get its results is being implemented. Nowadays, only the requirements treatment phase is implemented, but we are working in order to include in NDT-Tool the whole process of NDT.

4   Conclusions and Future Works

This paper has presented a very general vision of NDT, a new methodological proposition to get requirements and design models in a systematic way in web information systems. A general description of web methodologies and their general development process has been offered. Also, some important aspects in this general process like the communication with users or the dependency in the conceptual model has been analyzed. After that, bottom-up and top-down development processes have been compared and some advantages and disadvantages have been enumerated. Base on this comparison, a global vision of NDT has been shown. Finally, a short presentation of NDT-Tool, the NDT case tool, has been done. One of the most important advantages of NDT is that it has being applied to several real examples, like the system to manage information about historical inheritance in Andalusia or the system to manage public subventions in the public cultural administration in Andalusia. These and other projects have been developed in collaboration with public and private companies getting very good results. As a future work, we want to finish developing the NDT process and, obviously, to implement completely NDT-Tool in order to cover the whole NDT life cycle.

References

1   Barry, C. & Lang, M. *A Survey of Multimedia and Web Development Tecniques and Methodology Usage.* IEEE Multimedia. April-June 2001, 52–56
2   Cachero, C. , Koch, N. *Conceptual Navigation Analysis : a Device and Plataform Independent Navigation Specification.* 2nd IWOST. June, 2002.
3   Escalona, M.J.,Mejías, M., Torres, J. Reina.A. *NDT: Una técnica para el desarrollo de la navegación.* Congreso IDEAS 2002. Cuba. Abril 2002

4 Escalona, M.J., Koch, N. *Ingeniería de Requisitos en Aplicaciones para la Web- Un estudio comparativo.* Department of Language and Computer Science. December, 2002.
5 Garzoto F., Schwabe D. and Paolini P. *HDM-A Model Based Approach to Hypermedia Aplication Design.* ACM Trnasactions on Information System, 11 (1), pp 1–26. 1993.
6 Insfrán, E., Pastor, O., Wieringa, R. *Requirements Engineering-Based Conceptual Modeling.* Requirements Engineering Journal, Vol 7 (1). 2002.
7 Koch, N. *A comparative study of methods for Hypermedia Development.* Technical Report 9905. Ludwig-Maximilian-University, Munich, Germany. 1999.
8 Koch, N. *Software Engineering for Adaptive Hypermedia Applications.* Ph. Thesis, FAST Reihe Softwaretechnik Vol(12), Uni-Druck Publishing Company, Germany. 2001.
9 G. Rossi An Object Oriented Method for Designing Hipermedia Applications. PHD Thesis, Departamento de Informática, PUC-Rio, Brazil, 1996
10 Vilain, P., Schwabe, D., Sieckenius, C. (2000). *A diagrammatic Tool for Representing User Interaction in UML.* Lecture Notes in Computer Science. Proc. UML'2000. York.
11 UWA Consortium, UWA Requirements Elicitation: Model, Notation, and Tool Architecture.

Essential Use Cases in the Design of Multi-channel Service Offerings – A Study of Internet Banking

Lia Patrício[1], J. Falcão e Cunha[2], Raymond P. Fisk[3], and Oscar Pastor[4]

[1] Faculdade de Engenharia da Universidade do Porto
Rua Dr. Roberto Frias, 4200-465 Porto, Portugal
lpatric@fe.up.pt
[2] Faculdade de Engenharia da Universidade do Porto
Rua Dr. Roberto Frias, 4200-465 Porto, Portugal
jfcunha@fe.up.pt
[3] College of Business Administration – University of New Orleans
New Orleans, LA 70148-1566, USA
rfisk@uno.edu
[4] Dept. de Sistemas Informáticos y Computación – Univ. Politécnica de Valencia
Camino de Vera, Apartado 22012, 46020 Valencia, España
opastor@dsic.upv.es

Abstract. This article presents the results of a qualitative study of a multi-channel bank. It aims at developing new methods of gathering user requirements for web interfaces, joining HCI and Marketing perspectives. The results obtained so far indicate that, as most of financial operations are functionally available in the different service channels, experience requirements become increasingly important. In this context, essential use cases are particularly valuable in improving the process of gathering customer requirements. As they allow the analysis of users' interaction needs in a channel-independent way, their use can improve decisions on what services are best suited to each channel, to effectively address customer needs across different interaction modes, and make an efficient allocation of resources among channels.

1 Introduction

The widespread commercial use of the Internet for self-service provision has created a new environment in which interfaces are designed for a wide set of potential customers, with diversified user and usage profiles, and little technology orientation. This situation has created an increased need for accurate methods of requirements gathering for wide and diverse groups of customers, which analyze the interface in the context of overall service provision.

This study aims at developing new methods of gathering user requirements for web interfaces, joining UCD and Services Marketing approaches. It started with a qualitative study of the customers of a multi-channel bank, which provides services through high street branches (BB), telephone (TB), ATM and the Internet (IB). The research work began with 14 in-depth interviews and 4 focus groups with bank customers, and 1 focus group and 3 in-depth interviews with bank staff, in an overall total of 49 interviewees.

Following qualitative methods, the sample of customers was not designed to be statistically representative of the population, but was purposefully defined according

J.M. Cueva Lovelle et al. (Eds.): ICWE 2003, LNCS 2722, pp. 468–471, 2003.
© Springer-Verlag Berlin Heidelberg 2003

to theoretical relevance of cases [1] of both users and non-users of Internet Banking. The interviews were transcribed and analyzed via the qualitative software NUD*IST (www.qsr.com.au/products/n6.html).The qualitative research aimed to elicit the potential factors driving or inhibiting the usage of Internet banking, which can be used for the identification of interface requirements. The results were also used to design a survey, with the objective of testing the generalization of the exploratory findings, and measuring the impact of the different influence factors on customers' decisions to use the Internet banking service.

2 Customer Experience Requirements and Internet Services

As the Internet becomes a mature technology, requirements gathering should include both technical and market requirements, and both Interaction Design and Marketing perspectives are needed [2]. HCI research has produced several measures of user interface usability. These studies have produced guidelines on the most important usability goals, such as time to learn, speed of performance, rate of errors, and user retention [3], simplicity, clarity of function, and visibility [4]. However, given the critical influence of perceived quality and satisfaction in the adoption and usage of new interfaces, it seems that further effort should be made to improve the methods of elicitation of experience requirements. Customer experience requirements are related to user experience goals, and differ from usability goals as they are concerned with how users experience an interactive product from their perspective [5].

Service quality research can also provide useful insights in the identification of customer experience requirements. The upsurge of the Internet has motivated several researchers to develop measures of web service quality, such as e-SERVQUAL [6] and Webqual [7]. Theses studies identified the dimensions of e-service quality in the customers' words, such as efficiency, fulfillment, reliability and privacy (e-SERVQUAL); ease of use, usefulness, entertainment and complementary relationship with other channels (WebQual).

In this study, it is clear that customers do not express their preferences for each channel so much with technology features and functionalities, but with the service experience they can get. In the customers' perspective, Internet banking is usually seen as a more efficient interaction in terms of higher accessibility, convenience, ease of use and time saving. IB also performs well in terms of usefulness of functionalities, quality and deepness of information, autonomy and feed-back control.

The perceived service experience appears to be a key determinant of IB usage. IB security concerns and the negative issues associated with new technologies in general seem to be the main reasons why non-technology customers avoid it. On the other hand, its positive performance in terms of efficiency seem to motivate time poor, technology oriented customers to use it, in spite of security concerns and a certain degree of depersonalization.

3 Essential Use Cases and Customer Experience Requirements

Use cases have been extensively applied in software development to describe the interaction between a user and an interface [8]. However, it is important to distinguish between concrete use cases, which assume a previously defined interface and interaction design, and essential use cases, which describe users' intentions of interaction, and system's responsibilities, in a technology free and implementation-independent way [9]. The Marketing framework, especially the Consumer Behavior area, also provides tools to categorize and understand experience requirements for the different essential use cases. In service provision, use cases may be characterized in terms of the **type of decision process**, which is related to *perceived risk*, *complexity*, and *frequency* [9]. On the other hand, several **stages of consumer decision and consumption process** can be identified: problem *recognition*, information *search*, *evaluation* of alternatives, product *choice* and product *usage* [9]. Identifying the type and the stage of consumer decision process to which a use case belongs may help in identifying the most relevant experience requirements.

In this study, data analysis and categorization allowed the identification of relevant use cases of interaction between the customer and the bank, the associated customer needs or requirements, and the channels regularly used in each case. The consumer decision framework provided tools to categorize essential use cases and to understand the most relevant experience requirements for each one of them.

The results indicate that each essential use case is associated with different experience requirements, which influence strongly interaction choice [11]. The **type of decision process** influences strongly channel choice, as it generates specific needs. In the interviewees' perspective, financial operations which are considered routine, unimportant, low risk, and well known by customers – such as current account transactions - are usually undertaken in the IB, or other automatic channel, although they are also available in the bank branch. For these kinds of financial operations, customers give priority to the efficiency attributes of the Internet, such as convenience, ease of use, time saving and accessibility. For complex, unknown, important operations - such as mortgage loans - customers prefer the personal interaction in the bank branch, as this channel is associated with mutual knowledge, individualized attention, and professional competence of employees, which customer's value in these situations.

The study results also show that, for the same financial product, customers use different channels according to the **stage of product usage.** Information gathering for decision or monitoring purposes may be performed through the Web, even for mortgage loans. However, negotiation and contracting are usually undertaken in the BB, through person to person interaction. The bank under study offers in-depth information, simulations, and pre-approval of mortgage loans in the IB service. But if some customers are able to search initial information in the Internet, they prefer to go to the bank branch when it comes to the evaluation of alternatives and negotiation.

Each essential use case has a specific set of functional requirements, which is well studied, given the long tradition of the banking industry. The development of new technologies has made it possible to satisfy these functional requirements through web interfaces, and has expanded the potential use of the Internet for service provision. However, it seems that, more than just making services functionally available in new channels, it is important to understand what customer experience requirements are associated with each essential use case, in order to understand what service channels are best suited to provide the desired service.

4 Conclusion

This study shows that customers justify their preference for or avoidance of Internet banking, not so much in terms of functional attributes and technology features, but essentially in terms of experience requirements and general needs in a channel-independent way. These results suggest that the elicitation of customer requirements in multi-channel service can be improved through the application of essential use cases. As they are technology-independent, they allow a better understanding of customer needs, which designers can then use to develop interfaces which address customer requirements and make the best use of system capabilities. With this approach, service providers can make better decisions on what services are best suited to the Internet channel, to effectively address customer needs and offer a consistent service across different interaction modes.

References

1. Strauss, A. and Corbin, J.: Basics of Qualitative Research: Techniques and Procedures for Developing Grounded Theory. 2nd edn. Sage Publications, Thousand Oaks (1998)
2. Norman, D. A.: The Invisible Computer, 3rd printing. The MIT Press, Cambridge, Massachusetts (1998)
3. Shneiderman, B.: Designing the User Interface: Strategies for Effective Human-Computer Interaction. 3rd edn. Addison-Wesley, Reading, Massachusetts (1998)
4. Nielsen, J.: Designing Web Usability: The Practice of Simplicity. New Riders Publishing, Indianapolis (2000)
5. Preece, J., Rogers, Y. and Sharp, H.: Interaction Design: Beyond Human-Computer Interaction. John Wiley & Sons, New York (2000)
6. Zeithaml, V. A., Parasuraman, A. and Malhotra, A.: Service Quality Delivery through Web Sites: A Critical View of Extant Knowledge. Journal of the Academy of Marketing Science, Vol. 30, No. 4 (2002) 362–375
7. Loiacono, E. T.: WebQual?: A Web site quality instrument. Unpublished doctoral thesis, University of Georgia (2000)
8. Nunes, N. J. and Cunha, J. F.: Whitewater Interactive System Development with Object Models. In: Harmelen, M. V. (ed.): Object Modeling and User Interface Design. Addison-Wesley, Boston (2001) 197–244
9. Constantine, L. L., Lockwood, L. A. D.: Structure and Style in Use Cases for User Interface Design. In: Harmelen, M. V. (ed.): Object Modeling and User Interface Design. Addison-Wesley, Boston (2001) 245–280
10. Solomon, M., Bamossy, G. and Askegaard, S.: Consumer Behaviour: A European Perspective, Financial Times Prentice Hall, Harlow (1998)
11. Patrício, L., Cunha, J. F. and Fisk, R. P.: Addressing Marketing Requirements in User Interface Design for Multiple Platforms, accepted for presentation in DSV - IS'2003 – 10th International Workshop on Design, Specification and Verification of Interactive Systems, Funchal (Madeira Island), Portugal, 4–6 June (2003)

Modelling Dynamic Personalization in Web Applications*

Irene Garrigós, Jaime Gómez, and Cristina Cachero

IWAD Group
Departamento de Lenguajes y Sistemas Informáticos
Universidad de Alicante. SPAIN
{igarrigos,jgomez,ccachero}@dlsi.ua.es
http://www.dlsi.ua.es/iwad/

Abstract. This article presents an extension of the OO-H conceptual modelling approach to address the particulars associated with the design and specification of dynamic personalization. We describe how conventional navigation and presentation diagrams are influenced by personalization properties. The main benefit is that personalization specification can be modified without recompile the rest of the application modules.

1 Introduction

Current Web Engineering approaches [5] help designers to make easier the understanding, development, evolution and maintenance of web applications. These methods are based on new constructors and hypermedial views [8,9, 2,10] that broach the problem of navigation/presentation of the user across the information space. We argue that new techniques to extend metamodels with personalization aspects are needed. This article presents how the *Object Oriented Hypermedia Method (OO-H)* [7,6,1] is extended to support dynamic personalization. We describe how conventional navigation and presentation diagrams are influenced by personalization properties. These properties are captured in the form of external files written in XML, that represent the rules. These rules, that form the variable part of the interface logic, will be treated at execution time by an engine included in the execution architecture. The support for this architecture is achieved by two models: A reference model, that also registers the user activity in the system. A user model that collects the needed information to personalize.

The remainder of the article is structured as follows: Section 2 shows the elements that support the personalization in OO-H. Section 3 presents the concept of association rules to support the specification of dynamic personalization. Finally, section 4 presents the conclusions and further work.

---

* This paper has been partially supported by the Spain Ministry of Science and Technology, project number TIC2001-3530-C02-02.

J.M. Cueva Lovelle et al. (Eds.): ICWE 2003, LNCS 2722, pp. 472–475, 2003.
© Springer-Verlag Berlin Heidelberg 2003

2   Personalization Support in OO-H

The architecture of OO-H has been extended to support dynamic personalization. More specifically, personalization properties are captured at navigation/presentation level and are reflected in their corresponding conceptual models (NAD, APD) by means of a set of association rules. In this way the design and the generation of the navigation logic is specified in two parts: a stable part, that is independent from the properties of personalization, and a variable part, that supports the treatment of these rules. Finally, a rule engine provides the context to interpret the generated rules at execution time. The support for this architecture is achieved by a *Reference Model* that allows to capture the relevant properties of personalization. Moreover, a *User Model* must be defined to support the personalization requirements.

In OO-H the *User Model* captures information about the features that the system believes the user has. The information that should contain this model depends on the personalization requirements that we want to support. In OO-H the user model is centered on the concepts of user and role, the same that in another hypermedial approaches [2]. For the provision of personalized views to the user, OO-H provides a basic user model which is constructed around a class named *User*, that provides the information and behaviour that must be inherited by every *<<actor>>* of the system. A user may not have a role associated, in this case s/he would be treated as an *anonymous user*. Moreover, a user can only have associated a role at the same time. This model can be enriched to support the desired personalization policy adding attributes, methods or links from the class User to the rest of the classes of the domain or the *OO-H Reference Model*, which is presented next.

In OO-H, a repository contains the initial set of basic elements of information on which the desired personalization policy can be established. This is what is called the *Reference Model*. A first version of this repository was presented in [4]. The current OO-H Reference model (see Fig 1) structures the modelling of personalization in OO-H in three parts: user profiles, context information and association rules. For the purpose of this paper we must pay more attention to the part B of Fig. 1, it is, to the association rules that are presented in depth in the following section. This type of rules allow to capture the personalization properties embedded directly in the models of OO-H.

3   Specification of the Personalization in OO-H

OO-H incorporates an external mechanism to model the personalization of the adaptive and proactive applications in form of association rules. An advantage of using these rules is that they are defined in external files and can be modified in an independent way from the rest of the application. The rules have been divided in three types:*Acquisition Rules*: in which the needed information for personalization is collected. *Personalization Rules*: support the action of personalization.

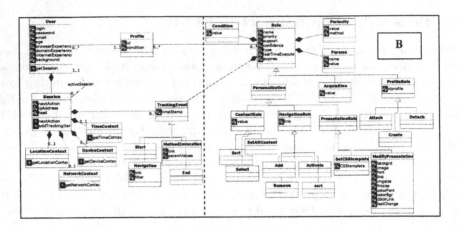

Fig. 1. Personalization Framework

As we have seen in the Fig. 1, this type of rules are also categorized, based on what we want to personalize, in:

-*Content Rules*: using these rules we can select *(Select)*, sort *(Sort)* or modify *(SetAttContent)* the content information of the application.

-*Navigation Rules*: With this type of rule we can *Add, Remove, Activate* or *Sort* any links in the user navigation.

-*Presentation Rules*: The possible actions that can be associated to this type of rule are: *SetCSSTemplate or ModifyPresentation*, according to wether we want to use a predefined template of presentation or we want to modify a specific value. We have a set of CSS templates, that can be associated to specific cases (as for disabled persons) captured in the *Reference Model* and a *Presentation Class* with presentation features. Moreover, in the *User Model* we can complete this Presentation Class with the features designed for a specific conceptual model. The rules permit the selection of a predefined template or the modification of specific features of the Presentation Class.

Profile Rules: With these rules we can associate *(Attach)* or disassociate *(Detach)* specific behaviours to user profiles, or we can create a new profile *(Create)*. OO-H supports the specification of these rules by means of an XML schema. It is important to note that the execution architecture of the generated applications from OO-H models allows to modify and reprocess this schema without recompiling the rest of modules. In the schema the different XML elements correspond to classes/attributes of the frame presented in Fig. 1. All the rules are ECA (Event-Condition-Action) rules [3].

4   Conclusions and Further Work

Web Engineering methods have to provide a well-defined software development process by which the community of software engineers can properly design powerful web-based applications in a systematic way. Our purpose has been to address these problems in the context of the OO-H conceptual modelling approach that has been successfully proven for the design of web applications. We focus on how to properly capture the particulars associated to the design of dynamic personalization. In order to achieve this goal, OO-H adds acquisition and personalization rules, which define the suitable semantics for capturing and representing the specific functionality of dynamic personalization. In this way, navigation and presentation models can be compiled to obtain an XML specification that represents the desired dynamic personalization. The final web application is viewed as a composition of a stable and variable part, where the variable part is interpreted by the rule engine to give personalization support. The main benefit is that personalization specification can be modified without need for recompiling the rest of the application modules. Others relevant contributions of this paper are the following: A user model that describes how the knowledge that the system has about the user is captured, A reference model that provides a way to extend the OO-H metamodel by means of a specific a set of information structures.

References

[1] C. Cachero, J. Gómez, and O. Pastor. Object-Oriented Conceptual Modeling of Web Application Interfaces: the OO-HMethod Presentation Abstract Model. In 1st International Conference on Electronic Commerce and Web Technologies (ECWEB'00), Greenwhich, London., volume 1875, pages 206–215. Springer-Verlag. Lecture Notes in Computer Science, 09 2000.

[2] S. Ceri, P. Fraternali, and A. Bongio. Web Modeling Language (WebML): a modeling language for designing Web sites WWW9 Conference. In First ICSE Workshop on Web Engineering, International Conference on Software Engineering, 05 2000.

[3] U. Dayal. Active Database Management Systems. In Proc. 3rd Int. Conference on Data and Knowledge Bases, pages 150–169, 1988.

[4] I. Garrigós, C. Cachero, and J. Gómez. Modelado Conceptual de aplicaciones adaptivas y proactivas en OO-H. In II Taller sobre Ingeniería del Software Orientado al Web (JISBD 2002), 11 2002.

[5] A. Ginige and S. Murugesan. Web Engineering: an Introduction. IEEE Multimedia Special Issue on Web Engineering, pages 14–18, 04 2001.

[6] J. Gómez, C. Cachero, and O. Pastor. Extending a Conceptual Modelling Approach to Web Application Design. In 12th International Conference on Advanced Information Systems (CAiSE'00), volume 1789, pages 79–93. Springer-Verlag. Lecture Notes in Computer Science, 06 2000.

[7] J. Gómez, C. Cachero, and O. Pastor. Conceptual Modelling of Device-Independent Web Applications. IEEE Multimedia Special Issue on Web Engineering, pages 26–39, 04 2001.

[8] N. Koch, A. Kraus, and R. Hennicker. The Authoring Process of the UML-based Web Engineering Approach. In Proceedings of the 1st International Workshop on Web-Oriented Software Technology, 05 2001.

[9] Daniel Schwabe and Gustavo Rossi. A Conference Review System with OOHDM. In First International Workshop on Web-Oriented Software Technology, 05 2001.

[10] Olga De Troyer and Sven Casteleyn. The Conference Review System with WSDM. In First International Workshop on Web-Oriented Software Technology, 05 2001.

Towards Self-Describing Web Services*

Phillipa Oaks

Centre for Information Technology Innovation - Faculty of Information Technology
Queensland University of Technology
GPO Box 2434, Brisbane, QLD 4001, Australia
{p.oaks}@qut.edu.au

Abstract. Self describing web services is a catchy phrase but it should mean more than having a description based on XML syntax. In this paper we take software engineering requirements for software interfaces and compare them to web service description specifications. The comparison shows that, at present, less information is associated with a web service than we expect for ordinary software.

1 Introduction

Web services are a new breed of Web application. They are self-contained, self-describing, modular applications that can be published, located, and invoked across the Web [1].

... agents provide service descriptions that tell how they can be used to accomplish other agents' *goals* [2].

... every information dependent resource, including enterprises, information services, application services, and devices, need to become augmented with machine processable descriptions to support the finding, reasoning about (e.g., which service is best), and using (e.g., executing or manipulating) the resource. The idea is that self-descriptions of data and other techniques would allow context-understanding programs to selectively find what users want, or for programs to work on behalf of humans and organizations to make them more scalable, efficient and productive [3].

Web services are a promising new technology for machine to machine interaction across application, enterprise and web boundaries. One of the reasons web services have gained so much interest and support over the last two years is that there are many existing branches of information technology that can be further developed within this new paradigm. Software engineering, components, component integration, distributed programs, grid computing, middleware, reusable

---

* This work was supported by the Australian Research Council SPIRT Grant "Self-describing transactions operating in a large, open, heterogeneous, distributed environment" involving QUT, UNSW and GBST Holdings Pty Ltd.

J.M. Cueva Lovelle et al. (Eds.): ICWE 2003, LNCS 2722, pp. 476–485, 2003.
© Springer-Verlag Berlin Heidelberg 2003

software, databases, knowledge representation, and other areas of computer science can contribute to web services.

The many sources of interest and contribution have led to a diversity of opinions and approaches on what web services can achieve, on what kinds of conceptual models can be used to describe web services, and also diversity in the approaches to implementation. Already there are competing standards and specifications being driven by various interest groups seeking to make a place for themselves in the web services arena. This leads to standards that either describe overlapping concerns, or are not integrated with one another, as was the case for software engineering in the mid 1990's [4].

There are many consequences of this diversity. There is no clear idea or agreement about what web services will be. Some see web services as the "dumb reactive" cousins of "intelligent proactive" agents. In this scenario, web services merely provide functionality to the agent, which uses and composes services to achieve its goals. Some describe "user facing" web services, these provide informational services via web pages (the stock ticker is a classic example). Others see web services as being able to invoke other (downstream) services themselves in order to provide composite and complex functionality. These interactive services, will have various levels of reactive and proactive functionality depending on the users' (human, agent, or other service) goals, and the interaction capabilities of both parties.

In addition, there is no clear idea or agreement about how web services will be used. At present there appear to be three ways to use web services. The first services made available[1] are rather simple, single function programs that can be invoked across the web. In the main, they are located by manually searching a UDDI[2] registry, and their invocation and use is pre-programmed by developers. The second type, are services that automate interactions between business partners who know each other and can agree on the syntax and semantics of the services up-front, similar to EDI. The third type, are "semantic web services" [5]. These are on the boundary between services, semantic web and agents. These web services of the future will provide complex functionality to previously unknown interaction partners. The exact nature of what they provide, and how to interact with the service will be contained within "self describing" machine readable documents [6,7].

The web services architecture is based on a "Publish, Find, Interact" model [8,9]. This model is insufficient for web services to progress towards automated service to service interaction. A more complex model that includes description, advertisement, discovery, evaluation and selection, initiation of dialogue, negotiation, configuration, interaction, and management is required. The first step is description. Web service descriptions must contain sufficient information to allow each step to proceed automatically.

As yet, there is no clear definition of what self description really means, but web services are still software. Therefore we can use the requirements for ordi-

---

[1] http://www.xmethods.com
[2] http://www.oasis-open.org/committees/uddi-spec/

nary software interface descriptions as the basis for requirements for web service interface descriptions. The reason for doing this is to ensure that the description of web service interfaces is at least as comprehensive as the description provided for other types of software. Web services operate in a complex environment and there should be more information about them provided to developers and users than for ordinary software.

In the next section we outline the requirements for software interfaces described in [10]. In section 3 we compare two prominent specifications for web service description (WSDL and DAML-S), against these requirements. We conclude with section 4.

2   Documenting Interfaces

In this section we give an overview of the interface documentation template presented in [10] and [11] and comment on how the sections apply in the web services context. These requirements have been refined over many years by the software engineering community. Each element is necessary to ensure that the developers implementing the interface, and third parties using the interface, can fully understand what the interface requires, what it provides and its constraints.

1. **Interface identity**: The most common means is to give a name to the interface and version numbers if appropriate.

   A unique identity for an interface is particularly important when many implementations of the same interface are expected or if different interfaces to the same service are provided for different classes of users. The identity can be used by service advertisements in catalogues and registries to indicate that the service complies with a particular interface.

2. **Resources provided**: These are the operations or methods provided in the interface.

   The description of resources should be sufficient to aid the discovery, evaluation and selection of services that meet the users' needs.

   Each resource needs to describe its:

   a) **Syntax**: The signature including its name and the logical datatypes of arguments.

   b) **Semantics**: A description of what happens when the resource is used i.e. what is visible to the user, and what are the restrictions on use of the resource. For example, the semantics describe the assignment of values to data that the user can access; changes in state, either to this, or another, element; the events signalled and messages sent by the resource; details of how other resources will behave differently when this one is used; and the execution style, whether the operation is atomic, interruptible or suspendible.

   The semantics of the operations is perhaps the most important part of the description in terms of enabling automated interaction. The semantics will be necessary in most phases from evaluation and selection to interaction.

c) **Usage restrictions**: Similar to pre-conditions, these state the assumptions about the environment that must be true, or describe the side effects of the operation. Exceptions should also be described here, detailing how errors are handled. For example, the number of retries or the meaning of returned status indicators.

3. **Locally defined datatypes**: This section describes how to declare variables, constants and literal values of the datatypes defined and used in the interface, and the operations, comparisons and conversions that can be performed on instances of those types.

   Datatypes in the web context can be viewed as both traditional programming language constructs and XML documents. In the case of XML documents, a reference to the document schema or a document template can be provided to allow creation of required documents or to enable understanding of the documents supplied by resources.

4. **Error handling**: The errors that can be raised by the resources on the interface and error handling behavior.

   This information will be necessary during the interaction phase to determine the cause of unexpected results.

5. **Variability provided by the interface**: Details of what configuration is possible, and range of allowable values for each configuration parameter should be provided. In addition, a description of how configuration affects the semantics of the interactions.

   Web service users will be of many different types, operating in different contexts, each with different capabilities. Consequently, web service descriptions must provide the facility to describe what can be configured and how that configuration can be achieved. In addition to operation attributes, there are other aspects of service delivery that could be configurable such as, the interaction mechanism or the security and transaction management protocols.

6. **Quality attributes of the interface**: Quality attributes include such things as the level of performance and reliability that the interface provides. Services may be selected based on their certified conformance to specific standards, or their ability to provide various quality of service attributes.

7. **What each interface element requires**: Either, specific named resources (described as above with syntax, semantics and restrictions), or other preconditions or assumptions about the environment.

   The usage restrictions (or non-functional requirements) of the operations will be used in the evaluation and interaction phases to determine if the constraints can be satisfied by the user.

8. **Rationale**: The motivation for the design, the constraints, compromises and alternatives considered.

   This is mainly for the benefit of developers implementing the interface.

9. **Usage guide**: the protocol of interaction or patterns of use for the entire interface.

   This information will be used during the interaction phase to ensure the correct order of interaction. This information could also be used to describe how to initiate a dialogue with the service, how to negotiate with or configure the service, and how to manage the operation of the service. Alternatively, the information may be used to select services that provide compatible interaction mechanisms.

The interface requirements described here can be considered the minimum requirements for the interfaces of web services. In the next section we use the template to determine how much of this information can be expressed using the current web-service specifications WSDL and DAML-S.

3   Evaluation of Standards in Terms of Interface Requirements

In this section we evaluate two web service specifications in terms of the interface documentation template introduced in section 2. The specifications are, the Web Services Description Language (WSDL) Version 1.2, W3C Working Draft 9 July 2002[3] and DAML-S 0.7 Draft Release[4].

3.1   WSDL Evaluation

WSDL is the primary specification for web service descriptions and it has achieved a high degree of acceptance. It provides a machine processable language, with XML syntax, for the description of web services.

1. Identity: No specific identity attribute is provided by WSDL. When registered in a UDDI registry as part of a UDDI tModel, a unique identity is assigned by the registry. The URI of the interface specification can be used as a unique identifier, however identical copies of the same interface with different URI's have to be treated as different resources.
2. Resources provided: A WSDL portType (interface) has a collection of operations (methods). Each operation has a set of input and output messages. Each message has one or more parts (parameters). Messages are defined outside of the operation, so in theory they are reuseable. Each message part has a name and a type. Although any type system can be used, XML Schema[5] datatypes are preferred.
   a) Syntax: Operation signatures are provided in XML syntax according to the WSDL 1.1 XML Schema specification, for example:

```
<message name="aNameMessage">
  <part name="firstName" type="xsd:string">
</message>

<operation name="printName">
```

---

[3] http://www.w3.org/TR/2002/WD-wsdl12-20020709/
[4] http://www.daml.org/services/daml-s/0.7/
[5] http://www.w3.org/XML/Schema

```
    <input message="aNameMessage"/>
    <output message="returnName"/>
  </operation>
```

    b) Semantics: WSDL makes no provision for semantics [12].

    c) Usage restrictions: Not supported.

3. Local data types: Defined using XML Schema complexTypes. No support for operations on the defined types.

4. Error handling: Not supported.

5. Variability: Not supported.

6. Quality attributes: Not supported.

7. Required resources: Input messages (as described above) are how required resources are described in WSDL. There is no support for semantics, usage restrictions or pre-conditions.

8. Rationale: Not supported, although could be added as documentation.

9. Usage guide: Not supported, although other specifications such as BPEL4WS[6] provide this kind of information for WSDL services.

3.2 DAML-S Evaluation

DAML-S provides several ontologies, based on the DAML ontology language, for describing the properties and capabilities of web services. DAML-S markup is intended to facilitate the discovery, execution and interoperation of web services [13]. DAML-S provides three sub-ontologies, each provides a different view of the service. The Profile describes three types of information including information about the organization providing the service, what function the service performs, and non-functional service characteristics. The Process Model describes how the service works in terms of its inputs, outputs, preconditions and effects. The Grounding describes how a service is used and provides a mapping from the the Profile and Process specifications to specific concrete protocols and message formats.

    In this evaluation we concentrate on the Service Profile, but describe elements from the Process model and Grounding when they provide more information. Although the various models provide a good separation of concerns they can be confusing when they appear to overlap. For example, the Profile describes parameters that have a name and an unspecified range. These Profile parameters make references to input and output parameters separately described in the Process model.

1. Identity: A Profile has a unique serviceName attribute.

2. Resources provided:

    a) Syntax: XML syntax is used with the vocabulary from the DAML and DAML-S specifications, for example:

---

[6] http://www-106.ibm.com/developerworks/webservices/library/ws-bpel/

```
<profileHierarchy:BookSelling
  rdf:ID="Profile_Full_Congo_BookBuying_Service">

  <!-- reference to the service specification -->
  <service:presentedBy
    rdf:resource="&congoService;#FullCongoBuyService"/>
  <profile:serviceName>
    Congo_BookBuying_Agent
  </profile:serviceName>

  <profile:input rdf:resource="#BookTitle"/>
  <profile:output rdf:resource="#ShippingOrder"/>

  <!-- specification of quality rating for profile -->
  <profile:qualityRating rdf:resource="#Congo-Rating"/>

  <!-- Preconditions and effects -->
  <profile:precondition rdf:resource="#AcctExists"/>
  <profile:effect rdf:resource="#BuyEffectType"/>
</profileHierarchy:BookSelling>
```

b) Semantics: The Profile provides the means to describe pre-conditions and effects. Processes can define conditions and condition effects for parameters. Other elements, such as computedInput and computedOutput, in the Process model can be used to give explicit semantics for specific items.
   Other aspects of semantics, such as events signalled and how other resources will behave differently are not supported.

c) Usage restrictions: Some support, but the property *domainResource*, that describes resources necessary for the task to be executed, has been deprecated.

3. Local data types: Most DAML-S objects are defined locally in DAML. Operations on data types are not supported.

4. Error handling: Not supported, although errors could be described in terms of *effects* as described in the Process specification.

5. Variability: Not supported.

6. Quality attributes: Various quality attributes can be defined for services, pre-defined attributes include *maxResponseTime* and *avgResponseTime*.

7. Required resources: Input parameters as described above.

8. Rationale: Not supported, although could be added as documentation.

9. Usage guide: The Process Control Model provides various control constructs including splits, joins, sequence etc. Composite processes can specify constraints on the ordering and conditional execution of sub-processes.

3.3   Summary

Table 1 gives a summary of the results of the evaluation. A "-" indicates no support, "+/-" indicates some support and "+" indicates reasonable support for the item.

Table 1. Summary of evaluation results

	WSDL	DAML-S
1 Identity	-	+
2 Resources provided		
2a Syntax	+	+
2b Semantics	-	+/-
2c Restrictions	-	+/-
3 Local Datatypes	+/-	+/-
4 Error handling	-	-
5 Variability	-	-
6 Quality	-	+
7 Resources required	+/-	+/-
8 Rationale	-	-
9 Usage guide	-	+

Both specifications rate well on providing the syntax of operation signatures. Unfortunately this is just about all that WSDL does provide. This means that all the processes of discovery, selection etc. must be based on operation signatures, which is clearly inadequate for all but the most simple services. To progress beyond manual discovery, selection and pre-programmed interaction, WSDL needs to be expanded to include the other aspects of interface description, or other specifications (such as BPEL4WS) covering those aspects must be developed.

DAML-S provides a better interface description for semantics and the usage guide. The main problem areas are error handling and configuration. Errors are inevitable, and interfaces must declare what errors are possible and how they are handled, neither specification provides primitives for this kind of information. The lack of error handling, which is essential in production systems, may be a reflection on the immaturity of the specifications or a deliberate attempt to reduce their complexity. In either case, this issue must be dealt with before widespread commercial use of web services is possible.

Although there is no support in DAML-S for the definition of operations on locally defined data types, this is typical of ontology definitions. Ontologies focus on describing elements in terms of their relationships, rather than on how instances of the elements can be used.

4   Conclusion

The evaluation of the specifications reveals that web service interfaces created with WSDL and DAML-S provide much less information than is usually expected for software interfaces. It is not reasonable to expect services to operate in a complex environment like the web, and at the same time provide less information about them than is necessary for ordinary software.

The evaluation also shows that WSDL and DAML-S overlap in some areas, for example they both describe the syntax of operations very well. Although some work is being done in DAML-S to align these two specifications [13], further effort should be directed at making web service interfaces more comprehensive.

In the future when web services engage in automated ad-hoc interaction, they will also need to describe the domain they operate in and the products they deal with. They will need to detail their security and authentication policies, transaction management procedures, and the interaction mechanisms they support. Web services will be self describing when they can do all this as well as provide the basic information discussed in this paper.

References

1. Tidwell, D.: Web services : Education : Tutorials web services – the web's next revolution (2000) Available from http://www-105.ibm.com/developerworks/.
2. McDermott, D., Burstein, M.: Overcoming Ontology Mismatches in Transactions with Self-Describing Service Agents. In: Proceedings of SWWS' 01 The First Semantic Web Working Symposium, Stanford University, California, USA (2001) 285–302 Available from: http://www.daml.org/services/daml-s/2001/05/, (20 September 2001).
3. Sheth, A., Meersman, R.: Amicalola Report: Database and Information Systems Research Challenges and Opportunities in Semantic Web and Enterprises (2002) Database and Information Systems Research for Semantic Web and Enterprises. Invitational Workshop Sponsored by NSF CISE-IIS-IDM, Co-Sponsored by EU Thematic Network OntoWeb. In cooperation with VP-Research and LSDIS Lab, University of Georgia. April 3 - 5, Amicalola Falls and State Park, Georgia. Organizers: Amit Sheth and Robert Meersman. Available from:http://lsdis.cs.uga.edu/SemNSF, (14 December 2002).
4. Moore, J.W.: Fundamental Principles of Software Reuse (1997) Eighth Annual Workshop on Institutionalizing Software Reuse (WISR), held at the Ohio State University. Available from: http://www.umcs.maine.edu/%7Eftp/wisr/wisr8/wisr8.html, (11 January 2003).
5. Bussler, C., Fensel, D., Payne, T., Sycara, K.: Tutorial (T3): Semantic Web Services (2002) More information available at: http://www.daml.ri.cmu.edu/tutorial/iswc-t3.html, (15 October 2002).
6. Fensel, D., Bussler, C.: The Web Service Modeling Framework WSMF (2002) to appear in Electronic Commerce Research and Applications. Available from: http://www.cs.vu.nl/~dieter/wese/wsmf.paper.pdf, (30 September 2002).
7. Sollazzo, T., Handschuh, S., Staab, S., Frank, M.: Semantic Web Service Architecture - Evolving Web Service Standards toward the Semantic Web. In: Proc. of the 15th International FLAIRS Conference, Pensacola, Florida, AAAI Press (2002) Available from: http://www.citeseer.nj.nec.com/sollazzo02semantic.html, (24 September 2002).

8. Hugo Haas (Activity Lead): Web Services Activity Statement (2002)
   http://www.w.org/2002/ws, (12 March 2002).
9. Bussler, C., Fensel, D., Maedche, A.: A Conceptual Architecture for Semantic Web
   Enabled Web Services. SIGMOD Record, Special Section on Semantic Web and
   Data Management **31** (2002)
10. Clements, P., Bachmann, F., Ross, L., Garlan, D., Ivers, J., Little, R., Nord, R.,
    Stafford, J.: Documenting Software Architectures: Views and Beyond. Addison-
    Wesley, Boston, USA (2003) ISBN 0-201-70372-6.
11. Bachmann, F., Bass, L., Clements, P., Garlan, D., Ivers, J., Little, R., Nord, R.,
    Stafford, J.: Documenting Software Architecture: Documenting Interfaces. Techni-
    cal Note CMU/SEI-2002-TN-015, Carnegie Mellon Software Engineering Institute,
    Pittsburgh, PA (2002)
12. Booth, D.: Semantics and WSDL (2002) Available from:
    http://www.w3.org/2002/09/wsdl-semantics-dbooth/semantics_clean.htm,
    (12 December 2002).
13. Martin, D., Burstein, M., Lassila, O., Paolucci, M., McIlraith, S.: Describing Web
    Services using DAML-S and WSDL (2002) DAML-S Coalition working document;
    August 2002. Available from:
    http://www.daml.org/services/daml-s/0.7/daml-s-wsdl.html, (19 January
    2003).

User Profiling Capabilities in OOWS

J. Fons[1], F.J. García[2], V. Pelechano[1], and O. Pastor[2]

[1] Department of Information Systems and Computation – Valencia University of Technology
{jjfons,pele,opastor}@dsic.upv.es
[2] Department of Computer Science – University of Salamanca
fgarcia@usal.es

Abstract. Personalisation and adaptation capabilities are significantly presented in today web applications. User profiling and user modelling are key activities to achieve the required personalised and adaptive levels in web domains. Adaptive hypermedia systems offer an adequate solution to this demand, but we argue the need to approach these issues from the beginning of the software life cycle. Object-Oriented Web-Solutions Modelling (OOWS) is a UML-based Web Engineering method to develop web applications that is strongly based on conceptual modelling techniques. OOWS has abstract primitives that allow the specification of the user profiles from the very first step of the application life cycle. This paper introduces how OOWS supports the user profiling activities that are the basis to develop personalised and adaptable web applications for specific user requirements.

Keywords. User profiling; Personalisation; Adaptable web applications; Conceptual modelling; Web Engineering.

1 Introduction

Traditional web sites consist of fairly static information. The WWW currently are formed by several millions of information pages across millions of web sites, and nowadays there are more than 500 millions of regular users from all walks of life with varying degrees of computer expertise, a wide range of interests and preferences, and a multimodal access representations or differing capacities to make use of them. Offering the right information for a particular web site user is one of the most interesting challenges of the Web Engineering.

Adaptive Hypermedia [2], content personalisation [16] and user modelling [11, 20] areas have presented a number of potential solutions to reduce the information overload by automatically learning about likes and dislikes of individual users in order to personalise the information retrieval, the services behaviour or the navigation.

User profiling and user modelling are key activities to achieve the required personalised and adaptive levels in web applications.

User profiling is the process of identifying and categorising the user audience of a Web site, gathering statistics on them. People from the different profiles, which are identified in a concrete web system, may perform similar tasks on the site; however,

J.M. Cueva Lovelle et al. (Eds.): ICWE 2003, LNCS 2722, pp. 486–496, 2003.
© Springer-Verlag Berlin Heidelberg 2003

the exact goals may change slightly, and their concerns will differ. So, it is important to understand the differing needs of these groups of users, otherwise the site may succeed with one group, but fail with another.

All the information about of each individual user of the web site (interests, navigation, environment...) is stored in its user profile. We call user model to the explicit representation of the properties of a particular user [9]. The goal of user modelling is to create systems that are adaptive to an individual's needs, abilities, and preferences. The user model should be central to the design process and substantially influences the basic functionality of web applications [18], because the user model is the source for personalising the content and navigation.

For this reason, we claim that the personalisation and adaptive issues in web applications should be approached from the beginning of the software process in the Web Engineering methods, i.e. from the requirements elicitation and especially in conceptual modelling.

Object-Oriented Web-Solutions Modelling (OOWS) [13, 14] is a UML-compliant [12] Web Engineering method (developed by the OO-M Group at Valencia University of Technology) to design web applications that is strongly based in the conceptual modelling techniques.

The aim of this paper is presenting how OOWS supports user profiling through a set of conceptual models and abstract primitives, this way, this method deals with the design of personalised and adaptable web applications.

The rest of the paper is organised as follows. Section 2 gives a general overview of the OOWS method. Section 3 focuses in the OOWS primitives that allow the user profiling. Section 4 presents a comparison with related works. Finally, section 5 provides remarks and further work.

2 OOWS Overview

OOWS is an extension of the OO-Method approach [15] that allows web applications development. OOWS enriches OO-Method with a navigation and presentation models to capture navigational and user interface aspects.

The software production process comprises two major steps: *specifying the system* and *developing the solution*. At first, a full specification of the user requirements is built in the *specifying the system* step. A strategy oriented towards generating the software components that constitute the solution (the final software product) is defined in the second step.

In order to make easier the explanation of the primitives that contribute to the user profiling modelling in the next section, we are going to present the specification step in a deeper way now.

2.1 Specifying the System

This step includes requirements elicitation based on use cases and scenarios (see detailed information in [8]) and system conceptual modelling activities. When dealing with the conceptual modelling stage, the abstractions derived from the problem space are specified in terms of their classes, structure, behaviour and functionality.

OOWS uses UML-compliant diagrams to represent the required conceptual information in five models: the *Object Model* that is represented by means of a class diagram; the *Dynamic Model* that is used to specify valid object lives and interobjectual interaction; the *Functional Model* that captures the semantic associated to the changes of state of the objects motivated by the services occurrences; the *Navigational Model* that specifies the navigation semantics associated to the system users using a UML notation too; and the *Presentation Model* that uses presentation patterns to specify the format of the output presentation.

The navigational Model is built using five main basic abstraction primitives: Navigational Map, Navigational Context, Navigational Link, Navigational Class, and Navigational Relationship.

The Navigational Model is essentially composed of a set of Navigational Maps that represents the global view of the web system for every potential end-user. It is represented by a directed graph in which the nodes are the Navigational Contexts and the arcs are the Navigational Links defining valid navigation paths.

A Navigational Context permits the definition of the content of user interactions units. It is composed by Navigational Classes and Navigational Relationships.

A Navigational Class defines a view of an object model class, and the Navigational Classes are connected by Navigational Relationships that describe valid navigation paths over object relationships.

There are Navigational Contexts of two kinds: *exploration contexts* that can be reached at any moment, independently of the current context; and *sequence contexts* that can only be reached by following a predefined sequence of Navigational Links.

3   User Profiling in OOWS

OOWS supports user profiling in the conceptual modelling phase by the different models that have been presented [1]. The overall models have to express the relevant information that allows creating a user profile. We have to act in three levels [17].

- *Content level*: which information is available for every kind of user, and also which information has to know the system about the different kinds of users.
- *Navigation level*: which links are available for every kind of user.
- *Presentation level*: how the information is shown to every kind of user.

In order to make a conceptual model of a web application, taking the user profiling capabilities, the steps that should be done are:

1. Find the user types that represent all the end-users of the web application.
2. Express every possibility of changing in the user type.
3. Model a view of the system for each user type, including the content, the navigation and the presentation levels.

3.1   Modelling User Types

The first activity in user profiling is to know the user audience of the system. In order to perform this activity we should gather all internal information on the users, including user feedback, survey results, customer support information, market research and so on.

All the information gathered should be analysed before creating realistic profiles for each segment of the user audience. The result of this analysis is a diagram representing all the user types (so called agents in OO-Method and in OOWS too) for the web applications.

Each user type represents a group of end-users that share all the properties and characteristics in the web applications at content, navigation and presentation levels.

It would be very interesting that the identified agents would be able to relate themselves by generalisation/specialisation relationships. This situation makes easy modelling the views of system for each user type presented in the system, because all the things modelled for an agent will be truth for a more specific one applying the substitution principle.

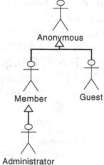

Fig. 1. Agent diagram

For example, the Figure 1 shows an agent hierarchy that expresses a typical situation in web applications. There exists an Anonymous agent that represents the most generic user type in the system, which is characterised because it has a very limited access to the system. Two new subtypes appear as direct descendants of the Anonymous agent: the Member agent and the Guest agent, which have a more specific behaviour in the system, but every end-user that belongs to one of these categories, can perform every Anonymous agent's behaviour. Finally, a new user type appears, the Administrator agent, which is a specialisation of the Member agent.

The agent diagram (see Figure 1), uses a UML-like notation where the agent is represented by the actor stereotype (with a stick man icon), and the relationships among agents is represented by the generalisation/specialisation connection.

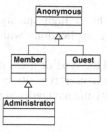

Fig. 2. Piece of the class diagram related to users

In order to register the information for each individual profile, this agent diagram is directly mapped to a class taxonomy in the class diagram of the OOWS approach. In this way, it is possible to provide more detailed information for a specific user that can be relevant to personalise the system. Fig. 2 shows the piece of the class diagram related to the users for the example illustrated in Figure 1. This information plays a very important role to achieve individual personalisation and adaptation.

3.2   Changing User Types in Navigation Models

Frequently in web applications an end-user can change its system view. For example, an end-user enters at the system as an anonymous user, but when the user needs more privileges or a specialised access, it authenticates itself and gains the proper level at the web system. To represent systems that define an intrinsic way of promoting the interactive user, OOWS allows specifying a UML State Transition Diagram (STD) attached to the Navigational Model[1]. This STD help us to model valid interactive user type changes during navigation. The STD states represent the possible types of users in the system, while the transitions express valid user type changes[2].

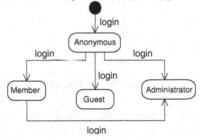

Fig. 3. Example of state chart expressing valid user type changes

Figure 3 shows an example of every possible user type change in a particular web system. In this example, by default, a user must be authenticated as an Anonymous[3]. Then, he can only *login as* a Member, Guest or Administrator user types, and being Member he can authenticate as Administrator.

3.3   Designing Personalised Views

According to [17], we only build high quality personalised and adaptable web applications if we design those applications with flexibility and extension in mind from the beginning.

Till now, we have identified the type of users that can interact with a web system, but we have to design for each user type its content, navigation and presentation properties. To do that, we specify the navigational and presentation model.

---

[1] If this STD is not specified, users can change their interactive type with no restrictions.
[2] Every change of user needs an authentication (login).
[3] A login and a password are not necessary.

The *navigational model* is made up of a navigational map for each identified agent. A *navigational map* represents the global view of the system for this group of end-users. This map is composed by a set of navigational contexts (depicted as UML packages stereotyped with the «context» reserved word) related by navigational links (depicted as arrows) defining the navigational (structure) personalisation for this type of user.

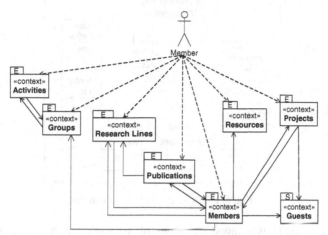

Fig. 4. Example of navigation map

For example, Figure 4 shows the navigational map for an anonymous agent of a web system. This map contains the navigational contexts that can be accessed by users of this kind and the valid navigational paths (sequence of contexts) than an anonymous user can follow. In the same way, a navigational map is built for each type of user, personalising its navigational capabilities.

Now, the navigation contexts are defined according to the user type that leads the navigation map. Each navigation context includes a configuration of navigation classes and navigation relationships that represents a view of a subset of the object model. This view expresses the attributes and the operations that are allowed for this user type, providing personalised access for this type of user.

Figure 5 shows the Members context from the point of view of an anonymous user. In the current case appears four navigation classes: the Member class, which is the *manager class* of this context (the main class of this context), and the WorkOn, Entity and RGroup classes, which are the *complementary classes* (contributing to give additional information).

Besides, in this example three navigational relationships appear. The first two (depicted with dashed arrows) are *contextual dependency relationships,* causing an object retrieval of the related instances (using a structural relationship, i.e. association, aggregation, composition, specialisation/generalisation). In the example, they relate the Member class with the WorkOn class and that WorkOn with the Entity. The last one is a *context relationship* (also a unidirectional binary relationship, depicted with a solid arrow) that relates the Member class with the RGroup class. Relationships of this kind act as contextual dependency relationships and they also define a navigation capability to a *[target context]* in the map (in this example, to the [RGroup] context).

Both kinds of relationships are defined on existing classes and class relationships from the class diagram, assuring full compatibility between the models of the conceptual modelling.

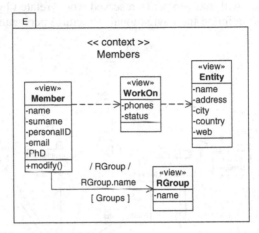

Fig. 5. Example of navigation context

Navigational contexts express the content personalisation for a type of user. Finally, for the presentation information we have to define the *presentation model* of the OOWS approach. This model allows specifying abstract presentation requirements of a web application related to each navigational context. Figure 6 shows an example of a navigational context with presentation information for the anonymous type of user.

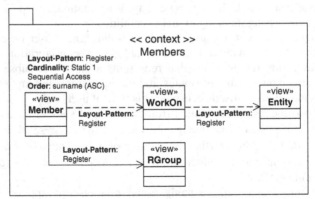

Fig. 6. Presentation information for a specific navigation context

4   Related Works

Nowadays, the approaches that address some kind of personalisation vary widely [16]: from single page generation strategies to complex content-based prediction systems, data mining, machine-learning algorithms... Most of these approaches consider personalisation and adaptation issues from an implementation perspective.

However, we consider the customisation issues in general should be treated from the conceptual modelling tasks inside of well-defined software engineering methods. Now, we are going to compare the personalisation issues presented in OOWS with other interesting conceptual modelling based Web Engineering approaches (WSDM [5], OOHDM [19], WebML [3], OO-H Method [7] and UWE [10]).

The Web Site Design Method (WSDM) is a user-driven approach that comprises three main phases: user modelling, conceptual design and implementation design. In the user modelling stage, the potential users of web site are identified and classified, this way for each potential user profile are systematically gathered and a class diagram of user profiles is built. The navigational model consists of a set of navigation tracks, each one specified for a particular user perspective. Every navigation track comprises three layers: context, navigation and information; this approach achieves very hierarchical web application compared to the flexible structured derived from the OOWS navigation model. On the other hand, WSDM defines its own graphical notation for the objects of the navigation model, and this fact is a very important drawback compared to OOWS, for example, which is UML-compliant. Lastly, the WSDM implementation design step looks for creating a consistent look and feel for the conceptual model, but this step is not very rich in recommendations, in this sense OOWS has a rich pattern-based presentation model and a generative approach for the automatic final product generation.

Object-Oriented Hypermedia Design Method (OOHDM) presents four activities: conceptual modelling, navigation design, abstract interface design and implementation. The notation of OOHDM is close but not completely compliant to UML. This method has been extended to specify personalised web systems by defining different scenarios according to user profiles or preferences [17]. One of the most representative differences with OOWS is that OOHDM does not allow objects to offer services to the users of application.

WebML is a specification language that gives a good basis for specifying different aspects of a web application such as content structure, page composition, navigation, presentation and personalisation. This language has its own graphical notation (not UML-compliant) that includes an explicit notion of group and user, where group describe sets of users with common characteristics (agent in OOWS), while users denote individuals. WebML is data-oriented while OOWS is object-oriented. This difference could be important when applications grew in size and complexity.

OO-H Method and OOWS share the same conceptual model, OO-Method [15], and also both have the goal of allowing an automatic web application generation. The main difference between OO-H Method and OOWS is that OOWS is a full OO-Method extension that includes the functional specification completely, meanwhile OO-H only specifies the interface. Another difference appears in the navigation model, more specifically in the concept of node. OO-H Method associates a different navigation access diagram with each user-type, but the nodes (navigation classes) are limited to present information of only one class, whereas nodes in OOWS (navigational contexts) can work with views of several classes, showing a more appropriate information for the user in every moment. OO-H Method is now being extended with an adaptation model to specify adaptive and proactive personalised web applications [6].

The UML-based Web Engineering (UWE) is a key reference of an engineered approach to the development of web applications with a special focus on personalisation and adaptation issues. It is based on the so called Munich Reference Model that describes the navigation mechanism of a web application. This model presents a three-layer structure (run-time layer, storage layer, within-component layer) that includes the needed functionality to support user modelling and adaptation aspects. UWE is a highly relevant reference in order to extend OOWS with the adaptive model, but also OOWS can contribute with a solid full life-cycle engineering process with automatic code generation capabilities.

5 Conclusions and Further Work

In this paper, we have presented how OOWS, a web application production process, deals with the user profiling activities in order to achieve personalisation and adaptation issues in web systems.

We have argued that our proposal allows the specification of the user profiles from the conceptual modelling at the beginning of the application life cycle. This way, our approach deals with other important research works that defend a more engineered treatment of the customisation issues in comparison to the most extended approach that considers the user profiling from an implementation point of view.

In order to achieve this goal, OOWS presents a set of UML-compliant abstract primitives that appear in the different models of its specification systems phase. Essentially, the user profiling primitives allow modelling the different user types that represent the allowed groups in the web systems, modelling the possible user type changes and modelling the content, presentation and navigation capabilities for each group. Limiting to the notation proposed by the UML instead of introducing a new notation has the advantage of using a well-known standard and that UML is supported by many case tools. UML is extended to model the navigation and the presentation according to the UML extension mechanisms.

With these arguments we can say OOWS supports the specification and design of personalised and adaptable systems, but actually this method fails in individual personalisation support. For this reason, according to [4], OOWS deals with the so called adaptable hypermedia systems but does not support the so called adaptive hypermedia systems.

Further work is mainly directed to define a new model in the conceptual modelling phase that gives an adequate support of adaptive properties but assuring a full compatibility between this new adaptation model and the other models used in the process of conceptual modelling in OOWS.

Acknowledgements. Research supported by a CICYT Project (ref. TIC2000-1673-C06-05), a Government of Castile and León Project (ref. SA017/02) and a MCYT Project (ref. TIC2001-3530-C02-01).

References

[1] Abrahão S., Fons J., González M., Pastor O. Conceptual Modeling of Personalized Web Applications. In *2nd International Conference on Adaptive Hypermedia and Adaptive Web Based Systems, AH2002*, Lecture Notes in Computer Science. LNCS 2347. Springer Verlag (2002) 358–362.

[2] Brusilovsky, P.: Adaptive Hypermedia. *User Modeling and User-Adapted Interaction*, Vol. 11 (2001) 87–110.

[3] Ceri, S., Fraternali, P., Paraboschi, S.: "Web Modeling Language", (WebML): A Modeling Language for Designing Web Sites. In *Proceedings of the 9ᵗʰ International World Wide Web Conference WWW9*, Elsevier (2000) 137–157.

[4] De Bra, P.: Design Issues in Adaptive Web-Site Development. *Proceedings of the 2ⁿᵈ Workshop on Adaptive Systems and User Modeling on the WWW* (1999).

[5] De Troyer, O. y Leune, C.: WSDN: A User-Centered Design Method for Web Sites. In *Proceedings of the 7ᵗʰ International World Wide Web Conference WWW6*. Elsevier (1997) 85–94.

[6] Garrigós, I., Cachero, C., Gómez, J.: Modelado Conceptual de Aplicaciones Adaptivas y Proactivas en OO-H. In *Proceedings of the 2ⁿᵈ Taller de Ingeniería Web – Webe02*. El Escorial – Madrid (Spain). http://www.dlsi.ua.es/webe02/programa.htm (2002).

[7] Gómez, J., Cachero, C., Pastor, O.: Extending a Conceptual Modeling Approach to Web Application Design. In *Proceedings of Conference on Advanced Information Systems Engineering (CAiSE)*. Lecture Notes in Computer Science. LNCS 1789. Springer Verlag (2000) 79–93.

[8] Insfrán E., Pastor O., Wieringa R.: Requirements Engineering-Based Conceptual Modelling. *Requirements Engineering* Vol7, N. 2 (2002) 61–72.

[9] Jameson, A., Paris, C., Tasso, C.: Preface. In A. Jameson, C. Paris, C. Tasso (Eds.), *User Modeling: Proceedings of the Sixth International Conference UM'97*. Springer-Verlag. (1997).

[10] Koch, N.: Software Engineering for Adaptive Hypermedia Applications. PhD. Thesis (2000).

[11] McTear, M.: Special Issue on User Modeling. *Artificial Intelligence Review Journal*, Vol. 7 (1993).

[12] OMG: OMG Unified Modeling Language Specification. Version 1.4. Object Management Group Inc. http://www.omg.org/uml (2001).

[13] Pastor, O., Abrahão, S. M., Fons, J. J.: Building E-Commerce Applications from Object-Oriented Conceptual Models. *SIGecom Exchanges, Newsletter of the ACM Special Interest Group on E-commerce*, Vol. 2, N. 2 (2001) 28–36.

[14] Pastor, O., Abrahão, S., Fons, J. J.: An Object-Oriented Approach to Automate Web Applications Development. In K. Bauknecht, S. K. Madria, G. Pernul (Eds.), *Electronic Commerce and Web Technologies, Second International Conference, EC-Web 2001 Munich, Germany, September 4–6, 2001, Proceedings*. Lecture Notes in Computer Science. LNCS 2115. Springer Verlag, (2001) 16–28.

[15] Pastor, O., Gómez, J., Insfrán, E., Pelechano, V.: The OO-Method Approach for Information Systems Modelling: From Object-Oriented Conceptual Modeling to Automated Programming. *Information Systems*, Vol. 26, N. 7 (2001) 507–534.

[16] Riecken, D. (Guest Ed.): Special Issue on Personalization. *Communications of the ACM*, Vol. 43, N. 8 (2000).

[17] Rossi, G., Schwabe, D., Guimarães, R. M.: Designing Personalized Web Applications. In *Proceedings of the Tenth International World Wide Web Conference WWW10*, Hong Kong, (2001).

[18] Scharl, A.: A Classification of Web Adaptivity: Tailoring Content and Navigational Systems of Advanced Web Applications. In S. Murugesan, Y. Deshpande (Eds.), *Web Engineering. Managing Diversity and Complexity of Web Application Development.* Lecture Notes in Computer Science. LNCS 2016. Springer Verlag, (2001) 156-169.
[19] Schwabe, D., Rossi, G.: The Object-Oriented Hypermedia Design Model. *Communications of the ACM*, Vol. 38, N. 8 (1995) 45–46.
[20] User Modeling Home Page. http://www.um.org/. (2002).

Towards a Common Metamodel for the Development of Web Applications[1]

Nora Koch and Andreas Kraus

Ludwig-Maximilians-Universität München,
Oettingenstr. 67, 80538 München, Germany
www.pst.informatik.uni-muenchen.de
{kochn, krausa}@informatik.uni-muenchen.de

Abstract. Many different methodologies for the development of Web applications were proposed in the last ten years. Although most of them define their own notation for building models such as the navigation, the presentation or the personalization model, we argue that in many cases it is just another notation for the same concepts, i.e. they should be based on a common metamodel for the Web application domain. In addition, tool-supported design and generation is becoming essential in the development process of Web applications due to the increasing size and complexity of such applications, and CASE-tools should be built on a precisely specified metamodel of the modeling constructs used in the design activities, providing more flexibility if modeling requirements change.

This paper presents a first step towards such a common metamodel by defining first a metamodel for the UML-based Web Engineering (UWE) approach. The metamodel is defined as a conservative extension of the UML metamodel. We further discuss how to map the UWE metamodel to the UWE modeling constructs (UML profile) of the design method which was already presented in previous works. The metamodel and this mapping are the core of the extension of the ArgoUML open source CASE-tool we developed to support the UWE design notation and method.

1 Introduction

The Web Engineering field is rich in design methods such as OOHDM, OO-H, UWE, W2000, WebML or WSDM [2,5,9] supporting the complex task of designing Web applications. These methodologies propose the construction of different views (i.e. models) which comprises at least a conceptual model, a navigation and a presentation model although naming them differently. Each model is built out of a set of modeling elements, such as nodes and links for the navigation model or image and anchor for the presentation model. In addition, all these methodologies define or choose a notation for the constructs they define.

---

[1] This research has been partially supported by the EC 5th Framework project AGILE (IST-2001-32747) and by the German BMBF project GLOWA-Danube.

J.M. Cueva Lovelle et al. (Eds.): ICWE 2003, LNCS 2722, pp. 497–506, 2003.
© Springer-Verlag Berlin Heidelberg 2003

We argue that although all methodologies for the development of Web applications use different notations and propose slightly different development processes they could be based on a common metamodel for the Web application domain. A metamodel is a precise definition of the modeling elements, their relationships and the well-formedness rules needed for creating semantic models. A methodology based on this common metamodel may only use a subset of the constructs provided by the metamodel. The common Web application metamodel should therefore be the unification of the modeling constructs of current Web methodologies allowing for their better comparison and integration.

Metamodeling also plays a fundamental role in CASE-tool construction and is as well the core of automatic code generation. We propose to build the common metamodel on the standardized OMG metamodeling architecture facilitating the construction of meta CASE-tools.

A very interesting approach in terms of metamodeling for Web applications is the metamodel defined for the method W2000 to express the semantics of the design constructs of this method [2]. This metamodel is an extension of the UML metamodel complemented with Schematron rules for model checking. The CADMOS-D design method for web-based educational applications [8] defines another metamodel. It provides a UML visual representation of the modeling elements, but does not establish a relationship to the UML metamodel. Other approaches, such as the Generic Customization Model for Ubiquitous Web Applications [3] or the Munich Reference Model for Adaptive Hypermedia Applications [6], define a reference model for such applications, providing a framework for understanding relationships among entities of those specific Web domains.

As a first step towards a common metamodel we present in this paper a metamodel for the UWE methodology, which could then be joined with metamodels that are/will be defined for other methods. It is defined as a conservative extension of the UML metamodel [10]. This metamodel provides a precise description of the concepts used to model Web applications and their semantics. Our methodology UWE is based on this metamodel including tool support for the design and the semi-automatic generation of Web applications. We further define a mapping from the metamodel to the concrete syntax (i.e. notation) used in UWE. The description of the complete metamodel and the details of the mapping to the UWE notation are not within the scope of this paper (published as a technical report [7]).

The paper is organized as follows: Section 2 gives a brief introduction to the UWE methodology. In Section 3 we propose a metamodel for the UWE methodology. This metamodel is specified in UML. In Section 4 we discuss how the metamodel elements can be mapped to the UWE notation. Finally, some conclusions and future work are outlined in the last section.

2   UWE Methodology

The UWE methodology covers the whole life-cycle of Web application development proposing an object-oriented and iterative approach based on the Unified Software

Development Process [4]. The main focus of the UWE approach is the systematic design followed by a semi-automatic generation of Web applications.

The notation used for design is a "lightweight" UML profile described in previous works, e.g. [5]. A UML profile is a UML extension based on the extension mechanisms defined by the UML itself with the advantage of using a standard notation that can be easily supported by tools and that does not impact the interchange formats. The UWE profile includes stereotypes and tagged values defined for the modeling elements needed to model the different aspects of Web applications, such as navigation, presentation, user, task and adaptation aspects. For each aspect a model is built following the guidelines provided by the UWE methodology for the systematic construction of models. For example, a navigation model is built out of navigation classes, links and a set of indexes, guided tours and queries. The navigation classes and links are views over conceptual classes. Similarly, the user is modeled by a user role, user properties and associations of these properties to the conceptual classes. Currently, an extension of the CASE-tool ArgoUML [1] is being implemented to support the construction of these UWE design models.

In   Fig. 1 we give an example for the UWE design models of a Conference Management System application. On the left side the conceptual model is depicted from which in successive steps a navigation model is systematically constructed. On the right side we show the result of the first step in building the navigation model.

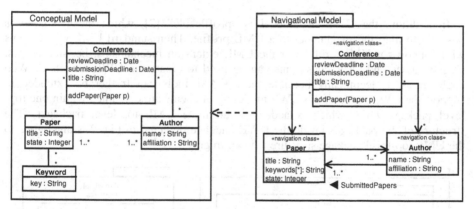

Fig. 1. Example for UWE design models of a Conference Management System

The semi-automatic generation of Web applications from design models is supported by the UWEXML approach [5]. Design models delivered by the design tools in the XMI-Format are transformed into XML documents that are published by an XML publishing framework.

3   UWE Metamodel

The UWE metamodel is designed as a conservative extension of the UML metamodel (version 1.4). Conservative means that the modeling elements of the UML metamodel are not modified e.g. by adding additional features or associations to the modeling element *Class*. All new modeling elements of the UWE metamodel are related by inheritance to at least one modeling element of the UML metamodel. We define for them additional features and relationships to other metamodel modeling elements and use OCL constraints to specify the additional static semantics (analogous to the well-formedness rules in the UML specification). By staying thereby compatible with the MOF interchange metamodel we can take advantage of metamodeling tools that base on the corresponding XML interchange format XMI.

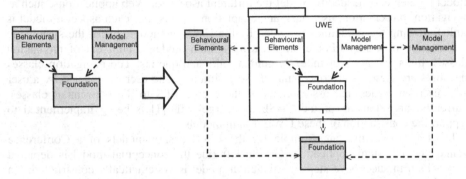

Fig. 2. Embedding of the UWE metamodel within the UML metamodel

In addition, the UWE metamodel is "profileable" [2], which means that it is possible to map the metamodel to a UML profile. Then standard UML CASE-tools with support for UML profiles or the UML extension mechanisms, i.e. stereotypes, tagged values and OCL constraints can be used to create the UWE models of Web applications. If technically possible these CASE-tools can further be extended to support the UWE method. All UWE modeling elements are contained within one top-level package *UWE* which is added to the three UML top-level packages. The structure of the packages inside the UWE package depicted in Fig. 2 is analogous to the UML top-level package structure (shown in gray).

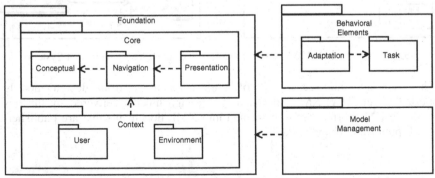

Fig. 3. Package substructure of the UWE metamodel

The package *Foundation* contains all basic static modeling elements, the package *Behavioral Elements* depends from it and contains all elements for behavioral modeling and finally the package *Model Management* which also depends from the

Foundation package contains all elements to describe the models themselves specific to UWE. These UWE packages depend on the corresponding UML top-level packages.

The UWE *Foundation* package is further structured in the *Core* and the *Context* packages (see Fig. 3). The former contains packages for the core (static) modeling elements for the basic aspects of Web applications which are the conceptual, navigation and presentation aspects. The latter depends on the *Core* package and contains further sub-packages for modeling the user and the environment context. The *Behavioral Elements* package consists of the two sub-packages *Task* and *Adaptation* that comprise modeling elements for the workflow and personalization aspects of a Web application respectively. All together one can say that the separation of concerns of Web applications is represented by the package structure of the UWE metamodel.

In the following sections we focus on the *Navigation* and *Presentation* packages of the *Core* package; for description of other packages see [7].

3.1 Navigation Package

The basic elements in navigation models are nodes and links. The corresponding modeling elements in the UWE metamodel are *NavigationNode* and *Link,* which are derived from the UML *Core* elements *Class* and *Association,* respectively. The backbone of the navigation metamodel is shown in Fig. 4. The *NavigationNode* metaclass is abstract which means that only further specialized classes may be instantiated; furthermore it can be designated to be an entry node of the application with the *isLandmark* attribute. The *Link* class is also an abstract class and the *isAutomatic* attribute is used to express that the link should be followed automatically by the system and not by the user. *Links* connect a source *NavigationNode* with one or more target *NavigationNodes* as expressed by the two associations between *Link* and *NavigationNode.* Note that this is an extension to the semantics of links in HTML where only one target is allowed (unless some technical tricks are employed). The associations between *Link* and *NavigationNode* are purely conceptual because we reuse the structure defined in the UML *Core* package where *Classes* are connected to *Associations* via *AssociationEnds.* For further details see the UML specification [10].

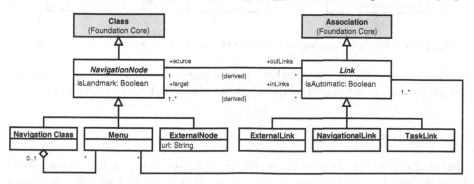

Fig. 4. UWE Navigation package – Backbone

The *NavigationNode* is further specialized to the concrete node types *NavigationClass*, *Menu* and *ExternalNode*. The *NavigationClass* element connects the navigation model with the conceptual model as described in the next paragraph. It may contain a *Menu* that contains *Links* to *NavigationNodes*. We also distinguish the following types of links that are specializations of the class *Link*:

- the *NavigationLink* is used for modeling the (static) navigation with the usual semantics in hypermedia applications and may contain one or more *AccessPrimitives*, such as *Index*, *Query* and *GuidedTour* (these classes are not visualized in Fig. 4 due to space problems).
- the *TaskLink* connects the source node with the definition of a part of its dynamic behavior specified in a UWE task model; and
- the *ExternalLink* links nodes outside the application scope, the so-called *External Nodes*.

Fig. 5 shows the connection between navigation and conceptual objects. A *NavigationClass* is derived from the *ConceptualClass* at the association end with the role name *derivedFrom* – or – one could say that there may exists several navigation views on a conceptual class. The *NavigationClass* consists of *NavigationAttributes* (derived from the UML *Core* element *Attribute*) which themselves are derived from *ConceptualAttributes*. An important invariant is that all *ConceptualAttributes* from which the *NavigationAttributes* of a *NavigationClass* are derived, have to be *ConceptualAttributes* of a *ConceptualClass* in the transitive closure of the *ConceptualClass* from that the *NavigationClass* is derived. This can be formally expressed as an OCL constraint.

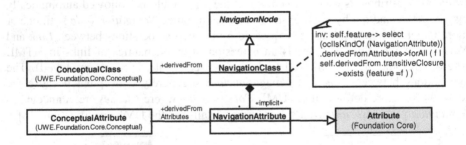

Fig. 5. UWE Navigation package – Connection between navigation and conceptual objects

Further it is possible to specify what types of access primitives should be used for navigation links with a target multiplicity greater than one. For more details see [7].

3.2   Presentation Package

The central element for structuring the presentation space is the abstract class *Location* (see Fig. 6). The presentation sub-structure is modeled with the specialized class *LocationGroup* that consists of a list of sub-locations whereas presentation alternatives between different *Locations* are modeled with the class

LocationAlternative; optionally a default alternative can be specified. Finally, the "atomic" subclass *PresentationClass* contains all the logical user interface (UI) elements presented to the user of the application. It is derived from exactly one *NavigationNode*. The user interface elements are for example *Image*, *Text* or UI group elements, such as *Collection*, *Anchor* and *Form*. How these elements are related to *Link* and *Index* can be seen in the complete description of this package [7]. Further we use a ternary association for expressing link-sensitive presentation, i.e. when following a link from one *NavigationNode* to another we can specify the *PresentationClass* which should be presented to the user depending on the link chosen.

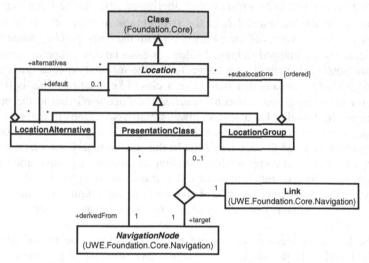

Fig. 6. UWE Presentation Package – Backbone

4   Mapping to the UWE Notation

Metamodels define the concepts and their relationships used in the modeling activities of a certain domain – Web Design in our case – whereas designers build application models using a concrete notation, i.e. the concrete syntax.

One way of mapping a metamodel to a concrete syntax often found in literature is to extend the UML syntax in a non-standard way. This means for example that instead of using the built-in extension mechanism of the UML new graphical symbols are introduced or existing symbols are decorated or its shapes are changed. This could technically be easily achieved e.g. using ArgoUML [1]; by using the NSUML Java framework one can make ArgoUML work with the extended UML metamodel and customize the graphical appearance of all modeling elements. The drawback of this approach is on the one hand that the syntax and semantic of the new notation has to be documented thoroughly. On the other hand the corresponding metamodel interchange format is no longer the same as the UML interchange format. The consequence is that one can no longer use tools which rely on the UML XMI format.

We chose to map the metamodel concepts to a UML profile. A UML profile comprises the definition of stereotypes and tagged values and specifies how they can be used by OCL constraints (i.e. well-formedness of a model). With appropriate tool support a model can be automatically checked if it is conform to the profile. The definition of a UML profile has the advantage of being supported by nearly every UML CASE-tool either automatically, by a tool plug-in or passively when the model is saved and then checked by an external tool.

A simplified version of the mapping rules is the following:

- Metamodel classes (e.g. *NavigationClass*) are mapped to stereotyped classes. The name of the class is mapped to the name of the stereotype and the inheritance structure is mapped to a corresponding inheritance structure between stereotypes.
- Attributes in the metamodel (e.g. the *isAutomatic* attribute of *Link*) are mapped directly to tagged values of the owner class with the corresponding name and type.
- Associations are mapped to tagged values or associations. Mapping to associations is only possible if both classes connected to the association ends are a subtype of *Classifier*, which means that they have a class-like notation. This is for example true for the aggregation between *Location* and *LocationGroup* in the presentation package. On the other hand we can always map associations to tagged values with the drawback of worse readability in the diagrams, e.g. the association between *NavigationClass* and *ConceptualClass*. In the case of binary associations we assign a tagged value to the corresponding stereotyped class of each association end.

We propose to resolve inheritance in the metamodel by repeating the mapping of attributes and associations for all subclasses, e.g. the *isLandmark* attribute of the abstract class *NavigationNode* which is also mapped for the subclass *NavigationClass*.

In the following sections we present the notation for some of the UWE models using the UWE UML profile. For more details about the mapping process refer to [7].

4.1   UML Profile for the Navigation Model

We use the simplified example of a conference management system presented in Fig. 1 to illustrate the mapping process and the notation of the UWE profile for the navigation model. The central element in the metamodel *NavigationClass* is mapped to the stereotype «*navigation class*» (see Fig. 5 and Fig. 7). The metaattribute *isLandmark* indicating that the *Conference* model element is an entry point is represented as a corresponding tagged value of the model element. Another tagged value *derivedFrom* is a mapping of the metaassociation between *NavigationClass* and *ConceptualClass*. As shown in the example for each model attribute the relation to the attributes of the conceptual model is specified by the *derivedFromAttributes* tagged value. The *keywords* attribute of the class *Paper* is a non-trivial example of this relationship, hence the *derivedFromAttributes* tagged value states that this attribute is related to the *key* attribute of the *Keyword* class in the conceptual model associated to the *Paper* class in the conceptual model.

As the metaclass *Link* is a subclass of the UML metaclass *Association* it is also visualized like a UML association. We decorate links with a stereotype such as for example «*navigation link*». Each link must have an explicit direction and multiplicities defined. For better readability the stereotype for links may be hidden when the context is clear.

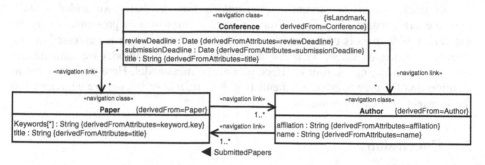

Fig. 7. Example for a navigation model using the UWE UML profile

4.2   UML Profile for the Presentation Model

The three specializations of the abstract class *Location* (see Fig. 6) are mapped to the corresponding stereotypes for the class elements *«location alternative»*, *«location group»* and *«presentation class»*. The presentation grouping expressed by the aggregation association of the *LocationGroup* element is mapped to aggregation associations of the *«location group»* classes where the aggregation is ordered and the association ends have classifier scope and multiplicity one. *LocationAlternatives* are mapped in a similar way, only that we express the default alternative by a tagged

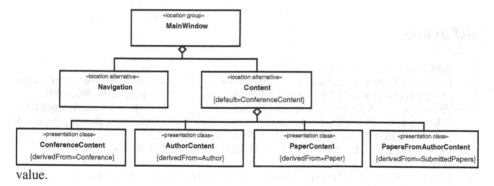

value.

Fig. 8. Example for a presentation model using the UWE UML profile

The relationship between *PresentationClasses*, *NavigationNodes* and *Links* is expressed by one tagged value of the *«presentation class»* element with the name *derivedFrom*. The value has to be the full qualified name of the corresponding *NavigationNode* for entry presentation classes corresponding to entry navigation nodes (i.e. *isLandmark=true*) or for not-link-sensitive presentation classes. In the case of a link- sensitive presentation the name of the corresponding *Link* is assigned to the tagged value. In Fig. 8 we give an example for a presentation model of the conference application example. The location group *MainWindow* divides the presentation space into the *Navigation* and the *Content* location alternatives. The possible alternatives are the presentation classes *ConferenceContent* (which is the default one), *AuthorContent* and *PaperContent*. For the latter we added a link-sensitive presentation class *PaperFromAuthorContent* which is presented when the link *SubmittedPapers* is used to navigate to the *Paper* node. This is expressed by the *derivedFrom* tagged value. As in the description of the metamodel we omit further details about mapping the user interface part of the metamodel. Here we only want to mention that the user interface elements (e.g. button, text or image) are aggregated to the *«presentation class»* elements.

5   Conclusions

In this paper we presented a metamodel for the UWE methodology and sketched the mapping to a concrete syntax (i.e. notation), the UWE notation defined as a UML profile. The UWE metamodel is defined as a conservative extension of the UML metamodel. This metamodel is the basis for a common metamodel for the Web application domain and for the CASE-Tool supported design.

In our future work we will concentrate on the further refinement of the UWE metamodel to cope with the needs for automatic code generation, especially for the dynamic aspects like tasks and adaptation. At the same time we will extend our tools: on the one hand we have to adapt the CASE-tool ArgoUWE to easily cope with a evolving metamodel and on the other hand our tool for the semi-automatic generation of Web applications UWEXML [5] has to be extended.

References

1. ArgoUML. www.tigris.org
2. Baresi L., Garzotto F., Paolini P. Meta-modeling Techniques meets Web Application Design Tools. Proc. of FASE 2002, LNCS 2306, Springer Verlag, pp. 294–307, 2002.
3. Finkelstein A., Savigni A., Kappel G., Retschitzegger W., Pöll B., Kimmerstorfer E., Schwinger W., Hofer T., Feichtner C., "Ubiquitous Web Application Development - A Framework for Understanding", Proc. of SCI2002, July 2002.
4. Jacobson I., Booch G., Rumbaugh J. The Unified Software Development Process. Addison Wesley, 1999.
5. Koch N., Kraus A. The expressive Power of UML-based Web Engineering. Proc. of IWWOST'02, CYTED, pp. 105–119, 2002.
6. Koch N., Wirsing M. The Munich Reference Model for Adaptive Hypermedia Applications. Proc. of AH'2002, LNCS 2347, Springer Verlag, pp 213–222, 2002.
7. Kraus A., Koch N. A Metamodel for UWE. Technical Report 0301, University of Munich, www.pst.informatik.uni-muenchen.de/publications/TR0301_UWE.pdf, 2003.
8. Retalis S., Papasalourus A., Skordalakis M. Towards a generic conceptual design meta-model for web-based educational applications. Proc. of IWWOST'02, CYTED, 2002.
9. Schwabe D., Pastor O. (Eds.). Online Proc. of IWWOST'01. www.dsic.upv.es /~west2001/iwwost01
10. UML, The Unified Modeling Language, Version 1.4. Object Management Group (OMG). www.omg.org, 2001.

The Spanish Morphology in Internet

Octavio Santana Suárez, José Pérez, Francisco Carreras,
Zenón José Hernández Figueroa, and Gustavo Rodríguez Rodríguez

Departamento de Informática y Sistemas,
Universidad de Las Palmas de Gran Canaria,
Campus Universitario de Tafira,
35017 Las Palmas de Gran Canaria, Spain
{OSantana, JPerez, FCarreras,
ZHernadez, GRodriguez}@dis.ulpgc.es
http://www.gedlc.ulpgc.es

Abstract. This Web service tags morpholexically any Spanish word and it gets the corresponding forms starting from a canonical form and from the flexion asked for. In the verbs, it deals with the simple and compound conjugation, the enclitic pronouns, the flexion of the participle like verbal adjective and the diminutive of the gerund. With the nonverbal forms, this web service considers: gender and number, heteronomy for change of sex, superlative degree, adverbiation and the appreciative derivation. In the tag and in the generation the prefixation is taken into account. It allows the manipulation of morpholexical relationships. It offers a global vision of the behavior and productivity of the Spanish words in the principal processes of formation (sufixation, prefixation, parasinthesis, suppression, regression, zero-modification, apocopation, metathesis and others which are unclassifiable and that generate alternative graphical forms). It includes the principal Spanish lexicographic repertoires. It considers 151103 canonical forms that produce more than 4900000 flexioned and derived forms and about 90000 morpholexical relationships are established.

1 The Spanish Morphology

As result of the work done by the Group of Data Structures and Computacional Linguistic of the University of Las Palmas de Gran Canaria (http://www.gedlc.ulpgc.es), a Web application has been created able to interpret and to handle with versatility different relevant aspects of the Spanish morphology. The application represents more a form to show the potentiality of a Web System of management of the morphology of the Spanish language than a finalist tool. This system allows its integration in other useful tools for the natural language processing like orthographic correction, advanced search information, text analysers, disambiguousers, lexicographical station, parsers, information extraction, text automatic generation, syntactic correction and extraction of summaries, among other applications, all of them aimed at offering interactive services distributed through Internet.

J.M. Cueva Lovelle et al. (Eds.): ICWE 2003, LNCS 2722, pp. 507–510, 2003.
© Springer-Verlag Berlin Heidelberg 2003

The automatized treatment of the Spanish morphology arouses great interest because it constitutes the first touchstone on which to construct any natural language processor and starts the way towards future Web services more specialized in the handling, learning and control of that great human potential –the language.

The available system in the Web tags any Spanish word identifying its canonical form, grammar category and the flexion or derivation that produces it, and is able to produce the corresponding forms from a canonical form and from the flexion or derivation asked for; both the recognition and the generation operate on a same data structure, to cross it in opposite senses implies that the tool works in one or another modality.

In the verbs, it deals with the simple and compound conjugation, the enclitic pronouns, the flexion of the participle like verbal adjective (gender and number) and the diminutive of the gerund. With the nonverbal forms, it considers: the gender and the number in the nouns, adjectives, pronouns and articles; heteronomy by sex change in the nouns; the superlative degree in the adjectives and adverbs; the adverbiation and the superlative adverbiation in the adjectives; the appreciative derivation in the nouns, adjectives and adverbs; the graphical variants in all the grammar categories and the invariant forms such as preposition, conjunctions, exclamations, words of other languages and locutions or phrases. As much in the tag as in the generation the incorporation of prefixes is discretionarily considered.

In addition it allows the recognition, the generation and the manipulation of the morpholexical relations of any word, it includes the recovery of all its lexicogenetic information until arriving at a primitive one, the management and control of the affix in the treatment of its relations, as well as the regularity in the established relation. It provides a global vision of the behavior and productivity of the Spanish words in the main processes of formation (sufixation, prefixation, parasinthesis, suppression, regression, modification-zero, apocopation, metathesis and nonclassifiable others that generate alternative graphical forms).

For the accomplishment of this work, a corpus of Spanish words with the lexicon of different dictionaries has been created: the *Diccionario de la Lengua Española de la Real Academia*, the *Diccionario General de la Lengua Española VOX*, the *Diccionario de uso del Español de María Moliner*, the *Gran Diccionario de la Lengua Española de Larousse*, the *Diccionario de Uso del Español Actual Clave SM*, the *Diccionario de Sinónimos y Antónimos de Espasa-Calpe*, the *Diccionario Ideológico de la Lengua Española de Julio Casares* and the *Diccionario de voces de uso actual* directed by Manuel Alvar Ezquerra. From 151103 canonical forms (which include about 15000 proper names and 9000 adjectives coming from participles of verbs not registered in the previous repertoires), they obtain more than 4900000 flexionned and derived forms (without adding the inherent extension to the prefixes and the enclitic pronouns) and around 90000 morpholexical relations are established.

The tagger allows the user to tag any Spanish word –it identifies its canonical form, grammar category and the flexion, derivation and prefix that affects to it. The tag is the first advisable step for the users of the system: on the one hand, it makes the entry flexible when allowing to have access to the rest of the available services without previously having neither morphologic nor grammar knowledge and, on the other hand, it identifies without ambiguity the different morphologic interpretations of the inserted form.

The verbal flexioner service allows the user to obtain, from a verb, the conjugation of a simple or composed tense, nonpersonal simple or compound forms, the flexion of the participle as a verbal adjective and the diminutive of the gerund. In addition, it is possible to select from three pull-down lists the valid combinations of one, two or three enclitic pronouns, so that the system incorporates them correctly to the required conjugated forms. The nominal flexioner service allows the user to obtain, from a noun, the changes of gender and number and the appreciative derivation for the selected gender and number. The adjectival flexioner service is similar to the one for nouns, although it adds the specific flexions of the adjectives: the superlative degree, the adverbiation and the superlative adverbiation. The flexioner of other forms service allows the user to obtain, from pronouns, articles, adverbs, prepositions, conjunctions, exclamations, words and expressions from other languages, changes in gender and number and appreciative forms when possible. In addition to the formation rules, the existing irregularities for all flexions are considered.

A important flexibility is the recognition of the existence of prefixes, discretionarily incorporated in the form to tag or to generate. It avoids, therefore, knowledge in this area –as to which prefixes exist in Spanish and which the rules of union and their irregularities are.

2   The Morpholexical Relations

The primary target of this service consists of obtaining a set of morpholexical relations between useful Spanish words for applications of processing of the natural language. In a synchronous study, and with the glance put in the automatic treatment of the morphology with computer science means, the formal or theoretical aspects do not have to agree with the strictly linguistic ones. There exist Spanish words that maintain a strong semantic and functional relation –the same that appears in the derivative or prefix level–, and that cannot take derivation or prefixation, although yes a formal relation through other stages in the evolution of the languages exists, that is why it is considered necessary to include them –*agua* with *acuoso*, *vejiga* with *vesical*, *conejo* with *cunicular*. This concept must be restricted to avoid to arrive at the concept of related notion –*blanco* with *albura*, *sólido* with *endurecer*, *niño* with *pueril*–, that is why a criterion of historic-etimologic confluence is applied. It is obvious that, for the speaker, and therefore for computer science *acuario*, *portuario* and *campanario* must be places equally related to *agua*, *puerto* and *campana*. So, it is necessary to pass to another level beyond morphology level, in order to resolve linguistic barriers that they would prevent to treat relations beyond the derivation or the prefixation; the concept of morpholexical relation is extended in this way.

There is an option that facilitates to obtain the set of words morpholexically closer to the given one –its primitive, its derivatives and the derivatives from its primitive.

Another option serves to obtain the complete family of words with any morpholexical relation. These two possibilities allow in addition their graphical presentation.

Due to any Spanish word is admited as input by the morpholexical relations service, the request is previously treated by the tagger in order to apply the adequate relations on the canonical forms. If the entry comes from more than one canonical form with relations, the requested relations for each canonical form are obtained.

References

1. Alsina, R.: Todos los Verbos Castellanos Conjugados. 17th edn. Teide, Barcelona (1990)
2. Alvar Ezquerra, M.: La formación de palabras en español. 5th edn. Arco/Libros, Madrid (2002)
3. Alvar Ezquerra, M.: Nuevo diccionario de voces de uso actual. Arco/Libros, Madrid (2003)
4. Carreras, F.: Sistema Computacional de Gestión Morfológica del Español (SCOGEME). Ph. Degree Thesis directed by O. Santana and J. Pérez, Universidad de Las Palmas de Gran Canaria (2002)
5. Casares, J.: Diccionario Ideológico de la Lengua Española. 2nd edn. Gustavo Gili, Barcelona (1990)
6. Corripio Pérez, F.: Diccionario Práctico. Incorrecciones: Dudas y Norma Gramatical. Larousse Planeta, Barcelona (1995)
7. Diccionario de la Lengua Española. Edición electrónica. Electronic edn. 21.1.0, Real Academia Española and Espasa Calpe, Madrid (1995)
8. Diccionario de Uso del Español Actual. Clave. Electronic edition, SM, Madrid (1997)
9. Diccionario de Uso del Español de María Moliner. 2nd edn. Electronic edn., Gredos, Madrid (2001)
10. Diccionario General de la Lengua Española Vox. Electronic edn. Biblograf, Barcelona (1997)
11. Gran Diccionario de la Lengua Española. Larousse Planeta, Barcelona (1996)
12. Gran Diccionario de Sinónimos y Antónimos. 4th edn. Espasa Calpe, Madrid (1991)
13. Gómez Torrego, L.: Manual de Español Correcto, 10th edn. Arco/Libros, Madrid, (2000)
14. Real Academia Española: Esbozo de una nueva gramática de la lengua española. 1st edn. Espasa Calpe, Madrid (1989)
15. Santana, O., Carreras, F., Hernández, Z., Pérez, J., Rodríguez, G.: Manual de la conjugación del español. 12790 verbos conjugados. Arco/Libros, Madrid (2002)
16. Santana, O., Pérez, J., Carreras, F., Duque, J., Hernández, Z., Rodríguez, G.: FLANOM: Flexionador y lematizador automático de formas nominales. Lingüística Española Actual, Vol. XXI-2, Arco/Libros, (1999) 253–297
17. Santana, O., Pérez, J., Hernández, Z., Carreras, F., Rodríguez, G.: FLAVER: Flexionador y lematizador automático de formas verbales. Lingüística Española Actual, Vol. XIX-2, Arco/Libros, Madrid (1997) 229–282
18. Santana, O.; Pérez, J.; Losada, L.: Generación automática de respuestas en análisis morfológico. Estudios de lingüística, Universidad de Alicante, Vol. 14, (2000) 245–257
19. Seco, M.: Diccionario de dudas y dificultades de la lengua española. 9th edn. Espasa Calpe, Madrid (1991)

Morphoanalysis of Spanish Texts: Two Applications for Web Pages

Octavio Santana Suárez, Zenón José Hernández Figueroa, and
Gustavo Rodríguez Rodríguez

Departamento de Informática y Sistemas de la Universidad de Las Palmas de Gran Canaria,
Edificio Departamental de Informática y Matemáticas, Campus Universitario de Tafira, 35017
Las Palmas de Gran Canaria, Spain
{osantana, zhernandez, grodriguez}@dis.ulpgc.es
http://www.gedlc.ulpgc.es

Abstract. The applications described here follow up the works performed in the recent last years by the Data Structures and Computational Linguistics Group at Las Palmas de Gran Canaria University. These works have been developed about computational Linguistics and, as one of their results, some tools for morphologic identification and generation have been released. This work presents the use of those tools as parts of new applications designed to benefit from the great linguistic information flow from Internet. Two kinds of applications are identified, both according to the interactive grade of the linguistics studies to be done, and two prototypes, named DAWeb and NAWeb, are developed with special attention to their architecture in order to maximize the efficiency of both. Analysis modes include: neologism detection, word use (qualitative and quantitative measurements) and some syntax aspects like lexical collocations or prepositional regimes.

1 Introduction

This work describes two computer applications developed by the Data Structures and Computational Linguistics Group at Las Palmas de Gran Canaria University. These applications follow up the previous works about computational linguistics performed by the Group in the last few years. As a result of those works some tools for morphological identification and generation of Spanish words have been released; several of these tools can be used on-line from http://www.gedlc.ulpgc.es. This work intends to apply those tools as part of new developments designed to get at the big flow of linguistic information of Internet documents. The results can be named as "tools for morphological analysis of web pages.

The study of the use of the language can be done in two ways: intensive, of a single or few documents, in order to identify concrete characteristics, or extensive, of a great mass of documents in order to obtain patterns frequently used. So two applications were developed, named DAWeb (Web Downloader and Analyzer, in Spanish "Descargador y Analizador de Web") and NAWeb (Web Browser and Analyzer, in Spanish "Navegador y Analizador de Web").

J.M. Cueva Lovelle et al. (Eds.): ICWE 2003, LNCS 2722, pp. 511–514, 2003.
© Springer-Verlag Berlin Heidelberg 2003

2 DAWeb

DAWeb is oriented to the massive analysis of documents from one or various websites. Formally, it can be compared to a downloader program; with the difference that it does not save the retrieved documents locally, but only the results of the performed analysis. Internally, DAWeb is organized into three modules: Configuration Module, Document Retrieval Module and Analysis Module. The Configuration Module serves to define an "Analysis project", specifying the set of URLs to explore, criteria to discard URLs, morphological analysis options, number of threads to use and, optionally, times to running the project.

2.1 Document Retrieval Module

The Document Retrieval Module consists of one Distribution Module and a variable number of Retrieval Modules interacting with Internet. The Distribution Module coordinates the work of the Retrieval Modules and prepares the results obtained by them to be used by the Document Analysis Module. It takes URLs from the "pending URLs list" and assigns them to idle Retrieval Modules, if any. Each Retrieval Module tries then to get the document tied to the URL assigned to it. When all Retrieval Modules are busy or all pending URLs are assigned, the Distribution Module waits for results. When a Retrieval Module gets a document, the Distribution Module adds it to the "retrieved document queue" to be processed by the Analysis Module, extracts the URLs contained in the document and adds them to the "pending URLs list", but only when they are not there, they were not there previously and they do not match the critera to discard URLs. If a Retrieval Module reports a fail, the Distribution Module analyzes the problem and decides whether to repeat getting the document later or discard the URL, annotating the case in the "log list". The work of the Document Retrieval Module ends when the "pending URLs list" is empty and all Retrieval Modules are idle.

Each Retrieval Module is a HTTP (HiperText Transfer Protocol) component running on an independent thread. The number of active Retrieval Modules can be fixed in the range one to ten (default number is five). This configurability produces a great adaptability to changing circumstances of the net.

2.2 Document Analysis Module

The first step when analysing a web page is to extract the text contained in it. Text extraction task is performed by a one pass syntactic parser that consists of an automaton driven by the characters sequence in the document. The automaton searches the text for the HTML (HiperText Mark-up Language) tags to discard or change them in order to obtain the text of the document free of marks but with a minimum structural information.

The core of the Document Analysis Module is a Morphological Recognition Tool that takes a word and returns a list of possible base forms, inflections, and grammatical values for it. The Morphological Recognition Tool was originally designed to identify single words. When the target is the analysis of texts this ratio can be improved taking advantage of the fact that a normal text is mainly composed using a small set of words that are repeated many times. Consequently, a special Morphological Recognition Improvement Tool using an ultra speed hashing structure to save information about each word when it first appears during the document analysis process has been developed for this work.

The results of performed analysis are structured into a hierarchy derived from the pair domain-page and organized by the different kind of programmed analysis. This hierarchical structure is saved to disk in a suitable format to be easily studied later.

3 NAWeb

The major differences between the architectures of DAWeb and NAWeb are the substitution of the Document Retrieval module by a TWebBrowser component that encapsulates the features of Microsoft Internet Explorer, and the inclusion of modules to classify and show the results in an interactive way.

Due to its interactive orientation, NAWeb looks like a typical web browser with additional features. Its main window is divided into three zones: the menu and toolbars zone, up, the views & annotation zone, in the middle, and the results zone, in the bottom. Both the views & annotations and the results zones are organized by means of multiple pages to allow a better analysis.

There are six pages in the views & annotations zone. All but the last one show a different view of the document (web page) retrieved from Internet. The first page shows the web page as it can be seen on any web browser. The second page shows the "pure" text of the document, free of HTML tags. The third page shows the HTML code for the web page. The fourth page shows the "lemma" view of the text, a list view of all the words in the text joined with the results of its morphoanalysis identification. the fifth page shows the information header of the document. The sixth page is an edition area where the user can do annotations and transfers information about the document.

The results zone shows results of analysis arranged by different criteria, each in a different page. As in the views & annotations zone there are six pages. The first page shows the words in the document distributed into six lists by their grammatical category (verbs, nouns, adjectives...). The second page shows the base forms of the word sorted by frequency, direct and invert alphabetical order and length. The third page shows the words in the document sorted by the same criteria and for distance respect to the selected one; two possible metrics of distance can be chosen: Levenshtein Distance (DL) or Largest Common Subsequence Distance (SCML). The fourth page shows, on the left, general information about the words in the document such as repetition grade and global category distribution; on the right, the outline view of the document is showed, this is a graphic representing the ratio of new words introduction. the fifth page shows complex and useful measurements of the spatial distribution/concentration of the words in the document and permits to compare similar patterns of distribution. The sixth page permits to locate repeated sequences of words by length and minimum frequency of apparition; this option is very useful for coocurrence studies.

4 Conclusions

The "Year 2000 annals" of the series "Spanish in the world" published by the "Instituto Cervantes" [8] points out the necessity of tools for intelligent information retrieval and analysis in order to increase the presence of the Spanish language on Internet. On the other hand, linguistic researchers need tools suitable to do larger and more accurate studies of the language and look at the web as a big source of documents for research. This work presents two tools that intend to fit these requirements: they are useful for linguistic analysis of information from the web, they can be used in the future as part of intelligent information retrieval systems adapted for Spanish documents, and further, they can serve other objectives as, for example, assistant tools for students of Spanish.

References

1. Santana, O., Hernández, Z. J., Rodríguez, G.: Conjugaciones Verbales. Boletín de la Sociedad Española para el Procesamiento del Lenguaje Natural, Nº 13, (feb. 1993) 443–450
2. Rodríguez, G., Hernández, Z., Santana, O.: Agrupaciones de Tiempos Verbales en un Texto. Anales de las II Jornadas de Sistemas Informáticos y de Computación, Quito, Ecuador, (Apr. 1993) 132–137
3. Santana, O., Hernández, Z. J., Rodríguez, G.: Reconocedor de Conjugación en Formas Verbales que Trata Pronombres Enclíticos, Lingüística Española Actual, Ed. Arco-Libros, Nº 16, (1994) 125–133
4. Alameda, J. R., Cuetos, F.: Diccionario de Frecuencias de las Unidades Lingüísticas del Español, Servicio de Publicaciones de la Universidad de Oviedo, (1995)
5. Santana, O., Pérez, J., Hernández, Z., Carreras, F., Rodríguez, G.: FLAVER: Flexionador y Lematizador Automático de Formas Verbales, Lingüística Española Actual, Ed. Arco-Libros, Nº XIX, 2, (1997) 229–282
6. Santana, O., Pérez, J., Carreras, F., Duque, J., Rodríguez, G.: FLANOM: Flexionador y Lematizador Automático de Formas Nominales, Lingüística Española Actual, Ed. Arco-Libros, Nº XXI, 2, (1999) 253–297
7. Millán, J. A.: Estaciones Filológicas, Filología e Informática, Seminario de Filología e Informática de la Universidad Autónoma de Barcelona, (1999) 143–164
8. Anuario 2000 del Español en el Mundo, Centro Virtual Cervantes, http://cvc.cervantes.es/obref/anuario/anuario_00

Agile Web Engineering (AWE) Process: Multidisciplinary Stakeholders and Team Communication

Andrew McDonald and Ray Welland

Department of Computing Science, University of Glasgow, Glasgow, Scotland. G12 8QQ.
{andrew, ray}@dcs.gla.ac.uk, http://www.dcs.gla.ac.uk/

Abstract. The Agile Web Engineering (AWE) Process is an agile or light-weight process that has been created to tackle the challenges that have been identified in Web engineering: short development life-cycle times; multidisciplinary development teams; delivery of bespoke solutions comprising software and data. AWE helps teams identify and manage the interactions between the business, domain, software and creative design strands in Web engineering projects. This paper gives an overview of the wide diversity of stakeholder roles reflected within AWE and how AWE tries to ensure communication between multidisciplinary sub-teams on large Web engineering projects.

1 Introduction

During September 2000 we decided to investigate traditional software engineering processes and methodologies and their application in Web engineering projects. From October until December 2000 we conducted a survey of commercial organisations involved in Web-based application development [7]. We carried out this survey by interviewing various different types of development stakeholder who contribute to the deliverables in a typical Web engineering project.

Across the seven organisations involved in our survey we concluded that in a development team of eight people: two will be from a technical or tradition software background; two will be from a creative design background; two will lead the team and the other two will be a domain and a business expert. Domain Experts are developer stakeholders who are responsible for issues associated with the application domain to which the Web application is being applied. Domain Experts are primarily responsible for the low-level integration and creation of content for Web applications. We believe that Domain Experts must be part of the Web development team. Business Experts are developer stakeholders who are responsible for business issues in the Web-based development team. Business Experts, in addition to providing content, are seen to provide guidance on achieving the business objectives of the Web engineering project. Business Experts are involved in contributing to the overall structure of the Web presence and in the high-level integration of data and software. We also view Business Experts as an essential part of any Web development team.

The multidisciplinary nature of Web engineering teams led us to think about how we could focus on the culturally diverse groups of people involved in Web engineering projects. This led us to consider an agile route [1] to solving the problems and is

J.M. Cueva Lovelle et al. (Eds.): ICWE 2003, LNCS 2722, pp. 515–518, 2003.
© Springer-Verlag Berlin Heidelberg 2003

sues a Web engineering process will have to tackle. We felt the agile approach best suited the challenges facing a Web engineering process. Particularly with the agile focus on: people and interactions over processes and tools; working software over comprehensive documentation; customer collaboration over contract negotiation; and responding to change over following a plan [3]. The wide diversity of disciplines and the large percentage of non-technical developers required to create the deliverables in Web application development make the agile route with its focus on people and interactions ideally suited to Web engineering [2]. In addition, the focus on working software, or working deliverables that satisfy business objectives, is something that is severely lacking in Web-based development processes [7]. The highly volatile nature of the markets and technologies in Web-based development, make an adaptive process that focuses on collaboration and responding to changing customer requirements, essential for success.

The AWE process provides a comprehensive framework for the development of Web products as described in full in our technical report [6]. This paper focuses on those aspects of AWE that deal with stakeholder roles and team communication.

2   AWE: Stakeholder Roles

The AWE Process identifies the *Stakeholder Roles* within the development team that need to be addressed during large Web engineering projects: *End-Users* represent all the users of the proposed system in a development project using the AWE Process; *Clients* represent the body or bodies who are paying for the project development; *Domain Experts* as discussed previously; *Business Experts* as discussed previously; *Software Engineers* lead responsibility for technical issues associated with the project such as Web application performance and version control; *Creative Designers* lead responsibility for aesthetic issues, such as screen layout, colour and font usage; and *Team Leaders* are responsible for team guidance and project management. Often these roles are misunderstood, and the responsibilities/roles of each stakeholder blurred. This often leads to some of the following fundamental mistakes during project development.

Validating the Web deliverables using the Client rather than a sample of End-Users. It is essential that project deliverables are validated against the business objectives using a sample of End-Users using proven well-understood techniques [8]. Often Clients are used to validate deliverables, unfortunately this can often lead teams to lose usability and business focus of the deliverables being produced [7], [9].

Lack of Business Experts and Domain Experts. Many organisations view the construction of Web-based applications as another software activity. Thus these organisations resource Web-based projects the way they would any other software development project. This often leads to the Software Engineer and Creative Designers making decisions regarding the product and its content, which they are not knowledgeable enough to do successfully in isolation from Business and Domain Experts.

Lack of co-operation/collaboration between Software Engineer and Creative Designer. In order to create the *browser experience* that best helps the project achieve its objectives it is essential both the Software Engineer and Creative Designer appreciate the contribution made by other roles in order to achieve the correct balance between function (usability) and form (aesthetic issues).

Poor leadership/management skills. Often if the Team Leader's background is in one of the other developer stakeholder roles, then the Team Leader can often be found to side with this developer stakeholder role during discussions/conflicts with other developer stakeholders. It is essential that the Team Leader be seen to be fair and always resolve conflicts in the best interests of the project in question.

AWE tries to address these issues by explicitly incorporating non-technical and technical stakeholder roles into the development team. The concept of small multidisciplinary development teams is something that Microsoft Solutions Framework (MSF) [4], [5] also advocates. However the cluster roles described in MSF [5] cover only those roles associated with traditional software development responsibilities, reflected within AWE's Team Leader and Software Engineer roles, together with consideration of usability issues. AWE goes much further to include roles reflecting the Business, Domain and Creative Design models in addition to those reflected in the traditional software development models. For a more detailed discussion of stakeholder roles reflected in AWE see our recent technical report [6].

3   Orthogonal Uni-discipline Developer Communication

One criticism levelled at other agile processes, is their inability to work beyond small teams of developers. We believe that AWE can scale beyond the limitation experienced by other agile processes. We use the term Orthogonal Uni-discipline Developer Communication to describe communication between similar types of developer on different teams working on the same project or Web presence. We believe that orthogonal uni-discipline developer communication will assist AWE in scaling to large numbers of developers due to the nature of large Web engineering projects.

Consider a large software engineering project to develop a new operating system. The developers will be split into smaller teams, with each team being challenged with a different type of problem. For example, one team will be responsible for the kernel, one team for the windowing system, one for device drivers, etc. Each team may be using similar technologies and techniques to build their respective deliverables, however every other team will view the deliverables primarily as a black box, through predefined interfaces, as each team will be working on a different type of problem space.

In large Web engineering projects, developers are often organised into a number of smaller teams, where deliverables are viewed as black boxes through pre-defined interfaces, just like large software engineering projects. However, each team will be working on similar types of problem spaces. For example, a large number of separate teams on the same Web presence will be concerned with Web-based sign-on, and will want to leverage the same development effort across multiple teams to achieve Web-based single sign-on. The goal being to reduce development effort and enhance the End-User experience across multiple team's deliverables for the same Web presence.

We envisage that each sub-team on a Web engineering project will include a number of different specialists. However, there will be a need for the specialists to communicate across teams, orthogonally to individual team structures. So, for example, all the creative designers will meet to coordinate design activities, the domain experts to coordinate their components, etc. AWE recommends that this structure be formalised by having a coordination team with a leader for each of the specialisations liaising with the respective specialists within the teams. For a more detailed discussion on orthogonal uni-discipline developer communication see our recent technical report [6].

4   Conclusions and Further Work

We have completed our first industrial trial of the AWE process in a global Fortune 500 Financial Service Sector Company. This trial focused on the introduction of an Evaluation Phase to the organisation's Web engineering development process during the evolution and maintenance of a retail Internet banking Web-based application. Unfortunately, it was not possible to comprehensively explore all of the features described in the AWE process, including stakeholder roles and communication on large projects, during our first commercial trial. However the first trial showed the business sponsors the merits of AWE's Evaluation Phase. As a result further consideration of other AWE features is underway on the largest Web-based and Object-based project in the group globally. We hope to be able to report regarding these trials in more detail late in 2003.

References

1. Beck K. et al.: Manifesto for Agile Software Development, The Agile Alliance, (February 2001), http://www.agilealliance.org/
2. Cockburn A.: Characterizing People as Non-Linear, First-Order Components in Software Development, Humans and Technology Technical Report, TR 99.05, (October 1999)
3. Fowler M.: The New Methodology, MartinFowler.com, (March 2001), http://www.martinfowler.com/articles/newMethodology.html
4. Getchell S. et al.: Microsoft Solutions Framework Process Model v. 3.1, Microsoft Corporation White Paper (June 2002)
5. Haynes P. et al.: Microsoft Solutions Framework Team Model v. 3.1, Microsoft Corporation White Paper (June 2002)
6. McDonald A., Welland R.: Agile Web Engineering (AWE) Process, Department of Computing Science Technical Report TR-2001-98, University of Glasgow, Scotland, (2 December 2001)
7. McDonald A., Welland R.: Web Engineering in Practice, Proceedings of the Fourth WWW10 Workshop on Web Engineering, 21–30, (1 May 2001)
8. Nielsen J.: First Rule of Usability? Don't Listen to Users, Jacob Nielsen's Alertbox, (5 August 2001), http://www.useit.com/alertbox/20010805.html
9. Ramsay M., Nielsen J.: WAP Usability Déjà Vu: 1994 All Over Again, Report from a Field Study in London, Fall 2000, Nielsen Norman Group, (December 2000), Page(s): 4. http://www.nngroup.com/reports/wap

Serverless Web-Multicast Chat System for Multi-users

M.A. Ngadi and Bernard S. Doherty

Computer Science Department,
Aston University,
Birmingham, United Kingdom
{ngadima,b.s.doherty}@aston.ac.uk
<http://www.cs.aston.ac.uk/>

Abstract. In this paper, we present the use of a Web-multicast chat system for collaborative work environment. Web-multicast is a concept that uses a Web-browser to communicate between multiple users. No Web server is needed for the communication. The system has the advantages of availability, portability, scalability, and performance. This paper describes the concept, implementation and some performance results.

1 Introduction

CSCW (Computer-Supported Cooperative Work) is a study on how people work together using computer technologies. CSCW applications have the potential to provide the environment needed for groups of diverse users to jointly accomplish their goals by sharing applications and exchanging messages [1]. CSCW have faced a number of issues such as:

- the applications are supported only for limited sets of users and limited range of platforms [2] [3],
- the applications are not scalable [4],
- the applications require adequate performance to support users' activities [5].

In this paper, we present the use of a Web-multicast chat system for the collaborative work environment. The system has the advantages of availability, portability, scalability, and performance. Web-multicast is a concept that uses a Web-browser to communicate between multiple users. The web-browser uses the multicasting method, and no Web server is needed for the communication. The rest of the paper is organised as follows. Section II explained the related work. Section III describes the implementation of CSCW application in Web-multicasting. Section IV describes some performance result. Lastly, Section V covers the conclusion and future work.

J.M. Cueva Lovelle et al. (Eds.): ICWE 2003, LNCS 2722, pp. 519–522, 2003.
© Springer-Verlag Berlin Heidelberg 2003

2   Related Works

In this section, we briefly review several related works that use multicasting on web browser for different applications. The Multicast Backbone (MBone) [6], the set of multicast-capable routers on the Internet, provides the infrastructure for efficient multipoint data delivery in the Internet. mMosaic [7] was one of the first tools for sharing web documents over the MBone. mMosaic is based on a modified version of the NCSA Mosaic browser, which processes incoming resources and multicasts them along with formatting instructions. WebCanal [8] is a proxy-based synchronous browser program written in Java. Changes in the current URL displayed by the master browser are detected by a proxy, which parses files to identify inline image, and transmits the data to the set of receivers. Since WebCanal operates only as a proxy, local control operations (such as Back and Forwards browser commands, and loading of local files) present difficulties. mWeb [10] is an ongoing project that uses the web browser as a multimedia slide presentation medium. mWeb is similar to WebCanal in that it is proxy-based and uses IP multicast to distribute web resources. Although, much work has been done with Web browsers, most has concentrated on real-time stream transmission using multicasting on the WWW. Little discussion has been found using the Web browser for cooperative work, especially in a learning environment. Thus, this paper has developed a prototype Web-multicast Chat System to increases the efficiency in a collaborative environment.

3   Implementation of CSCW Application

The application was developed using Java programming language to take advantage of it's platform-independent capability. Developing this application using multicast technology disassociates it from the need of a central server, thus preventing the situation of paralysing the whole system when the server breaks down. The system is built as a Java Swing applet. This application has used protocol LRMP [9] that provides a good choice for multicast environment. The benefits with the application implementation are it was reduced the network traffic by reducing the bandwidth consumption on the link from the server to the network and within the network.

4   Performance Result

The prototype was tested in order to test the efficiency of Web-multicasting to the collaborative work. All the testing have been done on open network using Windows 98 SE operating system and IE web browser. Fifteen PCs single processor with speed of 500MHz. The purpose of the testing is to show the factor that effect the response time to the end-user. The factors that affect the performance of Web-multicasting are size of the packet, number of recipient, network traffic, and capabilities of end-user's machine. In this paper, we show only the effect of packet size and number of user to the system. The factor has been chosen because these factors can be controlled more easier in the collaborative environment either by limiting the number of participant or limiting the size of packets.

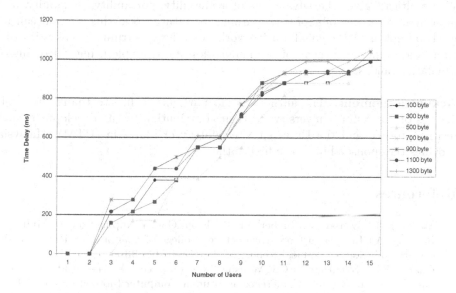

Fig. 1. Time Delay vs. Number of users with different packet size

Figure 1 shows the effect of number of users on the time delay with different packet size. It shows that the delay time is increasing with the increasing number of users. The graph also shows that the size of packet does not have much effect on the time delay at receivers. The packet size that tested is up to 1300 bytes. This size is approximately equal to 160 words. In chat system, the messages are normally small and 160 words are reasonable for the testing.

5 Conclusion

In this paper, we are concerned with the use of World Wide Web (WWW) in collaborative works environment. We present the concept of Web-multicast in this environment by developing Web-multicast chat system as a CSCW application prototype. Web-multicast is a concept that uses a Web-browser to communicate between multi-users. Some experiments have been done to test the implementation of a CSCW application in Web-multicast. The experiment also has carried out with the performance testing. In performance testing, two features are tested i.e. effect on time delay by data size and client size. From the testing, it shows that the delay time is increasing gradually with the increasing number of users. But, the size of data does not much effect on the time delay at receivers. From the test result, it shows that the Web-multicast method has a potential to provide an implementation of the collaborative work environment. The system gives a number of advantages such as providing an easy environment without need training, can be used in any platform, and give an adequate performance. As a summary, Web-multicast gives the advantages of availability, portability, scalability, and performance to the collaborative learning. In future work, this method can be used to implement the collaborative work for wider spectrum such as using different data types as a mean of communication, for example using video, audio, simulation, and images.

Acknowledgement. The authors would particularly like to thank their colleagues of the Aston University for their contribution to the development and testing process; and the University Technology of Malaysia (UTM), Malaysia provides the sponsorship to the first author.

References

1. Matta, I., Eltoweissy, M., Lieberherr, K.: From CSCW Applications to Multicast Routing: An Integrated QoS Architecture. College of Computer Science, Northeastern University. Technical Report – NU-CCS-97-09. **33** (1997)
2. Chaun, T.K.: Small group CSCW using Web resources: A Case Study. Proceedings of 8th International Conference on Human Computer Interaction and Special Session on Intelligent Tutoring and Learning Environments, Mahwah, NJ, USA.1 (1999) 788–92
3. Bentley, R., Horstmann, T., Trevor, J.: The World Wide Web as enabling technology for CSCW: The case of BSCW. Computer-Supported Cooperative Work, **6**(1997)
4. Matta, I., Eltoweissy, M., Lieberherr, K.: From CSCW Applications to Multicast Routing: An Integrated QoS Architecture. ICC '98. 1998 IEEE International Conference on Communications. Conference Record. Affiliated with SUPERCOMM'98. New York, USA. **2** (1998) 880–884
5. Ingvaldsen, T., Klovning, E., Wilkins, M.: Determining the causes of end-to-end delay in CSCW applications. Computer Communications. **23 3** (2000) 219–232
6. Erikson, H.: MBONE: The Multicast Backbone. Communications of the ACM. **37 8** (1994) 54–60
7. Dauphin, G.: mMosaic: Yet Another Tool Bringing Multicast to the Web. Proceedings of the Workshop on Real Time Multimedia and the WWW. (1996)
8. Liao, T.: WebCanal: A Multicast Web Application. Computer Network and ISDN Systems. **29 8–13** (1997) 1091–1102
9. Liao, T.: Light-weight Reliable Multicast Protocol. In ITSoftware. (1998)
10. Parnes, P., Mattsson, M., Synnes, K., Schefstrom, D.: The mWeb presentation framework. Computer Network and ISDN System. **29 8–13**(1997) 1083–1090

The Multimedia Home Platform (MHP) Framework for Web Access through Digital TV

Alberto Gil, José J. Pazos, Jorge García, Rebeca P. Díaz, Ana Fernández, and Manuel Ramos

ETSE Telecomunicación, University of Vigo, Vigo, Spain
agil@det.uvigo.es

Abstract. The DVB Consortium has recently published the MHP standard to regulate the execution of interactive applications in digital TV, including an Internet profile for web access. In this communication, that profile is analysed.

1 Introduction

Nowadays, digital technology is greatly enhancing traditional broadcasting: more channels in the same bandwidth, better image quality, hi-fi sound, etc. In the near future, watching television will be enhanced with a lot of amazing possibilities: complementary information to audiovisual contents, electronic program guides, selection of properties in configurable contents (language, camera angle or particularised advertisement), games, etc. These services are implemented by means of multimedia procedural applications being received in the digital transport stream. To guarantee competition (in order to reduce costs and prices), it is necessary to achieve compatibility in the computing platform that applications will find when they arrive at the digital TV set. The MHP standard [1] has been developed to standardize all necessary elements to promote compatible equipment and contents: the code of the MHP applications (Java), the execution context, the APIs supported in the SetTop box (STB), the life cycle of the applications, the signalling of the operator, etc.

But this standardization is not enough to achieve a successful integration of this new technology in the TV market. Content providers demand the introduction of new value-added services which users are willing to pay for, as Internet is. Besides, DVB considers it is necessary to equip digital TV with a "super teletext" system for applications or content providers to present structured stylised information to users.

So, MHP pays special attention to the specification of all necessary details to integrate in its computing model a mechanism to access to Internet or to browser over information structured in a similar way, adopting W3C standards as a starting point.

2 Internet Access through TV: The MHP Approach

We will concentrate on three different aspects of WWW browsing technologies:
- DVB has chosen the W3C *XHTML Modularization* standard to define DVB-HTML, the markup language that an MHP Internet browser must understand. It is composed of a set of modules that take into account the critical differences between computers

J.M. Cueva Lovelle et al. (Eds.): ICWE 2003, LNCS 2722, pp. 523–524, 2003.
© Springer-Verlag Berlin Heidelberg 2003

- and TV sets (computing power, screen resolution, viewing distance, etc.). A DVB-HTML application consists of a set of DVB-HTML documents forming a directed graph, and permits the service provider to send formatted and stylised data (several related DVB-HTML documents) in a packed and standard format. Even more important, the downloading, decoding, rendering and interaction processes of DVB-HTML applications must follow a well-defined life cycle in the user agent, which can be commanded from the content provider or by any other MHP application.
- In order to get a stylised rendering of a DVB-HTML document, the W3C CSS2 standard has been adopted. All the selectors defined in CSS2 must be included and a new media device is defined, *dvb-tv*, to identify tv-like devices: low resolution and computing power, limited scrollability, reduced interfaces, etc. Opacity is specifically addressed (and composition rules defined) as blending contents with background is a very frequent graphic operation in TV. A new *at-rule* is introduced (*@viewport*) where new pseudo-classes are defined to adapt to some parameters tv-related: device aspect (4:3, 16:9...), resolution, etc. Regarding fonts, only support for Tiresias type, plain, with four large sizes (24, 26, 31 and 36pt) is mandatory.
- MHP has adopted the W3C DOM and the ECMA ECMAScript standards to offer programmatic access to the internal logical structure derived from DVB-HTML documents, CSS2 decoration rules included. The fundamental structure has been extracted from the W3C DOM Level 2. The adopted events module defines mouse events as optional and includes new system events for the user agent to communicate life cycle transitions to the DVB-HTML application. A new kind of event (*triggers*) is defined for the user agent to deliver synchronization signals (in DOM events form) received from the service operator. All the interfaces must be offered as ECMAScript and Java interfaces, as well as an interface for scripts to access to all MHP APIs, which permits the implementation of hybrid applications that can divide their functionality between a declarative part (DVB-HTML containing scripts) and a procedural part (the Java code of MHP applications).

3 Conclusions

The MHP standard is the first attempt to standardize the computing platform of a STB with Internet access. The standard, quite ambitious, seems to be suitable for rendering documents specifically designed for this media. But Internet contents are more complex and heterogeneous, which may imply delays and differences in appearance of results in TV. The different evolving rate and life-span of TVs and computers will power technologies to particularize answers according to the client capabilities.

References

1. DVB Consortium: Multimedia Home Platform 1.1. *http://www.mhp.org*, (2001)

DEMOS Tools for Online Discussion and Decision Making

Rolf Luehrs[1], Juan Pavón[2], and Miguel Schneider[3]

[1]Technical University Hamburg-Harburg, Dep. for Technology Assessment, Schwarzenbergstr. 95, 21071 Hamburg, Germany
r.luehrs@tuhh.de
[2] Dep. Sistemas Informáticos y Programación, Univ. Complutense, 28040 Madrid, Spain
jpavon@sip.ucm.es
[3]Ibermática, Research & Development, Avda. Partenon 16-18, Madrid 28042, Spain
m.schneider@ibermatica.com

DEMOS provides an environment that assists the management of discussions and decision making through the web, especially when involving a large population (e.g., a community using the web to debate about city issues). It is based on the integration of three well-proven methods of social research: the Delphi method, Survey techniques, and Mediation method. These are supported by a set of tools (user interfacing, forum management, survey organization, text mining, and clustering), integrated in a layered architecture and adapted to multiple languages (the current version works on English, German and Italian web sites).

1   Introduction

DEMOS stands for Delphi Mediation On-line System*. The main objective of the project is to develop and evaluate new ways to support large-scale discussion and decision-making on-line. This is achieved by developing a novel participation methodology for on-line debate, combining three well-proven methods of social research: the Delphi method [1], Survey techniques [2], and Mediation method [3]. The result is an open web-based system with user-friendly and attractive interface, built on a modular software architecture, which allows DEMOS-based systems to be adjusted to the full range of processes for on-line debate. The approach and the system have been validated at two trial sites: the cities of Hamburg and Bologna.

The project is planned to make a substantial breakthrough in on-line consultation where currently no acceptable means exist to handle large-scale discussion processes and deliberative opinion formation. The DEMOS software architecture wraps, in a unified user interface, access to different tools such as survey organization, text mining, and group formation.

---

* The DEMOS Project (IST-1999-20530) is funded as a shared-cost RTD project under the 5th Framework Program of the European Commission (IST)

J.M. Cueva Lovelle et al. (Eds.): ICWE 2003, LNCS 2722, pp. 525–528, 2003.
© Springer-Verlag Berlin Heidelberg 2003

2   The DEMOS Process

A DEMOS process is always concerned with one main topic of discussion in a community of users on a limited timeline under the guidance of on-line moderators. To limit the debate to just one main topic is a conceptual decision derived from the general objective of the project to concentrate on deliberative discourses with potential impact on public decision-making process. It also serves to discourage debates from losing any sense of direction. However, in a DEMOS system several processes can be conducted in parallel and each of them split up into different subtopics during the course of the debate.

The basic process model comprises three different phases each with specific goals (see Figure 1): broadening, deepening, and consolidating the discussion.

The *first phase* has above all to initiate, facilitate and broaden the debate and subsequently to identify the most important aspects or subtopics of the chosen subject matter. Therefore the moderators have to analyze and cluster the (free text) contributions in order to find out the issues most participants seem to be interested in. The moderators are backed up by qualitative methods of content analysis. For instance, a text-mining tool can automatically group the text contributions once a set of categories (subtopics) are defined and illustrated by examples.

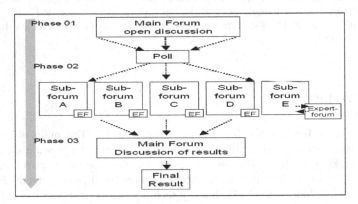

Fig. 1. The DEMOS process.

Additionally, the moderators have to summarize the discussion during the course of the first phase. These summaries consist of content and progress related parts and highlight and profile emerging lines of conflict according to the Mediation method. The first phase finally results in a set of proposed subtopics that can be more intensively discussed in separate discussion forums in the next phase. Since this procedure is relying on interpretations of the individual postings as well as of the entire discussion, the result may not exactly meet the preferences of the participants. At this point the Survey method comes into play in order to evaluate whether or not the proposed sub-forums meet the demands of the community and if necessary, to generate ideas on how to revise the list of subtopics.

The purpose of the *second phase* (deepening the discussion) is to intensively discuss specific issues in smaller groups of interested participants, while the main forum still catches those participants who want to discuss the topic on a more general level. Again the moderators have to summarize the developing debate on a regular basis and at the same time try to tease out and manage emerging conflicts. This is where the Mediation method comes in, as part of the moderator's task is to clarify how and to what extent people are agreeing or disagreeing and at the same time to reduce the distance between diverging positions by deliberative, moderated discourses. The result of the second phase should either be agreement (consent) or a rational dissent in the sense explained above. If required and appropriate, this opinion shaping process can be enriched and supplemented with expert knowledge by conducting Delphi surveys among a predefined set of domain experts. Delphi type studies can either be applied in the original fashion, e.g., to reduce the uncertainty with respect to future developments or in order to evaluate certain positions of the community from an expert point of view. Finally, the moderators close this phase with a summary of what was discussed so far, and once again ask the participants for their approval (survey).

The *third phase* (consolidating the discussion) reintegrates the sub-forums into the main forum by transferring the summaries and related survey results. Participants have the opportunity to see the particular subtopic as part of the general subject matter and a *big picture* will emerge. Participants have the last chance to comment on the main topic and the assembled results of the sub-forums and the community will be asked to rate the subtopics in terms of importance for the main topic that the DEMOS process was intentionally set up for. The final result will be a condensed document depicting both the results of a dynamic and deliberative discussion and the importance accorded to its different aspects in the view of its participants.

3   DEMOS Architecture

The main purpose of the DEMOS architecture is to implement efficiently the DEMOS social model and process. Note that there are strong requirements on the architecture concerning flexibility (therefore the modular approach, in order to be able to incorporate new functionality with minimum impact to existing modules), scalability (the system should work for a hundred of users, but grow to manage thousands; initially it is conceived to work at city level), and robustness (the system must be able to work without disruptions, and must be usable by a wide range of experienced and non-experienced users).

DEMOS system architecture is organized in several modules (see Figure 2), which provide the basic services that support the DEMOS process. All modules rely on the Argumentation and Mediation module (A&M) [4], which controls access to the repository of all the contributions that users may insert (i.e., it is a kind of forum manager). Users may participate in several forums, where they can read or put contributions about a certain discussion topic. Each forum has a moderator who has the responsibility for getting the discussion to some conclusion. In order to achieve this, the moderator can use DEMOS methodology with the tools that support it: Survey Module (SUR, supports the generation and distribution of questionnaires) and Subgroup Formation and Matchmaking (SFM, mechanisms for creating subgroups of users in a forum, which is essential for moving from phase 1 to phase 2 in the DEMOS process). These tools make use of Text Mining (TM) agents and User

Profiling (UP) agents. Finally, Graphical User Interface (GUI) provides a uniform access to users integrating the dialogue with the different modules (Figure 3).

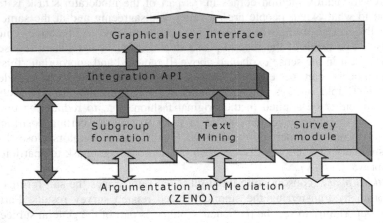

Fig. 2. DEMOS system modules

4   Conclusions

The innovative aspect of the DEMOS process is that a model of organizational workflow is applied to the broad public. The idea is to get together citizens interested in the same subject matter and to enable an organization-like interaction for the duration of the debate. This has been tested in the cities of Hamburg and Bologna in several debates during the period 2001-2003.

From the engineering point of view, DEMOS has shown the feasibility of integration of several tools for text mining, clustering, survey generation and management, on a common and customizable user interface. This way, DEMOS architecture shows its ability to evolve as it allows the addition of new tools supporting the participants in on-line debate and decision-making.

References

1. Florian, M. et al.: The Future of Security and Risks in Telecommunication – Expectations of Experts (TeleDelphi). In: Multilateral Security in Communications. Vol. 3. München; Reading, Massachusetts: Addison-Wesley-Longman (1999) 465–480.
2. Rossi, P.H. et al., eds.: Handbook of Survey Research, Orlando (1983)
3. Susskind, L. and Cruikshank, J.: Breaking the Impasse. Consensual Approaches to Resolving Public Disputes. New York: The Perseus Books Group (1989)
4. Gordon, T. et al.: Zeno: Groupware for Discourses on the Internet. Künstliche Intelligenz, 15 (2001)

Hera: Development of Semantic Web Information Systems

Geert-Jan Houben, Peter Barna, Flavius Frasincar, and Richard Vdovjak

Technische Universiteit Eindhoven
PO Box 513, NL-5600 MB Eindhoven, The Netherlands
{houben, pbarna, flaviusf, richardv}@win.tue.nl

Abstract. As a consequence of the success of the Web, methodologies for information system development need to consider systems that use the Web paradigm. These Web Information Systems (WIS) use Web technologies to retrieve information from the Web and to deliver information in a Web presentation to the users. Hera is a model-driven methodology supporting WIS design, focusing on the processes of integration, data retrieval, and presentation generation. Integration and data retrieval gather from Web sources the data that composes the result of a user query. Presentation generation produces the Web or hypermedia presentation format for the query result, such that the presentation and specifically its navigation suits the user's browser. We show how in Hera all these processes lead to data transformations based on RDF(S) models. Proving the value of RDF(S) for WIS design, we pave the way for the development of Semantic Web Information Systems.

1 Introduction

One reason for the popularity of the World Wide Web is that computer applications provide information for a diverse audience on different platforms worldwide and 24 hours a day and people find and view that information with easy-to-use navigation mechanisms. In the typical Web application the author carefully handcrafted a static collection of pages and links between these pages to present to the user information suited for navigation with a Web browser. The success has led to the desire to exploit this user-friendly paradigm in (professional) information systems. Not only has the typical Web application become data-intensive, using for example data generated from databases, but also information system developers want to extend their (traditionally non-Web) applications along the lines of the Web paradigm. This trend has caused the concept of Web application to evolve in the direction of the concept of Web Information System (WIS) [2], a software component that stores and manages information just like a traditional information system, but specifically uses the Web paradigm and its associated technologies. A specific class of Web technologies is that of the Semantic Web (SW) [1] initiative, specially targeting application interoperability. As we show in this paper, one of the SW languages, RDF(S) [3,12], offers effective support for the design of WIS.

The data in a WIS is retrieved from a heterogeneous and dynamic set of data sources and subsequently delivered as Web or hypermedia presentations to a heterogeneous group of users with different preferences using different platforms to view the presentations.

J.M. Cueva Lovelle et al. (Eds.): ICWE 2003, LNCS 2722, pp. 529–538, 2003.
© Springer-Verlag Berlin Heidelberg 2003

This poses new and different requirements for the design and development of a WIS: from handcrafting to engineering.

In our Hera [6] methodology we single out a number of characteristic aspects of WIS design:

- Most visible in WIS design (and missing in traditional non-Web approaches) is the need to automatically generate Web or hypermedia presentations for the data the WIS delivers. This includes that the system (instructed by its designer) decides on the navigation structure of the presentation, by describing the composition of the presentation objects (e.g. pages) and their connections (e.g. hyperlinks).
- A WIS includes a transparent repository of data obtained from different sources. The designer has to instruct the system how to search and find, retrieve, transform, and combine information. The aspect of integration is often disregarded in WIS design.
- Personalization is a prominent issue in WIS design: delivering the right data in the right way (e.g. device and connection) to the right user. Hera combines presentation generation with user adaptation [4].

Most WIS design methodologies focus primarily on presentation generation. A lot of models that consider adaptation do so only in the context of adaptive hypermedia documents. As notable exceptions among the Web engineering approaches we mention Object Oriented Hypermedia Design Model (OOHDM) [13], Web Modeling Language (WebML) [5], UML-based Web Engineering (UWE) [11], and eXtensible Web Modeling Framework (XWMF) [7]. For its RDF-based nature we consider the last one further. It consists of an extensible set of RDF schemas and descriptions to model Web applications. The core of the framework is the Web Object Composition Model (WOCM), a formal object-oriented language used to define the application's structure and content. WOCM is a directed acyclic graph with complexons as nodes and simplexons as leaves. Complexons define the application's structure while simplexons define the application's content. Simplexons are refined using the subclassing mechanism in different variants corresponding to different implementation platforms.

Hera uses a model-driven approach, specifying the separate aspects of the complete application design in terms of separate models, e.g. for presentation generation, integration, and adaptation. Similar to OMG's Model Driven Architecture, Hera distinguishes between Platform Independent Models (e.g. integration model, presentation model, and application model) and Platform Dependent Models (e.g. presentation model) but in the specific context of hypermedia. In this way if the targeted platform changes the specifications of the application logic remain the same.

The associated Hera framework implies a stepwise approach to get from data retrieval to presentation generation at the level of instances. Those steps constitute a sequence of data transformations that eventually produces the right data in the right format (e.g. HTML, WML, or SMIL). In the demonstrator for the framework we have used RDF(S) to specify the different models and XSLT [10] to transform the RDF data in order to generate the presentations in the right format.

2 Hera Methodology

From the gathering of requirements to the maintenance of the operational application, most information system design methodologies distinguish several phases in the design process. The development of a WIS is different in several aspects, and these aspects are the central focus of the Hera project.

Like other WIS methodologies Hera includes a phase in which the hypermedia (Web) navigation is specified. Hera considers navigation in connection to the data-intensive nature of the modern WIS in its *presentation generation* phase. Before, Hera's *integration and data retrieval* phase considers how to select and obtain the data from the storage part of the application. This includes transforming the data from these sources into the format (syntax and semantics) used in the application. Also, the handling of the interaction from users is specified: querying, navigation, or application-specific user interaction.

2.1 Model-Driven Transformations

Hera's target is to facilitate the automatic execution of the design: it should be possible to program the WIS in such a way that it can automatically execute the process specified by the design. Figure 1 shows how Hera typically views a WIS architecture:

- The *Semantic Layer* specifies the data content of the WIS in terms of a conceptual model. It also defines the integration process that gathers the data from different sources.
- The *Application Layer* specifies the abstract hypermedia view on the data in terms of an application model representing the navigation structure provided in the hypermedia presentation. It also defines the user adaptation in the hypermedia generation process.
- The *Presentation Layer* specifies the presentation details that (with the definitions from the Application Layer) are needed for producing a presentation for a concrete platform, like HTML, WML, or SMIL.

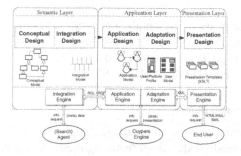

Fig. 1. WIS architecture in Hera

Hera uses several models to capture the different design aspects. Providing clear relationships between the different models, e.g. by expressing one model in terms of an other one, gives a major advantage: model-driven transformations. Populating the different models with data and then transforming them according to the relationships between the models leads to an automatic execution of the design at instance level, and ultimately to the production of the hypermedia presentation.

The models in the phase of integration and data retrieval obtain the data from the sources. In reaction to a *user query* a *conceptual model instance* is produced with the data for which the application is going to generate a presentation: see Figure 2.

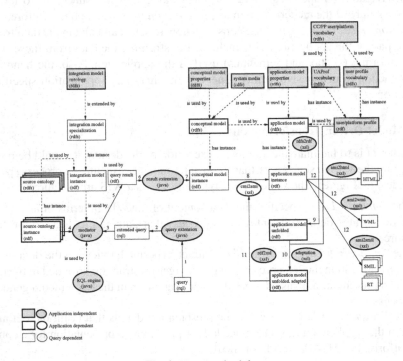

Fig. 2. Hera methodology

The models in the phase of presentation generation generate a hypermedia presentation for the retrieved data: see Figure 2. The result of the user query, represented by the *conceptual model instance*, is transformed into a presentation in the specific format of the user's browser (e.g. HTML, WML, or SMIL).

2.2   Software Demonstrator

The Hera demonstrator uses the example of the design of a virtual art gallery that allows visitors to create on-the-fly exhibitions featuring their favorite painters, paintings, and painting techniques. These hypermedia presentations are produced from the exhibits of different online museums and annotated with descriptions from an online art encyclopedia.

Our demonstrator shows that we have chosen in our methodology to use RDF(S) as the data format for the different Hera models. Hera's model instances are represented in plain RDF with the associated models represented in RDFS. RDF(S) is suitable, since it is a flexible (schema refinement and description enrichment) and extensible (definition of new resources and properties) framework that enables Web application interoperability. We reuse existing RDFS vocabularies like the User Agent Profile (UAProf) [14], a Composite Capability/Preference Profiles (CC/PP) [8] vocabulary for modeling device capabilities and user preferences. A disadvantage is the lack of proper RDF(-aware) transformation processors. Treating the models and instances as plain XML, the XSLT processor Saxon performs the different transformations based on stylesheets. For data retrieval we use RQL [9] and its java-based interpreter Sesame.

3   Integration and Data Retrieval

In the integration phase the designer defines and creates channels connecting the different data sources to the conceptual model. In the data retrieval phase the channels are used to obtain the data that correspond to the conceptual model.

3.1   Conceptual Model

The role of the conceptual model (CM) is to provide a uniform semantic view over the input sources. A CM (Figure 3 - top) uses concepts and concept properties expressed in RDFS to define the domain ontology.

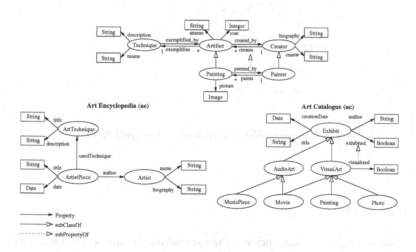

Fig. 3. Conceptual model (top) and integration sources (bottom)

There are two source ontologies (Figure 3 - bottom) that are integrated in the above CM. The first source is an online encyclopedia that provides data about different art pieces, offering their title, date of creation, author, used technique etc. Yet rich in content this source is purely text-based. So if one wants to obtain an actual image of a painting we have to consult the second source. This source represents an online multimedia catalogue of exhibits of different kinds including their digitalized versions.

3.2 Integration Model

The integration model (IM) links concepts from the source ontologies (Figure 3 - bottom) to those from the CM: a kind of ontology alignment. Hera provides an integration model ontology (IMO). A designer specifies the links between the CM and the sources by instantiating the IMO. The IMO of Figure 4 describes integration primitives used for ranking the sources within a cluster and for specifying links between them and the CM. The IMO uses the concepts of `Decoration` and `Articulation`. Decorations label the "appropriateness" of different sources (and their concepts) that are grouped within one semantically close cluster. Articulations describe the actual links between the source ontologies and the CM. They also specify the concept's uniqueness which is necessary to perform joins from several sources.

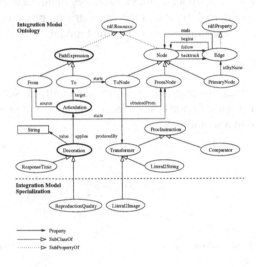

Fig. 4. Integration model ontology and its specialization

3.3 Data Retrieval

Integration is performed once, prior to the user asking the query. Data retrieval is performed for every query. The user query (in RQL [9]) is first extended to contain all relevant data needed in the presentation generation phase. The algorithm traverses the CM from the given concept(s) and adds all concepts and/or literal types reachable by following property edges in the CM graph. Subsequently, the mediator takes the extended query as its input, routes the appropriate queries to the sources, collects the results and assembles them into an answer which consists of a collection of tuples (in RDF terminology a bag of lists). Finally, the "flat" collection of tuples in the query result is transformed into a CM instance by adding the appropriate properties (such that it is a valid RDF graph).

4   Presentation Generation

In the presentation generation phase the designer assembles the retrieved data into a hypermedia presentation suitable for the user's display. Moreover such a presentation is personalized by considering the user preferences for the hypermedia generation.

4.1   Application Model

The Application Model (AM) represents an abstract specification of the presentation in terms of slices and slice properties. A slice is a meaningful presentation unit that groups concept attributes and/or other slices. Each slice is associated to a certain concept from the CM. There are two types of slice properties: slice composition, a slice includes another slice, and slice navigation, a hyperlink abstraction between two slices. The most primitive slices are concept attributes. The most complex ones are the top level slices that correspond to pages. A page contains all the information present on the user's display at a particular moment.

Figure 5 gives an example of an AM composed of two slices associated to two different concepts: `technique` and `painting`. Attributes are depicted with ovals, slice composition is described by the nested composition notation, and slice navigation is represented by arrows. If a slice contains another slice that is associated to a different concept a line labeled with the property name between the involved two concepts is used. In case that the cardinality of this property is one-to-many the `Set` unit needs to be employed.

The application model needs to take in account the user's device (e.g. PC, PDA, WAP phone). To personalize the presentation user preferences are also considered. The user/platform profile captures the device capabilities and the user preferences. The adaptation we consider in this paper is based on the conditional inclusion of slices (fragments) and slice navigation (link) hiding [4]. Figure 5 gives an example of a conditional inclusion of a picture based on the user's display capability to display images.

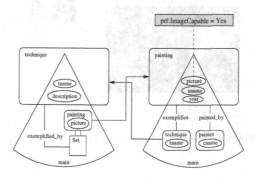

Fig. 5. Application model with adaptation

536   G.-J. Houben et al.

4.2 Presentation Data Transformations

The retrieved data (CM instance) will go through a number of transformations until it eventually reaches a form interpretable by the user's browser. The RDF/XML serialization of the proposed models and their instances enable the usage of an XSLT processor as the transformation engine. The most important transformations steps are: the application model adaptation, the application model instance generation, and presentation data generation.

After converting the AM to a template closer in form to an AM instance, the AM is adapted based on user/platform profile attribute values. Slices that have their appearance condition unfulfilled will be discarded and links pointing to them will be disabled.

In the second step based on the AM a transformation stylesheet is produced. Since the stylesheet is also an XML document, it was possible to write a stylesheet for the creation of another stylesheet. The resulted transformation stylesheet is used to convert the CM instance to an AM instance.

In the last step different stylesheets produce code for different platforms. This step uses a media-directed translation scheme where for each media appropriate code is generated, e.g. dates are displayed in italic, strings are represented with normal font, or images are refered with appropriate tags. Figure 6 exemplifies the same presentation for three different browsers: HTML, WML, and SMIL browsers. One should note the absence of pictures and the need to scroll the text in the WML browser presentation.

Fig. 6. Hypermedia presentation in different browsers

4.3 User Interaction

There is an increasing number of Web applications (e.g. shopping Web sites, conference management sites, community Web boards) in which the user interaction by only following links does not suffice. In the previous sections we saw the example of user queries that generate a hypermedia presentation. This section describes a more general form of user interaction in which in response to a user click on a button CM instances and their associated properties get created, deleted, or updated.

In order to exemplify the considered user interaction we extend our running example to a shopping Web site selling posters which are reproductions of the museum's paintings. The CM of the application is enlarged with the poster, order, and trolley concepts. A poster is associated (through a property) to the already existing concept of painting.

While browsing the generated hypermedia presentation the user has the possibility to order a number of posters corresponding to the currently displayed painting. This implies two modeling issues. First the AM needs to be extended with new navigational properties and possibly new slices that will model this user interaction. Second the callback function associated to this operation needs to be specified based on the current context and the existing hyperbase. The current context is given by the CM instances visible in a hypermedia presentation at a certain moment in time. The callback function is creating, deleting, or updating CM instances and their properties.

The extension of the AM by taking into account the newly introduced concepts modeling user interaction is a trivial process and will not be discussed further. Figure 7 depicts a snapshot of the CM instances during user interaction. The user has put into his trolley, trolley1, two orders, order1 and order2. The trolley and the two orders are instances that were created dynamically during user interaction. The first order, order1, refers to one copy of poster2 and the second order refers to two copies of poster1. Note that poster1 and poster2 are instances that exist independently of the user interaction.

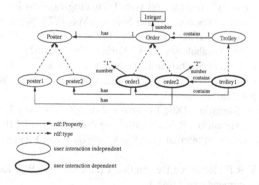

Fig. 7. Concept instance creation during user interaction

5 Conclusion and Further Work

Following the success of the Web, design and engineering methodologies for information systems have evolved in the direction of WIS engineering. Hera's model-driven approach uses Semantic Web technology, most notably RDF(S), to specify the design of a WIS. Its models define integration, data retrieval and presentation generation, but also aspects like user adaptation and user interaction. The choice of RDF/XML to represent the data models and their instances proved to be useful in the data transformations (using XSLT stylesheets). As we develop the Hera methodology by extending it with models for more aspects of the design, for example more advanced user interaction, RDF(S) is not sufficient anymore. Moreover, taking into account the extensions we had to make to RDF(S) we consider replacing it by a more powerful Web ontology language. Other research investigates the consequences in terms of (languages for expressing) transformations on models expressed using Web ontologies.

References

1. Berners-Lee, T.: Weaving the Web. Orion Business, London (1999)
2. Bieber, M., Isakowitz, T., Vitali, F.: Web Information Systems. Communications of the ACM **41(7)** (1998) 78–80
3. Brickley, D., Guha, R.V.: RDF Vocabulary Description Language 1.0: RDF Schema. W3C Working Draft (2002)
4. Brusilovsky, P.: Adaptive Hypermedia. User Modeling and User-Adapted Interaction **11(1/2)** Kluwer Academic Publishers (2001) 87–110
5. Ceri, S., Fraternali, P., Matera, M.: Conceptual Modeling of Data-Intensive Web Applications. IEEE Internet Computing **6(4)** (2002) 20–30
6. Frasincar, F., Houben, G.J., Vdovjak, R.: Specification Framework for Engineering Adaptive Web Applications. In Proc. The Eleventh International World Wide Web Conference (2002)
7. Klapsing, R., Neumann, G.: Applying the Resource Description Framework to Web Engineering. In Proc. Electronic Commerce and Web Technologies, First International Conference, EC-Web 2000, Lecture Notes in Computer Science, Vol. 1875. Springer (2000) 229–238
8. Klyne, G., Reynolds, F., Woodrow, C., Ohto, H.: Composite Capability/Preference Profiles (CC/PP): Structure and Vocabularies. W3C Working Draft (2002)
9. Karvounarakis, G., Alexaki, S. Christophides, V., Plexousakis, D., Scholl M.: RQL: A Declarative Query Language for RDF, In Proc. The Eleventh International World Wide Web Conference, ACM Press (2002) 592–603
10. Kay, M.: XSL Transformations (XSLT) Version 2.0. W3C Working Draft (2002)
11. Koch, N., Kraus, A., Hennicker, R.: The Authoring Process of the UML-based Web Engineering Approach. In Proc. First International Workshop on Web-Oriented Software Technology (2001)
12. Lassila, O., Swick, R.R.: Resource Description Framework (RDF) Model and Syntax Specification. W3C Recommendation (1999)
13. Schwabe, D., Rossi, G.: An Object Oriented Approach to Web-Based Application Design. Theory and Practice of Object Systems **4(4)** (1998) 207–225
14. Wireless Application Group: User Agent Profile Specification. WAP Forum (2001)

Development of an Application to Support WEB Navigation

Oscar Sanjuán Martínez, Vanessa Cejudo Mejías, Javier Parra, Andrés Castillo,
and Luis Joyanes Aguilar

Universidad Pontificia de Salamanca in Madrid
Paseo Juan XXIII, n° 3. Madrid. Spain
sanjuan@acm.org, vcejudo@upsaguate.org,
ljoyanes@upsaguate.org

Abstract. The Internet has evolved too rapidly, which has left us with no option but to leave many problems unsolved. In many occasions, this is due to the fact that this 'invention' was devised with a different purpose from what we understand as the Internet nowadays.

The Web aims to be a universally helpful utility.

Our Proposal consists of the development of a tool which makes the Web something more accessible to everybody, and it is aimed at solving language, understanding, and displaying problems, by building a new navigation interface based on icons.

1 Background

We are now witnessing the evolution of this universal instrument, which changes depending on users' needs. According to Ben Schnneiderman's words, the Internet is necessary as a means of achieving equality of opportunities. The information found on the Web is of growing general interest. Nowadays, there are many initiatives, which demand that both the contents and the design of Web pages from public entities are easily accessible [REVE02]. In order to permit equality of opportunities, Clement, A. and Shade, L.R. have pointed out seven major aspects: Transport Services, Devices, Software Tools, Contents Service, Server Access Forecast, Social Service, and Government.

Our tool stands out in the field of the software tools that aim the access to the Net to be improved.

2 What Is SAN?

SAN - Sistema de Ayuda a la Navegación (Navigation Support System)
San is a system that adds a new navigation interface to any Web page; an interface based on the use of icons which aims to:

J.M. Cueva Lovelle et al. (Eds.): ICWE 2003, LNCS 2722, pp. 539–542, 2003.
© Springer-Verlag Berlin Heidelberg 2003

- Facilitate access to the page contents by adding an icon bar that appears at the top of the page, in which, through the use of various icons, major topics are shown, along with the page resources.
- Filter information. Thanks to this navigation bar, we can view, in a quicker and more effective way, the contents and resources we need.
- Sort the information. The navigation bar will display the most important contents in the form of icons/ sounds, by means of a hierarchy of topics sorted in order of relevance.
- Soften language barriers. Icons are easily understood in any language, since they represent concepts, not words; thus, SAN could help to remove some of the linguistic obstacles that users encounter when navigating the Internet.

3 How Does SAN Work?

SAN interface is implemented separately from the page, and it does not modify it. SAN is able to dynamically generate the navigation bar and to incorporate it to the display of the Web. The SAN interface is made up of icons that mainly represent two things:

- Contents: That is, the most relevant concepts that the page refers to.
- Resources: Some specific elements that the page has, such as photos, files to be downloaded, and so on.

The navigation bar acts as a shortcut bar to the information that can be found on the page. When clicking one of the icons, the user can access either to that part of the Web where the concept is shown or to the resource in question.

4 SAN's Advantages

- The icons allow us to quickly perform Content based Navigation using the most universal language of all: images.
- SAN provides a faster, more intuitive navigation, since it synthesizes the contents of Web pages through the use of conceptual images. This allows the user to get an idea of the most relevant concepts of the page, with just a quick glance.
- It promotes the use of a universal language of icons, as well as its possible use as a standard.
- It allows for a faster navigational access, thanks to the discrimination of contents, leaving only those that are considered to be more relevant for the user.
- It organizes and structures the information of the Web site.
- It improves the usability of Websites.

5 Architecture and Operation

5.1 Architecture

The first version of SAN has a repository with all the icons, concepts, rules and relationships needed to infer the concepts from each page. The present technology used to develop SAN has been ASP pages, with COM components that embed the system's behavior and intelligence. SAN downloads the desired page and analyses it in order to locate the concepts that appear on the page. Such concepts are sorted in order of relevance and appearance on the page; this prioritized list will be considered as a basis for the generation of the appropriate icon bar.

5.2 Operation

After login in the system, a Web page informs the user about the virtues of SAN and will also allow to type the URL of the page the user wants to visit.

Once this operation has been completed, SAN takes over and generates the corresponding bar, as we will see in the example that follows.

When the user clicks one of the icons of the intelligent bar, SAN generates a link to the area related to the concept pointed out by the icon. The significant text will be highlighted in order to catch the user's attention.

If a link is chosen, the user will be transmitted to the corresponding URL and SAN will rebuild the icon bar, in order to adapt it to the contents of the new page.

6 Current and Future Work

It is our contention to make of SAN a pioneering tool for the humanization of the Internet, making it more accessible for everyone, specially for those who can obtain more benefit from it: the disabled, the children, or people who just want to have a different kind of approach to the Net.

We are nowadays working on a new version of SAN, a totally upgraded one, which aims at solving some of the problems encountered, and one that takes a completely different approach to the development of the system, but maintaining its original objectives.

Currently, we are working on an off-line version of SAN, that would work like a spider and that would generate a conceptual database of pages, which will allow SAN not only to analyze the superficial information of the Web page, but also to perform more in-depth searches.

Our more immediate goals are:
- Migrating to the new application model.
- Increasing the update capability of the database.
- Taking a close look at possible learning mechanisms.
- Carrying out some tests in order to evaluate the system in a real environment.
- Optimizing the system, so that it can be incorporated into a "home" environment, which allows us to make it accessible to the general public.

Bibliographical References

[BENS00] Shreiderman, Ben. : Universal Usability: Communications of the ACM: Embedding the Internet. May 2000 – Vol. 43 n° 5. Page 85

[CLEM99] Clement, A. Shade, L. R.: The Access Rainbow: Conceptualizing Universal access to the information Communications infrastructure. In Gurstein, M., Ed. Community Informatics: Enabling Communities with Information and Communications Technologies. Idea Publishing, Hersey; PA, 1999

[REVE02]Reventós, Laia.: El País: Ciberp@is: Info XXI: Administración.es, casi igual que hace un año. 19 December 2002, Page 5

Critical Information Systems Authentication Based on PKC and Biometrics

Carlos Costa, José Luís Oliveira, and Augusto Silva

DET/IEETA, Aveiro University, 3810-193 Aveiro, Portugal
ccosta@ieeta.pt, {jlo, asilva}@det.ua.pt

Abstract. This paper presents an access control model that dynamically combines biometrics with PKC technology to assure a stronger authentication mechanism to healthcare professional that can be used indistinctly in Internet and Intranets access scenario.

1 Introduction

Access control mechanisms are mostly related with the username and password association or with Public Key Cryptography (PKC). Despite these techniques are broadly used, the storage and handling of secrets, like PKC private keys, is yet a hard-worked problem. One solution can be provided by the usage of smart cards to store digital certificates and respective private keys with access provided by means of PIN code verification. However, when we are dealing with very sensible data it is mandatory to guarantee that the user is in fact who he claims to be, preventing the delegation of access to third persons. Our model proposes a new vision to integrate smart cards, digital credential, biometric fingerprint and user password, contemplating the indoor/outdoor access provenience. The main goal was the achievement of a flexible and robust security access system to verify and ensure that the users are in fact who they claim. The deployment scenario to this implementation was a mission-critical Healthcare Information Systems (HIS).

2 Developed Model

The first outcome of this system was the development of a web-based interface module to the HIS [1]. The *XML/XSL* technology was used to assure dynamic content creation and formatting, according to the user terminal and to the access privileges of different user profiles. Aspects of interface usability have also been matter of study in the implementation phase, aiming to create a flexible interface to distinct client terminals. The developed multi-platform interface integrates, in run time, the patient information retrieved from the HIS system with its images from the PACS [2], making these alphanumeric and multimedia data available in a unique Internet browser.

Because we are dealing with very sensitive information, the confidentiality, the users authentication and the log of events are crucial requisites. The data communication privacy is ensured with the adoption of protocols, like the HTTPS, to encrypt the data transferred between server and client. However, concerning access control the prob-

J.M. Cueva Lovelle et al. (Eds.): ICWE 2003, LNCS 2722, pp. 543–544, 2003.
© Springer-Verlag Berlin Heidelberg 2003

lem is a bit more complex. To cope with this we developed a dynamic access policy that contemplates the access source as well the type of authentication and identification provided. The core element of this system is an innovative Healthcare Professional Card (HPC) based in java cards (smart card) and PKC authentication.

In a PKC authentication, the user must sign the server challenge with their private key to prove the identity. This key must be kept in a secure place and the smart card appears as the best and flexible device to securely store these keys. In the proposed model, the smart card PIN results from the inside card processing of distinct elements and from a secret calculus formula that combines the user password with the biometric fingerprint template (a byte stream sequence). The fingerprint template used in the PIN calculus is securely stored inside the card and never leaves this device. The eventual attempt to use a live scan fingerprint capture does not result on a bit string exactly equally to the stored on the card [3] and consequently provides an erroneous PIN.

We realized that inside the institution the professional is authenticated through an HPC-Password pair, but to obtain a similar access level from a remote access our system contemplates and demands the use of the HPC-Password and fingerprint recognizing mechanisms. This idea is based on the assumption that inside de institution other persons and access control devices establish the necessary physical user identity control. Because this situation is not identical in an outdoor access, biometric recognition appears as fundamental element to enforce the identity of HPC owner.

The bypass to the biometric matching process dependents from the access provenience. The evaluation of indoor/outdoor situation is made by the server side, which will check the IP address of client workstation in the indoor access list. If the client, for instance, is not in the private departmental network, the server sends the encrypted information (date + provenience-flag + challenge) demanding the fingerprint match to the java card routine. At the end, the java routine just returns the signed challenge that will be sent to the server to provide user authentication.

3   Conclusion

In this paper we have presented an integrated access control model specially designed to information systems that handle sensitive data. The system provides a universal and robust PKC-based authentication, implements a flexible identification model including biometry as second authentication factor, allows high user mobility and copes well with the diverse kind of user interfaces.

References

[1] Bexiga, A., F. Augusto: IWBDC - Interface para Base de Dados Clínica, in Revista do DETUA. (2003) vol. 3 (8): p. 827–841. (in Portuguese)
[2] Silva, A., et al.: A Cardiology Oriented PACS. in Proceedings of SPIE. (1998). San Diego - USA.
[3] Riha, J., V. Matyas: Biometric Authentication Systems. Masaryk University Brno. (2000)

Electronic Patient Record Virtually Unique Based on a Crypto Smart Card

Carlos Costa, José Luís Oliveira, and Augusto Silva

DET/IEETA, Aveiro University, 3810-193 Aveiro, Portugal
ccosta@ieeta.pt, {jlo, asilva}@det.ua.pt

Abstract. This paper presents a Multi-Service Patient Data Card (MS-PDC) based on a crypto smart card and Web technology that integrates a new set of functionalities that allow handling well patient mobility.

1 Introduction

The world globalization process is increasingly promoting peoples' mobility, creating a higher dispersion of patient clinical records and forcing even more the healthcare providers to take measures to promote the share and the remote access to patient clinical data over the Internet. It is recognized today that Web-based technologies are a fundamental piece in the access to database and medical image systems. In this scenario, it is proposed and described a MS-PDC based on Web technology, Public Key Cryptography (PKC) and crypto Smart Cards that is unequivocally providing a way to store and transport patient's administrative and clinical data, handling well patient mobility and implementing an innovator vision of a virtual unique Electronic Patient Record (EPR).

2 Proposed Model

The patient administrative data and the emergency data are stored inside the card EPROM and structured following the G-8-Netlink specifications to ensure the PDC international interoperability [1]. On the Hyperlink area it is possible to store Web EPR locations [2]. We can see this feature as a mobile clinical patient homepage portal. This is achieved through a structured implementation of hyperlinks associated to remote clinical patient data, creating, by one side, a truly distributed EPR system and promoting, by the other, the idea of a virtual unique and universal EPR. When a patient goes to a healthcare provider and clinic data is produced, the institution can write on the card a digitally signed hyperlink referencing the local EPR information. The hyperlink dataset was defined in ASN.1 [3] and follows an ISO8825 data encoding implementation. Every pointer includes, beyond other fields, an electronic record address (URL), the issuer institution identification and digital credentials references, a relevancy factor indicator, as well important coded clinical details. They work as structured bookmarks that objectively provide the indexing, sorting, location and ac-

J.M. Cueva Lovelle et al. (Eds.): ICWE 2003, LNCS 2722, pp. 545–546, 2003.
© Springer-Verlag Berlin Heidelberg 2003

cess mechanisms to a distributed electronic patient record. Associated to every link it is appended the respective digital signature made using the institution private key. Due the smart card memory limitations many of the hyperlink fields are stored in a coded way and interpreted in run time by the browser API engine that converts and presents the card hexadecimal bit stream in a human legible form.

The remote access to distributed EPR locations and respective information systems is grounded on the presupposition that the system must proof, in a strong way, that patient is in fact on the remote place. The MS-PDC is supported by a cryptographic token, allowing the store and management of patient digital credentials. The confidence on security issues depends strongly on the trust we have on digital certificates, on private key storage and how it is verified that the correct person is the owner of the private key. Contemplating these demands, the PDC (hosted by a crypto smart card) implements card owner verification procedures. The first identity proof is related with the patient physical card possession. However, to access to local and remote patient data the authentication is made through the patient private key that signs a host-side challenge and proof the user identity. The user private key is unique and securely stored on the card protected by a PIN and/or biometric device. The PDC supports PIN verification but it is also prepared to acquire and store two distinct card owner fingerprint templates.

The system is supported by a Web portal that ensures the entire tasks related with the PDC issuing/revocation, patient digital credentials management and support, update of protected data and backup of information like the Hyperlink MS-PDC zone contents. Moreover, the URL of this PDC portal service is stamped on smart card front side and any institution or practitioner with the necessary credentials and a web browser client and a smart card reader can navigate inside the card contents making use of the API available in this portal.

3   Conclusions

The presented product represents a cost-efficient solution that enables high patient data mobility, implements a flexible and trustable model to index and access to distributed EPR information over open and heterogeneous environments as the Internet. Strong authentication enforcements, completely scalable and integrated utilization are other achievements of the proposal.

References

1. G-8-Netlink-Consortium: Netlink Requirements for Interoperability", v2.2, http://www.sesam-vitale.fr/html/projects/netlink
2. Costa, C., et al.: *New Model to Provide a Universal Access Mechanism to Clinical Data.* Technology and Health Care - IOS Press, (2001) vol. 9(6): p. 459–460.
3. ITUT02: ASN.1 encoding rules Specification of Basic Encoding Rules (BER), Canonical Encoding Rules (CER) and Distinguished Encoding Rules (DER),ITU-T Rec. X.690 (2002) ISO/IEC 8825-1:2002 (2002)

Publish-Subscribe for Mobile Environments

Mihail Ionescu and Ivan Marsic

Center for Advanced Information Processing (CAIP), Rutgers University
{mihaii, marsic}@caip.rutgers.edu

Abstract. The Publish-Subscribe paradigm has become an important architectural style for designing distributed systems. In the recent years, we are witnessing an increasing demand for supporting publish-subscribe for mobile computing devices, where conditions used for filtering the data can depend on the particular state of the subscriber (quality of the connection, space and time locality, device capabilities). In this paper we present a stateful model for publish-subscribe systems, suitable for mobile environments. In our system, the server maintains a *state* for each client, which contains variables that describe the properties of the particular client, such as the quality of the connection or the display size. The interest of each client can be expressed in terms of these variables. Based on the client interests, an associated agent is created on the server. The agent filters the data that reach the client based on the current client state. Experimental results show good performance and scalability of our approach.

1 Introduction

In a common scenario of a publish-subscribe system, publishers connect to a centralized server to publish events and subscribers connect to the server to establish connections (or subscriptions) in which they specify the set of messages they are interested in receiving. The job of the server is to match published messages with the subscribers conditions and deliver only the relevant messages to each subscriber. For example, a client can express interest about the companies DELL or IBM when the stock quote dropped under $100 with a query as this:

company ∈ {IBM,DELL} AND price≤100

A common characteristic of these systems is that the server does not maintain any state about the clients. The server keeps only the address of the client (usually an IP address) and the associated conditions. The condition is usually specified in a language based on first-order predicates and decides whether or not the message is to be sent to the particular client only based on the content of the message. The condition cannot effect any changes on the actual data that is transmitted.

The development of the mobile devices made an increasing demand to support publish-subscribe paradigm. However, the above publish-subscribe solution cannot be directly applied in mobile environments. The client should be allowed to specify how the conditions change depending on information like the quality of the connection or the space locality. We believe that the main differences between a classic publish-

J.M. Cueva Lovelle et al. (Eds.): ICWE 2003, LNCS 2722, pp. 547–550, 2003.
© Springer-Verlag Berlin Heidelberg 2003

subscribe system and a publish-subscribe system suitable for mobile clients are the following:

- *Stateful subscribers*

  The server must maintain a state associated with each subscriber. The state of the subscriber can change due to the subscriber's mobility and activities or due to external reasons, e.g., changes in the quality of the connection.

- *Rich language for expressing the conditions*

  The language in which the conditions are written should be able to allow the interaction with the content of the message and with the state of the subscriber and it should be able to modify the message content, according to the conditions.

In this paper we present a novel architecture to support the publish-subscribe mechanism for mobile devices that meets the above requirements. An important class of applications that might benefit from our approach is also described, and a motivational example is considered.

The paper is organized as follows. We first review related work in this area. Next, we describe our approach for supporting general publish-subscribe systems in mobile environments. We then present an example in detail, elaborating the process of creation and deployment of the conditions and finally conclude the paper.

2 Related Work

Content-based publish-subscribe systems are intended for content distribution over a communication network. The most important content-based publish-subscribe systems that we are aware of are GRYPHON [1], SIENA [2], ELVIN [4] and KERYX [3].

The subscription languages of the existing systems are similar to each other and are usually based on the first-order predicates. The filtering algorithm in these situations can be made very efficient using techniques such as parallel search trees [1] or other techniques. As a general observation, a trade-off between expressive subscription languages and highly efficient filtering engines is characteristic to these systems.

3 Stateful Publish-Subscribe Systems

In our system, the server maintains a state (profile) associated with each client. The state is an abstract concept and can be composed of any number of *variables*, which describe the properties of a particular client. The variables can be *static* (like the client's device capabilities, for example), or *dynamic* (the quality of the connection in a wireless network). In the latter case, the server has to monitor the values for the variables in order to comply with the client's conditions.

The architecture of the proposed publish-subscribe system is presented in Figure 1. The server publishes an interface, which indicates what variables from the subscriber state are available to be used as parameters in the conditions.

A subscriber uses the interface to construct one or more *conditions*, in a high-level language, and send these conditions (as a text file) to the server using a `setCondition()` command. Based on this information, the server generates an *agent*, which will be associated with this subscriber. Each time a message arrives at the server from a publisher, the associated agent for each of the subscribers is invoked to decide whether or not the message should be sent to the respective subscriber. If the message will be transmitted to the subscriber, the agent may also perform certain modifications of the data according to the user conditions. The reason for this may be to meet the network bandwidth constraints or the reduced display size. In our architecture, all of the messages are contained in a particular data type, called *UForm*.

4 Case Study: A Collaborative Graphical Editor

Here we present an example application that can benefit from the concept of stateful publish-subscribe systems. It is a multiuser graphical editor application, targeted for use in collaboration on a situation map, running on diverse devices, such as laptops or pocket PCs. In this case, each publisher is at the same time a subscriber.

We assume for simplicity that there are three types of objects that can be created: rectangles, circles and images. The user-defined policy (i.e., conditions) for distributing the messages is as follows. First the connection is considered to be of *good* quality if the available bandwidth is more than 100Kb/s, *average* quality if the bandwidth is between 10Kb/s and 100Kb/s and of *poor* quality when the bandwidth drops under 10Kb/s. If the client has a good connection it is interested in receiving notifications about all types of objects. If the connection quality is average, it is interested only in rectangles and images. Lastly, if the connection is poor, it is interested in rectangles only. In all cases, if the size of an object is greater than the size of the display available at the client site, the client is not interested in that particular object. The implementation of such a policy is shown in Table 1.

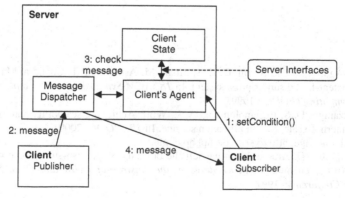

Fig. 1. The architecture of the proposed publish-subscribe system.

Table 1. The implementation of the user policy

public UForm testUForm(UForm uform)
{
if (getClientSize()<uform.getSize())
   return null;
if (getAvailableBandwidth()>=100.0)
{
       return uform;
}
if (getAvailableBandwidth()>=10.0)
{
If (uform.getProperty("typo")="rectangle")
   return uform;
	if (uform.getProperty("type")="image")
	   return uform;
	}
	
	if (uform.getProperty("type")="rectangle")
	   return uform;
	
	return null
	
	}

We do not expect each user to be able to generate the conditions, as presented in Table 1. Using a wizard with an appropriate graphical user interface, the application can generate automatically the conditions, based on the input from the user.

Because of the space limitation, we cannot present the detailed performance evaluation of our system. However, our tests show that the proposed architecture is scalable and perform very well under medium and high traffic.

5 Conclusions

In this paper we introduce the notion of stateful publish-subscribe systems and argue that the current publish-subscribe systems are not suitable for mobile environments. Our approach allows the conditions to interact with the current state of each subscriber and decide whether or not to send it to the subscriber and how to modify the message if necessary. Moreover, our approach can be incorporated in the current publish-subscribe systems in an incremental manner, by allowing for some of the subscribers to maintain a state at the server. Experimental results demonstrate good performance and scalability of our approach.

References

1. M. K. Aguilera, R. E. Storm, D. C. Sturman, M. Astley, and T. Chandra. Matching events in a content-based subscription system. In *18ᵗʰ ACM Symposium on Principles of Distributing Computing (PODC)*, 1999.
2. A. Carzaniga, D. S. Rosemblum and A. L. Wolf. Achieving scalability and expressiveness in an internet-scale event notification service. In *19ᵗʰ PODC*, 2000.
3. Keryx homepage, http://keryxsoft.hpl.hp.com
4. B. Segall and D. Arnold. Elvin has left the building: A publish-subscribe notification service with quenching. In *Proceedings of the Australian UNIX and Open Systems User Group Conference*, 1997.

Author Index